To Marilena—
a person who continues to care

A Question of Ethics: A Perceptual Query   44
A Few Fallacies   47
The Seven-Step System: A Logical Approach to Problem Solving
    51
I've Got a Hunch: Decision Making by Intuition   53
Pitfalls to Effective Decision Making   54
Creativity and the Individual   56
*A Box of Interest: How Burned Fingers Came to the "Aid" of
    Johnson & Johnson*   56
Experiential Exercise: We See, But Do We Perceive?   66

Chapter 3   The Need for Communication Skills: There's More to
                Communication Than Meets the Ear   69

The Nature of Communication   71
What Are Words Really Like?   72
*A Question of Ethics: A Frontal Attack—Is This A Kind of Sneaky
    Doublespeak Or What?*   75
Types of Communication   76
Silence Isn't Always Golden—Nonverbal Forms of
    Communication   81
*A Box of Interest: How to Talk to People Without Talking to
    People!*   81
What's the Meaning of This? The Barriers to Effective
    Communication   85
The Importance of Listening   88
*A Global Glance: Listen to These Words From a Japanese
    Communication Expert*   90
Developing Listening Skills   91
How to Break Down Communication Barriers   93
Experiential Exercises:
    Find the Four Cs of Written Communication!   108
    Whispering Sweet Nothings!   108

Chapter 4   The Dynamics of Small Groups: The Whole Is Greater
                Than . . .   111

Here a Group, There a Group, Everywhere a Group-Group   112
A Question of Ethics: Things Weren't Maxed, *Nor Have They Gone
    Well for Maxwell's Former Employees*   114
The Nature of Formal and Informal Groups   116
The Behavior of Groups   118
Informal Groups and the Grapevine   122
A Box of Interest: Spread the Word: Gossip Is Good   127
Group Problem Solving and Decision Making   127

Contents

Applications   xiii

Experiential Exercises   xv

To the Instructor   xvi

To the Reader   xxiv

Part One   Humans Are People   1

Chapter 1   An Introduction to Human Relationships in Organizations:
1 + 1 = Organization   3

Organizations and Human Behavior   6
A Small Dose of OB History   9
A Box of Interest: Farmers Have *Left the Soil*   10
A Global Glance: HRM in Action at This Plant   13
Individual and Organizational Needs   16
A Question of Ethics: Employee Pilferage—A Burning Issue   17
Decision Making in Organizations   18
Some Words to the Wise: Tips on How to Learn From This Text
19

Chapter 2   A Look at Human Perception: There's More to Perception
Than Meets the Eye   33

The Importance of Seeing What's Really There   34
Facts Versus Inferences   38
*A Global Glance: Is What You Think You See
What You Really Get?*   39
The Determinants of Perception   43

A Question of Ethics: A Perceptual Query   44
A Few Fallacies   47
The Seven-Step System: A Logical Approach to Problem Solving   51
I've Got a Hunch: Decision Making by Intuition   53
Pitfalls to Effective Decision Making   54
Creativity and the Individual   56
A Box of Interest: How Burned Fingers Came to the "Aid" of Johnson & Johnson   56
Experiential Exercise: We See, But Do We Perceive?   66

Chapter 3   The Need for Communication Skills: There's More to Communication Than Meets the Ear   69

The Nature of Communication   71
What Are Words Really Like?   72
A Question of Ethics: A Frontal Attack—Is This A Kind of Sneaky Doublespeak Or What?   75
Types of Communication   76
Silence Isn't Always Golden—Nonverbal Forms of Communication   81
A Box of Interest: How to Talk to People Without Talking to People!   81
What's the Meaning of This? The Barriers to Effective Communication   85
The Importance of Listening   88
A Global Glance: Listen to These Words From a Japanese Communication Expert   90
Developing Listening Skills   91
How to Break Down Communication Barriers   93
Experiential Exercises:
Find the Four Cs of Written Communication!   108
Whispering Sweet Nothings!   108

Chapter 4   The Dynamics of Small Groups: The Whole Is Greater Than . . .   111

Here a Group, There a Group, Everywhere a Group-Group   112
A Question of Ethics: Things Weren't Maxed, *Nor Have They Gone Well for Maxwell's Former Employees*   114
The Nature of Formal and Informal Groups   116
The Behavior of Groups   118
Informal Groups and the Grapevine   122
A Box of Interest: Spread the Word: Gossip Is Good   127
Group Problem Solving and Decision Making   127

A Global Glance: Worldwide Meetings—On Channel 3!   135
Really Small Groups—The Interview   136
Experiential Exercise: Examining Formal Work Arrangements
   151

Part Two   Leaders Need People   153

Chapter 5   Human Needs, Motivation, and Morale: Would a Carrot
Make You Happy?   155

The Importance of Needs and Motivation   156
Can You *Learn* To Need Needs?   159
The Priority of Needs   162
A Global Glance: Do Americans Work Too Darn Much?   164
The Maintenance of Motivation—Herzberg's Motivation-
Maintenance Model   167
The *Process* of Motivation   173
Behavior Modification Through Reinforcement Techniques   173
Are You Expecting? Let's Hear It for Vroom   176
*A Box of Interest: Carrots—Could They Turn the Stomachs of
Some Employees?*   178
The Relationship Between Equity and Motivation   178
Morale in Organizations   179
A Question of Ethics: Those Who Giveth Sometimes Taketh Away!
   180
What Are the Factors That Affect Morale?   182
Warning Signs of Low Morale   185
Evaluating Morale   187
Experiential Exercise: What Do You Need?   199

Chapter 6   Techniques of Leadership: Okay, People, Follow Me....
I Said, Follow Me! Aw, Come On, *Please* Follow Me!   203

The Functions and Characteristics of Leadership   204
Leadership Attitudes   209
A Global Glance: What Is the Right Stuff for a Global Leader?
   210
The Pygmalion Effect   215
Styles of Leadership   217
*A Question of Ethics: EI Can Backfire in an Environment of
Suspicion and Distrust*   221
Leadership as a Skill   227
A Box of Interest: Participative Leadership on the Rise   228

Development of Leadership Skills   230
The Need for a Supportive Organizational Culture   233
Experiential Exercises:
  What Do You Assume?   241
  What Can You Delegate?   244

Chapter 7   Quality and the Workplace: Total Quality to the Rescue
            247

The Concern for Total Quality Management   250
A Question of Ethics: Is Quality Going to the Dogs?   255
A Box of Interest: Teamwork Can Be Tricky!   259
Bouquets for Quality Companies   261
*A Global Glance: Japan's Biggest Import—American Managerial
  Expertise?*   262
Organizational Principles That Assist the Quest for Quality
  263
*Experiential Exercise: "Excuse Me, But Would You Mind Telling
  Me Your Mission?"*   276

Chapter 8   The Quality of Work Life: Does Anybody Really Care?
            279

Greater Concerns Over the Quality of Work Life   280
What Influences the Quality of Work Life?   281
Improving the Quality of Work Life   282
A Global Glance: Nothing Fishy Smelling About Skunk Works!
  288
A Box of Interest: Is This Job Ever a Pain!   290
Innovative Ways to Work   292
*A Question of Ethics: "Interim Assignments"—A License to
  Moonlight?*   298
*Experiential Exercise: What Dimension? Rotten to the Core—Or
  Enriched?*   313

Part Three   Constraints on Organizational Performance   315

Chapter 9   The Dynamics of Change: There's No Progress Without
            Change   317

The Effects of Change   318
Attitudes and Behavior in the Face of Change   319
*A Global Glance: EuroDisney at a Loss Over the French Reaction
  to Its Theme Park*   322

The Effective Introduction of Change—Change Management 327

A Box of Interest: Even a Boiling Kettle Couldn't "Unfreeze" This Little Bear   330

The Use of Organization Development (OD) to Effect Change 333

People and Productivity—The Managerial Grid   335

The Use of MBO to Effect Change   335

A Question of Ethics: Not Exactly What One Would Call "Country-Club Management"   337

Experiential Exercise: Is This Change Really Necessary?   347

Chapter 10   Cultural Diversity in the Workplace: Is It Back to the Drawing Board?   351

The Nature of Prejudice and Discrimination   354

A Box of Interest: Is the Accent on Foreign Hiring?   356

The Need for Objectivity and Sensitivity by Supervisors in Managing Diversity   362

A Question of Ethics: An Eye for an Eye, and a Bash for a Bash! 364

Legal Discrimination in Exceptional Cases   365

Reverse Discrimination—An Organizational Dilemma   366

You've Come a Long Way, Maybe! The Challenges Facing Women in the Workplace   368

A Global Glance: Childcare Around the World   374

Challenges Faced by Women Managers   378

Challenges Faced by Ethnic Minority Managers   382

Experiential Exercises:
   Upgrading Secretarial Positions?   393
   Don't Forget the Diapers!   394

Chapter 11   Organizational Challenges Faced by Older Workers and Those With Disabilities: Hire Them . . . It's Good Business 397

Employment Problems of the Aging   399

Attitudes Toward Older Workers   401

Assisting the Older Worker   403

Problems of Persons With Disabilities   408

A Box of Interest: What Can You Do to Prevent the Transmission of HIV?   411

Common Attitudes Toward the Physically and Intellectually Challenged   413

A Global Glance: Some People in the Netherlands Don't "Go Dutch!"   415

A Special Problem—HIV and AIDS   416
A Question of Ethics: "What? You've Got AIDS? Then We'll Change the Health Insurance Plan!"   419
Advantages of Hiring Persons With Disabilities   421
Managing Individuals With Disabilities   422
A Social Responsibility   425
Experiential Exercise:
    Birds Do It; Bees Do It; Can Aging Pilots Do It?   434
    A Quizzical AID to Enhanced Awareness   435

Chapter 12   Problems of Substance Abuse: Can They Just Say "No" to the High Life?   437

The Extent of the Alcohol Problem   438
The Trend Toward Rehabilitation   441
The Prevalence of Drug Abuse   442
A Global Glance: A Cross-Border Bust   445
The "Who" and "Why" of Substance Abuse   446
Organizational Approaches to Alcohol and Drug Abuse   449
The Establishment of Company Programs   450
A Box of Interest: EAPs Also Assist the Bottom Lines of Employers   453
Supervisory Responsibilities   453
Supervisory Guidelines   456
Recognizing Alcohol and Drug Abuse in the Workplace   456
Getting Tough with Substance Abusers: Employee Drug Testing   458
A Question of Ethics: Nothing Casual About Motorola's Anti-Substance Abuse Program!   461
Being Drug Free Is Good Business   463
Experiential Exercise: Don't Say Yes   472

Part Four   Organizational Health, Ethics, and Globalization   475

Chapter 13   Developing and Maintaining a Less Stressful Life: Stress Kills!   477

The Nature of Stress   478
Frustration—A Response to Stress   480
Reactions to Frustration   482
A Question of Ethics: Aim That at Me, You Little Squirt, and You're a Goner!   484
Burnout—The Disease of High Achievers   491

The Need to Manage Stress With Faith   493
Managing Career-related Stress   496
A Global Glance: Time Out for Stress Reduction!   498
Don't Bite the Hand That Needs You—Managing Stress Off the
   Job   506
A Box of Interest: Work It on Out!   512
Causing Associates to Become Distressed   514
Happiness and Success Are . . . ?   515
Experiential Exercises:
   Mechanisms for Personal Defense   525
   Are You a Candidate for Burnout?   526
   Are You an "A" or a "B"?   527

Chapter 14   The Challenges Facing Individuals in Organizations:
                 Without Individuals, Where Would We Be?   531

To Be or Not to Be? The Question of Conformity   532
A Global Glance: Don't Go There With an "Attitude"!   538
Do Employees Have the Right to Privacy?   544
A Question of Ethics: The Boss Is Watching!   545
The Challenge of Disciplining Employees   548
A Box of Interest: The "Opportunity" to Quit!   554
Challenges With One's Self   555
Have You Ever Considered Going Into Politics?   559
A Box of Interest: Is Whistle-Blowing by Modem the Answer?
   561
Experiential Exercises:
   Declining Ethics?   574
   How Willing Are You to Conform?   575

Chapter 15   Organizational Ethics and Responsibilities Toward Society:
                 It All Relates to the Bottom Line   577

Have Standards of Business Ethics Declined?   579
A Question of Ethics: Do Employees Have the Right to Feel Secure?
   584
Two Philosophies: Profit Quest Versus Social Accountability
   585
Areas of Social Responsibility   586
A Box of Interest: Ben and Jerry—Two Modern-Day Robin Hoods?
   592
Guide to Social Action   593
A Global Glance: Those Virtuous Europeans!   596
Experiential Exercises:
   Are You "Backlashing" Toward Business?   605
   The Commencement Speaker   607

Chapter 16   On a Global Scale: It's a Small, Small World   609

Opportunities and Challenges on a Global Basis   610
Organizational Cultures in a Global Environment   613
A Box of Interest: South of the Border . . . Down Mexico Way!
    614
A Question of Ethics: "If We Can't Sell It Here, Then Let's Sell It
    There!"   621
A Global Glance: Harley Does It . . .Toys 'R' Us Does It
    Why Can't Good Old Federal Express Do It?   624
Easing the Transition for Innocents Abroad   625
Repatriation—Returning Home   627
Experiential Exercise: A Cultural Quiz   637

Glossary   639

Index   653

Applications

1.1 Don't rock the boat   23
1.2 Whose organization is this, anyway?   24
1.3 The case of the uneven playing field   27

2.1 The friendly expediter   60
2.2 The case of the snapping judgments   62
2.3 The smelly case   63
2.4 Are you creative or mentally set?   64

3.1 "It's like cowabunga, dude, but it's not what I ordered"   102
3.2 The reticent subordinates   102
3.3 About as clear as mud   103
3.4 The Paragon Machine Tool Company   104

4.1 Who gets the office?   142
4.2 Meeting madness   144
4.3 We do it our way   146

5.1 The satisfied sales representative   193
5.2 No satisfaction   194
5.3 Moe graduates   195
5.4 "Give us more money!"   196—
5.6 "*Sure* I invite dissent."   197

6.1 What's Charlie's complaint?   237
6.2 The case of Incinerator 3   237
6.3 Banking on a solution at the data center   239

7.1 The Fosdick Generator Company and TQM   270
7.2 The dull letters case   272
7.3 Hot line to the top   272

8.1 The case of the unenriched retail operations   307
8.2 A "classless" society at Swindon   308
8.3 The child-care dilemma   309

9.1   But it's the all-American meal!   340
9.2   The Precision Parameter Company   340
9.3   The new broom case   342
9.4   Management by whose objectives?   344

10.1 William Johnson gets promoted   386
10.2 Promotion bypass   387
10.3 My rightful place   388

11.1 Loyalty or efficiency?   428
11.2 The disabled photography lab worker   430
11.3 The case of the forthright job applicant   430

12.1 The case of Johnny Ballantine   466
12.2 The producer who couldn't say no   467
12.3 Drug testing—solution or threat?   468

13.1 The rat race   519
13.2 A search for utopia   521
13.3 The case of the overworked American   522

14.1 Caught on two horns of a dilemma   567
14.2 A rebel with or without a cause?   568
14.3 We all want to march to different drummers   570

15.1 Whose responsibility is social responsibility?   599
15.2 Hiring and firing on the same day   601

16.1 "Why didn't they tell me it would be like this?"   630
16.2 "What we need is a consultant!"   633

Experiential Exercises

Chapter 2   We see, but do we perceive?   66

Chapter 3   Find the four C's of written communication!   108
             Whispering sweet nothings!   108

Chapter 4   Examining formal work arrangements   151

Chapter 5   What do you need?   199

Chapter 6   What do you assume?   241
             What can you delegate?   244

Chapter 7   Excuse me, but would you mind telling me your mission?
             276

Chapter 8   What dimension? Rotten to the core—or enriched?   313

Chapter 9   Is this change really necessary?   347

Chapter 10   Upgrading secretarial positions?   393
             Don't forget the diapers!   394

Chapter 11   Birds do it; bees do it; can aging pilots do it?   434
             A quizzical AID to enhanced awareness   435

Chapter 12   Don't say yes   472

Chapter 13   Mechanisms for personal defense   525
             Are you a candidate for burnout?   526
             Are you an "A" or a "B"?   527

Chapter 14   Declining ethics?   574
             How willing are you to conform?   575

Chapter 15   Are you "backslashing" toward business?   605
             The commencement speaker   607

Chapter 16   A cultural quiz   637

To the Instructor

The publication of the first edition of *The Human Side of Organizations* was the fulfillment of a five-year dream for me. I had long wanted to develop materials for my college students of human relations/organizational behavior that were not only practical but also interesting and enjoyable for them to read.

The response to the first five editions of *The Human Side of Organizations* has been extremely gratifying. The text, having been adopted by hundreds of colleges in the United States and Canada since its first edition, appears to have reached its intended audience.

One of my goals has continually been to avoid overloading students with the multitude of erudite theories that tend to turn off—rather than to excite—students facing their first course in organizational behavior, human relations, or industrial psychology. I've especially enjoyed reading the supportive fan mail sent to me by both students and faculty.

THE NEED FOR RESTRUCTURING AND RE-ENGINEERING

Restructuring and *re-engineering*—those are words that we've heard and read a lot lately. Recently we've seen numerous organizations jumping into the restructuring and re-engineering arenas, streamlining and redesigning their core processes in an attempt to make their organizations more competitive, efficient, and productive. There has also been a marked shift by American managers toward a concern for "total quality."

A textbook is, in a sense, somewhat like an organization, and an author had better behave like a professional organizational manager if he or she wants to create and maintain a quality textbook. Just as organizations find themselves in need of reorganization, so can a textbook. Considerable time and effort, therefore, went into analyzing the types of changes that had to be made to this— the sixth edition.

WHAT TO INCLUDE AND WHAT TO EXCLUDE

Based on suggestions of loyal users, I realized that it was time for me, too, to jump on the restructuring and re-engineering bandwagons and make some serious decisions as to what should be added and what pruned from the sixth edition. New concepts, terms, and processes, such as *total quality management* and *empowerment,* are continually developed by both practitioners and academics. Other concepts become outdated and are of less concern to modern managers. Adding information without trimming material of lesser importance would only intimidate many students if they had to buy a textbook resembling something approaching an encyclopedia.

Nothing was removed from this edition of *The Human Side of Organizations* without first consulting as many users as possible. However, as with any group of human beings, there is seldom absolute agreement. For example, some users feel quite comfortable teaching concepts that have become familiar to them. They tend to dislike seeing such material disappear from a textbook, even after the concepts become out of date. Therefore, recognizing the impossibility of pleasing everyone, I had to assimilate the variety of opinions and suggestions and make the most desirable decisions as to what to include and what to exclude from the sixth edition.

TOTAL QUALITY MANAGEMENT APPLIED

Before revising this edition, I decided to practice what I preach and use an important element of the process of *total quality management,* that is, to discover what customers—students and professors—want in a textbook. The result, with the assistance of my able and creative editors at HarperCollins College Publishers, is what I believe you will find to be a substantially improved textbook.

Most management courses cover organizational structure in depth. Prognoses of the future direction of organizations are generally included in texts in introduction to business and economics. In order to include as many as possible of the current trends and practices, therefore, individual chapters devoted exclusively to those two areas were omitted, and a new chapter devoted to a major concern of today's managers—quality management—was added. These changes, of course, were made based on input from users and reviewers of the fifth edition.

This edition also includes throughout the text both greater use of examples of global organizational behavior and increased emphasis on organizational ethics, two subjects of tremendous concern to organizational members today. Finally, the text has consistently been noted for its humorous, personal writing style that captures students' interest.

YOUR LOYALTY IS APPRECIATED

Something that is gratifying to me is the number of adopters of *The Human Side of Organizations* who have continued to use the textbook from its first edition to the present day. To me this is a sign that I have been on the right track with my efforts. If you are a first-time user or are considering adopting this edition, you should quickly discover why the text has appealed to instructors and students who have used it in the past.

The following sections provide you with an overview of the text's organization along with the principal features and improvements embodied in this edition.

ORGANIZATION OF THE TEXT

The Human Side of Organizations, Sixth Edition, is divided into four parts:

1. **Humans Are People**—four chapters designed to help the reader develop insight, sensitivity, and improved understanding of people—both leaders and operating employees—in organizations. Includes chapters that discuss an overview of organizational behavior, concepts of perception and decision making, communication, and small group behavior.

2. **Leaders Need People**—four chapters designed to assist organizational leaders in maintaining and improving the organizational climate. Includes chapters that discuss concepts of needs, motivation, and morale; leadership techniques; and the total quality management and quality of work life concerns of today's organizations.

3. **Constraints on Organizational Performance**—four chapters designed to assist present and future managers in understanding and dealing with forces that tend to constrict leadership activities. Includes chapters on managing change, culturally diverse groups in organizations, challenges facing individuals with disabilities (including AIDs) and the aging, and organizational problems associated with the abuse of alcohol and other substances.

4. **Organizational Health, Ethics, and Globalization**—four chapters designed to help readers understand how to manage stress, deal with the challenges facing individuals

in organizations, understand organizational ethics and responsibilities, and explore organizational behavior along global lines.

NEW AND UPDATED MATERIALS

Organizational trends continue to change quite rapidly. Consequently, a variety of up-to-date and practical materials have been added throughout the sixth edition. These include the following:

1. **Extensive emphasis on ethics throughout the text,** including such topics as misuse of company resources, employee "integrity tests," and international business standards. An entire chapter, Chapter 15, is exclusively devoted to the topic of ethics and its relationship to organizational behavior.

2. **Updated materials on global organizational behavior,** including an entire chapter, Chapter 16, "Crossing Cultural Boundaries," a topic integrated throughout the text.

3. **A new chapter on total quality management (TQM),** a topic that became one of the primary focuses of professional managers in recent years.

4. **A new chapter devoted exclusively to the quality of work life (QWL),** a current-day concern of organizational decision makers.

5. **Added sections in communications chapter** related to doublespeak.

6. **Added section in small groups chapter** related to "brainwriting," an offshoot of brainstorming.

7. **Motivation chapter reorganized** to include topic of morale, plus an added section related to performance-related payment plans.

8. **New material in leadership chapter** on employee empowerment.

9. **New material in chapter on prejudice and discrimination,** including L.A. police/Rodney King and Anita Hill/Clarence Thomas incidents.

10. **Expanded discussion of HIV and AIDS** and their relationship to organizational behavior.

11. **Expanded discussion of substance testing** in the workplace.

12. **New material on surveillance of employees.**

13. **Revised discussion of no-layoff policies** in organizations.

14. **Revised discussion of global organizational behavior.**

15. **A substantial use of real company examples** throughout the text, including Toys "R" Us, Western Electric Company, Merrill Lynch & Co., Johnson & Johnson, Ford Motor Company, General Motors, Eastman-Kodak, IBM, Caterpillar, Bethlehem Steel, Chevron Corporation, Pacific Bell, Kentucky Fried Chicken, Dow Corning, and Levi Strauss.

16. **Updated statistics and examples** throughout the text.

PEDAGOGY

Boxed Inserts

A popular feature, called "A Box of Interest," continues to be included in each chapter. The majority of the boxes are new to the sixth edition. Because of the current interest expressed by many users of the text in the topics of ethics and global organizational behavior, each chapter includes two additional boxes, "A Question of Ethics" and "A Global Glance," respectively. Each chapter contains at least three boxes, which typically present short stories, illustrations, or vignettes. These are taken from real-life situations intended to incorporate additional practical examples to enrich students' understanding of the chapter's concepts and to emphasize the importance of ethical and global concerns to today's organizational environment.

Experiential Exercises

Another feature of this edition is the experiential exercises that appear near the end of each chapter. These exercises are intended to provide the student with an opportunity to apply specific chapter concepts.

Applications

A variety of applications, or incidents, are included. Their use is intended to provide students with the opportunity to improve their organizational behavior skills through analysis of real-life situations.

New Cartoons, Tables, Figures, and Photos

A variety of new cartoons, tables, figures, and photos have been included to enhance student interest in the text matter. The various changes in design are intended to maintain the text's contemporary appearance.

Learning Objectives

Listed at the beginning of each chapter, objectives describe what students should learn.

Marginal Notes

These comments encourage students to ask questions and explore important ideas as they proceed through each chapter. In some cases, the marginal notes are intended to give the student a break and possibly the opportunity to enjoy a "chuckle."

Terms and Concepts to Remember

Placed in boldface within each chapter, important terms and concepts are repeated at the ends of chapters for additional reinforcement.

Discussion Questions

These questions cover the major topics of each chapter and test students' comprehension of the material.

Glossary

Key terms from each chapter and the page on which these terms are first introduced are listed and defined at the end of the book.

SUPPLEMENTS

A Revised Instructor's Resource Manual

Written by Connie Sitterly, Director of Management Training Specialists, CPCM, Fort Worth, TX, the instructor's guide includes a variety of materials designed to make the adopter's teaching experiences more effective. Some of its features include the following: a lecture outline, answers to end-of-chapter questions and experiential exercises, suggested responses to the applications section of each chapter, transparency masters and supplementary materials and teaching aids intended to enrich the instructor's utilization of chapter-related materials.

An Extensive Test Bank by Stan Kossen

An extensive test bank manual written by the text author is also available to adopting instructors. The test bank includes multiple-choice, true-false, fill-in, and essay questions.

Testmaster

The test bank is available on this highly acclaimed computerized test-generation system with full word processing capabilities. Harper Test produces customized tests and allows instructors to scramble questions and add new ones. The system is available for the IBM PC, XT, AT, PS/2, and compatible computers.

Grades

HarperCollins offers to adopters a grade-keeping and class management package for the IBM and compatible computers that maintains data for up to 200 students.

HarperCollins Business Video Library

Adopters of this edition may select from a variety of videos that are related to this text.

KUDOS

I want to thank the many individuals, both in industry and academia, who have provided me with assistance and encouragement during the revision of this book. I would especially like to thank the following people: Melissa Rosati, Pam Wilkie, and Mike Roche—all from HarperCollins—and Lori Jacobs, freelance editor, for providing me with the technical assistance and guidance necessary to develop a useful textbook. Thanks is also extended to Barbra Guerra, of A-R Editions, Inc., who did an outstanding job of coordinating the project.

I would also like to express my sincere gratitude to many who have helped me in the creation of this text. Many reviewers of the manuscript for this sixth edition or users of prior editions took the time to examine at least a part of the project and gave me good advice:

Kathryn Barchas, Skyline College
Larry Berthelsen, Odessa College
Stephen Branz, Triton College
Robert Brennaman, Cowley County Community College
Joseph Cantrell, DeAnza College
Barbara Ching, Los Angeles City College
Renee L. Cohen, Southwestern Community College
Mary Jane Dewe, Paradise Valley Community College
Bill Dow, College of St. Francis
C.S. "Pete" Everett, Des Moines Area Community College
Mike Farley, Del Mar College

Jan Feldbauer, Austin Community College
Pete Frigo, Moraine Valley Community College
Joe Galdiano, Normandale Community College
Larry Hill, San Jacinto College
Fayrene Hofer, College of the Sequoias
Don Hucker, Cypress College
Richard Immenhausen, College of the Desert
Alice Jacobs, Human Factors Consultant, Job Accommodation
    Network, West Virginia University
Art LaCapria, El Paso Community College
Tom Mason, Brookdale College
A. Ally Mishal, Stark Technical College
Erv Napier, Kent State University
Bob Redick, Lincoln Land Community College
Bill Roe, Nicholls State University
Nicholas Sarantakes, Austin Community College
David Sergis, Truckee Meadow Community College
Marilee F. Smith, Kirkwood Community College
Susan E. Somers, Quincy College
Bob Thomas, Roane State Community College
Joseph E. Thompson, Cuyahoga Community College
Terry Thorpe, Irvine Valley College
Ted Valvoda, Lakeland Community College
Bill Weisgerber, Saddleback College

And, as always, to the best judges of any text—my former students and the readers who have provided me with constructive criticism and lots of positive encouragement.

Stan Kossen

To the Reader

Every organization has many sides to it. You are about to explore one of these sides—the human side—of organizations. In one sense, an organization exists wherever there are two or more persons with mutual interests. For our purposes, the term organization can relate to business organizations, governmental bodies, social organizations, cause-oriented groups, and even family units.

CONFLICT—IS IT INEVITABLE?

Is conflict inevitable? Not in every instance. Yet, wherever there are two or more persons, potential conflict exists. But do people who have to make decisions (and who doesn't?) in this problem-beset world have to wait until after a crisis before they act? Wouldn't it be far more desirable if potential discord and organizational problems were anticipated and prevented? Perhaps problems could be prevented far more often if individuals in organizations could develop greater sensitivity toward *human* problems.

GUARD AGAINST SIMPLISTIC SOLUTIONS

Any book on human behavior in organizations shouldn't be a how-to presentation. Wish as heartily as we might, we are unlikely to discover ten simple rules that will enable us to resolve all problems that we confront. What should the book be, then? It should be a resource that will help you to develop a keener awareness of and sensitivity toward the needs, sentiments, and attitudes of individuals—including yourself—in organizations, to sharpen your perceptions, and to improve your ability to make effective decisions both on and off the job.

SOFT ON USERS

The computer software field is fond of the term *user friendly*. I think you'll find this book user friendly. It has been written at a level that you can understand with a minimum of effort, rather than one that tends to talk down to you. Managers of organizations in their communications—such as memos and letters—generally try to avoid appearing excessively complex. Likewise, a textbook needn't be excessively complex or scholarly to be useful. We've all read texts that were written in an overcomplex fashion that tended to discourage, rather than encourage, our interest in the subject.

BUILD A SOLID FOUNDATION

I recommend that, before you put this book down, you take a quick, but careful, look at the table of contents. It will give you an idea as to where you'll be going in your reading and also begin to build a framework on which you can attach your newly-acquired knowledge.

I also suggest that you take a good look at the *learning objectives* that are included at the beginning of each chapter. They are there to assist you. You probably would like to know where you're about to go in a particular chapter; the learning objectives help you find out. They also can serve as a checklist to enable you to see if you have studied the chapter well.

Key terms have been placed in boldface within the chapters. These terms are formally defined in the glossary, a section at the end of the textbook that you should likewise become familiar with.

Tickler questions and *sidecracks* have been placed in the margins of many pages. The tickler questions are intended principally to point up the importance of the paragraphs they represent as well as to serve as quick reference. The sidecracks are intended to serve as a change of pace and (I hope!) provide you with an occasional chuckle. Of course, studying should be serious business, but a sense of humor can help you immeasurably through the typical stresses associated with pursuing an education.

THIS BOOK IS FOR YOU

This text—*The Human Side of Organizations*—was written with college students in mind. Many of you who read this text may identify with management. However, you ordinarily will not begin your careers within managerial positions. As a result, you will have the employee's responsibilities of getting along with other employees (including your boss!), as well as working with and through individuals, both within and without the organizations. Even if your intentions do not include becoming a manager, you can benefit from this book. Although the expression may sound a bit trite, the application of good organizational behavior skills is the responsibility of everyone in an organization. It is hoped that the study of behavior in organizations will assist you in becoming more sensitive to human behavior, anticipating problems before they occur, and resolving them if they have already occurred.

Since I really wrote this book for you, I sincerely hope that you will find studying the sixth edition of *The Human Side of Organizations* a beneficial and enjoyable experience. Best of luck to you in your efforts!

Stan Kossen

Part One

Humans Are People

CHAPTER 1   An Introduction to Human Relationships
             in Organizations

CHAPTER 2   A Look at Human Perceptions

CHAPTER 3   The Need for Communication Skills

CHAPTER 4   The Dynamics of Small Groups

CHAPTER 1

An Introduction to Human Relationships in Organizations

1 + 1 = Organization

**When you finish this chapter,
you should be able to:**

1
Summarize the purpose of learning concepts of human behavior
as they apply to organizations.

2
Contrast formal with informal organizations.

3
Trace the history of organizational behavior.

4
Discuss current trends in the trade union movement.

5
Recognize how personal needs can affect the organization.

6
Explain the need for organizational order and predictability.

7
Describe the nature of decision making in organizations.

8
Apply some specific concepts for studying this text more effectively.

> The pertinent question is not how to do things right
> but how to find the right things to do. . . .

Peter Drucker, Management Philosopher

> Many people recognize that the quality of human relationships
> in offices, teams, and departments contributes
> to business success or failure.

Adrian Furnham, Management Writer

Have you noticed how every decade seems to bring with it mind-boggling events and changes that significantly influence organizational activities? For example, the 1940s were beset by a "hot" world war and shortages, followed by peace "breaking out" and "economic miracles" occurring in the 1950s in both Germany and Japan coupled with the beginning of the "cold war." The 1950s were also known for the Korean Conflict, "Ivy League" haircuts, the flight to suburbia by many Americans, and the omnipresent wood-paneled station wagon parked in the driveway of a white-picket-fenced "American dream."

The 1960s and the Vietnam War seemed to bring with them a revolution in many young people's thinking about sex, drugs, war, the environment, civil rights, and the so-called establishment. Hairstyles became long, the patience of law-enforcement officers became short, and demonstrations *for* civil rights and *against* war became commonplace.

Then the 1970s arrived, accompanied by a trend toward distrust of big government and a huge hike in energy prices. The evacuation of Indochina by the United States, the infamous Watergate scandal, and the resignation of President Nixon appeared to reduce faith in the capacity of the United States to influence world affairs.

The 1980s ushered in a severe recession followed by the longest peacetime economic recovery. The decade was later referred to as the "period of excess." Organizational managers began acquiring other organizations with increasing frequency, creating feelings of insecurity for their members and excessive debt for their owners. Householders, too, incurred debt in record amounts, assuming that their own economic situations would continue to get better and property values would always be moving up, up, and away!

Finally, the last decade of the century arrived—the 1990s—a period that has rivaled the 1960s with its pace of change. Heavy metal and rap music became "mainstream." "Japan-bashing"—blaming the Japanese for many of the economic woes of the United States—became fashionable. "Junk bonds," extensively used as leverage to acquire other companies during the 1970s and 1980s, became less fashionable, as did going into debt. The United States experienced the longest period of economic decline since the Great Depression of the 1930s and set a record of nearly one million bankruptcies in 1991. Attitudes swung from euphoria resulting from the Gulf War victory to pessimism accompanied by beliefs that the current generation of young people would be the first not to be as well-off as their parents. Experience suggests, however, that such pessimistic attitudes are quick to fade as economic conditions begin to improve.

Another significant event of the 1990s shocked Americans in early May 1992, when the United States seemed to experience history revisited with three days of rioting and vandalism in South-Central Los Angeles. At least 50 people were killed, 10,000 businesses looted and burned, 200 families made homeless, and nearly 14,000 jobs lost. Some observers believed that expanded efforts at aiding minority communities would result, while others were less optimistic.

Also during the 1990s, the face of Eastern Europe seemed to change by the hour as a result of Mikhail Gorbachev's efforts with *perestroika*. East and West Germany became one country, and the former Soviet Union became many. The disintegration of the Soviet Union resulted in the elimination of one of the world's two "superpowers." Western Europe's Economic Community (EC) attempted to become more united, and the former Federal Republic of Yugoslavia became less united with its bloody internal war. Imagine being a cartographer (mapmaker) during this period!

The United States has continued during the 1990s to be a world *military* superpower, but Japan has emerged as the dominant world *economic* superpower. However, even mighty Japan could not escape all the effects of the worldwide recession of the early 1990s.

What do all these incidents have to do with the study of organizational behavior? Historical events create innumerable challenges for organizational members. Certain events have caused many organizations to go out of business, while others have encouraged worldwide operations. Now Japanese crowd the large retail children's store, Toys "R" Us, which opened in the southwestern suburbs of Tokyo in the early 1990s. Former president George Bush was a guest at its opening ceremonies.

What sorts of organizations are likely to survive the continued challenges and changes? They are likely to be those that have the capability of providing customers with *quality* products and services. Of paramount significance, however, they are especially likely to be those whose managers have a concern for their employees—*people-oriented organizations*. One of the primary assumptions of this book is that *managerial concern for human beings is vital to the success of any organization.* The survivors are likely to be the organizations in which trust, positive attitudes, and an ample understanding of the human side of organizations exist. The development of an understanding of human behavior isn't easy, nor is the application of its concepts simple, but these activities are essential if organizational conflict is to be resolved, or better yet, prevented.

ORGANIZATIONS AND HUMAN BEHAVIOR

Is conflict inevitable?

Did you notice the subtitle of this chapter—"1 + 1 = Organization"? Whenever two or more persons have some mutual interest, an organization, in effect, exists. And whenever an organization exists, there is the potential for conflict resulting from myriad causes. Conflict isn't necessarily inevitable in every situation, but with the numerous differences among individuals, both in how they *perceive* and in the strengths of their *needs,* conflict among human beings is likely to be common in organizations. Considerable discord can also stem from difficulties in *communication,* for differences in the ways organizational members interpret words frequently lead to misunderstandings.

We can readily observe disharmony all around us, ranging from the relatively mild differences of opinion between two good friends to the brutal and destructive dissension among and within nations. Is all disagreement harmful? Not necessarily. Some types of conflict or differences of opinion can actually be beneficial to organizations by bringing fresh ideas to the surface and by discouraging complacency.

What Is Organizational Behavior?

Organizational behavior (OB), sometimes referred to as *human relations,* can be defined as *the study of the behavior of people and their relationships in organizations for the purpose of attempting to meld personal needs and objectives with the overall needs and objectives of the organization.*

How does OB differ from other behavioral sciences?

Organizational behavior as a field involves the application of skills garnered from the various behavioral sciences, such as psychology, sociology, and social anthropology. There is, however, a significant difference between OB and other fields. For example, psychology is concerned primarily with the scientific study of the behavior of individuals—why *people* behave as they do—and sociology emphasizes the scientific study of groups—why *groups* behave as they do. Social anthropology, a subfield of anthropology, is concerned with why *cultures* evolve and develop new customs, values, habits, and attitudes.

"Why" is a good
question, but *"what"*
helps get things done.

Organizational behavior is also concerned with the *why* of people and their groups, but it goes considerably further. In the study of OB, in addition to the *why,* we want to learn *what* can be done to anticipate, prevent, or resolve conflict among organizational members. The goals of an organization and the needs of its members are difficult to satisfy in an atmosphere of perpetual conflict.

In other words, our study of OB will be **action-oriented,** emphasizing the development of human relations skills for analyzing, preventing, and resolving behavioral problems within organizations.

What OB Is Not

The field of organizational behavior is significant because many problems and conflicts occur regularly among people in organizations. However, the intent of enhanced awareness of human behavior in organizations can easily be misunderstood. Its purpose is *not,* for example, to enable you to discover techniques for winning friends and influencing people through personality development. Nor is it intended to enable you to manipulate people as though they were puppets. Instead, its major objective is *to assist you in working more effectively with other people in organizations.*

Is *manipulation*
an OB skill?

You will soon discover, however, that the study of OB seldom provides the "correct" solutions to human problems, although an understanding of behavioral concepts should assist you in developing *better* solutions. Individuals who view events on a *two-valued* basis (a right-or-wrong, good-or-bad, one-answer philosophy) are often frustrated when they first confront a human behavior course and find that this narrow approach doesn't work.

Why study a field
without the answers?

There is a popular cliché that "working effectively with people is just plain common sense." The application of sound, people-oriented concepts to organizational behavior would seem to be plain common sense, but if this is true, why does there seem to be so much conflict in some organizations? The answer relates to the high degree of interdependence organizational members have with each other. Although

SOURCE: Reprinted by permission of UFS, Inc.

organizational members usually share certain common goals, they frequently must compete for limited organizational resources. Furthermore, value systems among organizational members may differ. Production managers, for example, may see a product primarily from the viewpoint of keeping production costs low, whereas marketing managers may see the same product from the standpoint of requiring features that appeal to the buying public, which may increase the production costs. Even members of the same department—such as those responsible for product development in a razor manufacturing company—may perceive things differently, some favoring the production and promotion of disposable razors while others favoring nondisposables. Working effectively with and through people, as you will see to a greater extent as you study this text, goes beyond mere common sense; it also requires an extensive understanding of the needs, values, and perceptions of human beings.

What Is an Organization?

In later chapters we'll discuss organizations in greater detail. For our purposes now, however, we should discover what is meant by the term **organization.** We've already learned that an organization can include two or more persons with some mutual interest. Any two individuals can experience some of the behavioral problems found in larger organizations.

Organizations can, however, be far more complex. If you have ever worked for an organization, you may have noticed something called an **organization chart,** which is really a guide to people's positions and their relationships in the formal organization. If you ever spend a fair amount of time in any organization, you're also likely to notice something called the informal organization, which encompasses the informal interaction that takes place among individuals in any group. These informal activities and relationships are not found in any company manual or organization chart. They could include cliques, those who cluster around the fax machine, and those who go out together for "happy hour."

Two Patterns of Structure

In any organization you'll usually find two principal patterns of structure, the *formal* and the *informal:*

1. The **formal organization** is the planned, or required, structure, and involves the official lines of authority and responsibility, ranging from the board of directors and president to the operative workers.

2. The **informal organization,** or emergent system, involves any natural self-grouping of individuals according to their personalities and needs rather than any formal plan.

As mentioned in the "To the Reader" section, for our purposes, the term *organization* can include not only business organizations but also governmental units, social organizations, cause-oriented groups, and even families.

A SMALL DOSE OF OB HISTORY

We needn't delve too deeply into the historical background of OB. However, some significant events are generally recognized as having influenced the greater human awareness that appears to exist today.

Industrialization—Farmers Leave the Soil

How ya gonna keep 'em down on the farm . . . ?

The stage was set for greater concern with organizational behavior at the beginning of industrialization in the mid-1800s, when farmers moved off the land and into towns in hope of improving their situations. Conditions in the early factories left much to be desired. Employees had to work extremely long hours for low pay, and were treated not unlike pieces of processed pigskin leather. Horrible working conditions persisted (some persons would argue that such conditions still exist in their organizations!) until the early years of the present century. There was little humane concern for the worker before the 1920s and 1930s. Managers tended to regard workers merely as factors of production fortunate to be employed.

Along Came Taylor, Gantt, and the Gilbreths

Not necessarily noted for his humanitarian views, F. W. Taylor entered the organizational scene in the early 1900s. He was concerned principally with efficiency and productivity in organizations and as a result became known as the **father of scientific management.** Systematically studying ways to improve productivity among steelworkers, he focused somewhat coldly on technical efficiency as an organizational goal, maintaining that, just as well-designed machinery could be made to operate more efficiently, so could people if their tasks were broken down into simple, repetitive, and specialized activities. The studies of Taylor and other proponents of scientific management, such as Henry L. Gantt and Frank B. and Lillian M. Gilbreth, did bring needed attention to the human being in organizations and were instrumental in the later development of the field of organizational behavior.[1]

Farmers *Have* Left the Soil[a]

There were 6,527,000 farms in the United States in 1938. There were fewer than one-third that number—slightly more than 2 million in the early 1990s. The nation's farm population plunged 24 percent to an estimated 4.6 million in 1990 from 6 million in 1980. Farm residents' share of the total population fell during the same period to 1.9 percent from 2.8 percent. The farm population has been going down since 1910 when it totaled 32 million, or 35 percent of the total U.S. population. Some of the reasons for the mass migration off the farm have been related to the waves of declared bankruptcies, especially by smaller farms, and the trend toward large agribusinesses and "factory farms" that are much more equipment intensive than labor intensive. So . . . how you gonna keep 'em down on the farm? You're not!

The scientific managers had much to learn about human behavior. Some significant errors in their reasoning included assuming that money would always motivate workers. They also assumed that workers would always act rationally, which has often proved to be an unsafe generalization.

Scientific managers also failed to anticipate the resistance that many workers would develop toward what were perceived as unrealistic standards. Workers were concerned that they would be fired if they *didn't* attain the higher standards. Some workers also feared that if they *did* attain these standards, then new and tougher ones would be established. These workers frequently believed that by not attaining new standards they would discourage managers from imposing higher standards (speedups) in the future.

Another shortcoming of scientific management was its failure to recognize the social needs of workers, that is, the need to feel a part of a group. Frequently, scientific managers would isolate workers and place them on a piecework type of compensation.

How About the Human Side of Organizations?
The excessive concern for production at the expense of the human element quite naturally brought about numerous organizational problems. As a result, an interest in the behavioral, or human, side of organizations developed in the 1920s.

Some research studies conducted in 1927 are said to have first established OB, then referred to as *human relations,* as a separate field. They were undertaken at the Hawthorne works of the Western Electric Company in Chicago by the late Elton Mayo (who became known as the **father of human relations**), F. J. Roethlisberger, and their colleagues at Harvard University.

Working conditions down, production up?

A series of studies involved altering the work environment of a group of production workers in the Relay Assembly Test Room. During the first study, the level of illumination within the work environment was periodically varied. During a follow-up study, 24 different working conditions were changed, sometimes improved and sometimes worsened. These conditions included rest breaks and workday length. However, to the researchers' amazement, production rates kept climbing and morale improved regardless of the changes made.

Many present-day students of human behavior are somewhat surprised at how basic the results of the study actually were. In short, the researchers discovered that when workers are treated like human beings rather than robots and when they have feelings of pride and personal worth on their jobs as well as the opportunity to get things off their chests, morale and productivity tend to rise.

A new expression was born out of the Hawthorne studies, the **Hawthorne effect,** which refers to *any improvement in worker performance that is the by-product of attention and feeling of self-worth.* The employees studied at the Hawthorne works had received more attention than a typical grandmother gives her grandchildren at Thanksgiving.

The Depressing Effect of the 1930s

What caused the workers' unrest?

The shock effect of the Great Depression of the 1930s, with almost 25 percent of the American labor force unemployed in 1933, stimulated the cohesiveness and militancy of labor union groups. Managers of the day discovered the need to develop an entirely new style of industrial relations. The antiunion efforts of industrial leaders seemed only to increase militant activities. The judicial and legislative branches of the government began to reverse their previously unsympathetic stance toward collective bargaining. Workers' sitdowns became common practice. In 1937, for example, the General Motors Corporation agreed to recognize the United Automobile Workers after employees had taken over the plant for almost three months.

A significant, albeit tragic, event occurred in 1937, when 10 persons were killed and 80 wounded during a Memorial Day clash between police and members of the Steel Workers Organizing Committee at the plant of the Republic Steel Company of South Chicago. Although the gulf between management and workers remained to some degree, this event and others like it began to set the tone for a new consciousness of the role of human beings in organizations.

Recent Trends in Organizational Behavior

It's easy to misunderstand the conclusions of past OB studies by assuming that researchers in the field claimed that happy workers were always productive workers. There may or may not be a relationship between happiness and productivity. A group of employees, for example, may be *happily* talking about yesterday's Superbowl game in the photocopying room, engaged in little in the way of production. Happiness alone doesn't beget productivity.

"I'm happiest when I'm loafin'!"

In recent decades, many managers have been "running scared" as a result of the competition brought about by Japan, South Korea, China, and other newly industrialized nations in world markets. New buzzwords and packages were created for many already established behavioral concepts. Let's take a look at some of the more common ones:

Human Resource Management (HRM). A modern and positive approach to organizational behavior is what is termed **human resource management,** which emphasizes empowering employees with the right to be involved in decision making in the organization. The approach attempts to cultivate workers' abilities and is likewise concerned with their personal needs.

Total Quality Management (TQM). Strongly influenced by the Japanese approach to management, American managers have become increasingly concerned with quality. Consequently, another word being kicked around organizational training sessions these days is **total quality management (TQM).** Simply stated, TQM means focusing all of a company's energies on improving the quality of its work. TQM is an ongoing process that requires all individuals within an organization to be motivated toward the goal of continuous improvement and meeting the needs of customers.[2]

Quality of Work Life (QWL). A related concept, **quality of work life (QWL),** also has become well-known among professional managers in recent years. QWL refers to how effectively the job environment meets the needs and values of employees. We'll explore TQM, QWL, and other current organizational practices in later sections of this text.

The Decline of Union Membership

A **union** can be defined as *an association of workers that has as its major objective the improvement of conditions related to employment.*

A
GLOBAL
GLANCE

HRM in Action at This Plant[b]

The Courtaulds Fibres Company in Grimsby, England, discovered the benefits of human resource management (HRM) in the late 1980s. Under Courtaulds' system, work has been rearranged to give downstream managers and supervisors more responsibility and to imbue all employees with a greater sense of commitment. According to Ashley Hall, a senior technician (the company's name for supervisor), "The management never used to appreciate the intelligence of the workers on the shop floor. They told them the bare necessities and did not want them to get involved with any decision making." The plant now attempts to involve workers in production changes and decision making more fully. Senior technicians are responsible for training employees to do each other's jobs. A goal is to enable employees to develop a common sense of identity with both each other and the company. Some employees opposed the change to HRM techniques at first. But things seem to be going fairly smoothly now, with favorable reactions from most of the employees.

The words *conditions* can represent anything from higher wages to a day off with pay on an employee's birthday. Unions exist in countries throughout the world. Union activity has long had a significant effect on organizations.

Trends in Union Membership.   What has been happening to labor union membership in recent decades? The 1980s were rough for unions, not only in the United States but throughout most of the free-market industrialized countries of the world. For example, the average share of trade union membership among total employees in 18 countries of the Organization for Economic Cooperation and Development (OECD) declined from 35 percent in 1980 to 28 percent in 1988.[3]

The aggregate figures, however, are a bit misleading. The decline in membership in the 1980s in highly unionized countries such as Italy, Australia, and the United Kingdom merely removed gains made during the previous decade. In reality, union coverage in the United Kingdom fell by only 3.3 percent and actually rose in both Italy and Australia. And among the OECD countries, unions are

TABLE 1.1   Degree of Unionization (as % of work force, 1990).

Denmark	80%
Belgium	75%
United Kingdom	43%
West Germany (prior to reunification)	42%
Italy	40%
Japan	27%
Netherlands	26%
United States	16%
France	10%

SOURCE: DGB (German Federation of Unions) and OECD (Organization for Economic Cooperation and Development).

generally stronger in the public than in the private sector, having grown from an average of 29.6 percent of total employment in 1970 to 38.1 percent in 1988.[4]

The United States Story. The United States provides a different story, however. Union membership as a proportion of the total U.S. work force has declined substantially during the past half century, from a peak of 35.5 percent in 1945 to slightly less than 16 percent in recent years. If government workers are excluded, less than 12 percent of the U.S. work force belongs to a union. In relation to other industrialized countries, the United States is now near the bottom of the union membership list (see Table 1.1).[5]

Success creates failure? Hmmm . . . Strange!

Some observers of the labor union scene contend that unions are weaker in the U.S. primarily because of their success in raising the wages of their members. The difference between union and nonunion wages, for example, is twice as high in the U.S. as it is in some other countries, such as Germany, the United Kingdom, and Australia.[6] The high union markup, it is argued, gives American employers the incentive to use hard-line techniques with union officials. Unions generally face less hostility from employers in countries where bargaining takes place for nonmembers as well as union members.

Fewer Smokestacks? Another general factor in the fall of union membership is believed to be the relative decline in the manufacturing and construction industries—so-called smokestack manufacturing. This trend should not be too surprising in light of the laborsaving technologies, such as **robotics,** that have been introduced in recent decades. *Robotics* is the use of mechanical equipment that duplicates human physical motions for the purpose of reducing or eliminating human labor. Such equipment can even exceed human physical motions.

The Trend Toward Harder-Line Bargaining. The trend toward a harder-line approach to bargaining with employee unions in the U.S. became evident after a strike called by the Professional Air Traffic Controllers Organization (PATCO) in August 1981 resulted in the firing of 11,500 controllers by the Reagan administration and the decertification of the union. Since then many firms, such as Greyhound Lines and Caterpillar Corporation, have threatened union officials with bankruptcy, plant relocation, or the hiring of replacement workers. Unions seem to have lost some of their punch in the 1990s. However, unions should not be considered dead yet. The declining trend could quickly reverse itself if employees generally believe that employers are taking undue advantage of them. A lack of concern for the quality of employees' work life prior to the 1930s was a principal reason for the rapid growth of labor unions in the first place.

Will there be a revival of unions in the 2000's?

OB—Here to Stay?

At times, the growing awareness of the human side of organizations has approached the proportions of a fad. At other times, a humanistic concern for the employee seems to have done some slipping and sliding, since not everyone is convinced of the usefulness of a positive approach to human behavior—after all, fear *does* motivate. An attitude that can still be felt around some organizations goes something like this:

"You're right. . . . Fear does motivate. I quit!"

> I'm not running a country club. My job is to make a profit. If my employees don't like the way I run things, they can go somewhere else. Love it or leave it, I say. There are lots of people eager to take their places!

There is also a potentially dangerous side effect that exists during periods when the dollar is "cheaper" in international markets. A lower-valued dollar makes U.S.-made products more competitively priced abroad, which could instill complacency in American managers. Despite such attitudes, however, too much irreversible change has taken place in our social structure for sensitive organizational members to ignore human factors.

Why aren't there rules of OB?

As we approach the twenty-first century, we see that OB is not yet, nor will it ever be, an absolute science. There are neither magic formulas nor lists of "10 simple rules" that can be applied to specific problems. Human beings can't be poured into test tubes like so many grams of a chemical for the purpose of controlled experiments. Firms that have appeared to be models of "excellence" in one period have turned out to be failures after a relatively short time. Consequently, there isn't likely to be complete agreement about which behavioral concepts are the most acceptable. Nonetheless, there are concepts that if learned and applied can aid us in preventing and resolving conflicts among people in organizations.

INDIVIDUAL AND ORGANIZATIONAL NEEDS

What is it that motivates you to work? Do you feel that unless you work, your needs for food, shelter, or a car will go unsatisfied? The income you receive for working helps to satisfy such material needs and wants.

Personal Needs Affect the Organization

How do your needs affect your work?

Individuals bring their personal needs to the organizations in which they work. These needs are partially material and economic, partially social and psychological. The personal needs of employees can have significant effects on the organizations themselves. For example, your personal needs strongly influence your motivation and attitude toward your job. Managers, especially, should attempt to understand human needs because they influence the attitudes and behavior of employees.

Organizations Need Order and Predictability

Can an organization survive without order?

Try to imagine any organization attempting to accomplish specific goals without some sort of order or guidelines. Freedom for all organizational members to do whatever they want may seem desirable in some situations, but most organizations, however progressive or enlightened, would find survival under such conditions extremely difficult. An organization without some structure can be compared to an airport that has no ground or air control over the airplanes using its facilities. Imagine the chaos that would result.

Why don't all rules seem reasonable?

Almost any well-run organization that you work for is likely to have a set of rules—sometimes called *policies, procedures,* or *guidelines*—designed not to restrict creativity but to assist its members in the accomplishment of organizational goals. You are also likely to find that most organizations have some rules that seem reasonable and others that appear ridiculous. Utopia is difficult to find. Since you'll probably never work for an organization that seems absolutely perfect, your next best approach when seeking a position might be to attempt to find one that provides you with a reasonable amount of satisfaction according to your own values. Organizations, like people, have personalities. You probably feel more comfortable around some types of personalities than around others.

Most well-managed organizations, therefore, will have some order and predictability, referred to—you may recall from an earlier discussion—as their **required system** (the formal organization). But, regardless of how energetically the management enforces and coordinates formal policies, the **emergent system,** or informal, types of behavior related to personal needs will tend to evolve. The needs of workers create many behavioral situations that can't be found in any company manual and should be handled on an individual basis.

Organizational Needs and Values Result in Organizational Culture
Organizations have what is referred to as an **organizational culture,** consisting of the values that its members—leaders and employees alike—bring to the work environment. One of the major purposes of this book is to expose you to some modern people-oriented concepts that when effectively applied can assist you in understanding, adapting to, and influencing the culture of organizations.

**A QUESTION
OF
ETHICS**

Employee Pilferage—A Burning Issue[c]

Twenty-five dead from smoke inhalation and 55 injured, all employees of a chicken-processing plant. Why dead and injured? One might say because chickens had allegedly been stolen from the plant.

The disaster occurred during a fire on September 3, 1991, at the Imperial Food Products plant in Hamlet, North Carolina. Investigators contended that management had bolted the emergency exits on the outside because of concern over employee pilfering. Investigators also testified that emergency lights, the alarm system, and the sprinkler system were all inoperative prior to the blaze. The exit doors had signs *on the outside* warning, "Fire door—Do not block." Yet, there was no marking on the inside. Employees told members of Congress that they were given no instructions on what to do in case of fire.

A Question of Ethics: Assume that you were the employer and you suspected that employees were stealing company materials. Do you feel that it is ethical to prevent employees from leaving the premises through the emergency exits? What might be a better solution to the problem of pilferage?

Who's responsible for
the organizational
culture?

As mentioned in the "To the Reader" section, the application of good organizational behavior skills is the responsibility of *everyone* in an organization. *Managers* have the primary responsibility for establishing and maintaining a favorable organizational culture, but the workers also have a strong influence over the culture and should share the responsibility for it. More will be discussed on the concept of organizational culture in a later chapter.

DECISION MAKING IN ORGANIZATIONS

How do you decide
how to make
decisions?

Regardless of your position in an organization, you have to make decisions in your daily activities. Your personal life is also beset by decision-making responsibilities. Any decisions that you make about human relations problems are strongly influenced by your past experiences, your perceptual skills, and your assumptions about a particular situation.

There are numerous ways to make decisions. Some are made on the basis of fallacious generalizations, snap judgments, intuition, and hearsay. More scientific and logical approaches are, however, available and should be followed. The next chapter discusses how your perceptual skills influence your decisions and suggests a more scientific approach to problem solving.

Rational Decisions Within the Limits of Time

Thinking it so doesn't
make it so.

In the everyday world of work we don't have endless amounts of time to spend analyzing problems. To save time in the longer run, we should attempt to gather as much useful information as possible (within the time available) about a specific problem before making up our minds. Before attempting to define a particular problem, we should try to see the situation as it *really* is and not as we *think* it is.

Situational Thinking

When confronting a particular problem, you should remember that each situation differs from others in certain respects. You may have previously confronted a similar problem, but chances are that it wasn't identical. For example, assume that you are a supervisor who must resolve a serious conflict between two subordinates. You recall how you resolved a similar situation in the past and decide to employ the same technique. Will it work? Perhaps. Perhaps not. Sometimes attempting the same solution will backfire because of the individual differences among the persons involved in the problem.

Therefore, when confronting problems you might do well to apply **situational thinking,** a method of confronting human relations problems by *drawing on past experience and knowledge but recogniz-*

ing that each situation is unique and may require a distinct solution. There's nothing particularly wrong with looking to the past for assistance, but you should recognize that the present and future aren't always identical to the past.

SOME WORDS TO THE WISE: TIPS ON HOW TO LEARN FROM THIS TEXT

If you've invested money and time in buying and reading a text on organizational behavior, you probably would like to recover your investment. Part of your return on investment includes being able to *apply* the concepts contained in this text, which can assist you in accomplishing many of your lifelong goals. While studying organizational behavior as a means of helping you to maximize your return, a few basic learning principles discussed in the following paragraphs could be well worth your while.

Do You Have a Motivated Interest in the Subject?

Will your interest level give you a high yield?

An enlightened philosopher once said, "There is no such thing as an *uninteresting subject,* only *disinterested people.*" Although most students identify easily with people-oriented material, it is essential that you have an interest in what you are learning. A lack of interest tends to result in a lack of learning. Interest can be generated more easily when you attempt to perceive a link between your studies and your daily activities.

Do You Make a Deliberate Effort to Remember?

Learning is typically not an automatic process; it takes some effort and concentration on the part of the would-be learner. To illustrate, some years ago television weather forecasters reported temperatures in both Fahrenheit and Celsius. Yet, even the most avid among weather watchers failed to grasp Celsius, a relatively simple and highly logical system. Their major difficulty was allowing the information to "go in one ear and out the other," so to speak, that is, not

Is tension *good?*

making a deliberate effort to learn the Celsius system. When you are too comfortable and relaxed, you may find yourself wasting a lot of your learning efforts. A reasonable amount of controlled tension can help you learn more effectively.

Do You Organize Your Studying Efforts?

Try to develop a workable system for organizing your studying activities. For example, clustering facts and concepts into meaningful categories can help you recall the learned material when it is needed.

Build the framing first.

Browsing quickly through the chapter prior to actually studying it, also reading each heading and subheading, provides a sort of frame work onto which you can build added knowledge once you begin to study the chapter. In addition, be certain to read the *learning objectives* that precede each chapter—they will furnish you with a clearer idea of what you are expected to gain from your efforts.

Do You Verbalize the Concepts Aloud?

You *recognize* but do you *recall?*

Recognizing previously studied material is typically easier than *recalling* and *reciting* it aloud to another person. However, what we really seek from our studying efforts is being able to *recall, recite,* and *apply*. To accomplish the latter three, review the material with another person. Ask each other questions related to the material. Answer the questions in your own words, which aids in transferring the material from your short-term memory, where it can be easily lost, to your long-term memory, where it becomes relatively permanent. Furthermore, if you are unable to answer your colleague's questions, you are unlikely to recall the answers at quiz or examination time, or when you need to apply the material to a real-life situation.

Could You Utilize a Tape Recorder?

Concepts on wheels!

Another way of verbalizing the concepts that you desire to learn, along with applying the concept of spaced repetition, is to use a tape recorder. Consider outlining your reading in question and answer form on an audio recorder. Later, while riding in your car, jogging, or doing routine chores around the house, you can play back your outline. The more exposure you have to the concepts, the easier it should be for you to recall them.

Are You Applying the Concept of *Spaced Repetition?*

Should you study until you drop?

Spaced repetition means reviewing material during relatively short study periods broken up by intervals of rest or diversion. Studying in short but frequent segments tends to reduce mental and physical fatigue and helps improve your long-term retention and maintain your motivation. Try to avoid studying to the point where little learning is resulting from your efforts.

Do You Attempt to Associate New Facts with Known Facts?

"Well, what do you know about that?"

Try to make an association between the new information you read and information that you already know. Doing so helps you to retain the new concepts. For example, you may have already learned about Maslow's motivational theories in a course in psychology. Relating what you already understand about motivation can make learning how it affects organizational behavior more meaningful.

Have You *Role Assumed* the Case Incidents?

An invaluable part of any study of OB can include the use of role assuming. Situations in a classroom aren't exactly identical to situations you may confront at work, nor can you acquire skills solely from lectures or books. You may have discovered that you can't become skillful in a sport, be it tennis, skiing, or wind surfing, just by reading a how-to book on the subject. You must practice.

A related old tale helps to demonstrate this concept:

> A confused-looking young violinist carrying his bass violin in New York City came across a taxi driver and asked, "Can you please give me directions on how I can get to Carnegie Hall?"
> The driver, without hesitation, quickly responded, "Practice, practice, practice!"

The same condition holds true for the study of organizational behavior. You must practice the application of effective OB concepts so that you can learn to use them skillfully. **Role assuming** is the concept of creating a more realistic situation, usually one of human problems and conflicts, and then acting out the various parts.

There's the tendency when asked what *you* would do about a given problem to respond, "Well, if I were Jennifer, I would . . ." In the real world of organizations you don't resolve problems this way; you must engage in certain types of actions usually involving face-to-face conversation and interaction. Role assuming should, therefore, closely approximate a real situation and afford participants the vicarious experiences that enhance their sensitivity, growth, and development.[7]

As a parting note to this first chapter, you might want to contemplate the words of the famous playwright, George Bernard Shaw:

> When I was a young man, I observed that one out of ten things I did were failures. I didn't want to be a failure, so I did ten times more work.

SUMMARY

Organizational behavior (OB), like other behavioral sciences, attempts to explain human behavior in organizations. OB, however, goes beyond explaining *why* individuals or groups behave as they do and strives to determine *what can be done* in a positive way about human behavior that may disrupt organizational objectives. It is also concerned with employee quality of work life (QWL), that is, how effectively the organization meets the needs of its employees.

The concern for human resources grew out of the industrialization movement. F. W. Taylor, the father of scientific management, emphasized technical efficiency. Greater human relations awareness resulted from the research studies at Hawthorne made by Elton Mayo, the father of human relations, and his associates from Harvard University.

To survive effectively, organizations require a reasonable amount of predictability and order. The organizational climate should be determined by an organization's managers; however, the application of organizational behavior skills is the responsibility of everyone in organizations.

Individuals attempting to resolve problems rationally should apply *situational thinking* and recognize the need for obtaining relevant information within the time available.

Applying the chapter suggestions on how to learn from this text can help to recoup your investment of money and time.

TERMS AND CONCEPTS TO REMEMBER

organizational behavior	total quality management (TQM)
action-oriented	quality of work life (QWL)
organization	union
organization chart	robotics
formal organization	required system
informal organization	emergent system
father of scientific management	organizational culture
father of human relations	situational thinking
Hawthorne effect	role assuming
human resource management	

QUESTIONS

1. Are all types of organizational conflict harmful? Explain.

2. What benefits can be derived from studying a subject, such as organizational behavior, that doesn't provide the "correct" answers to all behavioral problems?

3. What is meant by the statement, "The study of OB is action oriented"?

4. What is a significant difference between the *formal* and the *informal* organization?

5. What is the major significance of the Hawthorne studies?

6. On what does the *human resource management* approach focus?

7. What is the general nature of *TQM?*

8. What has been the trend of union membership in recent decades? What has caused this trend?

9. How do the personal needs of employees affect organizations?

10. What potential dangers can you foresee for an *excessively* ordered and predictable organization?

11. Do you feel that managers striving to accomplish their goals more effectively should attempt to prohibit the emergent, or informal, organization? Explain.

12. What is a major advantage of an experiential case incident approach to learning organizational behavior concepts over an approach that is limited to lectures alone?

13. What is the difference between *recognizing* and *recalling* previously studied information? Which is more important? Why?

APPLICATIONS

1.1 Don't Rock the Boat

Janet Yee, a lab technician at Medico Pharmaceuticals, Inc., asked to see Lionel Adams, her section supervisor. As she entered his office, she wondered if he would have the resourcefulness to attack her problem head on.

"What can I do for you, Janet?" Lionel asked.

"I've come up with a solution to the scheduling problem on the flu vaccine project. I think that if we just set up the batches differently, we can test the vaccine samples in less time than we're taking now. The time we'd save at the testing stage might put us back on track for the shipping deadline and—"

"That's fine, Janet," Lionel interrupted. "But you should be suggesting the change to Bill Mastrioni, your team leader, not me."

"That's just the problem, Lionel," Janet replied. "I've suggested my solution to him, and a couple of the other members of our team agree it's worth a try. But Bill rejected the idea before he'd even finished hearing it. All he said was, 'It doesn't sound like such a good idea to me, so forget it.' "

"Have any of the others in your group tried to approach him with the idea?" Lionel asked, checking his watch.

"No. You know Bill can be really unpleasant if he thinks he's being crossed. Nobody seems to want to take him on, and so we continue operating with a procedure that is delaying the whole project. I mean, what's the point of putting so much work and money into a new flu vaccine if it's not going to be ready in time for flu season?"

Lionel sat back in his chair and pondered what Janet had said. Then, glancing again at his watch, he said, "Janet, I believe in allowing my team leaders to run their own show. If I get involved here it will only create greater disharmony. It's *your* work team and *your* responsibility to get the job done. Bill can have a short fuse, I know. Still, I expect you folks to work out such matters among yourselves without rocking the boat unnecessarily. Now, if you'll excuse me, I'm running late for a meeting."

As Janet made her way back to her workstation, she thought to herself, "This is just crazy! They want us to do a good job and meet deadlines, yet they won't try anything new just because it might wound some guy's ego!"

Questions

1. Evaluate Lionel's response to Janet. How does he see his role in maintaining employee relations? What responsibility does Janet think Lionel should be taking? What role do you think Lionel should play? Why?

2. Whose responsibility is it to resolve this dispute? Why?

3. Is Janet's dismay at the apparently irrational behavior of her co-workers justified? What needs are at play for all the various characters in the case, and how have they affected each other's actions?

1.2 Whose Organization Is This, Anyway?

"I don't know what in the world could have made you people think that a nice, quiet, behind-the-scenes outreach project aimed at cosmetic companies and hamburger restaurants is the kind of activity this group should pursue. It doesn't take a rocket scientist to figure out that if we're going to save animals' lives, we have to make brutal, inhumane practices visible for all to see. Linda, how could you be so stupid? You just never seem to be able to get with the program!"

Linda Robinson's face burned as the humiliating words stung her one by one. This wasn't the first time Darcy Cantrell, assistant to the executive director of Humans for Animals, an animal-rights group, had lashed out at a task-force leader. Humans for Animals was dedicated to the principle that nonhuman species have an independent right to live free of exploitation for commercial, entertainment, or any other purposes. Darcy was deeply committed to her work, so much so that she often responded angrily when the results of the group's decision-making process did not conform to her sense of priorities.

Darcy's previous victim had been Darren Little, who headed the task force on protecting wild animals' natural habitats. His big mistake had been trying to coordinate an activity of Humans for Animals with a project that the Sierra Club already had up and running. Darren had figured that Humans for Animals would be able to work for wilderness preservation while achieving two additional ends: enhancing its public image through a connection with a better known group and avoiding duplicate programs. A higher public profile and one less program of its own would enable Humans for Animals to both raise and conserve precious funds for other activities; at the same time, the right of animals to live in their natural surroundings would be safeguarded. Darcy, as usual, disagreed.

"Darren, compromising with the mainstream is exactly what we *don't* want to do," Darcy had exploded, pounding her fist on the table. "I've been shouting myself hoarse trying to communicate the fact that it's going to take swift, decisive action to stop the forces that want to destroy animal habitats to make the world safe for strip mining! And I'm sure that's what our supporters want us to do. Granted, blockading the zoo on Children's Day—yes, I organized that on my own—wasn't exactly a public-relations triumph for us. Contributions have fallen off since then, and as a result we've had to drop our animal adoption project. Still, Darren, any fool could tell you and the other whiz kids on your team that it's crazy to alienate the more activist segments of the animal movement, even if they do offend some people. All you Einsteins should at least make an effort to keep that in mind."

Darren's fall from favor had occurred at last month's executive board meeting. The five task-force leaders had been there, as well as several other members of Humans for Animals and some observers from allied animal-rights groups. Today, the conference room was full once again, and it was Linda's turn to feel Darcy's wrath. The unfairness of Darcy's attack was especially wounding to Linda because she had worked nights and weekends to prepare her presentation. It outlined the Industry Task Force's plan to promote, among other things, the introduction of vegetarian items on fast-food menus and alternatives to animal testing of cosmetics. She and all the members of her team had spent weeks talking to corporate executives. She discovered that many of them agreed with her ideas but feared the adverse publicity that might result from trying to work with an organization known for its confrontational tactics. These conversations had convinced her that the task force could reach more of its goals faster if, in this case, it used a different approach, a more low-key one specifically tailored to businesses. She had never specifically discussed tactics with Darcy, but, as far as Linda could tell, "up against the wall" was Darcy's sole approach to everything.

It wasn't just the sacrifice of time that made Linda angry, even though it had come during a period when her husband was out of work and her family responsibilities were greater than usual. It was that she always worked so hard on her projects—always got them done on time and always achieved results—but never seemed to get any credit. Darcy worked nearly around the clock herself and didn't notice other people's office lights burning late into the evening. And as for the credit—well, Linda thought, Darcy sure knows how to put out a snappy press release and smile for the cameras when we're picketing a fur store!

This time, Linda decided she'd had enough of Darcy's bullying. The woman simply had no feelings at all. Linda's first thought was to go to Faye MacReady, the executive director of Humans for Animals and Darcy's boss, to ask her to do something about Darcy and the atmosphere that had developed in the organization. Everyone had taken to feuding with co-workers and belittling them in public. It was becoming hard to get anything done in a place where everyone seemed to be at everyone else's throat. Linda had to acknowledge that she herself had dressed down some colleagues in the past week or so, but she had been on a deadline with the task force's presentation, and shouting was the only way to accomplish anything. Faye had to be made aware of what was happening.

But with that thought, Linda's hopes sank. Why should it be necessary to make Faye aware of a situation that was painfully obvious? True, Faye had to travel a lot to raise funds, attend conferences, and make media appearances. Even when she was in the office, though, Faye often seemed to be "away." Staff memos went unanswered, reports languished unread, meetings were never scheduled, and names of co-workers were never learned or were quickly forgotten.

Linda pondered her options as she sat alone in her cubicle after the meeting. She decided to try to talk with Faye the next morning. But what would she bring to the discussion—a list of recommendations for organizational change or a letter of resignation?

Questions
1. Describe the culture of this cause-oriented organization, Humans for Animals. How do you think the culture developed? What would it take to change it?

2. Consider each character's view of the goals and needs of the organization. Do all the characters see these goals and needs in the same way? If not, exactly how do their views differ? What is the effect of each view on the organization?

3. Why did Darcy attack Linda's proposal? What does their confrontation tell you about their individual needs? If you were supervising both employees, what would you say to them to help them resolve their conflict?

4. How are decisions made at Humans for Animals? Is there a formal structure set up for decision making? If so, is it functioning as intended?

5. Suppose Faye MacReady sought out an expert on human resources management. What advice might that expert offer about the conflicts in the organization?

1.3 The Case of the Uneven Playing Field

"What we have here is the downside of downsizing," thought Chris Espinosa as he read the page for the third time. It was a copy of a memo from Rex Brown, chief operating officer of OmniPro, Inc., a large sporting-goods manufacturer, to Chris's supervisor, Joan Dudley-Haines, vice-president of marketing. A Post-It note was stuck on the copy: "Please let me have your ideas on this ASAP—JD-H."

Joan had hired Chris just three weeks earlier to take over OmniPro's customer-service department following the promotion of the previous department head. What Chris found on his arrival was a bare-bones staff and a suddenly rocketing work load. During the recent economic recession, OmniPro, like many other companies, had taken severe measures to cut costs, and a number of full-time positions had been eliminated. Now, with signs of recovery beginning to appear, consumers were opening their wallets and seemed to be ready to spend once again. OmniPro's sales were up strongly for the first time in seven quarters, resulting in additional customers and an increase in customer-service inquiries—more, in fact, than Chris's shrunken department could handle. Chris had discussed the situation with Joan, and they concluded that, given the company's emphasis on cost control, Chris would have to do the best he could with the resources he had. But that was before Rex Brown's memo.

Brown was not only OmniPro's COO; he was also chairman of the new Total Quality Management Committee, which comprised all the company's executive officers and vice-presidents. Brown had become a firm believer in TQM principles, and he established the committee at the top-management level to show his—and OmniPro's—total commitment to total quality. It was in his capacity as the TQM Committee chairman that Brown had written the memo to Dudley-Haines. In it, he emphasized that responsiveness to the customer is a critical TQM concept, and he expressed concern about several matters: Callers were having to wait as long as 15 minutes to get through on the company's "800" number; customer-service representatives were rushing callers off the telephone lines without fully answering their questions; written inquiries often were not answered for two weeks or longer; and representatives were not following through on problems to get them solved. Worst of all, some customers who telephoned were getting bounced around from one extension to another without receiving the information they sought. Brown stated that he viewed these difficulties with the utmost concern and urged that they receive prompt attention. There was no need for him to say more: To ensure the TQM Committee's clout, Brown had given it the responsibility to review all pay raises and bonuses for every department and work group in the company. Joan got Chris immediately on the case.

Chris was not altogether unhappy about Brown's memo. "Here," he thought, "is the go-ahead I need to request some additional customer-service staff"—something he had wanted to do almost from his first day at OmniPro. He knew his people were doing their best, but they were stressed-out and putting in too much overtime. More workers were the only solution to the problems Brown had described. Joan agreed. They both knew, though, that most of the other departments were working short-handed and that a number of department heads had already begun the hiring-request procedure. They also knew that the hiring process was long, with many approvals required along the company's chain of command, up to and including OmniPro's president. Nevertheless, Chris and Joan felt confident that given Rex Brown's preoccupation with customer service and TQM, their request for additional staff would be given top priority.

Six weeks went by, however, with no word of a decision about Chris's request for personnel. What he did find out was that Don DiBello, head of the sales department, had a new administrative assistant working in his group. Don hadn't even mentioned a hiring request at the department managers' meetings. How was he able to get additional staff so fast?

Chris decided to go straight to the source and ask Don. "Chris," Don explained, "there are formal procedures and there are . . . other ways of getting things done. You're new, so I'll fill you in. Joe Frank was an administrative assistant in accounting. Not long ago, I heard through the grapevine that he wanted out of that department, and his supervisor, Meg Warshawski, who's a friend of mine—we started out together in accounts receivable—wasn't all that eager to keep him around. Joe didn't have any particular department in mind that he wanted to transfer to, so I asked him, with Meg's permission, if he'd be interested in coming over to sales. He said okay. So a couple of weeks ago, Meg and I got together with Tina Rae, who works for Leah Scher, the human resources VP. Tina used her contacts to push Joe's transfer through, and now he's providing clerical support for one of our sales teams."

Chris could feel his irritation building. "It seems to me that if an employee wants a transfer and the supervisor agrees to it, the other department heads who have made staffing requests through the proper channels ought to have the opportunity to find out whether that employee would be interested in joining their group. Why do we have these procedures, anyhow, if not to allocate resources in a way that's both fair to everyone—managers and the rank-and-file alike—and beneficial to the company? Rex Brown is leaning heavily on my boss about customer-service problems, and she's leaning on me to straighten them out. I just can't do that without more people, and I don't get an even shot at the employees who are available. It's not right!"

"Look, it's a fact of life in organizations that things don't always happen by the book," Don replied. "But if you want to talk about allocation of resources, just consider how long it takes to get approval for a new hire and how much paperwork is involved if you follow the official procedures. I needed someone right away, and I got someone right away—to my mind, that's excellent resource allocation. And I can prove the benefit with this month's sales figures."

Chris was unimpressed. "Maybe it's excellent resource allocation for you," he said, "but it isn't for me or for any of the other managers who are desperate for staff. Somebody has to be the referee—somebody has to decide whose personnel requests should get priority. It shouldn't come down to who you're friends with in the company. I don't know many people here yet, but I can tell you for a fact that the COO happens to think that customer service is pretty important."

Don was starting to feel hot under the collar, too. "Rex Brown also happens to think that the bottom line is pretty important. My sales reps are 25 percent more productive now that they have a support person to handle their paperwork and keep track of their schedules. Brown came back from that executive retreat all gung-ho about TQM, but you can be sure he hasn't forgotten the lesson of the recession—without sales there's no money and no company, period! It's a safe bet that he won't be talking about TQM principles with the stockholders at the end of the year; he'll be talking sales and profits."

"And what do you think will happen to those sales and profits if the customers receive poor service and don't come back?" Chris retorted. "You're thinking short term. Customer service is this company's future."

Questions

1. Evaluate Chris Espinosa's and Don DiBello's arguments. Do you think one of them is right? Explain your answer.

2. Describe the formal organization and the informal organization at OmniPro. In what ways are they related to each other? What purposes does each fulfill?

3. If you were Rex Brown, what decision would you make about the staff increases?

NOTES

1. Frederick W. Taylor, *The Principles of Scientific Management* (New York: Harper and Brothers, 1911).

2. Mike Farrish, "World class performance through Total Quality Management," *Financial Times,* Management Consultancy Special Section, May 15, 1991, p. V.

3. Edward Balls, "Trends in Trade Union Membership in the 1980s," *Financial Times,* August 5, 1991, p. 4.

4. See note 3.

5. "Labour Negotiations—The Annual Ritual," *German Brief,* February 7, 1992, p. 11.

6. See note 3.

7. Adapted very loosely from *Keys to Efficient Learning,* distributed to faculty members of the Peralta Community College District Academic Senate, Oakland, California.

BOX NOTES

a. Adapted from Diane Crispell, "U.S. Farm Population Continues to Erode," *The Wall Street Journal,* June 15, 1992, p. B1.

b. Adapted from Michael Smith, "A Hands-On Role for Supervisors," *Financial Times,* February 1, 1991, p. 10.

c. Adapted from "U.S. Inspectors to help N.C. Push Work Safety," *The New York Times,* as reported in *The Stars and Stripes,* October 25, 1991, p. 4; and Colleen M. O'Neill, "North Carolina Fire Sparks National Outcry," *AFL-CIO News,* September 16, 1991, pp. 1, 12.

CHAPTER 2

A Look at Human Perception

*There's More to
Perception Than Meets
the Eye*

**When you finish this chapter,
you should be able to:**

1
Recognize the difference between a fact and an inference.
2
List the factors that influence what a person sees in a given situation.
3
List and describe at least five pitfalls in logical reasoning.
4
Summarize the seven-step system for problem solving.
5
Explain the nature of intuition in the decision-making process.
6
Describe the four pitfalls to effective decision making.
7
Describe how creativity can aid the problem-solving process.

> The senses do not give us a picture of the world directly; rather they provide evidence for checking hypotheses about what lies before us.
>
> *Professor Richard L. Gregory*

> Our minds are always mixing memory and desire.
>
> *Anonymous*

Have you noticed that many people tend to be enamored with the "correct" answers to questions? Quiz shows, for example, have long been a favorite of many television watchers. Question-and-answer parlor games, too, have been perennial best-sellers. Unfortunately, in the real world of organizations, especially their human side, absolute answers are not as clear-cut. "Facts" that at one time appear to be absolutely correct frequently turn out to be falsehoods.

Decisions have to be made daily in organizations. It is important for decision makers to perceive things as they really are in order to make accurate and useful decisions. We must continually be on guard against the tendency of believing that we see the "truth" in a human behavior situation before we've uncovered ample facts. Perhaps the late philosopher-mathematician Bertrand Russell hit the galvanized nail squarely on its round head when he said:

> Those who believe themselves to be absolutely right are often absolutely wrong.

In this chapter we are going to explore some of the major concepts of *perception* in the hope that an understanding of them will help you to perceive organizational situations more accurately. We will also explore some of the major *fallacies in logic,* a knowledge of which can aid you in avoiding some of the common pitfalls in perception and decision making. We will also look at a well-known method for solving organizational problems and making decisions, the *seven-step method.* We will conclude with an overview of the nature of *creativity,* a characteristic that can also aid substantially in the problem-solving and decision-making processes.

THE IMPORTANCE OF SEEING WHAT'S REALLY THERE

We've all observed how different individuals perceive the same situation dissimilarly. You have merely to take a ride in traffic on your mountain bike to observe some extreme differences in the perceptions of automobile drivers (and who knows what they're thinking about you!). Have you ever attended judicial proceedings and observed the pronounced differences in the perceptions of the same situations?

There's a Lot More to Perception Than Meets the Eye

There's a human tendency to believe that what *we* see is the truth. If there's a difference, it must be the other person who is off base. Many people, however, tend to perceive *what they want, or are set, to see, regardless of reality.* We call this type of perception **mental set.**

Why do we tend to have mental sets? A major reason is that we all possess **perceptual filters.** Each of us has **attitudes** about people and things. Our attitudes tend to decide for us what parts of our environment we allow our brains to interpret and what parts are filtered out. And since we all come from a variety of backgrounds, we tend to view the "real world" through our own set of perceptual filters. Shortly we will look at some perceptual exercises that help to illustrate how we see "what's out there" through our own personal filters. Try to keep in mind as you read through this chapter that we *see* with our eyes, but we *perceive* with our brains. And although we hate to admit it, far too frequently *reality* is completely different from what we see.

If we are going to confront problems among people objectively, we must attempt to develop the ability to see things as they really are, not as we are set to see them. Because of our deeply ingrained perceptual filters, we aren't going to find doing so a simple task. A prime (and dreadful-sounding) objective of this chapter is the *cleansing and confusing of your mind.* You'll see what is meant by this statement as we progress.

Why should you want your head dry-cleaned?

A Perceptual Enigma

Take a look at Figure 2.1. This illustration has been kicking around for some years, but it is still useful to prove some perceptual points. What do you see when you look at it? Most observers will see a woman. Approximately how old is the woman? Does she appear young, possibly in her twenties? Or does she look rather old, probably in her seventies? Or does she seem to be middle-aged? Make a decision before you read further.

About half of those who observe the picture will feel that the person is a young woman. Others will contend that she looks quite old. A few will say that she appears middle-aged. Still others will argue that *both* an old and a young woman appear in the sketch. Which did you see? Look at the picture again for a few moments to see if your original perception changes. If you saw the young woman, look for the older one. Did you see the older one first? If so, try to see the young one. *Both are actually there.* If you see only one woman, you may be experiencing some discomfort.

Figure 2.1 So, about how old is she?

If at first you observed only one woman, what might have been the reason? Could you have been mentally set to see only one? Why did you see only the young (or the older) woman at first? The point is that sometimes we don't immediately see the entire meaning of a situation; accurate perception may take some intense effort. Numerous organizational problems are the result of poor or incomplete perception.

Preset Judgments Can Sink Ships and Lose Legs

Have you ever known anyone whose mind seems to be already made up on a subject before he or she has gathered enough facts to make an accurate judgment? We're probably all guilty of some inflexibility at times.

Here's a short sea story about a sailor who didn't have the opportunity to make the same perceptual mistake twice. In 1912 a ship called the *Titanic*—named after a giant in Greek mythology—was proclaimed to be virtually unsinkable. Her builders were so *absolutely certain* (remember Bertrand Russell's advice?) of her indestructibility that they provided too few lifeboats for the passengers. The world was dismayed when the highly acclaimed vessel failed to complete her

Why did Captain Smith get that "sinking" feeling?

maiden voyage from Southampton, England, to New York. Captain Smith, the *Titanic*'s skipper, apparently set in his perceptions, perceived a small hunk of floating ice that, unfortunately, turned out to be a massive submerged iceberg. A fatal gash ended the voyage prematurely. The ship sank and took 1513 lives with her! How might this incident be related to problems of perception in organizations?

We've all probably read current examples in newspaper headlines that show the consequences of someone's not seeing what's really there. For instance, one recent headline revealed: "Doctors operate on wrong leg." In this incident, a 9-year-old boy who needed an operation to correct a deformed leg ended up with surgery on both legs because his two doctors first operated on the wrong leg. The doctors explained that they couldn't tell by looking which was the bad leg. Their false assumption caused them to lose their future rights to perform surgery in the hospital where this mistake occurred.

Judgments Should Leave Room for Error

We all must make judgments and decisions in our daily lives without being able to acquire all the facts first, but we should realize that sometimes our picture of reality will be accurate whereas at other Can you *really* size up a person right away? times it will not. Have you ever found yourself making judgments about other people based solely on their clothes? Retail sales personnel have sometimes lost sales and valuable commissions after assuming that a tattered-looking person couldn't afford the goods.

Do you tend to judge other people by their handshakes? A popular cliché states that "a *real man*" shakes hands with firmness and strength—not like a fish." However, within many cultures, both in the United States and abroad, a firm handshake is an indication of lack of warmth.

When dealing with problems of human relationships, make an effort to acquire relevant facts before making up your mind. False assumptions will usually result in false conclusions. Most of your judgments should be flexible and allow room for possible error.

Another Perceptual Puzzle

Are details important? Read the short sentence in the following insert. Have you read it? Okay. Now reread it and count—that's right, *count*—the number of times that the letter *F* appears. How many do you see?

> FINISHED FILES ARE THE RE-
> SULT OF YEARS OF SCIENTIFIC
> STUDY COMBINED WITH THE EX-
> PERIENCE OF MANY YEARS

Did you count the three *F*s? Many readers will; others will count four or five; still others will find six. Did you see them all immediately? If not, why not? Did you overlook half the letters—the *F* in the word *of*? Unimportant detail, you may say, but you were specifically requested to count *F*s, weren't you? In a human relations problem, could you afford to overlook 50 percent of the relevant details?

FACTS VERSUS INFERENCES

Most of us are fairly impressed by facts. There's nothing wrong with facts. Perhaps they deserve your respect. But are you clear about what a fact really is? Do you know the important distinctions between facts and inferences?

A Consensus Definition

A **fact** may be defined as *anything that we agree to be true.* If the general consensus of society is, for example, that the earth is flat, we could say that we have, according to our definition, established the fact that the earth *is* flat. Quite often a consensus is correct; occasionally it's not. For years no one saw anyone fall off the edge of the earth, yet people went right on believing that the earth was flat. The

Ball dropping expressly prohibited!

Catholic church once excommunicated a nice young Italian by the game of Galileo for refuting the established "facts" on the subject of the gravitational attraction of the earth's mass, that is, the law of gravity. So you can see that the consensus definition of a fact can often fall flat on its face, gravitationally speaking.

An "Actual" Fact

One of Mr. Webster's definitions of the word *fact* is the "quality of being actual." Without becoming excessively philosophical, when can we say that an event is "actual"? For example, is it a fact that John, an employee of your organization, has recently become lazy on the job? Or is his idleness something that you have observed and internally *feel* to be a fact? Is he actually lazy or have you inferred it? Perhaps John has some personal problems that have changed his normal behavior on the job.

Is Minneapolis a fact or an inference?

The point of this discussion is that it is important for you to differentiate between facts and inferences. Many facts are well documented, such as the population of Minneapolis, but such facts are really historical and change rapidly.

The fine line between fact and **inference** is difficult to determine, but the distinction is important. For example, assume that you are a floor manager in a department store. One of the salespersons

A GLOBAL GLANCE

Is What You Think You See What You Really Get?[d]

Those who feel it is important to "Buy American" do not find it so easy a task as might be imagined. Sometimes it's downright difficult to tell who makes what by the name and familiarity of the product.

Let's illustrate with a short quiz. Assume you want to buy American. Try your hand at the following matching exercise and see if you can determine the nationalities of the companies and products mentioned. Put the small letter of the nationality of your choice in the space to the left of the product. Answers are found below. Answers may be used more than once.

_____ 1. Bic pens are:	a. American
_____ 2. Godiva chocolate is:	b. Anglo-Dutch
_____ 3. Vaseline's owner is:	c. Belgian
_____ 4. Häagen-Dazs ice cream is made by a(n) _____ company.	d. Brazilian
_____ 5. Firestone tires are:	e. British
_____ 6. RCA televisions are made by a(n) _____ company.	f. Canadian
_____ 7. Atari video games are:	g. Czech
_____ 8. Jaguar cars made by a(n) _____ company.	h. French
_____ 9. Holiday Inns are owned by a(n) _____ company.	i. German
_____ 10. The parent of company Arrow shirts is:	j. Italian
_____ 11. The parent company of Braun household appliances is:	k. Japanese
_____ 12. Tropicana orange juice is owned by a(n) _____ company.	l. Korean
	m. Malaysian
	n. Mexican
	o. Saudi Arabian
	p. Swedish
	q. Swiss
	r. Thai

Answers: 1. h, Bic; 2. a, Campbell Soup; 3. b, Unilever; 4. e, Grand Metropolitan; 5. k, Bridgestone Corp.; 6. h, Thompson; 7. a, Atari Corp.; 8. a, Ford Motor Co.; 9. e, Bass; 10. h, Bidermann; 11. a, Gillette Co.; 12. f, Seagram Corp.

anxiously asks to speak with you. She states that she knows one of the other employees on the floor has stolen some money because she saw him take money out of the cash register and put it in his wallet. Is it a fact or an inference that the employee was stealing? Your assumptions as the floor manager might significantly influence your action in this case. True, taking money from the cash register and putting it in a wallet are suspicious behaviors, but is there any possibility that such activity could indicate something other than stealing? We can infer that a theft has occurred, but could we logically state our opinion as fact? Isn't it also possible that the employee was changing some of his own money?

Where is the line between fact *and* inference?

Table 2.1 summarizes some of the major differences between facts and inferences.

Probabilities and Certainties

Although it may sound strange, we could state that all facts are really inferences with differing degrees of probability. The nearer an inference is to certainty, the closer it is to being a fact. All this may sound a bit philosophical, but perhaps it could be made clearer with the use of a probability scale (see Figure 2.2). For example, we could state that the book you are reading at this moment has been made from poisonous paper. Is such a statement one of fact or inference? Is it possible that if you ripped off a corner of this page and munched on it you would expire? Certainly it is *possible,* but is it *probable?* Remember that almost anything can be said to be possible (could occur), but far fewer things are probable (are *likely* to occur).

If something is possible, *is it necessarily* probable?

Let's look at an example involving probability and certainty. Assume that you are a supervisor of a line of production workers. One afternoon while making your rounds, you observe something strange on the floor beside the workstation of one of your employees, Melvin. Upon closer scrutiny, you notice that the object on the floor beside Melvin's left running shoe appears to be the remains of a previously

TABLE 2.1   The Principal Differences Between Facts and Inferences

Inferences	Facts
1. Are made at any time—before, during, and after observation	1. Are established after observation or experience
2. Go beyond what you observe	2. Are confined to what you observe
3. Represent only some degree of probability	3. Are as close to certainty as anyone ever gets
4. Usually generate disagreement	4. Tend to get agreement
5. Are unlimited in number	5. Are limited in number

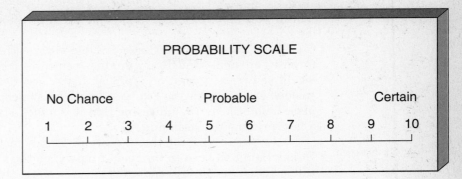

Figure 2.2 A probability scale.

smoked marijuana cigarette, an inference that would rank fairly low on the probability scale. Next you dutifully pick up the object, smell it, and decide that the possibility of the cigarette's being marijuana has moved up to about 9 on the scale. Should you reprimand Melvin for possession and use of marijuana on the job? You know for a "fact" that the cigarette is marijuana, but does your past supervisory training and experience tell you whether it is a fact or an inference that the cigarette belonged to Melvin? Where would you place the employee's possession and use on the probability scale? Is it likely that you could convince an objective grievance committee that the cigarette absolutely belonged to Melvin?

Fact or Inference?

Here's an incident based on a true experience uncovered by law-enforcement officers associated with Scotland Yard in England. The names of the individuals have been modified.

A law-enforcement officer is investigating the burglary of a house that had been empty during a previous weekend. The rooms had been freshly painted on Friday, so the occupants decided to rent a motel room rather than endure the smell.

Upon their return, the owners discovered that a window had been forced open and expensive pieces of silver and china were missing from a cabinet across the room from the window. The officer discovered a handprint on the fresh paint next to the cabinet, checked the print, and determined that it belonged to Slinky Sam, a person with a history of convictions for burglary.

Let's assume that we know this was not an "inside job," that is, the occupants of the home were not involved with the crime. Based on your understanding of facts and inferences and the probability scale, would you say that it is a fact or an inference that a burglary occurred in the house?

There were visible signs of forcible entry—the window had been forcibly opened—and the valuable items were missing. So where would you place a point on a probability scale—near 10, close to 0, or somewhere between the two extremes? Most people would probably place a point near 10, indicating that it is a fact a burglary took place, a fairly reasonable assumption.

All right, here's another question: Is it a fact or inference that Slinky Sam had been in the room from which the valuable items were taken? Most people will contend that it is a *fact* that Slinky had been in the room. Although it would certainly seem high on a probability scale that Slinky had been there, such was actually *not* the situation. Therefore, aren't we actually making an inference in relation to Slinky's presence in the room?

"How could Slinky's handprint have been on the wall if he hadn't been in the room?" you might ask. A good question. Here is what was alleged to have been the "true facts" in the case except for the individuals' names: Those investigating the burglary learned that a person known as "Dirty Larry" had attempted to pawn some items stolen from the house in question. After Larry was tracked down and caught with the stolen goods, he explained how Slinky Sam's handprint got on the freshly painted walls.

Larry had previously "cased" the house from which he later stole the goods and had discovered that the house would be vacant during the weekend. Larry then saw his past partner-in-crime, Slinky Sam, and informed him about the "opportunity." Sam, however, replied that he had decided to go straight; no longer would he participate in such nefarious acts. A violent argument ensued; Larry punched Sam, who fell backwards hitting his head on a radiator. The blow on the head was fatal.

Larry then got an unusually morbid idea. He amputated Sam's hand, wrapped it in plastic, and took it with him to the site of the burglary where he touched it to the wall in obvious places. Sam, as you can now visualize, was never bodily at the scene of the crime. To believe so is an inference, not a fact.

So you can see that even in cases where events seem 100 percent certain, we probably should still leave some room for doubt. Unfortunately, however, in the real world of organizations we don't have an endless amount of time to search for facts. Decisions have to be made. Within our limited time we must somehow attempt to make *certainties out of probabilities*. Yet we must remember to be flexible in our thinking and realize that what we believe to be a fact at this moment could turn out later to be not even a good inference. Leave some room for possible error and be willing to alter your approach when new "facts" are discovered.

THE DETERMINANTS OF PERCEPTION

Numerous factors influence your perception, that is, the way in which you see a particular situation. Among the more significant are:

What influences the mental photo you take?

1. Hereditary factors
2. Environmental background and experiences
3. Peer pressures
4. Projection
5. Snap judgments
6. Halo and rusty halo effects

Hereditary Factors

Who made the choice—you or your parents?

You didn't have much influence in the choice of your parents or grandparents. You may have been merely the result of a gleam in your father's eye. However, your forebears have had a considerable effect on who and what you are. In science courses you can learn in some detail how hereditary factors influence offspring. For our purposes, however, it's sufficient to understand that in addition to determining things such as the shape of your nose and the size of your feet, your parentage also determines your vision and color acuity. For example, if you are myopic (nearsighted), what you see without your glasses will differ from what a person with 20/20 vision sees. Or, like one out of about ten American males, you might have a color-weak tendency (popularly called *color blindness*) and you will see many objects differently from a person with normal color perception. Your vision and ability to perceive colors will often affect your eligibility for particular careers, such as those of airline pilot, commercial artist, or interior decorator.

Environmental Background and Experience

Environment probably has a greater influence on what you see in a given situation than anything else. For example, think about a baby girl deriving her necessary nourishment from her mother's breasts. If during her early years she continually hears from her parents such utterances as, "Those people are lazy . . . they don't really want to work . . . those people stink . . . those people are cheap . . . you can't trust those people," the infant has a good chance of emerging into adolescence with a firm belief in such statements. After all, parents do provide the infant with her needs, determine what is right and wrong for her, and are practically her complete frame of reference (her models) when she is in her formative stages.

Is a house always a home?

A Perceptual Query: How Many Times Greater Is a Company President's Worth Than Yours? Oh Yeah? Read On. You Might Be Surprised![b]

A QUESTION OF ETHICS

In 1992, the Wage and Salary Administration and Research Institute reported that top executives of U.S. companies made three times the income of their counterparts in Japan. Americans who headed companies with more than $80 million in assets received an average of $1.24 million per year, compared with $388,000 for the average president at similar-sized Japanese companies. Some did far better than the average. For example, Merrill Lynch & Co. Chairperson William Schreyer received a pay package in 1991 valued at $16.8 million in salary, bonus, and stock options.

What this boils down to is that if you happen to be earning $30,000 per year, the average president of a U.S. company is making 41 times more than you make. The study of executives of 1,000 major U.S. companies showed a range of salaries from $150,000 to $99.6 million. Not bad for a year's work, eh?

Unfortunately for the executives, however, stockholders began to grumble. In 1991, a group of U.S. shareholders produced a list of company executives they said were vastly overpaid based on their company's size and performance. The business press and some members of Congress began to question whether U.S. top executives are worth so much more than executives in other parts of the world. Regulations were passed by the Securities and Exchange Commission in 1992 that require American companies to disclose in unprecedented detail how much their top executives earn, as well as tell stockholders how those pay packages were determined.

A Question of Ethics: What do you think? Are some executives overpaid relative to their contribution? Should executives have to reveal their earnings?

Usually young persons will gravitate toward and identify with companions who share common beliefs and interests, and many of their early prejudices will tend to be reinforced. In the organizational world, however, continual agreement among managers or employees can lead to the stagnation of creative ideas. Educational experiences may change some beliefs but conversely can make individuals defensive about their existing beliefs. Did you perchance find yourself becoming defensive when you took any of the perception tests?

The way you perceive any situation is significantly influenced by your past experiences. For example, the next time you see the "How Many *F*s?" perception test, the chances are good that you will quickly see the "truth." Or think about how your prior experiences with people in authority affect your present perception. Unfavorable past experiences with bosses can significantly influence how you perceive your present boss.

Peer Pressures

How do your peers press you?

The effect that our peers or friends have on what we see is related to environmental experiences. Perception within groups is often different from individual perception.

An example of the **peer effect** took place in one of my classrooms during a discussion of an organizational behavior problem. After most of the students had developed firm opinions on the case, a latecomer entered the classroom. I decided to play a small trick to see if the late-arriving student would be influenced by what she believed to be the attitude of the other students. So I told her that the class members had considered the behavior of a specific person in the case to be ridiculous, and then I asked if she agreed. She responded with an emphatic, "Yes!" I then confessed that the class had *not* felt that the behavior was ridiculous. She then admitted that she hadn't even read the case but felt as if she should go along with the group. Perhaps our desire for peer acceptance influences our perception more than we sometimes realize. Chapter 4 will explore in greater depth the influence of small groups on the behavior of individuals.

Projection

"Say, Pete, that's not Paul you're talking about—that's you!"

"Everyone else cheats on expense accounts; why shouldn't I?" If you haven't already heard that question, chances are that one day you will. There is an unconscious tendency to attribute to others some of our own traits, faults, and motives, a characteristic called **projection.** But think quite seriously about a statement once made by the Dutch philosopher Baruch Spinoza: "When Peter talks about Paul, we often learn more about Peter than we do about Paul."

So if you assume, for example, that almost everyone cheats on expense accounts or examinations (or in politics!), might not your assumption be related to your own behavior or values? When approaching human behavior problems, be careful that your perceptions are not clouded by the projection of your own values onto another person's situation.

Snap Judgments

How might you avoid
snapping your
judgments?

Have you ever known anyone who exclaims proudly, "I can size up a person right away"? Most of us from time to time are guilty of making **snap judgments** before we have gathered enough facts to come to valid conclusions. Frequently we attempt to solve a problem before we know what the problem actually is. Here's an example of a supervisor named Carla who made a snap judgment at work. An employee, let's call her Anne, received a telephone call an hour before quitting time from a doctor saying that her son had just been hit by an automobile and was badly injured. The doctor requested that Anne come to the hospital immediately to be with her son. Anne looked for her boss, Carla, to ask permission to leave, but Anne could not find her. Anxious to see her son, Anne wrote a note informing Carla of the situation and suggesting that an hour's pay be deducted from her wages if necessary. Anne placed the note in Carla's incoming basket.

About fifteen minutes later, as Carla was returning from a meeting upstairs, she was stopped by Harry, one of Anne's co-workers, who told Carla that Anne had left work early. Carla was furious. "Why didn't she check with me before she left. I had something important I wanted her to do this afternoon. For that behavior she is going to be suspended for one week without pay."

Frequently, as in Carla's case, we attempt to solve a problem before we know what the problem actually is. Married couples who have lived together for many years are still learning about each other. So hold back a bit. How can you possibly make a valid judgment about a person or a human problem after only a minute or two of exposure to the situation?

Halo and Rusty Halo Effects

Another human tendency that affects perception has been labeled the **halo effect:** A person is good at one thing and so is assumed to be good at something else. The positive assumption, therefore, creates the halo.

For example, assume that you are a supervisor in a machine shop. Freddy Fnurd, an employee of yours, has been one of the best drill press operators in your section for over five years. A lathe operator is unexpectedly needed in another section. You recommend Freddy, assuming that he will also do well at the lathe. Freddy bombs! He may have excelled at one job, but he lacked the necessary skill or training to accomplish the other. Figuratively you had placed a halo over Freddy's head.

Another instance of the halo effect could occur if two of your employees have a violent fistfight on the job, and one is a personal friend with whom you regularly socialize off the job. Watch out for the tendency to place a halo over your friend's head by assuming that the other person must have been the cause of the conflict.

Some supervisors are guilty of what could be termed the **rusty halo effect.** For example, assume that there is a particularly incompetent man named Jimmy in your department who continually goofs in his job. You might place a rusty halo over Jimmy's head by assuming that he wouldn't do well in any job on which you might place him. When perceiving people, try to perceive them as they really are. Watch out for the tendency to place halos, shiny or dull, over their heads.

A FEW FALLACIES

In working with case materials or organizational behavior problems, you should make an effort to avoid the following pitfalls in logical thinking:

1. The fallacy of composition
2. The fallacy of division
3. *Post hoc, ergo propter hoc*
4. Wishing-it-were-so philosophy
5. Two-valued reasoning

We'll now take a brief look at each of these potential roadblocks.

The Fallacy of Composition

"Anybody can go to college if he or she really wants to. I didn't have any money, but I worked nights, lifted myself up by the bootstraps, and got a college degree. If I could do it, anyone can!" Is that statement necessarily true? What if a person has a disability or a large family to support and is living up to or beyond the limits of his or her income? What if a person hasn't had the good fortune to be born with great mental abilities? What about someone who came from an environment that discouraged intellectual growth? The exceptions could go on and on; in fact, the exceptions could become the rule!

If it's true for you, is it true for everyone?

"Why do I work? Simply because I need the money. After all, isn't that why everyone works? At least it should be the reason. I don't think Jennifer should be working here. After all, her husband makes good money so she doesn't even have to work." What's wrong with this statement? Once again, isn't the person assuming that what is true for one is true for all? Couldn't there be other reasons for working besides solely the quest for money? How about the need to socialize with others, or the need many individuals have to feel that they are making a contribution?

Unfortunately, however, there is the tendency to assume that what is true for one person or situation is therefore true for all persons or situations. If you were to make such an assumption, you might be guilty of employing the **fallacy of composition,** more formally defined as *the fallacy of assuming that what is true of a part is, on that account alone, alleged to be true also of the whole.*

There are, of course, generalizations that are true. For example, if one person were to puncture an artery and then bleed profusely, we would be secure in generalizing that all individuals would experience similar bleeding upon puncturing an artery.

Assume, however, that you are observing a parade, and there are three rows of tall persons standing in front of you. If you stand on tiptoe, you'll undoubtedly be able to see more of the parade. But if everyone stands on tiptoe, will anyone see any better? What was true for you alone wasn't necessarily true for all (except maybe those with tired arches!). So be on guard against the use of the fallacy of composition.

Fallacy of Division

"Milk is good for everybody, so it certainly would be good for all growing children." Such reasoning is an example of the **fallacy of division,** *the assumption that what is true for the whole is necessarily true for each of its parts.* A parent, for example, may have learned somewhere that milk is healthful for children, and, therefore, it must be good for her own child. However, some children are allergic to dairy products and break out in painful rashes upon ingesting them.

Here's an organizational example of the fallacy of division: Let's assume that a supervisor, Jill, recently completed a company-sponsored leadership training program. Jill learned that certain leadership techniques tend to increase the motivation and productivity of workers. If she assumes that results that are true in general will necessarily be true for every one of her subordinates, she may be applying the fallacy of division.

Be careful not to confuse the fallacy of composition with the fallacy of division; they are opposites. The fallacy of composition moves from the specific to the general, and the fallacy of division begins with a general statement and moves to the specific.

Post Hoc, Ergo Propter Hoc (The Fallacy of False Cause)

Of course, if you are a college student you speak and read Latin fluently and therefore know the meaning of the phrase **post hoc, ergo**

propter hoc. Literally (just in case you don't read Latin!), the words may be translated as, "after this, therefore because of this." The fallacy is formally defined as *the assumption that when one event precedes another, the first event necessarily causes the second.* A simpler way of illustrating the term is this: Event A occurs and is followed by event B. If you assume that in every instance event A is the cause of event B, you may be guilty of *post hoc* reasoning.

For example, assume that yesterday after a late dinner, you took a hot shower and immediately afterward streaked completely nude through your front entrance into the cool night air to sit on the edge of the cold, damp concrete curb. This morning you came down with a miserable head cold. Did event A—the act of running outside dripping wet after a warm shower—cause event B—the cold? Not necessarily. What usually causes colds? Air? Or is it viruses or germs? Besides, the incubation period for most colds is usually longer than one day. Perhaps you shouldn't have been so affectionate toward your sneezing friend two days ago!

Do showers cause colds?

However, if a police officer had arrested you while you were sitting bare-buttocked on the chilly concrete, we could perhaps be more justified in seeing a relationship between the two events—your lounging naked in public and your arrest.

Embarrassed?

Another organizational example: Assume that one of your subordinates is transferred to a different position within your department. Shortly thereafter the quality and quantity of her work begins to decline. What is the cause? Perhaps it is the transfer, but perhaps it isn't. Additional facts might indicate that she now has personal problems that bear no relationship to her new position. Once again, caution should be employed when making judgments about others. Perhaps there is no correlation between two consecutive events.

One more thing: Don't confuse *post hoc* with *ad hoc*. The latter literally means "for this" *Ad hoc* is a term often used to describe, for instance a committee (known as an **ad hoc committee**) that has been temporarily established to work on a specific task and is sometimes referred to as a **task force.**

Wishing-It-Were-So Philosophy

Have you ever wished upon a star?

We all tend to believe what we want to believe. If you have a vested interest in and are loyal to the company for which you work, you might believe that its practices are right regardless of how society perceives certain of its activities. Have you noticed how often environmentalists and individuals in the logging industry see things differently?

Let's look at an organizational example of **wishing it were so:** Assume that you are a manager who has developed a program designed to give your workers a better understanding of the importance of high profits to your firm. You feel that, given the information, they too will see the importance. You may be in for a surprise the next time that the wage contract comes up for renegotiation. *Wishing something to be true does not make it so.* Here's another example: A student openly copied from his neighbor's paper during a history examination. Asked why by the professor, the student answered, "You wanted the correct answer, didn't you?" When you are confronted with organizational behavior problems that present conflicting views, you should be careful not to make what *appears* to be the favorable decision by substituting *hope* for *logic,* as did the eager history student.

Two-Valued Reasoning

Can something be both good and bad?

Another pitfall to accurate perception is **two-valued reasoning,** the human tendency to believe that in any situation there is only "one correct side." To the person who engages in *two-valued reasoning,* situations are either right or wrong, good or bad, with no possibilities in between. You may know individuals whose philosophy can be expressed as, "We are right and they are wrong." Once you have dug more deeply into the problem, you will frequently discover that there is usually *more* than one right side to any problem. Organizational problems are seldom clearly divided into entirely right or entirely wrong positions. Be sure to look for those shades of gray in issues that seem to be clearly black or white.

Our language, unlike Asian languages, seems well designed for the limited, two-valued approach to reasoning. For example, we have no word in the English language for describing a woman's being "a little bit pregnant." In the English language, a woman is either pregnant or she isn't. We can, however, overcome the shortcomings of our language by applying **multivalued reasoning** to organizational problems; that is, by recognizing that in most situations there may be even *more* than two sides.

Can a situation have more than two sides?

THE SEVEN-STEP SYSTEM: A LOGICAL APPROACH TO PROBLEM SOLVING

There are numerous ways to approach problems. Some techniques are more effective than others. One widely followed approach is the

"After all, there's more than one way to skin a cat . . . "

SOURCE: From *The Wall Street Journal*—permission, Cartoon Features Syndicate.

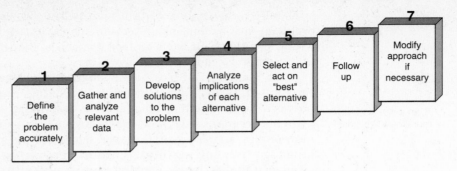

Figure 2.3 The seven-step system to problem solving

seven-step system (sometimes referred to as the *scientific method*) listed in Figure 2.3 and discussed in this section.

Step 1. What's the problem? Some persons dive energetically into their problems as would a hungry cougar in quest of breakfast. A far more effective approach to problem solving is first to *define the problem.* A wise maxim to remember is "A problem well-defined is a problem half-solved." Defining a problem accurately requires us to be objective—to see the situation as it *really* is, not as we *think* it is. Try not to let emotions or overeagerness cloud your perceptual filters. Being too anxious to define a problem, especially before gathering a sufficient number of facts, can result in developing a fantastic solution—but for the wrong situation! Far too often capable employees have been fired from their jobs or unjustly disciplined because the employer either hastily and wrongly defined a problem or came up with a solution before having a clear definition of the problem. Try your best to avoid the unscientific stance of "Don't confuse me with the facts—my mind's already made up!"

Step 2. What pertinent data can I obtain and analyze to verify the definition of the problem? Here's an important step. Rather than going off the deep end, try your best to uncover objective information relevant to the problem. For example, let's assume that one of your employees, Susan, has begun to be late on her weekly reports. Her personality also seems to have changed in recent weeks. You might define her problem as one of bad attitude. But think for a moment—is that really the problem, or merely a symptom? If you interview Susan, or even keep your ear tuned into the communication grapevine, you may find out that her changed behavior results from personal problems at home. So be sure to look for factual information about the *real* problem instead of making false assumptions. Verification of the problem is a necessary and critical part of this step. There's another old maxim worth remembering that warns, "That which can be asserted without proof can also be denied without proof."

Step 3. What are the available alternatives for solving the problem? Note that the word *alternatives* is in the plural form. There's seldom only one solution to a problem. Another wise person once said, "If you have only one alternative to a problem, you have not determined that there is a real problem." Often you will discover after developing alternative recommendations that your second or third solution appears more realistic than your first.

Step 4. What are the implications of your recommendations? This step is more important than it may first appear. Before actually carrying out any recommendations, you would be wise to *anticipate* the likely results of each recommendation. You may discover that some recommendations would create more problems than they resolve.

Step 5. Select and carry out your "best" recommendation. After evaluating all of your alternatives, choose the recommendation that, in your judgment, will best accomplish your desired objectives and *apply* it to the problem. However, don't forget the concept of situational thinking. You may have to alter your plans during your efforts. Will you be ready for such contingencies? Table 2.2 offers some guidelines that can help in selecting the "best" solution to a problem.

Step 6. Follow-up. The problem-solving process isn't complete yet. To make sure that your actions accomplish your objectives—that of resolving the problem—you should examine the situation carefully at a later (but not too late!) date.

Step 7. Modify when necessary. If, in your reexamination, you discover that your objectives have not been accomplished, you may have to study the problem and apply other alternatives to it. As Peter Drucker has suggested, "The importance of a decision is not the money involved but, rather, how fast the decision can be reversed if it is wrong."[1]

I'VE GOT A HUNCH: DECISION MAKING BY INTUITION

Should you ever arrive at conclusions on the basis of feelings rather than logic and facts? Doing so is termed **intuition.** Managers in organizations sometimes make decisions based on the feeling that they know something without the conscious use of reasoning.

TABLE 2.2   Guidelines in Selecting Among Alternatives

1. What will be the short- and long-term effects of each recommendation on the organization?
2. What human, financial, and physical resources would be necessary to carry out each alternative?
3. Will the benefits of my recommendations outweigh their costs?
4. What support will I need from my boss and employees to implement the best alternative?
5. Does my chosen alternative relate directly to the problem, or merely to a symptom of the problem?

Is making decisions by intuition a strictly chance situation?

Is it wise to make intuitive decisions? Surprisingly, a fairly large number of decisions made on the basis of "a hunch" are quite successful. However, is their success based solely on chance? Not likely, according to a number of psychologists who contend that many managers whose decisions seem to have been made "by the seat of their pants" are, in reality, drawing subconsciously on their past experiences and knowledge.[2] Both positive and negative past experiences can aid substantially in dealing with present situations.

A caveat is in order, however. Excessive reliance on intuition rather than logic and facts can be hazardous to your decision-making health. For example, hunch decisions that don't work are much more difficult to defend to your associates. Further, your moods, emotional states, habits, and prejudices can influence your conclusions, thereby leading you astray. Intuition is best used as a supplement to, rather than as a substitute for, logical means.

PITFALLS TO EFFECTIVE DECISION MAKING

Logical decision-making techniques, when applied properly, can be highly useful in problem solving and decision making. Also useful is a knowledge of what to avoid in those activities. Following is a brief discussion of four common pitfalls to which some organizational members succumb, especially those who consistently make bad decisions. Avoiding these traps should enhance your own problem-solving and decision-making activities.[3]

Making Unnecessary Decisions

Is making no decision a decision?

There are some instances when the best decision you can make is to make no decision at all. Some situations work themselves out through the passage of time, and unnecessary meddling can possibly create unwise risks. However, it is essential to be able to distinguish those situations requiring action from those that don't.

"Go on in, Harry—what are you waiting for?"

SOURCE: From *The Wall Street Journal*—permission,
Cartoon Features Syndicate.

Continually Putting Out the Same Fires

"Play it again, Sam."

Have you ever found yourself dealing with similar problems over and over, sometimes the result of your not having taken care of the problem properly in the first place? Some problems recur unless adequate procedures and policies are established for preventing or dealing with them. By anticipating certain types of problems, you can deal with them more effectively when they do arise.

Not Considering the Cost of Decisions

Is it worth the cost?

Sometimes the costs of a particular decision may be far greater than the value of the ultimate result. For example, the decision to buy an expensive mainframe computer would be foolhardy when a few less-expensive, strategically located computer workstations could suffice for the foreseeable future.

Putting Off the Decision

Decisions are not like good wine; they don't necessarily mellow with age. Sometimes organizational members prefer avoiding the difficult decision until they feel more in the frame of mind for such an activity.

Why not do it now?

Unfortunately, the unresolved problem may continually haunt the minds of such procrastinators. Decisions made promptly are often far more beneficial to the organization and can free the decision maker's mind to concentrate on other important tasks and responsibilities.

CREATIVITY AND THE INDIVIDUAL

Another concept related to problem solving and decision making is **creativity.** A creative mind can be tremendously effective in helping you develop sound alternatives to difficult problems. Let's take a brief excursion into the often-misunderstood area called creativity.

What Is Creativity?

Creative minds of the past have developed a variety of definitions for the term *creativity*. What do you think of when you envision a creative person? Is she or he one of those oddball types who don funny clothes, wear their hair either too short or too long, and work, live, and play in environments that look as though a hurricane recently struck? To many people, this is the creative person. But isn't it what individuals *accomplish,* rather than how they look, that makes them creative?

What, then, is creativity? Let's say that it's any thinking process that solves a problem or achieves a goal in an *original and useful*

A BOX OF INTEREST

How Burned Fingers Came to the "Aid" of Johnson & Johnson[c]

Imagination is a trait of the creative mind. Johnson & Johnson, one of the world's leading manufacturers of surgical dressings, was fortunate enough to have an employee with such a trait. Some years ago, one of Johnson & Johnson's newly-married employees had a wife who was learning to cook, and she was burning herself often in the process. The employee, using a bit of creativity, applied gauze to a role of adhesive tape. Whenever his wife acquired one of her burns, all she had to do was cut off a section and apply it to her wound. The employee then decided to present the idea to his boss, and the rest is history—the birth of what we now know as the Band-Aid.

way. But few ideas, if we really think about it, are 100 percent fresh and new. Creative ideas can also result from examining established ideas and methods and building on them. Creativity is also the ability to see *useful relationships among dissimilar things.* Try, if you will, to think of two objects or ideas that are not directly related but that could be synthesized into a third useful object or idea.

Why *reinvent* the wheel?

What Can Help You Become More Creative?

You don't need to be a genius to be creative. What you do need is to use your imagination. Problem-solving activities are often more effective when you allow your mind to run free, sometimes even allowing it to go off into what at first appears to be insane directions. But look for useful relationships among seemingly unrelated objects and you are likely to develop ideas and solutions to problems that you previously felt incapable of handling.

Can you imagine what you might accomplish by using your imagination?

We've already learned how preset notions can create barriers to accurate perception. A mentally set attitude tends to fog our perceptual filters, making creative activities much more difficult. Most people erect such barriers when approaching the nine-dot challenge illustrated in Figure 2.4. Here is what you're to do with this exercise: Try to draw four *straight* connecting lines through all nine dots without raising your pen or pencil. Cast off any preconceived notions, give it your best shot, and then check your answer on page 58 (Figure 2.5).

The creative person is characteristically *inquisitive* and *innovative,* is able to make *new applications of older concepts,* and is *receptive and open-minded to new ideas.* The negative person—the individual who feels that new ideas won't work, even before they've been tried—finds being creative fairly difficult. Managers should encourage their subordinates to be creative in their activities.

Open your mind to the fresh air!

Figure 2.4 The nine-dot challenge.

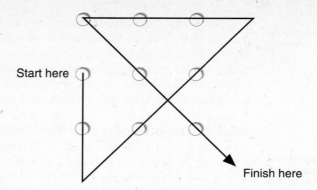

Figure 2.5 Solution to the nine-dot creativity challenge. Did you restrict yourself with artificial boundaries?

Most people, with sufficient desire and practice, can improve their creative ability. Why not give it a try? The feeling of having created useful ideas can even help improve your feelings toward your job and your personal life.

SUMMARY

Perception, by which individuals acquire mental images of their environment, is an important element of organizational behavior. You must be able to perceive organizational behavior situations accurately to be effective in preventing or resolving organizational problems. A major purpose of this chapter has therefore been to assist you in developing greater sensitivity of perception. Perception tests reveal that we don't necessarily see an accurate or complete picture of a situation immediately. An awareness and application of certain perceptual concepts, however, can sharpen your ability to see reality.

The differences between a fact and an inference aren't always clear. Facts can be said to be inferences that appear at higher points on a probability scale. So-called facts may be disproved by new evidence. Flexibility in making judgments is, therefore, essential.

Both heredity and environment influence a person's perception of a given situation. Perception is also affected by pressure from peers, the tendency to project one's own values onto others, snap judgments, and the halo and rusty halo effects.

An awareness of some of the major fallacies in logic can help you avoid some of the common pitfalls in reasoning and perception.

By using the seven-step method, intuition with caution, the guidelines for avoiding decision-making pitfalls, and a creative approach to solving organizational problems, you can reduce the number of your failures or ineffective efforts.

TERMS AND CONCEPTS TO REMEMBER

mental set	fallacy of division
perceptual filters	*post hoc, ergo propter hoc*
attitudes	ad hoc committee
fact	task force
inference	wishing it were so
peer effect	two-valued reasoning
projection	multivalued reasoning
snap judgments	seven-step system
halo effect	intuition
rusty halo effect	creativity
fallacy of composition	

QUESTIONS

1. Explain in your own words the meaning of the statement made in the chapter, "False assumptions will usually result in false conclusions." Can you also provide an example?

2. Give two examples of organizational behavior problems that can develop as a result of your perceiving inferences as though they were facts.

3. Explain how heredity and past experience influence perception. How might education alter perception?

4. Would your perception of a politician whom you and three close friends had watched on television together be any different if you had watched the person alone? Why or why not?

5. Give three examples of the halo and rusty halo effects that you have personally observed.

6. Determine the fallacies in the following statements:
   a. "You're lucky to have an Asian working for you. They're good workers."

b. "We recently hired a graduate of Sage State University, and he is the sloppiest employee I've ever seen. That's the last time I hire anyone from *that* university."

c. "We never had those types of problems in the Plating Department before we sent Sam Jones, the supervisor, to that supervisory management training program. I think we've had quite enough human relations nonsense around here!"

d. "Labor unions are harmful to a free-enterprise system and should be outlawed before it's too late!"

e. "Of course I'm aware that Clarence has had no training or experience in management, but I'm certain that he'll be able to handle that supervisory job. After all, he *is* my son."

f. "Low tuition is why many students don't do well in college. If we were to raise tuition, students would be willing to study harder and get better grades."

7. When attempting to solve human problems, why is step 4 of the seven-step method, *considering the likely results of each alternative,* so important?

8. Give an example of when the decision to do nothing about a problem in an organizational setting might be the best decision.

9. How would you describe the concept of *creativity*. What are the characteristics that aid a person in being creative?

APPLICATIONS

2.1 The Friendly Expediter

Teresa Gomez has been Section A expediter for eighteen months. Her job is to make pick ups and deliveries between Section A and other areas of the plant twice daily. While her exact route is determined by the needs of the sections that she serves, usually she makes ten stops in four different buildings on each run. Teresa is considered to be an exceptionally attractive and witty woman who often stops to interact and joke with co-workers whom she encounters on her route. While her co-workers regard her as fun loving and pleasant to deal with, Eddie Washington, her supervisor, has questions about why she is often late returning from her runs.

One day, Teresa's name came up while Eddie was having lunch in the cafeteria with several other supervisors from some of the sections that she services. "I can sure tell when your expediter, Teresa, is in our area. She's like a traveling comedy show!" remarked one of the supervisors.

"Yes," said another, "she loves to have a good time on the job! Does she do a pretty good job for you?"

"Well," Eddie responded, "she does seem to take longer than necessary to make her runs. She leaves about 9:30 A.M. and doesn't return until almost lunch time. But she seems to be getting the job done."

"Not on my end, she isn't," said the supervisor from Section B. "We've been waiting for parts to come in from the dock for two days. They claim the parts were sent, but there's no sign of them. And now no one seems to know what's become of them."

"Maybe she forgot them here in the cafeteria during her breakfast break," laughed another.

"Her breakfast break?" Eddie asked.

"Sure. She stops in the cafeteria every morning while she's here in Building C and has a big breakfast at about 10:00 A.M. I see her here every day when I take my morning coffee break. But don't be too hard on her, Eddie," he continued. "All those expediters are a bit flaky—if they had anything on the ball, they wouldn't be expediting, would they?"

Eddie called Teresa into his office when he returned from lunch. "What's this I hear you're eating breakfast in the cafeteria every morning on your run? Is it true?"

"Well, yes," said Teresa. "I'm over in Building C anyway, so I take my break while I'm over there. I'm in and out in fifteen minutes, my allotted break time. The lady in the cafeteria knows I don't have much time, so she always has it ready for me when I come through. It makes more sense to take my break while I'm there than to return and then go all the way back there for a break. Besides, if I don't take a break during my run, I'd have to take it first thing when I arrive or just before lunch, which doesn't make any sense."

"I'll decide what makes sense and what doesn't," Eddie responded angrily. "Your attitude is beginning to be a real problem. Other supervisors are complaining that you disrupt their areas when you come through, and now I hear that the parts you were supposed to have delivered to Section B have never arrived. They were ready two days ago!"

"Wait a minute, Eddie," Teresa said. "Those parts for Section B did arrive on the dock. I checked. But I haven't received them for delivery. You can check my delivery registers if you don't believe me. If you ask me, they were misplaced somewhere on the dock, and now they're trying to pass the blame off on me."

"Perhaps if you took a more business-like attitude, these accusations wouldn't arise."

"Look, Eddie, I enjoy my work, sure. But an expediter's job requires that other people stop what they're doing to take delivery or give me things to expedite. I know I get more cooperation from people because of my lighthearted attitude than I would by being hardnosed. I think I've taken a creative approach by joking around and being friendly, and I can cite lots of cases where people have gone out of their way to have things ready on time for me, because it's me!"

Questions

1. What perceptual influences have affected Eddie's understanding of the facts in this case? Do you think he sees the facts objectively? Explain.

2. What inferences have been made about Teresa? What examples of fallacies can you find in this case?

3. What do you make of Teresa's claim that she is being "creative" in her approach to her job?

2.2 The Case of the Snapping Judgments

News Item, Houston. A short circuit fought off more than 60 police officers along the Houston ship channel before it was finally subdued. Plainclothes and uniformed officers spent the predawn hours chasing what they thought was someone peppering them with gunfire from atop one of the tanks. One officer said he had been shot in the heel of the shoe. Another graphically described slugs slamming into a road paved with oyster shells. Police threw themselves to the ground with each loud crack.

Fire trucks stood ready and police lobbed tear gas bombs into spots where they thought the sniper was hiding. In the first light of dawn two sheriff's deputies and four journalists came upon the culprit—in a 1-inch piece of pipe. The "shots" were nothing more than the popping noise produced by water dripping through an opening into a conduit pipe, seeping through insulation tape, and shorting out a piece of no. 8 electrical wire. "I just goofed," said electrician R. A. Graves, who was called in to silence the wire. He said he forgot to put a plate on the outside of the pipe that keeps the wire inside waterproof. The ricocheting noises that sent police scurrying for cover in the dark of night were produced by the outside pipe's vibrating against the adjacent conveyor belt with each pop. The plate that was missing from the pipe cost $8.50. The personnel used to hunt down the "sniper" cost Harris County and the city of Houston an estimated $9000.[4]

Questions

1. What appears to be the main problem in this incident? How might the problem have been avoided?

2. List at least five types of activities entailed by certain jobs that would tend to cause some people to perceive negative situations where none actually existed.

3. How might this incident relate to your particular job?

2.3 The Smelly Case

Akio Yamashio, division manager of Ajax Perfumes, was reviewing the production records for its best-selling product, Smelnise. The information covered the last quarter and revealed decreased production during the last two months. When Akio compared the Smelnise results with those of other Ajax perfumes, he noted that Smelnise had the lowest production record. Akio knew that Smelnise production was now considerably below planned goals. Akio sat back in his padded executive chair, propped his feet on his spacious mahogany desk, loosened his tie, and began to reflect on this production problem.

Three months ago the production responsibilities for Smelnise had been assigned to Lori Pearlman. Lori had been with Ajax since graduation from Quality University with a major in chemistry. Lori had taken top honors in a class of 64 students, and her last two years at the university had been paid for by a grant she won for her persistence, accuracy, and attention to detail on a chemical research project for the university. During the past three years at Ajax, Lori had headed a small laboratory group validating ingredients for the various Ajax products.

The laboratory group headed by Lori Pearlman was considered a hard-working, well-organized team. It was the group's task to receive samples from each batch of ingredients used in all Ajax perfumes. Before each batch could be released, the laboratory technicians performed standardized tests on the samples and completed a validation form that was then presented to Lori for her review and signature. Lori personally participated in some validations and periodically repeated the validation tests to confirm the technicians' results. Group morale was good; work performance was timely and accurate, and coordination with other departments at Ajax was favorable. The validation laboratory generally performed well above expectations, with Lori receiving credit for the satisfactory performa~~ Her results had made her a prime candidate when Akio Ya~~ was searching for a Smelnise production supervisor.

As Akio continued to reflect on the production proble~ dered if he should again confer with Lori. During thei~ ence, she had mentioned a need for retraining some controllers and subordinate supervisors. The interphone buzzer interrupted his thoughts.

"Mr. Yamashio, this is Edwardo over in the warehouse," the interphone announced. "Our inventory of Smelnise is getting low. Can you push up the production before marketing gets on our tail?"

Akio Yamashio dispatched Edwardo with assurances that he would check into the matter and get back to him. As he clicked off the interphone, he knew he would have to stop reflecting and start acting. He had a problem that needed solving now.

Questions

1. What was the probable reason for Akio Yamashio's selecting Lori Pearlman as the production supervisor of Smelnise?

2. What pitfall of logical thinking may be involved if Akio Yamashio blames the lagging production on Lori Pearlman? Explain.

3. What would be the quickest way for Akio Yamashio to replenish the inventory temporarily?

4. Using the seven-step method, define the steps necessary for Akio Yamashio to find a long-range solution to Smelnise's production problems.

2.4 Are You Creative or Mentally Set?

Here's a corny riddle intended to stretch your creative muscles: If the removal of a growth in the abdomen is an appendectomy and the removal of a growth in the throat is a tonsillectomy, what's the removal of a growth on the head?

Try to overcome any present notions you might have and creatively come up with an answer to the question. You can check your answer in the notes section.[5]

NOTES

1. Harvey Gittler, "Decisions Are Only as Good as Those Who Can Change Them," *The Wall Street Journal,* October 7, 1985, p. 24.

2. Weston H. Agor, *Intuitive Management,* (Englewood Cliffs, N.J.: Prentice-Hall, 1985).

3. Adapted from Don Caruth and Bill Middlebrook, "How To Make a Better Decision," *Supervisory Management,* July 1981, p. 17.

4. Adapted from a true incident that occurred some years ago in Houston, Texas.

5. Answer to Application 2.4: *A haircut!*

BOX NOTES

a. Adapted from "So You Wanna 'Buy American,' Eh?," *The Stars and Stripes,* February 19, 1992, p. 16.

b. Adapted from William Power and Michael Siconolfi, "Merrill Pays Its Chairman $16.8 Million," *The Wall Street Journal Europe,* March 23, 1992, p. 9; Martin Dickson, "A Check on the Boss's Cheque," *Financial Times,* March 31, 1992, p. 18; and "Boardroom Sweets," *Time,* October 26, 1992.

c. Adapted from Robert H. Waterman, "Strategy in a More Volatile World," *Fortune,* December 21, 1987, p. 125.

EXPERIENTIAL EXERCISE

We See, But Do We Perceive?

Take a look at these two illustrations. What do you see?

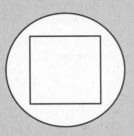 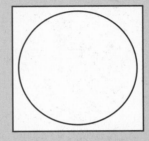

The square on the right is obviously larger in area than the one on left, isn't it? How about the circles? Which looks larger in circumference and diameter? The one on the right? Not so! If you measure them, you'll see that they are identical in size. Now take a look at the illustration below. What do you see?

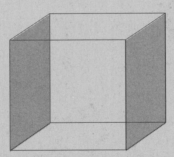

You should, if your brain is perceiving accurately, see alternating faces of a box, sometimes viewing it from the front and at other times viewing it from the top. Our brain receives a lot of information at any given time, and it tries to make sense of this information by limiting and organizing sensory input. Our brain, naturally, tries to help us function, but it sometimes plays tricks on us by creating distortions or inaccuracies in what we see. However, the brain does permit most people to switch back and forth between the sets of images.

Questions
1. Which was easier for you to perceive accurately—the illustrations here or Figure 2.1?
2. How do these exercises relate to the perception challenges you face in everyday life?

CHAPTER 3

The Need for Communication Skills

There's More to Communication Than Meets the Ear

When you finish this chapter, you should be able to:

1
Identify the essential ingredients of effective communication.
2
Summarize the main characteristics of words.
3
Summarize the major forms of communication.
4
Describe the nature of nonverbal forms of communication.
5
Identify the principal barriers to effective communication.
6
Explain how active listening habits benefit the organization and its members.
7
List five types of listening responses.
8
Contrast open with closed questions.
9
Understand the principal methods for overcoming communication barriers.

Human beings create the symbols of communication,
and then they cannot understand the symbols they create.

Anon.

God gave us two ears and only one mouth.
In view of the way we use these, it is probably a very good thing
that this is not reversed.

Cicero

A young woman named Sandy once had an embarrassing communications experience while employed by a drugstore. A middle-aged man with a fairly thick foreign accent approached her, wanting to make a purchase. To Sandy, his request sounded as if he wanted to buy something for "breath control" for his wife. Always quick and courteous, Sandy immediately handed him a container of Binaca breath spray. With a quizzical look on his face, the man asked, "Hjow doz me vife use diz fur 'breadt conetrol'?" Sandy smartly answered, "She merely sprays once or twice in her mouth as needed." The man looked at Sandy in utter disbelief and asked to speak to the manager. Sandy pointed out the manager, and the man went to him. A few minutes later Sandy's boss came over and exclaimed, "Sandy, I know you meant well, but that man wanted something for 'birth'—not 'breath'—control!"

Sandy's awkward experience helps to illustrate an important concept; *communication* can take place in a variety of situations, but for communication to be *effective* there must be *understanding*. One of the major causes of problems in organizations today is the lack of effective communication. Often supervisors *assume* that they've communicated when they make oral statements to their subordinates. And frequently they are virtually positive that they've communicated after transmitting a message in writing. Naturally, one does have to make certain assumptions in this world to function, but as one manager wryly puts it, "When you <u>ass</u> <u>u</u> <u>me</u>, you often make an *ass* out of *u* and an *ass* out of *me!*"

Organizations cannot function effectively when communication skills are lacking among their members. The current chapter will therefore consider some of the major facets of communication and will examine the characteristics of words, the need for established feedback mechanisms, and the means of overcoming common barriers to communication. We shall also explore some of the significant aspects of nonverbal communication and the importance of listening.

THE NATURE OF COMMUNICATION

We're continually bombarded by various forms of communication in our day-to-day activities. Not only are there thousands of radio stations and hundreds of television channels attempting to communicate with the nation's citizens each day, but also newer forms of communication are now competing for attention. We now can receive calls on our cellular telephones while driving to work and receive printed messages on our portable fax machines while driving home from work. Our voice mail systems can receive communications when we are away.

However, are all of these sophisticated electronic devices necessarily communicating with us when their electrical impulses are functioning and our ears and eyes are tuned in to their messages? Not necessarily. Even though we may hear or see a transmitted message, there is an essential ingredient of communication that is needed to make it effective: *understanding.*

What Makes Communication Communicate?

Whether we're talking about a radio station, a fax machine, or about you within your organization, *three essential ingredients* are necessary for effective communication to take place:

What are the essential ingredients of effective communication?

1. A sender
2. A receiver (listener)
3. An understood message

A Two-Way Process

Communication, therefore, can be defined as *a two-way process resulting in the transmission of information and understanding between individuals.* Note the two-way nature of communication. It's virtually impossible to know for certain how effectively you've communicated without some sort of **feedback,** the process through which the originator of a message learns the response to his or her message.

"Pregnant" with fragrance!

For example, if you were to say to your boss, "Susan, those [the flowers on the desk] sure are fragrant," and she looks up and asks, "Who told you I was pregnant?" have you communicated? Yes, but not as you intended. However, the opportunity to receive instant feedback when you heard Susan's words enables you to correct the misunderstanding. Try to avoid **one-way communication** as much as possible.

Responsibility for Effective Communication

Who's responsible?

Who has the responsibility for ensuring that effective communication takes place? Both the *sender* of the message and his or her *listener* share the responsibility. As in the case of the radio station previously mentioned, the listener has to be tuned in to the message and understand it before effective communication results. You, however, have a considerably advantage over the broadcasting medium in your efforts to communicate. You can discover immediately if the receiver is tuned in. How? Remember the word *feedback? By asking certain questions* you can discover if the receiver actually understood your message. If you are on the receiving end of the communication, by *restating what the speaker said* you can often determine whether you understood the message. (Later in this chapter we discuss some key techniques for asking questions.) Even a person's *facial expressions* can give you an indication of his or her reaction to your words.

It's a *two-way* process.

In a sense, both you and your boss, Susan (or anyone else, for that matter), are simultaneously *producers* (senders) and *consumers* (receivers) *of communication.* You produced and sent Susan a message, but you also consumed and received a message from Susan. The importance of **two-way communication** for overcoming misunderstandings can't be overstressed. Wouldn't you agree?

WHAT ARE WORDS REALLY LIKE?

We usually expect to have some difficulty when we talk with people whose language is different from ours. Misunderstandings seem likely in such instances. Unfortunately, however, we really don't have a completely common language with anybody, whether they are citizens of the good old U.S.A. or not. A big part of our communication problem is caused by the characteristics of the symbols we use in much of our daily communication. These **verbal symbols** are called *words* and can be used in either oral conversations or printed messages.

Are Words Things—Or Are They Merely Words?

Is a dictionary a source of the "correct" meaning of words?

Let's assume you and I were face to face, and I used a word that you didn't understand. The best place to find the "true" meaning of the word would, of course, be the dictionary. Or would it? Would a dictionary really tell you what *I* mean by words? Not necessarily. Most lexicographers (dictionary authors) contend that the book they prepare is merely a history book, one that shows how *some* words have been used at particular times and in certain contexts. You can probably think of numerous words that you use daily that are understood but are not in the dictionary.

Words as Inexact Symbols

Can you write down the meaning of the word *fast?* Think for a moment. Does the word imply motion, as in the case of a fast runner? Or does it imply lack of motion, as in a fast color or in she stands fast? Isn't our little four-letter word also related to eating habits, as in the case of a person who fasts during a holiday, such as Lent? What about the expression, "He was too fast on the first date"? A complete dictionary will offer at least 50 different meanings of the word *fast*. The same can be said for such words as *wind, wing, run, lie, air,* and many others. How, then, can we determine the true meaning of words?

First you have to get out of your head the notion that words have *absolute* meanings. The word is not the thing; the word is merely a symbol that represents different things to different people. Words are, in effect, like containers that attempt to transport something to someone else. The true meaning of a word isn't in the word itself or in the way the listener interprets the word. Words in themselves have very imprecise meanings.

Then just where is the meaning of the word?

The meaning of a word is therefore in the mind of the *sender* of the word and is carried by the word to the receiver. There are believed to be about 600,000 words in the English language. An educated adult in daily conversation uses about 2000, of which the 500 most commonly used have 14,000 dictionary definitions. Do you really think that you can guess the right meaning every time?

"George, will you please throw me down the stairs my hat? George, put me down! Help!"

Consequently, if we want to discover the meaning of a speaker's words, the only way to be certain is to *ask* her or him what they mean when we are in doubt. Instead of wondering what the *words* in a message mean, a better approach is to wonder what the *speaker* means. A corny story might help to illustrate this point:

"Now," said the village blacksmith to the apprentice, "I'll take this iron out of the fire, lay it on the anvil, and when I nod my head, you hit it." The apprentice did so, and now he's the village blacksmith!

You can lessen the chance of communication failures between you and others by following two rules:

1. Don't assume that everyone knows what you are talking about.
2. Don't assume that you know what others are talking about without asking them questions to make certain.

The blacksmith erroneously made the first assumption, and the imperceptive apprentice made the second!

Words with Regional and International Meanings

Sometimes the *meanings of words are regional* and vary significantly in different parts of the United States and in various nations of the world. For example, if you ever receive a package from Germany marked "gift" with a bottle of liquid inside, you would be ill-advised to drink it. The word "gift" in German means "poison"! Here's another example: Some British people traveling in France became red in the face after discovering what they were really saying when they asked if there were *"preservatifs dans le gâteau."* To the French those words mean, "Are there condoms in the cake?" Words that are identical in two similar Latin-based languages can sometimes create challenges. For example, *"Voce me deixou embaraçada"* means "you have embarrassed me" in Portuguese but "you've made me pregnant" in Spanish.[1]

A "gift" that remembers!

The Development of New Meanings

Words develop new meanings with the passage of time. Almost every decade brings forth myriad new meanings for old words. Often the parents of college or high school students can't understand the conversations of their offspring. Many popular songs have contained words with specific meanings only to some listeners. Various ethnic groups have also been a fertile and creative source of new meanings for old words.

Language just keeps "hip-hoppin'" along!

Word Interpretation Is Affected by Doublespeak

Which would you rather have happen to you—to be "fired" from your job or to be "offered a career-change opportunity"? Which would you prefer—to be "laid off," or to be "excessed" or "transitioned," because the company you've been working for is being "right-sized" or "re-engineered," or is "rationalizing marketing efforts"? If you had participated in the Gulf War, which would you have preferred to hear—that your organization's "massive bombing attacks" killed "thousands of civilians" or that your "force packages" successfully "visited a site" and "degraded," "neutralized," or "sanitized" targets?

Our house was burned down by a "friendly fire"!

Such is the world of **doublespeak,** a term applied to the use of words that are evasive, ambiguous, or stilted for the purpose of deceiving or confusing the reader or listener. The ethical use of doublespeak is highly questionable, but many organizational managers make use of it as a means, they hope, of softening the harsh blows of reality and to cover up bad news or mislead the public.

William Lutz, author of the book *Doublespeak,* provides numerous examples of the use of doublespeak. He cites such companies as Chrysler Corporation, which once initiated a "career alternative enhancement program" and in the same corporate breath threw 5000 people out of work. Another example occurred when National Airlines had the unpleasant task of informing its stockholders that they had earned $1.7 million from insurance payments after a Boeing 727 crash that resulted in the death of three passengers. According to

Lutz, the annual report of the company indicated that the income resulted from the "involuntary conversion of a 727."[2] So when you hear high-flown phrases, try to uncover the real intent of the sender of the message. (See the box, *A Question of Ethics,* for additional examples of organizational doublespeak.)

A QUESTION OF ETHICS

A Frontal Attack—Is This A Kind of Sneaky Doublespeak Or What?[a]

"Consumer Alert," "Citizens for Sensible Control of Acid Rain," and "National Wetlands Coalition"—nice sounding names that you feel you could trust, right? Not according to Mark Megalli, a researcher with a consumer advocate group. He says that these organizations, and many more like them, are "front groups" with deceptive names or misleading goals. Megalli further suggests that their intention is to confuse the public and win benefits through lobbying. Megalli contends that there are numerous groups with socially responsible names funded by some leading American corporations that seek to convince journalists and the American people that they represent something other than the usual corporate interests. He says, "The reason is simple—it's easier to believe disinformation when the disinformation is coming from an apparently disinterested party." The public tends to be skeptical of groups like the Tobacco Institute and the American Petroleum Institute. The so-called front groups use names that indicate a general concern for the public interest, employing doublespeak buzzwords such as "sensible," "responsible," or "sound" that hide the groups' real purpose and their business connections. Careful, you guys: although George Orwell might take notice of your clever use of doublespeak, you could anger Ralph Nader who might form a front group to end all front groups!

A Question of Ethics: Why might the general public perceive the "front" organizations mentioned here as having a different purpose from what is really intended?

The Development of New Words

New words are continually derived as a result of the development of new industries or fields, as in the case of the words *astronaut* and *space shuttle,* which emerged from space exploration, or *DOS, PC, laptop, notebook,* and *palmtop,* derived from the computer/word processing field. Each trade or profession tends to develop its own specialized or technical language, typically known as *jargon.*

Tone Affects Meaning

A difference in tone can change the meaning of words. "John, you've been doing a hell of a job around here," is a phrase that could convey praise or blame, depending on the tone of the speaker's voice.

In summary, therefore, there are six important factors about the meanings of words that we should remember.

1. Words have many meanings.
2. Words sometimes have regional meanings.
3. Words develop new meanings.
4. Word interpretation is affected by doublespeak.
5. New words are continually derived.
6. A difference in tone can change the meaning of words.

TYPES OF COMMUNICATION

Have you ever been around newborn babies? They're highly skilled communicators of a sort. At a typical 2:00 A.M. feeding time, the "little darlings" leave no doubt in their parents' minds what the message is: "Waaah! Waaah! I'm starved! I want my milk! And I want it now! Waaah!" This is another example of one-way communication, a type of communication that is not recommended to you as effective organizational behavior.

Many types of communication affect you as an organizational member. Understanding them should enable you to put them to more effective use. The forms of communication that we'll now examine are:

1. Formal and informal
2. Upward, downward, and horizontal
3. Spoken and written
4. Electronic
5. Nonverbal

Formalities, Formalities

One way of looking at communication is at both its formal and informal sides. **Formal communication** is the official communication that travels through the structured (formal) organizational network (see Figure 3.1). An example of formal communication would be your request for the purchase of some special equipment through your boss, who then seeks official approval from her or his boss.

Informal communication, on the other hand, is the real workhorse of message networks, one that can either help or hinder an organization's efforts to achieve its goals. Informal communication travels through a channel often referred to as the **grapevine,** a network that is usually much quicker than official channels. Wherever there are people, the grapevine is right there alongside them. The grapevine is the primary means for transmitting **rumors,** statements or reports whose truth cannot be verified by any known authority. More simply, rumors are statements that are generally, but not always, incorrect. We'll look at informal communication and the grapevine in more depth in Chapter 4 when we discuss their relationship to informal groups.

There's much more than grapes on the grapevine!

What Goes Up Must Come Down . . . and Around

As a member of any organization—a work, social, or family group— you must function in a world of symbols. Assume, for example, that you're a supervisor. You're likely to be bombarded continually from all sides with communications. You receive directives from your bosses, memos from other department heads, and both requests and complaints from subordinates. The nature of the communications coming toward you and radiating outward from you may be *upward, downward,* or *horizontal.*

No fun feeling like a funnel.

Upward Communication. Let's continue assuming that you're a supervisor. You've probably found that *upward communication* has been a continual problem. This type of communication flows up the organizational structure. Far too many managers think that they know precisely how their subordinates feel about a particular situation. "My people love working here," some bosses may boast. Then, to their complete surprise—Zaaap!—five people announce that they are quitting. "I can't understand it," a perplexed manager mutters. "They all seemed so happy here. I can't understand what went wrong."

"Well . . . I really thought they loved me."

As you can see in Figure 3.1, some of the principal formal types of upward communication in organizations include suggestion systems, open-door policies, listening, employee grievances, morale surveys, labor news publications, exit interviews, and observation.

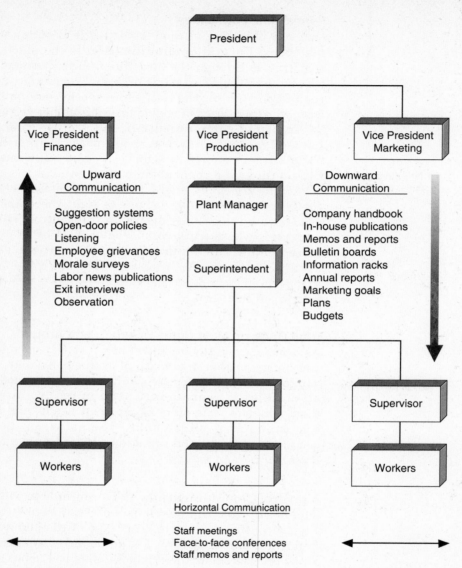

Figure 3.1 Formal channels of communication

Downward Communication. Communication that conveys messages from higher to lower levels of an organization is called **downward communication;** it, too, is difficult at times. Employees typically receive such a tremendous amount of downward communication that they often engage in **selective reception,** that is, they hear or see the information they are set to hear or see and tune out much of

Can you be both tuned in and tuned out at the same time?

the rest. Anyone who has regularly attempted to convey information to others recognizes how difficult the process is. All groups seem to include a certain number of individuals who fail to get the word. Do you remember our earlier example of how Susan was set to hear the word *pregnant* rather than *fragrant?*

Referring once again to Figure 3.1, you can see that some of the more prevalent forms of downward communication include company handbooks, in-house publications, memos and reports, bulletin boards, information racks, annual reports, marketing goals, plans, and budgets.

The Filter Factor. Unfortunately, one of the most prevalent problems in organizations is the **filtering** of communication. Filtering is the straining out of ingredients essential to understanding as communications rise up to management levels or travel from management down the organizational hierarchy to workers. We'll examine various methods for minimizing some of those difficulties in later sections of this chapter. In the meantime, take a look at Figure 3.2 for a graphic example of how our perception tends to filter out certain aspects of communication.

Should you strain not to strain out relevant info?

Were you able to read the word in Figure 3.2? If not, go back and fill in the open spaces to prevent the background from confusing your interpretation of the symbol.

Horizontal Communication. Another type of communication, one that permits managers on the same level to coordinate their activities more effectively, is called **horizontal communication.** Organizations in which supervisors have little or no opportunity to communicate with other supervisors on the same level often experience such problems as *duplicated efforts, ineffective use of resources, lack of coordination,* and even *destructive interdepartment rivalry.*

"But you didn't let me know!"

Considerable time and effort can be saved by horizontal communication because teamwork between departments can exist without their members having to refer every matter through a higher level of management. But beware! Horizontal communication, too, can create problems, especially if the bypassed boss feels that his or her decision-

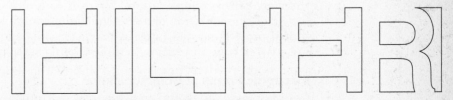

Figure 3.2   An example of filtering. Can you read the word?

making power (authority) has been reduced. It's a good idea to inform your boss of any communication that might affect him or her. If you don't, you could place that person in an uninformed and embarrassing position.

Spoken Versus Written Communication

Verbal communication can be either *spoken* (oral) or *written*. Which do you think is better for transmitting messages effectively? Both forms have their advantages and disadvantages, and organizational members usually use each type regularly.

Spoken Communication. A principal advantage of spoken communication over written communication is that spoken messages allow you to receive *instant feedback*. With written communication, feedback may be delayed or even nonexistent. Face-to-face types of oral communication, for example, enable you to *observe* at a glance how your audience is reacting to your message. You can also *ask questions* to make certain that you've been understood or that you understand what the other person has said. Telephone conversations, although not face to face, have some of the same advantages as face-to-face communication. You can also ask questions and receive immediate responses from the person at the other end of the telephone line. Furthermore, much information can be derived by carefully listening to the tone and inflection of the other person's voice.

Another potential advantage of spoken over written communication is *speed*. With face-to-face and telephone communication you can usually transmit your ideas directly to others without having to take the time necessary to write a memo, a letter, or a report. Watch out, however, for the tendency to shoot the breeze during oral communication transactions, a practice that sometimes offsets the potential savings in time.

Faster than a speeding fax machine!

Written Communication. In spite of the many advantages of spoken communication in organizations, it can't, of course, completely take the place of written communication, which also has its advantages. A key advantage of written communication is that it provides a *permanent record* or *reference*. It is also typically given *more thought* than spoken communication. Written communication also helps to provide *documentation* of a transmitted message, which can be important if proof is needed later. We'll cover some suggestions on improving written communication in an upcoming section of this chapter.

Electronic Forms of Communication

Cellular telephones and videophones, fax machines, voice mail systems, and computer networks—all instruments of communication—

have proliferated in organizational environments in recent years. They augment the already-existing forms of electronic communications such as standard telephones, telexes, photocopying machines, and executive information systems (EIS). All of these instruments are purchased at considerable expense by organizations to make it easier and faster for people to communicate with each other. (See *A Box of Interest* for an example of how electronic communication has changed the nature of communication in many organizations.)

SILENCE ISN'T ALWAYS GOLDEN—NONVERBAL FORMS OF COMMUNICATION

"I can see what's on your mind."

Most of the time when you think of communication you probably think of either *spoken* or *written words,* that is, **verbal communication,** but these are only two types of communication. Another type of communication, called **nonverbal communication,** relies on factors other than verbal symbols, as typified in Figure 3.3.

Take the time some day to observe closely someone else's communication. You're likely to find that a small proportion of the sender's

A BOX OF INTEREST

How to Talk to People Without Talking to People![b]

Here's the new communications trend of the 1990s. *Keeping out of touch*—with voice mail. Many people in organizations these days aren't communicating with each other anymore—they're merely downloading information. Thanks to the modern concept of voice mail, or voice messaging, where oral messages can be left on a central recording device to be retrieved by the recipient at a later time, organizational members can now save exorbitant amounts of time that used to be spent on talking about weather, baseball, and lunch or in correcting each other, arguing, or merely engaging in ritualistic small talk. In fact, some "communicators" over voice mail now save up their incoming messages and then return the calls during hours that they know they will be reaching the other people's voice messaging systems. So, in reality, no dialogue takes place among live human beings. A growing number of Americans have come to prefer voice mail to actual voices!

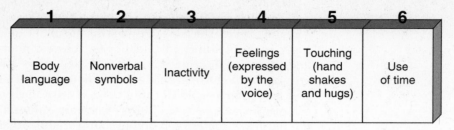

Figure 3.3 Various forms of nonverbal communication.

communication consists of spoken words; the person's voice and facial expressions make up much of the rest. Skillful communicators usually recognize that much more goes into any conversation than verbal symbols, or words. Let's now take a brief look at some of the more common nonverbal forms of communication.

The Body Speaks!

Whether you realize it consciously or not, you're communicating each time you make a gesture or glance at a person. The motions people make with their bodies (or sometimes don't make!) often communicate messages. **Body language** isn't always accurate or effective, but it is communication nonetheless. For example, assume that after you arrive at your job one morning, you pass a co-worker in the hallway who gives you an unusual glance, or at least a glance that appears to you to be strange. You might wonder for the rest of the day what that glance meant. Some employees seldom greet others then they pass in hallways or work areas. Instead, their faces seem frozen. Sometimes a person might feel that a frozen stare is an indication of displeasure.

Once again, a word of warning: Some people are misled by body language. We already are aware that we have plenty of difficulties interpreting correctly the verbal symbols of others, even when we've had training in listening. We can also be easily misled by body language. For example, your listener's crossed arms may not necessarily mean a lack of receptivity to your message. Instead, it could merely mean that the person feels cold.

Nonverbal Symbols Also Speak

Certain types of **nonverbal symbols** communicate special messages. For example, the way *space* and *height* are used in office situations can tell us something about the patterns of authority among the various employees. If you observe two department managers, one with office space twice as large as the other, you might safely assume something about their relative authority in the organization. Executive suites are seldom found in the basements of office buildings. In

When a body . . . sees a body . . .

our culture, *higher* is assumed to be better than *lower*. Have you ever heard of anyone aspiring to descend the ladder of success?

Personal appearance also communicates. Your clothing, hairstyle, use of makeup and perfume, and even your briefcase are likely to "say" something to others that is related to those people's values and cultural experiences.[3]

Status symbols tend to be visible indicators of an individual's rank in an organization. Items that might appear trivial to an outsider, such as a telephone or wastebasket within easy reach, can have an important influence on the morale of employees. Some executives would prefer a rug on their office floors or a cellular phone in their cars to a pay raise. Any items that people perceive as significant can serve as symbols of status among organizational members. What are some of your favorite status symbols?

"Look at me . . . I've got my own wastebasket!"

Inactivity Silently Says a Lot

Assume that you, a supervisor in an organization, are habitually cordial toward your employees each morning as you arrive on the job. You seldom forget to say hello to anyone. However, one morning you wake with pressing problems on your mind, problems that demand your immediate thought and attention. As you pass the receptionist on that particular morning, your mind might be millions of light years away, and you hardly notice him. Have you attempted to communicate anything to the receptionist? No, not consciously; yet you might have communicated something. The person might start wondering, "What did I do? Why didn't the boss say 'Good morning' to me today?"

How does lack of activity communicate?

Another form of inactivity includes the failure to compliment individuals on the quality of their work. Many employees feel that their superiors comment on their performance only when they've done something wrong. You will find that one way to influence favorably fellow employees or subordinates in your organization is *to recognize and acknowledge good work when you see it*. If you only communicate with the workers when they've done something wrong, they'll soon feel that they're not appreciated in your organization. As V. Wilcox wryly stated, "A pat on the back is only a few vertebrae from a kick in the pants, but is miles ahead in results."

Even Your Voice Has Feelings

"I can feel it in your voice."

A person's voice is an important element of communication. Much of what your listeners interpret comes from the sound of your voice. In fact, that's the main thing your listener interprets when you use the telephone. The voice is also a critical part of any face-to-face communication.

Tone, volume, pitch, rate, and inflection all significantly influence how you come across to others. These elements tend to reveal whether or not you're sincerely interested in those with whom you carry on conversations.

We usually aren't very aware of the way our own voice sounds to others. You could gain some personal insights by recording your voice on a tape recorder, preferably by role playing with another person. A video cassette recorder would be even better since it combines the elements of sound and sight. Such activity could aid you in determining what vocal changes you need to make.

For example, as you listen to playbacks of your own voice, does it seem too loud or overpowering? Or is it too soft and difficult to understand? Do you tend to speak in a dull monotone? Do you use adequate inflection and enthusiasm when talking? Is your rate of speech either too fast or too slow? Try to avoid coming across as a fast-talker, the type who tends to be distrusted by his or her audience. Too slow a rate of speech, on the other hand, tends to make holding the listener's attention more difficult. By understanding the strengths and weaknesses in your vocal patterns and by regularly practicing better techniques, you should be able to improve your vocal skills substantially.

Touching—Communicating with Handshakes and Hugs

Touching is another form of communicating. Let's start with handshakes. Americans are sometimes accused of being a nation of snap-judgment-makers. Frequently, one will hear the statement, "That person has a handshake like a dead fish." Standards for "proper" handshakes vary, however. If you travel to different parts of the world, you'll quickly discover that not all the world's citizens shake hands like your fellow Americans. Nor do all Americans shake hands identically. Remember that some persons will make judgments based on your handshake, which to them may communicate something significant.

Put 'er there, fellah.

In many of the Latin countries, handshakes are quite soft and gentle, without the vigorous up and down movements common in the United States and Germany. In northern European countries such as Germany, you might frequently suspect that you're in a contest of brute strength with a native handshaker who seems to be testing his or her grip on your hand. In France, if your right hand or arm is occupied holding packages, you may shake hands with your left hand without being regarded as impolite. Some people while reclining at a Riviera beach even use their feet!

Care to arm wrestle?

Shake a leg?

As we have already noted, various cultural groups, both in this country and abroad, have different norms regarding touching. For example, some American business people are frequently shocked

"We can't go on meeting like this!"

when they observe the "bear-hugging" that goes on between business people in Mediterranean cultures. To a Greek business person, for example, the lack of a warm hug by an American counterpart could be regarded as a cold or unfriendly gesture.

The Use of Time

My time is your time.

Your attitude toward time and the way you use it may also communicate messages to others. Concerned organizational members seldom arrive late for appointments. Those who do arrive late to work, meetings, or appointments often create a bad impression on those who must wait for them. People who expect you to arrive at a specific time will sometimes postpone other projects in anticipation of your arrival. Any time spent waiting for you is wasted time for them—they could have been doing other things. To avoid this problem, plan to arrive at least ten minutes before you're scheduled to arrive. If you must travel by automobile, allow for possible delays, such as those caused by traffic congestion. Struggling through highway traffic when you're late for an appointment can create additional tensions and frustrations that can do little but detract from your objectives. Those who try to get to appointments precisely on time tend to be late since they frequently don't allow for those omnipresent surprise factors.

WHAT'S THE MEANING OF THIS? THE BARRIERS TO EFFECTIVE COMMUNICATION

"I didn't hear you say that." "Oh, is *that* what you meant?" "Gosh, I'm sorry. I thought you meant . . ." "I'm afraid you must have misunderstood me. What I said was . . ." Unfortunately for the sake of understanding between individuals, these statements are uttered far too frequently within organizations on a typical day.

In this section we look at some common stumbling blocks to effective communication. An understanding of the principal communication barriers can assist you in avoiding or overcoming them in the future. These barriers result from eight factors, as illustrated in Figure 3.4.

We'll now examine each barrier separately.

Receiving Is Deceiving—Perception

"See what I mean?"

Do you remember our discussion about the many factors that influence our *perception?* As we learned, seeing things as they really are rather than as we are set to see them isn't an easy task. Our past experiences, our present moods, our attitudes, our peers, and much more—all these factors significantly influence how we interpret a

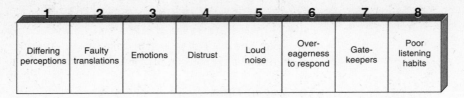

Figure 3.4 Causes of barriers to effective communication.

given message. Familiarity with the determinants of perception helps you to recognize that not everyone is likely to interpret your messages in the manner you intend, nor will you necessarily "read" the messages of others correctly. Once again, remember the importance of feedback in effective communication.

It Doesn't Make Sense—Faulty Translations

Say what?

Sandy's dilemma cited at the beginning of this chapter illustrates our next barrier to effective communication, *faulty translations*. We frequently misinterpret others because of ineffective listening habits or a preset attitude toward them. As a result, we sometimes miss the sender's intended meaning. We'll cover ways to overcome this and other barriers to communication later in this chapter.

Emotions as a Block to Clear Thinking

Control loss loses lots!

We've all seen people in an emotional state who afterward apologized by explaining that they didn't mean their earlier comments. You should try your best to control your emotions since a loss of control often results in a loss of respect by the receivers of your communication. Make every effort to maintain a calm, positive, and friendly atmosphere in your interpersonal relationships even if others approach you in an excessively hostile manner. Equally important in our conversations with others is that we attempt to avoid causing our listeners to feel either embarrassed or pushed.

That's the Last Time I Trust HIM! Developing Credibility Gaps

Credibility gaps are quite common between managers and workers in organizations. To prevent the cynical distrust of the communication that flows throughout an organization, you should remember that *words do not substitute for action*.

Assume, for example, that one of your subordinates, Ms. Anne Earnest, complains to you about the excessive glare of the sun shining through her office window. She informs you that the blinding sun reflecting off her desk makes work extremely difficult, if not virtually impossible. If you promise to remedy the problem but fail to do anything about it, you're likely to discover that Anne will tend to disbelieve many of your future statements.

You say it, but will you do it?

Some managers feel that a simple statement such as, "I'll see what I can do about the problem," will placate their employees. However, when dealing with others you should be aware that they'll frequently remember the promises you've made. The chasm of disbelief widens with each failure on your part to deliver what you promised.

I Can't Hear You Above That Infernal Noise!

Loud noise is a fairly obvious barrier to effective communication. For example, if you are trying to convey some important information to another person, you're likely to experience substantial difficulty if the setting has noisy machinery, equipment, or people in the background. Modern, open offices frequently obstruct effective conversations because of the overspill of noise from adjacent offices. There also may be a certain degree of self-consciousness in talking with others when you feel that you can be overheard by others.

Noise, in the communication process, is broadly interpreted and can be defined as anything—whether in the sender, the medium of communication, or the receiver—that hinders communication. An effective communicator will attempt to select a setting that is conducive to effective communication and eliminate or reduce the factors that obstruct the transmission of messages.

Overeagerness to Respond

Have you ever been around individuals who have the tendency either to finish your sentences for you during a thinking pause or to interrupt you in the middle of your sentences? How do you personally feel about such actions? Probably not so great. Yet, do you find that you, too, occasionally interrupt others?

Why do we interrupt or finish other people's sentences? One of the reasons may be related to our ego need for **self-esteem** (to be discussed in more detail in Chapter 5). We may feel the need to show the other person that "we know," that they're not telling us something that we don't already recognize.

Gary: "Harry, you look . . ."

Harry: "Marvelous?"

Gary: "Not quite, Harry, I was going to say 'sick.'"

In some cases the inclination to interrupt may be related to our impatience. For example, are you a high-achieving, busy type of individual who often feels short on time? If so, you may find that your intense preoccupation with progressing to something else may create a barrier to effective communication between others and you.

Open the Gate, Please!

The filter factor!

In some organizations there exist barriers to communication, called **gatekeepers.**[4] These are individuals who determine what information is received by key decision makers. They may or may not be actual decision makers themselves; sometimes they are assistants or secretaries of the person with whom you would like to communicate. Gatekeepers tend to screen information and decide on their own what should be passed on to others. What can you do when confronted with a gatekeeper? Breaking through the gate usually requires a certain degree of political astuteness if it is to be accomplished without creating additional barriers between you and the gatekeeper. You should try your best to maintain a cordial relationship with the person, hoping that his or her attitude will become more receptive. Even if the person continues to feel the need to be a roadblock, it is advisable to let those whom you would like to contact know that you would like to meet with them. Doing so, however, is not without some risk. You could anger the gatekeeper. Some people overcome the roadblock created by the gatekeeper by writing a memo to the person they want to contact expressing the importance of a meeting. A memo is also sent to the gatekeeper so that he or she will feel included in the communication.

The next barrier to effective communication—poor listening habits—is extremely important and, along with methods for asking questions, will be covered in the following section.

THE IMPORTANCE OF LISTENING

We usually tend to believe that we've understood another person's message merely because we've heard it, a notion that is often many kilometers away from reality. Unfortunately, most people have had little formal training in the area of **listening,** an important element in effective communication.

Think about your educational experiences. You've had courses in writing, reading, and possibly even speaking. But have you ever had a course in listening? If you're typical of the population, probably not, even though we spend more time in a listening mode than in any of the other processes of communication—speaking, reading, and writing.

A growing number of private organizations and schools have become increasingly aware in recent years of the need for training in listening. A number of training videos and materials have been developed by institutions, private firms, and associations. The purpose of this section is to present some significant—but often ignored—concepts designed to develop better listening habits.

Let's Hear It for Listening

Management will find it difficult to receive feedback from employees without developing improved techniques of listening. Often, however, rushed and harried supervisors feel that they just can't find enough time to listen to employees. Some supervisors, however, discover that time spent on effective listening can be as valuable as an investment in more efficient equipment and can save them a scarce and valuable resource—time.

Of course, effective listening habits are important for *all* organizational members, not only managers. Every employee should learn the techniques of better listening *to maintain good relationships* with those who deal with their organizations. Furthermore, *costly accidents* and *expensive errors* can often be avoided when employees listen to their supervisors and co-workers. Effective listening habits can also *prevent misunderstandings and rumors* from developing in an organization.

What are the benefits of effective listening?

There are other important reasons for acquiring effective listening habits. Five additional ones are cited in Table 3.1.[5] Think about how you might employ each of these in your day-to-day activities.

The Verbal Cocoon Problem

Judging from how often important feedback is filtered or misdirected, you might think that some supervisors in organizations were wrapped in *verbal cocoons,* from which they tend not to emerge, especially during their face-to-face interactions with others.[6] Effective listening is *not* a simple or passive activity; it requires a concentrated effort and a certain amount of tension. Managers who have the **verbal cocoon problem** tend to be non-stop talkers, seldom allowing new ideas to penetrate their encased world. In effect, cocoon listening prevents the penetration of unwanted information.

Unwrap your cocoon!

TABLE 3.1   Significant Concepts Related to Listening

1. People perform better when they know others listen to their opinions and suggestions.
2. Attention paid to small complaints often prevents their blossoming into big grievances.
3. Managers who don't obtain as many relevant facts as possible often make poor decisions.
4. Managers who jump to conclusions often lose the respect of their subordinates.
5. Listening requires giving full attention to the speaker; it is impossible to listen intelligently while the mind is preoccupied with something else.

The cocoon listening problem frequently exists when managers perceive their role as authoritative, one that involves the initiation of action and decision making. To have to engage in a less conspicuous activity, such as listening, sometimes bruises managers' egos, especially if they feel that they only have control of a situation when they are doing the taking. Such listening habits create a safe, nonthreatening way of avoiding the risk of new ideas. However, if you were to

A GLOBAL GLANCE

Listen to These Words From a Japanese Communication Expert[c]

Hirotaka Takeuchi, a professor from Hitotsubashi University in Japan, had a few interesting things to say about communication differences between Americans and Japanese when he participated in a special program for global managers at the University of Michigan's business school. He said that there are reasons other than unfamiliarity with English why Japanese speak much less than their American counterparts at meetings. Takeuchi revealed that unlike Americans, who like to jump in and grab control of a meeting, the Japanese prefer to wait and listen. He also explained that the higher their rank, the more they listen. Takeuchi wryly added that the Japanese have a saying: "He who speaks first at a meeting is a dumb ass." Takeuchi further advised, "If you are with a Japanese who speaks fluent English, you may be dealing with the wrong person. You are probably dealing with an *eigo-ya,* an English specialist, who doesn't know much else." His final bit of wisdom was that the Japanese will probably never be talkative like many American managers.

Takanaka-san, one of the Japanese managerial participants at the program, added: "We are a homogeneous people, and we don't have to speak as much as you [Americans] do here. When we say one word, we understand ten, but you have to say ten to understand one."

Perhaps their views may be true today. But cultures change. Who knows what the Japanese will be like in the future now that their young people are singing and dancing to American-style rap and hip-hop music? Besides, have you ever observed a rap singer who appeared to be listening?

ask some satisfied employees what they like most about their supervisors, frequently they would say, "I like my boss. My boss *listens* to me."

Whether you are a manager or a worker, either on or off the job, other individuals may approach you with their personal problems. When they do, is that the time to tell them that you, too, have similar problems? Put yourself in the shoes of the other party. When you have a personal problem that you want to discuss with someone else, do you really want to hear about *his* or *her* problem? Does hearing about the other person's problem necessarily make you feel any better? Usually not. Often you're more concerned, consciously or subconsciously, about having the opportunity to get things off your own chest.

Effective listening by organizational members can be a form of **preventive maintenance.** Just as lubrication can prevent friction and the resulting wear and tear of machinery, so can effective listening prevent friction and problems of human relations from developing in your organizational and personal life. Offering advice to a troubled person is often unnecessary. For persons who have complaints or difficulties, the mere act of finding an empathetic listener (one who attempts to put himself or herself into the speaker's shoes), frequently helps them to get things off their chests and possibly to see problems more objectively on their own.

Do troubled people want to hear *your* problems?

How is listening a form of *preventive maintenance?*

DEVELOPING LISTENING SKILLS

Listening is a skill to be developed, and the knowledge of how to make certain *listening responses* and how to *phrase questions* can greatly assist you in conveying to speakers that you're interested, attentive, and wish them to continue. Let's first examine some effective ways to elicit responses from your speakers.

Listening Responses

Listening responses should be made *quietly* and *briefly* so as not to interfere with a speaker's train of thought. As with any tool, responses can be misused, ineffective, or counterproductive. Responses are likely to be manipulative and unreal if they are not genuinely sincere. Responses are usually made when the speaker pauses. Five types of listening responses are:

1. The nod—nodding the head slightly and waiting
2. The pause—looking at the speaker expectantly, but without doing or saying anything

3. The casual remark—"I see"; "Uh-huh"; "Is that so?"; "That's interesting."

4. The echo—repeating the last few words the speaker said

5. The mirror—showing your understanding of the speaker by reflecting what has just been said; "You feel that . . ."

Phrasing Questions

Occasionally, a supervisor may notice that an employee's behavior or work habits have changed significantly. If a dependable employee with a record of good work suddenly starts coming to work drunk or having accidents on the job, the change may be a signal that a personal problem exists. Personal problems that affect an individual's performance on the job should become the concern of the employee's supervisor, who may be able to offer assistance when he or she discovers the nature of the problem. However, merely asking the worker, "Is there anything wrong, Joe?" will frequently elicit a negative response. There are far more effective ways of phrasing questions to enhance the possibility of receiving a more complete response. Questions may be phrased as **open questions** or as **closed questions.** Open questions usually generate better responses than do closed questions.

A question is *open* when phrased in such a way that it can't be answered with a simple yes or no. For example, "Joe, I've noticed some changes in your work lately. What seems to be happening?" The questioner who asks an open question, exercises patience, and says nothing until Joe finally responds often discovers that Joe will be far more likely to express his inner feelings about a personal problem.

Why do open questions elicit greater response than closed?

A question is *closed* when it is phrased in such a way that it can be answered yes or no. Here's an example: "Joe, do you have a problem?" Too frequently the answer to a question phrased like this will be no.

Psychiatrists and counselors regularly employ the open-question technique. Can you really imagine a psychiatrist saying to his or her patient, "Mrs. Jones, do you have a problem?"

As a supervisor, you could use the open-question technique effectively when trying to discover an employee's attitude about a change in the organization. If you ask, "Betty, do you feel the recent change in your duties is fair?" she is likely to say yes because of the natural status barriers between employee and supervisor. However, if you ask, "Betty, how do you feel about the recent changes in your duties?" you will more than likely find out some of her real attitudes.

Practice formulating questions by using the open-question technique. You may be surprised and pleased with your results. The following *key words* help determine whether a question is open or closed:

OPEN	CLOSED
Who	Is
What	Do
When	Has
Where	Can
Why	Will
How	Shall

Table 3.2 provides a useful summary of some of the principle "do's" and "don'ts" of listening.

HOW TO BREAK DOWN COMMUNICATION BARRIERS

In this chapter you've learned quite a lot about the nature of communication. These insights are useful, however, only in their *application*. As an effective member of any organization, it's essential that you be able to overcome the many communication barriers that continually confront you. In this section we'll cover some of the major precautions that can be taken and approaches used to help minimize communications breakdowns. You can:

TABLE 3.2   Some Do's and Don'ts of Listening

Do's	Don'ts
1. Show interest.	1. Argue.
2. Express empathy.	2. Interrupt.
3. Be silent when silence is needed.	3. Engage in other activities.
4. Eliminate distractions by holding telephone calls and choosing a quiet place to talk.	4. Pass judgment too quickly or in advance.
5. Allow adequate time for discussion.	5. Jump to conclusions.
6. Take note of accompanying nonverbal cues.	6. Let the other person's emotions act too directly on your own.
7. When you are unsure of what was said, restate what you think you heard in the form of a question.	
8. When you feel that something is missing, ask simple, direct questions to get the necessary information.	

SOURCE: Arthur G. Bedeian, *Management* (Chicago: The Dryden Press, 1986), p. 533.

1. Obtain feedback.

2. Encourage upward communication.

3. Use face-to-face communication where possible.

4. Avoid credibility gaps.

5. Anticipate and squelch rumors.

6. Write for understanding (deliver messages with a K.I.S.S.).

7. Watch your timing.

8. Be sensitive to the needs and feelings of others.

The following discussion will explain these guidelines.

Be Hungry for Feedback

How do you feel about it?

Too frequently we believe that we've communicated with others only to find ourselves sinking in a sea of misunderstanding and conflict. As has already been stressed in this chapter, feedback—finding out the receiver's response to your communication—helps to reduce misunderstandings. Some of the following recommendations for overcoming communication barriers concern the concept of feedback.

Upward Communication: May We Suggest Suggestion Systems?

To encourage upward communication, some organizations have developed formal **suggestion systems,** a well-intentioned feedback mechanism that can be either used or misused. An example of such misuse was once found in one of the largest printing plants in the Pacific Northwest. Employees passing through a particular corridor of the building could see, very firmly attached to a wall, a wooden box with the words *EMPLOYEE SUGGESTIONS* affixed to its side. Once, out of curiosity, an employee opened the unlocked lid. The suggestion box looked more like a garbage receptacle than a mechanism for generating feedback. Inside the dusty container were unsightly hunks of well-masticated stale chewing gum, along with crumpled old cigarette and gum wrappers! What might the employees have been attempting to suggest to management?

Do litterbugs use suggestion boxes?

The employees seemed to feel that there was little use in placing anything other than garbage into the box since, in the words of one of the employees, "Management would only put our suggestions in the wastebasket anyway!"

The usefulness of suggestion systems is doubted by some students of communication. They argue that management's requirement that suggestions be *written* may discourage the presentation of useful ideas by employees who lack either the inclination or the ability to put their suggestions into writing.

Why should recognition be given to the submitter of suggestions?

However, if management does decide to employ a suggestion system, it should give recognition to the submitter, whether or not the idea is accepted, to encourage the flow of useful ideas and employee gripes upward in the organizational chain of command. An employee usually feels that he or she is entitled to know why suggestions are rejected. Numerous firms provide not only *explanations in writing* to the employees but also *face-to-face discussions* of the reasons for the rejection or acceptance of ideas. Others present *cash rewards* to employees who offer cost-saving ideas. However, a suggestion system will soon be viewed by employees as a farce if the suggestions are not acknowledged by management.

Open Up, Boss, I Know You're in There!——Open-Door Policies

Let's continue with our discussion of upward communication for the purpose of minimizing communication barriers. Some managers assume that if they haven't personally heard derogatory remarks from employees, there must be little, if any, dissatisfaction among the employees with the company's policies and procedures. If much communication weren't filtered out so often, many managers would quickly discover that numerous employees detest their managerial intestines!

Aware of the problems of upward communication, many well-meaning managers inform their employees that they believe in an **open-door policy** and that any time employees want to see them, all they need do is drop in.

In too many cases, however, an open-door policy really means that the door is open for managers to walk out. Usually few, if any, workers feel inclined to walk through their bosses' so-called open doors because they sense various psychological or status barriers between the managers and themselves. Even where open-door policies have been announced, many employees have found that upon attempting to walk through the "open door" they have been stopped and asked, "Do you have an appointment with Mr. Lockout?"

For whom is the door *really* open?

If managers really want to discover how their subordinates feel about the operations of an organization, they must walk through the open portals themselves and engage in some observant exploration, an activity referred to by such organizations as Hewlett-Packard (HP) as MBWA, or **Management by Wandering Around. MBWA,** enables managers to make themselves available for informal discussions with employees.[7] Many managers seldom engage in MBWA, instead tending to keep themselves comfortably insulated from their employees.

Our pessimistic view of open-door policies isn't intended to suggest that they should never be attempted. Some managers are very effective in persuading employees that an open door actually exists.

When management's attitude is credible, an open-door policy can, in many instances, be used as an effective tool. For example, at Levi Strauss & Company, the open-door concept has allegedly worked so well that employees refer to it as the "fifth freedom."[8]

Let's Face It——Face-to-Face Communication Really Works

Why are face-to-face communications usually more effective?

Face-to-face communication is felt to be more effective than written orders in reducing misunderstandings because the sender can receive feedback immediately and discover if he or she has been understood. The impersonal character of a memo or letter can be easily misunderstood, especially when information of a negative nature is being conveyed.

While employed as a sales representative for an office products company, a person we'll call Victor Vendor discovered that personal meetings with his customers, rather than impersonal written communication, more effectively resolved problems or conflicts that had developed between them and his company. By asking certain questions and by listening empathetically to the answers, Vic regularly discovered that the problems seemed to diminish.

Avoid Credibility Gaps

What may happen when action doesn't follow words?

We've already talked about the importance of avoiding credibility gaps between you and others in your organization. Let's assume that you're a middle-aged crazy bent on masochistic self-destruction. You decide that one way to accomplish your perverted goal is to develop an organizational climate in which your employees *distrust* you. How might you accomplish this bizarre objective? An effective way would be to make commitments or promises to others and then do nothing about them!

Since the chances are that your reasoning processes exceed those of the character just illustrated, you should remember an important point mentioned earlier: To prevent the cynical distrust of the statements you make to others, always keep in mind that *words do not substitute for actions.* Also, remind yourself that if you want to communicate effectively with and influence others, such as employees, with your messages, you must be able to get them to be willing to do the following:

1. Hear what you say.

2. Believe what you say.

3. Be willing to act on what you say.

Once you have lost your credibility, your employees are much less inclined to do these three things.

Write Right——Say It with a K.I.S.S.

A young college student, Miss Ima Anxious, while enrolled in her first course in college English, was required to study and learn the definitions, spelling, and usage of ten pages of vocabulary words each week. As a serious student of the English language, Ima was quite proud of her scores on the weekly tests. In fact, she felt that she should display her newfound knowledge by using the words in a term paper assignment modestly entitled, "The History of Insurance." So she began: "As the adoption of the Constitution gave birth to a fairly sound financial system in the United States, conditions for corporate enterprise were copiously ameliorated."

"Copiously ameliorated"? What was Ima actually trying to say? Didn't she mean "greatly improved"? Apparently clarity wasn't the major concern of a conscientious first-year student who wanted to parade her scholarly knowledge.

Far too frequently, written communications within organizations appear to have been prepared by ambitious students like Ima. Some years ago while in the U.S. Navy I discovered that a memo was referred to as a promulgation. Another example of poor word choice once existed in a naval barracks where posted neatly over a drinking fountain was the notice: "Expectoration into drinking apparatus is expressly prohibited." About nine out of ten persons who were asked the meaning of the word *expectoration* didn't have the foggiest notion of its meaning. One person thought that the word might mean "to urinate"! A curious sailor decided to investigate its meaning, opened Mr. Webster's famous (but wordy!) book, and discovered that one definition of the verb to *expectorate* is "to spit." Perhaps the simple admonition, "Don't spit in the fountain!" would have sufficed.

A manager with a large insurance company once said that he believed all communications should be delivered with a **K.I.S.S.,** which meant "Keep It Simple, Stupid," or more tactfully, "Keep It Short and Simple." Perhaps you should ask yourself, "What is the major objective of any communication that I desire to make to others?" Communication isn't effective unless there is *understanding,* which should be a major goal of any communication. Don't overcomplicate your messages. If there were a fire in your office or plant, you probably wouldn't exclaim, "It is mandatory that we attempt to extinguish the portentous pyrogenation." You would be understood much more readily if you merely shouted, "Let's put out the fire!"

Here's a sampling of what one manager actually stated in a letter: "I should be gratified by your willingness to aid in this endeavor." Wouldn't the following be a much simpler way to convey the same meaning? "I'm glad you want to help."

Would a fire chief shout, "Extinguish the pyrogenation!"?

Written communication, before it can be understood, must *attract the attention* of those to whom you are aiming it. Imagine seeing this notice tacked to a bulletin board:

MEMORANDUM TO ALL EMPLOYEES CONCERNING
REGULATIONS AND RESTRICTIONS APPLICABLE
TO EQUITABLE ALLOCATION OF VACATION
PERIODS FOR THE YEAR 1995

Would you really expect many employees to spend much of their valuable coffee break perusing such a memo? A simple and readable title would be apt to attract the attention of the employees, as in the following example:

MEMORANDUM

TO: ALL EMPLOYEES
FROM: PERSONNEL DEPARTMENT
SUBJECT: VACATION SCHEDULES, 1995

Can you foresee how the four C's can aid you?

Virtually any correspondence or memo can be improved by applying what we'll term the "four C's of written communication." The four C's stand for *C*-omplete, *C*-oncise, *C*-orrect, and *C*-onversational. Use the checklist in Table 3.3 to help determine whether your written communications are likely to accomplish what you want them to.

Watch Your Timing

There's no time like good timing.

Assume that one evening you finally made the decision to ask your boss on the following day for the raise in pay that you feel is long overdue. All night you tossed and turned in bed trying to frame the most tactful and persuasive plan for the pay increase.

The next morning, however, you observed that your boss scarcely noticed the employees and appeared to be extremely harried upon her arrival at work. Nonetheless, your mind is set; your courage is at its peak. You bravely walk through the "open door" of your boss's office, and politely, but firmly, ask for a raise, and suddenly—BANG!! You feel as though you're reliving the 1906 San Francisco earthquake. Your boss shouts, "Can't you see I have some important things on my mind?" You realize that you must have picked the wrong time for the right question, and that you completely forgot to interpret her body language.

What is the best time for important communications?

Optimum timing is as important as your choice of words in many situations, whether you're talking to parents, children, friends, superiors, subordinates, or customers. The best time to attempt to convey important communications face to face is *when your message is com-*

TABLE 3.3   The Four C's of Written Communication.

C-omplete
   Have you provided all the necessary facts?
   Have you answered all the receiver's questions?
C-oncise
   Have you avoided unnecessarily long and complicated words?
   Have you said what you wanted in one page or less?
   Are your paragraphs short and easy to read?
   Have you avoided "hiding" important information, such as *where, when,*
      and *at what time* a meeting will be held?
C-orrect
   Have you checked your correspondence for accuracy?
   Are your commitments in agreement with company policy?
   Have you checked your grammar, spelling, and punctuation?
   Have you eliminated strikeovers and sloppy corrections?
C-onversational
   Have you written in a friendly, receptive manner?
   Will your writing style evoke the response you want?
   Have you avoided excessively complicated and flowery phrases?
   Have you avoided words and expressions that are likely to antagonize your
      reader?
   Have you put life into your writing through the use of *active* verbs?

peting the least with other situations affecting the listener. However, your message is most likely to be considered and listened to when it provides a *solution to a problem* affecting the receiver.

Be Sensitive to Feelings and Needs

Empathetic speaking and listening are also essential for effective communication. Some speakers create communication barriers because they seem to lack the understanding that some words or phrases are felt to be derogatory and offense to others. Some people, however, feel that extreme sensitivity to words is ridiculous. Regardless of how you feel personally, an important point is to try *to know your audience* and *be sensitive to the needs and feelings of your listeners* when you speak and listen; otherwise, you may short-circuit important communication networks.

"Don't use language like that around me!"

Along the line of concern for the feelings of others, try to remember what we discussed about impatience. Attempt to develop the ability not to interrupt. Instead, concentrate on listening instead of thinking only of your next response. Most people usually appreciate being listened to. Don't you?

SUMMARY

Communication, a two-way process imparting information and understanding between individuals, requires a *sender,* a *receiver,* and an *understood message* to be effective. Words facilitate communication but do not themselves have meaning. They are like containers; their meaning is in the *user.* When in doubt about the meaning of a word, ask the user what he or she means.

Communication failures are reduced when we neither assume that everyone else know what *we* are talking about nor that we know what *others* are talking about without asking them questions to make certain. The meanings of words are not always clear since words often have many meanings, and both new meanings and newly derived words can arise. Meaning can also vary according to region, and as a result of doublespeak and tone of voice.

Communication in organizations may be classified as upward, downward, and horizontal; formal and informal; spoken and written; electronic; and verbal and nonverbal (including body language) forms of communication.

Barriers continually develop, thus making effective communication more difficult. Among the more common communication barriers are differing perceptions, faulty translations, emotions, distrust, loud noise, overeagerness to respond, gatekeepers and poor listening habits.

Understanding the techniques for overcoming communication barriers can reduce their number. You can improve communication by obtaining feedback, encouraging upward communication, using face-to-face communication where possible, avoiding credibility gaps, writing for understanding, watching your timing, and being sensitive to the needs and feelings of others.

TERMS AND CONCEPTS TO REMEMBER

communication	body language
feedback	nonverbal symbols
one-way communication	status symbols
two-way communication	credibility gaps
verbal symbols	gatekeepers
doublespeak	listening
formal communication	verbal cocoon problem
informal communication	preventive maintenance

grapevine

rumors

upward communication

downward communication

selective reception

filtering

horizontal communication

verbal communication

nonverbal communication

listening responses

open questions

closed questions

suggestion systems

open-door policy

MBWA (Management by Wandering Around)

K.I.S.S. concept

QUESTIONS

1. How would you define *communication?*
2. What ingredients are necessary for effective communication to take place?
3. Why is communication said to be a two-way process?
4. Describe six characteristics of verbal symbols, that is, words.
5. What is meant by the statement, "Words are like containers"?
6. Evaluate the following statement: "The best place to look up the true meaning of a word that you don't understand is the dictionary."
7. Compare and contrast formal with informal types of communication. To which type does the term *grapevine* relate?
8. How does selective reception relate to downward communication?
9. What are some of the advantages and disadvantages of written and spoken forms of communication?
10. Give some examples from personal observation of the principal types of nonverbal communication.
11. Describe the major types of communication barriers and discuss techniques for overcoming them.
12. Why do some managers figuratively seem to encase themselves in a cocoon when their subordinates talk to them?
13. Explain the statement, "Words do not substitute for action."
14. What is meant by the concept of a *gatekeeper?* What can you do when confronted by one?

15. What are some of the benefits, both to the organization and to its members, of the application of effective listening habits by managers and subordinates?

16. Explain the various processes by which feedback can take place in organizations. How might they be misused?

17. Why will relating your own problems probably not comfort a person who has approached you with a personal problem?

18. Give two examples of open and closed questions. Why do open questions generally elicit greater response?

APPLICATIONS

3.1 "It's Like Cowabunga, Dude, But It's Not What I Ordered"

Customers of Tubular, Inc., which sells surfing and skateboarding equipment and apparel, frequently place their orders by telephone. You, the office manager, have received increasingly more numerous complaints about the shipment of *unordered* goods to your customers.

After a detailed study, you discover that the major problem is that incorrect information, such as item numbers, sizes, quantities, and colors, has been entered into the computerized ordering system by the telemarketing personnel who answer customers' calls.

Questions

1. What seems to be the major problem in this case?

2. What could you do to correct the problem?

3.2 The Reticent Subordinates

Jennifer O'Keefe is the food-services manager for Wonderworld, a resort hotel and theme park in Orlando, Florida. She sent a memo to her staff two weeks before the usual end-of-the-month staff meeting requesting topics for discussion at the upcoming session.

As of two days before the scheduled meeting, none of the employees had submitted any topics, so Jennifer assumed that the meeting might as well be canceled.

Questions

1. Does the absence of submitted topics necessarily mean that the employees would have nothing to say if the meeting were held as scheduled? Explain.

2. If the meeting were conducted, how might Jennifer elicit comments from her subordinates?

3.3 About as Clear as Mud

Les Mudd has worked for the I&S Brock income-tax preparation service for six years. Based in the Pacific Northwest regional office, Mudd was promoted after three years to supervisor and to the position of manager about five months ago. Face-to-face communication has been the normal practice at Brock for as long as Mudd has been with the company, although he typically felt ill-at-ease when interacting with his associates. Although knowledgeable about taxes and accounting, he lacked confidence in his ability to communicate well with others. However, he was an important link between upper management and the 15 supervisors in the regional office.

Mudd was happy about a recent policy change that came down from the vice-president for consumer tax services. Mudd received a memo indicating that all future directives were to be communicated in writing as a means of eliminating misunderstandings. Mudd said to himself, "My job is going to be a lot easier now that I don't have to deal with the supervisors face to face."

A few weeks later, Mudd received a telephone call from Samantha Santana, a human resource manager, requesting that he come to her office. The following conversation took place in Santana's office:

Santana: Les, I'm sorry to tell you this, but there have been a number of complaints from Kahaled Al-Masri, one of the supervisors, about your memos being unclear. Some bottlenecks have arisen in processing customers' electronic tax refunds, and Kahaled says it's because of the ambiguous way that you wrote the directives.

Mudd: That's ridiculous, Ms. Santana. I knew exactly what I meant by the memos, and there's no reason why Al-Masri shouldn't have, too.

Santana: Well, Kahaled said the memos were unclear and wondered why you seldom made any visits to the main floor anymore. He says it seems that you almost never leave your office in the annex.

Mudd: Visits to the main floor? The word I got from the consumer-tax VP was that all communication in the future was supposed to be in writing, and that's exactly what I've been doing. I don't understand why you are coming down on me merely for doing what I was told.

Questions

1. What seems to be the problem in this case?

2. What is your reaction to a company policy that establishes "management by memo"?

3. What are the comparative advantages and disadvantages of written and face-to-face communication?

4. What should Santana do about this situation?

3.4 The Paragon Machine Tool Company

The Paragon Machine Tool Company was started 17 years ago as a small company producing items for local businesses in the Dallas/Fort Worth area of Texas. Paragon continued modest in size until about four years ago when one of Paragon's managers made some business contacts in Spain, France, and Italy. These contacts, coupled with the relative cheapness of the dollar during the late 1980s and early 1990s, resulted in an increased demand for Paragon's products.

The stamping department, previously managed on a somewhat casual basis by Peter Vacher, the supervisor, found itself under substantial pressure to increase productivity. There were eight employees in the department accountable to Peter Vacher, six working the day shift and two working the second shift. All of the personnel in the department, including the supervisor, were union members.

Joe Martino, a journeyman, had been with the company for 17 years. Martino was classed as an "old-timer" by almost everyone in the plant, and he had seniority over all the personnel in his department. However, he wasn't classified as a supervisor.

Peter Vacher was considered by most of the people in his department to be quite capable. However, the general belief among the people in the department was that Vacher never seemed very happy. On numerous occasions Vacher had complained vehemently about how poorly organized the management was. On one occasion he had said to Nat Carson, an assistant who worked second shift and attended day classes at a nearby college, "As supervisor, I get it from both sides. I'm not supposed to get too friendly with the workers, but the management doesn't really accept me as a part of the management team either. Those "empty suits" won't even supply me with any cost information. The only way I can get it is to scrounge it out of Nora Johnson, the procurement manager. How in the world do they expect me to be cost-conscious if I don't even know anything about costs! Actually, Nat, management won't confide in any supervisor who came up through the ranks."

A month later, Betty Hanson, who was one of the two production managers, telephoned Vacher and asked him to come up to her office right away.

Hanson: Hi, Pete! Have a chair, will you?

Vacher: Thanks, Ms. Hanson. What can I do for you?

Hanson: Well, at a recent meeting the estimator revealed that he was having a difficult time trying to determine accurately just how much he should charge for labor for each job, since he doesn't have any labor time standards to go by. What I want you to do, Pete, is to go back to your department and establish some time standards for the various operations in the stamping department. Then submit a report to me by tomorrow morning at 9:00 A.M.

Vacher: All right, Ms. Hanson. I'll see what I can do.

Vacher went back to his department to speak to Martino.

Vacher: Joe, they're on our backs again. Now they want to know how long it takes you guys to complete your jobs. Will you please determine some sort of standard time for completing each of the different types of jobs you do? I've got to have this information before 9:00 A.M. tomorrow so I can give it to the "efficiency expert."

Martino: What's the matter with those crazy people upstairs? What do they think we're trying to do—put something over on 'em? Okay, I'll get something for you right away.

About half an hour later, Martino placed the report on Vacher's desk. After the second shift crew reported to work, Martino complained to Hank Willows, the night shift senior worker, about his being required to establish the new time standards.

Martino: For some reason, Pete asked me to establish time standards for our operations in this department. I wrote down the new standards on this piece of paper for you, and be sure you don't go *under* it. Those characters upstairs are trying to check up on us, and if we put out too much work, we'll work ourselves plumb out of work. So what I did was set a standard that we can do real easy. So don't work too fast or you'll foul things up. Tell the "professor," your assistant, about this.

Willows: Sure will, Joe. I've seen this happen before in other shops. If you set the standard too high, they'll always expect you to make it, and then they'll really come down hard on you if you don't. Don't worry about a thing!

Later that evening, Willows told Nat Carson, his assistant, to slow down, that a standard had been set, and that he was not to attempt to "work us out of work." Carson accepted the order reluctantly.

The regular hours of the night shift were from 4:00 P.M. until 11:00 P.M.. At about 9:00 P.M., the night after the standards had been established, production in the department halted.

Willows: Well, Nat, let's go home. We've done all we have to do, and if we do any more we'll go over the standards.
Stossen: Go home? It's only 9 o'clock. We shouldn't go home yet.
Willows: Don't worry, Nat, there aren't no supervisors on the night shift, so who's gonna know?
Stossen: If you don't mind, I think I'll stick around a while longer. I don't want to jeopardize my job. I've got two more years of college, and I don't know any other job where I could make this kind of money and work hours that will enable me to finish school.
Willows: Heck, there's plenty of jobs where this one came from. Okay, suit yourself. But don't do any work. That's an order!

Every night thereafter Carson took a textbook to work with him and studied from approximately 9:00 P.M. until 11:00 P.M.

Questions

1. What do you feel are the major problems in this case? What are some possible solutions?

2. Why do supervisors sometimes feel that they are caught between "a rock and a hard place," being neither managers nor workers?

3. Evaluate the leadership techniques of Vacher. Should he have established the time standards himself? Why or why not?

4. What was your evaluation of the approach that Carson took?

5. If you had been Carson and a manager made a surprise visit one evening at 9:30 P.M. after Willows had departed, what would you say to him?

6. What action would you take if you were a manager who dropped in one evening and observed that Willows was absent and Carson was studying?

7. Explain the following statement: "Followers tend to follow as they are led."

NOTES

1. James Morgan, "As They Say in Europe—Watch Your Tongue!," *Financial Times Weekend,* January 25/26, 1992, p. VIII.

2. Jeremy Gaunt, "Why Corporations Use Doublespeak," *San Francisco Chronicle,* November 13, 1990, p. C3.

3. Charles Batchelor, "No More than a Whisker Away from Success," *Financial Times,* November 1, 1991, p. 14.

4. Stan Kossen, *Creative Selling Today,* 3rd ed. (New York: HarperCollins, 1989), pp. 233–234.

5. Adapted loosely from "Leader's Guide," a pamphlet that the film *Listen Please* (Modern Management Films), Bureau of National Affairs, Washington, DC), no date.

6. As adapted from Wendell Johnson, "People in Quandaries," by Corinne Geeting, in *The Dynamics of Assertive Listening,* November/December 1980, pp. 16–17.

7. Tom Peters and Nancy Austin, "A Passion for Excellence," previewed by both authors in *Fortune,* May 13, 1985, pp. 20–30; and Douglas T. Hall and James G. Goodale, *Human Resource Management* (Glenview, IL: Scott, Foresman and Company, 1986), pp. 582, 583.

8. Thomas J. Peters and Robert H. Waterman, Jr., *In Search of Excellence* (New York: Warner Books, 1984), pp. 121, 122.

BOX NOTES

a. Adapted from "Groups are corporate wolves in sheep's clothing, activists say," *United Press International* as reported in *The Stars and Stripes,* December 23, 1991, p. 17.

b. Adapted from Ellen Goodman, "Phones Now Used to Avoid Talk," *The Stars and Stripes,* January 6, 1992; and Della Bradshaw, "Calls by a Voice From the Post," *Financial Times,* April 16, 1991, p. 10; and "Calls By a Voice From the Post," *Financial Times,* April 16, 1991, p. 10.

c. Jeremy Main, "How 21 Men Got Global in 35 Days," *Fortune* (International Edition), November 6, 1989, pp. 57–61.

EXPERIENTIAL EXERCISES

Find the Four Cs of Written Communication!

Write a business memo of approximately 100 words in your normal writing style. Then reread the guidelines for effective writing cited in Table 3.3, "The Four Cs of Written Communication." What proportion of the relevant guidelines did you apply? Which ones might you have applied but overlooked? Rewrite the memo and modify the lines that do not conform to the guidelines.

Whispering Sweet Nothings!

Have you ever played that silly little group game of whispering a phrase or sentence into the ear of the person seated beside you, who then passes the message on to the person beside him or her, and so on, until the message has been transmitted to everyone in the room? The results are sometimes startling. Let's see how the concept works with your own group. Your class facilitator will whisper a message into the ear of one member of your group, who will then pass it on.

Questions

1. What does this exercise help to illustrate?

2. According to the chapter, how can you know how effectively you've communicated with another person?

CHAPTER 4

The Dynamics of Small Groups

*The Whole Is
Greater Than . . .*

**When you finish this chapter,
you should be able to:**

1

Describe the purpose and nature of formal and informal groups

2

Recognize the types of group member behavior associated with small groups

3

Understand how informal groups utilize the grapevine

4

Summarize the advantages and deficiencies of group decision making

5

List and describe the principal types of interviewing styles

6

Summarize the suggestions for conducting and participating in interviews

> Groups, like individuals, have shortcomings. Groups can
> bring out the worst as well as the best in people.
>
> *Irving L. Janis, Author*

> The best way to get a good idea is to have a lot of ideas.
>
> *Linus Pauling, Chemist*

Greta Garbo, glamorous Swedish-born film actress of the 1930s, and
Howard Hughes, famous industrialist of the 1960s and 1970s, had
something in common. Both became world famous as a result of their
group activities, and both became obsessed in their later years with
the desire to avoid groups.

Although named best actress of the first half of the century by a
Variety poll in 1950, Greta Garbo withdrew from most public contact
and became renowned for her statement, "I want to be left alone." And
Howard Hughes, noted for his flight of a twin-engine Lockheed around
the world in three days and 19 hours in 1938, as well as for his gigantic
industrial empire, seemed almost to become a figment of the journalis-
tic media's imagination, so rare were his public appearances in the latter part of his life. It's lucky that Garbo and Hughes never fell in love
and married, since their talents in the area of group dynamics and
interpersonal relations seemed to leave much to be desired.

A large body of theory related to the dynamics of group behavior
has developed. Our approach here will not be to explore each theory
in depth, but, instead, to try to glean from past research those ideas
that can be applied in a practical manner to the everyday organizational behavior of small work groups.

We'll walk alone together!

HERE A GROUP, THERE A GROUP, EVERYWHERE A GROUP-GROUP

Few of us ever find ourselves in the position of being able to avoid
other people as Garbo and Hughes did. How much time, for example,
are you able to spend alone each day? Probably very little.

The chances are quite good that you're a member of a wide variety of groups, such as household, school, social, religious, and work
groups. For most of us, being a member of groups is as normal as the
daily ebbing and flowing of the oceans' tides. In short, being a member of a group or groups is usually a basic part of much of our lives.

Just WHAT Is a Group?

Do you remember our mentioning in Chapter 1 that whenever there
are two or more persons there is, in effect, an organization? The same

premise holds true for our meaning of the term **group.** Although not all scholars agree on the precise definition of a group, for our purposes we'll define the term as *two or more individuals who interact personally, or through communication networks, with each other.* Groups usually share (or are supposed to share) similar goals, experiences or needs.

Based on our definition, then, a husband and wife, an assembly team in a factory, and even the members of a large multinational corporation could be considered groups. Although it is apparent that groups vary in size, our principal focus in this chapter will be on the behavior and problems associated with smaller groups, those that interact on a face-to-face basis rather than through official interoffice or interdivisional communication networks.

Were Adam and Eve a group?

Just WHY Is a Group?

What causes people to join groups? Years ago, social scientists believed that people were a lot like sheep and therefore had a "flock instinct" not unlike that of their woolly, four-legged cousins. Most social scientists today reject this theory and believe that people tend to join groups for reasons such as those cited in Figure 4.1. We'll look briefly at each of these factors.

Security. Have you ever noticed that when you're home alone at night you feel somewhat different from when you're there with someone else? Do the squeaks and creaks in the dark recesses of the house sound much louder and spookier when you're alone? Does the presence of another person (or even a pet) tend to give you a greater feeling of security? The need for **security** is an important reason why people form such groups as neighborhood watch groups, unions, rifle associations, industrial cartels, medical associations, and so on.

In an organizational setting, forming a *buying committee* could enable individuals who are responsible for making organizational purchases to feel more secure. A buying committee is an ongoing, established group whose function is to determine the best sources for

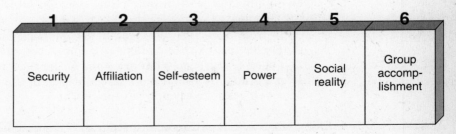

1	2	3	4	5	6
Security	Affiliation	Self-esteem	Power	Social reality	Group accomplishment

Figure 4.1 Reasons why people join groups.

the organization's purchases. Each member of the committee may feel more secure in his or her buying decisions since the *responsibility* for a bad decision is *shared* with others. No single member of the group is solely responsible for the group's actions.

Affiliation. Don't you generally prefer to be with other people who share your interests and values? This tendency—termed **affiliation** —is another reason why people generally want to be a part of a group. Some people join computer support groups to share ideas, knowledge, and software. Some people join Edsel owner clubs to

---

A QUESTION OF ETHICS

Things Weren't *Maxed,* Nor Have They Gone *Well* for Maxwell's Former Employees[a]

The late, great Robert Maxwell was a publishing tycoon with a flamboyant flair for publicity. He also had a tenacious grip on the door of secrecy that blocked public scrutiny of his personal financial condition until his sudden and mysterious death near the Canary Islands in November 1991. Well-known, however, was his use of leverage and heavy bank borrowing to finance his many corporate acquisitions. Not so well-known were activities that the *Financial Times* has referred to as "the ruthless and systematic looting of pension schemes in the Maxwell business empire by the late Mr. Robert Maxwell."

It has been revealed since Maxwell's death that much of the money he acquired for expansion and acquisition came from his employees' pension funds, and now more than 30,000 employees and pensioners have found their retirement prospects jeopardized. At the time of this writing it appears likely that the employees may find themselves facing their declining years with neither the monies that they were promised as a condition of loyal employment nor the sums they contributed to the pension plans themselves.

A Question of Ethics: Maxwell's employees, of course, belonged to a group. What are some of the reasons why people form groups—reasons that will be lacking in the lives of Maxwell's employees and pensioners?

share their feelings of owning a "successful failure." And others join singles clubs to share themselves with other singles! Managers sometimes join service groups, such as Kiwanis, to be able to exchange ideas (and business cards) with other managers in the locality. Engineers may join engineering societies, insurance risk managers may join associations of risk managers, procurement managers may join associations to share ideas on purchasing, and so on. Some organizational members may affiliate with others at work on an informal basis, perhaps regularly eating lunch together or playing softball together on company teams. People tend to affiliate more with groups that they join voluntarily than with groups to which they are formally assigned.

Self-Esteem. Membership in some groups tends to affect its members' feelings of **self-esteem,** or worth. For example, imagine being a part of the management team of a company on the verge of bankruptcy, alleged by the popular press to be responsible for the mismanagement of its resources. Wouldn't your feelings toward yourself, as well as those of others toward you, be higher if, instead, you worked for a high-technology company that was considered one of the most innovative, progressive, and profitable in the industry? Membership in certain groups can therefore provide individuals with *good feelings about themselves* they might otherwise lack.

Power. "In numbers there is strength," advises an old adage. Being a member of a group, therefore, helps individuals to acquire strength, that is, **power,** which is difficult if not impossible to attain alone. Power is defined as *the possession of control, authority, or influence over others.* Membership in a union or employee association, for example, provides workers with influence—the bargaining strength—that they lack as individual employees.

Social Reality. Another purpose of groups is to establish and test **social reality.** For example, when several individuals have similar attitudes about perceived unfair treatment by their boss, they tend to feel more secure in their beliefs because of the consensus of opinion that develops. The group members create, in effect, their own reality regardless of how accurate their perception of the situation may be.

Goal Accomplishment. Mountain climbers, basketball players, and astronauts—like the members of any work unit—generally function in groups. The group enables its members to *accomplish their goals* more readily because of the variety of skills and knowledge that can be collectively provided.

Just HOW Is a Group?

In basic mathematics, we learn the whole of an object is *equal* to the sum of its parts. In group relationships, however, the whole is often *greater* then the sum of its parts. This concept is termed **synergism** and can be defined as *the interaction of two or more independent parts, the effects of which are different from that which would be attained by each part individually.*

"You mean . . . 2 + 2 can equal 5?"

There is more information in a group than in any of its members. Thus problems that require the utilization of knowledge should give groups an advantage over individuals. Even if one member of the group (for example, the leader) knows much more than anyone else, the limited unique knowledge of lesser-informed individuals could serve to fill in some gaps in knowledge. For example, a skilled machinist might contribute to an engineer's problem-solving and an ordinary worker might supply information on how a new machine might be received by workers.

Let's look at another illustration. For example, the interaction of two separate departments, say, sales and manufacturing, can have a synergistic effect on customer satisfaction. Assume that salespeople promise customers their purchases will be delivered by a certain date and quality of the finished product will be of a particular standard. If the manufacturing department cooperates by meeting deadlines and quality standards, customer satisfaction is maintained or enhanced. Of course, if such cooperation and coordination are lacking, the synergistic effect on customers' attitudes will be adversely affected.

THE NATURE OF FORMAL AND INFORMAL GROUPS

Groups tend to be a basic part of organizational life. Regardless of the type of group we might discuss, most work groups have split personalities, so to speak. They have their *formal,* or *required,* side, and they have their *informal,* or *emergent,* side. Let's examine the principal differences between the two.

The What and Why of Formal Groups

Most formal groups are **formal, or required, systems.** The required system consists of individuals who are positioned and coordinated by management for the purpose of attaining predetermined organizational goals and objectives. Assume, for example, that you own a bicycle and roller skate sales and rental shop and employ five people to help you achieve your planned objectives. Your organization has to have some sort of formal structure to achieve your goals of selling bicycles and roller skates, providing service, and making a profit.

Why must we be so formal?

The formal system, therefore, provides some degree of *order* and *predictability* in an organization. You assume, for example, based on your planning, that Suzy, Joe, and Karen—your staff of salespersons—will be on the job promptly at 9:00 A.M. each morning, as will Frank and Ernestine, both service repair workers. Your work group couldn't function effectively without a formal—that is, required, planned, or orderly—system.

Formal organizations, then, exist for a variety of reasons. Basically, formal groups:

1. Facilitate the *accomplishment of goals* much less haphazardly than do informal ones.

2. Facilitate the *coordination of the activities,* or *functions,* of the organization.

3. Aid in the *establishment of logical authority relationships* among people and positions.

4. Permit the application of the concepts of *specialization* and *division of labor.*

5. Create more *group cohesiveness* as a result of a common set of goals.

The Informal Group Emerges

In Chapter 5, we'll examine concepts related to human needs and motivation, concepts that are significant to the topic of small group behavior, especially to its informal aspects. Let's return for a moment to your bicycle and roller skate sales and service shop. Whether you are what your employees consider a good or a bad boss has little effect on the existence of an informal organization. You, as owner-manager of the shop, can create a formal work group, but you *cannot* eliminate an informal one as long as you have an organization. The **informal, or emergent, system** evolves in one form or another regardless of your personal wishes, although you can *influence* its activities and behavior.

Why Informal Groups?

We've already discussed the reasons why groups generally form, as well as the major purposes of formal groups. Many of the same reasons apply to *informal groups.* Don't informal groups also have goals and objectives? Don't most individuals have various sorts of psychological and social needs that require satisfying? Unfortunately, the required system seldom satisfies all individual needs. So informal groups—the emergent system—come galloping to the rescue of small group members. But are informal groups a good or a bad thing?

Are they good—or are they bad—or both?

There's little doubt that informal groups sometimes create problems for organizations. They *transmit false information* (rumors) through the grapevine, *resist change, cause excessive conformity* to group norms, and sometimes even *develop goals that conflict* with those of the formal organization. The members of the group may ostracize or exclude an employee from social interaction. For example, a person whose work pace is faster than the norm for a particular group might be looked upon as a "ratebuster" who is trying to "show up" the other group members.

The informal organization can, however, perform a variety of positive and useful functions. As already mentioned, informal groups help the individual members *satisfy psychological and social needs.* In large plants and offices, a person could feel merely like an employee number instead of a human being if it were not for the opportunity to socialize and interact with other members of the group.

THE BEHAVIOR OF GROUPS

The whole is different from the sum of its parts.

Groups, it has been observed, are dynamic. Managers often express amazement at the "strange" behavior of some employees when they are grouped together. It's important to realize, however, that all sorts of factors can influence behavior in groups, such as the membership of the group itself, the cohesiveness of the group, the work environment, and the grapevine as a means of informal communication among group members. Let's now take a brief look at the first three of these.

The Influence of Group Members

Groups, as we know, are a lot like individuals. Both groups and individuals have distinct needs, personalities, and beliefs about what constitutes acceptable, or so-called normal, behavior. But individuals often undergo a kind of metamorphosis when they become part of a group, and their concepts of what ought to be may be altered along with their personalities.

Group standards, known as **social norms,** have a powerful influence over the group member who wants to be accepted by peers. The shy, retiring, high school youth, for example, who seldom asserts him- or herself when alone in an unfamiliar crowd may suddenly become boisterous and obnoxious when with friends. Most of us have read about the antisocial activities of youth gangs or observed the loud and aggressive behavior of packs of youths who, as individuals alone, would seldom behave in such a manner.

Here's another example of the influence of groups: An action-packed, highly emotion-charged movie about teenage violence, *The*

Warriors, when first shown in theaters was blamed for inciting violence among young people. Immediately after the film's showing, many in the audience ripped out theater seats, then ran shouting toward the restrooms crazily ripping out urinals and sinks. Imagine if one of the "urinal rippers" had been given a private showing of the film in the theater. Is it likely that the person's violent behavior would have been the same without the group present?

As we've already discussed, the group has a powerful influence on its members by providing them with power and security, and hence feelings of strength. Labor unions, as well as employer and medical associations, are vivid examples of groups that offer some degree of power and security to their members.

Some years ago, Professor Solomon Asch conducted an experiment—now referred to as the **Asch conformity studies**[1]—that helps to illustrate how people tend to conform to group standards as a means of being accepted. Asch gathered several groups of eight persons to participate in the experiment. The eight persons sat in a row and were asked to judge the length of various lines. However, only one person out of each group of eight was ignorant of the fact that the others had been told by Asch to conspire against the one. They were told to state the wrong answers in a confident manner two-thirds of the time. The "innocent victims" in each group had to make their choices last. About 40 percent of the time, the unknowing individuals went along with the incorrect decisions of the group, admittedly because they didn't want to look silly in front of their peers, and not because they truly believed the group's answers.

Conformity can make an Asch out of you!

Certain individuals within a specific group may also have a significant influence over the group's members. An obvious example is a supervisor, a **formal leader,** who has been officially delegated particular rights, or authority, over his or her subordinates. In many groups there may also emerge an **informal leader,** a person who is able to influence other group members because of his or her age, knowledge, technical or social skills, or physical strength. In a sense the informal group itself can assign a leadership role to a person who would be quick to refuse a formal leadership position.

The Cohesiveness of Groups—Sticking Together

Another common characteristic of group behavior is an emotional attraction and closeness, or **group cohesion** that members have for each other and their group. Groups provide the mechanism for giving people a sense of both identity and unity, something referred to as a feeling of **belongingness.**

Are we together or not?

Some groups are highly cohesive. Their members stick closely together in spite of pressures to reduce their emotional ties. Other groups consist of members who couldn't care less about unity, solidarity, or group cohesiveness. They don't really feel part of a team. These people are merely a collection of individuals who may officially be members of the group but whose needs are not satisfied by the personal interaction with the group's other members.

For example, you may have observed some professors who are members of a group, such as a psychology department, but who seldom interact with other department members. They feel little unity or personal identification with their cohorts. Yet there are other individuals, such as members of a sales force that is widely dispersed geographically, who share a feeling of camaraderie and mutual identity. Sometimes, groups that weren't the least bit cohesive suddenly attain tremendous unity upon recognizing an external threat of some sort. A historic example was the unified U.S. backing of "Desert Storm" military intervention against Iraq in 1991.

Professor John B. Minor suggests that three major factors influence the degree of unity of a group:

What tends to influence group unity?

1. The predominance of certain kinds of social motives or needs

2. The capacity of the group to provide emotionally for its members

3. The existence of a shared goal[2]

Watch out though! Group cohesion can be tricky. Individuals, for example, may develop cohesiveness either *in harmony* or *in conflict* with the goals of the formal organization. Subgroups or cliques may form within a group. Certain members of a group may develop cohesion against other group members and ostracize them based on their sex, race, age, or physical characteristics.

Some groups may be reluctant to accept new members. They view anyone not a part of their established group as an outsider. Let's assume that you have been assigned to a department where such cohesion exists. What should you do? Some authorities suggest that you recognize this as a natural process in many group situations, and that you be patient about winning acceptance of the group's members.[3]

Work Arrangement Influence on Informal Groups

How might the arrangement of work influence informal grous?

Studies made by Michael Argyle indicate that the formal arrangement of the physical work flow influences the nature of the informal group. According to Argyle, employees who work side by side on assembly lines seem not to develop a group feeling; they tend to feel isolated from their fellow workers. Such a lack of group cohesiveness,

Argyle contends, can provoke absenteeism and unfavorably affect job satisfaction, turnover, and productivity.[4] All of these factors, of course, can have adverse effects on the quality of the work done. To overcome such problems, some firms have restructured their assembly lines to include *worker teams* or *quality circles*. Some firms have also designed office layouts that create more interdependency and effectiveness of employees. Such factors as the location of desks influence group members' ability to satisfy belongingness needs as well as their status in the group. A later chapter will discuss morale problems in greater detail.

A Balance Between Task and Maintenance Activities

Groups, as we know, are formed to accomplish goals. A balance between two types of activities—*task* and *maintenance*—is essential if the group's goals are to be accomplished.

What might an imbalance cause?

Task activities are specific behaviors that directly affect goal accomplishment, such as processing letters or operating a fax machine. **Maintenance activities** are related to the social and emotional needs that employees bring to the job, such as the opportunity to "clown around," or joke from time to time. Any effort by a manager to squelch the satisfaction of such needs can upset the balance between the two factors and adversely affect the group's performance.

Cultural Diversity In Groups

In an earlier period, white male corporate culture was the norm in American organizations, but the workplace is becoming less a melting pot and more a mosaic. According to the Bureau of Labor Statistics, the white male share of the U.S. labor force will drop to 39.4 percent by the year 2000 from 48.9 percent in 1976, while the share of women and people of African, Hispanic, Asian, and Native American origin is expected to rise.[5] Consequently, work groups of the future will increasingly reflect what is referred to as **cultural diversity,** which means that group members will be even more varied in their beliefs, value systems, behavior patterns, and even thought characteristics.

This diversity can influence the cohesiveness of groups because of the mind-set and prejudices some group members have toward others. For example, behavior common to white cultures may appear exaggerated when performed by members of another cultural group. If a white male pounds on a table to emphasize a point, he may merely seem assertive. If an African American does the same thing, he may seem aggressive and hostile.[6]

Furthermore, members of different cultures frequently have different ways of responding to certain behavior. For example, some ethnic groups tend to react negatively toward structure. Others may

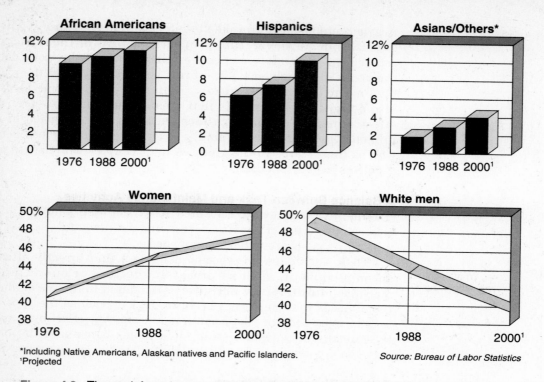

Figure 4.2   The work force is changing, minorities and women represent a growing share while the white male share is declining.

interpret eye contact as intimidating. And within each culture there also exists diversity. For example, any cultural group has members who dislike being praised in front of their peers and others who don't mind at all. Managers must learn to function in more culturally diverse settings. Such diversity can actually enrich the effectiveness of groups when properly handled. Chapters 10, 11, and 12 deal extensively with such diverse groups as ethnic minorities, women, people with disabilities, the aging, and those with substance abuse problems.

INFORMAL GROUPS AND THE GRAPEVINE

In Chapter 3 we learned that informal communication travels through a channel typically referred to as the **grapevine,** the real workhorse of message networks. We also learned that the grapevine is the means for transmitting **rumors,** *statements whose truth cannot* *be verified by any known authority.* The grapevine has a significant effect on any organization and should, therefore, be well understood by organizational members.

The Nature of the Grapevine

The grapevine, as part of the *emergent,* or *informal, organization,* exists out of the personal needs of employees. Let's now find out what grapevines are really like.

Grapevine Communication Is Fast. First let's think about how *formal communication* is developed. Ideas have to be crystallized, organized, and frequently put into writing. They then have to be transmitted to others, often through the various layers of the *formal organization.* However, *informal messages* traveling through the *informal organization,* that is the *grapevine,* are fast. They need not travel through a formal hierarchy. Professor Keith Davis, well known for his extensive research in the area of informal communication, has expressed the following about the grapevine:

> Being flexible and personal, it spreads information faster than most management communications systems. With the rapidity of a burning power train, the grapevine filters out of the woodwork, past the manager's office, through the locker rooms, and along the corridors. Its speed makes it quite difficult for management to stop undesirable rumors or to release significant news in time to prevent rumor formation.[7]

Grapevine Communication Is Oral. Unlike most formal communications, messages transmitted through the grapevine are generally *oral* rather than written. This factor contributes to the speed at which they travel. The grapevine is also an excellent means for managers to transmit information that they prefer to be "off the record."

Grapevine Communication Thrives on Insecurity. Another feature of grapevine communication is its tendency to be used more extensively by organizational members when they feel insecure about various situations. For example, *out-of-the-ordinary information,* such as an impending plant relocation or closure, or a company restructuring, often causes organizational members to be extremely active on the grapevine, typically transmitting rumors in the process. Imagine, for example, the grapevine communication and rumors that must have thrived on the insecurities among BankAmerica employees when company officials announced in March 1992 that as many as 12,000 jobs would be eliminated within three years following the

"Wow! Look at that message move!"

"Off the record, I would like to say. . . ."

"I'm insecure. Let's talk."

company's takeover of Security Pacific Corporation.[8] Employees of many firms, such as Exxon, IBM, and General Motors, experienced such insecurities during the economic recession of the early 1990s.

Grapevine Communication Is Extensive When People Don't Have Accurate Information. Rumors tend to fly through the informal organization when organizational members *lack facts.* For example, take the case of an employee, Michael, who injured his finger on a machine this morning. Harriet, who works near Michael, merely told Shayne during a coffee break that Michael was *hurt* while working on his machine, but failed to give Shayne any details. Shayne, in turn told three other persons that Michael had received *a serious injury* on the job, and within a half an hour the rumor spread that Michael was *critically injured* and not expected to survive. You can see, therefore, that managers must attempt to influence the grapevine and "rumor mill" by making certain that employees have accurate facts.

Squelch rumors with the truth.

Grapevine Communication Is Extensive When People Relate to the Situation. If organizational members have no interest in, or don't relate to, the information traveling through the grapevine, they are unlikely to pass it to others. Of course, the converse holds true. For example, assume that the 6 o'clock news reports there will be a significant cutback in defense spending during the next year. Engineers and, of course, others who work for companies in defense-related industries would probably relate to such news. They may deduce that their companies are likely to require substantially fewer engineering activities in the future, and, therefore, some of the staff is "certain" to be laid off. Rumors related to "impending layoffs" could start spreading among engineers throughout many organizations.

Engineering a rumor?

Chains Required for Grapevine Communication

How does the grapevine actually work? What are the typical *networks* through which informal messages pass from person to person? There are four generally accepted patterns, or *chains,* that characterize the grapevine, as depicted in Figure 4.3.

Single-Strand Chain. The simplest, and least common, pattern of grapevine communication, is termed the **single-strand chain,** which is the transmission of informal messages from one person to the next person in the chain. For example, Marilena recently walked by a manager's office and overheard someone say that a key senior executive was likely to be dismissed in the near future. Marilena, in turn, passes the information on to Jeremy, who tells Cameron, who relates it to Stan, who tells Jan, and so on.

"I tell you, you tell her, she tells him, and so on."

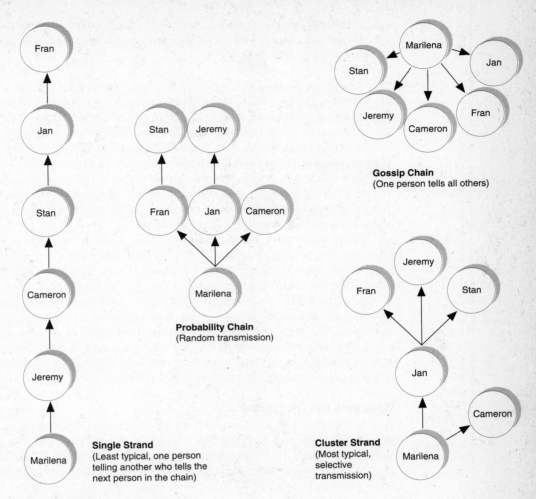

Figure 4.3 Grapevine chains.

Gossip Chain. A second grapevine network is termed the **gossip chain.** As with the single strand, the gossip chain is not particularly common, since it exists in those rare instances in which only *one person passes the information on to everyone else.*

Probability Chain. Substantially more common than the two grapevine networks already discussed is the **probability chain,** which exists when *information flows through the informal organization on a random, or unpredictable, basis.* Referring again to Figure

4.3, the first person, Marilena, passes the message by chance to Fran, Jan, and Cameron. Then Fran and Jan randomly pass the message on to Jeremy and Stan.

Cluster Chain. By far the most common grapevine network is the **cluster chain,** in which *individuals are selective regarding to whom they pass on information.* For example, an individual may tell something to one or more persons who may merely keep the information to themselves or pass it on to a few other persons. As you can observe in Figure 4.3, Marilena tells Cameron and Jan. Cameron, however, does not pass the information, but Jan, in turn, tells three others. Because of the tendency for an individual to pass information to more than one person, we can see that it often takes very few persons to transmit a rumor to a large number of people.

Those who pass information on in a cluster fashion are often *selective* in their approach. They may tell others not to tell anyone else. If anyone abuses their confidence, he or she may not become privy to certain informal communication in the future.

A fairly useful rule to follow is this: *Don't tell anyone anything that you do not want passed on to others.* Saying to your receiver, for example, "Be sure not to repeat what I told you," is no assurance of confidentiality. Many people on the receiving end of so-called private information have the tendency to promise to tell no one else and later tell the people they told not to tell anyone else!

"Remember, don't tell anyone, and if you do, be sure to tell them not to tell anyone!"

Managing the Grapevine

A supervisor once asked, "How can I get rid of the grapevine?" to which he received the reply, "You can't." If it is true that the grapevine cannot be eliminated, what can managers do about it? Primarily, they should recognize that the grapevine provides the organization with substantial benefits. For example, it provides employees with a *release of tensions,* an outlet for pent-up emotions. The mere opportunity for employees to get things off their chests informally often eliminates the likelihood of explosive reactions later. In addition, the grapevine provides management with *feedback,* an opportunity to find out how employees feel about the organization.

If you can't lick it, influence it!

Rumors, however, frequently become a thorn in the side of organizations in which trust is lacking between managers and their associates. Whereas rumors may be difficult to eliminate entirely, their frequency tends to be reduced in organizations whose *employees are kept well informed* and whose managers see to it that *credibility gaps are rare.* Managers have to be sensitive to potential rumors so that they can be squelched before causing damage to the morale of organizational members.

Spread the Word: Gossip Is Good[b]

The office grapevine is 75 to 95 percent accurate and provides managers and staff with better information than formal communications, according to a study cited by *CPA/Administrative Reports*.

The rumor mill is busier today than ever. For one thing, computer networks have given middle- and lower-level managers access to a plethora of information, while the era of corporate restructurings and takeovers has "made people increasingly nervous—and more receptive to believing and starting rumors," says Arnold Brown, a New York consultant. Another factor that heated up the rumor mill in recent years: the move of many corporate headquarters from urban to suburban and rural locations. Employees in isolated settings talk less to outsiders and more to each other.

Rather than ignore or try to repress the grapevine, it's crucial for executives to tune into it, consultants say. That can help managers uncover attitudes, problems, and ideas. Moreover, suggests Mr. Brown, executives should "identify the key people in your company's grapevine and, instead of punishing them, feed them information." He adds: "When a company issues a press release, it knows what newspapers to contact, so why not know your internal media?"

GROUP PROBLEM SOLVING AND DECISION MAKING

Quite customary in many organizations is **group decision making,** an activity based on the old adage that "two heads are better than one." Although many decisions are made as a result of one-to-one interaction between two individuals, a considerable amount of decision making in today's organizations takes place in **meetings.** Most meetings are intended to accomplish either of two objectives: (1) to provide information or (2) to solve problems. Let's take a brief look at some of the group dynamics and characteristics of such activities.

Planned and Unplanned Agendas

When managers call meetings for the purpose of providing information or for finding solutions to specific problems, they generally have a good idea of what should be covered during the meeting. In other words, they typically have a **planned agenda.** The planned agenda is useful in that it serves to guide the group's activities toward a preestablished goal. A planned agenda can help prevent a lot of scarce and valuable time from being eaten up needlessly.

Although an agenda may be planned, one of the potential pitfalls of any meeting is the possibility that a **hidden agenda** will surface. A group member's hidden agenda is basically the attitudes and feelings that he or she brings to the meeting. The hidden agenda may be "planned" in advance of the meeting, or it may emerge spontaneously as the result of a disagreement with ideas expressed or a distrust of the people conducting the session. In some instances, the person with the hidden agenda, either consciously or subconsciously, tries to place obstacles in the path of the planned agenda. A chairperson should weigh the validity of any hidden agendas that crop up and try to prevent them from sidetracking a meeting too far from its original purpose.

What are you hiding up your sleeve?

Brainstorming

A group activity that many have found useful for arriving at creative solutions to problems is **brainstorming.** In a brainstorming session, group members express themselves freely, regardless of how crazy or wild their ideas may appear to the other group members. The usual guidelines for brainstorming sessions are that (1) everyone is encouraged to participate, (2) a large number of ideas are to be generated, (3) group members listen to and build on others' ideas, (4) wild, creative ideas are encouraged, (5) the atmosphere is free from criticism or evaluation, (6) no idea or thought is squelched by either the idea's originator or the group members, and (7) all presented ideas are recorded.

Don't knock it!

Brainstorming sessions have proven helpful in generating a large number of potentially useful ideas. In a freewheeling session useful ideas tend to build on less useful ones. For example, the name of a new product could be developed by a group of individuals who say aloud every name that comes to mind during the session. After a long list of names is developed and recorded, an analysis is made, the choice is narrowed down, and the "best" one is selected.

Brainwriting

Another small group idea-generating technique utilizes features of brainstorming and is referred to as **brainwriting.** As with brainstorming, people build on each other's ideas.

How is brainwriting employed? Group members generally sit around a table and each person writes his or her ideas on a piece of paper. Papers are then placed in the middle of the table. Participants examine the papers other than their own and try to build on the presented ideas. After a preset time, the papers are collected and ideas are clarified and evaluated.

Could brainwriting reduce the chances of brainwashing?

Although brainwriting tends to result in fewer ideas, there are some significant advantages to the process over brainstorming. With brainwriting:

1. The activity of writing tends to result in more complete and better thought-out ideas.

2. Domination of the idea-generating process by a few members is less likely.

3. Socializing and the wasting of time are more difficult.

4. Emotionally charged or controversial topics can be handled more easily.

Deciding the Delphi Way

No peeking!

An approach to group decision making that contrasts with brainstorming and brainwriting is the **Delphi method.** Unlike brainstorming, the group members do not meet and interact with one another. Instead, each participant in the decision-making process is given a problem or a questionnaire to work on *independently*. Each person's analysis and suggestions are then distributed to the other participants without their knowing whose ideas they are reading. Each participant then revises his or her own original decisions and resubmits them to a coordinator. The process can be repeated until a desired conclusion is reached.

Although the Delphi method tends to take more time than other group decision methods, it has the advantage of being able to involve people who are separated geographically in decision making. This method also helps to avoid some of the negative influences associated with group decision making, which will be discussed shortly.

Deciding with Quality Circles

The subject of quality has practically become an obsession with some managers in the 1990s. **Quality circles (QCs)** are sometimes utilized to aid in achieving quality standards. A QC is a group of rank-and-file workers with a common concern that meets to exchange information for mutual improvement. It generally consists of five to ten members. The use of quality circles is closely related to total quality management, a topic to be discussed in greater detail in Chapter 7.

Let's Form a Committee

In some organizations, difficult decisions are often "referred to committee," either an *ongoing,* standing committee, or an *ad hoc* committee, one established to handle a specific situation. A **committee** can be defined as *a group of two or more persons who officially meet together for the purpose of considering issues or problems related to the organization.* In some instances, an ad hoc committee is referred to as a **task force.**

Sometimes task forces are mere *dummy groups,* set up merely to "park good company soldiers who are temporarily out of a job, but whom the company doesn't want to lose."[9] The group's ideas, which weren't intended to accomplish much, end up fading away.

Occasionally a task force is established as a *setup* by a manager who is trying to gain a high profile and establish a track record. To attract attention, the manager establishes a task force to study a problem, the answers to which she or he already has. The true intent of such a task force is for the manager to push her or his idea to gain recognition for future personal benefit, such as a promotion or pay raise.

"Look at what I already knew!"

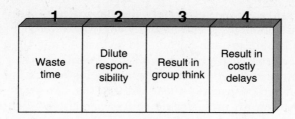

Figure 4.4 Dangers inherent in the group decision-making process.

Many people, however, hold the view that committees, when properly administered, are useful. They feel that committees can result in better decision making since—as with brainstorming—two heads can be more effective than one. They also argue that a greater input of ideas can occur in committee meetings, with one idea perhaps rising out of others. Further, several people with different types of knowledge, abilities, and experience might be able to see more facets of a particular problem than could one person.

Deficiencies in Group Decision Making

Although creative ideas do result frequently from group decision making, there are inherent dangers to the process that one should continually guard against. Such dangers are itemized in Figure 4.4. Let's look briefly at each.

Wasters of Time. If meetings are not well planned, they are potential *time wasters*. A manager and his or her subordinates can find much of their time wasted through discussions of trivia, topics that do little to further the organization's goals and objectives. One critic of committees, the late Dutch-American historian Hendrik van Loon, had this to say about committees:

> Nothing is ever accomplished by a committee unless it consists of three members, one of whom happens to be sick and another absent.

Diluted Responsibility. Another danger inherent in the use of group decision making by committees is that it tends to *dilute responsibility*. Since decisions are arrived at by group consensus, no one person can be blamed for a bad decision.

Groupthink. A further potential problem of group decision making lies in what has been called **groupthink,** *the process of deriving negative results from group decision-making efforts as a result of in-group*

Eleventh
Commandment: Right
or wrong . . . Thou
shalt stick together!

pressures.[10] We've already discussed the nature of group cohesion. Oddly enough, it can actually contribute to poor group decision making. Some groups become so cohesive that their tendency to agree interferes with critical thinking. People do tend to be influenced by their peers. Therefore, the attitudes and influence of some group members, especially those with status, can sway an entire group into pursuing an undesirable course of action. Such closely knit groups can be said to suffer from the *illusion of unanimity:* No one wants to break up the cohesiveness of the group. The group members become the victims of groupthink.

The misjudged sounds
of silence!

Group leaders sometimes encourage groupthink at meetings—particularly when they've arrived at specific decisions before the meeting even begins! The other members are there merely to rubber-stamp predetermined decisions. Group leaders may also assume that silence on the part of the participants means consent to or agreement with decisions actually made unilaterally by the leader.

On January 28, 1986, the space shuttle *Challenger* exploded immediately after liftoff, killing six astronauts and New Hampshire school teacher, Christa McAuliffe. Investigations later suggested that the concepts of groupthink may have come into play and that NASA had abandoned "good judgment and common sense" related to safety problems that caused the explosion.[11]

Costly Delays. Group decision making can also result in *costly delays.* Other tasks must be neglected while committee members are in session, and sometimes important members arrive late or are absent altogether. There also tends to be more indecisiveness rather than candid and creative thought among committee members as they try to arrive at reasonable decisions and conclusions. The German philosopher Friedrich Nietzsche long ago warned about group behavior, stating that "madness is the exception in individuals but the rule in groups." In far too many cases, he seems to have been right!

Meetings of the Minds—Avoiding the Pitfalls

In spite of the many potential pitfalls inherent in group decision making, it is likely to continue playing an important role in many organizations. When its limitations are recognized and sessions are properly planned, group decision making can lead to good ideas. Let's look briefly at some suggestions about holding meetings that can reduce some of the potential problems associated with group decision making.

Don't fall into the pits!

Have a Good Reason. It is estimated that the typical manager spends more than one-third of his or her work day at meetings, most of which, according to a survey by Goodrich and Sherwood Company, are a waste of time.[12] If this is true, rather than squandering time unnecessarily, meetings should be called only when there's a good reason to have one. Some meetings appear to be called more out of habit than necessity. ("Why did I call a meeting? Because we always have meetings on Fridays, that's why.") Why call a meeting if you don't have a specific agenda? When you have the responsibility for calling meetings, be certain that you have a planned agenda, which can go a long way toward preventing considerable scarce and valuable time from being eaten up needlessly. As can be viewed in Figure 4.5, meetings are generally held for any of the following three reasons:

Can't I just relax?

1. To present information to the attendees.
2. To receive feedback from the attendees.
3. To solve problems and make decisions.

Respect Time. Try to avoid scheduling open-ended meetings; they tend to drag on and on due to the lack of time pressures. Instead, establish precise times for meetings to begin and end. Let participants know that you expect them to arrive at meetings promptly. Waiting for participants can waste considerable time. Be sure to start meetings on time. If participants know from experience that your meetings always begin 15 minutes late, they may feel that there is no particular reason for them to be there on time.

"You can always tell when the boss wants a brief meeting."

SOURCE: From *The Wall Street Journal*—permission, Cartoon Features Syndicate.

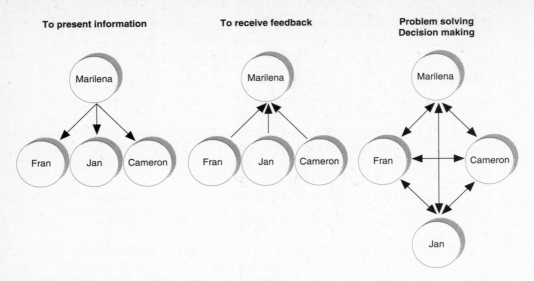

Figure 4.5 Typical reasons for conducting meetings.

Be Creatively Brief. Some managers schedule meetings just before lunch—say, 11:00 A.M. to noon—or during the hour just prior to quitting time. The theory behind this scheduling is that participants usually aren't eager to sit in a meeting during their lunch hour or on their own time. One manager keeps his meetings short by conducting them in a room with no chairs. He feels that the less comfortable the setting of a meeting, the more quickly participants will want to take care of the business at hand.

Recognize Effect of Physical Settings. The layout of the meeting room—that is, who sits where—can have a significant effect on the influence of some individuals on other attendees. For example, those who sit at the ends of the conference table are frequently perceived as having more power and influence than those who sit on the sides. People sitting side by side tend to have more difficulty seeing and communicating with each other. Tables designed so that everyone appears to be in an equal position, such as round tables, tend to encourage the free flow of ideas and discourage the domination of a meeting by one individual.

Clarify Responsibilities of Attendees. In many instances you're likely to be responsible for attending but not organizing or conducting a meeting. In such a case, you still have certain responsibilities. You can help make meetings flow more smoothly and waste less time if you:

1. Obtain an agenda of the meeting. Find out the meeting's objectives before attending it.

2. Prepare for the meeting. Obtain information that can enhance the meeting's outcome.

3. Participate at the meeting. Your ideas can build on those of other participants and contribute toward accomplishing the meeting's objectives.

4. Decide on a follow-up action. During meetings determine what your follow-up responsibilities are and decide when you will accomplish them.

5. Confirm follow-up action. Explain to the chairperson your understanding of your follow-up responsibilities to avoid going off in useless directions.

**A
GLOBAL
GLACE**

Worldwide Meetings—On Channel 3![c]

Many organizations are now using video conferencing to hold meetings among employees who are dispersed throughout the world, thus saving considerable time and travel expenses. The recession of the early 1990s motivated managers to look for ways to save money, so many of them leaped on the high-tech bandwagon of video conferencing. Transmission costs and hardware prices have plummeted with the increased demand so that a one-hour video conference between Los Angeles and Boston now costs about $20 an hour compared to $2000 not many years ago. Now executives can hold meetings anywhere in the world without having to leave corporate headquarters.

Computers are also getting into the act. Made available in 1993 was a desktop system that incorporated video conferencing into personal computers. Maybe one of these days you'll be cruising along the highway, parkway, or turnpike, laptop at your side, "attending" a video-conferenced meeting with the big chiefs situated at corporate headquarters in Kyoto, Japan. Oh, oh! And you're driving an American car!

The concept of video conferencing sounds great, but can you think of any possible advantages inherent in face-to-face conferences that are lacking in video conferencing?

TABLE 4.1 **Elements of a Good Meeting.**

Surveyed business leaders rated the following ingredients for a successful meeting on a scale of 1 to 10:

Adequate preparation	9.18
Agreement on follow-up action	8.86
Having an effective moderator	8.52
Staying on track	8.45

Table 4.1 summarizes the major elements of a good meeting, according to a Hofstra University survey of more than 2000 business leaders.[13]

REALLY SMALL GROUPS—THE INTERVIEW

Another aspect of small group behavior that receives considerable attention in management literature is the process of **interviewing.** For our purposes, interviewing can be defined as *the act of consultation between a manager and a present or past employee or an applicant for employment.* Most employees, whether managers or associates, are often involved in this form of interpersonal behavior, since interviews are used for a variety of purposes in organizations. The principal types of interviews are:

What are the main types of interviews?

1. Employment—to observe applicants for job openings
2. Appraisal—to review an employee's performance
3. Counseling—to aid employees with personal problems
4. Disciplinary—to discuss an employee's substandard behavior or performance
5. Grievance—to discuss an employee's complaints
6. Morale surveys—to discover employee attitudes
7. Exit—to assess reasons for employee terminations

Styles of Interviewing

What determines the style of interview that should be used?

The particular style of interview employed generally depends on the nature of the interview and the experience of the manager. As with most activities, interviewers (as well as interviewees) should alter their styles to suit the particular situation. The most commonly used styles include the *structured, unstructured, group,* and *stress* styles of interviewing.

Structured (Directive) Interviews. A **structured,** or **directive, interview** is one that usually follows a predetermined pattern. Frequently, a specific set of questions, taken from a detailed form, are asked of the interviewee. The form is a guide to what questions should be asked, and it helps keep the interview on track. Some interview forms include two sets of questions: (1) the specific questions to be asked during the interview, and (2) questions not asked by the interviewer but intended to help him or her interpret the significance of the interviewee's answers. These latter questions usually appear directly below the primary questions and are often highlighted in a different color to make them distinguishable. Some types of interviews—employment or disciplinary, for example—lend themselves to a fair degree of structure by their very nature, since interviewers usually know the specific ground they want to cover. Other types of interviews, such as counseling or grievance, are typically less structured.

Unstructured (Nondirective) Interviews. An **unstructured,** or **nondirective, interview** is one that attempts to avoid influencing the interviewee's remarks. Often a broad, general question is asked, and the interviewee is encouraged to answer in some depth. "How would you describe the perfect boss?" and "How did the problem between you and Cathy start?" are examples of such an open question. One manager asks job applicants to describe a typical day in their previous positions. During an unstructured interview, the interviewee tends to feel freer to express attitudes, desires, emotions, and problems. With certain types of interviews, such as grievance or counseling, the unstructured approach often serves as a beneficial safety valve by which employees can vent pressures or complaints. Inherent in such interviews, however, is the danger of getting sidetracked and wasting time on nonrelated topics, especially if the interviewee has a tendency to ramble.

"How do you feel about . . . ?"

Group Interviews. Another technique, the **group interview,** is adaptable to a variety of situations. In one variation, several managers, or members of a board or panel, observe, challenge, and pool their impressions of the interviewee. Applicants for positions with a high degree of responsibility, such as sales or executive trainees, may be subjected to group interviews. Some governmental jobs also require applicants for available positions or aspirants for promotion to go before a board or panel of interviewers.

In another variation of the group interview, several managers question and observe candidates for a particular position as a group. The group being interviewed may be questioned, observed, and assessed by the executive panel as the candidates interact with one another.

Whew! That turkey's cold!

Stress Interviews. The **stress interview** uses a technique whose merit has been widely debated. With this approach, the interviewee is intentionally placed in a tense—possibly even abusive—situation to see how she or he responds to stress. The theory underlying this approach is that during stress, the "true" personality of the interviewee tends to emerge. It is debatable, however, whether a person has one "true" personality. Most individuals tend to react differently at different times to similar situations, depending on their moods at the particular moment.

Hey! Why'd you punch me in the nose?

Managers who use the stress technique feel that by introducing tension into the interview through insults or extremely challenging questions, the applicant can be observed in circumstances other than artificial, courtship-styled behavior situations. A typical approach for inducing stress into an interview is for the interviewer to indicate that the applicant is obviously unfit and shouldn't be wasting the interviewer's time. The interviewer then observes the response of the applicant. Another interviewer intentionally and repeatedly blows cigar smoke in the face of the applicant seated directly across from him. The interviewer expects the applicant to be assertive and to request that he refrain from such activity. An inherent danger in this approach is that the applicant might develop negative attitudes toward the organization and interviewer that may be difficult to shake off later. A further danger is the possibility of a civil rights complaint of bias in hiring by a disgruntled applicant.

Guidelines for Conducting Interviews

Regardless of the type of interview, the manager should have patience, knowledge of questioning and listening techniques, an awareness of and a sensitivity toward nonverbal communication, and a basic liking and respect for people. Some types of interviews, such as *disciplinary interviews,* tend to be more effective when they take place out of earshot of others to prevent embarrassing the employee.

Although many managers go along with the suggestion that they should criticize in private and praise in public, the procedures of some companies and the contracts of some labor agreements require that a third party be present during any disciplinary interview. In the case of company policy, the purpose is to provide a witness in the event that the employee makes false accusations at a later time. Some union officials feel that a third party witness who is a union member is useful to help protect the employee against unfair treatment. In general, however, the *technique* employed by the interviewer is far more critical to the interview's success than its setting.

The following is a list of some guidelines for conducting more effective interviews:

What factors can improve your interviewing techniques?

1. Plan ahead. Know why you are there and what you want to accomplish. What do you want to find out?

2. Know something in advance about the person whom you are interviewing. Look at the person's application, personnel file, or any other relevant information before the interview.

3. Watch out for your own biases. Your task is to obtain information or provide assistance, not to feed your own ego.

4. Try to help the interviewee relax and feel confident enough to communicate with you.

5. Don't make the mistake of doing all the talking; encourage the interviewee to talk. You shouldn't be doing more than 25 to 30 percent of the talking.

6. Practice the concepts of good listening and phrasing questions.

7. Avoid questions that are likely to produce a biased answer, such as "How did you get along with your former co-workers?"

8. Don't fight the clock. Try to arrange for enough time to conduct the interview so that the session does not become tense.

9. Control the interview. Some small talk may help to relax the person you are interviewing, but, in general, attempt to guide the interview in the direction of your objectives.

10. Never argue. Arguments usually prevent the attainment of your objectives.

11. Look beyond the employee's words. Is there an ulterior meaning that has not surfaced?

12. Maintain your alertness at the end of the interview. Much can be learned after the first good-bye.

Guidelines for Being Interviewed

So far we've examined the interviewing process mainly as a tool of management. But almost everyone—both workers and managers—is interviewed periodically. So let's step now into the shoes of the person on the receiving end of an interview. How might you, for example, improve your image when being interviewed? The following guidelines could help you:

How to succeed at being interviewed by trying.

1. Try to determine in advance why you are being interviewed and be prepared for the types of questions that will be directed at you.

2. Be prompt. Arriving late can get you off to a bad start.

3. Make certain that your appearance is appropriate for the particular situation.

4. Bring something to do in case you have to wait to be interviewed. Writing a letter or reading a book can help you relax.

5. Don't be overanxious to answer questions. Give complete, but brief, responses. Don't ramble.

6. Listen carefully to the interviewer. If you don't understand a question, don't fake the answer. Ask for clarification.

7. Don't overreact to questions. They may merely be a part of a stress interview intended to test your ability to handle difficult situations.

8. Be certain to take with you any background, reference, or statistical material you might need. If you are being interviewed for a job, do you have a résumé, or summary, of any data you might need?

9. Be polite and courteous throughout the interview. Don't forget to thank the interviewer for his or her time, shake hands, and say good-bye.

SUMMARY

Everyone is a member of a variety of small groups. Organizational members should try to gain an understanding of the working of group behavior, both formal and informal, because of its significant influence over them. Managers, too, have an influence over the small group. Work groups strongly influence the behavior and performance of their members in either positive or negative ways. Groups as well as individuals function more effectively when a balance exists between task and maintenance activities.

Informal groups often utilize the grapevine for their informal communications. Although the grapevine can be used to spread harmful rumors, it can also be utilized in ways that benefit the organization. Group decision making has its advantages and disadvantages. Managers who conduct meetings will accomplish goals more readily with planned agendas. Brainstorming, brainwriting, the Delphi method, quality circles, and committees are some of the ways in which small groups are utilized for decision making.

Another aspect of small group behavior is the interview. We examined the structured, unstructured, group, and stress types of interviews. An understanding of effective interview behavior can be helpful to both managers and workers.

TERMS AND CONCEPTS TO REMEMBER

group

security

affiliation

self-esteem

power

social reality

goal accomplishment

synergism

formal (required) system

informal (emergent) system

social norms

Asch conformity studies

formal leader

informal leader

group cohesion

belongingness

task activities

maintenance activities

cultural diversity

grapevine

rumors

single-strand chain

gossip chain

probability chain

cluster chain

group decision making

meetings

planned agenda

hidden agenda

brainstorming

brainwriting

Delphi method

quality circles (QCs)

committee

task force

groupthink

interviewing

structured (directive) interview

unstructured (non-directive)
  interview

group interview

stress interview

QUESTIONS

1. Evaluate the following statement: "Formal groups, by their very nature, restrict our freedom. This would be a far better world in which to live and work if formal groups didn't exist."

2. It has been said that informal groups help individuals satisfy their psychological and social needs. How might an informal group have the reverse effect, that is, create dissatisfaction in an individual group member?

3. How does the concept of *synergism* relate to group behavior?

4. Why might a person not want to be accepted by a group?

5. What are social norms? In what ways might they make a supervisor's job easier? More difficult?

6. What did the Asch conformity studies help to illustrate?

7. Why do members of groups develop group cohesion?

8. Why should there be a balance between *task* and *maintenance* activities among group members?

9. What are the major characteristics of the *grapevine?*

10. Which is the most common of the grapevine chains? How does it work?

11. Is group decision making better than individual decision making? Explain.

12. Is *groupthink* a positive or a negative concept? What causes groupthink to occur among group members?

13. What are the usual guidelines that should be applied to *brainstorming* sessions?

14. How does the *Delphi method* of group decision making differ from brainstorming and brainwriting?

15. Assume that you are conducting a planned meeting with a tight agenda, and one of the attendees interrupts you to ask some questions about parking problems in the company lot. You don't have time during today's meeting, let's assume, for a discussion of this problem. What would you say, assuming that you don't want to alienate the person?

16. What might be some ways, not discussed in the chapter, in which *stress* could be brought into an interview?

17. What are some occupations in which stress interviews might be applicable? What sort of stress questions might be asked during the interview?

APPLICATIONS

4.1 Who Gets the Office?

Kevin Kucharski, a manager with Wontech, Inc. in Dallas, Texas, is in charge of four sales representatives whose job is to telemarket Wontech's products. Kucharski has a private office, and the four telemarketers each have a cubicle outside of Kucharski's office. Interpersonal relationships among the group members have consistently been harmonious until recently.

About a month ago, Wontech was acquired in a leveraged buyout by Universal Sales, Ltd., a British company attempting to get a marketing foothold in the United States. Universal's senior managers, in an attempt to reduce overhead costs, decided to downsize by closing Kucharski's office and consolidating it with a branch in Houston, Texas. As an attempt to soften the blow of closing down Kucharski's office, one of Universal's managers told Kucharski that instead of an office and four cubicles, he would be assigned two offices and three cubicles, thus providing one member of his staff with a private office.

Kucharski hadn't anticipated any particular problem regarding the assignment of the office. However, he soon discovered that three of the four telemarketers—Christopher, Yuri, and Lydia—were spending considerable time arguing over who should be assigned to the second office. Kucharski wanted to make a decision that wouldn't upset the other two too much.

While contemplating his decision, Kucharski heard a knock on his office door. Three of his four associates were there. One of the employees, Christopher, asked if the three of them could see him about the new office assignment. Kucharski invited them in.

Christopher spoke first:

"Mr. Kucharski, I've been with this department the longest time, and based on my seniority I believe that I should be given the office."

Yuri, another of the three, anxiously interrupted and said:

"Mr. Kucharski, I agree with Christopher that seniority should count in the assignment of the office, and I've been with the company longer than Lydia. Only one week, but it's still longer. Do you remember that I worked in another department for six weeks before being transferred to your department?"

Lydia, the last of the three, angrily exclaimed:

"Mr. Kucharski, women have always gotten the short end! I feel that seniority is an old-fashioned way of assigning things. True, you two have been here longer, but I think the office should be assigned on the basis of merit. I've consistently had the best sales performance of anyone in our department. I also have more direct contact with clients on company premises than you two. I recently had a job offer from one of our competitors, and I just may take it if I don't get the office."

Questions

1. What should Kucharski say now?

2. How should Kucharski determine which employee should be assigned the office?

3. How can Kucharski prevent the three associates who will not be assigned the office from becoming excessively disgruntled?

4.2 Meeting Madness

The Super Stress Surgical Instrument Company is a medium-sized firm located in an industrial park on the outskirts of Madison, Wisconsin. The company is principally involved with manufacturing surgical instruments and supplies for medical doctors and hospitals.

About a year ago, Mona Stephanian, age 23, niece of the firm's founder, Marshal Stephanian, was hired to replace Frank Salizzoni, quality-control supervisor, who had reached the age of retirement. Mona had recently graduated from the University of Wisconsin, where she had majored in industrial engineering.

Phillip Castellano, age 54, is the production manager of the Prosthesis Department, where artificial devices designed to replace missing parts of the human body are produced. Phillip has worked for Super Stress for fifteen years, having previously been a production line supervisor and, prior to that, a worker on the production line. Phillip has completed almost two years of college, acquired mostly by attending occupational night courses at a local community college.

From their first meeting, it seemed as though Phillip and Mona could not get along together. There appeared to be an underlying animosity between them, but it was never too clear what the problem was.

Grover Garvin, age 45, is the plant manager of Super Stress. He has occasionally observed disagreements between Mona and Phillip on the production line. Absenteeism has also risen in Phillip's department since Mona was hired as quality-control supervisor. Grover recently decided to write a memo calling for a meeting of all nine supervisory personnel in the production and quality-control departments. The memo was worded as indicated in the accompanying example:

Grover opened the meeting by explaining why he had called it, and then asked Phillip for his opinion of the problem. The following conversation took place:

Phillip Castellano: That wonder girl you hired is too eager to find fault in our department. Until she was hired, we hardly ever stopped production. And when we did, it was only because of a mechanical malfunction. But "meticulous Mona" has been

---

TO: All Supervisory Personnel,
       Production and Quality
       Control Departments
FROM: Grover Garvin
       Plant Manager   _____ PLEASE RESPOND
SUBJECT: Clarification of   _____ NO RESPONSE NECESSARY
       Work Roles

I would like all of you to meet with me on Friday, July 8, at 9:00 a.m. in Room 23, at which time we will attempt to straighten out any misunderstandings and differences that seem to exist among Production and Quality-Control personnel.

Respectfully submitted,
Grover

---

	stopping everything if one defective part comes down the line.
Mona Stephanian:	That's a lie, Phillip. You know darned well . . .
Phillip Castellano:	Grover, our quality hasn't changed one bit. It's still the same consistently good quality it was before she came, but all she wants to do is hassle us.
Mona Stephanian:	May I say something? Phillip, you never have accepted me right from the beginning. I can remember some of the snide remarks and wisecracks you used to make behind my back. I heard them quite clearly!
George Daskarolis: *(Mona's Assistant)*	I have to back up Mona, Grover. I think that everyone knows that the rules permit quality control to shut down production if rejects exceed five an hour. This is all Mona has been doing.
Phillip Castellano:	Now listen to me! Mona starts counting the hour from the moment she gets the first reject. Frank never really worried about that obsolete reject rule when he was supervisor. She wants my department to look bad! Isn't that true, Lloyd?
Lloyd Cunningham: *(Phillip's Assistant)*	It sure is, Phillip. Every time that lady halts production, she costs the company money, and the workers aren't able to earn their bonuses.

Twenty minutes later Mona and Phillip were still lashing out at each other. Grover decided that ending the meeting might be the best move for now. He promised to send out a memo clarifying the matter some time next week.

Questions

1. Should Grover have called a meeting to solve this problem? Why or why not?

2. How do you feel about the rule calling for production to halt if there are more than five rejects in an hour? Should it have been enforced? Explain.

3. Identify where, if at all, group cohesion exists among the members of the meeting group.

4. What do you feel is the major problem in this case? The solution?

4.3 We Do It Our Way

Medical Claims Processing, Inc. (MCP) is a company that was established by three computer specialists to serve federal and state government medical care programs. MCP was an immediate success. After fewer than five years in business, the company was employing 1000 people. Most observers felt that opportunities for continued growth would easily parallel the expanding public demand for adequate medical care. MCP was viewed as exemplifying the "state of the art" in computerized processing of medical claims.

Jon Rotenstreich, president of MCP, decided to explore systematically commercial opportunities to apply the company's technology to medical claims processing for unions and large corporate employee groups. Jon felt there would also be opportunities for selling consulting services to medical providers such as insurance companies, hospitals, and clinics. For example, the MCP computers accumulated facts on health care usage that could be useful to the health care industry in planning and pricing health services.

To capitalize on this unique business opportunity, Jon selected Jeff Sharp for this new assignment. Jeff had served for one year as a long-range planner analyst and was now promoted to director of marketing research and was authorized to hire a staff. Jeff prepared personnel requisitions for a start-up staff, including two project managers and one statistical analyst. The Human Resources (Personnel) Department initiated recruiting through its usual sources. Jeff found this process too slow, however, so he contacted two colleagues whom he had known while at Wharton School of Business, Steve Fenn and Dave Marcus, and sold them both on the benefits of joining MCP. Steve and Dave had recently completed M.B.A. degrees and felt that the rapidly expanding health care field might be a good place to start their careers. Jeff then arranged a transfer for Sandra Johnson, whom he knew for her excellent statistical experience in the long-range planning department.

One week after Steve and Dave accepted the positions as project managers, a woman telephoned to request an interview with Jeff Sharp. Judy Angelli had learned of the job opening from the placement office at San Jose State University. She told Jeff that she had an M.S. in statistics and was finishing an M.A. in health care services. The graduate studies in health care services was a new program. Jeff liked her background and decided to interview Judy, even though he had filled all budgeted jobs.

While studying at Wharton for his Ph.D. in business administration, Jeff became enthusiastic about participative management concepts. Now, as a director of marketing research who was running his own department for the first time, Jeff was going to practice participative management. He decided to implement this concept by scheduling a group interview. Jeff, Steve, and Dave would group-interview Judy Angelli.

The interview began at 10:00 A.M. and continued through lunch. The following are a few exchanges from the interview:

Jeff: Judy, the three of us represent the marketing research department of MCP. We have a mandate to identify marketable expertise now in MCP or available to MCP. We will identify demand, research the opportunity thoroughly, and prepare proposals for the sale of consulting or data to health providers. As you can see, our objectives are broad, and we are exploring new territories where no one has walked before. Steve and Dave were my research assistants while we were all attending Wharton Graduate School of Business just over one year ago. When I got this promotion a few weeks ago, I called them immediately because of my confidence in them.

Steve: We all think alike. Some of our brainstorming sessions are truly exciting.

Judy: I've been a research assistant at State University for Professor Hill. I enjoy the research environment—you know, all the freedom and challenge. I'm an independent person. Professor Hill and I couldn't agree on methodology for research, so he suggested I should seek other employment. I guess someday I'll be able to finish my second master's degree.

Jeff: Perhaps I told you on the telephone that we don't have budget approval for more than two project managers.

Judy: Yes, you told me. However, I felt that if I could meet you for an interview you would be impressed.

Dave: We have more statistical work already than Sandra can handle. Maybe we could get approval to hire Judy as a statistical analyst.

Judy: I don't want a clerical job. I want a management job. You know what I mean. With all my education I'm ready for real responsibilities.

Jeff: The pay would be less, but in this fast-growing company there's a shortage of good management candidates. There will be lots of opportunities.

Approval was granted to add one statistical analyst. Judy accepted the offer because she wanted to work and the starting pay was considerably more than she had earned as a student research assistant.

The group—Jeff, Steve, Dave, and Judy—began to function as one happy family. Sandra was a 9-to-5 person. She was well regarded by the group for her ability, but they all agreed her future was limited to that of analyst. The group dressed more casually than all other departments in corporate headquarters. Since they were in research, each member decided to arrive at the office about mid-morning, then work until well past dinner. After those long hours, stopping for pizzas and beer was a favorite way for the group to unwind.

Four months after Judy joined the department she confronted Jeff with a demand for a pay increase. Jeff decided to meet with Harriet Morrison, vice-president of the Human Resources Department, to resolve the pay demand. The following is part of the conversation that took place between Jeff, Judy, and Harriet.

Harriet: Would you like to fill me in on this situation?

Jeff: Judy demands that her pay be increased to meet Steve's and Dave's—something to do, she said, with equal pay. She also demands overtime pay for the past four months. Judy knows that we are not clock punchers. We have always included Judy in our evening brainstorming sessions because she has some good ideas. Now she wants to be paid like a clerk for overtime hours.

Judy: That's unfair. You promised me that I could get ahead. Steve and Dave have less education and less background in health care than I do. I've been managing projects the same as Steve and Dave; yet their pay is $950 more per month than mine. I make the same salary as Sandra, and she only has a B.A. and doesn't have the potential I have.

Jeff: Lately Judy has been out of control. Last week she wanted to send an invitation to a meeting to the heads of sales and the computer group. She even wanted to have an agenda, something we just don't do. I told her I'd send the memo. Next thing I knew she'd called a meeting with these two other department heads. Frankly, it made me look bad.

Judy: The idea of developing a client newsletter as a marketing piece was mine, and you agreed it was a good one. Why should you take credit for my idea? If I don't get the same pay as Steve and Dave, I'll file a charge of discrimination.

Harriet interrupted the meeting to excuse Judy and continued discussing the resolution with Jeff. The two-party discussion continued as follows:

Jeff: I guess Judy doesn't fit my group. I don't like threats. I've been fair and open with her. I'll send out a memo requiring neckties and fixed hours, and I guess I'll fire her for insubordination.

Harriet: Maybe we're moving too fast. Before any action is taken, I want to review Judy's job description. She said she's managing projects. Is she?

Jeff: Only with my close supervision. Not like Steve and Dave. They show more initiative.

Harriet: Could I read the job descriptions you agreed to write for each of your new people?

Jeff: You can't describe research in a job description. My people are creative, not like the rest of the company. We don't bother with job descriptions.

Questions

1. Do you feel the group interview as used in this case is a good selection tool? Why or why not?

2. Is Jeff's small group an "island" where casual attire, flexible hours of work, and unstructured jobs are justified because its members are in research?

3. Do you feel it is important that a member of the group be a statistical analyst or a project manager but not both? Explain.

4. Should participative management include group interviews, meetings without agenda, and "one happy family" relationships? Explain.

5. What is the major problem in this case? The solution?

NOTES

1. Solomon E. Asch, in Darwin Cartwright and Alvin Zander, eds., *Group Dynamics: Research and Theory,* 2nd ed. (New York: Harper & Row, 1960), pp. 188–200.

2. John B. Minor, *The Challenge of Managing* (Philadelphia: Saunders, 1975), p. 123.

3. Wendell L. French, Fremont E. Kast, and James E. Rosenzweig, *Understanding Human Behavior in Organizations* (New York: Harper & Row, 1985), p. 255.

4. "Newsletter/Social Science," *Intellectual Digest,* March 1973, p. 72.

5. Audrey Edwards, "Cultural Diversity in Today's Corporation: The Enlightened Manager," *Working Woman,* January 1991, pp. 45–60.

6. Jolie Solomon, "U.S. Melting Pot Boils Over in Workplaces: Office Conflict Often Starts With Cultural Misunderstanding," *The Wall Street Journal,* September 13, 1990, p. 14.

7. Keith Davis and John W. Newstrom, *Human Behavior at Work,* 8th ed. (New York: McGraw-Hill, 1989), p. 375.

8. "BankAmerica Plans to Cut Up to 12,000 Jobs in 3 Years," *The Wall Street Journal Europe,* March 20–21, 1992, p. 13.

9. "The Meeting Pitfall," *World of Work Report,* February 1985, p. 8.

10. Irving L. Janis, *Victims of Group Think* (Boston: Houghton Mifflin, 1972), p. 9.

11. *The World Almanac and Book of Facts 1992,* (New York: Pharos Books, 1991), p. 451.

12. Walter Kiechel III, "The Politics of Innovation," *Fortune / International Edition,* April 11, 1988, pp. 87–88.

13. Adapted from Harrison Conference Services/Hofstra University survey of more than 2000 business leaders as reported in *USA Today / International Edition,* March 28, 1989, p. 20.

BOX NOTES

a. Adapted from "Maxwell's Pensions," *Financial Times,* February 7, 1992; Tom Bower, "A Mirror on Maxwell," *Financial Times,* December 13, 1991; and Norma Cohen, "Maxwell's Paupers," *Financial Times,* February 1/February 2, 1992, p. IV.

b. Norman R. F. Maier, "Assets and Liabilities in Group Problem Solving: The Need for an Integrative Function," in J. B. Ritchie and Paul Thompson, *Organization and People,* 3rd ed. (St. Paul: West Publishing, 1984), p. 186.

c. Adapted from Glenn Rifkin, "Market Place—Signals of a Boom in Video Meetings," *The New York Times,* October 8, 1991, p. I-4.

EXPERIENTIAL EXERCISE

Examining Formal Work Arrangements

During the next week or so observe carefully in one of the departments where you work the formal arrangement of the physical workflow. (If you are not currently employed, ask an acquaintance if he or she can arrange for you to visit his or her office or plant.) How does the arrangement contribute to, or detract from, employee feelings of group cohesiveness? Are employees able to interact with each other based on the location of work stations or desks? How does the existing layout affect the status of the group members?

Part Two

Leaders Need People

CHAPTER 5   Human Needs, Motivation, and Morale

CHAPTER 6   Techniques of Leadership

CHAPTER 7   Quality and the Workplace

CHAPTER 8   The Quality of Work Life

CHAPTER 5

Human Needs, Motivation, and Morale

Would a Carrot Make You Happy?

**When you finish this chapter,
you should be able to:**

1

Recognize the importance of understanding concepts of needs and motivation.

2

Describe a basic model of motivation.

3

Explain the nature of four common learned needs.

4

Explain the differences among the motivational theories of
Maslow, Alderfer, and Herzberg.

5

Understand the use of four principal techniques of reinforcement
used in behavior-modification activities.

6

Understand the nature of expectancy theory.

7

Describe how equity theory can motivate employees.

8

List and describe the principal factors that influence morale.

9

Recognize the major warning signs of poor morale.

10

Describe the various methods for measuring or evaluating morale.

> If companies are to survive, they will have to change from management by movement to management by motivation.

> *Frederick Herzberg, Management Theorist*

> If you treat people well and they have the responsibility and authority, they'll produce. People should be incentivized and excited about what they're doing, and they'll perform well.

> *Alan G. Hassenfeld, CEO, Hasbro Corporation*

An employee, whom we'll call Christopher Chan, was assigned by his boss, Lydia Lanigan, the task of completing a report by the following Monday morning. Unfortunately for Christopher, he had put off preparing his final draft until late Sunday evening. A tumultuous thunderstorm was brewing outside while Christopher was in the process of inputting report data into his trusty personal computer. Suddenly, Christopher heard a deafening clap of thunder roaring through the atmosphere, and all lights in the house went dark. Christopher stumbled toward the kitchen, where he fetched a candle, and returned directly to his computer. The monitor was completely blank, without even a comma displayed on the screen.

Christopher, although not technically minded, but a bright young high achiever nonetheless, realized without hesitation that something was amiss. He had an unsatisfied *need:* electricity. Christopher's life would undoubtedly continue without his high-tech electronic marvel, but he had a work goal that was important to him, and his PC could have assisted him considerably in his quest. Many things we think of as needs, such as Christopher's "need" for electricity and a PC, are actually *wants,* but we have been conditioned to feel them as needs. For example, everyone *needs* food to sustain themselves, but would our friend, Christopher—even if he perceives himself as a gourmet—absolutely need (or merely *want*) a Japanese dinner of *nigiri, hosomaki, temaki,* rice, and seaweed?

How do your *wants* differ from your *needs*?

THE IMPORTANCE OF NEEDS AND MOTIVATION

All of us have needs. Although we might be able to survive without such gadgets as video telephones and digital compact disc players with random-access programming, we wouldn't survive for long without food, drink, sleep, air to breathe, and appropriate atmospheric conditions. A **need,** in effect, gives a person a feeling of *deprivation,* that something is missing from his or her life, at least at the moment. The missing things may be physiological (food and drink), security (medical insurance), social (friends), or psychological (self-esteem, status, and feeling of achievement). When you are deprived of various things, something to drink, for example, you feel a type of tension that moves (motivates) you to engage in activity intended to quench (satisfy) your thirst. Certain types of deprivation on the job can also influence your attitude—that is, *morale*—at the workplace, a topic that will be covered in a later section of this chapter.

Needs and Motivation

An awareness of the concept of needs, important for various reasons, is especially important for a greater understanding of your own behavior and the behavior of others with whom and through whom you work. If you ever become a manager or supervisor, you'll discover that an understanding of the needs of your associates will greatly facilitate your attempts to motivate them. Employees and family members also can benefit from a knowledge of needs concepts.

Why learn about needs?

Needs are also called motives because they *move* or *motivate* us to act. Is the concept of **motivation** clear to you? Try to remember as we use the term in this text that motivation means *the various drives within, or environmental forces surrounding, individuals that stimulate them to behave in a specific manner.*

If You Are a Manager

Managers get things done with and through people, and an understanding of concepts of motivation and human needs is essential if management is to be effective in accomplishing organizational goals with and through their associates. Managers should attempt to avoid the all-too-common mistake of assuming that everyone is motivated by the same incentives. One person, for example, might feel motivated by the opportunity to have more responsibility on the job; others may be frightened at the mere mention of such prospects. It is essential, therefore, that managers who want to establish and maintain an organizational climate that motivates employees continually remind themselves that different employees have different mixes of needs, wants, and goals.

Is *work* a nasty four-letter word?

Traditional managers believe that most people dislike work and will be best motivated by fear and financial reward. Such managers believe that since most individuals must work, they will respond more productively when the fear of suspension, demotion, or dismissal hangs over their heads. Fear can motivate in the *short run,* but often in the *long run* it merely motivates individuals to seek employment elsewhere.

The modern approach to motivational management makes greater use of positive environmental factors, such as recognition,

How does the modern
manager differ from
the traditional one?

status, and empowerment, than of the negative factors preferred by the traditional manager. Modern managers also recognize that they can have a significant effect on creating an environment that provides employees with positive *expectations* for accomplishing the *outcomes* (rewards) they desire. Managers who fail to recognize such environmental factors frequently have *morale* problems among their employees.

If You Are an Employee

How can you as an employee benefit from an understanding of needs and motivational concepts? The knowledge of what motivates a particular type of behavior can enhance your understanding of yourself and others. You should find that you become less irritated with the behavior of others when you're able to understand it. You may find it easier to solve problems between you and your boss or your co-workers if you have a better understanding of what motivates people.

If You Are with Family or Friends

The same premise can hold true for you if you are married, a parent, or even among friends. All behavior tends to be caused, and an understanding of some of the causes can help you anticipate, prevent, and resolve human problems in a variety of situations.

Knowledge Can Be Misused

Don't misinterpret the purpose of understanding human behavioral concepts. Individuals in organizations, for example, don't have the spare time to sit around in official ivory towers passing the hours merely contemplating their organizational navels, so to speak, and discussing theory among themselves. Most organizations don't, and indeed couldn't, cater to such academic pastimes.

Should organizational
members be
concerned with theory?

Who wants to be a
puppet?

Nor should we use an understanding of human behavior to manipulate others, a practice that has dire connotations. Any tool can be used or misused. The major purpose of an improved understanding of motivation is to assist us in working *positively* with and through individuals in organizations. Other purposes are likely to be counterproductive.

A Motivation Model

Look at Figure 5.1, a model of the motivation process. As you can see on the left side of the model, a *felt need* creates *tensions*. Tensions *motivate* a person into making *efforts* to reduce or eliminate the tensions. The individual's past and present *environmental experiences* influence the direction that efforts take.

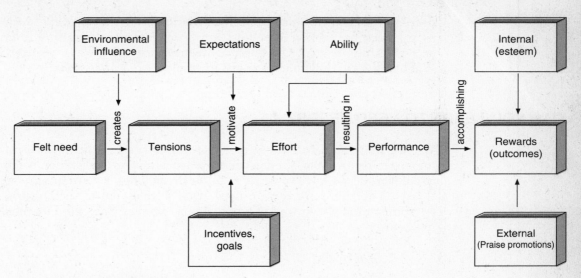

Figure 5.1 A motivational model.

A case of model
behavior.

For example, let's look at the case of Henry, a devout vegetarian, who typically downs his cauliflower with nothing less than the best brand of bottled mineral water. Let's assume that Henry has been stranded for five days on a desert island with no food and very little to drink. Exceptions would probably be made to Henry's usual manner of satisfying his basic needs if, upon being rescued, the only food and drink available were a lamb chop and a glass of ordinary tap water.

As with Henry, any person's environment tends to shape his or her needs. Note also in the model that *expectations* likewise influence effort. A person may not even bother to make an effort if he or she believes desired outcomes are unlikely or impossible. Managers, however, can influence employee expectations in a variety of ways, such as by *offering incentives* and *establishing goals jointly*.

Continuing with our examination of the motivation model, *ability* then blends with the person's *effort* and results in a certain level of *performance*. Unfortunately, however, performance alone doesn't always enable individuals to satisfy their needs and attain their wants, especially when their skill levels are deficient or their prior training is inadequate.

What do you need?

On the far right portion of the model are the *rewards,* or *outcomes,* that result from achieving the motivated activity. Outcomes may be derived from the person's *external environment* and take the form of praise, promotions, or financial rewards from the boss. An external environmental outcome could also be approval from one's peers. Outcomes can also come from the *internal environment,* such as the personal feeling of self-esteem or achievement resulting from accomplishing a goal. Of course, outcomes are not always positive. When negative, they tend to result in employee *dissatisfaction.*

CAN YOU *LEARN* TO NEED NEEDS?

We are motivated to satisfy many of our needs in quite a natural manner. For example, we don't have to learn how to sleep when we're tired. Nor, do we have to learn to eat or drink when we are hungry or thirsty. Yet, there are certain needs that develop out of the cultural environment of which we are a part. Four commonly accepted learned needs are:

1. Approval
2. Achievement
3. Competence
4. Power

Keep in mind that these are learned needs and, as a result, can vary substantially in intensity among different individuals.

The Need for Approval

We learn early in life to behave in a certain way with our parents, and later with out peers, in order to obtain their *approval.* As already suggested, people vary in the intensity of their **approval needs,** but researchers Crowne and Marlowe discovered that *people who have a high need for approval* tend:

What does a high need for approval mean?

1. To be more likely to conform to group standards.
2. To learn more rapidly when consistent approval is given for correct performance than when nothing is said.
3. To experience difficulty acting in an independent, self-assertive fashion because they fear disapproval.[1]

Can you visualize how these characteristics might influence the manner in which a manager assigns tasks to his or her associates?

The Need for Achievement

Why do some people seem to have such strong desires to achieve while others seem content with mediocre accomplishments? The answer relates to **achievement needs,** which also vary with the individual. Psychologists contend that the achievement need, as with most learned needs, is developed quite early in life. People whose parents were high achievers tend also to be achievement-oriented and to like hard work. Parents typically are a child's first role models. Achievement-oriented parents tend to reinforce achievement behavior by encouraging their children with recognition and praise when they do well.

David C. McClelland has made significant contributions to the study of achievement needs. His findings suggest that the *strength* of the achievement need in any given situation is dependent on three factors:

What determines its strength?

1. The *expectation* of success
2. The value of the *outcomes* (rewards and incentives) to the person
3. The feeling of *personal responsibility* for the achievement[2]

The Need for Competence

Some people have acquired the need to do high-quality work. To such individuals, mastery of their jobs and excellence in their task performance are important because of the personal satisfaction they derived from doing a good job. Managers who have strong **competence needs** tend to be *impatient* and *difficult to work with* since they often feel their associates should share their same high concerns for quality work. Managers with this trait should attempt to recognize the dangers associated with this need and develop and apply adequate organizational behavior skills.

Are you impatient to be competent?

The Need for Power

Power is another learned need that is strong in some individuals. **Power needs** relate to a person's desire to *possess control, authority, or influence over others.* Individuals whose need for power is low tend to feel uncomfortable and out of place in certain types of occupations, such as law enforcement, lion taming, and, without doubt, bullfighting. Power often accompanies certain types of positions in organizations. A chief executive officer, for example, by the very nature of his or her position in the organizational hierarchy, has more power than a first-line supervisor. Some individuals, even when they lack **position power,** are able to influence others through **charismatic authority,** the ability to influence others because of *personality traits and mannerisms.* A later chapter discusses charismatic authority in greater depth.

"I have you under my spell."

Implications for Management

An awareness of the nature of learned needs and an understanding of which needs are inherently strong and which weak in specific employees can aid the manager in both selecting and placing employees on the job and in assigning them tasks. *Challenging projects,* for example, could be assigned to employees high in *achievement needs. Exacting work* could be assigned to employees high in *competence needs.* Employees with strong *approval needs* should receive *consistent feedback and constructive comments* on their performance. Those with high *power needs* might be put *in charge of others.*

Everybody has a separate body.

However, guard against a simplistic application of these concepts. As has been repeatedly stressed thus far, you should remind yourself continually that individuals vary, and each individual is a reservoir of a complex blend of several needs, each working either in harmony or possibly in conflict with each other. Persons with strong power needs, for example, could create more harm than good for a department if they don't receive proper management training prior to being assigned a position directing the activities of others. Human behavior, as we'll learn shortly, can also be *modified* to some degree. Employees low in achievement needs might be encouraged to *change their behavior* if incentives that seem important to them are offered.

A variety of motivational theories have been espoused over the years, and—as you might imagine—there's much debate among behavioral scientists about whose motivational theory is the most reasonable. The following sections discuss some of the principal theories, in spite of certain shortcomings, that have especially made their mark on the field of organizational behavior.

THE PRIORITY OF NEEDS

One of the best-known contributors to the area of motivational research is A. H. Maslow, who categorized needs into an *order of priority* (**hierarchy of needs**) in his book, *Motivation and Personality.*[3] Maslow suggested that human needs can be assigned to *various levels,* and that each level of need has to be gratified to some extent before the next level assumes importance. Maslow developed a concept that distinguished five levels of human needs, ranging from basic, lower-order needs to social and psychological needs of a higher order (see Figure 5.2):

Are you satisfied? Then, move on!

1. Basic physical needs
2. Safety and security needs

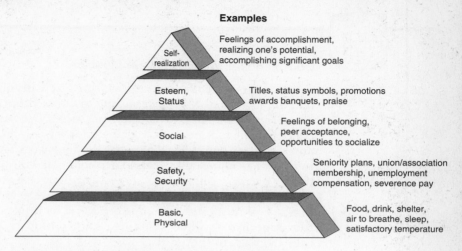

Figure 5.2 Maslow's hierarchy-of-needs concept.

3. Social needs

4. Self-esteem, status needs

5. Self-realization needs—the need for feelings of accomplishment

Maslow contended that as physical through esteem needs are satisfied, they cease to motivate. Lower-order needs don't become unimportant, but higher-order needs achieve greater significance for the individual as his or her basic needs become satisfied. Maslow also suggested that higher-order needs, such as self-realization, become even more important after they have been satisfied.

Here's an example of satisfied lower-order needs becoming less important: Take the case of an employer who pays his or her employees more than the prevailing industry rate. The employer may feel that the employees are satisfied and wouldn't think of withholding their services by going on strike. However, can you think of what might become more important to employees as their basic needs become relatively satisfied through the receipt of ample income? Perhaps various **employee benefits** such as a group health plan, a center for social activities on the company's premises, or even such reflections of status as a title, a thermostat control in an employee's own office, or a private assistant rather than the use of a steno pool.

Perhaps the hierarchy-of-needs concept helps to explain the behavior of young people who appear to their parents not to appreciate the many material things with which their elders have provided them.

Is money the sole motivator?

Do Americans Work Too Darn Much?[a]

Some Japanese leaders have accused Americans of being lazy and unmotivated. Not so, according to Juliet Schor, author of *The Overworked American: The Unexpected Decline of Leisure.* Schor contrasts American working efforts with those in numerous European countries where the 35-hour work week and four to six weeks of annual vacation are common. Unlike the hours of their European counterparts, reveals Schor, the working hours of Americans are already longer than they were forty years ago. She says that if present trends continue, by the end of the century Americans will be spending as much time at their jobs as they did back in the 1920s.

Schor contends that the cost of employee benefits has contributed toward this trend. She points out that such costs are directly related to the number of people employed. Some employers find it cheaper to have one employee work 70 hours per week, even with overtime pay, than to employ two people for 35 hours a week. She adds that this results in greater work loads for those employed accompanied by higher rates of unemployment.

Some Europeans would disagree with the assertion that employee benefits are the cause of increased working time. European companies also pay employee benefits. Schor does point out that there are two other factors accounting for the difference between American and European working hours. First, trade unions have not declined in Europe to the same extent they have in the U.S. in recent decades, thus providing European workers with greater collective bargaining strength. Second, Schor says, "European workers have successfully articulated a vision of a more leisured society. That vision is still missing in America, not only in the workplace, but in the home as well."

Numerous youngsters haven't felt the necessity to be particularly concerned about the satisfaction of their basic needs; food has always been on the table. Other social and ego needs, such as those for love, close friends, and self-respect, have become more important to them.

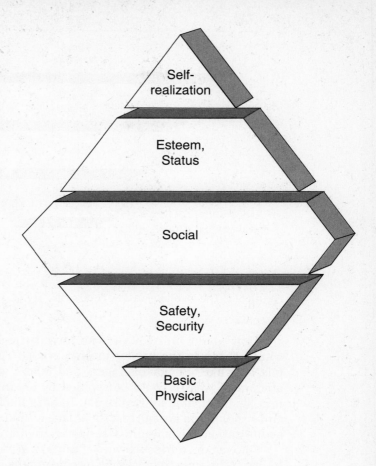

Figure 5.3 The pregnant Maslow needs mix.

Some Exceptions to Maslow—The Pregnant and Inverted Maslow Needs Mixes

Earlier we mentioned that there were exceptions to the concept that as lower-order needs become satisfied, higher-order needs assume greater importance. In fact, Maslow's needs mix (see Figure 5.2) probably applies more to people in lower-income groups than to society in general since their basic needs for food and shelter are often poorly satisfied. A fairly large proportion of the population, on the other hand, can be characterized by the **pregnant Maslow needs mix,** as illustrated by Figure 5.3. The strongest needs of this group tend to be social, with esteem and safety-security needs next strongest, and self-realization and basic physical needs least important (since they are already reasonably well satisfied).

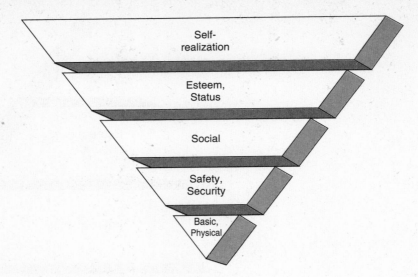

Figure 5.4 The inverted Maslow needs mix.

How about individuals who have little in the way of economic want—those in the higher-income groups? What would their needs mix look like? Senior managers and others who have acquired a fair amount of wealth could be typified by an **inverted Maslow needs mix,** as illustrated by Figure 5.4. If, as is likely, their physical, safety, and social needs are fairly well satisfied, then esteem (status) and self-actualization needs would assume far greater importance.

Once again, a friendly word of caution: Watch out for two-valued reasoning. All people from specific income groups wouldn't necessarily have the same shaped pyramids. Each person is a unique being with his or her own personal needs. Nor would a person's needs mix necessarily remain constant. Changing values would tend to change the mix over time.

Another Exception—Alderfer's ERG Theory of Needs and Motivation

Clayton Alderfer, after observing what he believed to be shortcomings of Maslow's hierarchy of needs concepts, developed a modification of the theory. Known as the **ERG theory of needs,** Alderfer's research offered three basic human needs: *Existence, Relatedness,* and *Growth* (see Figure 5.5). The first level, **existence needs,** includes physical and material human wants, such as food, water, pay, decent working conditions, and safety-security factors. **Relatedness needs** involve one's relationship with others (being accepted, for example), both on and off the job. The last level, **growth needs,** combines the desire for self-esteem and self-realization.

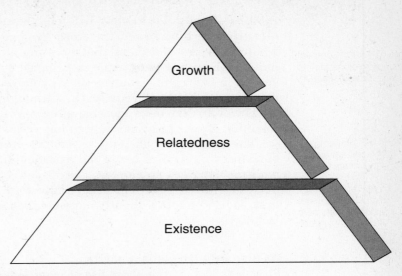

Figure 5.5 Alderfer's ERG model.

Five into three—and
no ladder.

One distinction between Alderfer's ERG and Maslow's priority-of-needs theories, therefore, is in the former's condensation of the five need levels into three. A more significant difference is that Alderfer's research, as already suggested, didn't assume that a person climbs the ladder of needs in an order of progression. Instead, hypothesized Alderfer, any or all three of the levels might be significant at any given time. He also suggested that the *less* relatedness needs (relationships with others) are satisfied, the *more* important the existence needs (physical/material) become, the opposite of Maslow's conclusion. Alderfer differed in another way from Maslow by contending that the *less* the growth needs (self-esteem, self-realization) are satisfied, the *more* important relatedness needs become. The burden, therefore, appears to be on you to decide which of the two theories seems to have the greater merit.[4]

THE MAINTENANCE OF MOTIVATION—
HERZBERG'S MOTIVATION-MAINTENANCE MODEL

Work environment plus
hygiene factors equals
zero effect.

Frederick Herzberg, a well-known management theorist, is best known for another theory of motivation, the **motivation-maintenance model.**[5] Herzberg's research indicates that *two sets of factors* or conditions influence the behavior of individuals in organizations. The first set provides an almost *neutral* feeling among the workers of an organization. Withdrawing these factors—called **maintenance,** or **hygiene,**

Work environment minus hygiene factors equals *dissatsifaction.*

factors—from the workplace will tend, however, to cause *dissatisfaction.* Herzberg borrowed the word *hygiene* from the medical field, where it refers to factors that help maintain, but not necessarily improve, health. For example, a hygienic activity that you regularly engage in is brushing your teeth. Why do you do so? To *maintain* the existing condition of your teeth. Although your mouth feels a lot fresher and is far more kissable after you've brushed your teeth, the condition of your teeth hasn't been improved, merely maintained.

Work environment plus motivational factors equals *satisfaction.*

Work environment minus motivational factors equals *zero effect.*

The second set of factors, termed **motivational factors,** or **satisfiers,** is said to *cause* job satisfaction, the factors serving to *motivate* or *satisfy* employees. The absence of satisfiers, however, will not cause dissatisfaction. The terminology may seem confusing at first, so let's go into a slightly more detailed explanation of each set of factors.

Maintenance (Hygiene) Factors

First let's look at the short list of what Herzberg calls maintenance, or hygiene, factors:

1. Company rules and policies
2. Quality of supervision
3. Interpersonal relations with superiors, subordinates, and peers
4. Salary and certain types of employee benefits
5. Working conditions and job security

According to Herzberg's research, maintenance factors such as these don't necessarily motivate workers in organizations. Can you figure out why? Mainly, such factors don't create satisfaction, although their presence helps to prevent dissatisfaction. But here's the rub: The absence of maintenance factors can lead to dissatisfaction among employees.

An illustration that might be meaningful to you may make the concept clearer. Assume that while attending college you live with your parents, who have provided you with a regular, generous allowance. Your father, a supervisor in an automobile assembly plant, has been laid off as a result of a slowdown in operations. Regretfully, he has to suspend your allowance. Having taken the allowance for granted, you might find that the removal of the allowance (a maintenance factor) creates a feeling of *dissatisfaction* in your mind (and wallet!), although the allowance did have a somewhat neutral effect on your behavior when you had received it.

Maintenance factors in formal organizations include sick leave, vacation, health and welfare plans, and most other personnel programs. Some managers have convinced themselves that a good employee benefit program will motivate workers. Instead, such programs are usually taken for granted and (like your allowance) merely maintain, but don't create, satisfaction.

Are you surprised at Herzberg's findings that working conditions aren't considered motivators? It's probably true that many employees would prefer working in a pleasant environment. But a sparkling new plant seldom substitutes for jobs that people enjoy, or for employee feelings of achievement and recognition. We've all probably seen organizations that function in rundown buildings yet morale and productivity are high. Herzberg contends that people's attitudes toward their jobs far outweigh the importance of *working conditions* or environment.

Another factor that at first glance might seem to be a motivator is *supervision,* which Herzberg lists under the heading of maintenance factors. Using a parent-child analogy, Herzberg reasons that a parent doesn't cause a child to grow; it's the nourishment provided by the food given to the child that does. Like a parent, the supervisor doesn't motivate the worker but merely *influences the environment* that causes the employee to feel motivated from within. Some students of motivation view Herzberg's argument as a distinction without a significant difference. The important aspect to recognize, whether you prefer to place supervision under a maintenance or a motivational heading, is that supervisors *do* significantly influence the various motivational factors that we are about to discuss.

Motivational Factors (Satisfiers)

Now let's take a look at a completely different set of factors. The following list includes what Herzberg calls *motivational factors,* or *satisfiers:*

1. Achievement
2. Recognition
3. The job itself
4. Growth and advancement possibilities
5. Responsibility

What motivates you?

Factors like these are said to motivate individuals. However, the absence of such satisfiers will not necessarily cause employee dissatisfaction. Let's see how each of these motivators might affect you and other organizational members.

Achievement is important to many employees. Is it to you? Achievement means feeling that you've accomplished a goal, that is, you've finished something that you've started. Some work situations provide this feeling; others, such as assembly-line work, often make feelings of achievement difficult.

Recognition is appreciated by many employees. It gives the employee a feeling of worth and self-esteem. Don't you like to know how you stand in a work situation? When you and other employees know how you are doing, even when the results aren't completely satisfactory, you at least know that your boss is concerned about you. There's a tendency for managers to overlook the need for giving employees feedback on their performance. Some managers feel that it's unnecessary to say anything to an employee when a job has been done well. "Charlie knows he does good work" is a far too typical managerial attitude. Charlie, like most employees, might not be certain how his boss really feels about his performance without some form of overt recognition.

"Tell the court, . . . is this, or is this not,
the carrot your employer dangled in front of you?"
SOURCE: © Leo Cullum 1992

The job itself is a highly important motivating factor. Have you ever thought why some employees are chronically late? In many cases it's because they dread—either consciously or subconsciously—going to their 9-to-5 jobs. They derive little satisfaction from their monotonous jobs and as a result would like to be able to say, as that defiant country song puts it, "Take this job and shove it!" People who like their jobs tend to be far more motivated to avoid absenteeism and lateness.

Growth and advancement possibilities also serve to motivate. In a sense, these are like the old carrot and a stick philosophy. Don't you, like many employees, tend to move in directions that help you obtain the "carrot," for example, a promotion with more salary? However, managers must keep in mind that if employees never get to "taste the carrot," but only feel the "stick," then their interest in carrots will tend to fade. Motivational tools should never be used to manipulate people. They should be used sincerely, with the employee's as well as the organization's interests in mind.

Responsibility is another factor that motivates many employees. Let's assume that, for example, you are a key person in a team project requiring critical input from you at 9:00 A.M. tomorrow. Let's also assume that you feel sick this evening. You may forego taking sick leave even though you don't feel well. Even the behavior of some so-called troublemakers in organizations has been modified after they have been given added responsibilities.

Some Final Words on Herzberg

Perhaps with an understanding of the theory of motivational and maintenance factors you can see that employers who attempt to increase the motivation of employees by raising their pay may be in for a disappointment. Workers, once they become accustomed to the new level of income, are likely to perceive it as a maintenance factor. Once a pay raise becomes a regular part of a salary or wage, it usually does little to provide additional motivation. People tend to be far more motivated by what they are *seeking* than by what they *already have*.

Remember, too, that we have been discussing theory. An important consideration to keep in mind is that an *employee's* perception of a motivational factor is of far greater importance than the *manager's* perception of it. A factor that merely maintains one person may motivate another.

Not every behavioral scientist fully accepts Herzberg's concepts. Yet, his research does help to reinforce our awareness that some factors in a work environment tend to motivate many employees, and others—even though they seem positive, like paid vacations—have little effect on an employee's motivation and productivity.

Care to caress a carrot?

Never satisfied?

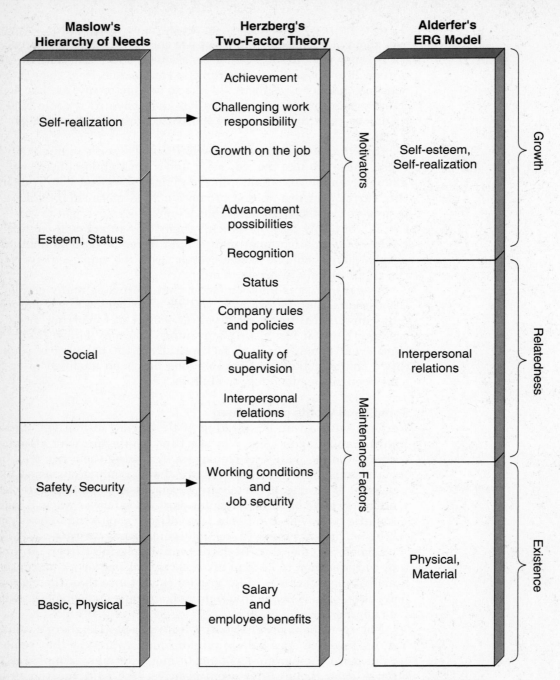

Figure 5.6 A comparison of the motivational theories of Maslow, Herzberg, and Alderfer.

Finally, see Figure 5.6 for a graphic comparison of the Maslow, Herzberg, and Alderfer theories of motivation.

THE *PROCESS* OF MOTIVATION

Thus far we have been discussing motivation by focusing on the perceived internal needs and expected outcomes of the individual, frequently referred to by behavioral scientists as *content theories of motivation.* Managers, however, cannot always pinpoint an individual's internal needs and expected outcomes accurately. Furthermore, the intensity of needs and perceived outcomes varies widely among employees. Imagine, for example, the difficulty you might have trying to measure your employees' need for prestige if you were a manager. Attempting to do so would be difficult.

Increasingly popular in recent years is a second set of motivational theories, termed *process theories,* which are concerned with how to relate content variables (human needs and outcomes) to particular actions of the individual. Three major process theories are the *reinforcement, expectancy,* and *equity theories,* each of which will be discussed in the following sections.

BEHAVIOR MODIFICATION THROUGH REINFORCEMENT TECHNIQUES

Although some managers shy away from the concept of *behavior modification* because of its appearance of being manipulative, the approach has been increasingly used by managers in numerous firms in recent years. **Behavior modification** is the *influencing of behavior through the use of positive or negative reinforcement techniques.*

Do you sometimes find yourself repeating behavior that brings pleasure and avoiding behavior that displeases you? To do so is quite natural. In effect, the *consequence* of certain actions tends to lead to similar actions being repeated (or avoided) in the future. This behavior is termed the **law of effect** and is a major component of what is referred to as **reinforcement theory.** B. F. Skinner, a well-known behavioral psychologist and researcher in the field of behavior modification,[6] is considered by many to be the "father of reinforcement theory."

Managers in the process of motivating employees may draw on reinforcement theory for assistance. Four principal techniques of reinforcement are termed:

1. Positive
2. Escape and avoidance
3. Extinction
4. Punishment

Each of these reinforcement methods can be used to *shape,* or *influence,* human behavior. Their application is explained in the following paragraphs.

Positive Reinforcement

"Play it again, Sam."

When a manager creates an external environment that *encourages a repetition* of certain employee behavior, he or she is utilizing what is termed **positive reinforcement.** We've already learned from the discussion of content theories of motivation that people feel the need for recognition and self-esteem. A manager could link those needs to the process of motivation and positive reinforcement by sincerely praising employees for work well performed. Employees who feel their efforts are appreciated by the boss typically desire to continue performing well because of the satisfaction they receive from the recognition and praise.

Escape and Avoidance

"There must be some way out of here!"

Another method managers can use to influence employee behavior is **escape reinforcement.** As with positive reinforcement, this somewhat negative technique is intended to motivate a person into performing in a favorable manner *to escape from, or avoid, a particular situation.* For example, let's take the case of a person whom we'll call Jeffrey. Assume that Jeffrey was hired and placed in an unpleasant entry-level job. He has been told that if he performs satisfactorily in his job, he is likely to be promoted to a more desirable position within six months. Jeffrey is a high achiever whose qualifications exceed those necessary for the entry-level job. Consequently, he will probably be motivated to do a good job now as a means of avoiding, or escaping from, a position he'd prefer not to have.

You can see, therefore, that escape reinforcement accomplishes the same results as positive reinforcement but by concentrating on the avoidance of a negative outcome.

The State of Extinction

Much of what we've learned thus far about reinforcement theory relates to the concept of **conditioned response,** *the learned or acquired reaction to a particular stimulus.* Ivan Petrovich Pavlov, the late Russian physiologist, is best known for his contribution to this concept. Experimenting with dogs, he originally rang a bell in their presence. The bell, of course, merely attracted their attention. Pavlov noticed, however, that the dogs would salivate when put in front of meat powder. He then discovered that after a while the sound of the bell would cause the dogs to salivate if food was consistently placed in front of the dogs as the bell was rung. Eventually, the food would not even have to be present to cause the dogs to drool, just the sound of the bell.

Ring around the collie!

Pavlov carried his experiment one step further. He learned that even though he *conditioned* the dogs to salivate merely at the ringing of a bell, this response ultimately resulted in **extinction** after repeated *non*reinforcement (no food present when the bell was rung), thus causing the dogs' response to decrease and ultimately to disappear.[7]

How does the concept of extinction relate to organizational behavior? Consider this example: Assume that a new employee named Carol consistently made suggestions to her boss, Harold, on her previous job. Harold, fond of the concept of positive reinforcement, always praised her for presenting ideas, even if they were unusable. Carol was later transferred to a different department where her current boss, Adam, seems indifferent to her suggestions, seldom uttering much more than something like, "Hmm, that's interesting, Carol. I'll look into it and let you know what I think." However, because Adam never actually follows up with a response—positive or negative, *extinction* begins to affect Carol's flow of fresh, new ideas. She tells herself, "Why should I come up with good ideas for the department if they're of no consequence to Adam? To heck with it. I've got better things to do with my time than wasting it making suggestions to a deaf ear!"

"Good, Carol!"

"Sure, Carol."

How Effective Is Punishment?

Punishment reinforcement is a type of behavior modification that most employees would prefer not to experience. It is also the one type that managers tend to dislike having to apply. The basic purpose of punishment reinforcement is to *withhold rewards,* or *outcomes* from the employee because of past undesirable behavior. Theoretically, the employee, if aware in advance of the negative consequences associated with punishment, will comply with existing standards. Or, also in theory, employees punished for undesirable behavior will avoid such activities in the future.

That's the basic theory behind punishment, but what's the reality? Professor Irwin L. Goldstein suggests that punishment doesn't always reduce the likelihood of the same response recurring.[8] He reveals that frequently the person's behavior has been positively reinforced prior to the punishment and will continue even if punishment is likely. For example, employees might believe that not wearing safety goggles is more comfortable than wearing them and, consequently, will wear them only in the presence of the supervisor, even if they are aware of the punishment associated with not wearing them.

Further, managers are not always consistent in the way they apply punishment, far too frequently ignoring certain types of punishable behavior. Goldstein also points out that a by-product of punishment may be the creation of an unpleasant and demotivating working environment accompanied by hostile attitudes toward the boss and organization from which the punishment came. The question arises as to whether punishment really results in desirable behavior. Perhaps punishment should be used only when there are no other alternatives available. Positive attempts at correcting undesirable behavior tend to have far more lasting effects on most employees.

"I'll become hostile, boss!"

How Important Is Timing?

The timing of reinforcement for behavior modification is extremely important. In general, reinforcement should take place as soon as possible after the desired response or it tends to lose its effect. More on timing will be discussed in Chapter 12, which discusses the use of discipline.

(One year later): "What's this for, boss?"

A caveat: As already mentioned, behavior modification is believed by some managers to be a form of manipulating others. In reality, the process *is* a form of controlling the behavior of others. Control, of course, is a legitimate function of management. However, as with any tool, its misuse will tend to be counterproductive over time. If employees, for example, feel that they are being "messed around with" and manipulated, they may respond in negative and reactive ways. Any manager using reinforcement techniques should employ them in a sincere manner that shows a genuine interest in both the employees and the organization.

ARE YOU EXPECTING? LET'S HEAR IT FOR VROOM

Another well-known theory of motivation—the **expectancy theory**—also leans heavily on the carrot/stick approach. Victor Vroom is credited with having popularized expectancy theory.[9] Others, such as Lyman Porter, Edward Lawler, and Richard M. Steers, have expanded and refined Vroom's concepts.[10] Our goal isn't to examine their views in depth but to provide a basic understanding of the motivational concept.

It's What's Up Front That Counts!

We've already talked about how unsatisfied needs tend to create tensions that cause activity designed to satisfy those needs. Expectancy theory takes a slightly different approach to motivation. Expectancy theory proponents don't say that needs are unimportant. They stress, however, that motivational behavior is also the result of how people perceive a situation, what they expect from it, and what they believe will result from specific types of behavior.

Do You Expect You'll Get It?

What do you expect?

Expectancy theory suggests that people behave in a certain way because they *expect* certain results from that behavior. For example, what is your motive for studying this text? Are you doing it because you don't have anything else to do? Probably not. Instead, you're probably motivated to study because you *expect* certain results from your behavior. For some individuals the expected outcome may be a promotion; for others it may be the feeling of achievement or power that added knowledge gives; for still others it may be a means to an end—college credits leading toward a degree.

Every person has his or her own personal expectations. According to expectancy theory, each person's estimate of the probability of a specific outcome is what motivates him or her to behave in a particular way.

You'll Get More Pay If . . .

Concerned with declining profits and increased competition, International Business Machines Corporation (IBM) went through extensive restructuring during 1992. IBM became a staunch proponent of expectancy theory by telling employees that, based on their performance in 1992, ten percent of them would receive flunking grades, which would be the first step toward dismissal. They were also told that another ten percent, perceived by their bosses as "superstars," could earn bonuses of $50,000 or more based upon their performance.[11]

Senior vice president Walton E. Burdick, one of the designers of the IBM **performance-related payment plan,** or **incentive payment system** (as such systems are sometimes called), believes that methods for evaluating and rewarding employees should reflect the "ingrained culture of individualism fostered by American companies." As the Box of Interest, "Carrots—Could They Turn the Stomachs of Some Employees?" suggests, not all students of employee motivation agree. Some observers feel that incentive systems can actually demotivate more employees than they motivate. What do you think?

A BOX
OF
INTEREST

Carrots—Could They Turn the Stomachs of Some Employees?[b]

Is it possible that a performance-related, or incentive, payment system, could actually *demotivate* the majority of employees in an organization? Although some companies, such as IBM and Lincoln Electric Company, disagree, a growing minority of firms are putting their performance-related payment systems out to pasture and adopting more egalitarian approaches based on teamwork, in which peer pressure, rather than the carrot and the stick, serves to motivate.

A number of managers these days feel somewhat like Professor Derek Torrington of the University of Manchester Institute of Science and Technology, who has this to say about the incentive systems: "They're like illicit love affairs. When you're not personally involved in one, you feel you're missing out on something marvelous. When you are involved, you spend most of the time being miserable!" W. Edwards Deming, a quality-management expert, contends that rewarding employees on the basis of merit "nourishes short-term performance, annihilates long-term planning, builds fear, demolishes teamwork, and nourishes rivalry and politics." On the other foot, there are supporters of performance-based systems who feel that the "star system" is as logical as Darwin's theory of natural selection and that employees become complacent without it. Companies that are rooting for teamwork include Ford Motor Company, General Motors, and Eastman Kodak.

THE RELATIONSHIP BETWEEN EQUITY AND MOTIVATION

Employees, of course, want their needs satisfied. But they generally want something else as well. They expect to be treated fairly in the way workloads are assigned and rewards are distributed. Developed by J. Stacy Adams, **equity theory** focuses on the concept of fairness. Illustrated in Figure 5.7, it looks at the tendency for employees to compare the fairness of what their jobs require them to do (called *inputs*) with what they receive in exchange for their efforts (called *outputs*).[12] As with Vroom's theory, equity theory deals with *expecta-*

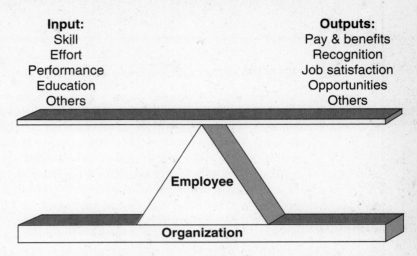

Figure 5.7 The equity theory of motivation assumes a balance of employee inputs and outputs as compared to others.

tions, primarily what people expect to get from their jobs. Employees whose expectations aren't met tend to become dissatisfied, as when they perceive that they are responsible for more tasks than reflected by the size of their paychecks. Their dissatisfaction can result in lesser motivation or, in some instances, the mere acceptance of things as they are, sort of a resigned *C'est la vie,* or *Asi es la vida* attitude.

"I want what *he's* worth!"

Employees also expect equity in relation to other employees. For example, an employee may experience a decrease in motivation upon discovering that he or she receives less income for performing comparable tasks. A related theme of the women's movement in recent decades has been "equal pay for equal work." Equity, or fair treatment, in work organizations relates not only to *pay,* but also to such factors as vacations, work assignments, and recognition. The elements may be either tangible or intangible, external or internal.

"You're just too good to me."

If an employee believes he or she is being treated *too* fairly—that is, receiving outcomes higher than the inputs—the employee tends to move toward a balance by either rationalizing, being more productive, or producing better quality work. Punishment, as well as rewards, can relate to equity theory.

MORALE IN ORGANIZATIONS

We've already learned that needs can influence the motivation of employees. Unsatisfied needs, of course, can adversely affect employee *morale.* And it follows that low employee morale can negatively affect

Those Who Giveth Sometimes Taketh Away![c]

A QUESTION
OF
ETHICS

Bitter conflict developed between management and the employees of Caterpillar after collective bargaining talks between union and company representatives collapsed on October 31, 1991. At the time, Caterpillar was the world's largest heavy-equipment manufacturer and a major industrial exporter.

After a five-month strike by its 12,600 employees, Caterpillar's management decided to open the plant gates to non-union replacement workers. Employees had been striking because they perceived that Caterpillar's management planned to reduce benefits, such as paid-in-full medical insurance premiums and negotiated collective bargaining practices. Management contended that it had to reduce the company's expenses in the name of "global competitiveness." However, one union official argued that "global competitiveness was merely a code name for bottom-line greed."

Many workers felt torn between their loyalty toward the company and their loyalty toward their union. Union officials feared that management could easily replace employees because of the high rate of unemployment in the area. So after company representatives and union officials met for two days in mid-April 1992, the union officials agreed to give up their five-month strike, and company representatives agreed not to hire replacement workers.

However, employees were turned away at the gate when they returned to work. Management argued that certain technical processes had been changed and reevaluation was needed to determine how many of the returning workers would be required in the future. A week later, however, most strikers were allowed to return to work.

What effect do you think management's actions and the loss of wages for five months had on employee morale and company results? Many workers felt demoralized and said that they would do the minimum required instead of pitching in to improve production. And management representatives reported that declining output and sales during the first six months of the year led to a net loss of $185 million. Organizational conflict can, indeed, be costly.

A Question of Ethics: From an ethical standpoint, how do you feel about management's turning away returning workers after union officials called off the strike? Do you feel that employees were behaving unethically by intending to work at a minimum level? What effect do you think the recession during this period had on employees' decision to give up their five-month strike?

productivity and quality management. Much organizational strife is often an indication of sagging morale among employees. The A Question of Ethics box, "Those Who Giveth Sometimes Taketh Away!" provides a vivid example of what can result from perceived unsatisfied needs and low morale in an organization.

However, unsatisfied needs is merely one category of factors that affect the morale of employees. The remaining section of this chapter discusses the factors that affect morale, reveals the major warning signs of low morale, and explains some common methods for evaluating morale.

Morale Defined

What is this thing called morale?

To influence employee morale, a manager must first understand what it is. **Morale,** however, is an elusive concept, not easy to define, control, or measure, yet exerting a strong influence over the atmosphere of any organization. Morale refers to employees' *attitudes* toward either their employing organizations in general or toward specific job factors, such as supervision, fellow employees, and financial incentives. It can be ascribed to either the *individual* or to the *group* of which he or she is a part. For our purposes, we shall define morale as the *atmosphere created by the attitudes of the members of an organization.* It is influenced by how employees perceive the organization and its objectives in relation to themselves.

Morale and Productivity

Generally speaking, there tends to be a direct relationship between high productivity and high morale. Under conditions of poor morale, favorable output is difficult to sustain for long periods. Profits are usually adversely affected when poor morale reduces productivity.

Lower profits can mean fewer wage gains in the future. A full and cumulative circle might then occur since wages can influence morale.

High morale, however, doesn't necessarily cause high productivity; it is merely one, albeit an important, influence on total output. For example, a group of workers could be happy as a result of the social relationships that they've developed on the job, but they may be so busy clowning around that their productivity is low. Their morale is high because of the *lack* of effective leadership. Clearly, for high morale to affect productivity favorably, it must be accompanied by reasonable managerial direction and control.

"I'm happy doin' nothing!"

WHAT ARE THE FACTORS THAT AFFECT MORALE?

The attitudes of employees are significantly influenced by the ways in which they perceive a number of important factors:

1. The organization itself
2. Their own activities, both on and off the job
3. The nature of work
4. Their peers
5. Their bosses
6. Their role expectation
7. Their self-concepts
8. The satisfaction of their needs

Let's briefly examine each factor.

The Organization

How might the organization affect morale?

The *organization* significantly influences workers' attitudes toward their jobs. For example, the public reputation of the organization, especially an unfavorable reputation, can adversely affect the attitudes of employees. An oil company, for instance, that is responsible for a serious oil spill drastically affecting the environment may receive negative publicity damaging to employee morale. Morale can likewise be influenced negatively when a company fails to anticipate market trends and therefore experiences a rapid decline in the demand for its products and in its profitability. The employees of a public agency or school whose reduced public support has caused severe cutbacks in budget and capabilities might also experience poor morale. Employees whose companies have been the victims of hostile takeovers may fear that their jobs are in jeopardy and, therefore, experience declining morale. Organizations whose policies, rules, and procedures are perceived as excessively restrictive may develop discontented employees.

Employees' Activities

Workers are the product of their *total environments*. The workers' relationships with their families and friends can significantly influence their behavior and attitudes on the job. Most organizations feel that employees should have the right to their own personal lives. However, when their activities off the job affect their performance on the job, managers should have both the responsibility and the prerogative to discuss such activities with employees. Some organizations offer employees counseling on problems ranging from marital difficulties to drug abuse.

Could marital spats affect morale on the job?

The Nature of Work

What, in addition to money, do people want from their jobs?

Historically, work has tended to become increasingly specialized and routinized while the worker has become progressively better educated. Many behavioral scientists contend that workers' current values and attained levels of education have led them to expect considerably more than just high pay and material prosperity from their work.

Many types of jobs, however, seem to lead to boredom and alienation. A recent investigation by the Institute of Manpower Studies reveals that one of the major reasons people quit their jobs is because of *boredom*. The study indicated that the following elements led to the feeling that jobs were boring:

1. Employees lacked autonomy and control over the sequence of tasks or pace of work.

2. Employees were not assigned ample responsibility to carry out their jobs adequately.

3. Jobs lacked variety and challenge.

4. Employees' skills were not being fully used.[13]

Peers

How are workers influenced by their associates?

The emergent, or informal, system in an organization can also significantly affect morale. Assume, for example, that you're a worker whose previous attitude toward company policies has generally been favorable. However, as a member of a group, your attitude toward a working condition could be swayed by the collective attitudes of your cohorts or union. A condition that formerly didn't disturb you may suddenly have adverse effects on your morale because of the *influence and pressure of your peers.*

Leadership

Who has the main
responsibility to
maintain morale?

Management, from the CEO to first-line supervisors, sets the tone and has the primary responsibility for establishing a healthy organizational climate. Consequently, the *actions of managers* exert a strong influence over the morale of the work force. High rates of turnover, for example, often (although not always) indicate ineffective leadership. In later chapters we will examine some ways in which management can improve and maintain morale.

Role Expectation

We've already discussed how people tend to assume different roles in different situations. Morale problems often arise when employees have one set of expectations of how their managers should behave and the managers have another. A concept related to this problem is **role expectation,** the way in which individuals are *mentally* set to perceive the behavior of others.

For instance, some managers believe that they will be more effective if they minimize the psychological distance between their associates and themselves. However, if the role expectation of the employees is such that they expect their bosses to keep their distance, attempts at closeness may be difficult if not impossible. Psychological distance is related to feelings of trust, and if a group of employees has a deep-seated distrust of authority, managers will find it difficult to foster closeness and participation. In such an atmosphere, situational thinking and sensitivity are important.

Shouldn't rules affect
the boss, too?

Role expectation can also create morale problems when employees feel that rules should apply not only to themselves but also to their bosses. For example, employees would probably feel that a rule prohibiting the use of a photocopying machine for personal use should apply equally to everyone. If managers openly use the machine for personal copying but employees cannot, the disregard for organizational rules can create role conflict and discontent among employees, who will feel that rules are being applied in a discriminatory fashion.

Concept of Self

How do *you*
feel about *you*?

The *self-concept* of workers (that is, how they perceive themselves) also tends to influence their attitudes toward organizational environments. For example, individuals who lack self confidence or who suffer from poor physical or mental health frequently develop morale problems.

Personal Needs

How employees' *personal needs* are satisfied can significantly influence their morale. Paychecks and employee benefits, for example, help to satisfy personal needs. Although increases in pay don't neces-

When might a
paycheck influence
morale?

sarily motivate employees to increase productivity, paychecks can be a source of poor morale, especially when paychecks are compared by employees doing similar work or with those of workers in other firms in the same industry. Employees can become disgruntled when they feel that their paychecks aren't in line with the current industry rates or aren't keeping up with rising prices.

WARNING SIGNS OF LOW MORALE

Morale in organizations is something that managers often take for granted. Morale frequently isn't noticed unless it is poor or until something has gone awry. Far too often, managers do not recognize how badly morale has deteriorated until they are faced with serious crises. Deep organizational scars result from ignoring the warning signs of deteriorating morale.

Perceptive managers are continually on the lookout for clues to the state of morale. Among the more significant warning signs of low morale are *absenteeism, tardiness, high turnover, strikes and sabotage,* and *lack of pride in work.* Let's take a brief look at each of these factors.

Absenteeism

What might cause high
absenteeism?

If a person enjoys certain sports, he or she will often exert the effort necessary to participate in them. Similarly, if workers enjoy their jobs, they will usually exert the effort necessary to do what is expected of them. However, the nature of work and the workers themselves have changed. As a result, some industries have developed severe morale problems, evidenced by high rates of *absenteeism.*

Absenteeism has been especially acute in certain industries, such as automobile manufacturing. Some American automobile plants have experienced as much as 20 percent absenteeism on some Mondays and Fridays. Temporary replacements tend to cause total costs to rise and productivity to decline.

A certain amount of absenteeism, of course, is unavoidable because of sickness, family crises, and other valid reasons. However, absenteeism on certain days tends to be indicative of employees' negative attitudes toward their work. Absenteeism is most common on Mondays, Fridays, workdays before and after holidays, and the day following payday. If as a manager you ever discover abnormally high absenteeism on these days or, for that matter, on any day, an investigation of the causes of the absences would be in order.

Which are the
"popular" days for
absenteeism?

Some managers evaluate absenteeism statistically. The U.S. Department of Labor suggests the following formula for computing *absenteeism rates:*

$$\frac{\text{Number of workers lost through job absence during period}}{\text{Average number of employees} \times \text{number of workdays}} \times 100 = \text{rate}$$

For example, if there were 350 employee days lost during a particular month with 22 scheduled working days at an organization employing 600 workers, the rate of absenteeism for the month would be:

$$\frac{350}{600 \times 22} \times 100 = 3\%$$

Tardiness

Tardiness is a form of absenteeism that can create problems for organizational managers, especially in departments in which one person's activity is dependent upon another's. Excessive tardiness, like absenteeism, is a warning sign of low morale. Workers who dread their jobs aren't eager to arrive early or even on time. However, those who derive substantial satisfaction from their jobs or feel that they'll benefit from making an effort will often arrive on the job early.

Better late than miserable?

High Turnover

In every organization some employees leave and others are hired. When the *turnover rate*—that is, the amount of movement in and out of an organization—begins to rise abnormally, another warning sign of poor morale could be flashing before the eyes of management. The U.S. Department of Labor suggests the following formula for computing *turnover rates:*

$$\frac{\text{Number of separations during the month}}{\text{Total number of employees at midmonth}} \times 100 = \text{turnover rate}$$

For example, if there were 30 separations during a particular month, and if there were 400 employees at midmonth, the rate of turnover would be

$$\frac{30}{400} \times 100 = 7.5\%$$

High turnover is costly because of the need to train inexperienced new personnel, plus the added expense of employee benefits and the additional paperwork associated with hiring new employees.

Some managers may feel that morale is always satisfactory when turnover ratios are low. However, turnover ratios tend to be lower

When might low
turnover not indicate
high morale?

during periods of economic recession when jobs are scarce. When economic conditions return to normal, disgruntled employees often begin to seek employment elsewhere. Ratios and costs then begin to rise.

Strikes and Sabotage

Strikes and *sabotage* are extreme examples of discontent in the work force and are costly in both human and economic terms. Although strikes have declined substantially in frequency from what was seen in previous decades, they continue to be an economic burden. Strikes accounted for slightly more than 6½ million lost worker days in 1990. Sabotage has sometimes resulted in product defects that have proven embarrassing to manufacturers. For example, there have been occasions in which disgruntled automobile workers have allowed loose nuts to remain in the doorframes of cars, allowing them to become irritating rattles for their future owners.

Lack of Pride in Work

In some industries in the United States there has existed at times a far-too-widespread "Who cares?" attitude. Observe, for instance, the debris floating in our lakes and oceans, plastic objects sometimes unmercifully choking fish and mammals. Some social observers contend that such attitudes and values exist especially in those organizations that lack the opportunities for employee job satisfaction.

The failure to take pride in one's work knows no bounds. Any type of job, industry, or country can be afflicted with the malady. Possibly as a result of intense competition from quality Japanese, Korean, and German products, there have been some signs of quality improvement in recent years.

"What's wrong with
tattered jeans behind
the teller's counter?"

When lack of pride exists, it can also take the form of a general deterioration of an employee's appearance. An individual with low morale, for example, may neglect his or her grooming by not getting regular haircuts, by not taking care of uniforms or clothing, and by lowering standards of personal cleanliness.

The problems of lack of pride and low morale in organizations are serious and can have dire effects on an organization's productivity. If North American firms are going to compete effectively for world markets, their managers have to develop innovative solutions to the problems of the discontented worker.

EVALUATING MORALE

To improve morale, managers must first attempt to determine what is causing poor morale. In the following section we will discuss some of the ways in which management can measure morale.

Statistical Evaluation

One way to measure morale is to evaluate actual results. **Absenteeism and turnover records** can provide useful information. For example, assume that during the past four years, the absenteeism rate in your organization rose from two to seven percent. Taken alone, these figures wouldn't be absolute proof that morale had deteriorated. Combined with the results of other techniques of evaluation discussed in the following sections, however, these statistics could give you a fair indication of morale trends and of potential problems.

Employee Counselors

How might employee counselors measure morale?

In some organizations there are **employee counselors** whose principal function is to assist employees with their problems and complaints. For example, the Xerox Corporation has staff members known as employee relations managers with whom employees, it is hoped, can feel free to discuss their problems in confidence.

Counselors are in the position to discover morale problems early. A snag can arise, however, if management regards the counselor as a source of information and the word gets out that he or she is a "lapdog" or "spy" of management. Counselors quickly lose effectiveness when employees distrust them.

Observing and Listening

What might a sudden change in the behavior of an employee indicate?

Another approach to uncovering what is bothering workers is so obvious that it is often overlooked. Alert managers can usually perceive when employees are behaving differently simply by *observing and listening*. A sudden change in the behavior of a particular employee is often a clue that something might be worrying him or her. For example, perhaps the employee doesn't hear you when you speak and sometimes appears to be in a fog. Perhaps the employee has recently come to work with what seems to be alcohol on his or her breath or seems irritable much of the time. An increase in the frequency of accidents may also be a sign of a morale problem.

Far too frequently managers don't even listen to the response after they have asked their employees how things are going. We've already discussed in Chapter 3 the importance of guarding against the "verbal cocoon" problem to be a more effective listener. One of the most effective means of discovering why employees are discontented is to *ask them* and then *listen* actively and carefully to their answers.

Regular Buzz or Gripe Sessions

What is the purpose of buzz sessions?

If managers have established a climate of trust and open communication, a fairly effective means of determining what is disturbing the employees can be the regular use of **buzz, gripe,** or **deep-sensing**

sessions. Some organizations allocate specific times each week—say, Fridays from 9:00 to 9:30 A.M.—for meetings during which employees are given the opportunity to air their concerns. Much can be learned about employee attitudes from the use of this technique when the psychological distance between managers and workers is not excessive. A feeling of mutual trust is essential.

Morale Surveys
Morale surveys are used by some managers to explore in great depth specific attitudes and opinions of employees. Various names have been attached to such surveys, including *attitude, opinion, employee,* and *climate surveys.* In general, there are two types of morale survey techniques: **interviews** and **questionnaires.** Table 5.1 presents five examples of typical employee attitude survey questions.

Interviews. In Chapter 4 we discussed some of the more common techniques of interviewing. Two of them—*interviews with current employees* and *exit interviews*—can aid in uncovering employee attitudes.

The process of interviewing current employees about their attitudes is useful but has its shortcomings. Employees who fear possible reprisals tend to conceal their real opinions and, instead, answer questions according to what they think the boss would like to hear.

The **exit interview** explores the attitudes of employees who leave the organization. It helps the interviewer to find out the employee's attitudes toward the organization and especially why he

What good does it do to interview someone who's through?

TABLE 5.1   **Sample employee attitude survey questions.**

	Agree strongly	Agree somewhat	Do not know	Disagree somewhat	Disagree strongly
1. If one of my good friends were offered a job here, I would say take the job—this is a good place to work.	☐	☐	☐	☐	☐
2. Employees in this organization are treated with respect.	☐	☐	☐	☐	☐
3. I agree with the changes made here during the past year.	☐	☐	☐	☐	☐
4. I think management could do much more to make my work more satisfying.	☐	☐	☐	☐	☐
5. Management should trust the workers to do the work instead of supervising so closely.	☐	☐	☐	☐	☐

or she might be dissatisfied with the organization. This approach also has its limitations since some employees fear that honesty may cost them a favorable letter of recommendation. The interview approach, however, does have the advantage over the questionnaires of permitting greater interviewer sensitivity toward and interaction with respondents.

Questionnaires. A second and more widely used method of surveying attitudes is the **questionnaire.** Of the two principal types of questionnaires, the **descriptive** asks open-ended questions; the other, the **objective,** asks multiple-choice questions. The objective questionnaire is more common because it is simpler and costs less to administer to large groups. Some questionnaires are a combination of the descriptive and objective types.

The following are some specific suggestions about the use of surveys:

What are some tips on the use of surveys?

1. Efforts should be made to *create a positive and trusting attitude among employees* toward the survey.

2. The survey should have the *active support of the senior managers.*

3. *Questions should be carefully framed* to avoid any built-in biases of management.

4. To obtain more candid answers, the *identity of the respondent should not be required.* Managers should be more interested in *what* the attitudes are than in *whose* attitudes they are.

5. It is best to let employees *know the results* of the surveys as soon as possible.

6. *Management action,* based on the survey results, should be taken and communicated.

7. Data should be *compared* from year to year to ensure that improvements are being made.

Some organizations employ a *postexit questionnaire* in lieu of, or in addition to, an exit interview. This type of questionnaire is felt to elicit more objective responses since it is mailed to the employee some time after his or her termination. Since emotions have probably subsided and the employee is likely to be firmly entrenched in another job, the postexit interview responses tend to be more honest. Once again, not requiring the identity of the respondent tends to elicit even more candor.

Why is the supervisor a key person in administering surveys?

Attitude surveys can be a useful management tool when conducted properly and regularly. If improperly administered, surveys can cause employees to feel suspicious or distrustful of management, and they will not answer the questions candidly. A final important point: Supervisors must be told the purpose and value of surveys. Since supervisors will be administering the surveys, they can make or break the efforts.

SUMMARY

In this chapter we discovered the importance of needs and motivation and their relationship to morale. An understanding of human needs is especially important to managers, who have the vital responsibility of establishing an environment that not only motivates others but also helps to maintain their morale in a positive fashion. Employees and individuals in family and social situations can also benefit from an understanding of needs and motivational concepts.

Felt needs create tensions that motivate a person into making efforts to reduce or eliminate the tensions. Some needs are somewhat basic and internal to the individual, such as the physical need for food. Others are cultural and learned, such as approval, achievement, competence, and power.

Theories of motivation discussed in the chapter were Maslow's hierarchy- or levels-of-needs concept, Alderfer's ERG theory, and Herzberg's motivation-maintenance model, each of which is considered a *content theory* of motivation. We also examined *process theories* of motivation, such as reinforcement, expectancy, and equity theories.

Managers should guard against the tendency to assume that the same factors will motivate all individuals. Motivational influences are highly personal. Each employee in an organization is unique and will thus respond uniquely to specific motivational attempts.

Morale, a condition related to the attitudes of employees, can be influenced by factors both *on and off the job*. Managers should continually be on the lookout for the *warning signs of poor morale* to prevent the deterioration of a healthy organizational climate. Among the more important signs of worsening morale are *higher rates of absenteeism, tardiness, turnover, strikes and sabotage,* and *lack of pride in work*.

Morale can be measured and evaluated in ways ranging from *informal observation to formal morale surveys*.

TERMS AND CONCEPTS TO REMEMBER

needs

motivation

approval needs

achievement needs

competence needs

power needs

position power

charismatic authority

hierarchy of needs

employee benefits

pregnant Maslow needs mix

inverted Maslow needs mix

ERG theory of needs

existence needs

relatedness needs

growth needs

motivation-maintenance model

maintenance (hygiene) factors

motivational (satisfier) factors

behavior modification

law of effect

reinforcement theory

positive reinforcement

escape reinforcement

conditioned response

extinction

punishment reinforcement

expectancy theory

performance-related payment plan

incentive payment system

equity theory

morale

role expectation

absenteeism and turnover records

employee counselors

buzz (gripe or deep-sensing) sessions

morale surveys

interviews and questionnaires

exit interviews

descriptive questionnaires

objective questionnaires

QUESTIONS

1. Why does a need typically have to be recognized before it will motivate?

2. In your opinion, what is the distinction between a *need* and a *want?*

3. Why is an understanding of the process of motivation especially important to managers?

4. Can we "learn" to need something? Explain.

5. List and explain the five levels of needs that Maslow indicated exist in human beings.

6. How does Alderfer's ERG theory of needs and motivation differ from Maslow's?

7. Explain why, according to Herzberg's two-factor model, maintenance factors do not necessarily motivate workers.

8. Why did Herzberg categorize working conditions as a maintenance, rather than a motivating, factor?

9. The late Sam Walton, a business pioneer who built Wal-Mart into the nation's largest retail chain, preferred to have the people working for his company known as "associates," not "employees." Relating Walton's philosophy to Maslow's and Herzberg's motivational theories, to which type of need(s) did he seem to be attempting to appeal?

10. Explain the differences among positive, escape, extinction, and punishment types of reinforcement techniques.

11. What are the dangers associated with the use of punishment as a reinforcement technique?

12. Why is the timing of reinforcement techniques important?

13. What is a major difference between Vroom's theory of motivation and those of Maslow and Herzberg?

14. According to equity theory, what sort of *equity* do employees want?

15. What are some possible exceptions to the generalization that productivity tends to follow morale?

16. Explain the following statement: "Employee perception tends to influence morale."

APPLICATIONS

5.1 The Satisfied Sales Representative

The Shifting Sands Mutual Insurance Company is a medium-sized concern situated in Portsmouth, Virginia. Bermuda Schwartz, a district manager for the Shifting Sands Company, is currently in charge of ten insurance company sales representatives whose principal responsibility is to sell all lines of property and casualty insurance to individuals and to business firms.

The sales representatives are paid a guaranteed sum of $2200 per month, which is actually a draw on (is deducted from) future commission sales. They receive a flat percentage of all new and renewable insurance premiums.

Sammy Sereno, one of the ten sales representatives directly responsible to Schwartz, has been with Shifting Sands Mutual for slightly more than fifteen years. During his first ten years, Sereno was highly ambitious and energetic and built up a substantial volume of business, most of which has been renewed automatically each year. Last year, Sereno devoted much of his time to his favorite hobbies, sailing and scuba diving, and as a result produced very little new business for the firm. In spite of his current, relatively leisurely life, his personal income before taxes last year was almost $110,000. Sereno is married but has no children. He and his wife are seriously considering the adoption of a Bosnian orphan.

Last week, while analyzing the previous year's production figures, Schwartz noticed that Sereno ranked last among the ten sales representatives in the production of new business. Because of his large volume of renewable sales, however, Sereno ranked third in total earnings.

One of Schwartz's primary responsibilities is to motivate his representatives to acquire new business continually since old accounts are sometimes not renewed because of the dissolution of customers' businesses, the death of customers, or the clients' moving out of the Portsmouth area and obtaining their insurance elsewhere.

Questions

1. Assuming that you are Schwartz, how would you attempt to motivate Sereno?

2. What would you do if Sereno said to you, "I'm tired of busting my back canvassing my territory for new business"?

5.2 No Satisfaction

Zoltran Hartfelt shocked the business world by announcing yesterday that he was resigning his position of chairman of the board of Polor Micronics after only eight months. In an interview with the press Mr. Hartfelt told reporters that the job wasn't personally challenging.

His resignation capped a 20-year career with Polor Micronics, Mr. Hartfelt served as Polor Micronics' president and chief executive officer for two years.

In his interview Mr. Hartfelt said that his promotion gave him little in the way of satisfaction. "The chairman's job at Polor Micronics," Hartfelt explained, "is more of a statesmanlike post of making speeches and shaking hands. That's all right for some people," Hartfelt added, "but I'm an operations man and a doer, and the chairmanship just wasn't enough of the kind of work that gives you the possibility to create things. The chief executive pretty well runs the entire show at Polor Micronics."

Mr. Hartfelt, who has an architectural background, added, "I've been a creator all my life and I just don't want to forget how to be a builder."

Questions
1. Zoltran Hartfelt, even though he achieved one of the highest positions possible with any major corporation, was not satisfied. Which of Maslow's need concepts seem to have been frustrated? Why?

2. What conditions at Polar Micronics might have existed for Mr. Hartfelt that could have changed his attitude toward his position as chairman of the board?

5.3 Moe Graduates

Moe Tivait was a senior in high school when he began working for the Peach Company. The work was seasonal, beginning just prior to the harvest and ending in early December. For six years Moe was called back each season to work in the factory. Each year the plant manager put Moe on a different job, often with different crews and even occasionally assigning him to do one-person tasks. Moe's activities included driving small trucks and fork lifts, operating conveyor units, feeding the processing hoppers, fumigating, and performing numerous general labor tasks.

Moe was well liked by the plant manager, and the production supervisors generally sought him for their crews. His co-workers found him amiable, hardworking, and a credit to any crew. Moe's work did not go unrewarded, and by the fourth year he was at the top of the pay scale for seasonal workers.

Moe started college during his second year at the Peach Company. During the off-season he attended day classes, and during the harvest season he attended night college. Only a few co-workers knew of his academic pursuits since he rarely discussed his personal activities with his supervisors.

Late in November of Moe's sixth season with the Peach Company, the plant manager asked him if he would like to work full time. By then, Moe could handle nearly any production job in the factory. He knew all the procedures for moving the raw product in and the packaged product out; he was extremely proficient in operating and repairing production equipment; and he enjoyed offering suggestions to improve production. The plant manager knew Moe had been married the previous Christmas, and he was afraid he might lose Moe to another employer.

As Moe mulled over the manager's offer, he thought about his experience and long career with the Peach Company, the degree in environmental sciences he would receive in January, and the baby he and his wife were expecting in late spring. Moe needed to review his goals in light of this offer from the Peach Company.

Questions

1. Applying the concepts of motivation discussion in the chapter, describe the motivational pattern that is displayed by Moe over the six-year period.

2. What motivational factors should the plant manager consider in convincing Moe to accept his offer?

3. What should be the manager's response if Moe tells him that he wants a better job than he has had during the past six years?

5.4 "Give Us More Money!"

Productivity had fallen to a new low among the 20 mechanics in Eddie White's department. He knew that part of the problem was due to the high employee turnover experienced among his workers. Several of his staff were new to the company, replacing mechanics who had quit. Even among the remaining well-trained workers who had been with the company for some time, absenteeism was high, and people didn't seem to put out their best effort.

Six months ago, Eddie had decided to do something about his group's productivity problems. Eddie, a recent college graduate, decided to institute some of the motivational techniques he had learned in his organizational behavior and supervision classes. First, he started competition among the workers that would yield recognition to high achievers. He decided to allow the workers to take more responsibility for the jobs the department had to handle, reasoning that this would induce the workers to show greater pride in their work. He also developed a new training program that would allow the mechanics to advance in their skill levels. But as Eddie reviewed the last month's production figures, he had to admit that the results had been poor.

Eddie had encouraged his subordinates to make suggestions for improving the department's performance, but with little success. When he tried to pin one worker down, the mechanic responded angrily at Eddie personally. Most of the workers just shrugged their shoulders and evaded the issue. Finally, Jeff Coluntuno, one of Eddie's better workers told him, "If I told you what I really think about this place, you'd probably fire me on the spot." This gave Eddie the idea of instituting an anonymous suggestion box. He told his workers that they should feel free to make any suggestions they wanted without fear of reprisal.

A week later, as Eddie opened the box, he was again disappointed. Only four of his mechanics had bothered to make suggestions. They were as follows:

"The pay here is lousy. If you want us to do a better job, pay us a living wage."

"We have to pay for our own health insurance benefits here, and I, for one, can't afford it. Dick, who left here for another job, gets free health insurance where he works now."

"The shop is cold all winter. If we close things up and try to get warm, there's no ventilation. How can a guy work when he can't breathe?"

"I don't give a hoot for your contests and classes! I have a family to feed and look after!"

Questions

1. Why do you think Eddie White's ideas were unsuccessful?

2. Did he perceive the workers' needs in the same way that they themselves did? White was attempting to use which needs as motivators? Which needs were most important to the mechanics?

5.5 *"Sure* I Invite Dissent."

A new employee named Kelli Sullivan was told by her boss, Fred Inouye, to feel free to disagree anytime she desired. Inouye told Sullivan, "I invite dissent in my department. That's the only way to obtain fresh ideas!"

Sullivan, fresh out of college, eager to contribute her ideas, and high in competence needs, found herself disagreeing with Inouye's suggestions on three occasions during her first week of employment. Each time she disagreed, Inouye would react strongly, openly making fun of her ideas in front of the other department members. Sullivan soon developed second thoughts about the benefit to her offering suggestions. "If Mr. Inouye is going to treat me like that every time I come up with a fresh idea, the heck with it! I'll just keep it to myself. I don't have to take that stuff from him!"

Questions

1. What concept of behavior modification relates to Ms. Sullivan's dilemma? Explain.

2. What concept of needs and motivation might account for Inouye's behavior toward Sullivan? Why?

3. How might a manager apply the concept of extinction in a manner that eliminated undesirable employee behavior?

NOTES

1. Research by D. P. Crowne and D. Marlowe, in *The Approval Motive: Studies in Evaluative Dependence* (New York: Wiley, 1964), as reported in and adapted from Gardner Lindzey, Calvin S. Hall, and Richard F. Thompson, *Psychology* (New York: Worth, 1975), p. 354.

2. David C. McClelland, *The Achieving Society* (New York: Van Nostrand, 1961).

3. Abraham H. Maslow, *Motivation and Personality* (New York: Harper & Row, 1954).

4. Clayton P. Alderfer, *Existence, Relatedness, and Growth: Human Needs in Organizational Settings* (New York: The Free Press, 1972).

5. Frederick Herzberg, *Work and the Nature of Man* (Cleveland: World Publishing, 1966).

6. B. F. Skinner, *About Behaviorism* (New York: Knopf, 1974).

7. Philip G. Zimbardo, *Psychology and Life,* 10th ed. (Glenview, IL: Scott, Foresman & Company, 1979), p. 67.

8. Irwin L. Goldstein, *Training in Organizations* (Monterey, CA: Brooks/Cole, 1986), pp. 73–74.

9. Victor H. Vroom, *Work and Motivation* (New York: Wiley, 1964).

10. Lyman W. Porter and Edward E. Lawler III, *Managerial Attitudes and Performance* (Homewood, IL: Dorsey Press and Irwin, 1968) and Richard M. Steers and Lyman W. Porter, *Motivation and Work Behavior,* 3d ed. (New York: McGraw-Hill, 1983).

11. Laurance, Hooper, "IBM to Cut 7,000 Jobs in Europe Next Year in Reorganization Bid," *The Wall Street Journal Europe,* September 6–7, 1991, pp. 1, 4; "IBM to Cut 20,000 Jobs Next Year," *The Stars and Stripes,* November 28, 1991, p. 18; "'Surplus' Workers Told to Find New IBM Job or Take Package," *The Stars and Stripes,* April 12, 1992, p. 17.

12. See note 10.

13. Diane Summers, "Why Employees Leave Their Jobs—Pay Is Not a Factor," *Financial Times,* July 10, 1991, p. 12.

BOXED NOTES

a. J. F. Ross, "Why Americans Work Too Much," *San Francisco Chronicle,* February 10, 1992, p. E4.

b. Adapted from Andrea Gabor, "Merit Raise Is Out in U.S., Teamwork In," *Herald Tribune International,* January 27, 1992, pp. 1, 9; and Michael Dixon, "A Good Way of Demotivating the Majority," *Financial Times,* January 17, 1992, p. 1.

c. Adapted from "Most Workers at Caterpillar Reject Its Call to End Strike," *The Wall Street Journal Europe,* April 7, 1992, p. 3; James B. Parks, "UAW Holds Line Against Caterpillar," *AFL-CIO News,* January 6, 1992, p. 5; Martin Dickson and Barbara Durr, "Playing for High Stakes on the Picket Line," *Financial Times,* April 9, 1992, p. 15; Barbara Durr, "Caterpillar Bars Door to Returning Strikers," *Financial Times,* April 16, 1992, p. 6; and "Caterpillar Inc. Posts $53 Million Loss in 2nd Quarter," *The Wall Street Journal Europe,* July 17–18, 1992, p. 4.

EXPERIENTIAL EXERCISE

What Do You Need?

This exercise is designed to help you to understand Maslow's motivational theory and to recognize how priorities of needs differ among various individuals.

Instructions:

1. Read the following story and then determine the order in which you would make your requests.

2. Form a small group of about five participants and attempt to reach a group consensus on the "correct" order in which requests should be made. Attempt to convince others in your group of your point of view.

3. How did the outcome—the group's ranking—compare with Maslow's hierarchy?

4. How do you account for the differences among individual group members regarding their initial rankings of needs?

STORY

You were sailing with a crew of five from San Francisco, California, to Sydney, Australia. Your boat sank during a turbulent storm and you were the sole survivor. You were rescued by a wealthy and eccentric recluse named Isolando, who lives on a small island with a small group of his followers. Since the island is uncharted, there is little chance of your being rescued.

Isolando, who discovered the island ten years earlier with his small group of followers, informs you that you are welcome to his island and all your needs and wants will be satisfied—all you have to do is request what you want. Below are listed five types of requests you may make. Rank them in the order in which you would make them.

Your Requests	Group's Requests	
_____	_____	Companionship of others
_____	_____	The ability to determine your goals and strive to achieve them
_____	_____	Food, drink, shelter, sex
_____	_____	Recognition and attention from others
_____	_____	A set of guidelines describing how life on the island is structured.

CHAPTER 6

Techniques of Leadership

Okay, People, Follow Me. . . .
I Said, Follow Me!
Aw, Come On, Please *Follow Me!*

**When you finish this chapter,
you should be able to:**

1
Restate in your own words the difference between leadership and management.
2
Contrast X, Y, Derived X, and Selective X-Y theories of managerial attitudes.
3
Explain the relationship of the Pygmalion effect to
a manager's assumptions about subordinates.
4
Contrast three major styles of leadership.
5
Describe the Vroom-Yetton continuum of manager-subordinate involvement.
6
Identify three skills that are fundamental for effective management.
7
Summarize four ways in which managers can improve their leadership skills.

For the 1990s we need leaders who are more sensitive to the global perspective, cultural differences, and the diversity of the work force.

Keshavan Nair, Author

Leadership is the art of changing a group
from what it is into what it ought to be.

Anon.

Assume that you've been placed in a room with five other persons who were chosen at random to work on the solution of a particular problem. An interesting phenomenon would probably unfold. If your group is typical, you'd soon discover the emergence of an *informal leader,* a person who would most likely be able to influence the other members of the group in certain ways. Your group, therefore, is an organization from which a leader has evolved.

Why do organizations develop leaders?

Organizations tend to develop *leaders,* that is, people who influence others. Can you imagine how difficult the fulfillment of organizational goals would be if there were no specified individuals with the authority and responsibility to plan, organize, coordinate, lead, and control their activities?

THE FUNCTIONS AND CHARACTERISTICS OF LEADERSHIP

Is there a simple definition of *leadership*?

Perhaps we'd better attach a meaning to the term *leadership,* which has no simple definition applicable to all situations. As you will shortly discover, there are a variety of leadership styles that may be applied effectively to different situations.

Leadership Defined

Is leadership manipulative?

As illustrated in Figure 6.1, the term **leadership** has been described by Catt and Miller as "the ability to influence the activities of others, through the process of communication, toward the attainment of a goal."[1] This definition might strike you at first as being somewhat manipulative, but think carefully about your own behavior with close friends or with your parents. To accomplish some of *your personal goals,* don't you regularly try to *influence their behavior* toward accomplishing something specific? Basically, the attempt to *influence behavior* is a key element of leadership. Your objectives don't have to be insidious or negative when leadership techniques are being employed.

Also, note the word *communication* in the definition. Leadership requires you to provide others with direction, and direction takes

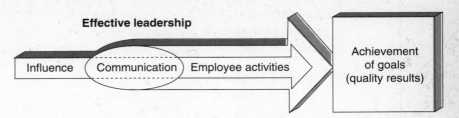

Figure 6.1 Leadership—the ability to influence others, through communication, toward goal accomplishment.

place through communication. If you can't communicate your plans—as outstanding as they may be—your associates are unlikely to carry out your directives.

The Difference Between Leadership and Management

It is perhaps not obvious that there's a significant difference between *leadership* and *management,* although these terms are frequently used interchangeably. *Leadership* deals *directly* with people and their *behavior;* it's only one aspect of management. *Management,* a broader concept *includes* the activity of *leadership* but may also involve *non-behavioral* functions that don't directly or immediately affect others. Ultimately, **management** is a process of planning, organizing, coordinating, leading, and controlling the activities of others.

Perhaps the following illustration will make the distinction clearer. Assume that you are an office manager with a staff of seven employees who perform a variety of clerical duties. One of your responsibilities is to respond to prospective customers' requests for additional information about your company's products. Forms that potential customers can complete and mail to your company are printed in trade journals. Each day your department receives a large number of the forms requesting additional product information. You must assign the task of responding to the requests to certain employees in your department. When you walk over to Harry's desk and say, "Harry, would you please respond to these 25 requests for information?" you are involved in a *behavioral leadership function;* you are influencing Harry's behavior *directly* and *immediately.*

Now let's assume that morale problems have developed in your department. Three of your employees have complained about receiving inordinate amounts of work assignments and feeling excessive pressure to get the work out. You have decided to make a thorough analysis of the way in which you have been assigning work. You then will develop a plan for scheduling work assignments on a more equitable basis. The *planning* activity that you will do is an example of *management* conduct. You are to engage in a function (planning) that

What's the difference between *leading* and *managing* Harry?

doesn't immediately or directly affect Harry or your other employees. Let's now turn to an examination of some significant organizational leadership concepts.

Formal Leadership

Where do formal leaders come from?

A person may be promoted or transferred to a position of formal leadership from *within* an organization or may be recruited specifically for the particular position from a source *outside* the organization. To ensure the future availability of leaders from within the organization, management development, or succession, programs are often provided.

The formal leadership of an organization can generally be discovered by looking at a company's **organization chart.** Organization charts are formal documents that serve as guides to authority relationships established in organizations. They also show official titles that have been assigned to managers.

Time out for some clarification of terms: Three words used regularly around work organizations and related to leadership are *authority, responsibility,* and *accountability.* Each term is significant to the formal organization but has a distinct meaning.

authority = "right" or "power"

Authority is the *right or power delegated to people in an organization to make decisions, act, and direct others to act.* It is also sometimes referred to as *empowerment* (a term to be discussed in greater detail later). For example, a supervisor might have the *authority* to schedule the work of others, determine who works overtime, approve vacation schedules, and authorize certain purchases. Authority, therefore, is something that is passed down—that is, *assigned* or *delegated*—to people by their bosses.

responsibility = "duty" or "obligation"

responsibilities = "assigned duties"

Responsibility, on the other hand, is *not* a right; it is a *duty.* It is the *obligation someone has to perform assigned work or to make certain that someone else performs it in a prescribed way.* The plural term **responsibilities** usually refers to the specific *tasks* or *duties* that have been assigned to an employee to perform.

accountability = "answerability"

Accountability is the *answerability of an employee to his or her boss.* Bosses, of course, are answerable to their bosses. (The term *accountability* is sometimes used interchangeably with *responsibility.*)

Try to visualize that authority and accountability flow in different directions. As you can observe in the simplified organization chart in Figure 6.2, authority flows *downward* from the president to the workers. For example, let's assume that Ms. Ton, the company president, has delegated to Mr. Gonzales, the plant manager, the right to make decisions necessary to run the plant. Furthermore, Ton has assigned Gonzales the responsibility to operate the plant in a profitable manner. Let's also assume that Gonzales delegates work-scheduling

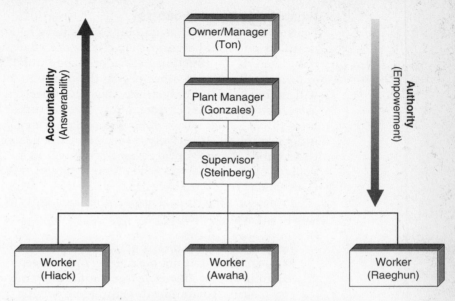

Figure 6.2 Accountability flows upward; authority flows downward.

Organizations have their ups and downs!

duties to a supervisor, Ms. Steinberg, and that Steinberg has organized her department into a team. She has empowered the workers in her team to conduct scheduling activities on their own. Keep in mind that accountability flows *upward.* Therefore, the workers are accountable to Steinberg for the results they achieve with their scheduling activities. Steinberg is accountable to the plant manager, Gonzales, for the results related to the scheduling activities in her department. And Gonzales is accountable to Ton for the overall results achieved in the plant.

How Important Are Leaders?

A preoccupation with the topic of leadership has become noticeable in the business press in recent years. Some management authorities contended that the United States had not a shortage of *management* but, instead, a shortage of *leaders* in contemporary organizations. They also contended that corporate America had been on the receiving end of an onslaught of challenging changes, such as global competition, takeover threats, rapid technological change, revolution in management-labor relationships, and fears that the United States was declining as an international economic powerhouse. Such factors, it has been argued, greatly increased the need for corporations to evolve and adapt. As a result, the need for unusually creative leaders to deal with these challenges became significant.[2]

Wanted: Creative leaders!

What Makes People Leaders?

What does a leader
need to be a leader?

Neither the titles that some individuals have been assigned nor their positions on formal organization charts are what make some individuals leaders. To function as leaders, they must have an *emotional appeal* that instills in other people the desire to follow them. Leaders will be able to lead only when they can effectively influence people *over extended periods of time.* Many famous titular heads of countries have fallen or have been forced to resign after losing their ability to influence others effectively, especially after losing the confidence of their public. Leaders everywhere are much more likely to retain the support of their followers when their behavior sets a good example for their followers.

Professor Robert J. House of the University of Pennsylvania has this to say about leaders.

> They tend to have more energy than most people, and they're a little smarter, but not outright geniuses because geniuses don't communicate well with lesser minds. They have a high level of social skills: communication, problem solving, the ability to clarify and negotiate. We call it dominance—social assertiveness, but in a good cause.[3]

Although the primary responsibility of leaders is to achieve the objectives of their organizations, they are less likely to do so if they don't also meet the needs of their followers. Even in military organizations, where the formal organization can be extremely significant, we can find numerous examples of designated leaders who have lost their ability to influence their subordinates effectively. There are historic examples of second lieutenants, for example, who have shouted "Chaaarge!" at the tops of their lungs as they rushed frantically up a hill, but the gold-plated bars on their neatly laundered battle dress didn't guarantee that their troops would follow; sometimes they didn't!

Charismatic Leaders

Some people are able to influence others substantially, at least in the short run, as a result of their having what is termed **charismatic authority,** a topic we touched on briefly in Chapter 5. The word *charisma,* stemming from Greek, represented a divine element of some sort. Here's a more up-to-date definition of charismatic authority that will suit our more modern tastes: It is the *power and ability developed by some individuals to influence and win the devotion and respect of others.* It is the power that emanates from a special quality of personal magnetism or charm that some individuals appear to possess.

Individuals with charisma may be designated formally as leaders, or they may completely lack any formal authority within the organization. They are people who enjoy power and influence over others because of their ability to inspire personal trust and confidence. Followers tend to identify with them.

Both John F. Kennedy and Ronald Reagan were charismatic leaders. President Kennedy especially seemed to have the ability to inspire the youth of the United States during his short tenure as president (although he tended not to be perceived in the same charismatic manner by much of the business community). President Reagan with his special type of personal magnetism was able to retain his popularity through far more of his second term than were most of his predecessors. Sometimes referred to as "the great communicator," Ronald Reagan greatly enhanced his public image through his polished ability to communicate. He was even tagged by the media as the "Teflon president" because mistakes and inconsistencies in his behavior seemed neither "to stick to him" nor to have an unfavorable effect on his prolonged high level of popularity. However, his successor, George Bush, seemed to lack charisma, continually having to do battle with what was referred to as the "wimp factor."

What gave Presidents Kennedy and Reagan "charisma"?

Leadership in a Global Environment

Many organizations today operate along *global* lines, rather than solely in their home countries. As a result, some managers may find that they are leading people in cultures completely different from the culture they are accustomed to. Because of the increasing importance of global organizational behavior, an entire chapter—Chapter 16, "On a Global Scale"—is devoted to this subject.

Leadership—When a Company Gets "Lean and Mean"

Companies restructured their operations with increasing frequency during the "double-dip" (some dared call it "triple") recession of the early 1990s. A result was the need for many leaders to deal with demoralized employees who feared the prospect of being laid off. This is a special challenge for leaders and is discussed in more detail in Chapter 13.

I'm sorry, Slim, but we're slimming down.

LEADERSHIP ATTITUDES

The perceptual tests we examined in Chapter 2 showed us that our perception is not always accurate. Perceiving drawings and photographs, however, is often far less hazardous than perceiving human beings. Have you ever noticed that some managers tend to perceive

What Is the Right Stuff for a Global Leader?ᵃ

Why is the "failure rate" of international personnel transfers by U.S. companies so high—about 30 percent—compared to failures of less than five percent for Japanese firms that send their employees abroad? One of the factors contributing to the high rate of dismissal and recall of American expatriates could be training. European and Japanese companies make greater efforts to prepare employees for a new culture and business environment, with 69 percent of European firms and 57 percent of Japanese firms providing advance training. In the United States, only 32 percent of companies provide their employees with training before assigning them overseas.

What preparation should a manager have to be effective in a global environment? Human resource management skills—especially those related to managing people from other countries—are essential, along with the ability to handle unfamiliar situations. Also helpful is a global outlook rather than one oriented only toward the United States.

Knowledge of languages is likewise important. Stuart Hammer, Ford of Europe's director of education and training, says, "Inability with languages has always been a disadvantage for the international manager."

A different view appears to be held by the Economic Intelligence Unit (EIU) of the Ashridge Management Research Group, located in the United Kingdom. According to one of EIU's reports, "The only effective way to develop international skills and perspectives is through direct international experience, either through participation in international task forces or, more importantly, through working and living abroad." EIU adds, "Such experiences open people's minds to the fact that things are done differently elsewhere and encourage them to think in a wider context."

Both views have their merit. As is usually the case, a combination of training and experience is often the best teacher.

their employees in positive or favorable ways and others in negative or suspicious ways? If you were a manager, how would you perceive the people who work with you? Read through the following sets of statements labeled "Theory X attitudes" and "Theory Y attitudes." Which of the two sets of attitudes seems to fit your conceptual scheme toward others?[4]

THEORY X ATTITUDES

1. Most employees dislike work and will avoid it whenever they can.

2. Because most people dislike work, they have to be pushed, closely supervised, and threatened with punishment to get them to help achieve the objectives of the organization.

3. Most people are basically lazy, have little ambition, prefer to avoid responsibility, and desire security as a major goal.

4. The typical worker is self-centered and has little concern for organizational goals.

THEORY Y ATTITUDES

1. Most people find work as natural as play or rest, and their attitude toward work is related to their experiences with it.

2. People don't have to be threatened with punishment to be motivated to assist an organization to accomplish its goals. They will be somewhat self-directed when they are able to relate to the objectives of the organization.

3. Within a favorable organizational culture, the average person learns not only to accept but also to seek responsibility.

4. A large part of our working force has the ability to exercise imagination and creativity on the job.

With which set of statements did you feel more in agreement: X or Y? Would you personally be considered an X-rated or a Y-rated person if you were a manager? Read on for a better understanding of the implications of X and Y types of attitudes.

X and Y Labels

What is all this X and Y stuff?

Don't be confused by the letters *X* and *Y*, which are merely labels assigned by Professor McGregor to two general ways in which workers may be perceived by managers. **Theory X,** as you may have discerned, takes a somewhat pessimistic view of humanity. **Theory Y,** in contrast, begins with the premise that workers will do far more than is expected of them if treated like human beings and permitted to experience personal satisfaction on the job. Theory Y does *not* represent the extreme—backslapping managers who bend over backward to be regarded as nice guys.

If your set of attitudes falls into Theory X, you fit into the pattern of the more *traditional manager.* Theory Y, however, is the result of newer and more *positive assumptions* that many managers have developed in recent years. An increasing number of leaders have discarded the traditional attitudes. Since your beliefs significantly influence the way you work with and through people, as well as their feelings of motivation, an understanding of the two views is important.

Is Reality Selective X-Y?

Do you recall our discussion of two-valued reasoning in Chapter 2? This concept was described as the tendency to perceive things as either right or wrong, good or bad. We concluded that labeling people or objects in a two-valued fashion could be injurious to one's perceptual health. Presentations of McGregor's X-Y theories run the risk of implying that managers are entirely one type *or* the other. But is that reality? Are a manager's assumptions about people likely to be so fixed and clear-cut?

How do you personally perceive people? It's likely that your perceptions fall into neither an X nor a Y category but are *selective.* Isn't it more likely that you get that X feeling about some people or groups and a Y feeling about others?

How do prejudice and discrimination relate to "Selective X-Y"?

Think for a moment about people who are prejudiced toward certain types or groups of people. They are X-oriented toward these people, yet Y-oriented toward the types of people with whom they identify. In other words, such individuals are what could be called **Selective X-Y** in their attitudes toward others. Can you imagine how these assumptions could influence a manager's process of selecting new employees?

Let's look briefly at an organizational example. Assume that Carlos, a supervisor, tries to practice a Y-oriented managerial approach. In reality, however, Carlos perceives some of his subordinates in a positive, Y-oriented way and others in an X-oriented way. He has discovered that some employees prefer closer supervision and do not want to assume any more responsibility than they already have. They've even admitted that their real interest is their paycheck and that they couldn't care less about what happens at work. These experiences have made Carlos *Selective X-Y* in his approach to his subordinates.

In summary, most of us are *selective* in our assumptions about individuals and groups. That is, the assumptions we make toward others tend to vary with our present notions and our past experience with similar types of individuals and groups. Unfortunately, those who have learned to regard others in a preconceived manner may be making assumptions that stray from reality. Naturally we should attempt to avoid unrealistically negative assumptions about others, since—as we'll see shortly—such assumptions can actually create the types of behavior in others that we don't want.

Derived X Theory

Many managers believe (or at least hope!) that their approach to leadership is the "correct" one. Many managers are sincerely interested in adopting a more positive stance in their managerial activities, but, unfortunately, their previous experiences have caused them to develop an attitude that we'll call **Derived X,** or the **I've-been-burned theory.** The following illustration should make this theory clear: A single person falls deeply in love but soon thereafter is abandoned and deeply hurt. The individual who has been ditched may have had optimistic and positive attitudes about love, but if such disappointing experiences recur regularly, the person may *shift* to a Theory X position in future relationships.

You people are deriving me X!

The same holds true for managers, who might try to maintain optimistic and positive attitudes toward subordinates but be "burned" in the process. The following is a list of attitudes that can be *derived* from negative experiences with employees:

DERIVED X (THE I'VE-BEEN-BURNED THEORY)

1. I want to feel that people are conscientious and find work a natural activity, but I've been burned too many times by some of my employees.

2. I've given my subordinates the chance to make decisions and to assume responsibility, but I've been burned too many times. They've simply taken advantage of me.

3. I've tried to create an atmosphere of growth and development for my subordinates by giving them the freedom to make mistakes and to fail, but I've been burned too many times. They haven't grown and developed; they've merely made mistakes and failed.

4. I've tried to get workers to participate in planning activities for achieving organizational goals, but I've been burned too many times. They're more interested in paydays than in accomplishing organizational goals.

If you find yourself shifting from a Y position to a Derived X, you could probably benefit from an attempt to analyze your own situation thoroughly. Could your shifting attitude possibly be caused by present notions about your subordinates? Are you truly concerned about your employees, and are you really trying to do something for them, or is your concern merely lip service? Remember that you're likely to be judged more by your behavior than by your words.

Of course, a manager must be realistic. You're likely to be burned occasionally. And there are undoubtedly some workers who aren't self-directed and self-controlled. Some workers do prefer security over responsibility. There are also employees who prefer to seek satisfaction during their leisure time and who merely look at their jobs as a means to non-work-related ends. But in spite of these realities, try to retain a certain degree of sensitivity. Be realistic in your feelings but sensitive in your behavior. You must have a certain amount of trust in subordinates; you can't search all workers as they leave the premises each day. Few people want to work in an atmosphere of suspicion.

Traditional Leadership

Have you ever had a boss who was a negative leader? This type of boss attempts to motivate through fear and feels that workers must be *forced* to cooperate and produce, mainly because, "People are just no damn good!" Managers who exercise *negative leadership,* a more traditional approach toward subordinates, tend to engage in excessively close supervision and find it difficult to delegate work. As a result, much of their time is spent "putting out fires," so to speak, and checking the work of subordinates, instead of carrying out essential management functions, such as planning, organizing, coordinating, leading, and controlling.

Fear and Motivation

Workers who operate in an aura of fear may be productive in the short run, but in the long run their morale is likely to be adversely affected, to the predictable detriment of the quantity and quality of their output. Often subordinates who work under negative leaders devote much of their time to trying to protect themselves from the boss by keeping unnecessary records in case they must prove later that "It wasn't my mistake, boss!" Workers on the receiving end of negative motivation may appear to be cooperative but are often searching for the opportunity to "put one over" on their supervisors. Turnover ratios of company personnel tend to be considerably higher in organizations in which the climate is filled with tension and fear, thus substantially increasing the training and operative costs of the work unit.

Modern Management

Modern managers have learned that the application of more positive techniques of leadership is more effective with subordinates. *Positive*

Are you positive?

leaders assume that most people will want to do good work if shown the reasons for their efforts. Such managers attempt to increase, rather than decrease, the satisfaction of their subordinates. Being positive doesn't mean that you're "soft" in your application of discipline. You can be positive and still be firm in your application of company policies and rules. An important point, however, for the positive leader is to treat employees with fairness and respect.

Positive leaders attempt to *explain why* a job is to be done rather than to *coerce* a person into doing it. Effective leaders soon learn that a positive approach results in the expenditure of even less time and involvement since their subordinates feel that they can use their own initiative without the fear of failure and the need for covering up mistakes.

You might be productive for both a positive and a negative leader, but to whom would you be most likely to say, "Take this job and shove it!" if a better opportunity came your way? From whom would you be most likely to get more job satisfaction over the long run? When you become a leader, will you recall these concepts? Keep in mind that concepts not applied are quickly forgotten.

Some further suggestions for effective leadership can be viewed in Table 6.1.

THE PYGMALION EFFECT

Once upon a time, there was a sculptor named Pygmalion who had some unconventional tastes. He was a young man in Greco-Roman mythology and classical literature made famous by Ovid in the *Metamorphoses*. According to Ovid, Pygmalion created an ivory statue

TABLE 6.1   Seven Guidelines to Effective Leadership[5]

1. *Trust your subordinates.* You don't expect them to go all out for you if they think you don't believe in them.
2. *Develop a vision.* Some executives, suspicions to the contrary, realize that planning for the long term pays off. And people want to follow someone who knows where he or she is going.
3. *Keep your cool.* The best leaders show their mettle under fire.
4. *Encourage risk.* Nothing demoralizes the troops like knowing that the slightest failure could jeopardize their entire career.
5. *Be an expert.* From boardroom to mail room, everyone had better understand that you know what you're talking about.
6. *Invite dissent.* Your people aren't giving you their best or learning how to lead if they are afraid to speak up.
7. *Simplify.* You need to see the big picture in order to set a course, communicate it, and maintain it. Keep the details at bay.

representing his ideal of the perfect woman. Apparently, Pygmalion wasn't too attracted to the organic women of his time, because he fell madly in love with his statue and wished mightily for it to become real. In his desire for his ivory work of art he was handily assisted by Venus, who made the creation come to life. As you might imagine, Mr. Pygmalion was enthralled by the opportunity to have a real living being for a change!

George Bernard Shaw, sensing the potential for a hit, based his play *Pygmalion* on the concept presented in Ovid's work. Musical comedy writers later seized on Shaw's story and set it to music, thereby creating *My Fair Lady*. In the play, Professor Higgins believes that he can create a "duchess out of a flower girl." His unabated faith and patience finally transform the poor, ill-mannered Cockney flower girl, Eliza Doolittle, and she appears proudly in high society, speaking with a refined British accent to discuss "the rain in Spain" and how it "stays mainly on the plain."

This little Pyggie didn't take her for granite!

What Do You Expect?

The works of Ovid and Shaw have an important application for organizational members. Out of these stories developed a concept termed the **Pygmalion Effect,** also known as the *self-fulfilling prophecy,* according to which *the expectation of an event can actually cause it to occur.*

This concept may at first appear to border dangerously on the *wishing-it-were-so philosophy* discussed in Chapter 2. We all know that wishing or expecting the hole in a doughnut to become two ounces of solid gold isn't likely to make it so, nor will wishing or expecting to "win big" on the state lottery garner you $2 million. However, one person's attitudes and expectations toward another often create near-miraculous transformations. For example, let's assume that you are a manager who has substantial faith in an associate named Santiago. Let's also assume that you demonstrate your faith through both *action and words* (a Theory Y orientation), often employing *supportive body language and positive verbal comments.* Isn't your positive attitude likely to be felt by Santiago? In fact, it may become self-fulfilling. The contrary holds true, too. If you have negative expectations of Santiago (i.e., you are X-oriented toward him), your feelings would probably be communicated to him and might result in less than satisfactory performance. He would be performing "down to your expectations."

"When I wish upon a lotto. . . ."

What do you expect from Santiago?

How About Toward *Your* Boss?

Most discussions of the Pygmalion Effect refer to its downward influence, that is, the effect of expectations on subordinates. However (although at times you may doubt it!), doesn't your own boss also

Do bosses *really* have feelings?

have feelings? If the positive or negative expectations of a manager can influence subordinates' behavior, couldn't it also be true that employees' expectations can affect a boss's behavior?

Let's look at an academic example first. Let's assume that a young man named Homer had a lot of bad experiences with authority in the past. It seems as though most of Homer's high school teachers hassled him in a manner that he felt was unfair. He also had a few "misunderstandings" with the law. Currently, however, he's a first-year student at a local college. Homer knows darned well that he has the ability to succeed in college, but he also knows that the wise-act professor up there in front of the class is going to hassle him just as his teachers did in high school. Homer's not going to let those "overeducated water buffalos" get on his case, however.

Unfortunately, but quite predictably, Homer's hostility and negative expectations are felt by the professor, who asks herself, "Why is this fellow reacting to me in such a negative fashion?" There is a good chance that the professor will start responding negatively to the hostile student, who can then say to himself, "Those teachers are all alike; I knew darned well she'd give me static."

However, let's assume instead that the professor, like you, knows something about human behavior. Instead of overreacting to Homer's protestations and negative attitudes, she says to herself, "I'm not sure why this young man is reacting to me in such a negative fashion. Undoubtedly he has his reasons. However, I know why I'm here: To help him and the other students in the class. I'll try not to let my disappointment show. I'll give him positive reinforcement when he deserves it, and I'll make a special effort not to place him in potentially embarrassing situations and therefore live down to his expectations. Based on my past experience with students who came across similarly, I expect that he will perceive me as I really am—a concerned instructor—within a couple of weeks."

Some important points in our discussion of the **Upward Pygmalion Effect** are these: If you are a manager, try not to let your associates have a negative Pygmalion effect on you. Try to maintain positive expectations (our old friend, the Y orientation) toward them. If you are not a manager, realize that your attitudes toward your boss—or anyone, for that matter—can be self-fulfilling. If you approach others with a positive attitude and high expectations, you could be pleasantly surprised at the results.

STYLES OF LEADERSHIP

Designating leaders as positive or negative is one way of classifying leadership. Another way is to classify leadership styles by the philosophy of the leaders. Three styles can be distinguished: autocratic, participative, and free rein.

As a potential leader in organizational situations, you may have already recognized the value of encouraging employees to participate in making some of the decisions that affect the achievement of organizational goals. However, you probably find that your approach must, at times, be decisive and direct, and that you cannot always afford the time that the participative approach to leadership requires.

A Major Problem

Many leaders face the problem of balancing the two values of participation and decisiveness. What sort of leader do you as an employee prefer? One who *tells* you what to do? One who *asks* for your opinions and advice? Or one who *presents you with a task* and permits you to perform the job *without direct supervision?*

There isn't one approach to leadership that neatly fits every situation. Before we can decide when to use a particular style of leadership, we should explore some of the major characteristics of the three principal forms, as illustrated in Figure 6.3.

Is there a "best" style of leadership?

Autocratic Style

Managers who employ **autocratic,** or **authoritarian,** styles of leadership could be termed *tellers.* Autocratic leaders usually feel that they know what they want and tend to express those wants as *direct*

"I'm the boss! You do what I say!"

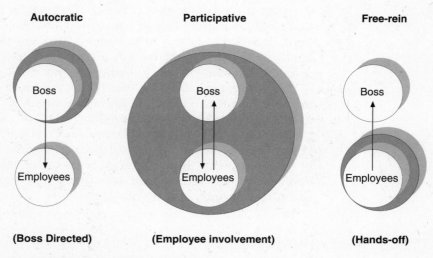

Autocratic   Participative   Free-rein

Boss   Boss   Boss

Employees   Employees   Employees

(Boss Directed)   (Employee involvement)   (Hands-off)

Dark shading is the decision-making area

Figure 6.3 Three styles of leadership.

orders to their associates. Autocratic leaders usually *keep decisions and controls to themselves,* since they have assumed full responsibility for decision making. Autocratic leaders usually *structure the entire work situation* for their workers, who merely do what they are told, that is, follow orders.

Autocratic Pros. Although in general the autocratic form of leadership is looked upon as negative, once again things are not all black or white in the real world of organizations. Many autocratic leaders have been successful in accomplishing goals. To be successful, however, autocratic leaders must have *broad and diversified backgrounds.* They must also have employees who *expect and want* their leaders to give them *strong direction.* Workers who are either somewhat *submissive or prefer not to be responsible* for participating in planning and decision making tend to respond positively to boss-centered leadership. Also, a more directive leadership is often welcomed by employees whose *job responsibilities are not clearly defined* or who *lack sufficient knowledge and training* to perform their jobs without assistance.

Some leaders are what is referred to as *benevolent autocrats.* Such leaders still retain absolute decision-making power, but they attempt to provide *positive rewards* to employees who follow their directives. These leaders also tend to be supportive of their employees. Some employees respond favorably to benevolent autocratic leadership.

Is there a place for autocracy?

In some situations a manager may have little choice but to apply autocratic leadership. For example, during an emergency or crisis, there is rarely sufficient time to assemble the group for a question-and-answer session. If the building were burning, it's doubtful that an effective manager would say to his or her employees, "People, we've got a problem. The entire second floor of our factory is engulfed in flames. The ceiling of this room should collapse within five minutes. What are your suggestions regarding the resolution of this problem?" Instead, the manager would probably shout, "Hey! The building's on fire! Everybody get the heck out of here right now!" It is doubtful that even so autocratic an approach would evoke much resistance from employees.

When might you use the autocratic approach?

The autocratic approach might also be used during an emergency occasioned by the breakdown of machinery with which the manager is familiar. Time being extremely critical in such situations, the manager might well use a directive approach to leadership.

And the Cons? The autocratic style of leadership is typically more X-oriented since managers who use this approach frequently feel that the individual employee lacks the capability of providing constructive input. Autocratic leadership has the potential for creating problems

What may happen with receivers of X?

of both morale and production in the long run. It also fails to develop the workers' commitment to the objectives of the organization. Employees on the receiving end of autocratic leadership frequently lack information about their functions and fear using their own initiative in their work. Furthermore, individual growth and development are far more difficult to attain within an autocratic framework.

Participative Style—Involving Employees

In recent years, **employee involvement (EI)** has been the hot buzz word within managerial circles. It actually is a newer term for another approach to leadership termed the **participative,** or **democratic,** style. Leaning toward a Y-oriented approach to leadership, this style assumes that individual members of a group who take part personally in the decision-making process will be more likely, as a result, to have a far greater commitment to the objectives and goals of the organization.

The participative approach doesn't necessarily assume that leaders make no decisions. On the contrary, leaders should understand in advance what the mission and objectives of the organization are so that they can draw upon the knowledge of the members of the work group.

Effective managers who use the participative approach in planning, effecting change, or resolving problems will customarily meet with affected workers and inform them fully of the problems, needs, and objectives of the organization. Then the participative manager will ask for the group's ideas about implementing the change.

"What are *your* ideas on this project?"

Professors John R. Turney and Stanley L. Cohen contend that a certain degree of structure is necessary even when the participative style of management is employed. They cite the example of a manager of an engineering design group who, during an open staff meeting, asked for employee assistance in planning a reorganization. After discussing his plans and objectives for change, he asked the employees to think about the implications of the change for a week or so and then let him know their concerns and recommendations. The manager received no response whatsoever.

Is structure compatible with a participative approach?

The manager still believed in a participative approach, but realized that after such a dismal response he had better change his tactics. He then asked each department to appoint a representative. He conferred with each representative to outline what reorganization issues needed to be worked on and what sort of information would aid him. He also requested that they meet for two hours a week for three weeks and then present their findings in four weeks. The manager discovered that by structuring the participation process he could obtain a large assortment of helpful ideas needed for the reorganization.[6]

Bethlehem Steel is one of many American companies attempting to utilize the EI concept. Its employee involvement program at the

Burns Harbor plant near Lake Michigan is part of a broad effort to push down through the organization the level at which decisions are made. All of the plant's 4600 hourly employees have attended a three-day course on EI and on teamwork. At first, both union officials and some managers were suspicious of the program, the former believing it was an attempt at employee attitude manipulation and the latter believing it was not far removed from a form of communism! One manager stated, "For managers who are used to the control mode, it is a very frightening thing."[7] The "Question of Ethics" points out some of the dangers associated with an EI program when managers distrust their employees and hesitate to give up some control.

A QUESTION OF ETHICS

EI Can Backfire in an Environment of Suspicion and Distrust[b]

One of the latest managerial fashions, employee involvement (EI), has failed in many U.S. companies, reports three researchers from Carnegie Mellon University. According to the trio—Maryellen Kelley, Bennett Harrison, and Lan Xue—"EI not only fails to help efficiency in many companies, but actually appears to hurt it."

Why should this be? After all, the EI technique has worked well in many Japanese companies, so why not among U.S. firms? Bennett Harrison believes that part of the reason may lie in the tendency of American managers to work more in their own self-interest. American workers, much less stupid than sometimes believed by their managers, see the EI programs as bureaucratic devices for tightening—not sharing—management control. Many American managers, it is believed, rather than empowering employees and sharing authority, prefer to hold on to their power. Japanese bosses, on the other hand, seem to have greater *trust* in their underlings. Initiating an EI program in an environment where management trust in employees is lacking is unlikely to generate trust in the reverse direction.

A Question of Ethics: How do you feel about some managers' use of techniques, such as EI, for the purpose of maintaining greater control over their employees?

The Pros of Participative Leadership. The participative approach tends to be extremely effective in numerous situations. Workers like to feel that *their ideas are important* and tend to feel considerably *more committed to changes* in which they have participated. Workers also develop *greater feelings of self-esteem* when they feel that they have been trusted to make competent decisions. Often the *combined knowledge and experience* of the members of a group exceed those of the leader. Furthermore, problems worked on collectively often give birth to *new ideas,* created as a result of the interpersonal exchange.

On the other hand, let's assume that you're an inexperienced manager in an organization contemplating a change in a particular production process. Human beings tend to resist change, even when a new situation is easier or more efficient. There is no labor law, however, that requires you, a manager, to do any more than merely notify workers of their new duties as a result of the change. If you do follow such a direct, nonparticipative approach, what might be the reaction of the workers? In many industrial situations where change is forced upon others, the equilibrium of the group members is so upset that excessive conflict has developed, made manifest by such activities as wildcat strikes, boycotts, slowdowns, and so on. Might there not be more effective ways to develop group commitment to organizational objectives?

And Now the Cons. The participative approach makes certain assumptions that, when false, can result in complications for the organization. For example, this approach assumes a considerable *commonality of interest* between the managers and their employees. However, in any group some individuals may be genuinely uninterested in their jobs, especially those who perceive their position merely as means to other, more satisfying, ends. They thus prefer not to expend any energy on participative decision making. Furthermore, employees in the organization *must be receptive to the participative approach.* Some workers might perceive the managers as ill qualified if they have to consult with the "lowly" workers. Other employees might perceive the participative approach as an attempt to manipulate them.

The participative approach also assumes that workers have the *necessary knowledge and skill* to participate in the decision-making process. If knowledge and skill are lacking, managers may find that they must either be bound by bad decisions or override the decisions of the group, thus detracting from the participative approach.

Some managers *feel uncomfortable* using a participative style, especially those leaders who haven't developed an open climate of trust and confidence in their work groups. Other managers hesitate to use participative leadership for fear that *control* over their followers *will be lost.* However, participation by workers often eliminates feelings of hostility and opposition and, instead, creates a climate of

What assumptions does the particiative approach make?

What problems can the participative approach create?

SOURCE: FRANK & ERNEST reprinted by permission of NEA, Inc.

cooperative attitudes that tends to *enhance* managers' influence over their employees. Often managers wish to exercise a power over their employees that they don't really have. Through participation, managers *do give up* some of their authority, but they *gain* far more control by using positive forces within the group.

Free-Rein Style

Another approach to leadership is called **free rein,** or **laissez-faire.** This approach does *not* mean the *total* absence of leadership. It does mean the *absence of direct leadership.* The free-rein leader, of course, should work through organizational goals. However, with this approach, a task is presented to group members who ordinarily work out their own techniques for accomplishing those goals within the framework of organizational objectives and policy. The leader acts principally as a *liaison* between outside sources and the group and ascertains what necessary resources are available to them.

When is the free-rein approach applicable?

Would a Theory Y type manager always use a free-rein style of leadership? You might think so at first glance, but it's not necessarily so. Managers still need to work with employees to establish objectives that are in harmony with organizational goals. Employees, even when under a Theory Y manager, are seldom free to engage in any type of activity they might want.

In some instances a free-rein approach to leadership degenerates into chaos. In others, the absence of direct leadership is appropriate. For example, the director of a science laboratory or medical clinic doesn't have to be involved in every decision made by the scientists or doctors. Such professionals usually have the knowledge and skill to accomplish their tasks without direct supervision. The director might present a task to a scientist who would then decide how to accomplish the organizational goals.

Free rein is also often found in educational settings. A dean seldom tells professors how to perform their jobs. The dean usually tells them what subjects they are to teach; the methods of carrying out the objectives of the institution are generally decided by the professors themselves.

Empowerment is another often-heard term these days that relates directly to the free-rein approach to leadership. Basically, empowerment is providing employees with *higher degrees of involvement* and *greater authority to make decisions on their own.* Professors David Bowen and Edward Lawler suggest that applying the concept to the workplace does not mean adopting an either/or approach to *empowerment* versus *control.* They point out that there are degrees of empowerment, which increases as additional knowledge, information, power, and rewards are pushed down the organization.[8] In spite of feelings of reticence among some managers about "giving up" some of their power, the trend toward empowering employees seems to be upward among American corporations. A survey of 476 Fortune 1000 companies found that the proportion of firms that had some employees in self-managed work teams had increased from 27 percent to 46 percent during a recent three-year period.[9]

Meant for power!

So Which Is the Best Style of Leadership?

As you may have determined from our discussion, there isn't necessarily one "best" style of leadership. In some instances employees should be encouraged to participate in making some of the decisions that affect the achievement of the organization's goals. In other cases, however, a decisive and direct approach is preferred because of time pressures or the nature of the work group. The "best" style of leadership for a given situation depends on three important factors:

What does the "best" depend on?

1. The situation
2. The type of followers
3. The type of leader

Situational thinking revisited

To be an effective leader, therefore, you should tailor your style to fit these variables. This style of leadership is sometimes referred to as **contingency,** or **situational, leadership.**

A leader's conduct during an emergency, for example, might vary substantially from his or her conduct during normal working conditions. Furthermore, leaders may sometimes use *positive* and at other times *negative* techniques of leadership. Effective leaders may find that in some situations an *autocratic* form of direction is most effective and in other situations that *participative* or even *free-rein* approaches are useful. Some leaders are designated as such by the *formal* organization; others develop their influence over members of their groups naturally and *informally* because of such characteristics as age, seniority, knowledge, education, and popularity.

Should Leaders Get Close to Their Associates?

A situation that some leaders find difficult is that of deciding how friendly or close they should be to their associates. **Psychological distance** is the term used to denote the mental attitudes of supervisors toward their employees from the standpoint of the closeness of the working relationship. The greater the psychological distance, the more remote the managers are from their employees.

For example, believing that familiarity breeds contempt, some managers avoid becoming close to their employees, contending that too much closeness leads to loss of respect and control. Other leaders try extremely hard to be one of the gang with their employees. Still others attempt to strike some sort of balance between the two extremes.

Which approach is best? There isn't complete agreement, but the more modern approach to management suggests that a minimum (but not complete elimination) of psychological distance is the most effective. The important factor is that supervisors should be genuinely interested in their personnel and operate in a manner that achieves intended objectives.

Does distance beget respect?

Managers who aren't afraid to get to know their associates as human beings and who are seen as human beings themselves actually tend to gain respect and control. Managers who are willing to be close to some of their employees must be careful, of course, that *all* their employees are treated fairly and without favoritism. Managers will lose a substantial degree of effectiveness if associates think that all an employee needs to obtain special favors is to be "a friend to the boss." To be close to employees requires a reasonable amount of confidence, not only in yourself but also in your employees.

A parallel can be found in the U.S. Navy, which has both seagoing divisions and air force squadrons. In general, the official policy of the navy has been that officers should not fraternize with or become close to enlisted personnel. On navy ships, for example, special areas have been designated "Officers' Country" in which enlisted personnel are forbidden. Even gangways, or exits from ships, have been segregated.

In the air force divisions of the navy, however, the officers—many of whom are pilots—seem to favor less psychological distance from their personnel. One of the principal reasons given is that the pilots' success in flying their airplanes is greatly dependent upon the mechanical services provided by their staff. Many officers state that they are able to fly with a greater feeling of security when they treat enlisted personnel as human beings. Maybe managers in civilian organizations should behave more as though their own lives depended on the activities of their employees!

Supervisors should, however, guard against appearing to be *excessively familiar,* which can sometimes lead to problems when discipline is to be administered or less pleasant tasks assigned. Extreme remoteness, on the other hand, can create artificial barriers between managers and workers and result in less effective interaction and communication. Once again, leaders should attempt to use *situational thinking* and develop the ability to know which approach enables them to accomplish specific organizational goals while also satisfying employees' social needs.

Participation—It's a Matter of Degree

Another way of looking at leadership styles relates to the *degree* to which a manager is willing to share decision-making and problem-solving activities with associates.

A model developed by professors Vroom and Yetton shows various styles of leadership ranging from *no participation* from employees to *the leader carrying out alternatives that were generated by the group.*[10] Table 6.2 shows the various leadership possibilities on a continuum, with styles ranging from style I to style V. As in our previous discussion of leadership styles, the Vroom-Yetton model also calls for a *situational,* or *contingency,* approach. The best style of leadership, according to Vroom and Yetton, depends on the answers that a manager might find to a number of questions, such as:

1. How critical to the success of the activity is acceptance of the manager's decision by employees?

2. Is conflict among employees likely to result from the manager's decision?

3. Does the manager have enough data and information to make an effective decision on his or her own?

4. Do associates have enough data and information to make a useful contribution to the decision-making process?

5. Do associates relate to the goals associated with the decisions that must be made?

6. Is the definition of the problem clear to all involved with the decision-making process?

Some Final Conclusions on the "Best" Style of Leadership

From our discussion of leadership, we should realize that a major difference in styles of leadership is in the *amount* of decision making done by the leader. The autocratic leader need not be a dictator or a Marine drill sergeant but can be a Theory Y type of leader who has followers who require more direction. A participative leader *shares* decision making with the workers but also reserves *final* decision-making authority. A free-rein leader allows workers to make decisions and serves mainly as a *resource person* for empowered associates.

TABLE 6.2   The Vroom-Yetton Continuum of Manager-Employee Involvement

I	II	III	IV	V
The manager solves the problem and makes the decision alone.	The manager gathers information from employees but actually makes the decision alone.	The manager shares the problem with each employee but actually makes the decision alone.	The manager shares the problem with employees as a group but actually makes the decision alone.	The manager shares the problem with employees as a group; the group generates and evaluates alternatives; and the manager implements the decision developed by the group.

How permanent is
education?

Remember, however, that formal education can become outdated rapidly. Some scholars contend that the knowledge acquired from a formal education will be obsolescent within seven years. Therefore, people never really become "educated"; they are always "pursuing an education." Regardless of the validity of these views, change in our society *is* occurring so rapidly that many people are overwhelmed by it. For example, individuals who have not purchased an automobile for several years may feel intimidated by some of the newer models. Some dealers require the purchaser to endure a two-hour lecture on how to operate and interpret the numerous computerized controls. One luxury model even has five control lights devoted solely to the braking system. Some employees who have had little exposure to computers or information processors may also feel intimidated when their organizations acquire such equipment, even though its software is advertised as "user friendly." In a later chapter we'll explore in some depth the problems that rapid change can bring to members of organizations.

LEADERSHIP AS A SKILL

Some people seem to have a knack for leading others, but fortunately most good leaders are not born but made. Effective leadership, as with good listening habits or a good tennis serve, is an activity that is usually developed.

Necessary Skills and Knowledge

A competent manager requires skill and knowledge, neither of which is inborn; they are acquired and developed. For example, assume you currently work in the sales department of an office equipment manufacturing company and aspire to be a manager. What skills should you acquire?

What skills does a manager need?

In general, anyone with managerial aspirations should attempt to develop the following skills: *Technical skills, human resource management skills,* and *conceptual,* or *administrative skills.* Now let's see how these three skills will help you become a manager.

A BOX OF INTEREST

Participative Leadership on the Rise

Not many years ago, American managers in the auto manufacturing industry were not too keen on the use of *participative leadership.* All this is changing. Supported by the United Auto Workers union officials, managers have modified their attitudes at Ford, General Motors, and Chrysler, where *EI (employee involvement)* programs have proliferated in recent years.

Becoming increasingly common at the so-called Big Three auto makers is the use of self-managing work teams. The team concept is spreading rapidly in other industries as well, such as aerospace, electrical equipment, electronics, food processing, steel, paper, and even financial services.

Adopting work teams is a radical departure from the past, since it typically means wiping out tiers of managers and tearing down bureaucratic barriers between departments. Dr. Carl Hahn, head of Volkswagen, points out that many employers have yet to dismantle the old demarcations that still characterize the work force. Hahn warns that "the internal world of the company could no longer be one of 'upstairs and downstairs.' Instead," he recommends, "employers must create a climate in their companies that permits all staff to contribute to the success of the business." Hahn suggests that "all workers be brought closer to the creation and management of resources and be invested with a sense of ownership through increased participation and responsibility."

Technical Skills

As a potential manager, you should have **technical skills**—the knowledge and ability necessary to perform the particular task or type of activity required by your job. Let's assume that you are currently a microcomputer salesperson. You must certainly have the technical knowledge to decide which types of hard- and software are best suited to the specific needs of your customers. After you become a sales manager, you'll still need the technical knowledge necessary for training your sales force and resolving technical problems. However, as you rise in the organization you are likely to have less need for technical skills than when you were an operating employee. You will tend to lean more on your subordinates for technical assistance. The amount of technical knowledge necessary for a managerial position depends principally on the nature of the specific managerial position.

Human Resource Management Skills

If you become a manager with the office equipment firm, technical skills are likely to be useful but will be less important than *human resource management skills*—the behavioral skills of being able to *work effectively with and through people*. We've already discussed a number of attributes that are essential for competent managers, such as perceptual, communication, listening, empathetic and motivational skills. The ability to plan, interview, coordinate, and control are also necessary managerial skills.

For example, proficient managers are more likely to perceive subtle changes in the behavior of their employees, changes that could cause serious problems if not dealt with immediately. Moreover, skilled managers are able to communicate orally, in writing, and by electronic means, such as by computer modems or fax machines, with fewer misunderstandings. The most significant reasons why many managers fail to achieve their organizational objectives is not necessarily because they lack technical skills but because they lack human resource management (people-oriented) skills.

Conceptual Skills

Conceptual, or **administrative, skills** become increasingly important as individuals ascend the organizational ladder. These skills entail the ability to *conceptualize,* that is, to think abstractly and see relationships between seemingly disparate entities. Many managers need the ability to analyze current problems and anticipate and prevent future ones. They must often plan for longer time periods. They must also be able to plan and coordinate the overall operations of an organization and its personnel. Senior executives of multinational corporations may have to judge the effects of currency fluctuations on future profits and decide whether to shift funds from one country to another as a hedge against value loss. All of these activities require the ability to think abstractly.

In summary, therefore, human resource management skills are important, regardless of your managerial level in an organization. Figure 6.4 shows how, as you rise, the importance of technical skills diminishes and that of conceptual skills increases. A challenge experienced by many individuals who come up through the ranks is making the transition from an operating employee with highly developed technical skills to a manager who suddenly needs a high degree of human relations and conceptual skills. Learning as much as you can about management processes and techniques before you become a manager can ease any transitional difficulty you might experience.

DEVELOPMENT OF LEADERSHIP SKILLS

How can you develop leadership skills?

Skill in leadership doesn't usually develop by accident; it can be acquired and perfected by trial and error, formal education, on-the-job experience, and supplemental reading. Whatever techniques are used to develop leadership skills, potential managers develop best in a growth atmosphere that allows them the freedom to make mistakes.

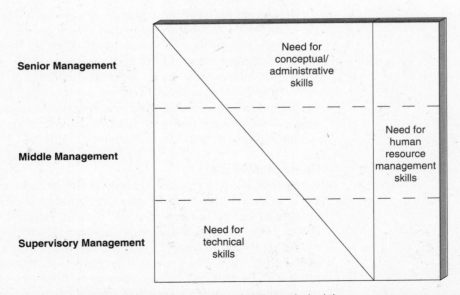

Figure 6.4 Managers need three types of skills: technical, human resource management, and conceptual. Technical skills become less important and conceptual one more important as managers rise in the organization.

Trial and Error

As with any skills, leadership skills can be developed with ordinary *practice* and through *trial and error on the job.* Although many highly skilled managers achieved their positions and developed their abilities in such a random fashion, more systematic approaches are currently used. Let's turn to some other ways in which managerial skills can be developed far more rapidly and with much less happenstance.

Should skill be developed by chance?

Formal Education

Formalized education can make your work and personal experiences more meaningful and your trials less filled with error. Courses in human relations, organizational behavior, management, personnel management, business, and the liberal arts frequently enable individuals to advance more rapidly in organizations.

On-the-Job Experience

Reading about leadership and observing managers can certainly give you insights on how to be an effective leader. However, these activities cannot substitute for actual on-the-job experience. Well-organized firms usually have formalized *management development programs* designed to assist and accelerate the development of the skills of employees with apparent managerial potential.

Some organizations have discovered the hard way that they had failed to groom anyone for unexpectedly vacated managerial positions. Other, more farsighted firms have initiated formal company programs to develop managers.

What are some on-the-job experiences that help to develop managerial skills?

Assessment centers are used by some organizations to help decide which employees are management material. They also help determine the training and development needs of specific employees. An assessment center isn't a place; it's a method. A group of employees is given a variety of simulated job experiences, tasks related to their future success as managers. Trained observers watch and evaluate how the participants handle themselves, then write a report summarizing the participants' strengths, weaknesses, and probable success as managers.

Coaching is another widely used on-the-job technique that provides potential managers with useful experiences and helps them develop necessary skills. Typically, an experienced and skilled person—usually a manager—is assigned to a lesser-skilled employee. As with athletic teams, the coach is responsible for developing the employee. Coaching is considered a fairly effective management development tool because of the close and regular contact an employee has with a manager who provides continual feedback on the employee's progress. Coaching should really be an ongoing aspect of any manager-employee relationship and needn't be a formalized program.

Understudy assignments are related to coaching, but differ in this manner: The lesser-skilled employee is assigned to an experienced manager and is groomed to take over the manager's job. Some organizations have formal policies indicating that managers cannot be eligible for promotions unless they have developed someone to take over their positions. For example, Alfred P. Sloan, Jr., while head of General Motors, believed that a primary duty of any executive is to develop a successor, preferably one more capable than him- or herself. Not all organizations seem to agree, however. Many companies have acquired the reputation of enlisting the service of executive "headhunters" who raid other corporations to fill senior-level executive positions. However, such organizations are the exception, not the rule, and the majority of managerial and supervisory positions are not senior level in nature. Consequently, the policy of internal management development programs and promotion from within continue to retain considerable merit.

We touched on only a few of the on-the-job experiences that assist in developing managers. Other types include *job rotation* and *horizontal promotions* intended to provide more diversified experiences for potential managers. The techniques available are limited only by the imagination and creativity of those who are responsible for management development programs.

Supplemental Reading

Not all organizations have formalized management development programs, especially the smaller ones. Regardless of what provisions have been made by an organization for human resource development, the major burden of the development of managerial skills rests on *individual organizational members themselves.*

One way for potential and current managers to maintain their acquired educations is to continue reading regularly after their formal training and classroom education have ceased. Some organizations today even provide their managers with "reading breaks," said to be far more healthful than coffee and cigarette breaks! Publications such as *Business Week, The Wall Street Journal,* and *Fortune* frequently present case histories of other firms, knowledge of which can often assist managers in their own organizational activities. Each year numerous books on businesses and economics are published. Well-rounded managers, however, will attempt to supplement their acquired educations by reading books other than those related only to business or government. A novel way to "read" books these days is to buy or rent "books on tape," which enable you to listen to a variety of materials while commuting during rush-hour traffic.

Read any good books lately?

THE NEED FOR A SUPPORTIVE ORGANIZATIONAL CULTURE

As is the case with people, organizations are unique. Likewise, each has a set of values. As mentioned in Chapter 1, the values that influence the environment in which people work is called the **organizational culture.** An organization's culture is what influences how leaders and other employees function; some organizations provide employees with a supportive environment in which they have plenty of opportunities to participate and make decisions, and others are restrictive and tend to suppress creative talent.[11]

Employees are better able to develop leadership skills when their own managers provide a positive organizational culture, or atmosphere, for growth. To develop into leaders, individuals must first learn to make decisions. In an organizational culture that fosters growth, associates are given decision-making responsibility and a reasonable amount of freedom to carry out that responsibility. Not all employees have the opportunity to make decisions, however. The value systems of some organizations don't allow employees the **freedom to fail.** Certainly, employees shouldn't make an excessive number of mistakes, but some employees seldom feel free to make decisions because of the probable consequences of their mistakes.

Managers, in a sense, are teachers. One of their chief responsibilities is to educate, train, and assist others. If managers want to create a culture that encourages initiative and decision making in their employees, they should be cautious when handling the mistakes made by conscientious employees.

SUMMARY

The term *leadership* has no catchall meaning but can be described as the ability to influence the activities of others, through the process of communication, toward the attainment of a goal. Accountability accompanied by authority (empowerment) enables leaders and other organizational personnel to make decisions and carry out their responsibilities more effectively.

Management, which includes the activity of leadership, is a broader concept and may include *nonbehavioral* activities. Leadership *directly affects the behavior* of individuals in organizations.

Leaders are not true leaders unless they have an *emotional appeal;* that is, they must have both *followers* and the *ability to influence people* over extended periods of time. Some individuals seem to possess a special charm, power, and ability to influence and win the devotion and respect of others, known as *charisma.*

Leaders may be classified according to their attitudes toward associates as *positive (Theory Y)* or *negative (Theory X),* and by their style of leadership, either *autocratic, participative,* or *free rein.* Many leaders are more likely to be selective in their perception of associates (*Selective X-Y*). Leaders who feel "they've been burned" by associates may develop an attitude termed *Derived X.* The best type of leadership in a given situation depends upon three major factors: the *leader,* the *followers,* and the *situation.*

A manager's expectations related to employees can often cause the expected behavior or event to occur, termed the *Pygmalion Effect*. In addition, the modern approach to management suggests that a minimum of *psychological distance* is most effective when dealing with associates.

Professors Vroom and Yetton developed a model that shows various styles of leadership, ranging from *no participation* drawn from associates to *the leader carrying out alternatives that were generated by the group members*.

To be effective, leaders need three major skills: *technical, human resource management,* and *conceptual skills.* Leadership skills can be developed through *trial and error, formal education, on-the-job experiences,* and *supplemental reading.*

Managers, in a sense, are educators and trainers; they therefore have the responsibility to groom others for leadership positions. Individuals tend to develop leadership traits more rapidly in a supportive *organizational culture* that gives them a reasonable amount of freedom to carry out their assigned responsibilities.

TERMS AND CONCEPTS TO REMEMBER

leadership

management

organization chart

authority

responsibility

responsibilities

accountability

charismatic authority

Theory X

Theory Y

Selective X-Y

Derived X (I've-been-burned theory)

Pygmalion Effect

Upward Pygmalion Effect

autocratic (authoritarian) leadership

employee involvement (EI)

participative (democratic) leadership

free-rein (laissez-faire) leadership

empowerment

contingency (situational) leadership

psychological distance

technical skills

human resource management skills

conceptual (administrative) skills

organizational culture

freedom to fail

QUESTIONS

1. What is the major distinction between *leadership* and *management?*

2. How do the terms *accountability, authority,* and *responsibility* differ in meaning?

3. What helps to determine whether a person is an effective leader?

4. How would you describe the "special charm" that people who develop charismatic authority seem to have? How might charisma be misused? Do you feel that virtually anyone could develop charisma? Why or why not?

5. What is the relationship of the Selective X-Y Theory concerning managerial attitudes to Theories X and Y?

6. What tends to cause a person to adopt a Derived X approach? How might this condition be avoided?

7. What are some of the probable consequences of workers operating in an aura of fear?

8. How does the Pygmalion Effect work?

9. Describe the circumstances in which the three major styles of leadership might be used effectively. Describe some situations to which they might not be applicable.

10. What determines the "best" style of leadership?

11. Is an autocratic style of leadership always counterproductive? Explain.

12. Describe the five styles of leadership related to employee participation developed by professors Vroom and Yetton. Give examples of when you might use each of the approaches.

13. What are some of the major advantages that result when a manager learns how to delegate effectively? With so many advantages associated with delegation, why do so many managers fail to do it?

14. Why do technical skills become less important as a person rises in the organizational hierarchy?

15. What are human resource management skills? Why are they important for managers at all levels of the organization?

16. Describe some of the ways in which managerial skills can be developed and improved.

APPLICATIONS

6.1 What's Charlie's Complaint?

John Zamora is a dock supervisor for a large freight line. Charlie Williams works for John as a dockworker. One morning, in an attempt to discourage what John felt was too much goofing off by Charlie at work, John made a comment about Charlie's being lazy to one of Charlie's co-workers, Jimmy Paige. In fact, John really criticized Charlie for being a regular goof-off. Jimmy and Charlie are good friends, and Jimmy told Charlie what John had said.

Later that afternoon, around 2:30 P.M., John was watching Charlie and the rest of the crew on the dock. Charlie appeared to be taking it easy again. However, at one point he seemed to be having some difficulty with a particularly bulky piece of freight. John happened to be walking by and gave Charlie a hand putting the piece on a cart since no one else was close by. John then returned to the office for most of the remainder of the afternoon.

The next morning Charlie filed a formal complaint with a union representative because his supervisor, John, had performed work that a management-labor union contract stipulated was reserved for union members.

Questions

1. What appears to be the problem in this case?

2. Why do you think Charlie filed a formal complaint? Do you feel he has reasonable grounds for a complaint?

3. What could have been done to prevent this problem from happening?

6.2 The Case of Incinerator 3

Charlie Cashew, the site manager for Whiting-Forrest Waste Management Systems of Huntsville, Alabama, had reason to suspect that one of the firm's incinerators was defective and should be inspected immediately. However, the company was busy with Saturday overtime to handle a freight-train load of medical waste from hospitals in New York and New Jersey. Neither a service technician nor an insurance company inspector was available to take a look at incinerator number three until Monday.

Cashew directed his immediate subordinate, Freddy Filbert, to ask two employees in his department to go into the servicing compartment of the incinerator to check it. Filbert asked Pete Kahn and Nancy McNutt, who operated machinery used to compact recyclable materials, to enter the compartment, a space barely large enough for a medium-size person to crawl through.

Kahn and McNutt strenuously objected to being told to perform the task, arguing that it was beyond the scope of their duties and was extremely dangerous. Moreover, because their training did not include hazardous materials, they were not familiar with the health and safety procedures the company used for potentially harmful refuse such as medical waste, which was burned in incinerator three. They flatly refused Filbert's request and asked to see Cashew, the site manager.

Filbert first telephoned Cashew and then went with Kahn and McNutt to Cashew's office, where the following discussion ensued:

Cashew: What in bloody heck's with you two prima donnas? I understand you didn't follow Filbert's order to inspect the incinerator.

Kahn: That's not our job; we're compactor operators, not monkeys. Besides, it's too darned risky. Those incinerators get white hot when they're fired up, and who knows what kinds of stuff are in those containers the hospitals ship down here for us to burn.

Cashew: There's no danger. And nobody's going to turn on the incinerator while you're in there.

Kahn: How do we know that? Here's another thing: There's not much air in that compartment. What if we fainted?

Cashew: Fainted? That won't happen, but if it does somebody will get you out.

Kahn: That's what you say. But I'm telling you right now, we're not going into that stuffy tin can!

Cashew: Listen, Kahn. You and McNutt are going into that incinerator compartment whether you like it or not. And to prove that this company isn't run by chickens, I'm going to go in first. If you don't follow me, you two are through with this company. And for all that back talk you gave me, even if you do come with me you both have earned unpaid holidays for three days starting tomorrow!

Questions
1. Define the problem in this case.
2. Evaluate the solution pursued by Cashew.
3. How would you have handled the problem if you had been Cashew?
4. Should a manager prove to subordinates that he or she is not "chicken"?

6.3 Banking on a Solution at the Data Center

Fourth Interstate Bancorp has a computer center in Rapid City, South Dakota, that is the size of a typical city block. The facility handles a large proportion of the data-processing operations for Fourth Interstate's 154-branch network in five Western states.

The employees have been assigned specialized duties in the particular sections of the data center in which they work. Using the latest computer equipment, the different sections handle such tasks as processing credit card accounts, servicing mortgage loans, inputting and updating customer information files (CIFs), and generating reports.

A number of problems have developed in recent months. For example, almost every day some sections are extremely overloaded with work, while employees in other sections are sitting around with little to do. When the work load is excessive in some sections, employees tend to become harried and tense, a situation that has led to a fairly high number of complaints within the bank. On numerous occasions, CIFs were updated with incorrect information, and reports have been coming out late or incomplete.

Questions

1. If you were the data-center manager for Fourth Interstate Bancorp, what would you do to resolve the problems?

2. What style of leadership would you apply? Why?

NOTES

1. Stephen E. Catt and Donald S. Miller, *Supervisory Management and Communication* (Homewood, IL: Richard D. Irwin, 1985), p. 65.

2. Kenneth Labich, "The Seven Keys to Business Leadership," *Fortune/International Edition,* October 24, 1988, pp. 54–62.

3. Walter Kiechel III, "The Case Against Leaders," *Fortune/International Edition,* November 21, 1988, pp. 116–117.

4. This concept was originally developed by Douglas McGregor, late professor of industrial management at Massachusetts Institute of Technology. See *The Human Side of Enterprise* (New York: McGraw-Hill, 1960).

5. See Note 2 above.

6. John R. Turney and Stanley L. Cohen, "Participative Management: What Is the Right Level? Need for Structure," *Management Review,* October 1980, p. 69.

7. John Gapper, "Blasts of Hot Air Help to Clear the Atmosphere," *Financial Times,* January 15, 1992, p. 9.

8. Christopher Lorenz, "Nuts and Bolts of Giving Power to the People," *Financial Times,* September 21, 1992, p. 14.

9. Sharon Cohen, "Workers Happy to be In Charge," *San Francisco Examiner,* December 2, 1990, p. D-1, D-4.

10. Victor Vroom and Philip Yetton, *Leadership and Decision Making* (Pittsburgh: University of Pittsburgh Press, 1973).

11. Brian Dumaine, "Creating a New Company Culture," *Fortune/ International Edition,* January 15, 1990, p. 55; and Christopher Lorenz, "A Cultural Revolution that Sets Out to Supplant Hierarchy with Informality," *Financial Times,* March 30, 1990, p. 12.

12. Adapted from Stan Kossen, "Assumptions about People," *Supervision,* (St. Paul: West Publishing Company, 1991), pp. 320–322.

BOX NOTES

a. Lisa Wood, "Search for 'Worldly-wise' Company Executives," *Financial Times,* April 9, 1991, p. 15; and Gilbert Fuchsberg and Tim Carrington, Global Managing—As Costs of Expatriates Rise, Companies Select Them More Carefully," *The Wall Street Journal Europe,* January 10–11, 1992, pp. 1, 20.

b. Michael Dixon, "Jobs: Trendy Schemes for Involving Employees Seem to have Counter-productive Effects," *Financial Times,* February 22, 1991, p. I.

c. Adapted from John Hoerrom, "The Payoff from Teamwork," *Business Week/International Edition,* July 10, 1989, pp. 34–42; and Michael Cassell, "VW Chairman Calls for Change in Work Attitudes," *Financial Times,* April 29, 1992, p. 12.

EXPERIENTIAL EXERCISES

What Do You Assume?

This exercise is intended to help you to become more aware of the assumptions you make about others and their attitudes. There are ten sets of statements below. Read each set. Then assign a weight from 0 to 10 to each statement in the set based on the relative strength of your belief in each statement. *The points assigned for each pair must total 10.* For example in set No. 1, the strength of your belief in the *a* statement may indicate a weight of 7, with a weight of 3 for the *b* statement, for a total of 10.

Be as open and honest as you can. Try not to respond as you *think* things are or should be. This exercise is not a test. There are no right and wrong answers. The exercise is designed to aid you in learning more about yourself and the assumptions that you make about others.

1a. It's only human nature for people to do as little work as they can get away with.   X _____

 b. When people avoid work, it's usually because their work has lost its meaning.   Y _____

2a. If employees have access to more information than they need to do their immediate tasks, they will usually misuse it.   X _____

 b. If employees have access to any information they want, they tend to have better attitudes and behave more responsibly.   Y _____

3a. One problem in asking for employees' ideas is that their perspective is too limited for their suggestions to be of much practical value.   X _____

 b. Asking employees for their ideas broadens their perspective and results in the development of useful suggestions.   Y _____

4a. If people don't use much imagination and ingenuity on the job, it's probably because relatively few people have much of either.   X _____

b. Most people are imaginative and creative but may not show it because of limitations imposed by supervision and the job.   Y _____

5a. People tend to lower their standards if they are not punished for their misbehavior and mistakes.   X _____

b. People tend to raise their standards if they are accountable for their own behavior and for correcting their own mistakes.   Y _____

6a. It's better to withhold unfavorable news because most employees want to hear only the good news.   X _____

b. It's better to give people both good and bad news because most employees want the whole story, no matter how painful.   Y _____

7a. Because a supervisor is entitled to more respect than those below him or her in the organization, it weakens his or her prestige to admit that a subordinate was right and he or she was wrong.   X _____

b. Because people at all levels are entitled to equal respect, a supervisor's prestige is increased when he or she supports this principle by admitting that a subordinate was right and he or she was wrong.   Y _____

8a. If you give people enough money to feel secure, concern for such intangibles as responsibility and recognition will be less.   X _____

b. If given interesting and challenging work, people are less likely to complain about such things as pay and supplemental benefits.   Y _____

9a. If people are allowed to set their own goals and standards of performance, they tend to set them lower than their manager would.   X _____

b. If people are allowed to set their own goals and standards of performance, they tend to set them higher than their manager would.   Y _____

10a. The more knowledge and freedom a person has regarding the job, the more controls are needed to keep him or her in line.   X _____

b. The more knowledge and freedom a person has regarding the job, the fewer controls are needed to ensure satisfactory performance.   Y _____

Instructions: Subtract the smaller number in each set from the larger number. If the net amount relates to the X statement, indicate the value by drawing a small dot above the corresponding number on the X side of the continuum below. If the net amount relates to the Y statement, indicate the value by drawing a dot on the Y side of the continuum. For example, if in set No. 1 your X response was 7 and your Y response was 3, your net amount would be 4 related to the X statement. You would then place a dot over the corresponding number (in this case, 4) on the X side of the continuum.

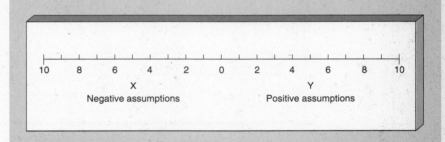

The validity of this exercise depends largely on your ability to respond accurately to the statements above. If most of your dots are clustered on the right (Y) side fo the continuum, the chances are fairly good that your assumptions about other people in general lean toward the positive. If, on the other hand, most of your dots are clustered on the left (X) side of the continuum, you could probably benefit from determining ways in which you could improve your attitudes toward and assumptions about others.[12]

What Can You Delegate?

In the spaces provided below, first list your job responsibilities, then decide which of those duties you might delegate and to whom. Finally, analyze if any additional training is necessary for the delegatee to be able to perform the tasks successfully.

My Duties	Delegate? (Yes/No)	To Whom?	Type of Additional Training Necessary?
1. _____	_____	_____	_____
2. _____	_____	_____	_____
3. _____	_____	_____	_____
4. _____	_____	_____	_____
5. _____	_____	_____	_____
6. _____	_____	_____	_____
7. _____	_____	_____	_____
8. _____	_____	_____	_____
9. _____	_____	_____	_____

CHAPTER 7

Quality and the Workplace

*Total Quality
to the
Rescue*

**When you finish this chapter,
you should be able to:**

1

Trace the background leading to the recent organizational emphasis on the management of quality.

2

Explain the general purpose of the total quality management (TQM) process.

3

Describe eleven significant elements in the total quality management (TQM) process.

4

Explain the nature of the Baldrige Award for quality.

5

List and describe significant principles of organization.

6

Recall the major benefits associated with the delegation process.

7

Explain what determines the optimum number of persons who should report to one manager.

—In the search for quality there's no
such thing as good enough;
there's never a finish line.

K. Theodor Krantz, President, Velcro USA

—The Japanese were very creative in the application
of the things they learned here [the U.S.]. We brought back
what we saw in Japan and tried to execute them mechanically.

Larry Spiegel, director of lean manufacturing,
General Motors Cadillac Division

"Made in Japan." Believe it or not, this phrase was synonymous with *poor quality* for the first two decades after World War II. What happened to change that image? Scholars tell us that the Japanese didn't *just study* management techniques first developed in American universities—they *applied them!* And what admiration and adulation Americans bestowed upon the Japanese during most of the 1970s and part of the 1980s for the effectiveness and efficiency, as well as the quality and uniqueness, of their products. Articles in the popular and management press showered awesome quantities of praise upon the Japanese and their deft approaches to management and production.

But watch out! Hardly anything remains constant in the real world of global competition. As Japanese firms made greater and greater inroads into the American marketplace, flooding shopping malls and city centers with camcorders, TVs, VCRs, and watches, some Americans got nervous. As the Japanese automobile manufacturers snatched larger and larger segments of the automobile market out of the hands of American manufacturers, some U.S. politicians and industrialists became angry. And as some Japanese leaders seemed to develop an economic superiority complex, attitudes of the average American toward the Japanese changed rapidly.

Do you recall, for example, the uproar that developed in 1992 after some prominent Japanese leaders ridiculed the quality of American products and the skill level of American workers? Americans, in general, were quite offended. They vented their anger by verbally bashing Japanese society. Some individuals became so incensed that they even bashed Japanese-made cars—not only verbally, but *literally*—with sledge hammers!

In spite of such defensive behavior, however, a poll conducted for The Associated Press by ICR Survey Research Group indicated that a large proportion of Americans *also* harbored serious doubts about the quality of American-made products, especially cars.[1] And a *New York Times* editorial by A. M. Rosenthal suggested that the Japanese might even be partially right about U.S. illiteracy, because only 20 percent of Americans are able to use bus timetables, and, therefore, many U.S. workers would be likely to experience difficulty in following work manuals. Only 22.5 percent of Americans reportedly can figure out a restaurant tip. According to the report, 44 percent can't even locate information in an almanac.[2]

So what should be done? Bash more Japanese-made cars? Stop using vcrs? Fortunately, many American managers and employees have gone beyond the defensive stage, recognizing that the very survival of their firms in a highly competitive global marketplace depends on their ability to provide quality products and services at reasonable prices. Therefore, an increasing number of organizational members have become extremely concerned—practically obsessed— with the concept of *quality*.

This chapter focuses on such concerns. It explores the highly significant topic of quality and discusses a currently popular approach to achieving and maintaining a quality-minded attitude among all employees—*total quality management (TQM)*. Also included are some organizational principles that can aid in establishing and maintaining quality organizations.

The following chapter, Chapter 8, continues along a related line with a discussion of quality as it applies to the work environment itself (*quality of work life*), another meaningful concern of professional managers in recent years.

Why Utilize Total Quality Management (TQM)?

One of the major reasons that business firms exist, as we know, is to make a profit. Many business managers see a positive relationship between increased quality and increased profits. As a result, many organizations in North America and Europe have jumped on the TQM bandwagon in recent years and have begun utilizing the TQM process. This relationship has been substantiated by a British Research organization, the Economist Intelligence Unit (EIU). EIU examined more than 3000 businesses in North America and Europe and found that every two percent improvement in a company's quality rating tended to result in a one percent *increase in its return on investment.*[3] Figure 7.1 illustrates the relationship between quality rating and profit.

As Table 7.1 suggests, there are other important reasons for employing the total quality management process. Competition has become intense in recent years from companies located in China, Japan and in the Pacific Rim. Many firms employ TQM in the hope that the process will *assist them in being more competitive*. And, as we'll see shortly, the activities involved in the TQM process, when

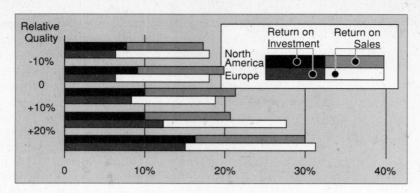

Figure 7.1 How quality is linked to rates of return.

effectively employed, should assist companies in enhancing their effectiveness in utilizing resources, in improving customer satisfaction, and in enriching the quality of employee work life.

THE CONCERN FOR TOTAL QUALITY MANAGEMENT

*Quality here!
Quality there!
Quality everywhere!*

"Total quality management," "total quality commitment," "quality circles," "continuous quality teams," "quality control," "quality councils," "quality of work life." These are only a few of the fad-approaching, quality-oriented expressions that have been leaping out enthusiastically from management articles in recent years. Concerns for quality are nothing new. Inspectors of products, sometimes referred to as "efficiency experts," "quality control managers," or "quality assurance specialists," have long been observed on the shop floor. *Quality circles* have also been popular with many organizations for over two decades. However, the need to compete with companies on a global basis has shattered the complacency of many American managers, who have jumped gingerly onto a crowded bandwagon called *total quality management*. The term "total quality management" has become one of the hottest managerial "buzzwords" of the 1990s.

What Is Total Quality Management (TQM)?

The long recession of the early 1990s caused many American managers to run somewhat scared. The process of **total quality management (TQM)** became a major part of the reorganization and restructuring programs of a substantial number of organizations. What is TQM? It is important to recognize that it is *not* a program with a beginning and an end. Instead, it is an *ongoing process,* one that

TABLE 7.1   **Reasons Why Firms Utilize the Total Quality Management (TQM) Process**

- To increase their return on investment
- To survive and compete against intense competition from China, Japan and other Pacific Rim countries
- To enhance their effectiveness in utilizing resources
- To improve customer satisfaction
- To enrich employee morale and quality of work life

requires everyone in an organization to be motivated toward the goal of *continuous improvement* and to be oriented toward meeting the *needs of customers*. In simple terms, TQM involves focusing all of a company's energies on improving the quality of its activities. Figure 7.2 summarizes the essential elements of the TQM process. Each element is discussed in the following sections.

No energy— no quality!

Provide a Supportive Organizational Culture

What would you guess is the central ingredient in the TQM process? If you guessed a *supportive organizational culture* (or peeked at Figure 7.2!) you're on the right track. The importance of a supportive organizational culture was discussed in an earlier chapter. As you recall, organizational culture consists of the values that influence the environment in which people work. Employees bring their own values to the workplace, and these values significantly affect their behavior on the job and their attitudes toward quality.

"I just don't trust those 'cultured' organizations!"

Imagine what would happen in an organizational environment where employees have a high degree of suspicion and distrust of management. Can you visualize the difficulty that would exist in such an environment if senior management attempted to develop employee commitment to the total quality management process? However, employee values can and do change, and therefore, so can an organizational culture. As we shall see in this and subsequent chapters, there are numerous methods to assist employees in developing more positive attitudes toward the work environment and in becoming more conscious of the need for maintaining high quality standards.

Provide Management Commitment and Leadership

"TQM starts in the boardroom," asserts Paul Spenley, head of Pera International's quality management division, an organization that assists other organizations in implementing TQM methodology. When consulting with outside organizations, Spenley emphasizes his belief that "TQM must enjoy full and informed support from the highest level."[4] Most students of organizational behavior would agree,

No support at the top, nada at the bottom!

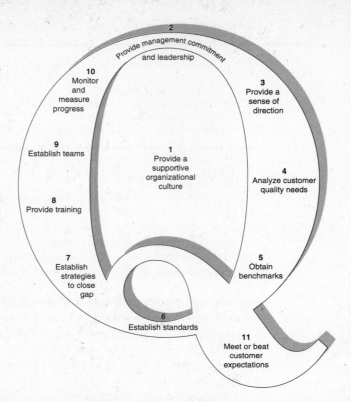

Figure 7.2 Significant elements in the total quality management process.

because it is at the higher levels of management where a commitment of the "top team" is developed and where the TQM process begins to be communicated throughout the entire organization. Senior management should also assume responsibility for providing an organizational *sense of direction* and for developing a *mission statement,* both of which are discussed in the following paragraphs.

Provide a Sense of Direction

W. Edwards Deming is considered one of the foremost experts in the area of industrial quality control, having been highly influential in advising Japanese managers attempting to rebuild their shattered economy after World War II. Deming insists that many firms fail to achieve excellence in quality and productivity because they *lack constancy of purpose or sense of direction.*[5] Strange as it may seem, Deming contends that some organizations fail because their employees (including some managers) are not clear as to why the organization is in business.

One way that many organizations attempt to provide a better sense of direction for employees is to establish and communicate a

If you don't know where you're going, you may end up somewhere else!

SOURCE: DILBERT reprinted by permission of UFS, Inc.

formal **mission statement,** sometimes referred to as a *vision.* A mission is a somewhat *general statement* that relates closely to the culture and philosophical objectives of an organization, that is, its purpose for existing.

Let's take a look at a real-world example of a mission statement to help clarify the concept. Safeway, a global food chain, provides us with a fairly typical mission statement. Safeway's stated mission is:

> To grow and prosper by being the best food retailer in terms of customer appeal, operating philosophy, and financial results.

Safeway breaks down its mission further by defining the key words in the statement:

Customer Appeal—We want to be known for providing superior quality, selection, and service at competitive prices in attractive facilities.

Operating Philosophy—We want our operations to be as efficient and cost-effective as any of our competitors' while maintaining a true concern for and sense of partnership with all our employees.

Financial Results—We expect each of our operations to produce targeted returns on current investment while generating opportunities for future growth and investment.[6]

Analyze the Customers' Quality Needs

Who are the real determiners of quality standards over time? That's right: the customers—those who purchase an organization's product or service. Therefore, another essential ingredient of the total quality management process is the need for organizational members to understand the quality requirements of customers and to be motivated toward satisfying those requirements.

If you don't,
someone else will!

What is likely to occur when there is a *gap* between the quality level your organization has achieved and the level your customers actually need? The answer is fairly apparent: If your organization doesn't meet the customer's standards, it will usually lose out to another organization.

IBM, although experiencing difficulty in recent years in the competitive computer marketplace, has long had the reputation for being concerned with the concept of quality as it applies to customers. The firm applies its philosophy by measuring quality both against its own established standards and against customer opinion. IBM's customers are canvassed twice a year to determine their level of satisfaction with the company's products and service. The results are quantified, and if they reach a certain numerical rating all employees receive a pay raise of between one percent and three percent.[7]

The term "customers" in the vernacular of TQM is broad and refers not only those who purchase goods or services from the organization—**external customers**—but also all people *within* the organization—**internal customers.** Why does TQM apply such a broad definition of customers? Think in these terms: If employees within an organization (internal customers) don't treat each other as customers and provide quality services to each other, then they are going to find it virtually impossible to meet the quality standards of external customers. Such activities as those that take place in a payroll department provide a "customer" service to employees. Virtually all functions in an organization should be considered a part of the total quality management process.

Obtain Benchmarks

To provide quality to customers, as we've just learned, we must know customer quality standards. But to compete in a global marketplace, we also must attempt to be familiar with the quality standards of our competitors. **Benchmarking** is another important element of TQM, one that assists organizations in learning about competitors' standards of quality. Benchmarking is the continuous process of obtaining accurate information about how others, such as competitors, handle similar quality problems. It involves comparing products, services, and practices against the toughest competitors or those recognized as industry leaders. The benchmarking activity has become a popular way of identifying organizational weaknesses, setting realistic targets, and improving performance. Ford Motor Company, in its quest to improve its performance, is said to use Toyota Motor Corporation as its benchmarking standard in just about everything—from quality to costs.[8]

Mark that bench
Tote that scale
Think about the client
And you'll never fail!

A challenge with benchmarking, of course, is *how* to obtain accurate information about competitors, particularly foreign ones. There are consulting services and publications that provide information. For example, one source of information is the American Quality Foundation, an organization that commissioned an international quality study. The study, based on questionnaires sent to 550 companies in Canada, Germany, Japan, and the United States, provides information related to the motor, computer, banking, and health care industries. The study generated a database containing 1.5 million pieces of information.[9]

Establish Standards

Another key requisite of the TQM process is to establish realistic **standards**. Standards basically are predetermined goals and objectives that employees are expected and able to meet. Graham Sharman, a senior partner in the consulting firm of McKinsey & Company, contends that senior managers should not be the ones to set quality

A QUESTION OF ETHICS

Is Quality Going to the Dogs?[a]

The customer, according to TQM, is supposed to provide the benchmarks for quality. Here's what could be considered an unusual mark on the old bench—boots made from the skin of dogs! Yes, you read it right. A company called Technica U.S. of Lebanon, New Hampshire, has been selling the boots for up to $350 to people who like to have humanity's best furry friend underfoot rather than trotting alongside.

"We're not dog killers," said Al Lavetti, V.P. of marketing and sales for the company. Lavetti points out that the skins and furs are imported from China, where the dogs were raised and slaughtered for food.

Wouldn't it be delightful if each purchaser of a pair of dog boots were provided with the dog's name? The purchaser could then say to his or her friends, "What do you think of my new Lassies? Don't worry, they won't bite."

A Question of Ethics: What do you think? Should products made out of the skins and furs of dogs be allowed or, instead, be given the boot?

"I wanna
do it
myself!'

improvement goals and objectives for lower-level employees. He feels that doing so is demotivating and ineffective. Sharman contends, "Over and over we find that, given some guiding principles or areas for improvement, they [lower-level employees] set much higher goals for themselves. Reward them for reaching their goals."[10] The concepts related to a participative style of leadership discussed in Chapter 6 could be applied effectively to Sharman's suggestions.

Unfortunately, there are some situations where the skill level and potential aptitude of existing employees prevent an organization from achieving desired standards. More will be discussed on this topic in the section on *continuous improvement teams.*

Establish Strategies to Close Gap

We've discussed the need for sense of direction—a mission. It is also important to develop quality standards that help close the gap between what *is* and what *should be.* To close this gap, effective **strategies** must be developed. Strategies are carefully thought-out decisions that help organizational members develop action plans for achieving the end results established by the mission statement.

Zap the gap!

Here's an illustration of a strategy: Let's assume that your organization develops and markets computer software systems. Let's also assume that some customers have had difficulty utilizing certain commands, partially because of their lack of willingness to spend sufficient time looking up the information in the user's manual. Your objective is to make it easier for end users to find information that explains how to use the software's commands. Your *strategy* is the decision to develop easier-to-access "Help" commands that clearly explain the hard-to-understand functions.

Provide Adequate Quality Training for All Employees

TQM is not a simple process. An organization's strategies will be difficult to put into action and its mission unlikely to be attained unless its personnel are trained in TQM. The type of training that is essential to an effective total quality management process includes training in TQM concepts, team building, problem solving, and statistical methods.

Good training
equals
better quality!

Just as Olympic athletes must spend considerable time training to improve their skills and enhance their performance, so must employees receive training that can lead to improved quality of work and greater productivity. Many organizations have found that empowering employees to analyze and determine their own training needs and to assist in the development of training programs can often heighten their desire to learn new skills. Of course, training has numerous objectives in addition to developing quality-conscious employees. These objectives include higher productivity, lower accident frequency, and improved advancement opportunities.

Training employees for *total quality* is not an easy task. As already mentioned, each employee brings to the workplace a set of values that may or may not already be in harmony with the organizational culture. For example, have you ever observed a person who carelessly threw a fast-food container on the ground or discarded soda or beer cans on the beach rather than taking them to a waste container? Such persons are not necessarily evil; often they have merely not developed a value system that helps them realize the effect of their actions on the environment and other people's enjoyment.

A similar situation exists on the job. There are employees whose value systems may not include what is necessary to enhance an organization's total quality management process. Furthermore, there are some cynics who believe that "you can't teach an old dog new tricks." However, if you've ever had an old dog, perhaps you've learned that such a belief is often unfounded. A more positive attitude is to recognize that although it may not be easy, change in employees' values can be encouraged. The concept of change is so significant that an entire chapter—Chapter 9—is devoted to the topic. At this point let's merely recognize that employee value systems are not likely to change overnight. Employees do tend to change, however, when they recognize the *need* to change and when they perceive how they themselves will *benefit* from changed attitudes and behavior.

And you can't trick an old *dog!*

Establish Continuous Improvement Teams

As mentioned earlier, TQM is *not* a program with a beginning and an end; it is an ongoing process, one that should involve everyone in the organization. As a means of sustaining this philosophy of permanence, many firms have established **continuous improvement teams (CITs).**

Continuous improvement teams are actually an outgrowth of quality circles, which were mentioned briefly in Chapter 4. Whether they are called quality circles, continuous improvement teams, or quality improvement teams, their goals are usually similar: to be concerned with improving quality in those areas where there is a gap between what *is* and what *should be.*

CITs are generally established first among middle managers, followed by the development of teams for assistant managers and supervisors. Team members meet on a regular basis, typically for about an hour each week. Teams are empowered with responsibility for identifying, analyzing, and establishing objectives for solving current quality and productivity problems. Quality objectives are aimed at both external and internal customers.

Don't just
CIT around,
do something!

Participants at the CIT meetings also conduct brainstorming sessions that help to establish standards, goals, and objectives for improving specific processes, products, and services. After careful analysis (a process that can take months to complete), the team decides on the methods necessary to accomplish goals and the ways results will be monitored. Team members should also be trained in measurement techniques and communication. Team leaders, often mid-managers or first-line supervisors but sometimes selected group members, help put recommendations into practice. In some cases, the position of team leader is rotated among members.

The success of teams is highly dependent upon four major factors:

1. A supportive organizational culture.

2. How team members perceive their managers.

3. The willingness of team members to share information.

4. The skill level and learning potential of team members.

The need for a supportive organizational culture has been discussed earlier. Resistance is likely to develop in a climate of distrust, especially if employees feel that the TQM process results in greater efficiency leading to employee layoffs. Employees tend to be more receptive to the TQM process when management sincerely conveys to them that jobs are relatively secure and that savings and productivity gains will be shared.

Teams tend to lose their effectiveness when individual members hesitate to share their knowledge. Read *A Box of Interest,* "Teamwork Can Be Tricky," for an explanation of this problem.

The skill level and learning potential of team members certainly have an influence on the success of the TQM process. Unfortunately, however, some organizations have found that the skill level of some of their operating employees is woefully inadequate. A National Association of Manufacturers' survey tragically brings this point home. The survey revealed that 30 percent of queried companies said they couldn't reorganize work activities because employees couldn't learn new jobs. Twenty-five percent said they were unable to improve product quality because workers couldn't learn the needed skills. These findings exist despite the fact that the average manufacturer in the study reported rejecting five out of every six candidates for a job.[11] Although these figures may be high for some industries, perhaps organizations will have to provide remedial education to bring some employees up to the required skill level.

Wanted on
nobody's team.

In spite of these discouraging findings, an increasing proportion of U.S. employers are using empowered continuous improvement teams: about one employer in five, compared to only one in 20 in the early 1980s. According to Charles Manz, a management professor and consultant, companies that utilize teams find that labor costs drop, morale rises, and signs of alienation ease.[12] Among the companies that use teams are TRW, 3M, General Electric, Dana, Hewlett-Packard, and IBM.[13]

A BOX OF INTEREST

Teamwork Can Be Tricky![b]

The use of teams has become a popular tool in organizations in recent years. Managers in some organizations have become enamored with what they've read about the success of teams in improving quality, cutting costs, and slashing the time it takes to bring new products and services to market.

Unfortunately, however, team members don't always practice teamwork, which can reduce their value as a part of the TQM process. Problems sometimes develop when specialists from different functions, such as design engineers and production people, get together. There often exist barriers of perception and communication between such types of employees. One large petroleum company, for example, found that some of the members of its continuous improvement teams were hesitant to share their knowledge with others on the team. "Knowledge is power" was a common belief, and to share knowledge was to share, or lose, power—a loss that apparently some team members did not want to experience. A large pharmaceutical company that rewarded employees on the basis of individual performance found a similar reticence among some employees to share knowledge and information.

Communication tends to be one of the biggest problems among teams. Numerous companies have found that sharing information among team members who are geographically separated has created a challenge. Some organizations have overcome this barrier by developing on-line computer information networks. Others have brought their teams closer together by the use of fax machines and telephones to enable more regular communication to take place among team members.

Measure and Monitor Performance

Where there's a gap, there's a need.

Why might there be a need for quality improvement? Usually the need exists because there is a gap between actual results and desired results. Can you visualize a type of skill that is necessary for those involved in determining what the existing gaps are and in measuring and monitoring performance? As a part of the TQM process, employees are usually trained in **statistical process control (SPC),** which involves the use of statistical techniques that aid in analyzing a process and its output and in determining the activities necessary for improvement, that is, eliminating any gaps.

It's what's up front that counts!

The tendency has long been for quality inspection to occur during and especially at the end of the production process. However, a concern for quality *after* something has been done can be expensive in terms of labor costs, scrap, and wasted materials. The TQM process emphasizes the need for *building quality into the product* in the first place rather than making quality control an "after-the-fact" phenomenon by inspecting, and then accepting or rejecting, the finished product. Building quality into the product also requires building quality-mindedness into every employee.

Employee progress in the TQM process should be monitored. Especially important is for employees to receive feedback regarding the quality of their activities. Providing feedback, that is, communicating results to organization members, is extremely important as a means of maintaining employee interest and enthusiasm in the process. Some organizations supplement the communication process by reporting the activities and results of continuous improvement teams in company newsletters.

Meet or Beat Customer Expectations

The final element—*to meet or beat customer expectations*—in reality states the major purpose of the entire TQM process. Of course, customers do have *expectations* from their purchases. Consequently, customers consider the quality that they receive to be paramount, and quality is a major factor influencing the reputation of organizations. Substantiating such attitudes toward quality, a recent Corporate Reputations Survey prepared by *Fortune* reported two factors that were the most significant ones related to a corporation's reputation. More than 8,000 senior executives, outside directors, and financial analysts were polled. The items that came up most frequently in the survey were *quality of management* and *quality of products and services,* the former cited first among 82 percent of those polled and the latter second among 63 percent.[14]

Quality 1st!

BOUQUETS FOR QUALITY COMPANIES

As the box *A Global Glance,* "Japan's Biggest Import—American Managerial Expertise?" indicates, the Japanese have been awarding prizes for quality to Japanese industry since the 1950s. American managers finally received a wake-up call in 1987 with the advent of the **Malcolm Baldrige National Quality Award,** an award that was named after a former U.S. Secretary of Commerce who was killed in a rodeo accident. Administered by an offshoot of the Commerce Department—the National Institute of Standards and Technology—two Baldrige awards are given each year in each of three categories—manufacturing, service, and small business.

Companies nominate themselves and must submit extensive application forms that describe a variety of their practices. (AT&T has an internal group of 12 consultants who assist divisions prepare for the award.[15]) The most-qualified firms are then selected and visited by an examination team that evaluates them in seven categories, each listed in order of priority in Table 7.2.

The award somewhat parallels the TQM movement, as it reflects the belief that customers provide the most important benchmarks of quality. Also considered important in the award are that all employees are involved and that each firm's mission includes striving for continuous, long-term quality improvement.

The award, however, is not without its detractors, some critics contending that the qualifying criteria ignore certain important areas, such as financial performance and superior product or service quality. Regarding the latter criterion, critics have cited General Motors' Cadillac division, which won the award at a time when surveys indicated that consumers did not rate its cars very highly.[16]

TABLE 7.2   Criteria for Winning Baldrige Award (in Order of Priority).

1. Customer satisfaction
2. Quality results
3. Human resource development and management
4. Management of process quality
5. Leadership
6. Information and analysis
7. Strategic quality planning

Japan's Biggest Import—American Managerial Expertise?ᶜ

W. Edward Deming, an American and one of the world's renowned experts on quality management, was imported, so to speak, by Japan after World War II to assist with the reconstruction of that devastated nation. His philosophy on quality management and techniques of statistical control was so well received by Japanese industry that the Japanese Union of Scientists and Engineers created in the early 1950s the now coveted *Deming Prize,* awarded annually for advances in product quality. The United States finally decided to reclaim some of the American managerial ideas that assisted Japanese industry so well by initiating, in 1987, the Baldrige award, which is discussed elsewhere in this chapter. A similar quality award was begun by the European Foundation for Quality Management in Europe in 1992, the first of which was awarded to Rank Xerox, the joint-venture office equipment group.

Deming is also well known for his explanation of the major causes of problems plaguing Western industry in his presentation of "Deming's Seven Deadly Diseases." These "lethal" diseases are the following:

1. *Lack of constancy of purpose.* Companies need a sense of direction—a mission and vision of the future.
2. *Emphasis on short-term profits.* Managers should not sacrifice long-term improvements in quality, products, and service for short-term improvements in dividend payouts.
3. *Annual performance appraisals.* Short-term performance reviews obstruct long-term planning and results.
4. *Excessive mobility of management.* Managers tend to job hop too frequently, a practice that is not conducive to long-range planning.
5. *Use of only visible figures.* Managers tend to consider only figures they can see and to ignore other important ones, such as the multiplying effect of a satisfied customer.
6. *Excessive medical costs.* Employee medical insurance benefits, due to skyrocketing hospital and doctor's costs, have become a severe financial burden on many organizations.
7. *Excessive costs of liability.* Especially in the United States, lawyers, who work on contingency fees, have created additional financial burdens on organizations.

A real
eye
opener!

Nonetheless, the Baldrige award, which is handed over by the U.S. president to up to six companies a year—has awakened many American managers to the need for greater attention in the area of quality management.

Quality—In Danger of Becoming a Scapegoat?

It seems to have become fashionable lately for the popular press to attack the concepts associated with total quality management. Reports have appeared revealing that a number of American managers have soured on some of the approaches to quality that were applied with startling success by many Japanese companies. They haven't necessarily decided that the systems don't work, but they believe that the approaches haven't achieved much in their own plants.[17]

A danger exists when managers observe a creative process that seems to work well in one culture and then attempt to transplant it mechanically to their own environment without understanding how cultural differences may affect the process. General Motors' executive, Larry Spiegel, stresses such hazards in the quote at the beginning of this chapter.

Quality should never become a dirty word in organizations. To attack and discard quality concepts could be akin to shooting one's self in the foot. A more positive approach is to attempt to understand one's own organizational culture before initiating such activities, to make certain that employees are prepared for such processes, and to tailor operations to fit the specific organization. The misapplication of such concepts by some organizations is no reason to discard ideas that are logically sound.

ORGANIZATIONAL PRINCIPLES THAT ASSIST THE QUEST FOR QUALITY

It's a matter
of principle.

A body of established organizational principles that has proven useful over the years can also serve as a useful adjunct to total quality management concepts. Their sound application can assist organizational members in their efforts to develop and maintain a quality organization. Some of these concepts are covered in the section that follows.

The Scalar Principle

The **scalar principle** asserts that the clearer the lines of authority and accountability between the point of ultimate authority (the boss at the top) and the workers at the bottom of the hierarchy, the more effective the decision making and communication within the organization will be. The principle implies that only rarely should this chain be broken.

For example, assume that a worker, Bill, has a complaint about a fellow employee, but instead of discussing the problem with you—his line supervisor—he leapfrogs (bypasses) the formal chain of authority and complains directly to your boss. Any direct action taken by your boss would tend to usurp the authority delegated to you. As a result, your future effectiveness with your departmental associates would probably diminish. Although numerous exceptions abound in organic forms of organizations, according to the principle communication and authority relationships should generally follow official channels, or problems related to our next principle, the *unity of command,* are likely to occur.

What problem can develop from ignoring the scalar principle?

The Principle of Unity of Command

The principle of **unity of command** states that problems of accountability and communication are reduced if subordinates report to no more than one superior. The implication of this principle is that orders from one boss may conflict with orders from another and thus place the subordinate in a difficult and awkward situation.

Why is it awkward to serve two masters?

Have you ever had to "serve two masters," that is, had one boss who regularly gave you orders to perform specific tasks and another boss who gave you conflicting orders? Such arrangements place subordinates in unnecessarily uncomfortable positions. What should you do when you find yourself in this position? One approach that tends to be more effective is to ask your direct superior what he or she believes you should do. Even if you are directly and equally accountable to both bosses, you might be able to resolve the problem by discussing your plight with each of them and suggest that they come to an agreement about how conflicting orders should be handled.

Will *dual command* always result in organizational problems?

Dual command is the term generally used to denote a situation in which one subordinate is accountable to more than one superior, a condition that should be avoided whenever possible. Dual command is fairly common in matrix organizations, where there is an overlay of managers from more than one group.

Delegation-by-Results Principle

Delegation is the act of *giving rights or assigning tasks and responsibilities to others.* Since most managers are concerned with *results,* it follows that *results* should be a major concern when *delegating* tasks to associates. However, some managers by abusing our next principle tend to hinder the accomplishment of adequate results by employees.

The **delegation-by-results principle** reveals an important ingredient of the act of delegating. It states that *any person to whom authority is delegated should be provided sufficient rights to accomplish expected objectives.* Managers and operating employees typically find themselves in awkward positions when they've been assigned specific responsibilities and accountability without having been empowered with ample authority to perform the assigned tasks.

For example, assume that you are the personnel director of an organization and your responsibilities include developing and administering a new training program for employees. You have the duty to make certain that the program succeeds, but you have been delegated no authority to order the usual types of equipment and supplies necessary for your program. Much of your time might be expended on trying to persuade "the powers that be" of the necessity of such normal expenditures. Your job could have been made much easier and more effective if you had been delegated ample authority along with a clear indication of its limits.

Why is responsibility
without authority
undesirable?

Another problem of responsibility without authority can arise for department heads whose primary responsibility is to ensure the profitable operation of their sections, but who haven't been delegated the authority to select their staff. In well-managed organizations, managers wouldn't necessarily recruit personnel for their departments themselves, but they would customarily have the authority to accept or reject anyone chosen for their sections by the personnel department. Supervisors who are responsible for employees whom they didn't originally choose are likely to have their morale and attitudes adversely affected.

In small organizations, delegation is less essential (sometimes not even possible), but in larger organizations delegation is necessary if managers are to perform their assigned responsibilities effectively. Delegation offers a number of benefits to both managers and their associates. Among the major benefits are that delegation:

1. Frees the manager to perform broader responsibilities and functions.

2. Enriches employees' jobs.

3. Provides employees with the opportunity to develop new skills.

4. Helps to groom employees for upcoming promotions.

Why aren't some
supervisors able to
delegate work?

1. Lack of confidence
in employees

2. Lack of confidence
in self

Even though the benefits of delegating are readily apparent, many managers find it difficult to assign responsibilities to others. These are sometimes the types of leaders who tend to perceive their employees negatively (the X or Derived X approach), have *little faith in their employees,* and feel that "if you want something done right, you've gotta do it yourself!"

In some cases managers who cannot delegate may actually *lack confidence in themselves,* fearing that they are giving something away that rightfully belongs to them. Often these are the managers who spend the last two hours each day in the office trying to determine what work they are going to take home that evening. Sometimes managers who are afraid to delegate *fear that their employees will show them up* by doing better jobs than they could. And in some cases, managers don't delegate because they simply *like doing the job.* They've always performed a particular task in the past, they do it well, and they feel comfortable continuing to do it themselves. Delegation, however, is essential for managers who want to be free for other more important managerial functions.

3. Fear of being shown up

4. Like performing certain tasks

Accountability-for-Results Principle

In Chapter 6, responsibility was defined as the obligation to perform assigned tasks. We also stated that accountability means that employees are answerable to their bosses. The **accountability-for-results principle** states that the obligations assigned to individuals by their bosses are absolute and cannot be totally passed on to others. In other words, if you have been given the obligation to perform a particular task, you are held accountable for the results even when you have shared this responsibility with one of your subordinates.

For example, on an aircraft carrier many people *share* the captain's obligation, or responsibility, for ensuring that the objectives of the ship and the navy are achieved. Nevertheless, even when the captain—let's call him Captain Sidney Sueno—is comfortably asleep in his cabin, he is *ultimately* accountable for the actions of the crew. If the ship runs aground, those who were piloting the vessel at the time of the mishap are accountable, but Captain Sueno, too, is accountable, for he has merely *shared* part of his responsibility with others.

"But I was sleeping!"
"Tough darts, Captain!"

In private organizations the presidents may not be fully aware of certain negligent acts on the part of their key executives, but the senior executives are still ultimately accountable for any organization-related actions of their subordinates. A supervisor may have assigned specific duties to his or her operating workers, but the supervisor continues to be accountable for the activities within the department.

Let's reinforce these concepts: Authority is the *right* that is *delegated,* or given, to others; responsibility is the *obligation* to perform specific tasks that are *assigned* to subordinates; and accountability is the *answerability* of employees to their bosses. We can *share our responsibilities* with others, but we *retain accountability* for the results (see Table 7.3).

The Principle of Exception

There's nothing particularly wrong with being a "firefighter," but the position descriptions of most managers don't cite the putting out of fires as one of their principle activities. Nonetheless, managers who have not

TABLE 7.3   Summary of Major Principles of Organizations.

Principle	Description
Scalar	Authority and accountability in an organization should flow in a clear unbroken line through the chain of command.
Unity-of-command	No employee should be accountable to more than one boss (desirable but not always feasible).
Delegation-by-results	Any person to whom authority is delegated should be given sufficient rights to accomplish expected objectives.
Accountability-for-results	Bosses are still held answerable for results even when authority to achieve objectives has been assigned to their subordinates.
Exception principle	Recurring activities and decisions should routinely be delegated to and handled by associates, and unusual nonrecurring decisions should be referred to a higher level.
Span-of-control	The larger the number of employees reporting to one manager, the more difficult it is for him or her to supervise effectively.

developed the ability to delegate discover that much of their time is spent on routine matters that should have been assigned to others.

Help prevent fires. Be a fire preventer, not fighter!

The managerial concept termed the **exception principle** is related to our discussion of delegation and has often been abused by "firefighter managers." The exception principle states that *regular recurring activities and decisions should routinely be delegated to and handled by employees and that unusual nonrecurring decisions should be referred to a higher level.* Some managers, apparently unaware of the exception principle, find themselves running from one crisis to another because they failed to spend enough time on the more important managerial functions of planning, organizing, directing, and controlling.

Many managers, although in general agreement with the exception principle, take mild exception to it. Such managers feel that they shouldn't delegate solely routine "grunt work" types of activities. Perceiving delegation as an employee development and job enrichment tool, they feel that challenging activities requiring a certain degree of stretching to perform should also be delegated to employees.

The Span-of-Control Principle
Have you ever been attempting to study when a few friends came over to chat with you? At such times it's difficult to carry out your objectives, isn't it? Just imagine if you were quite popular and had friends wandering into

your house about every fifteen minutes during the time you had allotted for studying. Would you get much homework done?

If you understand the schoolwork problem, you can probably understand the **span-of-control principle,** which refers to the number of subordinates that one manager can supervise directly. It's also called the *span-of-management* or the *span-of-supervision principle.* The principle asserts that the larger the number of subordinates reporting to one manager, the harder it is for him or her to supervise effectively.

Any manager has only so much available time and can attend to a limited number of activities during that period. How many persons should be accountable to one manager? Some authorities suggest that five to fifteen people are the most anyone can manage effectively. However, the precise number is debatable and depends principally upon the *type of organizational structure,* the *supervisor's ability,* his or her *employees,* and the *nature of the work itself.*

What influences your "span"?

Peter Drucker, the doyen of management pundits, has developed a related concept, **span of empowerment,** which suggests that the greater the degree of employee empowerment, the greater the number of employees can be supervised effectively, possibly well above twenty. In such a situation, contends Drucker, the leader's role shifts from controller to coach, or mentor.[18]

The following chapter continues examining current-day quality concerns with a discussion of some of the modern attempts to improve the quality of work life.

SUMMARY

Management fads come and go. However, one current consideration of U.S. managers that is likely to be around for awhile is the growing concern for quality. Numerous organizations have already trained, or intend to train, their personnel in total quality management, an ongoing process that focuses organizational members' energies on improving the quality of their activities. TQM uses a customer-oriented approach, recognizing that customers usually have the final say on acceptable quality, especially over the long run.

Although various organizations may apply variations of the TQM process presented in the chapter, a fairly typical application of the concepts includes eleven steps: (1) provide a supportive organizational culture; (2) provide management commitment and leadership; (3) provide a sense of direction; (4) analyze customer quality needs; (5) obtain benchmarks; (6) establish standards; (7) establish strategies to close gaps; (8) provide training; (9) establish teams; (10) monitor and measure progress; and (11) meet or beat customer expectations.

The Baldrige award is presented for quality and two are given each year in each of three categories: manufacturing, service, and small business.

Several organizational principles have been developed that, when effectively applied, can aid in establishing and maintaining a quality organization. Discussed in this chapter were the scalar principle, the unity-of-command principle, the delegation-by-results principle, the accountability-for-results principle, the exception principle, and the span-of-control principle.

TERMS AND CONCEPTS TO REMEMBER

total quality management

mission statement

benchmarking

standards

strategies

continuous improvement teams (CITs)

statistical process control (SPC)

Malcolm Baldrige National Quality Award

scalar principle

unity of command

dual command

delegation

delegation-by-results principle

accountability-for-results principle

exception principle

span-of-control principle

span of empowerment

QUESTIONS

1. What is the basic purpose of the process of total quality management?

2. Why is TQM considered to be a process rather than a program?

3. What is considered to be the number one ingredient influencing the success of the TQM process? Why?

4. What is the purpose of a mission statement?

5. Who are considered to be the ultimate determiners of an organization's quality standards? Why?

6. What is a major challenge associated with applying the concept of *benchmarking?*

7. What is the reason some managers believe that quality improvement goals and objectives should be set *by,* not *for,* lower-level employees?

8. Evaluate the following statement: "A sound training program, regardless of the ability of the trainees, will ensure the success of the TQM process."

9. What is the function of continuous improvement teams? What significantly influences their success?

10. What is meant by the phrase, "Quality should be built into the product rather than inspected after the product is built"?

11. What is the purpose of the Malcolm Baldrige National Quality Award? What are the two most important criteria in its set of standards?

12. What hazards might exist when the *scalar* and *unity of command* principles are abused?

13. Should anyone ever be accountable to more than one boss? Explain.

14. Why does a leader with responsibility but little authority find it difficult to function effectively?

15. Can employees ever be held accountable for responsibilities that were assigned to their boss? Explain.

16. How can the application of the *exception principle* aid both the leader and his or her associates.

17. What is the optimum number of employees that should report to one manager?

APPLICATIONS

7.1 The Fosdick Generator Company and TQM

Franklyn Fosdick knew there was something drastically wrong with his Little Rock Generator factory, but like many small business owners, he was too busy running around "putting out fires" to try to figure out just what the problems were and what should be done about them.

Fosdick felt something had to change, however, after his 12-year-old business had lost money for the fourth year in a row. He finally decided that he had to take some type of action if his firm was going to survive.

While attending a luncheon meeting of the local Rotary Club last Tuesday, Xavier Caliber, a fellow club member, suggested that he look into "this total quality management stuff that everybody's talking about these days." Fosdick had been receiving advertisements in the mail regarding seminars that were being offered at Eureka Springs, a nearby resort area where conferences and workshops regularly took place. One was going to be offered a week from this Thursday. Fosdick decided to go.

Larry Laud, the TQM workshop leader, was nearly evangelistic in his delivery. At one point he made the comment, "TQM, with its CITs [continuous improvement teams], SPCs [statistical process control], empowerment, and missions, is the greatest stuff since sliced bread." At times Fosdick wondered, "Is this guy for real?" However, he thought to himself, "I paid a lot of good dollars for this workshop, so I'd better get what I can out of it."

Laud, the leader, appeared to be well versed in the vernacular of TQM, although he admitted that he had never personally worked with any companies that had initiated the process. Nonetheless, he provided each workshop participant with a manual and an audiocassette that were intended to serve as guides for participants to set up their own TQM activities. Laud closed the session by saying, "When you people get back to your offices, review this stuff, apply it to your operations, and you'll be eligible to receive the Baldrige award in less time than it takes a kitty cat to lick its whiskers!"

One of the first things Fosdick did on the following Monday morning was to develop a mission. The mission statement that he developed was, "To be the greatest and most profitable generator manufacturer in the Southeastern states." Fosdick then called a meeting of the plant manager and the four supervisors and handed them a copy of his newly-developed mission statement. Fosdick told the managers that he had learned from the workshop that employees needed a sense of direction, and a mission statement was supposed to help them get it. He instructed each supervisor to convey the company's formal mission statement to every employee as soon as possible. He also directed the supervisors to convey to the employees that each department was now considered to be a team, and the teams would be competing with each other to achieve quality results.

Fosdick suddenly got an idea. He said, "I'm going to give each team a name, like the 'Panthers,' 'Killers,' 'Marauders,' and so on." Fosdick added that he would evaluate team results twice a year, and that the members of the best team would receive a cash bonus. He would also continue to provide bonuses based on each employee's individual results, as had been the situation in the past. Fosdick concluded by asking the supervisors to meet with their teams sometime that week and have team members develop lists of the expectations of the company's customers.

The supervisors returned to their departments. The approach of Jane Johnson, one of the supervisors, was fairly typical of the way TQM was introduced to "team members" in the company. Jane casually told each employee that the boss wanted everyone to know about the company's new mission. One of her employees, Dick van Brug, responded after hearing the mission by saying, "Great! But how's that going to pay for my baby's shoes?" Jane answered, "Come on, Dick. This quality business is a pet project of the boss. Let's humor him, and it'll all blow away in time."

Questions

1. What is your prediction as to the potential success of the TQM process at the Fosdick Generator Company? What are the reasons for your prediction?

2. What are some specific shortcomings in the way the TQM process was presented to the employees? What might have been a better approach?

3. If you had been brought in as an outside consultant, how would you have advised Fosdick about implementing TQM?

7.2 The Dull Letters Case

The Softford Insurance Company, a large organization headquartered in Bangor, Maine, has an information processing pool consisting of more than forty persons. Many of the company's letters are of a technical nature, dealing with such matters as subrogation, reinsurance, and co-insurance clauses. Most of the stenographers are not highly versed in the complexities of insurance jargon. In an attempt to improve efficiency, management established a system of standardized paragraphs covering nearly every topic about which customers or agents might inquire.

The information-processing clerks' new duties include reading the customers' questions and then inserting the "proper" paragraphs into form letters with standardized styles for opening and closing. The letters are then turned over to the supervisor for signature.

Absenteeism and turnover in the information-processing pool have been considerably higher than in any other department. The atmosphere among the employees appears to be extremely tense. Some employees frequently burst into heated arguments. Customers regularly complain about errors in their correspondence.

Questions

1. What appears to be the main problem?

2. Assume that you've been requested to provide advice on how quality, productivity, accuracy, and morale could be improved in the information-processing pool. What *specific* recommendations would you make?

7.3 Hot Line to the Top

My name is Cary Scrant. I'm a student studying business administration at a local college. Every summer since I was fifteen years old, I've worked at Greenleaf Nurseries, a large commercial grower of plant stock such as flowering perennials, shrubbery, and ornamental trees. The company sells to landscape contractors and retail garden centers. In my position, I am directly accountable to both the production manager and the distribution manager, and I feel that I get along very well with both. I think that I'm well liked and accepted by my fellow workers. I also happen to be the son of one of the owners.

Since the operation was relocated from Stockton to Lodi, California, there's been a decline in morale due mostly to the attitude of the production manager, Hiroshi Shingu. He rules the greenhouses with an "iron hand" and doesn't use any of the participative techniques of management that I am studying in college. His leadership is clearly autocratic. Mr. Shingu seems to resent any suggestions and has thus caused production to become less efficient. As a result, I've heard an increasing number of complaints from my co-workers. The other employees seem to feel that because I'm the son of one of the owners, I should be able to get some type of action.

I've had numerous conversations in the past with my father about various aspects of the company. My father welcomes these discussions and respects my ideas and suggestions. I've always been interested in the company, but my interest seems to be intense now. I see the inefficiencies in the ways things are done and can tell my father a fair amount about them during our discussions. I don't accept any information from my fellow employees as fact. If I don't already have firsthand knowledge of a problem, I check it out. I'm aware of the efforts of management to resolve problems and, on many occasions, have defended company actions and policies.

The general manager and the production manager are beginning to feel a certain amount of pressure from the top. I was recently called in to the general manager's office, along with the production manager, Mr. Shingu. The general manager came directly to the point. He doesn't like me to talk to my father about the problems at the nursery. He feels that neither he nor Mr. Shingu can be effective leaders if the employees have a hot line to the top.

I explained to them that I have observed a lot of waste and inefficiency in Greenleaf's operations. I also pointed out that the money the company makes provides the roof over my head, the clothes on my back, the food I eat, and the funds for my education. I know, although I didn't mention it, that I'll probably be employed full time by this company in the future, and I don't want my future livelihood jeopardized by the inefficiencies of the production manager.

The general manager receives information given to him by the production manager. He's not aware of everything that goes on in production; he has an office, a shipping department, and a sales force to oversee. Thus the time the general manager devotes to production is limited by his present span of control.

Questions

1. What appears to be the problem in this case: Is there more than one?

2. What should be done about this situation? By whom?

3. Has Cary made any inferences not based on fact? If so, what are they?

NOTES

1. "Quality of American Products Worries U.S. Citizens, Poll Says," *Associated Press,* as reported in *The Stars and Stripes,* March 2, 1992, p. 17.

2. A. M. Rosenthal, "Japanese Right on One Thing—U.S. Illiteracy," *The New York Times,* as reported in *The Stars and Stripes,* January 31, 1992, p. 13.

3. Paul Taylor, "Why Customers Must Come First," *Financial Times,* October 26, 1992, p. 8.

4. Mike Farrish, "World Class Performance Through Total Quality Management," *Financial Times,* Management Consultancy Special Section, May 15, 1991, p. V.; and Martin Dickson, "Total Quality: Bouquets and Barbed Ire," *Financial Times,* February 3, 1992, p. 10.

5. See note 3.

6. Mission statement provided by the public affairs department of Safeway Inc.

7. Alan Cane, "Temple Dictates New Catechism for Born-Again IBM," *Financial Times,* October 11, 1991, p. 25.

8. Paul Ingrassia and Neal Templin, "At Rebounding Ford, Picking a Chairman Is Next Big Challenge," *The Wall Street Journal Europe,* July 21, 1992, pp. 1–8.

9. Paul Taylor, "Keeping Up To the Mark," *Financial Times,* June 29, 1992, p. 7.

10. Graham Sharman, "When Quality Control Gets in the Way of Quality," *The Wall Street Journal,* February 24, 1992, p. 6.

11. John Cunniff, "Companies Leave Jobs Unfilled Because Applicants Lack Skills," *The Stars and Stripes,* January 21, 1992, p. 17.

12. Joann S. Lublin, "U.S. Bosses Find Poor Worker Performance Improves With Better Management Practices," *The Wall Street Journal Europe,* February 14–15, 1992, p. 9.

13. "How One Company Learned from Others," *World Monitor,* October 1991, p. 46.

14. Kate Ballen, "America's Most Admired Corporations," *Fortune,* February 10, 1992, pp. 30–48.

15. Dean McCauley, "Quality's Time May Have Come and Gone," *Contra Costa Times,* February 8, 1993, pp. 1C, 6C.

16. Martin Dickson, "Total Quality: Bouquets and Barbed Ire," *Financial Times,* February 3, 1992, p. 10; Martin Dickson, "Big Reshuffle Is Designed to Improve Company Efficiency," *Financial Times,* June 25, 1992, p. 4; and William McWhirter, "Who's in the Driver's Seat?" *Time International,* October 26, 1992, p. 54.

17. Amal Kumar Naj and Janet Guyon, "Some Manufacturers Drop Efforts to Adopt Japanese Techniques," *The Wall Street Journal Europe,* May 17, 1993, pp. 1, 5.

18. Christopher Lorenz, "Workers Happy to Be In Charge," *San Francisco Examiner,* March 30, 1992, p. 14.

BOX NOTES

a. Adapted from "Dog Boots 'Disgusting'," *The Stars and Stripes,* February 2, 1992, p. 7.

b. Adapted from interviews with various managers personally involved with continuous improvement teams.

c. Adapted from Charles H. Walden, "The Secret of Japan's Success," *Industrial Education,* November 1989, pp. 35, 36; Martin Dickson, "Total Quality: Bouquets and Barbed Ire," *Financial Times,* February 2, 1992, p. 8; and Paul Taylor, "Why Customers Must Come First," *Financial Times,* October 26, 1992, p. 8.

EXPERIENTIAL EXERCISE

"Excuse Me, But Would You Mind Telling Me Your Mission?"

As you learned from the chapter, one of the purposes of a mission statement is to assist employees in developing a sense of direction. However, as with any management tool, communication and understanding are necessary for it to be effective.

Here's an activity for you: Contact the public affairs director of three medium-to-large companies in your region and ask them to give you copies of their mission statements. Carefully read each statement first, then tell each public affairs director that you would like to perform a short experiment related to a college assignment. Request permission to ask three operating-level employees in the organization to relate to you what their company's mission is. What is the significance of the way each employee related his or her understanding of the company's mission?

CHAPTER 8

The Quality of Work Life

*Does Anybody
Really Care?*

**When you finish this chapter,
you should be able to:**

1

Summarize the specific factors that influence
the quality of work life (QWL).

2

Describe some of the more common techniques being used
to improve employees' quality of work life.

3

Describe some of the contemporary techniques of
job enrichment used by various organizations.

4

Identify some of the innovative programs currently utilized in the
workplace to enhance employee productivity and morale.

> The main reason American industry has lost
> competitiveness is distrust. We must go down
> the stairs to people.
> They won't come up to us.
>
> *Kan Higashi, President, NUMMI*

The year, 1936. The film, a classic satire of assembly-line work entitled *Modern Times*. A dehumanized Charlie Chaplin went mad after
monotonously tightening pairs of bolts hour after hour on the factory
floor. He left his work station and tried to tighten the factory supervisor's nose, fire hydrants, and the buttons on women's dresses.
Industrialists didn't laugh at what they saw. Instead, they reacted
defensively.

Has there been much improvement in the quality of life in the
workplace since the 1930s? Opinions vary. Much organizational strife
and conflict continue. We've already learned how costly such strife
can be from the box, "A Question of Ethics," in Chapter 5. As you
recall, a bitter labor battle between the employees of Caterpillar and
its management developed into a five-month work stoppage in which
the company experienced a net loss of $185 million for the first half of
1992 and the employees accomplished little.

Regardless of such isolated incidents, however, considerable
progress has been made in many organizations. Many managers, as
we learned from some of the previous chapters, *have* achieved a high
degree of enlightenment and sophistication in the area of organizational behavior. This chapter will describe some of the ways in which
contemporary managers are attempting to improve the *quality of
work life* of today's employees.

GREATER CONCERNS OVER THE QUALITY OF WORK LIFE

Although it's true that some employees do lack the necessary skills to
accomplish certain tasks, a fairly large proportion of today's work
force has attained higher levels of education than any in American
history. Increased achievements in education are typically accompanied by rising levels of expectation. Yet many observers believe that
the quality of jobs will decline steadily as newer positions offer
employees less challenge and ego satisfaction than existed in the jobs
being phased out. Thus an enormous challenge faces today's managers. Employee expectations that aren't fulfilled can cause job dissatisfaction and a weakening of the work ethic.

White-Collar Woes, Blue-Collar Blues

We learned earlier about needs and motivation. Employees, of course, aren't like robots—that is, mechanical objects—whose only human trait is caring about their paychecks. Most employees have a strong need for self-esteem and a sense of belonging. Without such satisfactions, many employees become bored, disgruntled, alienated, and sometimes even destructive.

Both blue- and white-collar workers today often feel alienated from their jobs. These feelings tend to result in increased alcohol and drug abuse, mental illness, shoddy work, lower productivity, pilferage, and sabotage.

Does Anybody Care?

Monotony gets boring!

Modern managers have become concerned about the declining *quality of work life,* and many are doing something about it. Numerous managers have discovered that the elimination of monotony on jobs is not as difficult as some more traditional managers apparently want to believe. New styles of thinking, however, are necessary for programs to succeed. Managers who resist new efforts on the ground that employees are treated too much like spoiled children should attempt to recognize that the prime aim of such programs is to make the *total organization* more effective, not solely to provide greater satisfaction to the workers.

A steadily increasing number of organizations are experimenting with or have adopted job enlargement and enrichment programs, team approaches, empowerment, flexible working hours, and a host of other techniques designed to improve workers' attitudes toward their jobs and thus improve productivity, product quality, profitability, and the quality of work life. In the remaining sections we discuss some of the major factors that influence the quality of work life, along with some specific suggestions for improving it.

WHAT INFLUENCES THE QUALITY OF WORK LIFE?

How's your QWL?

The quality of equipment, tools, and other technical and material factors influence the productivity of an organization. Also affecting productivity is the **quality of work life (QWL),** how effectively the job environment meets the personal needs and values of employees. Of course, a factor that enhances one worker's QWL might have little effect on another worker's QWL. There are some common features, however, that tend to directly influence the QWL in most organizations.

Richard Walton suggests eight major categories that together make up the QWL:[1]

1. *Adequate and fair compensation.* Is the employee's paycheck sufficient for maintaining a reasonable standard of living? Is the wage or salary comparable to amounts received by others in similar positions?

2. *Safe and healthy working conditions.* Is the work environment relatively free from excessive hazards that could cause employees injury or illness?

3. *Opportunity for developing and using human capacity.* How does the job relate to the employee's self-esteem? Does it permit the employee to use and develop his or her skills and knowledge? Does the worker feel involved and challenged?

4. *Opportunity for continued growth and security.* Are there opportunities for advancement, or is the job perceived as a path to nowhere? Does the job provide the employee with employment and income security?

5. *A feeling of belonging.* Does the worker feel a part of a team or, instead, isolated from the group? Are fellow employees supportive of each other or in a state of continual conflict? Is the work environment relatively free from destructive prejudice?

6. *Employee rights.* What sort of rights does the employee have? What are the standards of personal privacy, attitudes toward dissent, equity in the distribution of rewards, and access to grievance procedures?

7. *Work and total life space.* How does the job affect the employee's personal life roles, such as his or her relationship with family? Are overtime demands, travel requirements, and transfers perceived as excessive?

8. *Social relevance of work life.* Does the employee perceive that the organization is socially responsible? Does the organization produce a product or service that contributes to the employee's pride? Or does the organization engage in unethical activities? What are the organization's employment practices? Are they fair? How does the organization dispose of wastes?

IMPROVING THE QUALITY OF WORK LIFE

Earlier you learned that monotony on the job can result in boredom and reduced productivity. Technology in the United States and elsewhere has developed to an extent that has created numerous problems for managers and workers in organizations. An increasing number of firms have responded with more positive approaches to the human problems that result from a high degree of specialization. Let's now briefly examine some suggestions that you as existing or future managers might consider when you are modifying work environments in your organizations.

Enriching Jobs

A current catchall term for improving the QWL is **job enrichment,** a concept that can take a variety of forms. Job enrichment frequently involves greater use of factors that are intended to *motivate* the worker rather than only to *maintain* a satisfied feeling toward the job. (Remember Herzberg's motivation-maintenance model?) Basically, job enrichment is a form of *changing or improving* a job so that a worker is likely to be more motivated. It provides the employee with the opportunity for greater recognition, achievement, growth, and responsibility, the lack of which can cause worker alienation. In short, job enrichment involves modifying jobs so that they appeal more to employees' higher-order needs. An example of job enrichment would be to allow secretaries to sign their own outgoing letters and to be responsible for content and quality.

What actually enriches jobs?

The Core Dimensions of Jobs

What are the principal factors that tend to enrich jobs? J. Richard Hackman and Greg R. Oldham have identified five factors—termed **core job dimensions**—that they feel are essential ingredients of any job if the benefits of job enrichment are to be derived (see Table 8.1).[2] A brief discussion of each follows.

Task Variety. A significant core dimension of an enriched job is **task variety.** Basically, this dimension enables employees to perform a wide variety of operations requiring both *thinking* and *doing* types of activities.

TABLE 8.1   The Core Dimensions of Jobs

Factors that tend to enrich jobs include:

1. **Task variety.** Performing a variety of operations and procedures
2. **Task identity.** Completing an entire piece of work
3. **Task significance.** Believing that the work is important to others
4. **Autonomy.** Controlling decision-making opportunities
5. **Feedback.** Receiving information regarding level and quality of performance

Task Identity. A second core dimension relates to *performing an entire task* and is referred to as **task identity.** A job designed with this factor in mind allows the employee to have *a more complete job* with which he or she can identify, rather than a minute, repetitious job that seems to have little relationship to a whole. A later section of this chapter discusses the *whole job concept.*

Task Significance. Many people like to feel that the job they perform *has an impact on others.* They want to believe that their job is important and makes some contribution to the company and society. When a job offers this dimension, it is said to have **task significance.**

Autonomy. Many employees like to feel responsible for their actions. They prefer to have the *freedom to make decisions,* even when there is a chance of failure. Jobs that empower their holders with the right to make a variety of decisions without first having to consult a higher authority are said to have the **autonomy** dimension.

Feedback. "How am I doing?" is a question that many employees want answered. The **feedback** dimension exists in jobs where employees consistently receive information on how they are performing. Feedback includes constructive criticism as well as praise. An ideal time for employees to receive feedback is during their formal **performance appraisal interview.** The interview session also provides the manager with the opportunity to guide the employee toward establishing new goals and improving or modifying future performance.

Getting Loaded—Vertically and Horizontally

"Getting loaded" on the job is generally considered a "no no" in most organizations. However, an exception to this general rule has developed in organizations that practice types of job enrichment referred to as *vertical* and *horizontal loading.*

Pull/push!

As you can observe in Figure 8.1, **vertical loading** involves enriching the work itself by pulling down responsibilities from above and pushing certain tasks of a job down to a lower job classification. In other words, a manager analyzes what he or she currently does for the employees that could be delegated to the employees themselves. Are there tasks performed by employees *when the manager is absent* that they could do regularly? Could workers be empowered with *more responsibility* for deciding how things are to be done? Are there certain tasks that should be *pushed down* to a lower job classification? How could the employees be made to feel *more accountable* for their actions? Could some *controls be removed* without removing accountability?

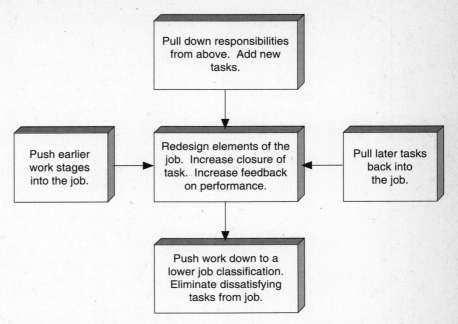

Figure 8.1   Enriching work through vertical and horizontal loading.

Push/pull!   **Horizontal loading,** as you can observe in Figure 8.1, actually enlarges the job by *pushing into it earlier work stages* and *pulling into it later work stages.* Could certain tasks that precede the work be made a basic part of the job for the purpose of making the work more meaningful and responsible and less monotonous?

Creating Whole Jobs

Vertical and horizontal loading results in what is often termed **job enlargement,** the process of *increasing the complexity of the job to appeal to the higher-order needs of workers.* Some managers currently believe that workers who have the opportunity to make greater use of their minds and skills are more able to help satisfy their personal needs for self-esteem and dignity.

Sometimes referred to as the *whole job concept,* this technique suggests that you, as a manager, attempt to give workers more complete, or whole, jobs to perform. The technique has a greater chance of success if you draw on employees' suggestions when trying to introduce greater challenge into jobs. Try to develop an environment in which employees are able not only to be actively involved in their jobs but also to participate in both *planning activities* and *evaluating the results* of their efforts.

All together now!

Rotating Jobs, Cross-Training, and Multiskilling

Job rotation is the *moving of people to different jobs on the same organizational level for short periods of time.* Providing employees with a variety of work experiences, many managers believe, can help reduce boredom for some employees. Job rotation can also provide employees with variety, along with broader knowledge and understanding of an organization's operations, which can help qualify them for promotions.

Some firms, such as Motorola, maintain planned programs of **cross-training** production workers so that they can easily rotate from one position to another. Also termed **multiskilling,** cross-trained workers at Motorola have received rewards of up to 27.5 percent more pay. Cross-trained employees have been found to have an improved understanding of the entire production process, which, at Motorola, resulted in a 77 percent fall in the defect rate over a 4-year period.[3]

There can be a short side to job rotation, however. A potential disadvantage is that some people may feel *less commitment* to specific positions, an attitude which, in some instances, can encourage *job hopping.* For many employees, though, the benefits of job rotation tend to outweigh any disadvantages.

Do Two "Dulls" Equal Job Enrichment?

"You've been washing forks . . . now wash knives!"

Since some jobs seem difficult to make interesting and challenging, job rotation seems like the ticket to the theater of job enrichment. But some critics ask, "Does rotating a person from one dull and unpleasant job to another dull and unpleasant job really enrich an employee's work environment?" Although job rotation would at least lend a certain degree of variety to an employee's organizational life, would his or her personal needs really be satisfied? Furthermore, certain employees, especially those who have been with an organization for a long time, may resist being placed in less pleasant jobs.

Some managers make unpleasant jobs *entry-level positions.* Employees can be told that the job is monotonous but temporary. Another possibility is to put dull jobs "up for grabs" each day. Sleepy or hungover workers may even prefer a day on a job not requiring much use of their minds. Another possibility is that those with physical or mental limitations might be given simple jobs. For example, deaf individuals hired as mail handlers can be effective workers since they tend to be less affected by environmental distractions.

A Liberal Lacing of Praise and Recognition

"But no *pats* on the *post!*"

Which do you prefer to receive from your boss: A kick in the posterior or a pat on the back? The latter, I'd assume. One of the important needs that employees generally have is for *praise and recognition.* We already discussed a more sophisticated term, *positive reinforcement,* in a previous chapter. Consistent and sincere praise and recognition for performance have a significant effect on employees' QWL. Employees tend to be far more motivated when they feel that their efforts are recognized and appreciated.

Positive reinforcement can be given through words, touch, and a variety of actions, such as favorable glances and smiles. The way you listen to another person, for example looking at the person attentively, can likewise be a form of positive reinforcement.

Providing Well Pay

"You mean time off for time on?"

Excessive employee absenteeism can be a serious problem for many employers. As a means of discouraging absenteeism and tardiness, some organizations provide an extra reward through a program of **well pay** for those who do show up for work as expected. Under this proposal, workers who put in a given number of days without being absent or late are given an extra day off. For example, Parsons Pine Products, one of the principal manufacturers of mousetrap bases in the United States, found its absenteeism rate dropped 30 percent and tardiness to almost zero after the firm initiated a *well-pay* plan. Parsons gives an extra day's pay at the end of every month to workers who are punctual.[4]

Building Responsibility into Jobs

Should bosses risk letting them take risks?

Managers should not be afraid to empower their employees with the right to make **risk decisions.** Delegation, as we've learned, can aid employees in their growth and development, improve their QWL, and, especially important, free the manager for other important tasks.

Providing Child Care for Employees' Children

And baby makes three.

Off-the-job concerns can certainly affect an employee's on-the-job morale, and small children are a major concern of today's employees. A large proportion of the work force requires some sort of child-care facilities for their small children. An increasing number of organizations have begun to recognize that establishing on-site child-care centers has improved employee morale, reduced absenteeism and lateness, and reduced turnover. Alternatives to such on-site centers are financial aid for child care, maternity/paternity leave for expectant and/or new parents, and flexible work hours to allow for the care of a sick child. Johnson & Johnson is at the forefront of a growing movement among American companies to provide better support for employees with family problems.[5]

Modifying the Work Environment

Some managers improve the QWL of employees by modifying the work environment. This activity is a broad one and could be applied together with all of our suggestions for improving jobs. Wherever possible, *teams* or *work groups* should be used. Smaller groups tend to be more cohesive than larger ones. Team members are usually more productive when they can participate in choosing compatible workmates for their groups. With effective leadership, teams tend to improve work standards and accept new processes more readily. Further, many employees like teamwork since it provides for more variety of tasks as compared to repetitive jobs on typical assembly lines.[6]

Workers generally prefer some degree of *social contact* with other employees. The opportunity for conversation, therefore, tends to enhance morale, especially on repetitive jobs that don't require much mental concentration.

A GLOBAL GLANCE

Nothing Fishy Smelling About Skunk Works![a]

The skunk is a bushy-tailed little creature indigenous to the new world. The odor from its fetid defensive fluids has not been reputed to be one of humankind's favorite scents, yet the atmosphere and results created by so-called "skunk works" have been appreciated by many managers. Skunk works is another of those management concepts that was supposed to have been invented in the U.S. but—as with many management concepts—was effectively applied by Japanese managers some years ago.

Here's what you should know about skunk works: A skunk works approach utilizes small teams of talented knowledge workers who are provided with virtually all the resources and empowerment they need to function as a smooth-running team. Team members are free to make decisions without outside interference, just as a skunk's space is usually not invaded by anyone familiar with its odoriferous capabilities. Skunk works teams often develop new products and innovations in a relatively short time because their activities progress unfettered by traditional functional barriers and organizational bureaucracy. Senior management merely reviews and approves, but *only* at key milestones.

So . . . what do you think? Smell better than you expected? Do you sense that more American organizations in the future will also be working the skunk?

Would you please turn off that bloody elevator music!!

Music can be an effective morale builder in some circumstances, but the captive audience—the workers—should participate in determining the types of music to be played.

Regular *rest breaks* have been known for some time to have beneficial effects on productivity. Some firms have recently introduced voluntary *exercise breaks,* which can be a healthy source of enjoyment, especially for workers whose jobs don't require much in the way of physical exertion.

Designing the Workplace Ergonomically

Ergonomics is another term that you're likely to hear around management circles these days. Ergonomics basically is designing products and workplaces in a way that makes them more suitable for employees. Examples include designing handles of tools so that fatigue is lessened during their use, designing chairs that reduce back strain, providing employees with computer monitors that ease eyestrain, designing computer software that is more user friendly, and installing proper lighting and ventilation equipment.[7]

Ooh, my achin' back!

The changing nature of work is bringing more attention to designing workplaces ergonomically. For example, **video display terminals (VDTs),** those glare-producing screens for personal computers, word processors, and work stations, have become increasingly common in the workplace in recent years. The National Academy of Sciences estimates that there are more than 50 million Americans who work on computers, and millions more work in systems paced or propelled by computers.[8]

An outgrowth of the increased use of VDTs has been protests from employees who complain about catching a "terminal disease" that causes headaches, deteriorating eyesight, and various aches and pains. Some studies have even linked miscarriages to their use.

"I'm suffering from *mouse elbow!*"

The future is likely to bring about an increase in the concern for VDT-linked injuries. An affliction that is apt to become better known among office managers is **carpal tunnel syndrome (CTS),** also known as *repetitive strain injury (RSI),* an inflammation of the tendons, nerves, blood vessels, and ligaments around the hand, forearm, and shoulder. CTS is caused by several types of repetitive motions, such as those made in front of a VDT. Similar injuries have long been common among workers in manufacturing, food processing, health services, and crafts, jobs that typically require excessive amounts of tapping, gripping, or twisting motions.

CTS now accounts for more than one-half of all reported work-related injuries. As a result, pressure has been exerted by concerned groups to encourage the redesign of jobs and equipment to reduce the problem of CTS. Additional pressure has begun in state legislative

Computer terminal?
I can't see
any terminal.

bodies. For example, both New York's Suffolk County and the city of San Francisco passed laws (in 1989 and 1991, respectively) requiring companies to schedule breaks at regular intervals, provide adjustable computer furniture, and hold training classes on the safe operation of computer terminals. Although both laws were late overturned in the courts, observers believe that there will be additional efforts to pass laws of this nature by various states and cities.[9]

Providing Wellness Programs

Healthy bodies make
for healthy bottom
lines!

Many organizations are realizing the dollars-and-cents value of fitness programs to them and their employees. An increasing number of firms now refer to their fitness programs as **wellness programs,** since they have discovered that physically fit employees generally have better attitudes toward their jobs, are more productive, have lower absentee rates, are in better control of their weight, experience less stress, enjoy reduced chances of heart attacks, and have an enhanced sense of well-being.

Some firms are now using incentives to encourage employees to exercise vigorously. Johnson & Johnson, for example, developed a fit-

**A BOX
OF
INTEREST**

Is This Job Ever a *Pain*![b]

Carpal tunnel syndrome (CTS), an inflammation caused by repetitive motions such as exist when using VDTs, has become a concern of many organizations. How will you know if you're getting CTS? Symptoms include a feeling of numbness or tingling in your hands, or aching pains in your arms when you use a keyboard or a steering wheel. What can you do to prevent or reduce the effects of CTS? When typing, keep your arms parallel to the floor. Screens are often too high, causing neck strain. Ideally, the screen should be positioned about ten to twenty degrees below your eye level. Filters can be installed over screens to sharpen clarity and remove glare. Don't use office chairs with long armrests that prevent you from moving up close enough to your screen. In addition, don't pinch a phone between your cheek and shoulder while typing, since that can cause you to type at an awkward angle and put strain on your tendons. Also, take a short break about every fifteen minutes.

ness program called "Live for Life." The plan helps workers stop smoking, control weight, manage stress, learn about nutrition, and detect high blood pressure. The employees earn "Live-for-Life dollars" for each mile they run, each aerobic dance class they attend, and so on. These "dollars" are good for spending at a "Live-for-Life store," carrying such things as gifts and personal items.[10] Some companies even provide courts for basketball, tennis, and volleyball and running tracks, showers, and locker rooms. Some organizations pay a portion or all of the fees for those who sign on for wellness programs.

If your organization doesn't yet have one, try your own wellness program—gradually at first, especially if you are out of condition—and you may find that you are experiencing one of the most enjoyable "highs" of your lifetime. If exercise seems boring to you, take a look at the suggestions in Table 8.2 for making the activity more satisfying.

Does QWL Have Its Limitations?

Most managerial programs, such as QWL and job enrichment, have their positive attributes along with certain limitations. Professor Webber warns us of five limitations inherent in job enrichment (see Table 8.3).[11]

Furthermore, not all employees necessarily want their jobs enriched. Some individuals, for example, believe that they don't want added responsibility. Their attitude is something like, "I do an adequate job. All I want is my paycheck, thank you!" Managers can't really force something "good" like job enrichment on employees if their needs and attitudes are not in harmony with such programs.

We examined individual differences when we discussed needs and motivation. Each employee differs, as you recall, in the intensity of his or her achievement and security needs. Also, some employees don't feel

TABLE 8.2   Suggestions for Making Exercise a More Enjoyable Activity.

1. Try to schedule your exercise program for the same time each day so that it becomes a habit, rather than a chore.
2. Vary the location and types of exercise you do so that you don't become tired of doing the "same old thing."
3. Exercise with a friend, but don't let either of you make the activity a stress-inducing, competitive one. Running three miles in 20 minutes every other day, for example, is better for you than running three miles in 10 minutes daily.
4. Don't exercise to the point of misery and pain. Stop when it no longer feels good to you. However, try to build up your endurance with a program of no less than 20 minutes of continuous exercise at least three times a week.

TABLE 8.3   Limits of Job Enrichment.

Everything has
its limits.

1. Applicable only where workers are and feel under-utilized.
2. Not all workers feel frustrated.
3. Some workers don't desire greater challenge.
4. Some workers distrust management's expansion of their tasks.
5. Not a substitute for unpleasant working conditions or poor benefits.

a strong need for interpersonal relations. Some employees prefer simpler, not more complex, tasks. Nor, as we learned from our study of perception, will every employee perceive job enrichment programs in the same light. Some may distrust management's efforts along such lines.

INNOVATIVE WAYS TO WORK

Because of the changing nature of workers and technology, as well as management's desire to improve productivity and morale, many organizations in recent years have experimented with a wide variety of work-related innovations. Some managers are proud of their successes with certain programs, whereas others have quickly abandoned similar programs because of the belief that they weren't accomplishing desired objectives. Regardless of some of these bad experiences, there is a variety of additional modern techniques intended to improve the quality of work life. Some of these are discussed below.

Sharing Gains

A rapidly expanding technique for improving the quality of work life of employees is **gainsharing.** Also termed **production-based compensation plans,** gainsharing plans are defined as organizational change programs of employee involvement, with an organization-wide financial formula.

Psst . . . Hey, boss! Wanna buy a good idea?

In simple terms, gainsharing involves providing employees with periodic cash bonuses for developing ways in which the organization can enjoy cost savings. The payouts are related to financial cost-savings formulas and vary widely among organizations, ranging from 20 percent to as high as 100 percent of the value of the cost savings. Payout typically is made to employees on a monthly basis. In a gainsharing plan the employer attempts to communicate clearly to employees the state of the business, asks for employee ideas, and seeks to jointly solve problems related to such factors as product quality and productivity.

Many organizations—large and small, manufacturing and service—have found that gainsharing results in cost reductions, along with fewer grievances, improved morale, and a better work climate. Gainsharing programs have also brought about improved labor-management cooperation as a result of labor and management working closer together. Some of the firms that use gainsharing plans include Hewlett-Packard, General Motors, Ford, and USX.[12]

Flex Your Working Hours

Can you imagine showing up for work at almost any time you want and leaving your job early or late, depending on your own personal desires? Alternative work schedules, known by a variety of names, including **flextime, flexible working hours,** and **glide time,** exist in many firms throughout the world. The variable-working-hour concept was first introduced by a West German aerospace firm in 1967.

Basically, flexibility wipes out the 9-to-5 syndrome faced by many employees and enables workers to enjoy hours that more closely match their personal life-styles. Workers must still work a preestablished number of hours, say, 40 hours per week or 80 hours over a two-week period. But the major difference between flextime and a conventional system of work hours is that flextime gives employees the freedom to choose, within certain limitations and usually with advance notice given to their supervisors, what times they begin and end their jobs each day.

What good is it?   **Lots of Benefits.** What are the benefits of flextime? For one thing, it tends to reduce traffic congestion during rush hours in crowded urban areas, which in itself makes going to and returning from a job less hectic for the worker. But the benefits are more far-reaching than the mere alteration of traffic patterns. Individuals under flextime can *take care of family and other personal affairs* more easily, which tends to *reduce absenteeism and tardiness* in organizations. For example, employees with children can arrange their hours to coincide with babysitting or school requirements, and employees who are morning people can start work at a time when they are likely to be *more productive.*

Hey! How come I gotta stay?   **And Some Disadvantages.** Flextime is not without its shortcomings. Some firms have found that flextime *requires a more elaborate record-keeping system* for keeping track of employee working hours, which tends to increase administrative costs. Some supervisors have also complained about *greater difficulty in coordinating employees* who start at varying times. And *morale problems could increase,* rather than decrease, in organizations in which some employees are *not* permitted to participate in the program because of the nature of

TABLE 8.4   Major Types of Flextime Programs.

1. *Daily flextime, fixed lunch, and core time.* The employee works a full number of hours each day, typically 8.
2. *Daily flextime, flexible lunch.* The same as type 1, but the employee has more choice regarding lunch.
3. *Weekly flextime.* Employees have to work the core hours each day, but do not work a fixed number of hours per day. Instead, they must work a fixed number of hours per week.
4. *Monthly flextime.* This is similar to type 3, except the employee must work a certain number of hours per month, rather than per week.

their jobs. In general, however, many firms, including Hewlett-Packard, Control Data, and Metropolitan Life, have found that flextime has improved morale, increased productivity, and given employees a greater sense of control over their own lives. Table 8.4 summarizes the main types of flextime programs.

Four/Fortying It—Compressing Your Work Week

Something known as the **compressed work week** has become popular with some firms in recent years. A typical approach is for employees to work Monday through Thursday (4 days) for 10 hours per day (40 hours total). Many employees like having the 3-day weekend that a 4/40 approach allows.

"Ten hours a day? I'm not a manager!"

One variation of the 4/40 approach offered by Chevron Corporation enables employees to work eight 9-hour work days, followed by one 8-hour work day. This plan provides employees with every other Friday off. Employees, therefore, have a normal two-day weekend, the next weekend providing them with three days off.[13]

Will all employees warmly embrace a compressed work week? Of course not. An employee's personal needs and values would influence how he or she felt about it. For example, someone who has a number of personal outside interests or a weekend job might prefer to be free on Fridays, Saturdays, and Sundays. A parent without a partner, on the other hand, could find it difficult to arrange suitable child care for such extended hours. Professor Andrew DuBrin's summary of the principal advantages and disadvantages of the compressed work week appears in Tables 8.5 and 8.6.[14]

Flexplace—Home Is Where the Terminal Is!

Can you visualize walking to work in 30 seconds each morning without having to struggle with the rush hour traffic, the usual babysitter problems, and the decision about what to wear? Imagine what society

A 30-second commute!

TABLE 8.5   Possible Advantages of the Compressed Work Week.

1. Improved performance and productivity because of less warm-up and phase-down time
2. Improved morale because of more time for outside activities
3. Reduced absenteeism since personal matters can be attended to on the extra day off
4. Enhanced recruiting because many potential employees find the prospects of 4/40 to be alluring
5. Lowered costs for lunches, gasoline, tolls, and carfare, and less wear and tear on streets and highways
6. Extra hours of work can be scheduled on minishifts over the long weekend, allowing for efficient use of equipment
7. Reduction of unemployment because 4/40 eliminates the need for overtime, and additional workers can be hired for the 3-day minishifts

TABLE 8.6   Possible Disadvantages of the Compressed Work Week.

1. Complains of fatigue by many employees, with little time for rest and recuperation
2. Difficulties encountered by working parents in making suitable child care arrangements
3. Lowered productivity because of less effective service to customers, especially on the days when most workers are off
4. Concern that the 4/40 approach will lead to employee and union demands for a 4/32, thus increasing the cost of operations
5. Concern that employees are likely to socialize more on the job because the workday is longer
6. A large increase in moonlighting (taking second jobs), creating problems of dual allegiance for employees

would be like if larger numbers of workers could work at home. Less highway traffic would mean less pollution and less energy consumed by the vehicles that don't pull out of their garages.

Such a scheme may sound a bit farfetched, but a concept that has begun to receive attention is **flexplace,** that is, companies allowing some of their employees to work at home instead of in an office or plant. In a recent year, a study by Link Resources indicated that roughly 9 million Americans work at least part of the week at home. About 3 million of them are employed by organizations and work between 8:00 A.M. and 5:00 P.M.[15]

Thanks to modern electronic wizardry, such as the computer terminal, some firms already have initiated **telecommuting** flexplace programs (also called *teleworking*). Pacific Bell, for example, has over 1500 telecommuting employees. Bank of America and Safeco Insurance Company have started pilot flexplace programs.[16] Steve Coulter, Pacific Bell's area vice president for San Francisco, points out that although telecommuting is not suited to all jobs or work styles, some studies have shown that it reduces overhead costs and increases productivity.[17]

"Boss, I'm calling in sick today; I've got a 'terminal' disease!"

Advantages of Flexplace. Flexplace offers a number of advantages, especially when computers are used. It can help to resolve problems associated with occasional labor shortages, as in periods when there is a tight supply of programmers and data analysts. It can also give more people, such as individuals with disabilities or those with small children, the opportunity to work. A work-at-home parent can be present when the kids get home from school. Employees also have less supervision, lower work-related expenses, and more flexibility. The cost of their work space at home is tax deductible. Employers require less office space, thus reducing overhead costs. Productivity and accuracy have also been found to be higher among flexplace employees.

Home sweet office!

Some firms require that their work-at-home employees work set hours, such as 9:00 A.M. to 5:00 P.M. Others provide their flexplace employees with a combination of regular and flexible hours. For example, an employee may have regular hours from 9:00 A.M. to 11:30 A.M. and from 2:00 P.M. to 4:30 P.M., with an additional three hours work to be done at the convenience of the employee. The only requirement may be that the work be submitted by the opening of the office the next day.

Disadvantages of Flexplace. Working at home does have some disadvantages. Company loyalty may be lacking in the employee who "telecommutes" rather than actually commuting to a company location where he or she has interaction with other employees and a boss. Work-at-home employees have less opportunity to take part in discussions and meetings with other employees, thus stunting their "political growth" within the company. Employees at home must develop self-discipline if they are not to be distracted by family demands, gardening projects, or fatigue. Supervisors sometimes resist managing "invisible" workers. Trust of employees is essential for flexplace to succeed.

"I'm lonesome!"

Union officials are somewhat skeptical of the programs. They envision the likelihood of exploitation, with violations of child-labor, overtime, and minimum-wage legislation. A "home worker's" children, for example, could be stuffing envelopes in violation of child-labor laws. Union leaders further find that isolated workers are more difficult and expensive to organize.[18]

Of course, flexplace can't be readily adapted to all types of jobs. It's especially suited to those tasks requiring computer terminals. Nor do all employees want to work at home. Some people work as much for the social interaction they receive on the job as they do for the money. Perhaps flexplace should be applied only when both the employee and the boss want it and when the work does not require the presence of a supervisor.

Contingent Employment

Another growing trend in employment is the use of **contingent workers:** temporary, part-time, and leased employees, as well as independently-contracted workers. According to a Conference Board survey, the contingent work force has become one of the fastest-growing sectors of employment in the United States and Great Britain since the 1980s and now accounts for more than 25 percent of civilian jobs in each country. Almost one-third of the contingent work force in the United States had short hours out of economic necessity rather than personal choice.[19] Some of the major types of positions in which *temps* are in demand are clerical/receptionists, secretarial/word processing, accounting/financial, data processing, and engineering.[20]

"Oscar, I'm reviewing your work record.
Are you full- or part-time?"

SOURCE: From *The Wall Street Journal*
—permission, Cartoon Features Syndicate.

"Interim Assignments"—A License to Moonlight?[c]

American managers have taken the brunt of criticism for some years now for their lack of inclination to look to the long term as their counterparts in Japan are wont to do. However, it now appears that this criticism may not matter so much any more because, according to recent reports, U.S. executives might not have the opportunity to look to the long run even if they wanted to. Because of the cost-cutting, downsizing, restructuring, and "leaning and meaning" activities that organizations have been putting their employees through during the past decade, a new type of manager seems to be evolving. The "Organization Man" of the 1950s and 1960s appears to be in the process of being replaced by the migrant manager and freelance professional of the 1990s.

Companies like PepsiCo are somewhat typical of the flock. The firm announced in late 1991 that it would "rightsize" its organization and reduce management and administration at its Frito-Lay unit by 30 percent—which meant 1800 higher-level jobs eliminated. IBM announced in mid-1992 that it would reduce its personnel by 50,000 people.

So white-collar folk at companies like these are finding themselves in a new role, not unlike that of the migrant farm worker who picks strawberries for awhile at one farm or orchard and then moves on to pick at another. The corporate "lifer," at least during the recent periods of slow economic growth, seems to be a dying breed.

Because of the lack of security associated with many white-collar positions today, numerous managers have taken to moonlighting, often running their own companies on the side. Sometimes their activities compete directly with those of their employer. In some cases, moonlighting activities take place in broad daylight on company time and with company resources.

A Question of Ethics: Because organizations tend to provide less security for their managers these days, should it be considered unethical for a person to moonlight on company time and with company resources?

"I need a part-time lover!"

In the past, temporary work was uncommon for executives. However, the organizational trend toward downsizing and restructuring during the late 1980s and early 1990s resulted in an increasing number of managers who had been laid off and were able to acquire only part-time work. In fact, a new breed of temporary employment agency for "flexecutives"—managers and professionals—now exists. But the agencies don't like the term "temp," preferring, instead, the more professional sounding "interim assignments."[21]

Is the use of part-timers good or bad? The answer to this simplistic question depends on the values of the person answering it. The good-siders contend that part-time and temporary work is highly desirable *for individuals who either don't want or don't need full-time work,* such as retirees, parents, and those with other interests. We know that people work for a variety of reasons, money being only one of them. Some persons—such as *mommy trackers,* want to be able to spend more time at home with their young children. Other individuals have a variety of *personal interests,* such as reading, writing, and bicycling, that are difficult to pursue when a person is locked into a 9-to-5 job. A part-time position, or temporary assignments obtained through agencies such as Manpower, enable a fairly large segment of American society to meet such personal needs.

Other proponents of part-time and temporary work are employers who contend that their use enables organizations to be more flexible in hiring. For example, employers can more easily meet the short-term need for additional production workers or temporary fill-ins for vacationing employees without hiring new full-time employees who would be difficult to discharge if the work volume subsided. Further, the use of part-time and temporary workers has proven a way to *avoid layoffs and the negative publicity* they sometimes generate in the community. One electronics firm, Tektronix, has discovered a novel way to improve productivity and company loyalty—the firm obtains permanent employees from the ranks of existing temporary workers.

What's the other side of the story? The bad-siders argue that *company loyalty* is practically nonexistent among part-time and temporary workers. Critics add that *company productivity* suffers, since a firm's productivity is affected by the employee's lack of experience with the employing firm. *Part-time and temp employees,* it is also argued, *suffer* since they typically receive lower wages and get no medical insurance, retirement benefits, or job security from their positions. For example, the median hourly wage for part-time clerical workers is only 65 percent of that for similar full-timers. Some critics fear that the lower pay and lack of benefits are creating a large group of second-class workers in the United States. (Interestingly, some temporary hiring agencies do provide benefits for employees who work a minimum number of hours per year.)

Unions tend to oppose the trend toward part-time and temporary employment since such employees are much more difficult to organize, thus contributing to the declining membership in unions in recent years. The previous strength of unions resulted from organizing full-time production workers. Union officials also argue that *employers can more easily discharge such employees without just cause,* since part-timers typically cannot follow established grievance procedures.

As you can see, and as is usually the case, there is more than one side to the issue. Travelers, a large insurance company, appears to view the positive side and favors "recycled retirees," that is hiring on a part-time basis employees who have retired from the company. No orientation is necessary, so training costs are minimal. Further, the retirees tend to be more dependable and loyal than the occasional

Can part-time workers support families part-time?

So who's right?
Ça depends!

temp might be. About 250 retired temporaries work at Travelers during any given week.[22] On the other hand, some pessimists, such as economist Richard Belous, warn, "If we make the labor market flexible but don't also make the social welfare system flexible, there are going to be lots of people falling through the cracks."[23]

Twinning It

*Surprise! You have just
given a berth to twins!*

Another novel idea that has caught on in some occupations and is likely to become more common in the future is a practice referred to as **job sharing,** or **twinning.** Under this system two workers divide one full-time job. Not only are the hours split but so are salary and fringe benefits. Job sharing is still available mostly at the clerical level. Most companies do not permit supervisors to share jobs because of the problem of having people report to two bosses.

Those who especially favor the twinning concept are mothers and fathers who want to spend more time with their families or on other interests without losing income. Others who lean toward job sharing are older people who want to retire gradually, those with physical limitations, and students.

Although twinning has the drawback of doubling an employer's training and personnel costs, the overall benefits seem to outweigh any disadvantages. For one thing, employers can more easily *achieve affirmative action hiring goals* by tapping labor markets previously inaccessible. Another major advantage, according to some studies, is that part-time workers tend to approach their work with far *more energy and enthusiasm* and put in more than a half-day's work in a half-day's time. *Absenteeism also tends to be reduced* since one of the "twins" can cover for the other in the event of illness or other emergencies.

Twinning has become increasingly prevalent in such fields as teaching, library and laboratory work, the professions, and in government. Some states such as Wisconsin and Massachusetts, encourage twinning among government employees.

Flexible Benefits

*"I'll have one
of those . . .
and one of
those . . . and . . ."*

A growing number of organizations now offer employees a **cafeteria-style benefit program** (also termed a **flexible-benefit plan**), in which employees can pick and choose a combination of insurance and other options best suited to their personal desires and individual and family situations. In a flexible-benefit plan, there typically is a "core" range of benefits in addition to salary, including a contribution to a retirement plan. Employees can then select options up to the value of a set allowance. Benefits might include such alternatives as child care assistance or legal fees. More than 60 per cent of the top 100

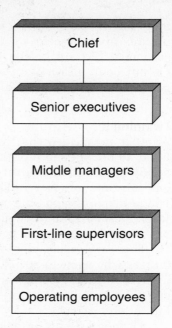

Figure 8.2 Traditional organizational structures.

American industrial companies are reported currently to offer flexible benefit programs to their employees.[24]

Many employees with grown children, for example, may feel less of a need for life insurance than employees with younger children. Others may prefer dental insurance over full medical insurance. Many employees like the feeling of being free to make their own choices among several benefit options. There is an inherent danger, however, that some employees with specific benefit needs may not recognize those needs at the time they select their benefits.

Providing Opportunities for Upward Assessment

Traditional managers have long believed that only bosses are entitled to assess the performance of their employees. The mere thought that employees should also have the right to appraise bosses tends to shake up the security of their managerial comfort zones. Contrary to such traditional beliefs, however, something called **bottom-up assessment** or **upward appraisal** has become increasingly common among American organizations.

Some organizations conduct bottom-up assessments on a one-to-one basis, that is, an individual employee answers a questionnaire related to the boss's performance, and both meet later to discuss the

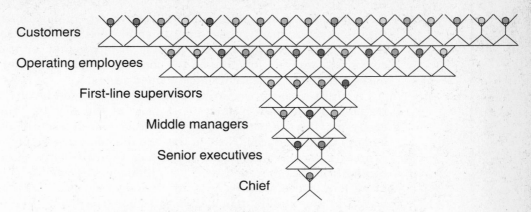

Figure 8.3 "Right-side-up" organizational structure.

findings. Another approach, which provides greater anonymity to individual employees, is for assessment to take place on a team basis, with a team facilitator preparing a summary of the findings for presentation to the manager at a follow-up team meeting.

Bosses who sincerely want to improve their leadership performance needn't feel threatened by the sessions. They should especially attempt to avoid any tendency to become defensive or adversarial toward employees who have expressed their real feelings. Sometimes seemingly insignificant employee comments can substantially improve a boss's relationship with employees. For example, a manager with a large book-retailing company discovered that he would occasionally turn and gaze out his office window when listening to a colleague who had dropped in to discuss something. The manager had no idea why he did it, nor was he aware of the negative impact the behavior was having on his employees. The upward appraisal system assisted him in breaking an offensive habit.[25]

"Hey, boss. Look at me. I'm over here!"

The "Right-Side-Up" Organization

Do you remember what the term *customers* means from our discussion of total quality management in Chapter 7? As you recall, in TQM vernacular *customers* means employees working inside the organization *and* purchasers of goods and services outside the organization. Management and quality analyst Phillip Richards feels quite strongly about the customer concept in TQM. Richards asserts: "Customers, including front-line workers, deserve their place at the top of the organization because without them everyone else would be looking for other employment."[26] Richards also suggests that the traditional organizational structure (see Figure 8.2), described by Max Weber in his classic writings on bureaucracy, is somewhat misleading. Richards feels that the traditional manner of portraying organizational structure is psychologically demeaning to employees. It fails to recognize that the employees who directly provide the goods and services to the customer—whether involved on the shop floor or the customer service desk—are the organization's most valued assets.

A **right-side-up organization,** therefore, would be one as illustrated in Figure 8-3. It shows customers at the very top, since they really provide the benchmarks for quality and determine over time what is to be produced. Next in line are the operating employees who *support* the customers. Such employees typically have more direct contact with purchasers than do the managers. *Supporting* the operating employees are the first-line managers who in turn are *supported by* the middle managers and senior executives. Upon careful analysis, it is not demeaning for the chief to appear on the bottom of the hierarchy, because he or she, not unlike Atlas in Greek mythology, carries the burden of the entire organization.

Of course, diagrams of an organization do not determine an organization's culture and success. However, if customers—both external purchasers and internal employees—can be convinced that management really values and needs their cooperation and assistance in the quest for continuous quality and that management truly supports them in the process, then positive customer participation in an organization's mission is more likely to exist.

You've Gotta Have Heart

Not all attempts at job enrichment, job enlargement, and innovative programs are successful. Some failures, however, are self-imposed. The ways in which new programs are introduced are as important as the programs themselves. Problems can develop when programs are poorly introduced or ill-timed as a result of the differing perceptions of organizational members. For instance, senior management may initiate a program that it believes will satisfy and motivate the workers. However, if the employees skeptically perceive the change as a management gimmick, the program is unlikely to succeed. Nor are all workers alike; some may not respond to programs in which others thrive.

Imaginative managers can develop many more innovations to make jobs more interesting, including temporary transfers and special projects. To be successful, however, job enrichment must have the *support of senior management* and likewise be *accepted by workers at all levels.* Considerable education of supervisors and employees is essential if programs are to succeed. Stumbling blocks exist when supervisors fear that such programs may threaten their own decision-making authority. Programs viewed by employees as deceptive management schemes designed solely to increase their work loads or

Without trust . . . ?

reduce the number of employees are also unlikely to succeed. A *climate of trust and understanding is essential* for the effective use of morale-building techniques.

SUMMARY

A major quality-oriented concern of managers today is that of initiating programs for improving the quality of work life (QWL). A number of these programs were discussed in the chapter, including vertical and horizontal loading, job enlargement, job rotation and cross-training, entry-level assignments, consistent positive reinforcement, well pay, building responsibility into jobs, child-care assistance, modifying the work environment, designing the workplace ergonomically, and wellness programs.

Most jobs have five core dimensions that are essential for job enrichment: *task variety, task identity, task significance, autonomy,* and *feedback.*

A number of innovative ways to work were also discussed. These included gainsharing, flexible working hours, the compressed workweek, flexplace, contingent employment, job sharing, and flexible benefits. The concept of the *right-side-up organization* was also presented.

Essential to the success of any or all of the programs that may be developed is *acceptance* by both workers and management, along with a *climate of trust and understanding* between them.

TERMS AND CONCEPTS TO REMEMBER

quality of work life (QWL)

job enrichment

core job dimensions

task variety

task identity

task significance

autonomy

feedback

performance appraisal interview

vertical loading

horizontal loading

video display terminals (VDT)

carpal tunnel syndrom CTS)

wellness program

gainsharing

prodution-based compensation
  plans

flextime (flexible working hours,
  glide time)

compressed work week

flexplace

telecommuting

job enlargement

job rotation

cross-training

multiskilling

well pay

risk decisions

ergonomics

contingent workers

job sharing (twinning)

cafeteria-style benefit program (flexible-benefit plan)

bottom-up assessment (upward appraisal)

right-side-up organization

QUESTIONS

1. What are the typical job characteristics that influence the quality of work life (QWL) of many employees?

2. Assume that you have been assigned the responsibility to develop a program intended to improve QWL in your particular field. What changes would you be likely to make?

3. Critically evaluate the following statement: "All individuals in organizations would prefer to have their jobs enriched."

4. What is *carpal tunnel syndrome?* Is there anything that can be done to avoid its symptoms?

5. What are the principal purposes of gainsharing? Has it been proven to be effective with organizations?

6. What is *flextime?* What are some of its principal advantages and disadvantages?

7. What are some of the benefits that result from job sharing, or twinning?

8. How would you feel about working for a company that uses the 4/40 approach?

9. What, in your opinion, is the reason why some union officials tend to oppose the use of flexplace (homework) and gainsharing instead of pay raises for their members?

10. In your opinion, does contingent employment have more in its favor or disfavor from the standpoint of the work force?

11. Can you think of any potential disadvantage to the cafeteria-style benefit program?

12. Why might some managers disapprove of a bottom-up assessment system?

13. What is the philosophy behind the *right-side-up* concept of organizational structure? How do you feel about it?

14. There have been surveys reporting that a large proportion of American workers are suspicious of management and have an "us-against-them" attitude. If this is true, what are the implications of the surveys for managers who desire to implement the TQM process or initiate a QWL program in their organizations?

APPLICATIONS

8.1 The Case of the Unenriched Retail Operations

Rosa Sierra had been in charge of customer service at the Big Valley Mall branch of All-Mart, a nationwide chain of discount department stores. Recently, she was promoted to assistant manager of All-Mart's Countrywood Center store. Her new duties include direct supervision of fifteen employees, among them cashiers and stock clerks. According to the grapevine, her predecessor, Benjamin Wassermann, was asked to resign because of both his inability to get along with others and the dismal record of mistakes in his area of responsibility.

Rosa believed she could make substantial improvements, although she knew that doing so wouldn't be easy. Wassermann's manner had created distrust of management, bitterness, and low morale among the employees. She reasoned, however, that good supervision would make a significant difference. What's more, Rosa felt she already had an important advantage going for her: The salary and benefits at All-Mart were better than those offered by other retailers in the community. Rosa was knowledgeable about company operations and therefore was confident that a fair and friendly supervisory style would turn things around. Her major objectives were to reduce the high employee-turnover rate the store had experienced during Wassermann's reign and to encourage greater employee attention to detail as a means of reducing the excessive number of mistakes that were plaguing All-Mart's Countrywood location.

During the first few months in her new position, Rosa had some success in reducing errors, but accuracy remained far below acceptable standards. Furthermore, absentee and tardiness rates actually increased, and two additional employees will be quitting next week.

Rosa has decided to solicit some employee input regarding the problems at the store. She is requiring each employee to submit a written report to her within two weeks explaining the excessive absenteeism, tardiness, and errors that have been occurring.

Questions

1. What indicators of low morale are apparent at the Countrywood Center All-Mart?

2. Why haven't Rosa's expectations—that a "fair and friendly" supervisory style would solve the problems—been confirmed?

3. What is your evaluation of Rosa's techniques for diagnosing the problems at the store? What techniques can you suggest that might bring about improved results?

8.2 A "Classless" Society at Swindon[27]

Honda, the Japanese automobile maker, has a manufacturing complex located in Swindon, a town about eighty miles west of London, England. There is a certain degree of uniformity in the appearance of the organization's employees since all 845 employees, from the receptionist to the president of Honda Motor Europe, wear standardized overalls at work.

Although employees are assigned to specific jobs, anyone in the organization may have to fill in on the production line when necessary, even the plant manager. No person in the plant is considered too senior or exempt for any reason from helping out on any task no matter how mundane it may be. The plant manager has neither an office nor a secretary, nor do any managers in the plant. There are no reserved parking spaces. Everyone eats in the same lunchroom and uses the same changing rooms. There are no position descriptions. No one is classified as a subordinate, worker or director—only "associates." Production workers work in teams of four. There are also fifty-two "Honda Circles," which are actually continuous improvement teams of six persons who meet regularly for the purpose of developing ideas for improvement in such areas as training, safety, and productivity.

Andrew Jones, the plant manager, contends, "Teamwork means that we reject class differentiation and job demarcation. We don't accept anyone as being more important than anyone else. If we are recruiting at a senior level, that recruit spends at least one month on the shop floor. So if you want high status, a secretary, and an expensive desk to keep everyone at a distance—don't come and work here."

In 1990, there was an intensive campaign by engineering unions in Great Britain to get domestic companies to move from a 40-hour work week to 39. Swindon's Honda employees were told that they could have even more and go from a 40 to 37-hour work week—without preconditions. Management reminded the employees that they were being given a 5.1 percent shorter work week at the same rate of pay. According to Jones, employees were asked, "Will you please make up the difference?" Jones asserts that ideas poured forth from employees with hundreds of small suggestions on ways work and efficiency could be improved.

In addition, working times were modified on Fridays for the two shifts so that the second shift could begin the weekend by 6:30 P.M. at the latest rather than the usual bewitching—but not so desirable—hour of midnight.

Questions

1. How do you feel about the so-called classless society that exists at the Swindon manufacturing complex? Do you feel that everyone would like to work in a similar environment? Why or why not?

2. Which factors that influence the quality of work life, as discussed in the chapter, appear to be present in the automobile manufacturing complex at Swindon?

3. Does the organizational structure at the plant seem to be traditional, "right-side-up," or a variation of the two? Explain.

4. In your opinion, why didn't production decline as a result of reducing the work week by three hours per person?

8.3 The Child-Care Dilemma

Bobbie Ann Clark burst through the front door of Medcheck, Inc., out of breath, her coat half unbuttoned, and her uncombed hair flying in all directions. She glanced frantically at the clock—it read 10:35 A.M.—as she punched one of the four flashing buttons on her ringing desk telephone. "Rene is going to have my head when she finds out I got to work late again," Bobbie thought as she took a call from an annoyed nursing home manager who had been trying to reach her since 9:00.

Rene Demetris, Bobbie Ann's supervisor, watched Bobbie's whirlwind entrance with dismay. Bobbie Ann was a valued employee at Medcheck, a fifty-person firm that reviewed medical claims forms for insurance companies to see that the charges submitted for reimbursement were reasonable and customary. Bobbie Ann examined claims fairly and thoroughly and, until recently, had had the lowest error rate in the company. Moreover, she was adept both at handling telephone inquiries from insurers and health care providers and at working with complex computer programs.

During the past couple of months, however, Bobbie Ann's behavior on the job had changed. She frequently arrived at work late or departed early, and her lunch breaks were stretching into the middle of the afternoon. Rene had also learned that Bobbie had agreements with several colleagues to cover for her absences by, in effect, splitting her work. It seemed to Rene that Bobbie Ann was trying to set her own hours, which did not conform to Medcheck's official 9-to-5 workday. Clearly, the time had come for a talk.

Rene asked Bobbie Ann to join her in her office. "It all began when the babysitter quit," Bobbie answered with a sigh when Rene asked about the erratic comings and goings. "First, I tried placing my son, Buddy, in a day-care center, but the only center that had room for him closes promptly at 5:30 P.M., and I couldn't get there in time to pick him up. That's why I was leaving the office early for a while. I knew I couldn't keep that up, though, so I made arrangements with a woman who watches four or five children at her house. The problem was that she lives way over in Brookdale; by the time I drove there to leave Buddy and headed back to Medcheck, it was already 9:00 A.M.

"When I realized that plan wasn't going to work out, either, I started to look for a new babysitter to stay with Buddy at home. The phone calls and interviews meant that I had to take extra-long lunch hours. Now I have a new babysitter, one Buddy and I like very much, but she has two children of her own in school, and they both came down with the flu last week. She's had to stay home with them while they're sick, and for days I've had to spend half the morning running Buddy around to whichever friend or relative can look after him for a few hours.

"Rene, I like it here at Medcheck, and I want to do a good job and follow company rules. But I love my son, too, and I want to do what's right for him. I'm at my wit's end with child-care problems. I firmly believe that a more flexible work schedule or some other alternative way of doing things is the only solution."

Rene promised that she would think about what Bobbie Ann had said—and she did, most of the day and all evening. Many of Rene's friends had similar difficulties. Moreover, Rene knew that as a single mother, Bobbie Ann needed to keep her full-time job and had less support to fall back on when problems arose. Rene was fully sympathetic. Still, she wondered what might happen if she allowed Bobbie a flexible work arrangement of some kind. How, for example, would Bobbie's co-workers react? Would it be fair to the men in the company? How would it affect the way she supervised employees? Could she sell the idea of flexibility to Medcheck's management? Rene went to sleep that night unsure what to do.

Questions

1. What would you do if you were in Rene Demetris's place? Explain the pros and cons of your decision.

2. If you were in favor of a flexible work arrangement in this case, what arguments would you use to persuade top management to adopt it? If you were not in favor of such an arrangement, what arguments would you use to support your position?

3. Is fairness an issue in flextime and similar arrangements?

4. How might Rene's supervisory methods and style have to change

if Bobbie Ann, and perhaps a number of her co-workers, adopted flextime, job sharing, telecommuting, or other nontraditional ways of working?

NOTES

1. Richard E. Walton, "Criteria for Quality of Working Life," in *The Quality of Working Life, Vol. 1,* eds. Louis E. Davis and Albert B. Cherns (New York: Free Press, 1975), pp. 91–97.

2. J. R. Hackman and G. R. Oldham, *Work Redesign* (Reading, MA: Addison-Wesley, 1980), pp. 77–80.

3. Norm Alster, "What Flexible Workers Can Do," *Fortune/International Edition,* February 13, 1989, pp. 36–39.

4. "Well Pay—Bonuses for Just Showing Up," *Time,* August 7, 1978.

5. Martin Dickson, "Dealing the Cards for Happy Families," *Financial Times,* April 22, 1992, p. 13.

6. "Management Discovers the Human Side of Automation," *Business Week,* September 29, 1986, p. 72; and Bob Shallit, "GM Tries Team Concept Near LA," *Contra Costa Times,* October 27, 1986, p. 19.

7. Stan Kossen, *Supervision, 2nd ed.* (St. Paul, MN: West Publishing Co., 1991), p. 500; and Diane Summers, "Software Suitability: The Human Factor, *Software at Work/Financial Times,* Autumn 1991, p. 25.

8. Bob Baker, "Computers Bring Stress, Job Isolation," *Contra Costa Times,* June 23, 1991, p. C–1.

9. Pamela Nakaso, "Pressure Mounts for Safe VDT's," *San Francisco Examiner,* October 23, 1990, p. C–1; Arlee C. Green, "VDT Workers Win Measure of Protection," *AFL-CIO News,* January 7, 1991, pp. 1–8; and Catherine Peckingham, "Ergonomics: Work-Related Illnesses," *Financial Times,* October 5, 1992, p. viii.

10. Brenda C. Coleman, "Workplace Fitness Programs Found to Be Effective," *Contra Costa Times,* February 23, 1986, p. 18D.

11. Ross A. Webber, *To Be a Manager—Essentials for Management* (Homewood, IL: Richard D. Irwin, 1981), p. 310.

12. Michael Shroeder, "Watching the Bottom Line Instead of the Clock," *Business Week/International Edition,* November 7, 1988, p. 88.

13. As related to the author by Donald Ledwith, a manager with Chevron Corporation.

14. Adapted from Andrew J. DuBrin, *Personnel and Human Resource Management* (New York: Van Nostrand, 1981), p. 254.

15. Ellen Graham, "Flexible Formulas," *The Wall Street Journal,* a special section on "Managing Change in the Workplace," June 4, 1990, p. R8; and Della Bradshaw, "Banking on Flexibility," *Financial Times,* May 6, 1993, p. 12.

16. Joyce Hedges, "Telecommuting Gets Legislative Boost," *Contra Costa Times,* June 10, 1991, p. 2–E.

17. Kathleen Sullivan, "Notions of Work Schedules Shifting," *San Francisco Examiner,* October 27, 1989, B–1.

18. "Labor Department Scuttles Homework Ban," *AFL-CIO News,* November 19, 1988, pp. 1, 7; and Ken Barcus, "Debate Over Doing Industrial Work at Home Heats Up Again," *Christian Science Monitor,* October 21, 1986, p. 5.

19. Andrew Mollison, "Work Force Shifts Toward Part-timers," *The Stars and Stripes,* November 20, 1991, p. 18; and David Goodhart, "Pleasing Most People Part of the Time," *Financial Times,* March 4, 1993, p. 12.

20. Bruce Nussbaum, "I'm Worried About My Job!" *Business Week,* October 7, 1991, pp. 94–104.

21. "USA Snapshots—Where Temps Are in Demand," *USA Today / International Edition,* November 8, 1989, p. 20.

22. See note 15.

23. Robert Kuttner, "The Labor Market is a Lot Looser Than It Looks," *Business Week /International Edition,* March 27, 1989, p. 10.

24. Andrew Jack, "Why It Can Pay To Offer a Choice," *Financial Times,* August 5, 1991.

25. Fiona Thompson, "Keeping Bosses Up to the Mark," *Financial Times,* February 10, 1992, p. 6.

26. Phillip Richards, "Right-Side-Up-Organization," *Quality Progress Magazine,* October 1991, pp. 95–96.

27. Adapted from John Griffiths, "Honda Reaches Accord in UK," *Financial Times,* November 9, 1992, p. 8.

BOX NOTES

a. John D. Trudel, "Tales from the Skunk Works," *Electronic Designs,* September 26, 1991, p. 54.

b. Adapted from "Spotting Symptoms," *USA Today/ International Edition,* June 28, 1989, p. 7.

c. Adapted from Bruce Nussbaum, "I'm Worried About My Job!" *Business Week,* October 7, 1991, pp. 94–104.

EXPERIENTIAL EXERCISE

What Dimension? Rotten to the Core—Or Enriched?

Review the core dimensions of jobs discussed in the chapter, then analyze the importance of each dimension to you. In the column titled "Desired Dimensions," rank how important each dimension is to you in any job you might hold, not your current job. Rank them in order of importance from 1 (the most significant) to 5 (the least significant). In the "Existing Dimensions" column, rank each dimension based on what their current strength seems to be on your existing job. Compare the two columns. How do you account for any differences that might exist? What specifically might be done to modify (enrich) your existing job so that it would be more satisfying to you?

Dimensions	Desired Dimensions	Existing Dimensions	Difference
Task variety	_____	_____	_____
Task identity	_____	_____	_____
Task significance	_____	_____	_____
Autonomy	_____	_____	_____
Feedback	_____	_____	_____

Part Three

Constraints on Organizational Performance

CHAPTER 9   The Dynamics of Change

CHAPTER 10   Cultural Diversity in the Workplace

CHAPTER 11   Organizational Challenges Faced by Older Workers and Those With Disabilities

CHAPTER 12   Problems of Substance Abuse

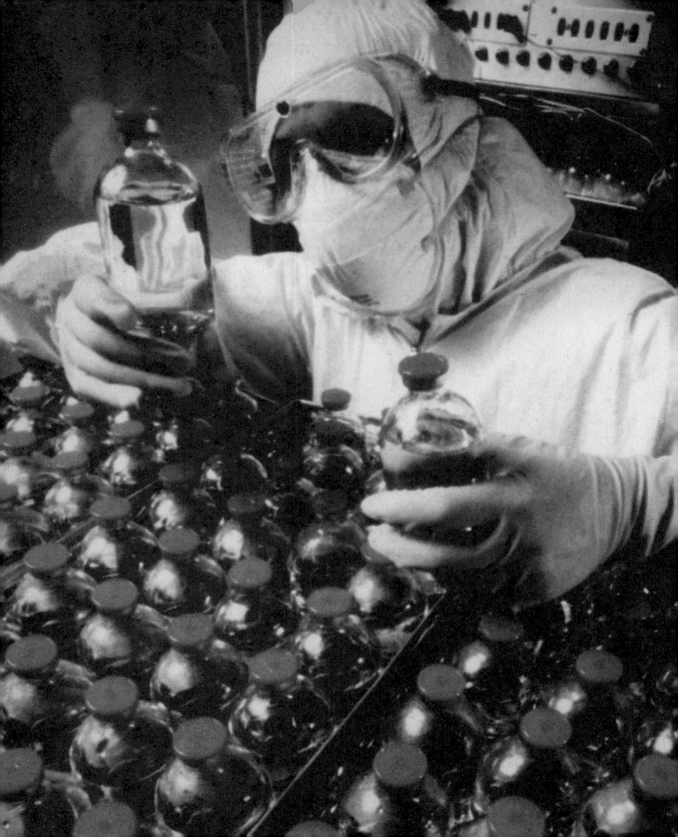

CHAPTER 9

The Dynamics of Change

*There's No
Progress Without Change*

**When you finish this chapter,
you should be able to:**

1

Explain the importance of managers anticipating
the need for change before crises arise.

2

List and describe the major causes of employee resistance to change.

3

Restate in your own words nine suggestions for managing change
more effectively.

4

Describe the nature and use of *organization development (OD)*
in effecting organizational change.

5

Trace the sequence of activities involved in *management by objectives (MBO)*.

> It is only an error in judgment to make
> a mistake, but it shows infirmity of character to
> adhere to it when discovered.
>
> *Christian N. Bovee*

> *Plus ça change, plus c'est la même chose.*
> (The more things change, the more they stay just as they were.)
>
> *Alphonse Karr*

"I just don't understand those jerks upstairs. First they tell us to drop everything—that job 4114 has to be done by Friday, and now they tell us drop job 4114 for now and get out job 4117 by Friday. When are those management people ever going to make up their minds?"

Attitudes like this are not particularly uncommon among employees in organizations. Introducing and administering change is probably one of the most difficult and challenging tasks managers must face, since employees, regardless of their positions or education, tend to resist alterations to their work environment. However, the administration of change is probably one of the most *important* tasks managers face, since conditions in the world of work seldom remain static. The sage Greek philosopher Heraclitus once said, "There is nothing permanent except change." He went on to declare, "You cannot step twice into the same river." One of his wise Greek friends, Cratylus, added, "And you could not step even *once* into the same river!" These are fairly abstruse remarks, so reread them if they didn't make sense immediately.

This chapter will introduce you to some of the principal challenges associated with any attempt to modify processes within organizations. This chapter is divided into five major sections:

1. The effects of change
2. The tendency to resist change
3. The effective introduction of change
4. The use of organization development to effect change
5. The use of management by objectives (MBO) to effect change

How are the words of Heraclitus and Cratylus related to the world of work?

THE EFFECTS OF CHANGE

Unfortunately, change often occurs only *after* managers recognize that conditions are in a state of crisis. A more rational and usually far less costly approach is for leaders to attempt to *anticipate* the need for change and to develop creative innovations *before* serious problems evolve.

The Need for Anticipation

Far too frequently, managers in organizations haven't set aside the time necessary for analyzing changing conditions or attitudes and have suddenly found themselves in the middle of severe complications. Managers, as we have noted, must learn to delegate routine matters so that they have time for planning necessary changes. The conditions that lead to poor morale can then be anticipated and prevented.

There is something of a paradox between the need for *continuity* and the necessity for *change* in organizations. For example, customers and employees usually prefer feelings of continuity in their lives, since such feelings enable them to have faith that events in the future will unfold in a predictable manner. Customers hope that a continued supply of materials at comparable prices will be available. Employees want their paychecks to be secure so that they will be able to continue to purchase the items they want and need.

However, in the real world conditions seldom remain static. Change is a basic part of any entity's existence. Work environments are continually modified. New production processes regularly are introduced. Organizational restructuring sometimes occurs. These are the types of activities that tend to upset some aspects of an organization's equilibrium and continuity.

Why should management anticipate the need for change?

Whenever possible, the need to change with the times (or even before!) should be anticipated, and management should attempt to implement these changes before the crisis state is reached. Otherwise, serious organizational behavior difficulties can result.

ATTITUDES AND BEHAVIOR IN THE FACE OF CHANGE

Why learn about the concept of change?

Regardless of our attitudes toward change, the likelihood of our having any success in preventing it is negligible. A safe prediction is that change *will* continue to take place all around us. Perhaps more rational than the attempt to prevent the unpreventable, therefore, would be the attempt to learn more about the change so that we can deal more adequately with its effects.

Why do so many individuals tend to fear and resist alterations in their environment? In the next section we will attempt to answer this question by examining some of the factors that commonly retard or obstruct the introduction of change. These factors are listed in Table 9.1.

Personal Attitudes

Change, of course, doesn't affect everyone in the same way. How individuals respond to particular changes is significantly influenced by

TABLE 9.1   Major Factors That Obstruct the Introduction of Change.

- Personal attitudes
- Training and environment
- Financial reasons
- Alterations in one's social life and status
- Habits
- Lack of recognition of need
- Fear of uncertainty
- Fear of change
- Lack of trust
- Myths

How is response to change influenced by personal attitudes?

their personal attitudes. Some individuals thrive on change whereas others react negatively to the mildest modification, even when it is beneficial. In general, people operate in a state of equilibrium. When this equilibrium is upset, there is a *tendency to resist the change.*

Sometimes individuals balk at change because they don't want to exert what they feel to be the *extra effort* necessary to learn new things. For example, let's assume that Lois De Domenico, an office manager, wants to surprise her assistant, Richard Kiwata, by loading the latest version of IBM's OS/2 operating system into his desktop computer. De Domenico believes that OS/2 surpasses Microsoft's current version of Windows in advanced features. However, Kiwata, who feels completely confident and comfortable with the existing version of Windows, may not be at all happy about his boss's attempt to improve his world of bits and bytes.

"But I love change . . . except when I have to change."

Training and Environment

Another significant influence on an individual's reaction to change is his or her background. According to some child psychologists, the first six years of a child's life are highly formative years that determine most of his or her later attitudes. *Religious and educational training* are a significant part of young children's backgrounds, both of which influence their perception and attitudes toward new and different experiences.

Does previous training always cause a negative reaction to change?

Like training, environment influences perception, which in turn affects people's attitudes toward any changes they may confront. For example, *leadership* is a part of the employees' *environment.* Consequently, the style of leadership received by employees can influence their attitudes toward the modification of work procedures.

Financial Reasons

Workers may not work for bread alone, but a major cause of their resistance to change is the *fear of losing their jobs,* their primary source of *income.* For example, when new and more efficient processes are introduced, or senior management announces plans for organizational restructuring, workers sometimes perceive the changes as a threat to their job.

Why might changes appear to threaten the pocketbook?

In some instances employees feel so threatened by changes that they attempt to sabotage new processes or products. There are situations, however, when an employee's fears are unfounded. In such cases, employee resistance to change can be lessened if the change is introduced with greater sensitivity by managers. Effective ways to introduce and manage change will be discussed later in this chapter.

Alteration in One's Social Life and Status

A result of change that is easily overlooked by managers is its effect on the *social life of employees*. For example, assume that you work in the personnel department of an organization and have been responsible for training new employees for the past three years. The head of your department recently decided to rotate work assignments among the various department members to "enrich" their jobs. You've been assigned to a position that consists of issuing parking permits and keys, assigning lockers, and making certain that the coffee break areas are amply stocked with supplies.

But . . . what will my neighbors think?

Some department members might welcome the change. However, many of your personal friends were aware of your previous responsibilities, and you perceive the change as a reduction of your **status;** that is, the perceived social ranking that you feel you have relative to your fellow employees. Sometimes seemingly insignificant changes can affect the self-esteem of employees or their standing with their co-workers, families, and friends. A person's *self-image* can be threatened by certain changes.

Some organizational changes require employees to move to a different community. Having to uproot one's family can influence an employee's morale, especially in the case of **dual-career families,** households in which both spouses have well-established positions with organizations. The wife or husband may have to give up her or his job to enable the other spouse to accept the new position. Furthermore, children must transfer to new schools, and the entire family must leave its friends behind and cultivate new acquaintances. To some, such situations are exciting and challenging; to others they are threatening.

Other types of changes can break up established patterns of *social interaction* or *conversation* on the job. A change from benchwork to assembly-line production, for example, might result in the elimination of an informal communications system among the employees. Such a change might be resented by some workers.

Habits

Have you ever tried to kick the smoking habit?

Do you ever feel you're in a rut? Do you travel to work or school in precisely the same way each day, after hurriedly devouring a break-

EuroDisney at a Loss Over the French Reaction to Its Theme Park[a]

What a time the Walt Disney Company had in its attempt to transplant a previously successful formula to a different cultural setting in France with a theme park called EuroDisney. The French have seldom been noted for their willingness to conform to other countries' standards. And this time was no different. French intellectuals confirmed this reputation by calling EuroDisney "a cultural Chernobyl," "a terrifying giant's step toward world homogenization," and "a horror made of cardboard, plastic and appalling colors, a construction of hardened chewing gum and idiotic folklore taken straight out of comic books written for obese Americans."

Whew! Quite a reaction, eh? And if that weren't enough, Disney's management had a challenge trying to get its European employees to accept the "EuroDisney look." The company has long had a strict dress code. It stipulates that employees must wear "proper undergarments"; that hair must not be bleached, tinted, frosted, or streaked; that moustaches and beards are not permitted; that "due to close contact with guests and fellow cast members, the use of a deodorant or antiperspirant is required"; and that "sunglasses are a block to interpersonal communication with the guests and should be avoided when possible." The length of fingernails and hair is limited. Staff are further told that "as a condition of your continued employment with EuroDisney, you are responsible for maintaining an appropriate weight and size."

Disney has had a Midas-like touch in the good old U.S. of A. However, in France the company had to weather harsh pre-opening disputes with French unions over its dress codes and with contractors over construction fees. Then the company was hit with a symbolic protest by French truckers and farmers who tried to block access to the park. As a result of less-than-expected attendance, especially by the French themselves, EuroDisney had to close one hotel and experienced a net loss during its first two years of operations.

fast identical to the one you ate the day before? **Habits,** those activities that we perform unconsciously as a result of frequent repetition, can make life less threatening and more comfortable. Sometimes, however, we become so accustomed to doing things in a particular manner that we fail to recognize that there may be better ways.

For example, many organizations require their field personnel to submit regular written reports to their managers. Over time new forms are developed that may partially overlap or even duplicate the older forms. The coincidence sometimes goes unnoticed. Employees who question their superiors about the necessity of such duplication may be told, "Well, we've always done it that way." Even when forms or processes are improved, they are often resisted—the old way usually seems more comfortable and predictable.

Here's a tricky example of how habits can influence our thinking and actions. Complete the sentence, "Never buy a pig in a _____." Your answer should be *poke,* which is an old southern expression for *bag.* Now quickly read and fill in the following sentences.

Don't poke the pig!

1. Never buy a pig in a _____.
2. A person with a cigarette will _____.
3. A person without money is _____.
4. A funny story is a _____.
5. A popular soft drink is a _____.
6. The white of an egg is the _____

How did you do? The first answer, as you already know, is *poke.* Number 2 is *smoke,* number 3 is *broke,* number 4 is *joke,* and number 5 is *Coke.* What was your answer to number 6? Did you say *yolk?* That's great . . . but you're wrong! If you said *yolk* you helped to illustrate the tendency we all have to get into habits that are difficult to break. Think again. Is the white of an egg really the yolk? Not at all; the yolk is actually yellow, and the white part is called the *albumen.* Can you see how habits can make it difficult for us to accept something different?

I was just yoking!

Lack of Recognition of Need—The "Boiled-Frog Syndrome"

Sometimes the need for change is hard to recognize because of the gradual way in which certain factors change. The **boiled-frog syndrome** helps to explain this concept. According to neurobiologist Robert Ornstein of Stanford University, if a frog were put in a pot of water and the water heated up slowly, the frog would not detect the gradual change in temperature and would thus remain in the pan

Or would you rather be a lobster?

until it boiled to death.[1] Sometimes managers, not unlike our ill-fated frog, are so preoccupied with day-to-day pressures that they don't see a gradual deterioration of certain conditions, such as employee morale, and therefore don't recognize the need for modifying existing conditions until after a crisis has erupted.

Fear of Uncertainty

Why do people tend to fear the unknown?

Fear of uncertainty is probably one of the basic causes of resistance to change. Change begets uncertainty, an uncomfortable situation to say the least. And uncertainty sometimes begets pressure to prevent change. Carefully read these words of warning by David McCord Wright from *Democracy and Progress:*

> From freedom and science
>   came rapid growth and change.
> From rapid growth and change
>   came insecurity.
> From insecurity
>   came demands which ended growth.
> Ending growth and change
>   ended science and freedom.

Employees often fear change because they don't understand how the change might affect them; they fear, quite naturally, the uncertainty associated with the change. For example, the cost-cutting efforts by General Motors created many uncertainties in the minds of its employees in 1992. The company's head at the time, Robert Stempel, announced in mid-1992 that additional plant closings would take place, but he refused to name any plant or say exactly when the plants would be closed. Fourteen of twenty-one GM plants were already scheduled to be closed and 74,000 employees cut by 1995, but the closure of at least four more assembly plants was yet to be announced. A few months later Stempel himself was sacked by a "boardroom coup" because of directors' impatience with Stempel's slowness in carrying out restructuring plans. Directors decided in late 1992 to eliminate a total of 120,000 jobs during the decade.[2] Imagine how employees in the remaining plants probably felt, wondering how the company's restructuring activities would affect their own jobs. Job security became a major issue to GM's employees in the 1990s.

The fear of uncertainty can also create difficulty in making risk decisions. There is the human tendency to prefer the *certainty of misery* over the *uncertainty of pleasure.* For example, some people will remain in undesirable situations that are familiar to them rather than risk changes that fail to provide them with a "guaranteed" result.

Insurance companies have capitalized on the fear of the unknown and the desire to reduce uncertainty. A businessperson who buys a building, for example, acquires a risk. There's the chance, or fear, that the building may be destroyed by fire or some other peril. The payment of a *certain* number of dollars—the insurance premium—transfers the burden of risk to the insurance company. In the event of fire, the businessperson is reimbursed for roughly the amount of the loss. Thus, the fear of uncertainty has been reduced.

Fear of Change

Is fear frightening?

The *fear* of change can sometimes be as upsetting as the change itself. In an organization, for example, the rumor of an impending layoff could cause premature resignations or other adverse reactions. People frequently react more to what they *feel* the effects of a change will be than to the change itself.

While co-editors of a U.S. Navy ship's newspaper, another young sailor and I once started a near panic by publishing a special April Fools' Day issue. Each article began with exaggerated statements about imminent changes and ended by saying that the article was false. Apparently many readers didn't glance at much beyond the first few paragraphs of each article. One article, for example, falsely reported that the ship, which seldom left its berth at New London, Connecticut, was to change its home port to Reykjavík, Iceland. Although few of the sailors were acquainted with Reykjavík, near panic ensued. Some individuals went so far as to cancel their upcoming weddings. One fellow was even in tears after reading the article.

President Franklin D. Roosevelt touched on this type of reaction in his inaugural address in 1933 when, referring to the numerous and recent bank failures, he asserted, "The only thing we have to fear is fear itself."

Lack of Trust

Resistance to change is likely to be significant in work environments where employees don't trust their managers. And conversely, managers are not likely to ask for employee participation in effecting change if they don't trust their subordinates. Theory X managers, as we've learned in a previous chapter, tend to make decisions themselves, which is likely to increase resistance to change.

The Effect of Myths

Why do myths make some people's lives easier?

Superstitious beliefs, or myths, can cause resistance to change in some individuals. For example, during the civil rights movement of the 1960s and 1970s, people who believed that particular ethnic groups were naturally lazy or unable to acquire skills resisted moves to integrate members of those groups into the work force. Their fear of change was exemplified by the construction workers from Seattle and Tacoma, Washington, who marched on the state capitol in Olympia in the late 1960s to protest the hiring of black trainees on public projects—all the while sporting tiny American flags on their hard hats!

The fear of *AIDS (Acquired Immune Deficiency Syndrome)* and *HIV (Human Immunodeficiency Virus)* has caused near panic among some Americans in recent years. (AIDS is a disease that reduces a person's natural resistance to certain other diseases. HIV is a virus that may lead to AIDS.) Some parents have demanded that children with AIDS be prohibited from attending schools with nonafflicted children. Many employers have refused to hire people known to have AIDS. Although some fears are genuine, many medical researchers have asserted that much of the public's attitudes are filled with myths and misinformation related to the ways in which AIDS is transmitted. The topic of AIDS will be discussed in greater depth in Chapter 11.

Another example of ungrounded belief existed in the bindery of a large printing plant where a worker operating a large paper cutter

"Never mind the facts of life! Learn all you can about the myths of life."

SOURCE: From *The Wall Street Journal*—permission, Cartoon Features Syndicate.

refused to use the safety feature designed to protect the operator's fingers. The man argued that he had faith that God would watch over him and protect him while he was operating the machine and, therefore, he didn't have to use the safety device. One day the cutter amputated his right hand.

President John F. Kennedy skillfully summarized the concept of belief in myths when he declared:

> The great enemy of the truth is very often not the lie—deliberate, contrived and dishonest—but the myth—persistent, persuasive, and unrealistic. Too often we hold fast to the clichés of our forebears. We subject all facts to a prefabricated set of interpretations. We enjoy the comfort of opinion without the discomfort of thought.[3]

THE EFFECTIVE INTRODUCTION OF CHANGE— CHANGE MANAGEMENT

How can change be introduced more effectively?

Now let's turn to the crux of the matter—the way in which change can be introduced effectively. We've already learned that many individuals have a tendency to resist change. Therefore, **change management,** that is, the manner in which managers introduce change, regardless of how ideal their intentions may be, largely determines the success of their efforts. By understanding and applying some basic concepts, managers can improve their track records. Some of the important considerations for leaders to keep in mind when introducing change are cited in Table 9.2.

TABLE 9.2   Guidelines That Assist in the Introduction of Change.

- Recognize the three-step nature of the change process.
- Stress the usefulness of the change.
- Be empathetic toward the feelings of those affected.
- Make certain that employees understand the nature and purpose of the change.
- Allow for employee participation when possible.
- Stress benefits.
- Provide economic guarantees where possible.
- Consider timing.
- Introduce the change gradually where possible.
- Introduce the change on a trial basis.

Change as a Three-Step Process

We've already examined how established habits tend to affect the manner in which individuals react to new things. A way to gain a better insight into what people go through when changing is to view the activity as a three-step process: (1) *unfreezing,* (2) *changing,* and (3) *refreezing,* as graphically illustrated in Figure 9.1.[4]

A 1971 Commerce Department study recommended a 10-year plan to turn the United States metric, since it was the only major nation that had not yet embraced the metric system. Most American manufacturers had already discovered the necessity to convert to metrics if they wanted to compete effectively in the "global village." The Metric Conversion Act was passed in 1975. Opposition by small firms, the general public, and many employees was so vehement, however, that Congress made the conversion voluntary. Even though American manufacturers have since largely converted, and consumers now routinely buy 2- and 3-liter bottles of Pepsi and Coke and their wine in 1.5-liter bottles, few Americans have traded in their miles for kilometers, their pounds for kilograms, or their Fahrenheits for Celsiuses.

Are we inching our way toward the metric system . . . or not?

Unfreezing. As our metric example illustrates, many employees find it comfortable and much less risky to maintain the established ideas and practices with which they are familiar. Unfortunately, such ideas and practices may be far out of tune with the realities of today's organizational world. People do change. However, before an employee will readily accept and effectively apply new methods, he or she must "unfreeze" the old. The first step in the change process, therefore, is

Throw away the old ice cubes!

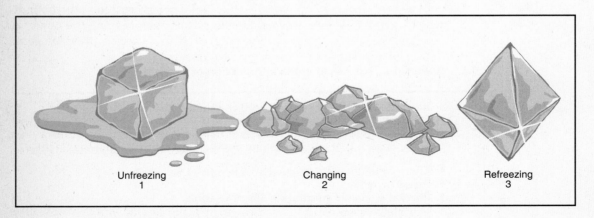

Unfreezing
1

Changing
2

Refreezing
3

Figure 9.1 Change as a three-step process.

unfreezing, discarding old ideas and habits in order to learn new ones. Many managers overlook this significant step when attempting to introduce change. People are likely to resist change until they are willing to unfreeze certain thought and activity patterns. Later sections will discuss in more detail specific techniques that managers can employ to assist in the unfreezing step.

Time for a change!

Changing. The next step in the process is **changing,** learning new ideas and habits so that the desired behavior can be employed. Continuing with our metric system example, a manager could present training sessions for employees unfamiliar with the metric system to enable them to feel more comfortable using it. Once they learn the system, they are likely to find it to be much simpler and more logical since it is a system based on tens, as is the U.S. monetary system.

For example, which would more likely be easier for a child (or an adult) to learn: That the boiling point of water is *212 degrees Fahrenheit* or *100 degrees Celsius?* That freezing is *32* degrees Fahrenheit or *0* Celsius? That a mile is *5280* feet or that a kilometer is *1000* meters? That there are *3* feet in a yard or *100* centimeters in a meter? Informal surveys of American college students have indicated that a surprisingly large proportion did not know how many feet there are in a mile or at what temperature water boils. A major point is this: People will be less willing to change and quite naturally tend to resist the "unfreezing" process if they are unfamiliar with the new alternatives.

Brr . . . back into the freezer!

Refreezing. The third step in the change process is **refreezing,** the attempt to apply regularly what one has learned. People can learn new ideas, methods, and systems. If they don't consciously apply them on a regular basis, however, they may soon forget them. For example, employees may once again feel uncomfortable with the metric system if they are trained in its use but seldom have the opportunity to apply it. The remaining portion of this section provides some useful suggestions for applying the change process.

The Change Must Be Useful

Then why change?

Any leader attempting to introduce change into the organizational environment should make special efforts to see that affected individuals understand its utility. Workers who see no valid reason for a new situation will tend to resist it. They may feel that change has occurred just for the sake of change rather than for any logical reason.

The Manager Should Be Empathetic

How do they see it?

A manager's perception of change in a particular work situation is not as important as the workers' perception of it. Managers should

A BOX OF INTEREST

Even a Boiling Kettle Couldn't "Unfreeze" This Little Bear[b]

Once upon a time there was a hunter who left a kettle of water on the campfire while he left for a few minutes. A bear crawled out of the forest and was attracted to the steaming kettle with its whistle incessantly singing. The bear grabbed onto the kettle and was badly burned. Instead of letting go of it the bear hugged it tightly, believing this was his only means of defense. The more the kettle burned the bear, the tighter he hugged it, and, of course, the tighter he hugged it the more it burned him.

How does this anecdote relate to organizational life? Some organizational members fear change so much that they prefer remaining where they are—holding onto the kettle, so-to-speak—even though outcomes are not what they desire. They refuse to "unfreeze" their habits and values. They tend to cling to that which is familiar rather than to experience growth and improve through change.

A discerning sage once said, "Although change alone does not beget progress, without change there can be no progress."

strive to employ *empathy* by asking themselves, "How might my subordinates view and react to this change?"

Here's an example of a situation in which an owner of a manufacturing facility—let's call him Sean—overlooked the need for putting himself in the shoes of his employees. After attending a management seminar that included a segment on the benefits of flexible working hours to both employees and employers, Sean decided to initiate such a program at his plant. He assumed that his employees would be grateful for their newly found freedom to determine their own working hours.

Instead, the employees perceived the change differently. They thought that the new program meant they would have to be working irregular hours in the future, such as early mornings and weekends. The employees complained to their union officials, and an unnecessary conflict was created.

The Change Must Be Understood by Those Affected

In Chapter 3 we discussed methods for ensuring more effective communication throughout organizations. As we discovered, any modification of the work environment tends to upset the equilibrium of

"I don't get it . . . so I
don't want it!"

those affected. Consequently, *clear and effective communication* of any change and its probable effects is essential if the work force is to accept it. Many changes are likely to be resisted naturally, but if changes are not understood by those affected, the chance of resistance increases considerably.

For example, assume that your company manufactures audiological support devices (hearing aids). As a result of the rapidly increasing number of older people in the United States, sales in your organization have been outstanding during the past three years and are expected to continue at a similar brisk rate. Your plant, situated at New Bedford, Massachusetts, is currently operating at the limit of its capacity. Output, however, has not been able to keep pace with current and anticipated demand.

You and the other managers of the organization decide to open another plant in Oakland, California, thus having production and marketing operations close to two major population centers. Since the expansion doesn't directly affect workers at the New Bedford plant, no official announcement is made to the employees there.

However, rumors start flying throughout the New Bedford plant. The employees believe that that purpose of the new Oakland plant is to replace the existing facility, not merely to supplement it. Morale rapidly takes a nose dive, and the union representatives call for a strike. Considerable damage is done to the morale of the employees before the facts of the move are made known.

Without understanding, people are likely to resist a new system even if it is simpler. We already learned about the unwillingness of many Americans to learn and use the metric system of measurement. You can see, therefore, when the reasons for an impending change aren't made clear by managers, distorted interpretations of its purpose and effect can easily result. Resistance to the change often develops because of a misunderstanding.

Employees Should Participate Where Possible

Perhaps you can now see that many of the concepts discussed in previous chapters can also be applied to the problems of administering change. For example, in our discussion of styles of leadership in Chapter 6, we suggested that a participative approach could be used effectively to develop support for organizational plans and objectives. When change is necessary, the use of *participation* can be especially helpful because it often cultivates greater commitment on the part of the participants. Employees tend to be happier to see self-imposed innovations succeed than those that they feel have been forced upon them.

Two heads are better
than none!

Ideas developed by the *entire group* (the supervisor and his or her workers) working together are frequently *more effective* and *creative* than those developed by one-person rule. (Do you remember the "syn-

How does getting it off your chest help?

ergistic effect" from Chapter 4?) Managers should therefore encourage subordinates to air their feelings, positive or negative, about proposed changes. Changes generally seem much less threatening when employees can discuss them openly.

Benefits Should Be Stressed

Hey, boss—what's in it for me?

"What's in it for me?" may seem like a selfish question, but it is likely to be on the minds of workers about to be subject to organizational change. A new process, for example, may be useful because it reduces labor, but how are the persons who had previously provided the labor likely to be better off? Might they not perceive the laborsaving process as a threat to their economic security? Do you recall the need for *security* in Maslow's level-of-needs concept? To optimize the acceptance of change, managers should try hard to show how the *persons affected by the change may benefit.*

Provide Economic Guarantees Where Possible

In some instances it might be possible to provide employees with **economic guarantees** as a means of increasing their willingness to adapt to new ideas and processes. For example, some organizations have developed formal "no-layoff" policies guaranteeing that no employee will lose his or her job as a result of the introduction of laborsaving equipment. Such economic guarantees tend to reduce opposition to new technology.

Another example relates to the resistance some employees might have toward being asked to relocate to another city. Guaranteeing the employee reimbursement for all expenses incurred as a result of the move, including assisting with the sale of his or her house, will often reduce some of the potential resistance to the change. Such economic guarantees may seem expensive for an organization, yet they may save money through reduced turnover of existing employees.

The Problem of Timing

When is the best time to introduce change?

The question of *timing* is as important in managerial activities as in athletics. Leaders should attempt to choose a good time for the initiation of any change. There is no one perfect time to introduce a modification into the work environment, but the best time is likely to be influenced by the current organizational culture, the nature of the change itself, and the type of industry involved.

Avoid Too Much Too Soon

Some years back, author Alvin Toffler introduced the term **future shock** into the American language. Toffler defined the term as "the dizzying disorientation brought about by the premature arrival of the future."[5] Another way of looking at future shock relates to the problem of our reaction to change that occurs more rapidly than we are able to absorb and cope with it. For instance, global events that unfolded during the past decade in such places as the former Soviet Union, former Yugoslavia, and former East Germany are practically boggling to the mind.

Why does gradual change tend to be more acceptable?

The concept of future shock applies to organizations as well. *Gradual change* is more likely to be accepted than excessively rapid change since individuals need ample time to become accustomed to new situations. Managers should guard against the tendency to introduce too much change too fast for employees to absorb and accept. President Bill Clinton appeared to learn this concept the hard way in the early months of his administration in 1993. He was accused by some critics of attempting to accomplish too much in too little time, and—as a result—seemed to accomplish very little.

Just Give It a Try

Sometimes new processes or ideas are more readily accepted if introduced on a *trial basis*. Employees can be told, for example, that a new reporting form will be utilized on a trial basis for three months and will be dropped if it proves not to be an improvement over previous reporting devices. The mere awareness that something new is not being unilaterally forced on employees often makes their accepting it easier.

Why might a *trial* basis work?

THE USE OF ORGANIZATION DEVELOPMENT (OD) TO EFFECT CHANGE

Another approach to organizational change that has received considerable attention from managers is **organization development (OD).** OD, a term that has become something of a catchall, is a process for effecting organizational change. It applies many of the concepts and techniques that have been developed in such varied behavioral fields as employee relations, sociology, anthropology, management training, organizational behavior, and clinical psychology. The total quality management (TQM) process discussed in Chapter 7 could be considered an application of the OD process.

The Rudiments of OD

In a nutshell, OD is *a group problem-solving process intended to bring about planned and orderly change for the purpose of improving the effectiveness of the entire culture of an organization.* Activities referred to as **interventions** are intended to aid organizational members in adapting to rapidly changing technology and to more challenging types of employees. Virtually any organizational problem can be a job for an **OD practitioner,** also known as a **change agent** or **OD consultant,** who attempts to *diagnose* specific problems, provide feedback to organizational members related to his or her findings, and then assist them in developing *strategies and interventions* for improving the total organization.

The OD Process

What is the process called "OD"?

To make the OD process clearer, we'll now trace it with an illustration. Assume that a key executive—let's call him Mr. Norman Conquest—learns that there is a specific problem with productivity in his organization. Mr. Conquest then contacts an OD practitioner, whom we'll call Cameron Cambio. Mr. Cambio could be a member of an outside consulting firm or an in-house consultant who is assigned to a human resource management (or personnel) department.

Mr. Conquest and Mr. Cambio then agree on the need for an **organizational diagnosis,** or **organizational analysis,** to uncover the causes of the productivity problems. The OD specialist, Mr. Cambio, is especially interested in the organization's cultural aspects, or norms, which tend to work to the detriment of the organization's formal objectives.

The practitioner attempts to *diagnose* the organization's sagging productivity through the use of surveys, personal interviews, and direct observation. Most OD practitioners attempt to remain detached during the entire process. They usually perceive their role more as a **facilitator**—a guide or a coach—than as a person imposing new systems on the organization.

After analyzing the gathered information, Mr. Cambio meets with Mr. Conquest and other managers for the purpose of providing **feedback** concerning the diagnosed findings. He may have discovered that employees' morale is low because they have little opportunity to share in decision making. The group members then attempt to decide which aspect of the problem demands priority attention. Guided by the practitioner, the group attempts to agree on **strategies** for dealing with the problem.

Remember that the OD practitioner typically doesn't impose personal strategies on the organization. However, he or she does provide the tools intended to assist the group in developing its own solutions. For example, the practitioner may present short lectures or exercises related to team building, management by objectives, or other methods for modifying less desirable behavior. In some cases, new training and development programs grow out of these sessions. Our practitioner, Cameron Cambio, might guide the group of managers into the use of the **grid organization development method** for analyzing existing managerial approaches to production and people, a variant of which will be discussed in the following section of this chapter.

PEOPLE AND PRODUCTIVITY—
THE MANAGERIAL GRID

People or productivity— what's *your* choice?

A widely used OD intervention in some organizations today was developed a number of years ago by researchers Robert Blake and Jane Mouton. Blake and Mouton contend that, to be effective, managers should have a concern for both *production* and *people*. The researchers documented the differences managers have in their attitudes toward these two factors. Some managers feel a high degree of concern for production and little concern for people. Others have a high degree of concern for people and little concern for production. And, as you might expect, the degree of concern felt by many managers fell between one extreme and the other.

The Nature of the Grid

The **managerial grid** was an outgrowth of Blake and Mouton's research. According to Blake and Mouton, a manager's attitude toward production and people could be illustrated graphically with the grid.[6] As a part of his or her organizational diagnosis, the OD consultant uses a questionnaire that was developed to measure a manager's current values, which are then positioned on the grid. A manager's position can fall into any of 81 positions. Figure 9.2 shows examples of 5 relative positions.

The grid, therefore, can be used as an OD technique to enable managers to become more familiar with their existing styles of leadership. This awareness then becomes a basis for determining what modifications in leadership attitudes might be made to improve managerial effectiveness.

THE USE OF MBO TO EFFECT CHANGE

Little happens in the absence of change. Plans can be carried out and goals accomplished only through activities intended to change things from the way they currently are to the way we want and expect them to be in the future.

Many employees fail to live up to the expectations of their bosses. Why is this? Frequently, it's because employees feel left in the dark. They're not the least bit clear on what managers expect from them; that is, what changes in their behavior and activities are necessary to meet their bosses' standards. We've seen in Chapter 3 that ineffective communication can cause organizational problems and conflict. And for a manager to communicate organizational objectives to employees so that employees understand them, accept them, and are willing to change their behavior, is far from simple.

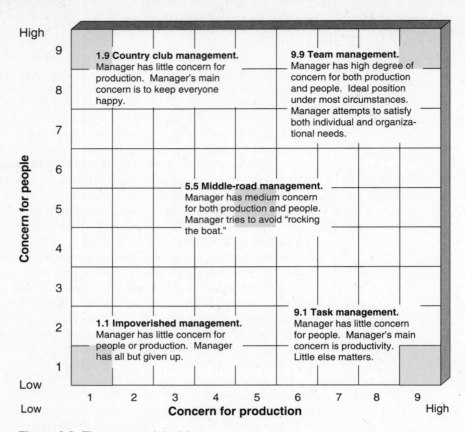

Figure 9.2 The managerial grid.

To overcome some of these difficulties and to facilitate employee acceptance of the need for change, an approach related to participative management—termed **management by objectives (MBO)**—is used by many modern managers. Sometimes referred to as *results management,* MBO's major focus is on involving managers and their subordinates *jointly* in developing *specific goals and objectives.* Naturally, estimates of future results must fit into the overall scheme of the organization's goals and objectives.

Now just what is it we want to accomplish?

Establishing objectives mutually, of course, isn't enough. A formalized MBO approach also involves developing specific *plans* for accomplishing the goals, which are either agreed upon and accepted by the manager or modified by the mutual agreement of the manager and his or her subordinates. The expected results that are agreed upon then become a guide for future employee performance.

What's our plan?

Some managers prefer to explain the MBO procedure in an understandable fashion that they refer to as the **RIO process** as

¡El RIO grande!

?

**A QUESTION
OF
ETHICS**

Not Exactly What One Would Call "Country-Club Management"[c]

During the early 1990s, things weren't going very well for many companies in the United States. Sales and profits were down and layoffs were up. Firms were getting "leaner and meaner" in many instances, with many employees feeling less secure about the future of their career. Some observers of the organizational scene thought that many employees were beginning to believe that being ethical was becoming too risky. Some employees felt that they were placed in positions where it was too dangerous to just say no to their bosses. What developed was a condition that consultant Barbara Ley Toffler calls the "move it" syndrome. This condition exists when the boss tells a subordinate to "move it—just get it done, meet the deadline, don't ask for more money, time or people, just do it!" In the vernacular of the managerial grid discussed in this chapter, some managers assumed a 9.1, task management, stance.

The boss doesn't necessarily come right out and tell the employee to be unethical, but frequently the lack of ethics has crept in because of the pressure to "move it or lose it"; that is, "if you don't get the job done, we'll find somebody else who will!" Some observers feel that this type of pressure has caused typically honest people just trying to hold their jobs to cross over ethical boundaries. For example, someone who is told that he or she must finish a project that normally takes four weeks in two weeks may sometimes feel compelled to stretch the usual standards of acceptable behavior.

A Question of Ethics: Assume that you have a good job and a promising career. Would you be willing to risk telling your boss no to an order that you knew was impossible to achieve ethically?

illustrated in Figure 9.3. Using this technique, for example, a middle manager and a first line supervisor could jointly develop lists of the specific areas of supervisory *responsibilities,* which represent the "R" in the RIO acronym. The "I" in RIO symbolizes *indicators,* which are documented existing conditions, such as the number of lost-time injuries in the supervisor's department. Both persons then mutually agree on measurable *objectives*—the "O" in RIO.

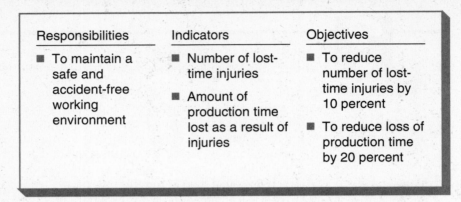

Responsibilities	Indicators	Objectives
■ To maintain a safe and accident-free working environment	■ Number of lost-time injuries ■ Amount of production time lost as a result of injuries	■ To reduce number of lost-time injuries by 10 percent ■ To reduce loss of production time by 20 percent

Figure 9.3 An example of the use of the RIO process with MBO.

Let's take a look at how we're doing.

The MBO and RIO processes require managers to provide employees with periodic feedback. The manager should meet regularly with employees to tell them whether progress has been made and whether objectives need *modifying*. One of the key advantages of MBO is that it creates a situation in which employees tend to feel greater involvement with their work. This participative approach to management also helps employees develop more positive attitudes toward their jobs, since they are able to participate in decision making that affects them directly. Of course, MBO is unlikely to succeed in a climate of distrust or when a manager fails to recognize and consider subordinates' needs in relation to the established objectives.

When applying the MBO process, a major challenge for the manager is to make certain that employees understand what constitutes realistic objectives. An objective such as, "I will work harder during the forthcoming year," or "I will perform better on my job," is certainly desirable but is too vague to meet the basic requirements for sound objectives. Why don't you take a look now at Table 9.3 where you can read a list of the essential ingredients of sound objectives used in the MBO process.

TABLE 9.3   Basic Requirements for Establishing Sound Objectives in the MBO Process.

Do your objectives meet these guidelines?

Objectives should:
• Be stated in terms of end results.
• Be specific and measurable.
• Be realistic and practical.
• Be attainable within a definite time period.
• Require "stretching" to motivate.

SUMMARY

Managers need to introduce change *before* conditions in the organization deteriorate to the crisis stage. They must realize, however, that change affects different individuals in different ways, and that people generally tend to resist changes. The reasons for such resistance are numerous, ranging from personal attitudes to habits to fear of change itself. Alert and cautious managers should attempt to familiarize themselves with the major causes of resistance to be able to manage change more effectively and beneficially for both management and workers.

The smoothness (or friction) with which managers introduce change is influenced significantly by their awareness and application of specific behavioral concepts. For example, the use of employee participation in planning changes tends to achieve greater commitment on the part of the participants. The techniques of organization development (OD) can assist managers who plan to initiate changes. Tools that can assist in effecting change and gaining greater acceptance of new ideas, processes, and goals include the managerial grid and management by objectives (MBO).

TERMS AND CONCEPTS TO REMEMBER

status

dual-career families

habits

boiled-frog syndrome

change management

unfreezing

changing

refreezing

economic guarantees

future shock

organization development (OD)

interventions

OD practitioner (change agent or OD consultant)

organizational diagnosis (organizational analysis)

facilitator

feedback

strategies

grid organization development method

managerial grid

management by objectives (MBO)

RIO process

QUESTIONS

1. How does the concept of future shock relate to organizational change?

2. How do personal attitudes influence attempts by managers to introduce change?

3. List some of your own experiences that might cause you to resist certain types of change.

4. How would your attitude toward a new laborsaving process differ if you were working part- instead of full-time?

5. What sort of changes in your job might affect your self-esteem and the esteem in which your family and friends hold you?

6. Why are habits once established so difficult to break?

7. What causes some people to hold steadfastly to myths?

8. How does the three-step change process relate to the concept of OD interventions?

9. Assume that you're a manager in a firm that plans to move to a new building in the suburbs. Outline some major considerations for effecting this change with a minimum of friction among employees.

10. Why might some workers view as threatening your decision to enrich their jobs?

11. What are some of the principal benefits derived from the application of the management-by-objectives process? How does the RIO process relate to MBO?

APPLICATIONS

9.1 But It's the All-American Meal!

News item, Miami: Inmates in the Dade County jail protested Thursday night when they were served hot dogs and green beans for dinner.

Some forty prisoners on the third-floor cell block pitched their plates onto the jail corridor. They complained that the menu had called for beef and noodles.

Questions

1. Since many of the inmates probably like hot dogs, what factors discussed in this chapter may have contributed toward their behavior?

2. How does this incident relate to the organizational world of work?

9.2 The Precision Parameter Company

The Precision Parameter Company is an electronics firm whose general offices are located in Sunnyvale, California. The firm has separate divisions located in Annandale, Virginia, and Tempe, Arizona, each involved with similar activities and employing approximately 175 to 200 people. The company is principally a manufacturer of components for electronics equipment, such as computer chips that turn personal computers into videophones.

Mary Levin, an in-house organization development practitioner, recently analyzed statistical data from each manufacturing unit and discovered a wide discrepancy between the activities of the Tempe plant and those of its Annandale counterpart. Ms. Levin discovered that at the Tempe plant:

1. The rate of employee turnover was nearly double.
2. The incidence of accidents on the job was 35 percent higher.
3. Absenteeism was three times higher.
4. There was 65 percent more tardiness.

Ms. Levin asked the plant managers of both locations to supply her with production figures and discovered that the Tempe plant also had:

1. Lower levels of production.
2. Higher levels of wasted materials and customer-rejected products.

Ms. Levin decided to call the two plant managers, Charles Drocco of Annandale and Jim Albritton of Tempe, to Sunnyvale for a conference. The following conversation took place during the meeting:

Ms. Levin: Gentlemen, each of us here is interested in furthering the goals and objectives of the Precision Parameter Company. I want you to know that I haven't called this meeting to criticize anyone, merely to uncover some information so that we can improve our operations at all of our locations in the future.

I personally feel that people are one of our most important resources. I also feel that we might be able to do a more effective job of managing if we know more about the attitudes of our employees at the production level, and so. . .

Mr. Albritton: Ms. Levin, with all due respect to you, ma'am, I know exactly what you're gonna say. I've been through sessions like this before with "*OverDose*" specialists and . . . well . . . they're all just about alike. They sit up there smugly in their office towers dreaming up new ideas. You're gonna tell me that my division isn't operating as efficiently as Charles', aren't you? Well, I wanna tell you this. His situation is completely different from mine. You can't get the same types of employees in Tempe that you get in Virginia. They're all either young people who have lost the good, old-fashioned work ethic that we all used to have, or they're old and ready to retire, rock back and forth in their chairs, and bask in the warm Arizona sun. I know those production employees. Heck, I used to be one of 'em myself. All they're interested in are their paychecks.

Ms. Levin: Jim, there certainly is the possibility that employment conditions are different in your area, but I want to assure you that I'm not here to criticize. Nothing is perfect, but perhaps we three can put our heads together and come up with some ideas on how we might improve things.

What I'd like is for us to attempt to develop materials that we might incorporate into an employee attitude survey. If we can find out what our employees like and don't like about working for Precision, then perhaps we'll be in a better position to manage more effectively and to retain valuable employees. Let's give it a good, positive effort. What do you say?

Questions

1. What is your reaction to the way in which Ms. Levin conducted the meeting?

2. What do Jim's statements reveal about his attitude toward workers in his plant? In what ways might he be contributing to the poor results at the Tempe plant?

3. Assume that you are Mary Levin. What broad areas of employee concern would you include in an attitude survey? Develop a list of survey questions that could apply to each of these broad categories.

4. How can the information uncovered in the survey help the managers improve working conditions?

9.3 The New Broom Case

One year ago, Chan C. Lee accepted the leadership of the sprawling Capital City Recreation District, which operates an extensive range of sports, arts and crafts, and health and fitness programs. Chan formerly headed a smaller recreation agency in a neighboring state, where he successfully kept within his budget while providing excellent services to the community.

In his previous position, Chan was responsible for a single park and several indoor and outdoor sites for specific athletic activities. Chan's new position in Capital City requires him to administer three parks, four recreation centers, and a number of smaller facilities scattered throughout the metropolitan area. These neighborhood facilities offer team sports as well as specialized programs such as ceramics instruction, ballroom dancing, and nutrition for weight control. The Capital City Recreation District has been functioning on a decentralized basis since its inception fourteen years ago. The recreation centers, for example, are considered separate from the parks even when they share the same location.

Chan recently received county board approval to reorganize the entire recreation district. He is taking advantage of the numerous retirements and resignations that have occurred recently to restructure each division, placing his personnel selections into key positions. New positions have been established and staffed from both inside and outside the district. Chan has combined the parks and recreation centers, apparently to deal more effectively with personnel who are trying to form a union.

The new centralization of the district will create greater supervisory control over the assignments and appraisals of instructors and members of the sports staff. In the past, people in these positions had personal contact, on almost a daily basis, with an activity coordinator. The coordinator worked under the guidance of the program director for the particular park, recreation center, or auxiliary facility. Now, with the reorganization, both the coordinator and the program director positions have been abolished. The program director has been replaced by an area manager with responsibilities at several sites, and the activity coordinators appear to be a thing of the past.

The general structure of the reorganization has been announced, but details and future plans are a matter of conjecture. Park superintendents, facilities managers, planning and development personnel, and other administrators are still feeling their way and apparently are not privy to the master plan. The instructors and sports staff have only recently learned of the changes, and, in general, they strongly oppose the plans for reorganization.

Questions

1. In your opinion, why didn't Chan C. Lee announce more details concerning his plans for reorganization?

2. Why do you think many of the instructors and coaches are resisting the changes?

3. At this late date, how can Chan C. Lee gain acceptance of the changes and attempt to raise the morale of the instructors and sports staff?

9.4 Management by Whose Objectives?

Andy Goren is director of human resources for Lester & Darby, Certified Public Accountants. L&D was experiencing a high rate of staff turnover. Resignations were frequent among high achievers, accountants who were no more than two or three years into their careers. Through exit interviews, Andy heard these sample statements:

1. "I never know what is expected of me."

2. "No one ever tells me if my work is good or bad."

3. "When I have a problem and want help, partners do not listen."

4. "Partners only worry about chargeable time (billable client services)."

5. "I want more personal opportunities to grow."

6. "I don't think anyone knows what this firm's objectives are."

7. "The partner in charge is a hard-X leader."

8. "L&D does not have a communications problem. They simply don't have communications!"

9. "Partners meet to discuss everything, real participative style, but we never get decisions."

There were no complaints about salaries, promotions, or the quality of training seminars.

Andy met with Ken Booker, the partner in charge, to review his findings and recommendations. Andy proposed that the firm adopt management by objectives (MBO). Ken reluctantly agreed to a trial MBO program. He said he feared that if young accountants were given a chance to set their own goals, they would "forgo profit and bankrupt the firm with their fun and games."

The MBO program was kicked off at a three-day partners' meeting. The partners explored firm objectives for auditing, tax services, and data processing consultation. The three-day debate about the firm's objectives was regarded by all partners as their most successful meeting ever. At the conclusion of the meeting each partner was given a list of six or seven accountants. The partner would serve as a sort of homeroom teacher, a counselor to the accountant. With guidance from a partner, each accountant would set his or her objectives (MBOs) for one year.

An announcement went out to the staff extolling the merits of MBO. The promise was clear that every effort would be made by the partners to create an environment that nurtured individual growth. A partner would meet with each staff member, one on one, to communicate what was expected of each person and to set MBOs.

Ken looked over his list of counselees. For his first counseling session he selected Sharon Chapman, an audit supervisor with four years of experience. Sharon held an MBA from Stanford University, had passed the CPA examination, and consistently received high performance ratings from all partners. Ken felt sure that Sharon would understand MBO and this would be an easy first experience at goal setting.

Ken and Sharon held a brief first meeting. Ken explained how the program would work, the advantages to the firm, and what would be expected of Sharon. A second meeting was scheduled to review Sharon's goals.

For the second goal-setting meeting, Sharon prepared her MBOs on a page as shown below. The handwritten entries are Ken's changes. Ken said, "With only 1300 hours of client work, you will not earn your salary. At this stage in your career you must spend your time on client auditing because you need to develop your technical skills. A few years from now you'll be able to spend time with client prospects and personnel activities. We're not interested in nonprofit volunteering." The meeting ended when Ken had completed his changes to Sharon's MBOs.

ANNUAL MBO PLAN

Activities	Hours	Ken's Goals for Sharon
Chargeable client services	1300	*1850*
Estimate time to complete client jobs		
Hold performance interviews with subordinate accountants at the end of each audit		
New client development	200	*0*
Entertain one client prospect per week		
Civic activities	100	*0*
Volunteer day per month to CPA Society's Minority Business Service		
Campus recruiting	100	*10*
Schedule 6 days of campus interviews		
Schedule 52 hours of interviews during student office visits		
Instructor at staff training school	40	*40*
Teach classes on inventories and CPA ethics		
Attend professional seminars	80	*80*
Attend CPA Society Personnel Seminar in May		

Attend Auditing Through Computers Seminar in August		
Attend Tax Reform Act Seminar in October		
Professional Reading	100	*100*
Read two technical books		
Personal (holidays, vacations, etc.)	200	*160*
In July raft the Colorado River with my husband	2000	*2240*

Questions

1. Does Ken appear to be an X-rated or a Y-rated manager? What has influenced your judgment?

2. Do you think MBO could solve the turnover problem? Why or why not?

3. Is self-fulfilling prophecy a problem in this case? Explain.

4. Is it important that Sharon is an economic (profitable) unit for her firm? Explain.

5. If you were Andy, what would be your advice to Sharon? To Ken?

6. Which goals do you think Sharon will achieve? Why?

NOTES

1. Dan Sperling, "We Need New Minds to Fix Old Problems," *USA Today/International Edition,* January 26, 1989, p. 2.

2. "GM Says It May Announce More Plant Closings in '92," *The Wall Street Journal Europe,* August 13, 1992, p. 3; and William McWhirter, "What Went Wrong?" *Time International,* November 9, 1992, pp. 40-46.

3. John F. Kennedy, Commencement address at Yale University, New Haven, Connecticut, June 11, 1962.

4. Keith Davis and John W. Newstrom, *Human Behavior at Work* (New York: McGraw-Hill, 1989), p. 294.

5. Alvin Toffler, *Future Shock* (New York: Random House, Bantam Books, 1970), p. 11.

6. Robert R. Blake and Jane S. Mouton, *Managerial Grid* (Houston, TX: Gulf Publishing, 1964).

7. Adapted from Harold R. McAlindon, "Toward a More Creative You: Stretching Your Mind," *Supervisory Management,* February 1980, pp. 29-34.

BOX NOTES

a. Michael Skapinker, "Europe Joins the Mickey Mouse Club," *Financial Times,* March 21-22, 1992, p. 8; George Will, "Disney 'Horror' Spells Hope for Europeans," *Contra Costa Times,* April 22, 1992, p. 13; Michael Skapinker, "Culture Shock for the Mickey Mouse Outfit," *Financial Times,* April 23, 1992, p. 13; and Peter Goldstein, "EuroDisney Says It Expects a Net Loss for Its First Year," *The Wall Street Journal Europe,* July 24-25, 1992, p. 10.

b. Adapted from Doug Hooper, "Making Changes," *Contra Costa Times,* June 8, 1983, p. 2E.

c. Adapted from Barbara Ley Toffler, "When the Signal Is 'Move It or Lose It'," *The New York Times Forum,* November 17, 1991, p. 13.

EXPERIENTIAL EXERCISE

Is This Change Really Necessary?

Analyze conditions on your job and develop some ideas for a change that is long overdue. Carefully answer the questions below related to your proposed change. If you currently do not work, or lack ample authority to carry out such changes, answer the questions based on the hypothetical assumption that you do have a job and do have sufficient authority.

If you have the opportunity before actually carrying out the change, gather in groups of five students who have also performed this exercise. Each person is to take a turn at presenting his or her proposed change to the other group members, who then provide feedback and a constructive analysis of the proposal.[7]

Nature of Change

1. How will this change improve the operation of the company and the quality of work life of the employees?

   _____

   _____

2. Has the change been thoroughly thought out, and is it the best of the alternatives available?

   _____

   _____

3. Does the change represent an emotional overreaction, or is it a necessary new direction? Explain.

   _____

   _____

4. Why is this change necessary?

   _____

   _____

5. Who will be affected by the change?

   _____

   _____

6. What are the long-range consequences of the change?

   _____

   _____

7. Is the change consistent with personal/organizational philosophy?

   _____

   _____

CHAPTER 10

Cultural Diversity in The Workplace

Is It Back to the Drawing Board?

**When you finish this chapter,
you should be able to:**

1
Contrast the difference between prejudice and discrimination.

2
Recognize the nature of prejudice.

3
Explain the importance of sensitivity and objectivity to supervisors of minorities and women.

4
Summarize the principal types of civil rights employment legislation.

5
Understand three major exceptions regarding discrimination accepted by the Civil Rights Act of 1964.

6
Recount the controversy surrounding the issue of "reverse discrimination."

7
Summarize the progress made and the challenges still faced by women in the work force.

8
Describe the nature of the comparable worth concept.

9
Express your views of the merits of a special "mommy track" for working mothers.

10
Describe the typical problems faced by women and ethnic managers.

> As African Americans, we have to be careful
> to avoid always seeing racism.
> Black people are spotlighted a bit more than whites.
> Our mistakes are amplified, but so are our successes.
>
> *Milton Irvin, Executive*

> For more women, earning as much as a man
> remains a distant dream.
>
> *Aaron Bernstein, Author*

Americans today live and work in a society that is more multicultural than ever before. Most observers of the American scene would agree that progress has been made in the area of civil rights and in the more equitable treatment of minorities and women—individuals who have received unfair treatment, especially in employment, in the past.

However, there are critics who contend that the United States has experienced some "slipsliding" in recent years. They argue that what is perceived by many minorities as a formidable struggle is not yet over. They point to statistics that reveal, for example, that African Americans are twice as likely as whites to be unemployed and several times more likely to give up looking for work. Those who do work earn less (between $580 and $907, depending on age and sex, for every $1000 whites earn). They assert that although the black middle class has tripled in number, the statistic is misleading: it is not uncommon for a middle-class white man, for example, to bring home $75,000 a year to a nonworking wife, while the typical black middle-class couple—say a nurse and a bus driver—scrambles to make do on two salaries of $30,000 each.[1]

Not solely a black or white issue.

The issue, of course, is not solely one of black or white. Newspaper headlines continue to reflect the view that there is still some distance to travel before a wide variety of individuals will have true equality and be accepted into the economic and social mainstream of American life, as reflected in these recent headlines from popular newspapers and magazines:

"Colleges Conduct Far Too Little Research on Issues of Great
    Concern to Hispanics"
"Glass Ceiling Stops Female Managers Reaching the Top"
"Airline Is Sued for Minimum Height Code"
"Asian Americans Seek Understanding—Feel Left Out of Race Debate"
"Anti-Semitic Cases Rise"
"U.S. Melting Pot Boils Over in Workplace"
"Gays 'Under Siege' as Violence Escalates"

"Campaign against Indian Nicknames Opens with Lawsuits aimed at Chiefs"

"U.S. Public Schools Biased Against Girls, Report Says"

Events seem to unfold with extreme rapidity these days. For example, Arthur Fletcher, chairperson of the U.S. Commission on Civil Rights and a crusader for civil rights for most of his life, commented on some of his fellow African Americans during an interview in December 1991 when he said, "It shocks me that blacks between 20 and 35 have no feel for the need of civil rights laws. They aren't even aware that it's not working the way it ought to."[2]

Fletcher was probably more than willing to eat those words when five months later, in early May 1992, three days of rioting and vandalism broke out in such cities as Los Angeles, San Francisco, Sacramento, Atlanta, Las Vegas, and New York. Violence erupted as a reaction to a jury verdict that acquitted four Los Angeles law enforcement officers accused of brutally beating an African American, Rodney King, after he was stopped for speeding on March 3, 1991. A home video tape made by an observer showed King receiving 56 baton blows. However, the jury verdict initially decreed that the officers were innocent of any wrongdoing and were merely acting within the scope of their authority and police department policy (However, two officers were later indicted in mid-1993).

California Governor Pete Wilson deployed about 2000 National Guard troops followed by hundreds of California highway patrol personnel on loan from other parts of the state. Former president George Bush placed 4000 army troops on alert to assist in restoring calm to the Los Angeles area. Some observers of the social scene believed that the violence was a reaction to pent-up frustration that developed because of reported increases in bias toward African Americans in hiring and layoff practices, reduced enforcement of established civil rights legislation, and presidential executive orders during the more conservative political climate of the 1980s and early 1990s. Also of no help to minorities was an ailing economy that saw many people who had been among the last hired to be the first fired.

Viewing things differently.

We learned in an earlier chapter that not everyone perceives situations in the same way. To further illustrate, one study indicated that the majority of white Americans—58 percent—believe that most African Americans have attained a level of equal opportunity.[3] However, only 28 percent of African Americans see things that way. Another study showed that 64 percent of whites believe that job opportunities for blacks are better than five years earlier, while only 39 percent of blacks agreed.[4] How do you personally perceive the equity situation? What are your beliefs about the current state of fair and equal treatment of minority Americans?

In this chapter we explore some of the principal organizational behavior problems concerning persons who receive *different treatment* for reasons unrelated to their employment situations. *Different treatment* is a more polite way of saying *discrimination*. Some individuals are treated differently principally because they're part of a **special employment group.** In our diverse society—although much progress has been made in recent decades—there still remain considerable prejudice and discrimination toward these groups. A word seldom used in the past—**xenophobia**—has become commonplace in newspapers in recent years. Xenophobia is *an unreasonable fear or hatred of foreigners or people who are different.*

In the first part of this chapter, we'll investigate the *nature of prejudice* and *discrimination* and discuss two broad groups that have been on the receiving end of both—*ethnic minorities* and *women*. We'll then examine some of the problems these groups face in organizations and offer suggestions to those who supervise them. And finally, we'll look specifically at the principal problems facing ethnic minorities and women managers.

The concepts presented in this chapter apply to the members of any groups that receive different treatment. In subsequent chapters we'll explore the specific organizational behavior problems of older employees, employees with physical and intellectual challenges, and employees with alcohol and drug abuse problems.

THE NATURE OF PREJUDICE AND DISCRIMINATION

If someone were to ask you if you were prejudiced, how would you respond? Regardless of your answer, the chances are that you have some prejudices; virtually everybody has.

Prejudice and discrimination aren't necessarily harmful. Some of your prejudices may even be quite reasonable, excusable, or justifiable. For example, perhaps you're "exceedingly discriminate" when it comes to food and drink. To illustrate, assume that every time you eat an egg or plain yogurt you become extremely ill. Although you aren't personally acquainted with every egg on the earth or every ounce of yogurt, your past experience has been such that your generalized aversion toward eggs and yogurt isn't particularly unreasonable.

Being prejudiced and discriminating about food and drink, however, is one thing. Prejudice and discrimination against human beings are quite another, and they are frequently characterized by erratic emotion, economic discrimination, and sometimes even senseless and bloody violence.

The issues of prejudice and discrimination have always been emotional ones, and your own background and experiences will influence your perception of them. Let's now turn to these two important topics by first defining them.

What Is the Difference Between *Prejudice* and *Discrimination*?

Prejudice is related to attitudes. It is basically an *internal* phenomenon that entails the act of *prejudging,* or *the making of judgments based on insufficient evidence.* If you understand and are reasonably well acquainted with something or someone, in effect you are not *pre*-judging.

Discrimination is the *result* of prejudice and is *external*. It is an *action directed either against or in favor of something or someone.* As you can view in Figure 10.1, attitudes can cause prejudice, which may lead to discrimination.

In many of our daily activities we make prejudgments about situations and people. In the real world of work, decisions must be made or organizations couldn't function. The pressures of time often don't permit the exploration of all available evidence. However, when we make judgments based on less than complete data, we should leave a margin for error in case the results differ from our expectations. We should at least attempt to withhold our judgments until after we've examined the best available evidence.

Are you ever likely to have all *the facts?*

Prejudice——An Acquired Habit

How do we acquire prejudice?

According to most studies, prejudice toward other human beings is not an inborn but a *learned response.* In short, we learn from others to use the mental shortcut of prejudice. As children, we go through stages referred to by psychologists as the *modeling-identification-socialization process,* and it is during this process that prejudice can be acquired.

Parents are believed to be the major teachers of prejudice, especially since their influence is greatest during the *modeling* stage, the period when children are under five years old. Modeling is a process in which young children *imitate* others, usually their parents.

As children grow older and attend school, they tend to be influenced by their peers. During this stage they *identify with,* not just

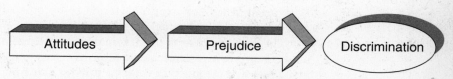

Figure 10.1 Attitudes can lead to prejudice, which may lead to discrimination.

A BOX
OF
INTEREST

Is the Accent on Foreign Hiring?[a]

More common these days is for U.S. companies to think globally when selecting leaders for coveted senior positions. A recent study conducted by Orban International, an executive recruiting firm, reveals that American corporations picked foreign executives for between seven percent and eleven percent of their high-level assignments in 1991, compared to only one percent of such placements in 1986. The trend appears to be significantly upwards.

Examples include Fritz Amman, president of American sportswear maker Esprit de Corp., who is Swiss; Eckhard Pfeiffer, chief executive of Compaq, a personal computer maker, who is German; and José Ignacio Lopez, a Spaniard, who was head of worldwide purchasing for General Motors until he switched to Volkswagen in 1993.

All is not paella and schnitzel for such culturally diverse transplants, however. One foreign executive, a Frenchman, had his promotion to chief operating officer blocked. Although he had worked at the organization's Midwestern headquarters for twenty years and held U.S. citizenship, he was still perceived as a foreigner when he talked. The company's top executives vetoed his promotion because they felt his accent "was an extra barrier to overcome." An American was chosen for the slot instead.

Experiences of foreign executives with New York firms are said to be different from those of such executives with companies located in small midwestern towns. Consequently, some observers of the global scene are warning foreign-born executives to think twice before accepting a high-level position in the United States.

imitate, their models, frequently the parent of the same sex. Once children are over nine years old, however, the parental ties begin to wear thin, and others begin to exert strong influence on their values. Peer acceptance, for example, tends to become all-important. At this stage *socialization* has taken place.

The role of parents is extremely significant in shaping the values of their offspring since, according to many child psychologists, our attitudes are strongly developed during the first five or six years of

"We don't discriminate on the basis of age, sex, religion, color or national origin—we just don't hire Scorpios."

SOURCE: From *The Wall Street Journal*—permission, Cartoon Features Syndicate.

life. Parents can therefore be effective teachers of prejudice. Yet by their words and actions parents can also teach their children to grow up in harmony with people of different races and backgrounds rather than to use prejudice as a means of resolving their own personal problems and feelings of insecurity.

Prejudice in Favor of a Group

How might you be "burned" by prejudice in favor of someone?

Prejudice isn't always directed *against* others; it can *favor* a particular group. For example, there are certain types of clubs or groups whose members regard one another as "brothers" or "sisters," even when they don't known one another. In some instances, the "brothers" have little in common other than their club affiliation, which creates a type of prejudgment *in favor* of some other individuals.

Sometimes people who belong to the same political party, have attended the same university, or belong to the same religious faith develop positive prejudgments about each other. These prejudices, too, may well be inaccurate, and managers should guard against succumbing to the "old-school-tie" and "old-boy-network" forms of prejudice, as well as to negative prejudices, when interviewing applicants for positions.

Preventive Prejudice

Individuals sometimes engage in an activity toward others that can be termed **preventive prejudice,** which means that they *prejudge the intentions of others and thus react first on the basis of an often unfounded belief that an action is going to be taken against them.*

Here's an organizational behavior example of preventive prejudice: Assume that the job performance of an employee named Jordan has not been up to acceptable standards in recent months. Jordan is actually considered to be quite a capable employee, but he is unfamiliar with some complex equipment that the company recently acquired. As a result, Jordan has made a number of mistakes in attempting to operate it.

"You can't fire me . . .
I quit!"

Jordan's boss, Joe Casco, recently commented about the quality of Jordan's work and indicated that he soon would be taking some action related to it. Jordan prejudged Casco's remarks to mean that Casco intended to fire him. Jordan decided that he would not wait for Casco to discharge him—he would quit first. Thus, Jordan's prejudgment caused him to react to what he believed would be an action, which was not based on reality. All that Casco had decided to do about the performance problem was to send Jordan to a training program sponsored by the equipment's manufacturer!

The "Oppressed Majority"

Who is on the receiving end of discrimination in America? One could argue semantically that there really is no such thing as prejudice against a minority in the United States since, collectively, all those who have been discriminated against have added up to a majority. Furthermore, the population growth of so-called minorities is increasing at a much more rapid rate than that of whites.[5] The terms *minority* and *majority,* however, aren't as important as the fact that numerous people in American society have been and, in many cases still are, discriminated against in employment as a result of the prejudiced attitudes of some members of organizations.

Who are the
"oppressed majority"?

The list of groups who have been on the short end of the employment stick is appallingly long and includes a wide variety of culturally diverse persons. Table 10.1 provides a summary of special employment groups who have been discriminated against in the past. As you can see from the list, almost anyone could find himself or herself on the receiving end of prejudice and discrimination.

TABLE 10.1   Special Employment Groups Who Have Experienced Prejudice and Discrimination.

- Abusers of alcohol and drugs
- African Americans
- The aging
- AIDS and HIV infected persons
- Alaska natives
- Asians
- Gays and lesbians
- Native Americans
- Physically and/or mentally challenged persons
- Hispanics (Spanish-speaking subgroups, such as those of Mexican, Puerto Rican, Cuban, and Central and South American descent)
- Immigrants (especially those with accents)
- Middle Easterners (such as Arabs and Iranians)
- Obese persons
- Religious group members
- "Excessively" tall or short persons
- Vietnam veterans
- Young persons seeking their first jobs
- Whites (reverse discrimination)
- Women

It's the Law

Organizational members should be aware of the various employment laws that affect the workplace today. Congress has passed some significant laws in recent decades. Special employment groups affected by such legislation are sometimes referred to as **protected classes of workers.**

In 1963, Congress approved an important law—the **Equal Pay Act**—forbidding sex discrimination in wage scales and attempting to guarantee that women doing the same work as men would be paid the same. (The act applied, however, only to employers covered by the Fair Labor Standards Act of 1935 and did not apply to women—or men—in administrative, professional or executive positions.)

One of the most significant acts of Congress is the **Civil Rights Act of 1964,** whose **Title VII** provides for equal employment opportunities. The act *prohibits employers, labor unions, and employment agencies from discriminating against persons on the basis of color, religion, sex, or national origin.* The act also established the **Equal Employment Opportunity Commission.** The **EEOC,** as it is typically called, has the responsibility for regulating employment practices of organizations under civil rights acts. Most federal contracts also have clauses requiring "acceptable" proportions of minority employees. Many firms are monitored by the Office of Federal

TABLE 10.2   A Summary of Key Employment Legislation Related to Discrimination.

Legislation	Purpose
Civil Rights Act of 1866	Establishes that all persons regardless of race shall have the same right to make and enforce contracts related to employment as enjoyed by white citizens.
Title VII. Civil Rights Act of 1964, as amended by the Equal Employment Act of 1972	Prohibits employment discrimination based on race, color, sex, religion, or national origin.
Civil Rights Attorney's Act of 1976	Provides that courts may allow prevailing party a reasonable attorney's fee in actions to enforce Civil Rights Act.
Executive Order: 11246 amended by E.O. 11375. E.O. 11478, and E.O. 12086	Prohibits employment discrimination by federal contractors and subcontractors on the basis of race, color, religion, sex, or national origin. Requires written Affirmative Action Programs (AAP).
Equal Pay Act of 1963 (a part of Fair Labor Standards Act of 1938) amended by the Fair Labor Standards Amendments of 1974	Requires employers to provide equal pay for substantially equal work regardless of sex.
Age Discrimination in Employment Act of 1967 (amended in 1978 and 1986)	Prohibits discriminatory employment practices related to persons age 40 and over.
Pregnancy Discrimination Act of 1978	Prohibits discrimination against women because of pregnancy, childbirth, or related medical conditions, especially in the area of benefits administration.

Contract Compliance to ensure that they have adequate minority representation.

A more recent act, **The Civil Rights Act of 1991,** vetoed by former president George Bush in 1990 but finally passed in 1991, reversed six Supreme Court decisions that civil rights organizations contended had weakened antidiscrimination laws on hiring and promoting.

Discrimination can be costly to organizations. For example, in 1986 USX Corporation lost a $3.3 million sex discrimination case to hundreds of women denied coal-mining jobs. The settlement was made after an eight-year court battle involving two USX mining districts in Pennsylvania and West Virginia with about a dozen mines.[6]

Although not widely known, concern for civil rights legislation didn't begin with Title VII. The **Civil Rights Act of 1866** established that *all persons regardless of race shall have the same right to make*

TABLE 10.2   A Summary of Key Employment Legislation (*continued*)

Legislation	Purpose
Rehabilitation Act of 1973 (amended in 1980)	Requires federal contractors to take affirmative action to hire ("reasonable accommodation") and advance in employment handicapped persons.
Vietnam Era Veterans Readjustment Assistance Act of 1972 and 1974 (amended in 1980)	Requires contractors to take affirmative action to hire disabled individuals and Vietnam era veterans.
Americans with Disabilities Act of 1990	Requires that private as well as federally financed employers provide persons with disabilities the same protection against discrimination as provided by other civil rights laws.
Civil Rights Act of 1991	Overturns several Supreme Court rulings that made it difficult for minority and female workers to gain legal remedies for workplace discrimination and expands rights of victims of sexual harassment and discrimination to sue for damages.

and enforce contracts related to employment as enjoyed by white citizens. Table 10.2 summarizes key employment legislation.

What good are laws?

Of course, legislation alone can't alter the feelings of hatred and xenophobia that some individuals have for others, but it can help to create a climate that makes the unfair treatment of human beings more difficult.

Religious Beliefs

A further challenge exists for employers in regard to days of worship and religious holidays of a small minority of a company's employees. Civil rights legislation also extends to those with different religious beliefs. Not only is it unlawful to discriminate against employees regarding conditions of employment, but civil rights legislation also requires that employers make *reasonable accommodation* for employees to practice their religion. Employers may allow such employees a flexible work schedule or provide other accommodations to enable them to practice their religion. However, employers are not required to make accommodations that would place undue hardship on the company or other employees.

"Boss, can I have the day off? It's Halloween!"

Sexual Preference

States have also become involved in the area of civil rights. A controversial area of special concern to many persons in recent years relates to the rights of homosexuals. Voters in Colorado, for example, approved an amendment to its constitution that banned protected status for gays and lesbians. The amendment, which passed by a 53 percent majority, took effect in January 1993. Threats of a national boycott of Colorado's tourism industry in protest of the new state law quickly followed. Meanwhile, as residents of Colorado were expressing their views at the ballot box, an anti-homosexual measure that was previously passed by Oregon citizens in 1988 was ruled unconstitutional by an appeals court. And in Minnesota, also in 1993, legislation was signed into law aimed at protecting homosexuals against descrimination in housing, employment, and education.

The controversy also spread to the United States military services as a result of President Bill Clinton's open support of civil rights for gays and lesbians during and after his presidential campaign. Although the majority of Americans polled after Clinton became president said that homosexuals should not be discriminated against in job opportunities, many military leaders vociferously opposed lifting the prohibition of homosexuals serving in the military. The issue of gay and lesbian rights is likely to be controversial for some time.

THE NEED FOR OBJECTIVITY AND SENSITIVITY BY SUPERVISORS IN MANAGING DIVERSITY

Many firms today utilize **affirmative action programs (AAP),** efforts by an organization to ensure equitable treatment of minorities and women in employment. The supervisory level is key to implementing such programs, especially in the areas of fair recruitment, hiring, and promotion practices. Senior management may recognize the need for fair employment practices in their organizations and approve such programs. However, such programs are doomed to failure if managers on the "front lines"—that is, the supervisors—are not aware of the means for *managing diversity,* an expression that has become the corporate watchword of the decade.

Let's examine some typical challenges faced by managers who supervise members of culturally diverse groups.

The Problem of Mental Set

Some supervisors are *mentally set* to perceive ethnic minorities, women, and the members of other special employment groups differently from the way they perceive white males in the same situation. For example, some supervisors perceive and stereotype certain individuals to be "good workers" and others to be "lazy and shiftless" solely because of their personal style, gender, or cultural background.

Supervisors should attempt to avoid such preset attitudes and to recognize that a wide degree of diversity also exists *within* each cultural group. Preset attitudes can produce an unhealthy environment, one that helps to create the very problems that some supervisors are set to see.

Double Standards of Supervision

Should white supervisors have separate standards for minorities and women?

Some supervisors who have had little or no experience in managing minorities and are concerned about not conveying a prejudiced attitude are sometimes uncertain about the best approach to follow. To avoid appearing prejudiced, some well-intentioned supervisors give "more than equal treatment" to members of culturally diverse groups. **Double standards of supervision,** however, are likely to backfire; supervisors should try to treat all their employees in a comparably fair and consistent manner. A minority employee, for example, might willingly accept no discipline for an infraction of a rule, but would he or she be likely to respect the supervisor who applied rules differently to different employees?

The Need to Provide Adequate Training

Most employees require training to improve and maintain their skills. Unfortunately, when an ethnic minority employee lacks certain basic skills, he or she may be perceived as inept and fired. A more creative approach, however, is to ensure that such employees (in reality, *all* employees) receive adequate training that can improve their job performance.

How can training help?

To illustrate, the four Sheraton Hotels in Hawaii have sometimes hired immigrants from the Philippines, Samoa, and the Micronesian Islands to fill labor-intensive functions such as housekeeping and laundry. However, most of the workers could not read and write above the fifth-grade level. As a result, employees had difficulty following hotel policies and interpreting operating manuals. Sheraton's human resources department managers produced a creative idea: They teamed up with the University of Hawaii and obtained a $182,000 federal grant to set up English and basic-skills classes. Within a year, six of the employees had been promoted to supervisory positions and several others had received high school diplomas. The trained employees were said to have become more productive and enthusiastic in their jobs than they were in the past.[7]

The Glass Ceiling

Let's assume that you are an ambitious person with aspirations to rise to a higher-level position in an organization. The position you assumed with a firm is typically considered to be one for "fast trackers," one

A QUESTION OF ETHICS

An Eye for an Eye, and a Bash for a Bash![b]

"America is a land of lazy illiterates producing nothing but shoddy products," states a Japanese business leader. "American workers should draw a mushroom cloud and put underneath it: 'Made in America by lazy and illiterate Americans and tested in Japan,'" retorts a United States senator. A University of Michigan study reveals that Japanese tend not to trust American workers employed by Japanese firms. The American Baseball Commissioner was hesitant to approve the bailout purchase of the Seattle Mariners baseball team by a Japanese businessperson who had lived in Seattle, Washington, substantially longer than the team's two previous American owners.

And so . . . the beat goes on. Xenophobic bashing during the early 1990s picked up steam in both Japan and the United States. Some of the bashing, however, went beyond mere verbal insults. Japanese Americans in Southern California became worried in early 1992 by the rash of hate mail, graffiti, and threats. Some Japanese automobile import dealers have received bomb threats and experienced vandalism, including bullets fired into their showrooms. A newspaper article told about a Japanese university president who went to Boston to celebrate a sister school agreement with a local college and was shot in his hotel room. Another article describes a Japanese businessperson who was stabbed to death less than a week after telling police his life had been threatened by a man who blamed Japan for economic problems.

Yet, each culture admires much about the other. For example, one study points out that Japanese people perceive Americans as friendly and admire the United States for its world leadership and opportunities for free expression. Americans, on the other foot, generally view Japanese as competitive, hard-working, and friendly.

A Questions of Ethics: In your opinion, is there any reasonable justification for bashing by Japanese or Americans, either verbally or physically? What are some potential dangers in the practice?

that typically leads to rapid advancement in the company. As time progresses, you observe that individuals who have less talent than you are advancing on the track at a more rapid clip. You're beginning to wonder if you've been "derailed." You might even become so dissatisfied with such a situation that you feel like quitting.

I'm sorry, but I don't do windows

Such is the plight of many minorities and women who discover that up to a certain point, ability and intelligence pay off. After that point, however, a *glass ceiling* seems to come between them and higher-level positions. A **glass ceiling** is a condition in which certain individuals, such as minorities and women, can see the next step up in a typical career path, but they never get invited to take it.[8]

LEGAL DISCRIMINATION IN EXCEPTIONAL CASES

Did you know that discrimination is legal in certain situations? Section 703 of the Civil Rights Act of 1964 exempts certain employment practices from the scope of Title VII enforcement. The major exceptions are the bona fide occupational qualification (BFOQ) exception, the testing requirement exception, and the seniority exception. We'll briefly look at each of these.

Bona Fide Occupational Qualification (BFOQ) Exception

Yes, according to Section 703(e) of Title VII, it *is* legal for an employer to discriminate against employees in hiring practices on the bases of their religion, sex, or national origin "in those instances where religion, sex, or national origin is a **bona fide occupational qualification (BFOQ)** reasonably necessary to the normal operation of a particular enterprise."

What do you think? Could a woman guard such offenders?

Can you think of an example in which the BFOQ clause might be applied? Here's an interesting actual case: A Supreme Court ruling upheld as a BFOQ a requirement that all guards be male in a male maximum security correctional facility in Alabama. The Court argued that female guards would not be practicable since 20 percent of the inmates were convicted sex offenders and would create an excessive threat to the security of female guards.[9] Can you think of any other BFOQ examples?

The Testing Requirement Exception

Here's another important exception to Title VII: Section 703(h) of the Civil Rights Act of 1964 authorizes the use of professionally developed ability tests if they are not "designed, intended, or used to discriminate." This may sound like doubletalk, but the **testing requirement**

exception can be used to discriminate in hiring practices as long as the tests are not used *intentionally* to discriminate for non-job-related reasons.

Stated differently, a test that is job related can be used to weed out those obviously unfit for a particular position. For example, a person who has applied for a position in an office may be asked to take a test that measures his or her ability to use a word processing system. Rejecting the person who fails a job-related word processing test is, in a sense, a form of discrimination. It is a legal practice, however, unless the test was designed to discriminate against a job applicant on the basis of race, color, sex, religion, or national origin.

The entire area of testing is complicated. Experts in the field contend that tests should be both *valid* and *reliable*. **Validity** means that the test measures what it was designed to measure, such as a person's ability to use a word processing system in specific ways. **Reliability** means that the test measures the same factors over and over, such as the ability to construct forms and letters. A major point is that tests should be used only when there is a high degree of certainty that they are *job related,* are *predictive of a person's future success* in a particular position, and *consistently measure the same factors.*

Tests can make some people testy!

Seniority System Exception

Another exception to the Civil Rights Act of 1964 can be found in Section 703(h), which is another provision that enables employers to discriminate if their intention is not to discriminate.

Organizations that have **seniority systems** provide a degree of security to employees who have been employed for longer periods of time. A seniority system refers to "a set of rules that ensure workers with longer years of continuous service for an employer a priority claim to a job over others with fewer years of service."[10]

A bit of LIFO—Last in, first out.

Seniority systems have occasionally discriminated against minorities in organizations that had to lay off people during periods of declining economic activity, or recessions. "Last hired, first fired," describes the condition that has affected minorities during such declines. The courts have generally ruled that this exception to the Civil Rights Act of 1964 is legal as long as the *intent* of the seniority provision was not to discriminate against minorities, women, or various ethnic groups.

REVERSE DISCRIMINATION—AN ORGANIZATIONAL DILEMMA

A young evening-session student named John was enrolled in a course on organizational behavior and once complained during a class discussion that he was being discriminated against in his efforts to become a firefighter. John, who was white, said that the city fire department had an affirmative action hiring program that favored minorities. John groused, "Why should I suffer for something I had nothing to do with?"

Offsetting Past Inequities Through Proportional Employment

John's plight is not an uncommon one. Although affirmative action programs (AAPs), as discussed in an earlier section, have as their objectives the creation of greater equity in employment, they have sometimes led to **reverse discrimination.** The challenge associated with an AAP is how to offset past inequities. In order to achieve a work force that is more representative of the surrounding community, many civil rights proponents advocate a program of **proportional employment,** hiring practices that attempt to match the percentages of particular groups in the local work force. If, for example, the local work force is ten percent Hispanic, then a firm's proportional employment goal would be ten percent Hispanic employees.

If 10 percent there, then 10 percent here.

Unwanted Problems Associated With AAP

The preferential hiring of minorities has sometimes resulted in human relations problems in organizations where it has been utilized. Resentment and bitterness have, at times, developed toward such programs among applicants for employment and existing employees. In addition, disgruntled white applicants or employees have occasionally brought discrimination charges against employers or institutions.

For example, there are a number of significant legal decisions related to the problem of reverse discrimination. One was *Bakke v. University of California Medical School at Davis* in 1978, in which Bakke accused the university of reverse discrimination and sued after being denied admission to medical school because quotas had been filled by minorities. The courts ruled in favor of Bakke and decreed the institution's *quota admissions system unconstitutional,* although affirmative action based on *goals* was upheld.

Quotas v. goals— a distinction without a significant difference?

Another case involved a Supreme Court ruling in 1989 in which white firefighters in Birmingham, Alabama, who claimed unfair treatment due to affirmative action programs, could seek redress under civil rights legislation. The firefighters claimed that the eight-year-old, court-approved AAP program aiming to increase the number of African Americans hired and promoted deprived them of promotions because of their white race.

President Bill Clinton also experienced some unwanted problems in this area during the early months of his presidency when, during June, 1993, he nominated law professor Lani Guinier for the position of assistant attorney general. He felt pressured to back down and withdraw her nomination after it was alleged that her academic writings advocated the use of quotas in hiring practices. Professor Guinier contended that her writings were misinterpreted by her critics.

The development of fair employment practices, as you can see, is not easy. A positive view of the challenge has been presented by an affirmative action consultant, Clint Bolick, who has asserted that "Companies should view and structure 'affirmative action' not as a zero-sum game in which one person's gain is another person's loss, but as a vital human resources process that expands opportunities for everyone."[11]

YOU'VE COME A LONG WAY, MAYBE! THE CHALLENGES FACING WOMEN IN THE WORKPLACE

Most observers of economic history would probably agree that the lives of many women have traditionally been filled with challenges. For many years, a primarily male-dominated society seemed to believe that "a woman's place was in the home." That view appears to have faded to a great extent. Blatant female stereotyping appears also to have diminished to some degree. For example, college textbooks have largely been "de-he'd," their authors finally recognizing that females as well as males read their books. Likewise, primary schools have cleaned up their acts by selecting books that avoid the "pink-and-blue syndrome," where "pink had always equaled 60 percent of blue." Businesses, such as Safeway Stores, have contributed toward a broader view of women by emphasizing their concern for fair employment practices and "gender equality."

On the One Hand . . . Progress

The U.S. Bureau of Labor Statistics provides some significant facts concerning increased female participation in the work force:

1. The average annual income of women age 25 or older with four or more years of college increased at a more rapid rate than the income of men of comparable age and education between 1968 and 1990.

2. About 69 percent of all women 18 to 64 in 1992 were either working or looking for work, versus 50 percent in 1979, 40 percent in 1969, and only 33 percent in 1950.

3. By the year 2000, nearly 80 percent of women of *working age* are expected to be in the work force.

4. By the year 2000, women will compose almost half of the *total work force,* compared to only 30 percent in 1950.

But on the Other Hand . . .

Yes, many barriers have been broken and progress has undeniably been made in recent decades. But men, put yourselves in a pair of women's shoes for a moment. If you were a woman, would you really be satisfied with the following statistics?

If you were an "average" full-time female worker, you would discover that the gap between men's earnings and your own had not really changed all that much since 1955. For example, in 1955, women earned slightly less than 64 percent as much as men. About a third of a century later, a woman's earnings have crept up to only 70 percent of the average man's income. That figure is the average for all women. For African American and Hispanic women, the percentage was only 62 percent and 56 percent, respectively, in 1990. (See Figure 10.2 for a comparison of average weekly earnings by men and women in selected occupations.)

Hang in there. We'll cite only a few more depressing (for women, at least!) statistics: Adult women with *four years of college* still earn only about $600 a year more than what an adult man with a *high*

Narrowing the gap—barely!

Figure 10.2   A comparison of relative earnings by men and women in selected occupations.

school education earns. A man with four years of college receives an average of $15,000 above what a college-educated woman earns.[12] And if that weren't bad enough, here's some more bad news: According to a report by the National Commission on Working Women, nearly twice as many women as men earn only the minimum wage or less. The report reveals that 40 percent of the female work force earns less than $10,000 a year, and 63 percent of all workers earning the minimum wage or less are women.[13]

Where's the gender equality?

Those shoes you're wearing, made out of genuine empathy, are probably beginning to hurt your feet, aren't they, men? Well, take off your unmasculine shoes now, relax your feet, tense up your minds a bit, and let's try to find out more about how women have been treated in the past and might be treated in the future. And women—wipe those smug looks off *your* faces. Unconsciously, you may be more guilty of sexism toward women than some *men!*

The Effects of Culturalization on Values Toward Women

We've already discussed the effect that our past experiences—our culturalization—have had on our perception and values. In the same way that "we are what we eat," psychologically our attitudes are conditioned by the nourishment that our minds absorb.

Although there have been substantial changes in the use of sexual stereotypes in grade-school primers, a large proportion of American adults were raised on a reading diet of little girls compartmentalized into inferior roles. These stereotypes were perpetuated by high schools not permitting young women to attend automobile mechanics, wood shop, and other trade classes. Many young women were instead encouraged to concentrate on courses in home economics.

Women were also believed not to "have a head" for science years ago. For example, Vera Rubin, who became one of three female astronomers in the National Academy of Sciences, was told when she requested a catalog for Princeton University's graduate school in 1947 that the school did not accept women in graduate physics and astronomy. In fact, Princeton did not accept women in graduate physics until 1971 and in graduate math programs until 1976. As researcher K. C. Cole has said, "It's difficult to make it to the top when they don't even let you in the door."[14]

Women didn't count!

We would like to believe our schools have made progress in the area of reducing sexist treatment of young girls. However, a recent study by the American Association of University Women contends that public schools continue to shortchange girls. The report, which gathered research material over two decades, examined the biases girls face from preschool through high school. Some of its findings were:[15]

1. Teachers give girls significantly less attention than boys.

2. Although the "gender gap" in math is declining, girls still are not pursuing math-related careers in the same proportion as boys are, and a large, and perhaps growing, gender gap persists in science.

3. Curricula often ignore females or reinforce stereotypes.

4. Most standardized tests are biased against girls.

Care to Compare Worth?

The Equal Pay Act of 1963 requires employers "to provide equal pay for substantially equal work regardless of sex." In other words, according to the law, a male secretary should not receive a higher salary than a female one. Sounds reasonable, *nicht wahr?* Most people would probably agree with the intent of the law.

Is comparable worth worth comparing?

A related hot issue in recent years has been that of **comparable worth,** which is defined as *the assertion that women should be paid as much as men for performing tasks in other occupations requiring comparable (not identical) skills, training, responsibilities, hazards, and effort.* The proponents of comparable worth want to reduce sex discrimination in employment by eliminating the pay gap between female-dominated occupations (such as elementary-school teaching, nursing, and secretarial work) and most other jobs. Opinions are mixed as to the desirability of the comparable worth concept. Some public employers such as the state of Washington and the city of San Jose, California, have enacted comparable worth statutes, but not without considerable debate and controversy.

The opponents of comparable worth argue that it "breaks the laws of supply and demand." They contend that higher salaries would mean fewer jobs in traditionally female occupations and would, therefore, hurt females in the long run. What do you think?

SOURCE: © 1992 by Gary Trudeau—permission, Universal Press Syndicate.

Fast Versus Mommy Track

What do you think of this idea to assist working mothers with small children—the establishment of a **mommy track,** an employment scheme that distinguishes between women who want to dedicate themselves to the job and those who want to combine career and children? Some companies have established such secondary tracks in recent years.

The mommy track concept was popularized by Felice Schwartz, a women's rights advocate, who points out that too many employers give manager-moms only two options: full-time work or no work at all. Schwartz says that, instead, companies should offer flexible working hours, part-time jobs, and job sharing for working mothers.

But wait a minute! There's a danger signal flashing in front of mommy's track. Could this approach be used by some employers to perpetuate their "glass ceiling" philosophy? Some observers fear that a secondary track—the one for mommy—is a giant step backward for women. For example, publisher Myrna Blyth is concerned that the mommy track "can be used as an excuse for employers to not treat women as equally as they should be treated." She fears that employers will not take mommy trackers as seriously as other employees.[16]

Other observers, such as lawyer Paul Sprenger, go beyond the morale issues and contend that a special track for women is illegal. Sprenger argues that an employer attitude such as "We didn't promote her because we felt she really cared about her kids" is the same as any other discrimination. Sprenger adds. "The companies may not even realize what they are doing is sex discrimination." If the courts agree with Sprenger, companies could be opening themselves up to Title VII civil rights violations by "mommy tracking" certain employees.[17]

Any tool's value is significantly related to the results it achieves. Mommy tracks are no exception: A mommy track is likely to be a useful and welcome addition to a firm that enjoys a positive organizational climate, but in an atmosphere of mistrust and suspicion, however, employees might perceive it as merely another management gimmick intended to perpetuate discriminatory policies.

Company Family Leave Policies

The role of women in the work force has expanded greatly during recent decades, and today in most American families both spouses work. Pressure has been building for some time for companies to adjust to the needs of American workers and their families by providing **family leave;** that is, time off for parents to care for newborn or adopted children and for family medical emergencies.

Company policies have varied greatly in the past, with few companies having offered parental leave. Many organizations ignored the

A mommy track to nowhere?

Take it, dad . . . if you dare!

father's role altogether in the childbirth process. Senior management likewise seemed to resist the demand for leave for fathers, since 62 percent of company executives were reported to have said that they believe it "inappropriate" for paternal leave to be taken.[18]

AT&T, however, appeared to want to jump on the family-leave bandwagon relatively early. In the late 1980s, its employees—both mothers and fathers of newborns—began to be allowed to take up to 1 year of parental leave. The company also permits leaves for employees to take care of ailing relatives. In addition, AT&T offers payments up to $2000 to employees who adopted children. The firm also established a $5 million fund to help support and establish child-care centers.[19]

Supervising Women Employees

Sound management concepts should be applicable to employees regardless of their sex. Because of past culturalization, however, women employees and managers have arrived on the work scene with built-in expectations, frequently negative ones. As we've already learned, negative expectations can beget negative results (remember the Pygmalion effect?). Today's supervisors must attempt to be sensitive to the special needs of all employees, especially to those who have only recently been able to take part in the mainstream of economic opportunity. Table 10.3 summarizes some guidelines that can assist supervisors in working more effectively with women employees.

What did you expect?

The Problem of Sexual Harassment

Late 1991, a judge named Clarence Thomas received a presidential nomination to become a Supreme Court Justice. The nomination hearings brought out an unexpected surprise: the issue of **sexual harassment** in the workplace. Professor Anita Hill's allegations that Judge Thomas had previously harassed her sparked memories of similar experiences among many American women, and the topic rose to the forefront of national issues. An awareness of the problem of sexual harassment had existed for some time, but the Professor Hill/Judge Thomas hearings seemed to raise the level of national consciousness as well as the degree of confusion over the issue of what actually constitutes sexual harassment.

The issue was kept alive and maintained the nation's attention the following year after Bob Packwood, Republican senator from Oregon, was accused of engaging in a pattern of sexual harassment towards women for twenty years. He was reported to have agreed that his actions had been "out of sync" with a long political career in which he had consistently practiced "gender neutral" policies. Two other senators, David Durenberger from Minnesota and Daniel Inouye from Hawaii, also faced allegations of sexual harassment in 1992.[20]

Childcare Around the World[c]

Nobody cares for children the way we Americans do, right? Well, that depends on how you look at it. Things have changed regarding family values over the years. While mothers in the 1950s were generally expected to stay at home to look after the children, today nearly two-thirds of them work. There has even been a revolution in the thinking of men, who generally have no difficulty with the concept of a "working mother" or "father." However, a revolution in thinking has taken place only recently in the United States regarding the provision of leave to allow workers to care for a newborn child. Until 1993, childcare was viewed mainly as a private affair.

Most other industrial nations, however, have long had family and medical leave legislation that guarantees employees jobs to return to after taking leaves. For example, Chileans are entitled to 100 percent of their pay for 18 weeks while taking family or medical leave. Jobs are guaranteed to be available for them upon their return. European Community (EC) countries are required to provide protection to pregnant workers. EC country employees are eligible *as soon as they start work* to receive a minimum of 14 weeks' pay at a level no lower than statutory sick pay. However, all EC countries except Britain, Ireland, and Portugal, provide employees with even *more generous* family and medical leave than the EC requirement. The German government, for example, requires employers to keep jobs open for three years for mothers or fathers who take time off to look after children. In addition to the job guarantee, the state will pay mothers or fathers nearly $300 per month childraising money for two years.

Nordic countries follow similar practices, with childcare leave and childcare facilities available to all who desire them. Although 40 percent of all childcare centers are private in these countries, the state pays between a third and half of the costs of the private facilities. Other countries, such as the Netherlands, France, and Belgium have similar provisions.

After debating the merits of family leave legislation since 1985, the United States Senate and the House of Representatives finally passed a national family leave bill in

1991 that requires employers with 50 or more employees to grant employees up to 12 weeks of *unpaid* leave for the birth or adoption of a child or for the serious illness of either the employee or an immediate family member. The legislation was vetoed by former president Bush in spite of several polls showing majority support for such policies. The bill became one of incoming president Bill Clinton's major priorities and was signed into law on February 4, 1993, eight years after having been first introduced by Representative Patricia Schroeder of Colorado.

The benefits of the United States' legislation contain a few "ifs." Employees are covered *if* they work for companies with 40 or more employees. *If* they have worked for these companies for a year. *If* they have worked at least 1,250 hours during the year. And *if* they are not considered critical workers in the top 10 percent of the company's pay scale.

Various polls suggest that harassment is not particularly unusual in the workplace. For example, in a recent survey conducted by the *New York Times* and CBS News, four out of ten women said they had encountered unwanted sexual advances or remarks from men they worked for. Few of the women reported the incidents at the time fearing that doing so would jeopardize their job.[21] Although laws are designed to protect both men and women from unwanted sexual advances in the workplace, studies show that the majority of victims are female clerical workers, usually single parents, who work for male supervisors.[22]

The safe path between flirtation and harassment, between welcome and unwelcome attention, is a rather fuzzy line, one that isn't always easy to pinpoint. As a result, some well-intentioned, but uncertain, men have taken to bluntly asking women "Where's the line?" in an attempt not to be perceived as intentionally harassing them. As shown in Table 10.4, the Equal Employment Opportunity Commission (EEOC) has attempted to establish acceptable guidelines to assistance organizations in dealing with this challenge.

You gotta draw the line somewhere . . . but where?

TABLE 10.3   Supervisory Guidelines for Supervising Women.

- Avoid what is termed *statistical discrimination,* the making of prejudgments about a person's potential performance in a higher-level job based upon statistical results in a lower-level job. Recognize that women have traditionally had higher turnover rates not because they are women but because they usually had been placed in dead-end jobs or had bumped against the "glass ceiling." Turnover rates have proven satisfactory for women in responsible "career-type" jobs.
- Don't assume that a woman works only for "pin money." The majority of today's employed women work out of economic necessity.
- Don't be more critical of a woman than you would of a man for making the same types of mistakes. Guard against the tendency to expect more than adequate performance from a woman or minority group member.
- Avoid calling women employees such names as "sweetie," "honey," "dear," or calling your secretary "my girl."
- Do light cigarettes, open doors, and help with coats if you like. People of either sex tend to respond favorably to politeness and courtesy.
- Avoid any activities that can be interpreted as verbal or physical sexual harassment. An increasing number of women have pressed charges under Title VII of the Civil Rights Act of 1964 and in civil law in recent years, claiming sexual harassment.

The Need for Organizational Policies and Training

Regardless of the "fuzzy logic" associated with sexual harassment today, managers must continually be on guard against engaging in any activities that could be construed as being either verbal or physical sexual harassment. Many companies have established polices and training programs for supervisors dealing with the problem.

For example, Honeywell, an electronics company, spells out specifically what it regards as unacceptable conduct. Such behavior as catcalls, sexual jokes, and reportedly looking a woman up and down are included on its "no-no" list. Sensitivity toward the issue has reached such intense proportions that Honeywell officials ordered the removal of some tasteful nude photographs from an art exhibit at its corporate headquarters.[23]

DuPont, a large chemicals company, is another firm that has shown its concern for the problem. The company has put more than 65,000 of its 100,000 U.S. employees through voluntary workshops on the topic of sexual harassment. The company also provides a confidential telephone "hot-line" that allows women to air their grievances with less fear of retribution from their bosses.[24]

Management must attempt to be sensitive to the legal and moral aspects of the issue. The Supreme Court ruled in 1968 that sexual harassment of an employee by a supervisor violates the federal law

TABLE 10.4   **Equal Employment Opportunity Commission Guidelines Related to Sexual Harassment**

Sexual harassment may occur when and employer or supervisor:

- Threatens the security of an employee's job or potential promotion because the employee objects to comments of a personal, sexual nature, such as touching, feeling, or demands for sexual favors.
- Withholds a promotion or pay increase, demotes, or discharges an employee because of acceptance or rejection of the employer's or supervisor's conduct.
- Makes sexual innuendos that interfere with the employee's work performance or create a hostile, intimidating, or offensive work environment (including unwelcome behavior from a fellow employee).

against sex discrimination in the workplace, Title VII of the Civil Rights Act of 1964, which prohibits racial and sexual discrimination. The Court also ruled that an employer's "lack of knowledge of harassment by a supervisor does not necessarily insulate that employer from liability."[25]

Can you plead ignorance?

Sexual harassment can be costly to firms in terms of lost productivity, turnover, absenteeism, and court costs. Persons who feel that they are victims of sexual harassment can file a charge with the Equal Employment Opportunity Commission and check with local authorities regarding applicable state laws.

Working the Nets—Networking for Women

As a means of fostering their career paths, many men have for years turned to "old-boy networks" that consist of their friends, acquaintances, and prior school chums. In recent years, women, too, have begun to recognize the usefulness of being "old girls." Many women have started linking with each other and forming women's networks.

"Don't call me an 'old girl'!"

Networking provides women with the means of sharing information that is withheld, often unintentionally, by males. Sometimes women's network groups are formed within organizations, such as the one established within the Equitable Life Assurance Company: They also may be formed outside of formal work organizations, as in the case of a Minneapolis self-help, job-counseling networking group called "All the Good Old Girls." The group boasts over 2400 career women who establish contacts with other women and offer seminars on topics such as speech-writing, managerial techniques, and job stress. Such women's networks help women establish executive contacts as many men have been able to do in the past.[26] Many minority groups also have established such self-help networks.

A Second Thought? Or Merely More Options?

Some women appear to be questioning whether being a full-time working wife is all that worth it. A *Time* magazine and Cable News Network poll in 1992 revealed some of those doubts: a majority, 82 percent, of women feel that they have more freedom than their mothers did. But only 39 percent said that the women's rights movement has improved their lives.[27]

Perhaps the following is part of the reason for changing women's attitudes: The mothers of today's typical working mothers used to put in a 25-hour workweek as a full-time housekeeping mom. Their daughters, however, have apparently been "liberated" to a 50-hour workweek, since many of them still accept the principal responsibility for domestic chores in addition to working away from home. However, younger and middle aged men tend to help with house work slightly more than older men. Perhaps what every working women really needs is a wife!

You call this liberation?

Changing women's attitudes seem to be causing a counter trend. In 1985, given the choice between having a job or staying home to care for the family, 51 percent of U.S. women preferred to work; by 1991 that number fell to 43 percent, and 53 percent said they would rather stay home. Karlyn Keen of the American Enterprise Institute views this self-questioning not as a sign of weakness but of strength. She contends, "It's saying, 'I have many possibilities, and this is just what I prefer.'"[28]

CHALLENGES FACED BY WOMEN MANAGERS

Cultural diversity has been noticeably missing from managerial ranks in the past. Both women and ethnic minorities have not been represented in proportion to their numbers. Many women continue to remain stuck in jobs with little authority and relatively low pay. Although the executive suite seems within their grasp, many women have found that barriers continue to keep them from higher positions. (Do you remember the "glass ceiling" mentioned earlier?) For example, as of 1991, according the U.S. Department of Labor, women accounted for only 6.6 percent of corporate executives, and minorities held a paltry 2.6 percent of executive jobs.[29]

In spite of these discouraging statistics, an increasing proportion of management positions in recent years have been filled by women and ethnic minorities. Women have especially made their presence felt in such industries as retailing, banking, and publishing. This is probably natural, since a higher proportion of *all* employees in those industries are women.

In this and the following section we look at some of the specialized managerial challenges that each of these groups faces, starting with the distaff side of organizations.

The Managerial Women

"Effective management favors no gender," to coin a cliché. To be an effective manager, a woman needn't "act like a man." But she does need to "act like a manager." The concepts of management and leadership previously discussed apply to any manager regardless of sex. Women managers do, however, confront some situations and problems that are unique to their sex. These problems concern her *employees,* her *peers,* and her own *bosses.*

"Yes, Sir, Ms. Callahan"—Dealing With Employees

Search and be destroyed?

As a woman supervisor, don't be *preset* to perceive that problems with your employees are caused solely because you're a woman. Often problems related to your sex will never arise unless you search too long and hard for them and thus create a self-fulfilling prophecy. Paranoia can be counterproductive. However, be prepared to deal with any problems that do arise.

Problems With Male Employees. As a female manager, you may find some males resent being held accountable to a woman. In some instances, either consciously or unconsciously, they might try to make you look bad, bypass your authority, or even give you the silent treatment. What can you do if confronted in such ways by employees? As with any problem, try to discover what the problem actually is. Talk openly with your associate and ask him to level with you. Remember that it takes time for any new manager to gain the respect of employees, so try to be patient and understanding of their attitudes. Don't be afraid to exert your authority, but try wherever possible to draw on the input and participation of all your associates to gain their confidence, respect, and commitment. Also remember the concepts of change discussed in Chapter 9. Your presence may represent a radical departure from the established order of things. Try, above all, to be firm, fair, and friendly in your dealings with employees.

Why might a male resent a female boss?

Problems With Women Employees. Some women employees firmly believe that they prefer male managers over females. This attitude shouldn't surprise us since male managers have, until relatively recently, been the only type that existed. As a result, women who blindly accept the traditional pink-and-blue syndrome may—like their male counterparts—resent the presence of a female superior. Some women employees feel that it lowers their own status to have to take orders from another woman.

Once, again, try to get such problems out into the open and discuss them frankly. Use the participative leadership style whenever possible and attempt to serve as a role model. Perhaps you can help them realize that their own chances for future advancement probably hinge on your success or failure. Be sure to attempt to understand why your employees feel the way they do. Your problems should be diminished if you display a genuine concern for their feelings and needs.

How can a woman boss gain the confidence of her employees?

Peers and Their Effect

Females and males have certain responsibilities toward each other in any organization if goals are to be accomplished with minimum difficulty. Some male managers feel that the woman manager expects special treatment, which shouldn't be the case. Of course, the male manager should be as supportive or critical of a woman as of a man. Furthermore, the woman should be able to open the door if she gets to it first. Regardless of sex, an important managerial characteristic is courtesy, so should it really be upsetting if a woman holds the door for a man?

A "hold-the-door-open" policy.

Most woman managers prefer not to be singled out as women. For example, at meetings, some conference leaders stress the fact that a woman is in the room. As a man, don't say, "Good morning, gentlemen—and lady." Be somewhat casual, and say something like, "Good morning, everyone."

Also, many women would prefer that men not apologize every time they utter a swear word. Most women today have heard the words and are no longer shocked by their sound. However, you might ask yourself, "Do I really gain anything by using swear words among *any* business associates?"

"Shoot! Oops, sorry, lady."

Although much less common than in the past, some men continue to use sexist terms for women, like "birds," "broads," "gals," and "dolls." More men today are sensitive to the effect of words on others. If, as a woman, these words disturb you, tactfully let the person who uses them know your feelings. Often the male has no desire to be offensive and doesn't realize that his choice of words offends.

Who pays?

How about the question of who pays the bill when male and female cohorts lunch together? One guideline is for the person who did the inviting to offer to pay. Sometimes, however, older men may insist on paying. If this happens, and you're a woman, you can say that you would like the next outing to be on you.

The great leap forward should be a giant step backward.

Another peer problem: At a meeting, what should the woman do if asked to perform secretarial tasks like recording the discussion or making and serving coffee? One suggestion is that when someone says, "Let's have some coffee," the woman shouldn't jump up, but, instead, merely continue sitting. If silence descends on the meeting, she might look at the person nearest the door. Another suggestion is to say, "Fine, I'll take notes this time, but why don't we rotate it from now on?" Or, "No thanks, I've already had my quota of coffee this morning—why don't you go ahead and have some?"

Female peers can also become obstacles to managerial progress for women. Some new female managers have been surprised to find their female colleagues engage in sabotage toward them. There may be a tendency for some women to be more jealous of one another than men are of their counterparts. Many women have not been raised to feel comfortable with assertiveness and competition, which sometimes makes them feel uncomfortable in the workplace where they are cultural norms. A possible solution is for women to attempt to accept other women's successes and not perceive them as a personal affront.

Even Women Bosses Have Bosses

Women who have moved up the organizational ladder sometimes face serious resistance from their male bosses, who may have difficulty accepting new female roles. Male bosses, as well as male peers, may perceive women as a new form of competition for positions on the increasingly narrow managerial pyramid. Or at the other extreme, overzealous bosses may promote women to responsible positions before providing them with adequate training and background, a procedure likely to scuttle a woman's chances of success in management.

Some less enthusiastic male bosses refuse to develop training programs for woman managers because of established beliefs that the woman will not remain for long on the job. What can you do about it if you—a woman—aren't receiving adequate training and development opportunities on your job? You can grin and bear it (that is, do nothing and suffer); you can seek out training and experience on your own, or you can explain to your boss how both he and the organization would benefit from your training. The latter approach is the most advisable. Let your boss know that you plan to remain with the organization and that you want to advance. Convince him that both he and the organization will benefit by having well-trained personnel such as you.

How does assertiveness differ from pushiness?

A Role Conflict?

Some people feel that a woman who desires to have equal opportunities *and* have her door held open or a bus seat offered to her is experiencing a *conflict in roles,* perhaps there is a role conflict; values, however, have been changing rapidly. Many young women today seem far more concerned about "job openers" than "door openers." A modern attitude among many young couples is that whoever is nearest a door opens it as a matter of courtesy. Some women contend that many men who open doors or insist on paying for the business lunch don't necessarily respect women; they open the doors and pay for the lunch out of habit, not respect. The problem of who opens doors is really a side issue and not necessarily one related to equal employment opportunities.

Now let's turn to a discussion of the challenges facing ethnic minority managers.

CHALLENGES FACED BY ETHNIC MINORITY MANAGERS

As a result of the successes of many affirmative action programs, along with the growing number of more experienced and better-educated ethnic minority members, minority managers are no longer a complete rarity in responsible managerial positions. Of course, every new manager has adjustments to make, but for many ethnic managers the adjustments are greater.

Those Darn Expectations Again

Decades of knee-jerk negative expectations by a large proportion of both nonminority and minority segments of society are difficult to eradicate, and as an ethnic minority manager, you may not be able to avoid being in the limelight. Some of your subordinates, especially those who have been culturalized to develop stereotyped perceptions of others, may unconsciously expect you to fail or may even establish a higher set of performance standards for you than they would for other mortals. When you goof, it may be perceived as a result of your ethnic background. When a white male boss goofs, however, it may be perceived as merely a human mistake. ('Tis human for white males to err, *n'est-ce pas?*)

Does mythology provide nourishment for the intellectually underfed?

Don't Live Down to the Expectations of Others

What can you as an ethnic minority do about the present negative expectations of others? First, don't live *down* to negative expectations. Remember that you, too, may be preset to expect others to perceive you differently—which will not always be the case. So you may be wasting time and energy expecting to be upset by a nonevent.

Live it up, not down*!*

Second, attempt to know your subordinates well, and let them get to know you. *Prejudice,* as we've concluded, is the act of *pre*judging. A fairly common thought of the prejudiced person who gets to know those who were previously unfamiliar is, "Hmm, this person seems different from most. . . ." Yet, *most* was usually something never really observed first hand.

Getting to know you can help.

Third, strive for excellence in your performance—as any manager should. Be familiar with modern managerial skills and theories. Upgrade your own skills by attending management seminars and

Keep it up!

classes. Read articles that broaden your knowledge and contribute toward self-improvement. Your image will tend to be higher in the minds of subordinates when your own self-image is high.

And finally, be fair and consistent in your dealings with all subordinates. Don't practice the same types of prejudicial activities that some white males did in the past. Above all, don't stoop to the level of anyone who might have "attacked" you. Any supervisor who gives subordinates equitable and consistent treatment tends to beget greater respect.

Be consistently fair.

SUMMARY

In the space of one chapter we can barely scratch the surface of the numerous complex problems created by prejudice and discrimination. We have, however, delineated the nature of those two concepts and have discussed the problems faced by persons in multicultural work environments who receive different treatment for reasons unrelated to their employment situations.

The word *prejudice* means to *pre*judge. A prejudgment is an attitude usually based upon insufficient facts or no facts at all. As mainstream Americans have learned more about the similarities, as well as the differences, between minority Americans and themselves, many of their fears and uncertainties have become allayed. Likewise, minorities and women must continue to prepare themselves for opportunities that may open up for them in the future.

Although much progress has been made in the past thirty years, prejudice and discrimination have not yet been fully eradicated from the workplace. A disquieting trend in the early 1990s has been the tendency toward xenophobia, which—it is believed by many observers—will be reversed as the American economy improves and offers more jobs to more people.

Many organizations have experienced gratifying results with their affirmative action programs and greater concern for gender equity. Not only have women and ethnic minorities generally been satisfactory workers, but through increased exposure to women and minorities, other employees have also found that much of their prejudice had been based upon ignorance and a lack of understanding.

Many myths, based on tradition and custom, have long surrounded women in the workplace. When women were typically limited to lower-level jobs, a rapid turnover of female employees was inevitable. Women are now being given more responsible positions in which they are interested in staying, which contributes toward stability of employment. Today a larger proportion of the female work force works to support completely, or in part, herself and her family. In addition, a greater proportion of the female work force has more education and different values and responsibilities.

Employers should be on guard against allowing their equal employment opportunity programs to "slipslide." We should keep in mind that historically any society with large numbers of people who feel alienated or oppressed has typically experienced violence, turbulence, and unrest. Few groups in the past have continued indefinitely to accept oppression without reaction or revolt. More fortunate individuals must strive to improve the lot of those less fortunate. As the late American president, John F. Kennedy, said in an address to Latin American officials, "Those who make peaceful revolutions impossible, make violent revolution inevitable."

TERMS AND CONCEPTS TO REMEMBER

special employment group

xenophobia

prejudice

discrimination

preventive prejudice

protected classes of workers

Equal Pay Act of 1963

Civil Rights Act of 1964—
    Title VII

Equal Employment Opportunity
    Commission (EEOC)

Civil Rights Act of 1991

Civil Rights Act of 1866

affirmative action program (AAP)

double standards of supervision

glass ceiling

bona fide occupational qualification (BFOQ)

testing requirement exception

validity

reliability

seniority systems

reverse discrimination

proportional employment

comparable worth

mommy track

family leave

sexual harassment

networking

QUESTIONS

1. What is the difference between *prejudice* and *discrimination*?

2. What seem to be the principal causes of prejudice? How can prejudicial attitudes be changed?

3. What are some examples of *preventive prejudice* that you have observed or read about?

4. Does an employer have to give a person time off for religious worship under *any* circumstances?

5. Read the following statements:[30]

> "I'm gonna stall a Clinton nomination for weeks and weeks and weeks and weeks and weeks because the nominee is a damn lesbian!"
> —*U.S. Senator Jesse Helms*

> "To say that because gays are coming in the military that the military's effectiveness will be destroyed, that we will no longer be the world's premier military . . . I do not believe that. I think it's a peripheral issue."
> —*Retired Admiral William J. Crowe Jr.*

What was your reaction to each of the above two statements? Can you explain why you reacted the way you did?

6. Why is the supervisor one of the key persons in determining the success or failure of an AAP?

7. Do you think that ethnic minorities and women should be satisfied with the progress they have made during the past thirty years? Explain.

8. What is the nature of the so-called glass ceiling? Whom does it affect? What effect might it have on the motivation of some employees?

9. What are the dangers associated with a supervisor succumbing to double standards of supervision?

10. What is a BFOQ? What are some exceptions to civil rights legislation that might fall under the BFOQ?

11. What should be a significant concern of any employer who uses tests as a means of screening applicants for employment?

12. What is a seniority system? How do you feel about its fairness?

13. How does the concept of comparable worth differ from the concept equal pay for equal work?

14. Some people feel that preferential hiring—that is, hiring minorities and women over white males—is necessary. Assume you personally oppose preferential hiring on the grounds that it is reverse discrimination: What other means would you recommend to offset the inequities of past unfair employment practices?

15. What is your attitude toward the establishment of a secondary "mommy track" for working mothers? Would such a program be possible in all jobs, such as a sales position that requires a person to be "on the road" about 50–70 percent of the time?

16. Is an act of sexual harassment easy to determine? Explain.

17. What is the purpose of networking? Do you feel that it is a worthwhile activity? Explain.

18. Evaluate the following statement: "Women would make far better managers if they would only learn to think and act like men."

19. Who is easier for a woman to supervise—men or women?

20. What is meant by the advice offered to minority managers, "Don't live down to the expectations of others"?

APPLICATIONS

10.1 William Johnson Gets Promoted

William Johnson, an African-American, is a former photocopy-machine repairperson who rose through an AAP promotion plan with the Kopy Kat Corporation. Johnson recently was promoted to a managerial position as supervisor of 22 repair technicians and clerical workers. Much to his dismay he has begun to receive resistance from some of the employees. All but two of his associates are white.

One of Johnson's principal assistants, Jerry Franklin, has really begun to get on his nerves. Johnson told his wife one evening, "Jerry is really getting on my case. He questions every decision I make. He wants to double-check everything I do. He acts like he's my boss, instead of the reverse. He's really getting to me."

An interesting sidelight to this incident is that Jerry Franklin worked previously for another African American and there was seldom any friction.

Johnson has heard through the grapevine that there is concern on the part of some of his employees that he is likely to give the two African Americans in his department favorable treatment. Florence Farber, Johnson's boss, recently confided in him that an employee even mentioned such concerns to her. The same employee questioned whether Johnson hadn't received his promotion as a result of special, "fairer-than-fair" treatment.

The results Johnson has been having when interviewing applicants for open positions also concerns him. On three occasions, applicants never returned for a second interview after realizing that their boss would be black.

Johnson is becoming increasingly concerned about his future relationship with his employees. He believes that he cannot allow them to continue questioning his authority. Johnson said to himself this morning, "I'm not going to tolerate any more static from these employees. I going to let them know who's boss around here!"

Questions

1. What seems to be the problem in this case?

2. What specifically should Johnson do to reduce his feelings of distress in his new supervisory position?

10.2 Promotion Bypass

Boris Brash is a branch manager whose Portland, Oregon, office has developed a reputation with the company for efficient operations. Recently, a division manager telephoned Brash about a new branch office that was to open within two months in Corvallis. The division manager informed Brash that senior management is highly pleased with the way the Portland office has been run in the past and would like him to choose someone from his office to manage the new Corvallis branch.

Brash agreed to find someone and started analyzing his personnel to determine who might make a good manager. He has narrowed the choice down to two persons within his office: Miss Zelda Zelous and Mr. Edgar Eager.

Both Zelda and Edgar are bright young persons in their early thirties. Each has a college degree from a nearby university. Zelda has been with the firm seven years and Edgar five years. Zelda usually seems more effective and tactful when dealing with customers, especially those with complaints, than does Edgar. Both, however, have low absenteeism records, and either one would probably make a satisfactory manager for the new Corvallis office.

Brash is reminded of some of the things that his father, a retired manager, had taught him. He recalls his father telling him that "women in general don't make good managers. They have those monthly ups and downs," which certainly would be detrimental to stability in the new office. "Most people prefer male supervisors. Women generally have babies and quit the company; they're not really interested in careers."

Brash wants to be fair. That night he ponders over in his mind which person should be chosen. "Zelda is a good, dependable worker," he muses, "but she probably would become oversensitive in a new managerial role and develop aggressive, pushy female tendencies."

Brash decides to choose Edgar. However, he doesn't want to upset or alienate Zelda, so he plans to invite her to his office tomorrow morning to explain the situation. He intends to tell her that the reason she wasn't chosen for the promotion is because she is the best person the office has, and that the Portland office just can't get along without her.

Questions

1. What sort of problems seem to exist in this case?

2. What do you anticipate might be Zelda's reaction to the reason Brash intends to give her: "Zelda, you weren't chosen for the promotion because you're the best person the office has"?

10.3 My Rightful Place

Tom Wack's secretary placed his morning mail on his desk and hurried from his office. Tom had no sooner started to read the top letter when he let out an emotional burst, "Get the attorney on the phone!" Before the lawyer's telephone number could be dialed, new instructions came: "Cancel that call!"

Tom's violent reaction was to a letter from the Ohio Commission on Human Rights, which notified the company of a complaint, reading in part: "Complainant was continuously denied promotions and salary commensurate with her job duties by the Respondents because of her sex. The Respondent company has placed males with less seniority and experience in positions of responsibility over the Complainant and have paid those males salaries far above what the Complainant receives, in addition to perquisites and bonuses inherent in managerial positions."

Tom was hurt deeply. How could Jane Spiegel do this to him? When Tom was hired as a salesperson in 1989, Jane was his secretary. She had three years' experience with the company and knew her job very well. During the years, as he moved up the management ladder, he promoted Jane at every opportunity. In fact, Jane was currently "the highest paid broad," as he put it, in his nationwide field distribution network. The only reason she was not higher in the organization was because she refused to relocate to corporate headquarters in Tallahassee, Florida. In 1991, Jane was offered a promotion to become Tom's national sales administrator concurrent with his move to national sales and distribution director. Jane had declined the move because her husband, whom she had recently married, was a bus driver who had 18 years' seniority with the city. She said, "Barney will not be able to find a secure, well-paying job in another city."

One year ago, Tom had promoted Jane to dealer relations coordinator at the Cincinnati distribution warehouse. Last month he considered Jane for promotion to manager in charge of the Cincinnati outlet. Of course, she would have been the only female manager in charge of warehousemen anywhere in the company. Because of the closing last month of the Tulsa warehouse, Jim Hansen was available for reassignment. There was concern that Jim would leave the company if he were assigned to a job in the Florida headquarters. Thus, Jim was transferred, and Jane did not get promoted to the number one job. However, Tom knew she expected that "chance of a lifetime," so he told her the lateral transfer of Jim would be temporary, perhaps six to twelve months. The promise was that when Jim was next promoted, Jane would become manager in charge.

Peter Paulson, director of personnel examined records and interviewed managers familiar with the Cincinnati situation. Peter's findings were as follows:

	Jane Spiegel's Record	Jim Hanson's Record
Hired	10/10/86 as Clerk Typist @ $1400 monthly.	2/4/90 as Credit Coordinator @ $2700 monthly.
Education	3 years as education major.	BA in business administration.
Age	38 years	31 years
Current status	Promoted to Dealer Relations Coordinator 1 years ago @ $2400 monthly.	Lateral transfer to Manager in Charge 1 month ago @ $3800 monthly.
Latest performance evaluations	"Very bright and ready for promotion"	"Excellent results" Manager in Charge, Tulsa
Career potential	Unwilling to relocate; ultimate potential is Manager in Charge, Cincinnati	Senior marketing and sales potential

Jane talked by telephone to female employees in five cities, telling them of her suit against the company and how she "plans to make waves." Within a week, five women told their bosses that they would file discrimination complaints if the company agreed to pay Jane "all the money she wants."

On a Friday, without requesting an excused absence, Jane was absent all day to review her case with the State EEO Specialist. On that date, the two data entry clerks phoned in "sick." Only Jane and the two trained data entry clerks could efficiently enter orders on the computer so that the warehouse crew could make dealer shipments. Orders were delayed and dealers were angered. When questioned by the manager, all three women said their absences were a "coincidence."

Choosing of sides started early. Everyone in the warehouse office seemed to be for Jane or against her. Women who were "for the company" stopped speaking to Jane and vice versa. Jane had for many months functioned as second in command. She had been there longer than anyone and knew the ropes better than anyone. Communication problems became so serious that operational efficiencies plummeted, and dealer complaints hit an all-time high.

Peter Paulson had placed all managers on notice, especially Jim Hansen and Tom Wack, that every precaution must be taken to assure the claimant-employee, Jane Spiegel, that she will not be harassed or subjected to reprisal. Under the law, she has that protection.

Jim and Tom met to explore strategies for correcting all operational inefficiencies. They found some problems that were clearly no fault of Jane. However, her attitude had caused serious dealer dissatisfaction. Jim and Tom decided to telephone Peter with this question: "We know we cannot harass Jane, but how far can she push us before we can fight back?"

Questions

1. What is the problem in this case?

2. What is your remedy?

3. In the complaint, Jane is arguing that her "rightful place" (but for discrimination, where she would have been) is to be promoted and that she receive the salaries, perquisites, and bonuses of managerial positions held by men of like seniority. Do you agree?

4. Should Jane insist that her husband relocate for the sake of her career? Why or why not?

5. Do you feel the men in the warehouse would object to working for a woman manager? Would your answer be different if half the crew were women?

6. Do you feel that women who are subjected to sex discrimination always file complaints? Sometimes file complaints? Very rarely file complaints?

7. Does Tom appear to be sexist? Explain.

NOTES

1. Tamar Jacoby, "A Portrait of Black and White," *The Wall Street Journal,* July 7, 1992, p. 10.

2. Janet Howells-Tierney, "Of Pride and Prejudice," *Sunday—A Stars and Stripes Magazine,* December 1, 1991, pp. 1, 4.

3. *The State of Black America,* published by the national Urban League, as reported in "State of Black America," *USA Today / International Edition,* January 26, 1989, p. 6.

4. Priscilla Painton, "Quota Quagmire," *Time,* May 27, 1991, pp. 42–46.

5. Tim Bovee, "Asians Led U.S. Growth in 1980s," *Contra Costa Times,* June 12, 1992, p. 2–B.

6. "Sex Bias Settlement OK'd," *Contra Costa Times,* December 7, 1986, p. 1–B.

7. Abby Livingston, "Cultural Diversity in Today's Corporation—What Your Department Can Do," *Working Woman,* January 1991, pp. 59–60.

8. Diane Summers, "'Glass Ceiling' Stops Female Managers Reaching the Top," *Financial Times,* April 9, 1991, p. 14; and Susan B. Garland, "Throwing Stones at the 'Glass Ceiling,'" *Business Week / International Edition,* August 19, 1991, p. 27.

9. David P. Twomey, *A Concise Guide to Employment Law: EEO & OSHA* (Cincinnati: South-Western Publishing, 1986), pp. 26, 28.

10. See note 9.

11. Clint Bolick and Susan Nestleroth, *Opportunity 2000—Creative Affirmative Action Strategies For a Changing Workforce,* United States Department of Labor, (Washington D.C.: U.S. Government Printing Office, 1988) p. 177.

12. Tom Bovee, "Income Gap Between Sexes Still Persists," *San Francisco Examiner,* November 14, 1991, p. E–1, E–4.

13. Diane Summers, "Great Expectations," *Financial Times,* November 18, 1992, p. 14.

14. 15. K. C. Cole, "Who Needs Women?" *Omni Magazine,* May 1987, p. 35.

15. "U.S. Public Schools Biased Against Girls, Report Says," *Los Angeles Times,* February 11, 1992, p. 12.

16. Barbara Reynolds, "For Women, Future Holds More Respect," *USA Today/International Edition,* April 12, 1989, p. 19.

17. Karen S. Peterson, "Problems of Singling Out Moms," *USA Today/International Edition,* March 16, 1989, p. 7.

18. "Family-Medical Leave Act Facts," *AFL-CIO News,* February 18, 1989, p. 5.

19. "Ma Bell's Family Way," *Time/International Edition,* June 12, 1989, p. 38.

20. Jurek Martin, "Sex-Case Senator Vows to Stay On," *Financial Times,* December 11, 1992, p. 8; and John Elson, "Conduct Unbecoming," *Time,* December 14, 1992, p. 32.

21. Martin Dickson, "Workplace Advances," *Financial Times,* October 17, 1992, p. 18.

22. Karen Shallcross Koziara, Michael Moskow, and Lucretia Dewey Tanner (eds.), *Working Women: Past, Present, Future,* (Washington, DC: Bureau of National Affairs, 1987), p. 388.

23. See note 21.

24. See note 21.

25. Stuart Taylor Jr., "High Court Rules Sexual Harassment Violates Law," *Contra Costa Times,* June 20, 1986, p. 1A.

26. Ed Worden, "Caucuses Help Women and Minorities to Help Themselves," *World of Work Report,* August 1981, p. 63; and "'Old Girls and Old Boys,'" *Time,* October 26, 1981, p. 68.

27. "Feminists Lose in Poll," *Stars and Stripes,* March 2, 1992, p. 6.

28. Ann Blackman, Priscilla Painton, and Elizabeth Taylor, "The War Against Feminism," *Time/International Edition,* March 23, 1992, pp. 42, 44.

29. Susan B. Garland, "Throwing Stones at the 'Glass Ceiling,'" *Business Week,* August 19, 1991, p. 27; and Torri Minton, "Cracking the Glass Ceiling," *San Francisco Chronicle,* November 6, 1991, pp. B1, B5.

30. "Helms Vows to Block Lesbian Nominee," *The Contra Costa Times,* May 8, 1993, p. 5; and John Lancaster, "Crowe Says 'Emotion' Fueling Anti-Gay Stand," *The Washington Post,* April 14, 1993.

31. "Labor Letter," *Wall Street Journal,* August 22, 1989, p. 1; and Diane Summers, "Secretaries No Longer Typecast by Executives," *Financial Times,* January 27, 1992, p. 6.

BOX NOTES

a. Adapted from Joan S. Lublin, "Going Global—More U.S. Companies Seek Out Europeans To Fill Top Positions," *The Wall Street Journal Europe,* May 25, 1992, pp. 1, 4.

b. Adapted from William D. Murray, "Racism Toward Asian-Americans Increasing, Commission Says," *Contra Costa Times* February 27, 1992, p. 3; Martin Dickson, "Play Ball! Means Several Things in Seattle," Financial Times, March 27, 1992, p. 6; and Beth Hughes, "Study: Japanese Don't Trust American Managers," *San Francisco Examiner,* November 2, 1989, p. C–1.

c. Adapted from David Goodhart, "Germany Raises Child Care Leave to 3 Years," *Financial Times,* August 15, 1991, p. 2; Jim Smolowe, "Europe—Where Children Come first," *Time International,* November 9, 1992, pp. 38, 39.; and Mike Hall, "Senate Passes Family Leave Bill," *AFL-CIO News,* October 14, 1991, p. 3.

EXPERIENTIAL EXERCISES

Upgrading Secretarial Positions?

According to a report in *The Wall Street Journal,* secretaries are in short supply. Although not all secretaries are women, a large proportion continue to be so. With more women entering the job market, many of them seek positions with more responsibility. Modern electronic office equipment can give them more time for new types of duties. More firms are reported to have given their secretaries higher-level responsibilities and duties, such as contract negotiation, budget, or engineering-related jobs.[31]

Contact the human resource directors or office managers of five well-known firms in your area. Tell them you are working on a project for a college course you are taking. Ask them the following questions:

1. In what ways have secretarial jobs within your organization changed during the past 5–10 years?

2. What, if any, higher-level duties and responsibilities have secretaries within your organization been assigned that were not typically assigned in the past?

3. Do your secretarial hires seem to want to take on responsibilities beyond those required for a typical secretarial position?

4. To what extent have secretaries with your organization been successful in making the transition to nonclerical managerial positions?

5. What proportion of the secretaries in your organization are men?

After you have obtained the information from the five organizations, analyze the data carefully. Do you see any positive trends developing in the companies surveyed? If you have the opportunity, compare your results with other members of your class.

Don't Forget the Diapers!

Some parents of small children have to engage in job-related overnight travel periodically. Parents—both mothers and fathers—who desire to maintain a better balance between family and business life, occasionally take their children with them on such trips. They feel that there are benefits to children in seeing that there is a real world out there. Parents are also able to spend some quality time with their children during the evenings.

A major challenge, however, for parents of tagalongs is finding someone to take care of their children while off on business. Many hotels have long provided cribs; some hotels have made arrangements with professional baby-sitting organizations to take care of children whose parents must be gone during the day.

Here's an activity for you: Contact five hotels in your area that typically cater to business travelers. Ask them the following questions:

1. Do you provide cribs for infants? Is there an additional charge for this service?

2. Do you have baby-sitting facilities? What sort? How can you assure me that the sitters are qualified? Is the sitter organization bonded?

3. Can you arrange to warm baby bottles?

4. Do you have a special children's menu available with room service?

5. What other services for children do you offer?

BusinessWeek

FEBRUARY 1, 1993   A McGRAW-HILL PUBLICATION $2.75

MANAGING AIDS

This is the story of how one mid-level executive at Digital Equipment struggled with managing an employee suffering from AIDS. It is a tale of fear and compassion, denial and hope, anger and humanity. It is a story that is being played out, in one way or another, in virtually every major American corporation.

PAGE 48

FRANK DALOISIO AND HIS MANAGER, JEAN LANGONE SMITH

CHAPTER 11

Organizational Challenges Faced by Older Workers and Those With Disabilities

Hire Them . . .
It's Good Business

When you finish this chapter,
you should be able to:

1
Understand some of the special types of employment problems faced by older
employees and those with disabilities.

2
Recognize the traditional prejudicial attitudes toward the
aging and those with disabilities.

3
Explain how aging trends are likely to affect employment practices.

4
Summarize some of the principal suggestions that can be
applied to assist the older worker.

5
Recognize some of the common myths associated with hiring
people with disabilities.

6
Understand employers' obligations related to people with HIV and AIDS.

7
Identify the advantages of hiring persons with disabilities.

8
Cite the problems associated with managing individuals with disabilities.

> The human being is by nature active
> and when inactive begins to die.
>
> *Erich Fromm, Psychoanalyst*

> We hire people because of their abilities,
> not their disabilities.
>
> *Donald Devey, IBM Executive*

A visionary once mused, "We're all middle-aged sometime—if we're lucky!" Unfortunately, however, good luck doesn't always accompany middle age, especially when the middle-aged person is out of work. The chances are fairly good that you—the reader of this book—are relatively young. Can you imagine, however, applying for a job and being rejected solely on the grounds that you are over 40 years old and thus too old to hire?

Also think about how you might feel if you had previously suffered an industrial accident, or had been born with an impairment, or had your right leg blown off by "friendly fire" while serving in the military during the Desert Storm crisis in the Persian Gulf, or had contracted AIDS as a result of receiving improperly screened blood during a blood transfusion—and people refused to enable you to engage in gainful employment. Would you feel such treatment to be fair?

Why must managers understand special employment groups?

In the previous chapter we examined some of the conditions and employment problems of minorities and women. Unfortunately, these are not the only special employment groups in our society. The organizational manager of today, facing additional social responsibilities and pressure, must understand and be prepared to deal with numerous *special employment groups,* especially since their members are also demanding what they believe to be basic rights in a society that refers to itself as "free."

In this chapter, therefore, we are going to examine two groups that far too often have been the forgotten humans in most studies of organizational behavior: the aging and those with physical or intellectual challenges, currently referred to as **individuals with disabilities**. Our discussion will also include a group that has been at the forefront of controversy and misinformation during the past one and one-half decades—those who have contracted the AIDS virus.

These groups by no means complete the list of those who are discriminated against solely because of conditions over which they have little or no control. They do, however, serve to illustrate for the student of organizational behavior the variety of problems with which organizational members are faced in the modern world.

EMPLOYMENT PROBLEMS OF THE AGING

Like it or not, we're all getting older. Aging is a condition that few of us can avoid experiencing and one most of us would prefer to avoid thinking about. Unfortunately, however, various forms of subtle **age bias** in employment have accompanied the aging process in American society. For reasons that we shall examine, older workers have regularly been discriminated against in the hiring, promotion, and retirement practices of many organizations. As evidence, the number of age discrimination cases filed in 1991 went up 12 percent over 1990 and was expected to continue to rise.[1]

The Graying of America

According to the U.S. Bureau of the Census, the fastest growing segment of the population in 1990 was adults and elders. By the year 2000, a predicted 36 percent of the population of the United States will be over 45 years old, as compared to 30.8 percent in this category in 1980. And by the year 2030, an estimated 21 percent of the population will be 65 and older compared to only 12 percent in 1986. Instead of being youth-oriented in the future, perhaps, as some individuals have prophesied, being 50 will become fashionable.

Fifty is only half way to 100!

Signs of such changes are blowing in the wind: For example, movie star Nick Nolte at age 51 was named *People* magazine's "sexiest man alive." Movie star/producer Warren Beatty became a "proud papa" at age 55. Even ex-Beatle singer/composer Paul McCartney is now over age 50. And the first wave of the 77 million baby boomers, who once admonished, "You can't trust anyone over 30," are now approaching the land of the "Big Five-O"![2]

The Variability of the Aging Process

The term **older worker** is one with little in the way of absolute meaning. If you were to choose 30 people at random, all 45 years old, you would quickly discover that not all of them have experienced the aging process at the same rate. Some members of your sample would appear trim, agile, youthful-looking, and topped with full heads of their own hair. Others might be plump, muscularly soft, a bit weathered and wrinkled, and sporting heads of hair imported from the Far East. A variety of factors, especially *heredity* and *past dietary* and *health habits,* significantly influence the aging process.

Do all persons age at the same rate?

What determines how old is "old"?

The *nature of a particular job* and the *industry* itself also influence how "old" a person is for a specific occupation. Baseball players, for example, are generally considered old if they are in their thirties, while corporate presidents are considered young when they are in their mid-forties.

One "young" old-timer was Harland Sanders, the goateed "colonel" who founded the Kentucky Fried Chicken fast-food chain, which now has over 6000 outlets in 48 countries. In spite of his years, Sanders never lost his sizzle and remained with the KFC Corporation as a $125,000-a-year consultant until his death at the age of 90.

Still lickin' fingers good at 90!

And that near-centenarian comic, singer, and movie star George Burns, who boasted that he was the only person to have played God in the movies and to have cut a country-western disc while in his 90s, signed a five-year deal in 1991 with the Riviera Hotel instead of one for ten years because he wasn't sure the resort would last until the year 2001! His contract was for 35 shows a year.[3]

Oh, my God! It's "Waylon" George Burns!

Who Are "Older" Workers?

Who are considered to be the older workers in the United States? Age, of course, is relative. Few people 40 years old consider themselves "old" or "older." The *older worker,* however, is officially defined by the **Age Discrimination in Employment Act of 1967,** as amended in 1978 and 1986, as age 40 and over. The "official" age of an older person is not as significant as the specific problems that many individuals experience merely as a result of their own advancing ages. Managers must recognize that, as another special employment group, older workers are protected by legislation and, as a result, are legally entitled to employment, proper placement based on physical limitations, adequate training, fair pay, impartial consideration for available promotions, and retirement assistance.

Forty years young!

The Problem of Job Loss for the Aging

There is an expression often uttered by older workers that stresses part of their plight: "Too old to rehire and too young to retire."

The problems of older workers are often disguised by unemployment statistics, which show that unemployment rates tend to *decrease* with age. This condition is not surprising since older persons generally have more *seniority* and thus are usually the last to be laid off. However, once out of work, individuals over 40 are likely to remain unemployed much longer than their younger co-workers. In fact, the likelihood of *long-term unemployment* actually tends to increase with age. From the age of 40, many unemployed workers often find job hunting a nightmare.

How is the problem of aging disguised by unemployment statistics?

Older women share the same unemployment problems that older men do—and then some. Older women face even greater barriers than men after age 40, their unemployment rates being one-third higher than men's. Older women remain out of work longer than older men. Income is also lower for older women.

Sounds like women aren't supposed to get old, eh?

Why is finding a new job so difficult when you are over age 50?

Another major problem for older persons, especially those over 50 years old, is that when they lose their jobs, they have difficulty finding others. A large proportion of workers not covered by employer-sponsored retirement plans, or who had pensions in companies that went bankrupt, face potential financial problems when they retire. They also face personal problems, including loneliness, loss of purpose, housing difficulties, failing health, and fear of death.

ATTITUDES TOWARD OLDER WORKERS

The aging often find it difficult to secure employment because of biased attitudes of some employers. Table 11.1 cites some of the more common myths and realities associated with the employment of older workers. Each of these is summarized in the section that follows.

Increased Costs of Employee Benefits

Why don't older workers necessarily increase costs?

An attitude toward the aging often expressed by employers is that operating costs rise when older employees are hired because of the increased expense for health and retirement plans. Not all employers, however, agree that costs necessarily rise; some contend that any increased cost in benefits is more than offset by savings in turnover and training costs plus not having to pay retirement costs until later. For example, a study of a large aerospace company found that when a worker retired at ages 50–54, it cost the company $40,000 per year for pension and health benefits. But if the worker left between 55 and 59, the cost declined to $30,000, and to only $23,000 if the worker

TABLE 11.1   **Myths and Realities Associated With the Employment of Older Workers.**

Myths	Realities
• They cost more in employee benefits.	• They may actually reduce total costs, especially related to turnover and training.
• They have fewer working years left.	• They tend to remain on the job longer than younger workers.
• They are physically too weak for certain jobs.	• They vary significantly in their physical capabilities, as do younger workers.
• They have higher rates of absenteeism.	• Their documented results indicate otherwise.
• They are *old* rather than *older*.	• People age at varying rates.

stayed until he or she was over 60. Costs declined partly because pension and benefits were paid out over a shorter period of time. Also, senior workers are less likely to have school-age children who use health benefits. In addition, the cost of training replacement workers is avoided when an older employee is retained.[4]

Fewer Working Years

Another cause of age bias is the assumption that younger persons potentially have more years remaining with a company; that is, a 25-year-old could potentially be with an organization for 40 years, while a person age 50 would ordinarily have only 10 to 15 years remaining at the most.

Why doesn't the younger worker necessarily have more potential years?

However, studies have consistently indicated that turnover rates are actually *higher among workers* 25 to 34 years old than among workers over 50 years old. Younger workers, often feel that they have less to lose by changing jobs, or even careers, early in their working years. The older individual is far more likely to finish out his or her career with a company than a younger worker. Furthermore, the average time that *all individuals* have held their jobs is only between 3 and 4 years.[5] In light of this information, 10 years is a fairly long time for a company to have the potential of a mature, trainable person, and that assumes at 50 the person becomes unable to work. Usually, such is not the case in the real world.

Physically Too Weak

Another attitude that has worked to the detriment of older employees is the belief that older workers are physically weaker than younger ones. Although this contention is often true, exceptions are numerous. Many members of society, including medical doctors, tend to try to force the aging into a preconceived role. After all, aren't old people *supposed* to be sick much of the time? There's a story, for example, of the man of 104 who, when he complained of a stiff knee, was told, "After all, you can't expect to be agile," and replied, "My left knee's 104, too, but that doesn't hurt."

What can be done when an older worker becomes weaker?

On occasions when an older employee has not had sufficient muscular strength for a specific job, some concerned managers have either *reassigned the person* to a different job within the organization, or *redesigned the job* to enable a physically weaker person to perform it.

Higher Rates of Absenteeism

There is also the belief that older employees have higher rates of absenteeism, another myth refuted by many managers. Studies have consistently shown that the older worker has a substantial lower absenteeism record than younger workers. McDonald's Corporation typifies the experience many companies have experienced with older workers. Stan Stein, McDonald's Senior Vice President for Personnel, declares, "There is no question that the company's extensive efforts to attract older workers is cost-effective. Older workers are reliable and enthusiastic, and provide a very settling influence on younger workers."[6]

Is absenteeism related only to bad health?

Factors far more significant than age influence the absence of employees from the job. Young workers are frequently absent for reasons other than those related to illness. An interesting study on absenteeism might be made, if one were inclined, at any afternoon game of the Minnesota Twins to determine the numbers of younger persons who were absent from work for reasons unrelated to their health! Furthermore, although older people might be marginally less fit or more prone to illness than a younger person, they are not away on maternity leave or at home nursing a sprain acquired during mid-management racquetball league competition.

Are *Old* Rather Than *Older*

Just because I'm older *doesn't mean I'm* old!

We know that people age at different rates. Some employers perceive applicants for employment as old when, in reality, they've merely lived more years than some people; that is, they are older. Other employers have begun to recognize the value of hiring the older worker. Partially as a result of a shortage of willing teenage help, Kentucky Fried Chicken and the McDonald's Corporation hire older workers. Other firms recruiting oldsters with positive results include Minneapolis-based Control Data Corporation, Georgia Power Company, Safeway Stores, Church's Fried Chicken, and J.C. Penney. These firms also seek such nontraditional workers as people with disabilities and homemakers, often for part-time and flextime work.[7]

ASSISTING THE OLDER WORKER

As with any organizational behavior challenge, managers must develop a high degree of *sensitivity* to and *understanding* of the problems of aging employees. Ours has been, and will continue to be in the foreseeable future, a work-oriented society, which in itself can place psychological stress on under- and unemployed middle-aged and older persons.

Legislation for the Older Worker

Attitudes toward the aging are changing. They are bound to, since between the years 1990 and 2000 the number of Americans aged 25 to 34 will shrink by 18 percent due to the low birth rates of the late 1960s and the 1970s. There are 77 million people who were born between 1946 and 1964 currently in or entering middle age and looking beyond. As mentioned earlier, by the year 2030 an estimated 21 percent of the U.S. population will be 65 or older. Even the number of people aged 80 or older is expected to skyrocket, from 6.2 million in 1987 to over 12 million in 2010.[8] The older worker in the future, instead of being pressured to take early retirement, is likely to be encouraged to work longer or begin a second career after retirement in light of the impending shortage of skilled labor predicted for upcoming decades.

Grayness is growing!

The passage of the *Age Discrimination in Employment Act* reflects this greater awareness of the aging process. With current population trends, larger proportions of the total U.S. population are likely to be included under the act in the future.

The basic provisions of the act are that:

1. *Private employers* of 20 or more persons, and *federal, state, and local governments,* regardless of the number of employees, may no longer refuse to hire qualified workers over 40.

2. *Employers* may no longer fire employees in this age group because of age alone, or discriminate against them in terms of salary, seniority, and other job conditions.

3. *Employment agencies* may no longer refuse to refer workers in this age group to prospective employers, nor try to classify them on the basis of age.

4. *Labor unions* with 25 or more members may no longer exclude those over age 40 from membership or refuse to refer older members to employers simply because of their age.

5. *Help wanted advertisements* may no longer include age specifications.

6. All organizations obligated under the act must post in conspicuous places the rights of employees or union members related to the act. (See Figure 11.1 for an example of an approved poster.)

The Need for Counseling and Guiding the Older Worker

Why is facing the aging process sometimes difficult?

The problems of the aging are further aggravated by the tendency of older people not to adjust readily to the realities of *changed conditions in the job market.* The necessity of having to face the problems of aging is something of a blow to the egos of many. Numerous persons do not want to leave the communities in which they have lived for many years even though the move may be necessary to obtain another job. The possibility of having to accept a job with less pay or prestige can also be mentally painful.

Persons 40+ Years Note!

The Federal Age Discrimination in Employment Act prohibits arbitrary age discrimination in employment by:

- Private Employers of 20 or more person

- Federal, State, and Local Governments, without regard to the number of employees in the empolying unit

- Employment Agencies serving such employers

- Labor Organizations with 25 or more members

Certain exceptions are provided.

If you feel you have been discriminated against because of age, contact the nearest office of the Wage and Hour Division, U.S. Department of Labor. It is important to contact the Division promptly.

If you wish to bring a court action yourself, you must first notify the Secretary of Labor of your intent to do so. The notice should be filed promptly, but in no event later than *180* days after the alleged unlawful practice occurred.

Questions on State age discrimination laws should be directed to State authorities. These laws may affect the *180* day time limit noted above.

Questions on Federal employment should be directed to the U.S. Civil Service Commission, Washington, D.C. 20415.

U.S. Department of Labor

Employment Standards Administration
Wage and Hour Division

Figure 11.1 An example of an approved poster related to the Age Discrimination in Employment Act.

For some older workers—as with any employees—having to develop new skills may seem threatening. Some older workers may not have worked in modern high-tech environments in the past. For them, a newer work environment can be a frightening experience, especially for the person who feels more confident working on familiar equipment. A mere glance at the 1044-page thick recent edition of

Mastering WordPerfect 5.1, designed for use with a word-processing system, can cause heart palpitations and shortness of breath!

There are some older employees who have been conditioned to fear high-technology electronic equipment, since it seems mysterious and complicated to the uninitiated. Managers must attempt to placate such fears by "selling" the benefits of new equipment or processes and by providing adequate training.

Some older workers not only resist opportunities to be retrained but also do not know how to seek jobs effectively. Consequently, to offset some of the natural attitudes of the aging, more attention in the future must be paid to the counseling and guidance of older employees to reduce their potential psychological fears.

Encouraging Multiple Careers

Someone once said, "To take work away from the worker is the cruelest thing society can do." Some years ago, Johns Hopkins University professor M. Harvey Brenner made a study that indicated that death rates rise with unemployment rates. His research pointed out that an increase of 1 percent in unemployment is associated with a 1.9 percent increase in the general death rate. His studies also showed that a 1 percent increase in unemployment is accompanied by a 4.1 percent increase in suicides and a significant increase in first admissions to mental hospitals and admissions to state prisons.[9]

Rather than giving older employees a gold watch, a rocking chair, and walking papers, an increasingly popular move for progressive organizations is to offer older employees "life planning" counseling programs that prepare them for **multiple careers.** Some organizations also assist their older employees through retraining and reassigning them to new positions within the company.

Age 55? Time to freshen up!

Management consultant Marc Michaelson suggests that people might have three or four careers during a lifetime, or at age 55 take a sabbatical from a company, go back to school, and then return to the company in a different position.[10] Often the opportunity for fresh challenges helps to enrich the lives of those who have been at the same position for many years, especially for those who have been in positions involving high degrees of stress or rapid obsolescence.

Easing the Transition Into Retirement

Many employees look eagerly toward retirement—the day when the boss will hand them a certificate symbolizing their years of dedicated service to the company. Unfortunately, however, retirement for many people has not turned out to be the enjoyable experience that they had expected. On the contrary, some workers who opted to retire early *to escape* the drudgery and boredom of work have discovered their retirement *to be* one of drudgery and boredom.

From ennui to ennui.

Myriad problems exist for many retired persons. Accumulated pensions, if any, have frequently not kept pace with rising prices. Mental and physical health also suffer for some retirees who are accustomed to being active and productive. Various medical studies have suggested that people who are healthy in old age will stay healthy longer if they work. Many people, regardless of their age at retirement, appear to be totally unprepared for the adjustments necessary to retire successfully. As a result, some organizations have developed special programs and counseling services for employees prior to retirement for the purpose of enabling them to make the transition into retirement a more satisfying experience. Let's look briefly at some of these programs.

Phased Retirement and Job Banks. One plan that can help ease the shock of moving from full-time employment to retirement is to allow older workers to engage in **phased retirement** (also termed *tapered retirement*). One way in which this approach is utilized is to enable workers—say, those over 60—to share their current jobs with another worker, thus reducing their average work week. Another approach to phased retirement is to allow older employees to be part of a **job bank** of experienced retired personnel who are subject to recall on a part-time or full-time basis during periods of peak work loads. Such employees, in effect, are on *standby*.

Travelers Insurance Company created a job bank in 1981 that allows its qualified retirees to work up to 960 hours per year—almost half-time—without having their pension incomes reduced. The employees fill jobs that previously were filled by workers from temporary employment agencies. The demand by supervisors for such reliable workers became greater than the available supply, so Travelers sponsored an "un-retirement" campaign to attract individuals who had retired from other companies. Travelers' job bank has grown to about 750 persons, of which approximately 250 are working any particular week in clerical, event coordination, research, and underwriting positions. Travelers also offers paid training in word processing and computer literacy for retirees with deficiencies in those areas.[11]

Counseling. Some companies attempt to help employees adjust to upcoming retirement decisions by offering employee counseling services. Corporate wellness programs, for example, could include workshops on life planning. Various organizations have developed preretirement planning programs that provide seminars and counseling on *social security, financial and estate planning, and other challenges associated with the aging process.*

Special Privileges. Some firms offer special privileges for older employees, such as free lunches, extra time off, or even a title like *senator*. Others keep retirees informed through company newsletters

Caution: The Psychiatrist General has determined that *no work* is dangerous to your health!

¡*Poco a poco*!

You can bank on older employees!

"Well, old-timer. Here's what I suggest. . . ."

"Why don't you just call me 'king'"?

and provide personal counseling throughout the retirement years. As we've already noted, some firms assist employees in changing to new careers that they can pursue elsewhere after retirement as a form of life enrichment. A few progressive firms have even established toll-free telephone numbers that can be called for assistance with medical and other insurance claims.

Social Activities. Many companies continue to show their concern for employees after their retirement by providing various social activities. Some companies make available certain facilities, such as a company clubhouse, to its retirees. Some companies sponsor monthly dinners, Christmas gatherings, and summer picnics for retirees.

"Twist again, like we last did in '62."

One More Time—We'll All Be Old Someday, If . . .

"If I'd known I'd live this long, I'd have taken better care of myself!"

As we've already indicated, larger proportions of our society are becoming older and members of the **third age** (individuals over 50 and under 75). This trend may portend a significant reduction in the long-standing emphasis toward a youth-oriented culture. Greater concern for solutions to the problems of the aging are more likely to come about when larger numbers of our population have to face such problems.

They helped us. Shouldn't we help them?

We sometimes forget that when we were infants, we couldn't have survived without the assistance of people older than ourselves. Unless Americans develop a greater awareness toward the aging U.S. population, older persons will continue to experience difficulty in adjusting to the problems of growing older.

Thus far, we've seen some of the difficulties that will have to be faced by many of us. There is another special employment group to which it is even harder for many people to relate—those with *physical and intellectual challenges*—commonly referred to in the past as the **handicapped.** Their problems, to be covered in the following section, should be understood by responsible organizational members.

PROBLEMS OF PERSONS WITH DISABILITIES

It's time to get comfortable.

People with **physical and intellectual challenges** used to be given little, if any, treatment in most texts on organizational behavior. Perhaps little was written about their employment problems for the same reasons that so-called normal persons tend not to look at another person's disabilities. Have you ever felt self-conscious when your eyes met those of a person whose face was scarred or mutilated? Perhaps we also tend to develop the same uncomfortable feelings when discussing the topic of persons with disabilities.

Many employers, for reasons that we shall examine, are afraid to hire persons with physical or intellectual disabilities. Yet in our society there are numerous individuals who have served in the military and lost a limb during armed conflict. For example, about 15 percent of the 3.1 million Vietnam veterans—about 477,000—experienced post-traumatic stress, and a substantial proportion of them are considered to have disabilities. A number of veterans of the Gulf crisis have experienced heart and intestinal problems, loss of memory, and fatigue, believed by some medical authorities to have been caused by prolonged exposure to chemicals and burning oil while serving in the Persian Gulf. Many other Americans have met with unfortunate accidents and may have to spend their entire lives in wheelchairs. Still others have become disfigured as a result of fires. Some were born with impaired vision or other disabilities. For many "challenged" persons, regardless of their condition, entry into the job market has been as difficult as for minority groups in the past.

Progress has been relatively slow.

People with disabilities continually encounter other forms of discrimination, such as those caused by architectural, transportation, and communication barriers and overprotective rules and policies. Unfortunately, people with disabilities, as a group, have long occupied an inferior status in American society, and have been severely disadvantaged vocationally, economically and educationally. Physical and mental challenges can result from a variety of causes. The principal ones are listed in Table 11.2.

It's the Law

Two principal laws assist individuals with disabilities. The first, the **Rehabilitation Act of 1973** (amended in 1980), is aimed at the public sector and affects all federally assisted programs and activities. The act introduced a new philosophy of hiring people with disabilities in the United States. It finally extended the concept of affirmative action to those with disabilities. Section 503 of the law states that firms with government contracts in excess of $2500 have significant

TABLE 11.2　**Principal Causes of Physical and Mental Disabilities.**

- Inborn (congenital)
- Accident
- Disease
- Birth injury
- Cultural or environmental deprivation
- The aging processes

responsibilities to people with disabilities. The law requires that efforts be made to select *qualified individuals with disabilities*. It also requires employers to attempt to make sure that employees with disabilities will be accepted by their supervisors and co-workers and receive promotional opportunities. In addition, **reasonable accommodations** are to be made by employers so that individuals with disabilities will not face insurmountable obstacles.

Section 504 of the act requires that organizations receiving government *grants* (as opposed to *contracts* in Section 503) must also adopt nondiscrimination policies related to employees with disabilities. An additional part of the act (originally controversial because of the cost of implementing it) is the provision that requires providing **physical access** for individuals with disabilities to public schools, colleges, community health and welfare facilities, and public transport and housing. However, it doesn't require that every building or part of a building be accessible, only the program as a whole. The act allows any person with physical or intellectual challenges who has been discriminated against to file a complaint with a regional office for civil rights.

Another significant law, the **Americans with Disabilities Act of 1990 (ADA),** broadens the scope of the Rehabilitation Act by requiring that *private,* as well as public, employers provide persons with disabilities the same protection against discrimination as provided by other civil rights legislation (See Table 11.3). The Equal Employment Opportunity Commission (EEOC) is responsible for implementing the intent of the ADA.

Who Are Individuals With Disabilities?

Accurate statistics on the number of persons with disabilities are scarce. However, estimates by the U.S. Department of Health and Human Services places the number of Americans with one or more disabilities at about 43 million, and this number is increasing as the

TABLE 11.3   Major Provisions of the Americans With Disabilities Act of 1990.

The Americans with Disabilities Act of 1990:
- Bans discrimination against persons with disabilities or with conditions that might be considered as limiting or causing negative public reactions.
- Requires employers, including unions, to modify the workplace and employment tests to accommodate persons with disabilities.
- Ensures that employees and dependents with disabilities have health insurance.
- Protects employees who are recovering from illness or drug dependency.

population as a whole grows older. One in eight Americans is believed to have some sort of physical or intellectual disability. An estimated 2.5 million individuals with disabilities in the United States are in wheelchairs.

When we use the expression *individuals with disabilities,* just to whom are we referring? The U.S. Department of Labor Employment Standards Administration defines an individual with disabilities as "any person who has a physical or mental impairment that substantially limits one or more of the major life activities of such individual, has a record of such an impairment, or is regarded as having such an impairment." Most persons with disabilities, however, are capable of working and are referred to as **qualified individuals with disabilities,** individuals who, with or without reasonable accommodation,

What qualifies an individual?

A BOX OF INTEREST

What Can You Do to Prevent the Transmission of HIV?[a]

According to Jonathan Cohn, director of the adult AIDS program at the University of Maryland, the following are some of the ways in which you can prevent the transmission of HIV, the AIDS virus:

1. Sexual abstinence.

2. Maintaining a monogamous sexual relationship.

3. Use of condoms when engaging in sex outside of a monogamous relationship.

4. Not sharing needles or syringes.

5. Scrubbing and disinfecting sharp instruments.

In a health-care setting, individuals should observe "universal precautions": Wearing gloves, masks, and eye and body protection in work activities in which employees might be sprayed, splashed or splattered with blood, bloody body fluids, semen, or vaginal secretions.

Workers should always wear gloves when they are doing procedures in which they might come in contact with blood or bloody fluids.

TABLE 11.4   Individuals Legally Considered to Have Disabilities.

- Sensory (vision, hearing, deaf/blind, speech)
- Motor (loss of limb, paralysis)
- Neurological functioning (mental retardation, mental illness, heart disease)
- General bodily systems (allergies, diabetes, heart disease)
- Multiple limitations (multiple sclerosis, cerebral palsy, muscular dystrophy)
- Dependency on alcohol and drugs (when they do not pose a direct threat to property or the safety of others in the workplace)
- Disease or infection (when it does not pose a health or safety risk to themselves or coworkers)

are capable of performing the essential functions of the employment position. Table 11.4 cites the types of persons considered to have disabilities under the Rehabilitation Act of 1973 and expanded in scope by the Americans with Disabilities Act of 1990.

The official definition of a person with disabilities is actually quite broad and includes certain persons who traditionally haven't been regarded as having disabilities, such as those with a disfiguring scar, a limp, or any person who would be treated as having disabilities. Some managers fear that legislation requires them to hire or retain all employees who may have alcohol or drug abuse problems or have a contagious disease, such as AIDS. However, as already indicated, the Americans with Disabilities Act specifically states that individuals need not be hired or retained when their current use of alcohol or drugs poses a direct threat to property or the safety of others in the workplace. Further, discriminatory actions can take place against individuals who are currently using *illegal drugs*. Nor must individuals with currently contagious diseases or infections be hired or retained when they pose a direct threat to the health or safety of other individuals in the workplace.

Only if no direct threat.

The ADA does not provide a *carte blanche* definition of disability. Characteristics such as blue eyes or brown hair are not considered to be disabilities. The same applies to trivial or minor impairments, such as an infected finger. The courts have further refined the definition of disability as not including pregnancy, left-handedness, fear of heights, and a mild case of cerebral palsy (that did not limit a major life activity).

Are Individuals With AIDS Really Disabled?

Not all authorities agree that *acquired immune deficiency syndrome (AIDS)* should be considered a qualification under disability laws.

Some persons argue that those with AIDS are not persons with disabilities since they usually function well until they can no longer work. However, contagious diseases have been considered disabilities for more than twenty years under Section 504 of the Rehabilitation Act of 1973. Furthermore, AIDS-infected persons and carriers of the virus HIV are often perceived by others in the workplace in a manner that makes "normal" functioning a rather difficult activity. This topic, to be discussed shortly, is charged with emotion, fears, myths, and strong opinions on various sides of the issue.

Let's now look at some of the traditional beliefs and prejudices about people with disabilities and then discuss what might be done to improve their chances for employment.

COMMON ATTITUDES TOWARD THE PHYSICALLY AND INTELLECTUALLY CHALLENGED

Why don't some employers hire the challenged?

Employers have given state departments of rehabilitation an assortment of excuses for not hiring people with disabilities. Among the more common defenses offered are that insurance costs will rise, such individuals are more prone to accidents, and they are more offensive to the public. Let's take a look at each of these reasons.

Increased Insurance Costs

According to representatives at the California State Department of Vocational Rehabilitation, a frequent excuse given by employers for not hiring individuals with disabilities is that their workers' compensation insurance premium costs will rise. Insurance rates, however, bear no relationship to the *hiring* of people with disabilities. Rates are determined by the nature of the industry and the accident experience of the individual firm.

Accident Prone

Another common belief about individuals with disabilities is that they are more likely to have accidents than nondisabled employees. Studies made by the California State Department of Vocational Rehabilitation do not support this belief. In fact, the safety records of those with disabilities who have been rehabilitated have been as good as or better than those of others.

Persons with disabilities tend to be more sensitive to and thus more aware of their limitations, rather like the person who has had a serious automobile accident. And like the person who has *seen* an automobile accident, co-workers will often be more cautious on their own jobs.

Offensive to the Public

Some employers shy away from offering positions to individuals with disabilities for fear that the person's appearance would be offensive to the public. When thinking about those with disabilities, far too many employers seem to have the image of the armless, legless, wheelchair-bound invalid. However, there are all sorts of degrees of disability; most are not as severe or as highly visible. Even those with severe disabilities are not necessarily a public relations liability. On the contrary, employers who have the reputation for being concerned about people often enjoy an enhanced public image.

As already mentioned, in the past individuals with disabilities were sometimes called *handicapped,* a word with unfavorable connotations to many people. Unfortunately, the word often conjures up an image of a wheelchair-bound person incapable of doing any type of work. In reality, however, most people who were considered handicapped had no desire—or need—to be "charity cases." Frequently, they were able and willing workers who had been deprived of opportunities because of misunderstanding and bias. In reality, most individuals considered handicapped are merely persons with *physical* or *intellectual challenges.* Besides, don't we all have to face physical and intellectual challenges of some sort on our jobs?

Or even better— "differently abled"?

Actually, the proportion of total jobs that require persons with unimpaired faculties is declining. Of course, good health, youth, and the use of all limbs and senses are unquestionably desirable. But for many jobs available today, demands are changing. Industrial, manual types of jobs are becoming less available, whereas the proportion of jobs in the service, professional, and technical occupations has increased. For example, an increasing percentage of those rehabilitated by the California Department of Rehabilitation go into clerical, sales, service, professional, technical, or managerial jobs.

This is not to say that those with limitations, or challenges, can't handle industrial jobs. In fact, most challenged people are well suited for jobs involving their bodies as well as their minds. Nearly 30 percent of California's rehabilitated workers are placed in industrial occupations.

Many recent high-tech developments have also opened up new career opportunities for persons with physical challenges. For example, individuals with hearing impairments can use the Telecommunication Device for the Deaf (TDD), which allows a person with a hearing impairment to communicate over the telephone with someone who has the same device at the other end. Another example of newer technology: computers with voice synthesizers that convert text into speech and actually "read" text aloud to workers with vision impairments.

Numerous companies have attempted to accommodate individuals with disabilities. Texas Instruments, for example, enabled an

**A
GLOBAL
GLANCE**

Some People in the Netherlands Don't "Go Dutch"![b]

A tiny country in Western Europe known as the Netherlands, with more than 11 million bicycles, 15 million pigs, 5 million cows, a human population of about 15 million, and a labor pool of only 6 million, has numbers of people approaching one million receiving disability benefits from the state. There are more than 800,000 people registered as being *arbeidsongeschikt,* or unfit to work in one way or another. An additional 100,000 have been joining their ranks each year.

Some observers feel that the situation is getting out of hand with some Dutch workers and employers abusing the system. The Dutch definition of disability is quite generous and includes not only victims of industrial accidents but also workers who suffer from stress, burnout, or serious emotional problems at work that make them unable to perform their jobs. Those considered disabled are entitled to receive benefits until age 65.

The Netherlands is viewed as a country with one of the world's highest standards of living, including high-standard working conditions and health care. Consequently, having so many people receiving disability benefits looks a bit suspicious. In reality, many employers that have experienced bad economic times have taken the more humane route of declaring employees "unfit" for either physical or psychological reasons rather than firing them. Another suspected factor contributing to high disability rates relates to productivity, which is reputed to be among the world's highest in the Netherlands. Employees who don't make the productivity grade are often shunted out the back door with disability benefits in their pockets. Many of them don't seem to mind, since their benefits equal 70 percent of their last salary, up to maximum of 45,000 guilders, which was equivalent to about $26,000 a year based on the value of the dollar in early 1993. Absenteeism is another Dutch "disease." Employees in the Netherlands are one-and-a-half times more likely to call in sick than their Belgian and German counterparts. The "disability" problem has become so acute that the Dutch Prime Minister, Ruud Lubbers, has threatened to resign once the total number of people drawing disability benefits reaches one million.

employee with almost no hearing capability to obtain a surgically implanted device that allows him to function normally both in person and on the telephone. GTE-Michigan worked out a method for magnifying the letters and numbers on the computer screen of an employee with a visual impairment so that words and phone numbers appear 2 inches high. AT&T has installed hands-free telephones for employees with motor disabilities. IBM has provided sight-impaired employees with talking computers and braille typewriters.

A SPECIAL PROBLEM—HIV AND AIDS

Prior to June 1981, those seven letters—HIV and AIDS—were virtually unheard of. The decade and one-half since 1981 have brought about a near panic among many members of the public related to possible contact with individuals who have the **human immuno-deficiency virus (HIV)** and **acquired immune deficiency syndrome (AIDS).** Each has emerged as a major world epidemic. According to the World Health Organization (WHO), between 10 million and 12 million adults and 1 million children are infected with the virus, 2 million people have developed AIDs, and more than 1 million have died. AIDS currently kills an estimated 100,000 people worldwide each year. It is now the second-leading killer among men ages 25 to 44, up from third in 1988, according to the National Centers for Disease Control. Projections for the year 2000 range from 30 million to 120 million people with HIV.[12]

Now number two.

HIV and AIDS—What's the Difference?
Confusion sometimes surrounds the difference between HIV and AIDS. The former is classified as infection with the virus. The virus inserts itself into certain human cells and in essence becomes part of a person's body. HIV can be carried for years before a person may encounter any feelings of illness.

AIDS is the name for the condition that occurs after the virus has gradually destroyed a person's immunity so that he or she is prone to life-threatening infections. Far more people are HIV positive than have been diagnosed with AIDS. No one can tell if a person is HIV-infected simply by looking. Some people feel that former NBA basketball star Magic Johnson's disclosure of his HIV-positive status has done a great service to blast through some of the myths associated with HIV.[13]

You can't tell by looking.

How Is the Virus Transmitted?
Opinions differ as to the transmittability of the virus. Most medical authorities currently contend that it is *not* transmitted through casual contact. However, even though a person may not feel ill, the

Not casually transmitted.

virus can be easily transmitted from one person to another through some specific ways. The four major ways in which the virus is presently known to be transmitted are:

1. Through "unsafe sex" (especially with drug abusers).
2. Through shared hypodermic needles.
3. By an infected mother to a fetus.
4. Through blood transfusions where screening procedures for the presence of HIV are inadequate.

One myth surrounding the virus is that only homosexuals can catch or transmit it. In reality, almost 40 percent of all reported cases have occurred among nonhomosexuals (heterosexuals).

Furthermore, the gender gap is closing fast, placing women at increasing risk of contracting the virus. According to the World Health Organization (WHO), half of the one million people infected during the first half of 1992 were women. And women in the U.S. now constitute the single fastest-growing patient group. According to Michael Merson, head of WHO's Global Program on AIDS, "By the year 2000, more than half of newly infected adults will be women."[14]

Affected by Prejudice and Discrimination

People with HIV and AIDS have been subjected to substantial prejudice and discrimination. Parents have refused to let their children go to the same schools attended by children with AIDS. Employers have refused to hire individuals with AIDS. And although AIDS is considered an illness, a growing number of AIDS patients have been denied medical coverage and reimbursement by health insurers and companies that maintain their own self-insured health plans. In spite of legislation to the contrary, many health insurance companies have violated their own industry guidelines by attempting to screen out homosexual applicants for individual policies. An attitude prevalent among some employers is, "There's no cure, so why spend thousands of dollars on useless experimentation?"[15]

What do you think?

The following section answers some of the critical questions associated with the employment of AIDS victims.[16]

What Are the Legal Aspects Associated With AIDS in the Workplace?

AIDS antibias laws have become prevalent in a number of major metropolitan areas of the United States in recent years. The purpose of such legislation is to ban housing and employment discrimination against people who are infected with the human immunodeficiency virus that causes AIDS and against those who suffer from related diseases. The Americans with Disabilities Act of 1990 extends coverage to individuals with unpopular contagious diseases, as does the Rehabilitation Act of 1973.

Antibias laws have sometimes aroused much ire among critics. Reverend Lou Sheldon, while statewide California director of the Traditional Values Coalition, stated, "AIDS laws serve only to promote and legitimize homosexuality by wrongly giving special civil rights protection to people who are gay." However, former President Reagan's commission on AIDS disagreed. A 1988 commission report stated, "As long as discrimination occurs, and no strong national policy is established, individuals who are infected will be reluctant to come forward for testing, counseling, and care."

Must an Employer Hire a Person With AIDS?

When is it a "direct threat"?

Do employers have to hire applicants for jobs if they have any stage of AIDS? The answer to this question depends on whether or not the person could reasonably be expected to perform the essential functions of the job. Those with more advanced cases of AIDS may be disabled to the point that normal job functions are beyond their abilities. The ADA approach to contagious diseases, including AIDS, is the same as that provided for drug and alcohol abuse. The employer may adopt a standard that disqualifies persons who currently have a contagious disease if they pose a "direct threat to the health or safety of other individuals in the workplace."

?

A QUESTION
OF
ETHICS

"What? You've Got AIDS? Then We'll Change the Health Insurance Plan!"[c]

The Americans with Disabilities Act of 1990 states that employers cannot discriminate against AIDS victims by changing pay and "other terms, conditions and privileges of employment." Perhaps some members of the Supreme Court had not yet had the opportunity to read the provisions of the act since all but two justices in November 1992 refused to hear the case of *McGann v. H&H Music,* thereby fulfilling a request by the Bush Administration that the highest court not disturb the 5th Circuit Court's decision.

John McGann, a warehouse employee for five years at H&H Music Co. in Houston, Texas, discovered in 1987 that he had contracted AIDS. McGann notified his employer, who at the time provided lifetime medical benefits up to $1 million for all employees. A few months later, H&H Music changed the health plan's provisions by reducing the ceiling on AIDS-related costs from $1 million to $5,000. Medical coverage was not changed for any other catastrophic illness.

Apparently ignoring the Americans with Disabilities Act provisions, the Supreme Court justices contended that another act, the Employee Retirement Income Security Act of 1974, does not prevent cost-cutting employers from reducing or eliminating coverage for any ailment, even if such changes hurt people with AIDS or other diseases. Oh, and by the way, John McGann didn't have to personally feel the rejections of either the Bush Administration nor the Supreme Court. McGann died in 1991.

A Question of Ethics: Employee health plans cost employers substantial sums these days. What do you think? Should employers be allowed to reduce costs by reducing or eliminating coverage on employee health plans?

What Risks Are There in the Workplace?

Medical authorities contend that there is no risk to co-workers or the public from normal social or work contact with an HIV-infected person. Certain types of jobs in the health care sector and in community, welfare, custodial, cleaning, and emergency services may involve contact with infected blood or other body fluids. In these occupations

Just be careful, as always.

there is risk from a variety of infections, such as hepatitis, and the usual precautions already in use are effective against HIV. In the case of accidents in the workplace involving blood spillage, the usual hygienic precautions will reduce the risk of blood-to-blood infections, including HIV.

What Can an Employer Do to Prevent Co-worker Pressure?

No easy answers to difficult questions.

The question associated with co-worker reaction to fellow employees with AIDS is a difficult one. The issue has been raised many times in school districts, with the most publicized instances being those in which children with AIDS have not been allowed to attend classes. The AIDS hysteria factor is real, whether it affects your children or where you work.

It is essential to take steps to avoid unnecessary alarm and allay fears. Information about AIDS and HIV should be provided to employees in advance of any organizational behavior problem arising. If a problem does occur, the manager should take prompt action to reassure employees in what may be an emotionally-charged situation. Face-to-face discussion of the general issues (but not the personal circumstances of a particular individual) is considered to be a desirable approach. Giving in to pressure from other employees and dismissing an infected employee could not only result in legal problems for the employer but also reinforce prejudice and fear in the employees and create additional problems in the future.

Training and Education of Employees Is Essential

Managers should not only know how to deal with problems if they arise but also how to discuss AIDS with their employees. Training and education are necessary. Managers should first look at their own attitudes and learn how to handle questions on sensitive subjects.

A little understanding should help.

An approach used by some organizations is for managers to conduct meetings with employees during which the policy dealing with the issue is explained. Literature is distributed, and a videotape on the subjects of HIV and AIDS can be shown. At the end of each session an evaluation form is distributed to employees, which helps managers judge the effectiveness of the sessions. The evaluation form can provide space for people to ask questions in writing that can be answered in follow-up discussions.

AIDS es SIDA en Español.

The National Centers for Disease Control (CDC) maintains a national AIDS hot line to assist any managers or employees who desire information about AIDS. The 24-hour-a-day hot line, which includes Spanish speakers and a computer telephone for the deaf, received more than five million AIDS questions during the first five years of its existence. After Magic Johnson's announcement that he is HIV-positive, the line received a flood of calls—500,000 in thirteen days. The AIDS hot line number: 1-800-342-AIDS.

The CDC also sponsors a program called "Business Responds to AIDS," which will help businesses establish workplace AIDS policies, train supervisors to deal with infected employees, educate workers and their families, and encourage community service.

ADVANTAGES OF HIRING PERSONS WITH DISABILITIES

Just *why* is it good business?

Hiring individuals with disabilities can be a good business practice principally because they often provide a readily available supply of trained workers, and employers' training costs are frequently reduced. In addition, employees with disabilities tend to have lower turnover and absentee rates, to be more efficient on certain jobs, and to elicit favorable responses from co-workers. Let's briefly examine these five reasons.

A Supply of Trained Workers

Employers concerned with assisting persons with disabilities should contact their state departments of rehabilitation where they can often locate well-trained workers. These are generally persons who have been evaluated medically, psychologically, and vocationally for the proposed job.

Reduction in Training Costs

Since many departments of rehabilitation also have training facilities, employers often discover that their own training costs are reduced.

Lower Turnover and Absentee Rates

Persons with disabilities generally appreciate the opportunity to work. As a result, turnover and absentee rates and, consequently, operating costs, tend to be lower among workers with disabilities since they realize that finding other employment can typically be a difficult process.

Greater Efficiency

In some cases, people with disabilities may even be more efficient than others on similar jobs. For example, a deaf employee could hold certain types of jobs without being distracted by the surrounding noise. Efficiency is, in part, influenced by motivation. As already mentioned, those with disabilities tend to appreciate the opportunity to work and are often highly motivated.

Positive Effects on Co-workers

Some employees have discovered that persons with disabilities improve the motivation of *other workers,* who develop a greater appreciation for their *own* situations. The "able" person may feel, "If a person with disabilities can do that sort of work, so can I."

MANAGING INDIVIDUALS WITH DISABILITIES

As we have already learned, legislation requires companies to hire and advance qualified individuals with disabilities. Legislation also requires employers to provide them with "reasonable accommodation." However, many companies have lagged far behind in their efforts to hire the physically and intellectually challenged person compared with their progress in employing ethnic minorities and women. As evidence, the unemployment rate for people with disabilities is said to be the highest of any special employment group, approximately 60 percent. A substantial proportion among those unemployed are considered employable. And two out of every three of the individuals with disabilities who are unemployed, according to a Louis Harris and Associates' poll, said they want to work.[17]

Let's now look at some suggestions related to the employment of people with disabilities.

Preemployment Physicals Can Be Preempting

What are the major purposes of requiring that applicants for employment be given physical examinations? There are two principal reasons: (1) To determine if the applicant has the *physical capabilities* necessary to perform the required tasks of the job, and (2) to protect the hiring organization against *future claims* based on a physical condition that existed prior to the employment.

Is the exam job-related?

Unfortunately, however, examinations have frequently been the source of discriminatory hiring practices against people with disabilities. Once again, as with examinations for any employees, it is essential that they be directly related to the requirements of the job and not to unrealistic standards serving only to discriminate.

The Need for Selective Placement

Selective placement is probably the most important first step in managing workers with disabilities. Selective placement means *matching* the physical abilities of the person who has disabilities with the physical demands of the job. The matching process can often be accomplished by *redesigning a job* so that it is more suitable and safer. This can be accomplished by a slight change in duties or machine controls, such as changing a lever from right- to left-hand operation or from hand to foot control (or vice versa).

Round in round and square in square.

Many disabled persons are highly motivated. Of course, motivation alone doesn't mean that they will have no problems performing certain tasks. A key factor determining successful performance of individuals with disabilities is ensuring that they are placed in a position that they are capable of filling. Inability to perform in one area, however, does not mean inability to perform in others.

Selective placement should also attempt to avoid the *glass ceiling syndrome* discussed in Chapter 10. Unfortunately, those with physical and intellectual challenges have had problems with upward mobility and advancement. Far too many managers perceive them as fitting into a particular job and unsuited for higher positions on the career ladder.

A supervisor should be involved with the personnel department to guide recruiters in their efforts to find a qualified person with disabilities. Job descriptions should be communicated clearly to the personnel department with all job requirements precisely stated so that a person with disabilities will not be misplaced and consequently more likely to fail. Creativity, as we'll see shortly, should be used when deciding which jobs can be handled by which individuals.

Integrating the New Employee

Although reasonable accommodations should be made so that employees with disabilities can perform their jobs satisfactorily, displaying favoritism toward them could cause other employees to become resentful. To avoid such undesirable departmental tensions, the supervisor should discuss with associates in advance any plans to hire people with disabilities. The supervisor should not only emphasize the company's legal and moral obligations, but also stress that new employees will be held to the same standards of performance as any other workers. The supervisor should also encourage existing employees to attempt to understand the challenges facing people with disabilities and to have patience with them.

Help your associates to help your associates.

Maintain a Normal Relationship

Supervisors themselves are often uncertain about the best approach to take when dealing with employees with disabilities. The sudden arrival of a person with disabilities can temporarily upset the established organizational equilibrium of your department. Experienced rehabilitators feel that supervisors should neither overemphasize, nor be overprotective of, a person's disability.

"Treat me as you would any human."

Supervisors should attempt to treat employees with disabilities as they would any other worker. Such individuals are generally aware of their own strengths and weaknesses and generally prefer not to be singled out as someone strange or different. Once disabled persons become a norm in the workplace, they are likely to be perceived by managers and fellow-employees in the more positive way that women and minorities are now perceived in many organizations. Employees with disabilities will start feeling more comfortable after their co-workers stop looking first at a person's handicap and instead focus on his or her talents.

Encourage Workers to Be Open

"Let me give it to you straight."

Physically and intellectually challenged employees should be encouraged to be natural and honest about their own disabilities. A self-conscious attempt to conceal the condition tends to accentuate it. Rehabilitators generally recommend that the person with disabilities attempt to clear the air by explaining what he or she can and cannot do to avoid the creation of an exaggerated situation.

Be Reasonably Accommodating

What is reasonable?

The Americans with Disabilities Act requires employers to make reasonable accommodations to the known limitations of a qualified individual with a disability unless it can be demonstrated that the accommodation would impose an "undue hardship" on the operation of the business. The legislation states that reasonable accommodation "may include such areas as job restructuring, part-time or flexible work schedules, acquisition or modification of equipment or devices, the provision of readers or interpreters, and other similar actions."

A number of companies have been active in accommodating people with disabilities, including Marriott Corporation, Toledo Edison Company, AT&T, Du Pont Company, and Hewlett-Packard. For example, a Marriott Corporation facility made modifications to the work environment that aided deaf and hard-of-hearing personnel. Employees working in its laundry room are alerted to the end of a wash load by flashing lights instead of a buzzer. The same Marriott laundry facility installed multicolored bins to make it easier for mentally limited laundry attendants to sort sheets and towels by size.[18]

Need Help? Here's an Accommodating Network

American and Canadian employers who need help in assisting people with disabilities can obtain it by phone from the President's Committee on Employment of the Handicapped (PCEH). The committee's Job Accommodation Network (JAN) provides free information on how new technologies can help as well as names and phone numbers of employers who have successfully developed programs of accommodation.

JAN has a plan that can!

JAN not only provides assistance to employers but also can aid employees, applicants for employment, trainers, and job-placement specialists. JAN is staffed by trained human factors consultants who analyze problems and make recommendations, drawing on a computerized data base of over 10,000 specific accommodations.*

JAN clearinghouse representatives disclose that most employees with disabilities require only minor accommodations. A JAN survey

*JAN can be contacted through the following telephone numbers: In Canada, voice or TDD, (1-800) 526-2262; in the United States (other than West Virginia), voice or TDD, (1-800) 526-7234; in West Virginia, voice or TDD, (1-800) 526-4698; commercial, (304) 293-7186.

of employers helped to dispel some of the myths associated with the costs of accommodation. Of the respondents, 31 percent stated that the accommodating changes cost nothing, 19 percent said the costs were $1 to $50, and 19 percent said the costs were between $50 and $500. Examples of typical low-cost suggestions made to employers include placing a desk on cinder blocks so a wheelchair can fit beneath it, training a mobility-impaired librarian to use a computerized catalog system, and installing a flashing red ceiling light in an office to warn a deaf employee about an emergency.[19]

Employees who feel that they are being unfairly discriminated against because of their disabilities and who cannot work out the problem through normal company grievance procedures can follow the Equal Employment Opportunity Commission's (EEOC) enforcement procedure outlined in Table 11.5.

A SOCIAL RESPONSIBILITY

One of the stated goals of the U.S. Congress is *to provide equal employment opportunities for all American citizens.* Sometimes the individuals who need the most assistance tend to be overlooked. Both private and public resources are needed to provide the necessary rehabilitation for persons with disabilities so that they, too, may live

TABLE 11.5   EEOC's Enforcement Procedure for Individuals with Disabilities.[20]

The EEOC enforces the employment section of the Americans with Disabilities Act (ADA) with the same administrative procedures it uses to investigate sex, race, age or other discrimination in employment. These procedures are outlined below.

   1. An employee or job applicant who believes he or she is the victim of job discrimination files a complaint with the EEOC or, alternatively, a state fair employment agency.

   2. The EEOC or state investigates the complaint to determine whether there is reasonable cause of discrimination. If the commission or state finds that the employer had violated the law, then it attempts to negotiate an agreement between the employee and employer.

   3. If conciliation fails, the employee can sue in federal court for equitable relief (back pay, reinstatement and injunctions against further discrimination).

Or—

   4. An employee can forgo the administrative route and proceed directly to federal court. The EEOC must issue a right-to-sue letter within 180 days of receiving the request to sue from the employee. The remedies are the same as in step No. 3.

---

as full a life as their abilities will permit. The major types of assistance needed by individuals with disabilities include medical examinations and treatment, guidance counseling, training, and placement.

In the short run, legislation such as the Rehabilitation Act and ADA place additional demands on the energies and time of today's managers, as well as on the purse strings of society. However, the long-term benefits to society as a whole are likely to be substantial. The hiring of people with disabilities can enable another group to participate in the mainstream of American economic activity. Persons previously unemployed can become taxpayers rather than welfare recipients. Further, people with disabilities can help to offset the nation's shrinking labor pool of qualified workers. Probably most important is that the hiring of people with disabilities enables *them* to develop a feeling of *contribution and self-respect*. Productive work is usually far more satisfying for people with disabilities than enforced idleness. If we ever feel that it's just too costly to aid individuals such as those with physical and intellectual challenges we ought to remind ourselves that:

There but for fate go we.

SUMMARY

In this chapter, we've examined the problems of two additional special employment groups—the *aging* and those with *physical and intellectual challenges*. Managers have increasingly responded to the needs and aspirations of groups who formerly were among the "forgotten humans." Government legislation and heightened awareness of the social responsibilities of organizations have substantially changed the traditional approaches to managing human resources.

The labor supply is expected to shrink in the future as the U.S. economy experiences healthy economic growth. The desire of an aging population to continue working, along with the desire of persons with disabilities to participate in the mainstream of American economic life, provides a "window of opportunity" for both employers and employees.

Older workers, defined as those over age 40 by the Age Discrimination in Employment Act of 1967, often experience difficulty obtaining employment when they lose their jobs, primarily because of the false attitudes held by some toward the aging.

Some of the ways in which a graying population can be assisted is through protective legislation, counseling and guidance, the use of multiple careers, and programs designed to ease the transition into retirement.

Individuals with disabilities seem to be receiving greater, although long overdue, attention in recent years through legislative efforts and employer assistance. Two pieces of legislation that affect individuals with disabilities are the Rehabilitation Act of 1973 and the Americans with Disabilities Act of 1990. In spite of these gains, however, unemployment rates among the physically and intellectually challenged continue to be among the highest of any segment of society.

Common myths associated with individuals with disabilities include increased insurance costs, tendency toward accidents, and an offensive appearance to the public. The special challenges associated with the *human immunodeficiency virus (HIV)* and *acquired immune deficiency syndrome (AIDS)* were also discussed in the chapter.

A concerned and informed management that prepares and trains *all* employees on the nature of accommodating people with disabilities is necessary if past inequities in employment practices toward the aging and individuals with disabilities is to be eradicated.

TERMS AND CONCEPTS TO REMEMBER

individuals with disabilities

age bias

older worker

Age Discrimination in Employment Act of 1967

multiple careers

phased retirement

job bank

third age

handicapped individual

physical and intellectual challenges

Rehabilitation Act of 1973

reasonable accommodations

physical access

Americans with Disabilities Act of 1990 (ADA)

qualified individuals with disablities

human immunodeficiency virus (HIV)

acquired immune deficiency syndrome (AIDS)

selective placement

QUESTIONS

1. What has been the trend in the United States related to the median age of Americans? What are the implications of this trend?

2. What determines how "old" a person is for a specific occupation?

3. Since unemployment rates tend to be lower for individuals over age 40 than they are for age 20, what special sorts of employment problems do the aging face?

4. Who tends to face greater burdens to employment—older men or older women? Why do you think this is the case?

5. What are some of the prejudices employers have developed against the aging? In your opinion, why have these prejudices developed?

6. How might the concept of multiple careers help the older person?

7. Why do some employees find it difficult to make the transition to retirement? What can be done to ease the transition?

8. What are the principal areas affected by the Age Discrimination Act?

9. Describe the major features of the Rehabilitation Act of 1973.

10. What is a major distinction between the Rehabilitation Act of 1973 and the Americans with Disabilities Act of 1990?

11. If you were physically or intellectually challenged, why might you react negatively to being considered "handicapped" or "disabled?"

12. What are some of the typical false viewpoints that some employers hold toward people with disabilities?

13. Under the Americans with Disability Act, is an employer required to hire anyone with AIDS or a drug or alcohol abuse problem? Explain.

14. What is the basic difference between *human immunodeficiency virus (HIV)* and *acquired immune deficiency syndrome (AIDS)?*

15. What are the principal ways in which the human immunodeficiency virus can be transmitted to another person? How can the chances of acquiring the virus be reduced?

16. What are some of the benefits that tend to result from hiring individuals with disabilities?

17. Evaluate the following statement: "You have to be careful when supervising people with disabilities. In general, because of their limitations, you can't assign employees with disabilities the same types of tasks or discipline them the same way you would normal people."

APPLICATIONS

11.1 Loyalty or Efficiency?

Joe Morales, a department head with the Phaseout Supply Company, currently finds himself in an uncomfortable position. He recently attended a meeting of all department heads that was conducted by the executive vice-president, Paula Pickwick. The department heads were informed at the meeting that a slowdown in the demand for

Phaseout's products required that the company be restructured and a number of employees be laid off. Ms. Pickwick told each department head that personnel budgets would have to be reduced by 15 percent.

Eunice Brown, another department head, shared Joe's dismay. While in the photocopying room, she saw Joe and complained, "You know what this means don't you? Pickwick's going after the older workers. It would have been a lot easier if she had said to cut five workers, rather than laying off people based on a percent of budget. I know that the only way to cut my department's personnel budget by 15 percent and still come close to meeting my departmental goals is to lay off the employees at the top of the pay range. I think Pickwick's idea is ridiculous!"

After Joe had looked over his own personnel budget, he could see that Eunice was right. To meet the targeted percentage reduction in his department, he had two main options. The first option would be to discharge Laura Sohoni, age 48, and Lewis O'Brien, age 55, both senior employees at the top of the pay range. Joe's second option was to discharge his five lowest-paid employees, each of whom was unmarried and had joined the company within the last two years.

Joe also had to consider that the nature of the work in his department was changing. Later this year his department was converting to computerized work stations, which would require additional training for the employees. Joe had already gotten some clues of potential resistance from some of the older employees who resented the proposed changes. Most of the younger employees, however, had learned something about computers in school and had little in the way of computer phobia.

As Joe analyzed his data again and again, he wondered how Laura, a widow and head of a household with three children, would survive if she lost her job. Laura had been with Phaseout for about six years, which was an insufficient amount of time for her profit-sharing retirement fund with Phaseout to be fully vested. At least Lewis, who had been with the company for 20 years, would be eligible to collect early retirement pay.

Joe found himself almost wishing that the company had a union contract that would automatically make the decision for him—one that would require the less senior employees to be laid off first. Joe felt, however, that he had to deal with the realities of the situation. He convinced himself that he really had only one choice if he was to reduce the personnel budget by 15 percent and still meet his department's goals. He decided to lay off Laura and Lewis.

Questions

1. Do you feel that age discrimination is an issue in this incident? Explain.

2. What would you have done if you had been Joe?

11.2 The Disabled Photography Lab Worker

When Kelly Darby was 15 years old, she was a passenger in a car that was involved in a serious accident. Her injury required the amputation of her left leg. Kelly was fitted with an artificial appliance that enables her to function nearly as well as anyone under most circumstances. She is currently 23 years old, married, and the mother of a two-year-old daughter. Kelly enjoys physical activity and spends weekends with her family bicycle riding and working in her vegetable garden.

Kelly, a high school graduate, learned about a year ago that there was a Department of Rehabilitation near her home where she could obtain assistance and training designed to aid her in preparing for a career position. For a number of years, she has had a strong interest in photography and was able to obtain training in printing and processing techniques through the department.

About two months ago, the department obtained a job for Kelly at the Color-Rite Photo Laboratory. Kelly was overjoyed with the opportunity and felt quite fortunate to be offered a job in an area in which she had interests. Her major hope, however, was that her co-workers would treat her as they would any other worker.

Unfortunately, Kelly's wishes have not come true. Most of her fellow employees seem to feel sorry for her and continually refuse to allow her to carry darkroom equipment or packages of photographic materials. Kelly has attempted to convey to her co-workers that she can carry whatever they can, but the other employees refuse to heed her requests.

Recently, Kelly has become quite moody on her job. She sometimes feels that she is being treated as if she were helpless or "some kind of a freak." Kelly has started getting into conflict situations with the other employees in areas that do not relate to her disability. Today, Kelly has felt especially depressed and believes that she has had it with her job. She has decided that she will tell her supervisor, Harry Harmony, that she intends to leave her job with Color-Rite.

Questions

1. What do you feel is the major problem in this case?

2. If you were Harry Harmony, what would you do about the situation?

11.3 The Case of the Forthright Job Applicant

HELP WANTED: Nationally known public relations firm seeks bright self-starter with 2-3 years PR or related experience for career spot. Work with variety of clients to create newsletters, press releases, full-color brochures. Also set up meetings, conferences, and media events for clients and assist in all office work. Successful candidate will have degree in journalism, communications, or English and demonstrated ability to write clearly and concisely under tight deadlines in fast-paced environment. Experience on daily newspaper and/or writing for advertising or broadcast industries preferred. Layout, design, or photographic experience a plus. Send resume and salary requirement to Human Resources Director, c/o Box 7886 CHRONICLE.

Human Resources Director
Box 7886 CHRONICLE
Dear Sir or Madam:

I am writing in response to your advertisement in yesterday's *Daily News Chronicle* for a journalism graduate with writing experience for a career position in public relations. I hold a B.A. degree in journalism from City University, where I was editor-in-chief of the weekly student newspaper during my senior year and an assistant to the director of alumni publications. In the latter position, I was responsible for editing and laying out articles for the quarterly alumni magazine, as well as obtaining color illustrations. After graduation, I worked for a year and a half as a suburban reporter for the *Riverton Post-Dispatch,* a daily newspaper in Miles County. I met an early-afternoon deadline every day for my assigned stories and often acted as photographer as well. My portfolio of more than 150 bylined articles for the *Post-Dispatch* is available for your review.

An award-winning three-part article I wrote about Genysus Computer Company's program to accommodate workers with disabilities brought me to the attention of the firm's corporate communications director. I joined Genysus two years ago as chief writer of the company's employee newsletter. Within six months, I had also launched a newsletter for Genysus's customers, increased the number and frequency of press releases, and helped produce a multimedia presentation about the company to be used at computer industry trade shows. I contributed to the redesign of the annual report to stockholders and had the idea to create an in-house "wire service" to distribute news bulletins about the company through its electronic mail system. In addition to my ongoing writing responsibilities at Genysus, I have continued to practice journalism as a hobby, contributing book and movie reviews to the local weekly newspaper in my community.

I am interested in the advertised position because I am eager to expand my experience beyond the computer industry. I am also attracted by the opportunity to arrange meetings and conferences, an area of communications that is new to me. My experience interacting with a wide range of people during my work as a reporter and cooperating with individuals at all levels of a major corporation has prepared me, I believe, for the type of interpersonal contact that conference planning involves.

I hope you will consider me for the advertised position, for which I am convinced I am qualified by my education and experience. I feel that there is another thing you should know about me: I have tested positive for HIV. My health is good, I have no symptoms of AIDS, and I am under the continuous supervision of a doctor. I am sharing this information with you because I do not want to feel that I have to hide from managers or co-workers in any way, and I do not want my HIV-positive status to become an issue in my employment later on. I prefer openness from the outset rather than concealment and fear.

I have enclosed a copy of my resume, which includes my salary requirement. Thank you for your consideration, and I look forward to hearing from you.

Sincerely,

I. M. Enniwon

Questions

1. If you were the human resources director who had placed this "help wanted" ad in the newspaper, would you hire I. M. Enniwon for the position? Explain your reasons.

2. If Enniwon were hired for the job, what preparations, if any, would you make for this person's joining your work force?

NOTES

1. As reported by Dan Rather on *CBS Evening News,* February 27, 1992.

2. Karen S. Peterson, "The Graying Years Are Often Golden," *USA Today/International Edition,* June 11, 1992, p. 1D, 2D.

3. "Burns, 96, in No Rush to Sign 10-Year Deal," *USA Today/International Edition,* November 2, 1991, p. 18.

4. Anthony Ramirez, "Making Better Use of Older Workers," *Fortune/International Edition,* January 30, 1989, pp. 107-111.

5. "Job Tenure," *Economic Road Maps, No. 1888* (New York: The Conference Board, October, 1980) p. 1; Jack Lesar, "Older Managers Do Better in Jobs Market," *San Francisco Examiner,* November 1989; and Diana Cornish, "You're Never Too Old to Take on a New Job. . . ," *Financial Times,* March 4, 1993, p. 11.

6. Kevin P. Hopkins and William B. Johnston, Project Directors, *Opportunity 2000—Creative Affirmative Action Strategies For a*

Changing Workforce, "Older Workers," (Washington D.C.: Superintendent of Documents, 1988), pp. 150.

7. "Service Firms Hire More Oldsters and Other Nontraditional Workers," *The Wall Street Journal,* August 11, 1987, p. 1; and see note 6 above, *Opportunity 2000,* 1988, pp. 148-151.

8. Ben Wattenberg, "Fewer People to Pick Up the Tab," *Martinez News-Gazette,* August 7, 1987, p. 2; and Emily T. Smith, "Aging: Can It Be Slowed?" *Business Week / International Edition,* February 8, 1988, pp. 42-48.

9. "Unemployment Spurs Death Rate," *Socioeconomic Newsletter* (White Plains: NY: The Institute for Socioeconomic Studies, September 1980), p. 3.

10. Katie Brown, "An Aging Work Force Requires Life Planning," *Business Times / Contra Costa Times,* December 2, 1985, p. 1.

11. Donald R. Johnston, "Retirees Work as "Temps' at Travelers Insurance," *World of Work Report,* August 1981, p. 57; and see note 6 above, *Opportunity 2000,* 1988, pp. 156, 157.

12. "Second-Leading Killer Among Young Men in America: AIDS," *United Press International* as reported in *USA Today / International Edition,* January 26, 1991, p. 10; "AIDS Toll Rises," *Financial Times,* February 13, 1992, p. 1; and Clive Cookson, "Grim Statistics Mask Advances," *Financial Times Weekend,* July 25/26, 1992, p. 8.

13. Marianne Restel, M.D., "Myths About Condoms," *Contra Costa Times,* December 23, 1991, p. 22.

14. Marilyn Chase, "WHO Says Women and Girls Have Become Group Most Vulnerable to AIDS Infection," *The Wall Street Journal Europe,* July 21, 1992, p. 3.

15. "Insurers Pass the Buck on AIDS Patients," *Business Week / International Edition,* March 28, 1988, p. 27.

16. Adapted from "Affirmative Action Flyer/Newsletter," No. 5-86, Peralta Community College District Affirmative Action Office, September 1986; James Bruggers, "AIDS: Legal Challenges Slow Passage of Anti-Bias Laws," *Contra Costa Times,* August 13, 1989, pp. 1-2; "Swamped Hot Line for AIDS May Be Expanded, CDC Says," *San Francisco Examiner* November 22, 1991, p. 2; and *AIDS and the Work Place—A Guide for Employers,* an educational booklet prepared and distributed by the Department of Employment of the United Kingdom.

17. Catherine Collins, "Fitness—Employers Find Those with Physical Handicaps Can Do a First-Rate Job," *Los Angeles Times,* May 21, 1989, p. II-1; and see note 6 above, *Opportunity 2000,* 1988, p. 100.

18. See note 6 above, *Opportunity 2000,* 1988, p. 121.

19. Information derived from an interview with Alice Jacobs, Human Factors Consultant, Job Accommodation Network, West Virginia University.

20. *ADA Compliance Guide—Monthly Bulletin,* Vol. 1, No. 2, May 1990, p. 5.

21. Lori Sharn, "Pilots: Don't Ground Us at 60," *USA Today/International Edition,* March 11, 1989, p. 3.

BOX NOTES

a. Adapted from "Q & A on AIDS," *Baltimore Sun,* December 22, 1991, p. 15.

b. Adapted from Ronald van de Krol, "Dutch Try to Turn Back a Wave of Job-Related Disability," *Financial Times,* August 16, 1991, p. 2.

c. Adapted from "High Court Says Law Doesn't Block Cut in AIDS Victim's Health Insurance," *Contra Costa Times,* November 9, 1992, p. 3.

EXPERIENTIAL EXERCISE

Birds Do It; Bees Do It; Can Aging Pilots Do It?

Airline pilots who fly jumbo jets typically are forced to "turn in their wings" and retire at age 60, yet many of them contend that they still have the "right stuff" and are capable of flying past that age. They cite such examples as Captain David Cronin, who guided a Boeing 747 back to Hawaii in 1989 after the fuselage ripped open and the jet lost two engines at 20,000 feet. Nine passengers were killed, but 345 survived. Cronin was forced to retire 1 month later when he turned 60.

Some people argue that people over 60 should not be flying wide-bodied jets since they are more susceptible to incapacitating medical episodes than people under 60. How do you personally feel about flying in a DC-10, Boeing 747, or Airbus with a pilot over age 60? Is there anything particularly wrong with that? Would your attitude differ if you had just read about a pilot age 62 suffering from a fatal heart attack while flying over San

Diego, causing a disastrous plane crash over a residential neighborhood? Perhaps it would; perhaps it wouldn't.

Here's a chance for you to conduct your own *un*scientific survey: Contact 10 persons under age 30 and 10 persons over age 50. Ask each of them the same two questions you just answered. Also ask each person how many years of schooling he or she has completed. Compare the results of your survey with the results obtained by other members of your class. What factors seemed to have influenced the responses you received from your surveyed groups?

A Quizzical AID to Enhanced Awareness

Answer either *true* or *false* to the following statements.

True False

_____ _____   1. A person is generally aware immediately after contracting an HIV infection.

_____ _____   2. There have been numerous reported cases in which the father and his wife's fetus were infected with HIV but the wife was not.

_____ _____   3. It is no longer considered safe to donate blood at blood banks.

_____ _____   4. Individuals with HIV infection are unlikely to develop AIDS.

_____ _____   5. HIV and AIDS are actually different names for the same malady.

_____ _____   6. AIDS is concentrated almost exclusively among homosexuals and people who share drug needles.

_____ _____   7. AIDS can be spread by shaking hands or by sharing cups, plates, or toilet facilities.

_____ _____   8. Food preparers or servers who may be infected with HIV pose a tremendous health hazard to customers or coworkers.

_____ _____   9. In the majority of work places, health care workers need take no protective measures because of the lack of risk associated with the direct contact with blood and other bodily fluids of HIV carriers.

_____ _____   10. Most health authorities contend that in the majority of occupations individuals infected by HIV or AIDS should be refused employment because of the risk associated with contact with their peers at the work place.

Instructions: Count the number of *false* responses. According to recent medical evidence published by the World Health Organization (WHO), each statement is false. Many myths and differences of opinion are associated with the HIV virus and AIDS. Belief in such myths is often the cause of prejudice and discrimination in the work place.

No Smoking
In These
Premises

**Under Penalty Of
Fine Or Imprisonment,
Or Both, By Order Of
The Fire Commissioner.**

CHAPTER 12

Problems of Substance Abuse

*Can They Just Say "No"
to the High Life?*

**When you finish this chapter,
you should be able to:**

1

Discuss modern organizational attitudes toward the problems of
alcoholism and drug dependency.

2

Explain some of the potential causes of alcohol and drug abuse.

3

Recognize the possible symptoms of alcoholism and drug dependency.

4

Describe management's responsibilities for establishing and carrying out
employee assistance programs.

5

Explain the importance of the supervisor's role in influencing the success of
the organization's employee assistance programs.

6

Review the guidelines for employers considering testing employees for drugs.

It's much easier to help a person who has been
on the job for nine years than it is to
hire and train a replacement.

Miriam Ingebritson, Clinical Consultant

Managers in organizations are continually faced with challenges, and many managers perceive challenges as an opportunity to overcome obstacles and accomplish goals. Unfortunately, however, organizational members have discovered that many of today's challenges are unrelated to the basic missions established by their organizations.

A significant and costly challenge has emerged in recent decades, one that is taking an inordinate amount of managerial time: the non-identical twin problems of alcohol and drug abuse among employees. These are relevant organizational behavior concerns that should be of no less importance to managers than are such problems as communication, motivation, and morale.

The current chapter presents a general overview of the nature and extent of the problems of alcohol and drug abuse and then examines the more successful approaches and guidelines currently being followed by some concerned organizations. Let's now examine how extensive the problems are.

THE EXTENT OF THE ALCOHOL PROBLEM

The problems of alcohol and drug abuse are considerable. Society, by both custom and law, defines what is meant by "drugs," and many authorities claim that alcohol, an intoxicant, should be classified as a drug, just like other types of stimulants, depressants, hallucinogens, and narcotics.

Alcoholism—A Major Health Problem

Alcoholism is recognized as a major health problem. It is currently one of the greatest killers in the United States. The National Institute on Alcohol Abuse and Alcoholism estimates that nearly *18 million persons* suffer from problems related to alcohol. Years ago, the typical stereotype of the alcoholic was the intoxicated derelict staggering clumsily through skid row. This view is *not* a realistic reflection; such persons are said to represent only three to five percent of all persons with alcohol-related problems in the United States.

A study of 212,802 junior high and high school pupils in 34 states by Parents Resource Institute for Drug Education indicated that smoking and drug use were on the rise in 1992 among young people. Among children in grades six through eight, usage was higher in all categories surveyed, the biggest increase coming in hallucinogens, such as LSD, and inhalants, such as air fresheners. Among high school students, usage was up in most of the substance categories, the biggest increases in the categories of inhalants and uppers. The National Institute on Alcohol Abuse and Alcoholism estimates that 4.6 million high school students, or about 30 percent, have alcohol-related problems—not quite the image of the "wino" or "street person" hunched in a downtown doorway.[1]

High-spirited young people!

The direction of alcohol use has become unclear in recent years. The proportion of Americans who drink peaked in the 1970s and then declined until 1991. The downward trend was partially attributed to the physical fitness craze, along with a highly effective campaign conducted by Mothers Against Drunk Drivers (MADD) and Students Against Drunk Drivers (SADD).

Down with beer! Up with celery!

However, after several years of declining alcohol and drug use among high-school and middle-school students, drinking and smoking rates have started to climb again. The increase in alcohol use was particularly noticeable among ninth-graders, 57.4 percent of whom reported drinking in a 1992 survey—up from 61.8 percent in 1989. "We haven't made a lot of progress," said Rodney Skager, the UCLA researcher who headed the survey.[2]

Another group that seems to be "hitting the bottle" with greater frequency is elderly people. Loneliness and isolation are believed to be driving older people to drinking, warned a congressional report in 1992. Alcoholism affects nearly 2.5 million elderly Americans, and up to half of all nursing home residents have alcohol-related problems, according to the report.[3]

The costs of alcohol abuse are shocking. Chronic liver disease and cirrhosis were the tenth leading causes of death in the United States in 1990. Drunk drivers were responsible for approximately half of the nearly 48,000 driving fatalities in the United States in 1990. Alcohol has been blamed for about 70 percent of the more than 5000 drowning deaths in 1990 and for about 30 percent of the more than 30,000 suicides. A Department of Justice study estimates that almost one-third of state-prison inmates drank excessively before committing rapes, burglaries, and assaults. And nearly half of the nation's homeless are said to be alcoholics.[4]

What Constitutes a Drinking Problem?

When might drinking be a problem?

We should be clear about what is generally meant by a drinking problem. In all cases related to alcohol abuse, a common factor is the unfavorable effect alcohol has on the *health* or *well-being* of the *drinker* and his or her *associates*. A later section of the chapter outlines in more detail the common signs and symptoms that frequently indicate a drinking problem (see Table 12.1). There is also a self-test in the Experiential Exercise at the end of the chapter that can help you examine the influence alcohol may have in your own life and work—and perhaps identify trouble areas you need to be aware of.

Alcoholic Defined

A person could experience some isolated instances of drinking problems without necessarily being an alcoholic. The term **alcoholic** generally refers to the person who *habitually lacks self-control in the use of alcoholic beverages,* or who drinks to the extent that his or her *health is adversely affected,* or that his or her *social or economic functioning is significantly disrupted.*

Drinking Problems Among the Work Force

People drink for a variety of social, cultural, religious, or medical reasons. Approximately 68 percent of American adults are said to drink at least occasionally. Unfortunately, some persons reach the stage where they feel that they cannot do without alcohol, and many such individuals are employed in industry. Experts warn that alcohol is the most common drug in the workplace—"the overwhelming drug of choice," as a Washington, DC-based specialist noted in 1991.[5] Because illegal drugs—such as cocaine and marijuana—have received so much media attention, and because substance abusers tend to use both alcohol and illegal drugs, companies risk underestimating the seriousness of alcohol problems among their employees. Recent figures show that this can be an expensive oversight. For example, productivity losses due to alcohol abuse are estimated to cost U.S. business about $60 billion a year—double the $30 billion in lost productivity due to illegal drugs.[6]

How extensive is the drinking problem?

The National Council on Alcoholism estimates that ten percent of the work force can be classified as alcoholics, with another ten percent borderline alcoholics. Studies indicate that there are variations within specific companies, ranging from as little as *three percent* of the employee population to as much as *twelve percent.* The Associated Builders and Contractors estimates that at least twenty percent of all construction workers in the United States have an alcohol or drug abuse problem.[7] A watchdog group, Public Citizen, reported that records it obtained from the Nuclear Regulatory Commission showed over 350 "safeguard events" reported by utilities during 1988, 1989, and 1990, many of which included alcohol or drug abuse at nuclear facilities.[8]

A nuclear cocktail?

Shhaay, fella, why's that other plane on our runway?

And here's a shocker: Three Northwest Airlines pilots were convicted in a recent year for having flown an airliner while intoxicated. One pilot admitted at the trial to having drunk seventeen mixed drinks and the other two to having shared six or seven pitchers of beer. One pilot received a sixteen-month sentence and the other two were given twelve months. How would you like your next flight to be in the not-so-friendly skies of intoxicated pilots?[9]

Pretty slick method of distributing energy, eh?

The infamous 1989 disaster, the Exxon oil spill, that occurred after the tanker *Valdez* struck a reef in Alaska's Prince William Sound and leaked eleven million gallons of crude oil into the clear, cool waters, was believed by many authorities to be alcohol-related. Although later acquitted, the ship's captain, Joseph Hazelwood, an alleged alcoholic, was found to have a blood-alcohol level 50 percent higher than the drunk-driving limit set by the Coast Guard for seamen operating a moving ship. An interesting sidelight is that Exxon supplied low-alcohol beer to tanker crewmen despite its policy of banning drinking aboard its ships.[10]

The nation's "big hangover."

The alcohol problem is costly to industry and society in terms of *lost work time* of employed alcoholics, *health and medical care expenses, property damage, wage losses,* and other costs associated with *traffic accidents.*

The National Council on Alcoholism has gathered the following information on alcoholism in industry:

1. The alcoholic employee is absent two to four times more often than the nonalcoholic.

2. On-the-job accidents for alcoholic employees are two to four times more frequent than for nonalcoholics. Off-the-job accidents are four to six times more numerous.

3. Sickness and accident benefits paid out for alcoholic employees are three times greater than for the average nonalcoholic.

4. The alcoholic employee files four times more grievances than nonalcoholic employees.

Easy to Cover Up?

Who, me? Never touch the stuff. Hic!!

Alcoholic employees can sometimes go undetected for years. Fellow workers cover up for employees unable to perform their jobs because of drunkenness. Even managers may be adept at concealing their alcohol abuse problems. Their secretaries or loyal associates may cover up for them. Alcoholics can be clever at inventing "credible" excuses when detected. "I must have a drink or two when I'm entertaining customers, of course."

THE TREND TOWARD REHABILITATION

Until the mid-1960s, alcohol abuse in the United State was customarily dealt with as a criminal offense. Although some states had enacted treatment legislation, those laws received scant attention and were largely ignored. In 1966, however, some significant court decisions stimulated a radical departure from previously held attitudes.

Since 1966, considerable progress has been made in the direction of treatment and rehabilitation. Employers have found that it is often more cost-effective to return an experienced worker to sobriety than it is to hire and train someone new. Changes in the law have also contributed to the rehabilitation trend. The Comprehensive Alcohol Abuse and Alcoholism Prevention, Treatment, and Rehabilitation Act of 1970, better known as the **Hughes Act,** created the **National Institute of Alcohol Abuse and Alcoholism,** which conducts research and provides assistance to managers in establishing alcoholism programs. The Rehabilitation Act of 1973 and the Americans With Disabilities Act of 1990 address employment issues involving persons with disabilities. In some instances, courts have ruled that individuals with alcohol problems are disabled; as such, they may be protected under these two laws.

Private employers, government, and the courts are not the only organizations that have influenced the developing view of alcoholism as a treatable disease rather than a criminal act. The American Medical Association has also played a major role. The association's *Manual on Alcoholism* states that "alcoholics are treatable patients. Because their illness is a chronic disorder with tendency toward relapse, it should be approached in much the same manner as are other chronic and relapsing medical conditions. The aim of treatment is then viewed more as one of control than cure."[11]

Note the use of the phrase *more as control than cure.* Both the American Medical Association and Alcoholics Anonymous take the position that a former alcoholic is never completely cured. The term **recovering alcoholic** is typically used. The American Medical Association further contends that the best reason to define alcoholism as a disease is that it is impractical to do otherwise. Calling alcohol abuse a moral problem tends to feed the guilt, fear, and anger felt by alcoholics, driving many of them deeper into alcohol abuse.

THE PREVALENCE OF DRUG ABUSE

Let's now turn our attention to the problems associated with **drug abuse,** or **drug addiction,** a condition that exists when the taking of drugs, whether prescribed or nonprescribed, legal or illegal, causes difficulties in any area of an individual's life. Years ago, the stereotype of the drug user was either of a glazed-eyed musician frantically beating his sticks on the tight skin of a drum or of a person who dwelled in a ghetto. Mass publicity on drug abuse has long since caused that stereotype to fade from view.

A Declaration of War?

No more, "Just say no"!

In recent years, the topic of drug abuse has become practically a national obsession. Legislation known as *The Drug-Free Workplace Act,* which applies to federal grantees and contractors, was enacted in

1988. Former President George Bush "declared a war on drugs" that included the sending of armed troops and financial aid to such countries as Colombia. Victory seemed close at hand, because the following year Bush triumphantly announced a sharp drop in illicit drug use. However, the victory appeared to be short-lived: the results of a national survey and a compilation of hospital reports made public in December 1991 indicated that drug use was on the increase again. For example, the number of people using cocaine in 1991 rose to 1.9 million from 1.6 million in 1990. The biggest gains, the reports showed, were among members of the middle class over age 35. The National Institute on Drug Abuse found that during the first half of 1991, emergency cocaine cases at more than 150 hospitals it surveyed around the United States were up almost 3000 over the number recorded in the same period the previous year.[12] The upward trend continued in the months that followed. According to figures from the Department of Health and Human Services, the number of people seeking care in hospital emergency rooms for adverse reactions to cocaine increased 13 percent in the third quarter of 1991; heroin-related emergency room visits increased 10 percent.[13]

Complicating the ongoing war on drugs are changes in public attitudes and drug-use patterns. Some critics recently contended that something is wrong with antidrug education because the percentage of people who think taking drugs is risky or harmful had been falling.

In 1988, for example, 84.9 percent of the population thought taking drugs was dangerous. That figure dropped to 80.6 percent in 1991[14]—the same year in which drug-related emergency room cases were on the rise. Moreover, it sometimes seems that no sooner is progress made in combatting one illegal drug than a different kind of substance abuse comes into vogue. Ethyl alcohol was the social drug during Prohibition, marijuana became the social drug of the 1960s and 1970s, and some observers feel that crack cocaine and possibly ecstasy—another so-called upper—have become the social drugs of the 1980s and 1990s. The drugs of choice and people's attitudes toward them may constantly change, but the problem of drug abuse appears to be continuing unabated.

What Is a Drug?

A **drug** may be defined as a *substance that has an effect upon the body or mind.* Many substances not usually considered drugs could be included in this definition, such as alcohol, caffeine, nicotine, cola, pollutants, airplane glue, and household chemicals.

We will concentrate on the types of drugs that can potentially create problems for organizations because of their capabilities to alter the minds of the users. The abuse of such drugs may also harm the body. The major types of drugs currently being used and abused include:

1. *Cannabis*—marijuana, hashish, and hashish oil
2. *Hallucinogens*—so-called psychedelics, such as LSD, mescaline, psylocybin, DMT, STP, MDA, and others
3. *Stimulants*—so-called uppers, such as cocaine (including "freebase" and "crack"), amphetamine, phencyclidine (PCP or "angel dust"), dextroamphetamine, and methamphetamine, that is, "speed," "ecstasy," or "crystals"
4. *Sedatives or depressants*—so-called downers, such as barbiturates, tranquilizers, and sleeping pills
5. *Narcotics*—opiates, such as opium, morphine, and heroin, that is, "smack"
6. *Androgenic anabolic steroids* ("steroids")—used by some athletes to stimulate muscle growth, and which have a variety of dangerous side effects
7. *Miscellaneous*—model airplane glue, gasoline, paint thinners, air fresheners, and others

Historically, the use of drugs has varied depending principally on availability and custom. The major problem among office and factory workers appears to center around the abuse of *stimulants* (uppers)

A Cross-Border Bust[a]

On February 4, 1988, federal grand juries in Miami and Tampa, Florida, returned indictments against General Manuel Noriega, president of Panama, charging that he had protected and assisted the Medellín drug cartel. Although believed to have aided the U.S. Central Intelligence Agency in the past, Señor Noriega seemed none too eager to cooperate this time.

So U.S. authorities decided to give Panama an early Christmas surprise by sending U.S. troops to invade the country on December 20, 1989. The troops succeeded in removing Noriega's government from power, but Noriega himself played hide-and-seek for a while, finally taking refuge in the Vatican mission. The U.S. forces, however, found a secret weapon to scare him out of the mission—loud, I mean **really loud**—rock-and-roll music.

The ruddy-faced leader finally surrendered on January 3, 1990. He was extradited to Florida on charges of drug trafficking. It was another successful drug bust—but one with a difference. It had involved the governments and armies of two nations, not to mention many casualties on both sides: 23 Americans killed, 312 Americans wounded, and hundreds of innocent Panamanians killed or wounded in the cross-fire that destroyed the peace of Panama City's streets.

While the hunt for Noriega—and his defeat by rock-and-roll—filled front pages in the United States for weeks, another story was there to be read between the lines. It was about the frightening reach of the international drug trade and its suspected role in events that finally led to the military invasion of one country by another. The Noriega affair raises troubling questions. Has global drug dealing grown to the point where it can affect the most critical decisions and actions of governments? If we don't fight drugs in our own homes, schools, and workplaces, is it possible that there could be more armed conflicts in our future like the one in Panama?

and *sedatives* (downers). Many purchasers of these drugs depend on them as an aid in making it through the workday.

Drugs and the Workplace

The owner of a small family-run business in the Midwest took a walk through his plant one day. He didn't know what to do with the suspicious-looking packet of white powder he found on his way through the building, so he called in the local police to take a look. An investigation revealed a ring of cocaine dealers operating out of the company's facilities. They were moving the drug inside the stuffed animals manufactured there.

This is a true story, and its meaning is plain: drugs can be present in any workplace—anywhere, anytime. According to figures from the American Council for Drug Education, 68 percent of drug users are currently employed.[15] Statistics also show that drug use or abuse is likely in some cases to affect job performance, especially absenteeism and employee turnover.

As evidence, a study of 2537 Boston postal workers published by the American Medical Association reported that 7.8 percent of postal employees whose urine tested positive for marijuana use had 55 percent more industrial accidents and 78 percent more absenteeism when compared to other employees. The 2.2 percent of postal employees whose urine tested positive for cocaine use had 145 percent more absenteeism and 85 percent more injuries than other employees.

"Next time I think I'll take my Roller Blades!"

In recent years there have been numerous documented cases of work-related accidents due to drug abuse, such events as a Conrail-Amtrak crash and a commuter plane crash. Even employees at some nuclear plants were reported as having been high on drugs while working with highly dangerous radioactive materials.[16]

Truckin' along the "high" way.

Drugs have also made inroads on alcohol as a factor in fatal accidents involving truck drivers, according to the National Transportation Safety Board. Accident investigators have found evidence that cocaine, amphetamines, and methamphetamine—all stimulants—have been used by truckers involved in accidents. Some truckers who must drive long hours and distances select drugs they think will help them make it through the night. A high percentage of accidents in which truckers kill themselves or others have involved the use of either drugs or alcohol, according to the Board.[17]

THE "WHO" AND "WHY" OF SUBSTANCE ABUSE

You Never Know Who It Might Be

What sort of conditions sometimes cause the disease?

The problems of alcohol and drug abuse can beset virtually anyone in an organization. Often some of the best and brightest of employees "catch" the contagious disease of addiction. Especially afflicted are those who feel that the occupational environment is *dispiriting and dehumanizing.* As a result, some employees may feel forced into the escapism of daydreams, drink, and drugs. If efforts at job empowerment and job enrichment are successful, perhaps some of these feelings will be eliminated or reduced.

Others who may use alcohol or drugs to excess are those with *financial or health problems,* either theirs or those of members of their family. Some individuals who know that they should stay away from alcohol—persons with ulcers, for example—profusely immerse their damaged surface tissue in straight whiskies, hoping to deaden the pain, at least temporarily.

A reversal of drug patterns occurred in 1989 when a United States Justice Department study found that in many U.S. cities, hardcore users of cocaine and heroin were as likely to be women as men. A dramatic increase was noted in the number of inner-city women abusing drugs, particularly crack cocaine. Some health officials believe that the increased use of substances by women is a major cause of the growing numbers of drug-addicted babies and cases of sexually transmitted diseases being reported in many urban areas. There are a reported 375,000 babies born annually who are addicted to drugs.[18]

Why is poverty not the sole cause of addiction?

At one time, sociologists believed that if poverty could be eliminated, drug abuse would naturally fade away. This notion was found to be erroneous: *affluent people,* also, are hit by the disease. Read what a Prudential Insurance Company pamphlet says about drug usage:

> In a world where changes are rapid and yesterday's faiths and values may erode, affluence allows the time and finances to support drug excesses. Loss of goals and drive can be by-products of affluence. When individuals no longer need to work in order to eat and clothe themselves, they may develop problems of leisure. If they have no viable goals, no motivation or drive to create, to study or help others, they may become bored or alienated, and vulnerable to the temptation of using chemical substitutes for productive living.[19]

The above words might well apply to the excessive use of alcohol.

Although large urban areas seem to be notorious for the greater availability of drugs, some surveys have discovered that the location and the size of a company makes only a minor difference regarding the extent of the problem.

What Causes Excessive Use of Alcohol or Drugs?

Not everyone uses alcohol or drugs for the same reasons. One of the more common reasons is *peer pressure,* the desire to be one of the group. The person who has never smoked marijuana, for example, may feel socially compelled to take his or her first puff on a joint as it is being passed from person to person. Or the young person whose discotheque friends take ecstasy with their techno sounds may feel peer pressure to do the same. The fear of the group's ostracism or disapproval often motivates some individuals, especially those searching for self-identity or acceptance, to establish their habits.

Many persons who abuse drugs have had previous *environmental experiences* that have disturbed them. Often they feel rejected or dominated by their parents. Some persons believe that their drug activities can provide them with an *escape* into a group that accepts—rather than rejects—them.

The consumption of alcoholic beverages has been firmly established in the American culture as a *social and business custom.* Although there are numerous exceptions to the stereotype, business executives are infamous for their two-martini lunches. And one of the first questions that hosts or hostesses often ask their newly arrived guests is, "What would you like to drink?" In some circles, the question, "Would you like to try some good stuff?" is substituted.

A salient point, therefore, is that society—that is, our culture—strongly influences our tastes and customs. Alcohol and drugs are not the root of the problem: Their abuse is an indication of other deep-seated complications and frustrations.

We've already pointed out how persons who perceive their *jobs as being dull* or who have *personal problems* often use drugs and alcohol as an escape. Some observers feel that *excessive economic security* and *leisure time* are among the paramount causes of abuse. Still others blame the *advertising industry.* They cite the prevalence of *television advertisements* promoting the "ethical" or "straight drug culture" on which millions of dollars are spent annually.

The Effect on the Bottom Line

Accurate cost data derived from drug abuse are still scarce. Yet ample evidence of the excessive economic costs of drug abuse is available. It has been estimated that drug abuse costs the U.S. economy well in excess of $100 billion per year, and this figure has been rising dramatically every year.

A costly habit.

Drug addiction can become an expensive habit. To support their habits, dependent employees often become *pushers,* or *junkies,* and sometimes inveigle *fellow employees* into narcotics addiction. Addicts are believed to be responsible for *stealing* billions of dollars in property each year from organizations and individuals. A large proportion of *shoplifting* is believed to be done by drug users, including some persons employed by the stores.

Costs have also soared as a result of *higher turnover* rates among addicted employees. Since many companies lack programs to deal with drug problems, most *employees are fired* when their habits are discovered.

Generally, however, most employees with drug problems are not fired specifically for drug use, which, unlike alcohol abuse, has a sort of *public invisibility.* An employee on drugs, for example, can coyly pop a pill into his or her mouth unnoticed by the boss and, conversely, the boss could do the same. (Do you remember how you used to slip chewing gum into your mouth in grade school?) Workers with drug problems, therefore, are fired more frequently for the *effects* of their habits, such as *high absenteeism, chronic lateness, sleeping or daydreaming on the job, and theft.*

For what reasons have

Increasingly, as a means of uncovering drug abuse on the job, more and more organizations have begun to utilize detection schemes that include urine, hair, and lie detector tests, drug-sniffing dogs, and even private eyes that spy on unsuspecting employees.

ORGANIZATIONAL APPROACHES TO ALCOHOL AND DRUG ABUSE

Until relatively recently, most managers seemed not to want to recognize that alcohol and drug abuse were organizational behavior problems in need of their attention. When cases did become known, they were often covered up until the employee could no longer function effectively on the job and had to be dismissed, which did little to correct the individual's problem. At long last, however, most authorities recognize that alcoholism and drug addiction are **treatable diseases** and therefore require medical attention or therapy, as do other diseases.

An increasing number of organizations—both private and public—have taken an active interest in attempting to reduce the prevalence of these two costly afflictions by developing employee assistance programs that offer help for alcoholism, drug abuse, and other behavioral problems and chronic illness. A large proportion of the Fortune 500 largest industrial corporations has established in-house employee assistance programs. Many executives believe that their businesses have actually saved money as a result of investing in such programs.

The Nature of Company Programs

What is the nature of current programs?

Organizations with established programs have attempted to steer clear of the traditional solutions of either firing the employee with a drinking or drug problem, giving sermons on the evils of excessive consumption of alcohol, or calling in the police to "bust potheads." Instead, modern organizations have concentrated on *counseling* the employee to seek treatment, generally with an *outside agency* while keeping him or her on the job. Although sympathetic understanding of the employee's problem is conveyed, the employee is told that deterioration of work habits, absenteeism, or other troubles created by alcohol or drug abuse will not be tolerated indefinitely. Typical programs, therefore, deal with three principal stages: *detection, treatment,* and *rehabilitation.*

THE ESTABLISHMENT OF COMPANY PROGRAMS

Rather than being allowed to develop haphazardly, an alcohol or drug program should have someone specifically assigned to establish and coordinate it. Individuals with experience in creating undertakings of this nature tend to feel that a new program should not begin with fanfare but should instead be introduced gradually and combined with other ongoing behavioral, medical, and counseling programs.

The key ingredients of any successful organizational program attempting to control drinking and drug problems are:

1. Knowledge of the need

2. Top management commitment

3. Workable disciplinary procedures

4. Effective referral process

5. Follow-up procedures

A Formal Statement of Policy

Why should a company policy be formulated?

Before a program is carried out company management should first establish a formal policy designed to deal consistently with the problems. The Kemper Insurance Group adopted their original policy in 1964; it covered only alcoholism. Their current policy—a broader one—has served as an industry model and now includes drug addiction and emotional disturbances as well.

KEMPER INSURANCE GROUP PERSONAL ASSISTANCE POLICY STATEMENT[20]

Policy. The underlying concept of Kemper's personnel policies is regard for the employee as an individual as well as a worker. Reflecting this concern, the company has devised a policy with six principles.

1. We believe that alcoholism, drug addiction and emotional disturbance are illnesses and should be treated as such.

2. We believe the majority of employees who develop alcoholism, other drug addiction or emotional illness can be helped to recover, and the company should offer appropriate assistance.

3. We believe the decision to seek diagnosis and accept treatment for any suspected illness is the responsibility of the employee. However, continued refusal of an employee to seek treatment when it appears that substandard performance may be caused by any illness is not tolerated. We believe that alcoholism, other drug addiction or emotional illness should not be made an exception to this commonly accepted principle.

4. We believe that it is in the best interest of employees and the company that when alcoholism, other drug addiction or emotional illness is present, it should be diagnosed and treated at the earliest possible date.

5. We believe that the company's concern for individual alcohol drinking, drug taking and behavioral habits begins only when they result in unsatisfactory job performance, poor attendance or behavior detrimental to the good reputation of the companies.

6. We believe that confidential handling of the diagnosis and treatment of alcoholism, other drug addiction or emotional illness is essential.

The object of this policy is to retain employees who may develop any of these illnesses, by helping them to arrest its further advance before the condition renders them unemployable.

The Need for Management Support and Employee Understanding

How can the program be communicated?

The cooperation of all levels of management—especially supervisory—is essential for the success of any employee assistance project. Managers can learn about the problems at *management training or development sessions.* Discussions should not focus exclusively on alcoholism and drugs but should emphasize factors that affect job performance.

Instead of holding special meetings to announce a new program, employees can be notified more subtly and less dramatically at other *normal functions,* such as at safety meetings where some persons with alcohol or drug problems are likely to be present.

Videos can be used to disseminate information effectively and can be publicized by notices in the cafeteria. *Literature* can be handed out at *meetings of employees* and placed on *bulletin boards* and in *pamphlet racks.* The organization's *company newsletter* can be another useful medium for enabling employees to become aware of the services available to them. However, management cannot expect all employees with problems to seek counseling on their own. Many will have to be referred by supervisors.

The Stigma of Alcoholism and Drug Programs

The words *alcoholic* and *drug addict* have disagreeable and frightening connotations to many employees. Company managers involved with the establishment of **Employee Assistance Programs (EAPs)** need to be concerned with semantics when determining what to call their plans. A key problem, therefore, is how to eliminate the stigma of such programs.

As we've already mentioned, the programs shouldn't be considered as something separate and apart from other medical and counseling services. Some employee relations directors feel that calling something an alcohol program gives it the kiss of death. Some organizations use broad titles such as "Employee Counseling Service" or "Employee Assistance Program," preferring not to stress solely the problems of alcohol and drug dependency. These programs frequently include assistance in a variety of other areas such as self-identity, health, marriage, and financial difficulties. Some firms even prefer to avoid any stigma that might be associated with the words *counseling* or *therapy*. To make it easier for employees to get advice on drug programs, some companies, such as Xerox, have established toll-free numbers that workers and their families can call to get advice on drug problems. These services guarantee privacy to employees. The hotline counselors attempt to encourage employees to seek help through EAPs or local clinical programs.

How can the stigma of programs be reduced?

Treatment and Recovery Services

The treatment of alcoholism and drug addiction is generally not the function of the employer. Instead, the coordinator of a program generally maintains *local consultants* or recommends *community resources* to the willing employee. *Alcoholics Anonymous* is reputed to be one of the best sources of therapy for the alcoholic, as are *Al-Anon* groups for families of alcoholics. For persons in need of drug therapy, there are various public and private nonprofit organizations whose services are available throughout the United States, especially in the larger urban areas. There now exist in some areas branches of Cocaine Anonymous, a national self-help group patterned on the principles of Alcoholics Anonymous. A drug-problem hotline—1-800-999-9951—exists to provide treatment referral and information.

Where does treatment generally take place?

Coverage in Health Insurance Contracts

Insurance companies seem to have developed a greater awareness that alcoholism can be treated, for many group insurance contracts now include coverage for alcoholism. Numerous labor-management-negotiated contracts also provide health coverage for the treatment of alcoholism as an employee benefit. This coverage is given on the assumption that reducing alcoholism problems may actually reduce insurance costs because the employee's health is likely to be improved after treatment. Some insurance companies also include coverage for drug-related medical costs in their insurance policies. Unfortunately, however, recent health care cost-cutting trends among employers could result in some slippage in coming years.

EAPs Also Assist the Bottom Lines of Employers[b]

Employee Assistance Programs (EAPs) have become increasingly prevalent in organizations in recent years. The United States has led the pack globally in their use. More than 75 percent of United States Fortune 500 companies now use EAPs, whereas only a mere 50 to 70 companies in the United Kingdom currently use them.

Richard Bickerton, an EAP consultant, suggests that the rise in the use of EAPs in the United States is due to "the increased recognition by employers that it's a way to restore productive workers in the most cost-effective way possible." For every $1 spent on EAP programs, return has been estimated to vary from $2.00 to $16.00—not a bad profit indeed.

SUPERVISORY RESPONSIBILITIES

How should supervisors handle abuse problems?

Once again, key persons in the determination of the success or failure of any program are supervisors. Supervisors, however, should *not* attempt to be amateur diagnosticians or counselors nor should they become involved in discussing illnesses that they are not qualified to handle. Instead, supervisors should approach alcohol and drug problems as they would any other erratic performance by employees.

Communicate Policies and Rules

Make it understood.

Supervisors should try to make certain that policies and rules related to substance use are clearly communicated and understood by employees. Employees should recognize that even though their company has an EAP, the purpose of which is to assist employees with problems such as substance abuse, they may be subject to immediate dismissal under certain circumstances, which we'll examine shortly.

Detect Symptoms and Document Employee Behavior

Supervisors, who in effect are monitors of the employees' work, should be trained to recognize the *symptoms* of alcohol and drug problems. As we have already learned, substance abuse problems are generally accompanied by *specific changes in work performance and dependability*. If you as a supervisor were to become aware of such changes, you should document in writing all incidents of unsatisfactory behavior.

Write it down.

Conduct a Disciplinary Interview

After detecting symptoms and documenting unsatisfactory performance, you should call in the employee, review the actual record, and inform the person that his or her performance *must improve*. Be certain to obtain an agreement related to a *specific time limit* for the improvement of the employee's performance.

Obtain an agreement.

After the disciplinary interview is over, you might ask the employee about any personal problems that could be affecting his or her job performance. Whether or not the employee admits to the existence of a problem, he or she could be told that the company has a confidential counseling service that can provide assistance. The employee might initially reject any suggestions to see a counselor, but the idea, nevertheless, has been planted in the person's head. People sometimes reconsider such advice.

Follow Up Where Necessary

As is frequently the case, the employee may conceal his or her personal alcohol or drug problem, refuse to see a counselor, but promise to improve work performance. The supervisor should continue after this meeting to keep written records of the employee's work performance. Personnel managers generally recommend that information only about job performance, not alcohol or drug use, be included in the employees' records.

Monitor performance.

If the deficiencies continue, a second meeting becomes necessary and the supervisor may need to use a more direct approach, perhaps something like:

> Peter, you promised me that your performance would improve. Instead it has continued to deteriorate. I've shown you specifically what I mean. You and I both know that such performance cannot continue. Consequently, I'm going to send you to see our company counselor (or doctor), and unless you and the counselor work out your problem, I'm afraid your job is going to be in serious jeopardy.

Another approach that has a significant impact on the employee is to say something like:

> Peter, we're going to ask you for your resignation (pause . . .), if you don't seek help related to your performance problems.

The above approaches may appear, at first glance, to be harsh and cold. However, they are intended to be an "attention-getting" process, sometimes referred to as **constructive coercion.** Motivation to seek help, of course, must come from within the drug addict or alcoholic. The employee must want to stop abusing substances for his or her *own sake* and not because of being *pushed* into it by others. Under the techniques discussed, the substance abuser is not being *forced* into action. Instead, he or she has a choice and should be made aware of the consequences of inaction.

Be on Guard Against the Sham Approach

"Sure, boss. Anything you say."

Even substance abusing employees typically want to keep their jobs. Consequently, as a means of placating their bosses, they may engage in what has been termed the **sham approach,** merely making the pretense of seeking professional help, without really being sold on the advantages of doing so. Supervisors must be on guard against such deception. Perhaps the employee is not yet convinced that a drinking or addiction problem actually exists. Unless there is a sincere interest in recovering, the employee is likely to continue the same substance abusing habits.

In other instances, the employee may sincerely want to recover but continues to abuse substances because of the difficulties associated with adjusting to a life without drugs or alcohol. Alcoholics and drug abusers have typically developed a physical response to their habits, one that is usually difficult for them to control. They cannot recover until they learn to live without the substance, not an easy task after they've crossed over that dangerous and thin line into dependency.

Should Employees Ever Be Discharged for Substance Abuse?

Organizational EAPs concerned with substance abuse are intended to assist, not punish employees. The major responsibilities of supervisors related to such programs are to detect abusers and attempt to refer problem employees to professional counselors.

A supervisor's sympathies are likely to be greater toward the employee who is truly willing to seek assistance. Are there any circumstances, however, that might call for immediate dismissal of the employee? The policies of many organizations state something like this:

> The conviction of employees on illegal drug traffic charges can constitute grounds of immediate termination. Furthermore, employees found to be involved in such traffic on company premises or during working hours will be terminated and reported to proper authorities.

Avoid traffic problems.

Most organizations feel they cannot condone the illegal trafficking of drugs on premises. However, the *use* of illegal drugs on premises is often another matter. The decision to refer the employee to a professional counselor or engage in disciplinary action is often dependent on which course of action is better for both the company and the offending employee.

As a means of avoiding the likelihood of being victimized by the sham approach, it is suggested that a specific probationary period be established for the substance-abusing employee. The employee may then have to be discharged if unsatisfactory job performance continues after he or she recognizes the substance abuse problem and understands the steps necessary for recovery.

SUPERVISORY GUIDELINES

Let's summarize some *specific guidelines* for supervisors to follow when they suspect an employee has an alcohol or drug problem:

- *Do* attempt to learn to recognize the symptoms of alcohol or drug abuse.

- *Do not* attempt to diagnose the employee's problem. Instead, show a genuine concern for the employee's problem and attempt to refer him or her to a company specialist qualified in such matters.

- *Do not* discuss drinking or drug problems with the employee; instead, focus on *job deficiencies* and *corrective action*.

- Never—repeat, *never*—accuse an employee of using drugs or being an alcoholic. If you do, you may open yourself and the company to a slander or defamation of character lawsuit.

- *Do not feel guilty* about referring an employee to staff specialists. Doing so is not an admission of failure in the way you manage your department.

- *Do* follow up after an employee both begins and completes rehabilitation to ascertain that he or she is following prescribed recommendations.

- *Do not* dismiss a previously satisfactory employee for deteriorating performance before giving the employee ample opportunity to seek assistance.

RECOGNIZING ALCOHOL AND DRUG ABUSE IN THE WORKPLACE

Pinpointing the specific symptoms of alcohol and drug abuse problems is not a simple task. A supervisor's main responsibility, therefore, should not necessarily be uncovering evidence of dependency on alcohol and drugs but instead be observing declining job performance. Yet there are certain behavioral patterns that some excessive users of alcohol and drugs display. These patterns can sometimes be spotted through simple observation. Increasingly, however, employers are taking more aggressive steps to ferret out substance abuse among their work forces. A growing number of companies, especially large ones with more than 5000 employees and those in businesses with the potential to affect public health or safety (e.g., transportation companies, utilities, hazardous-materials handlers), are adopting drug-testing programs.

Signs of Alcohol Dependency

The **signs of alcohol dependency,** unfortunately, do not always become manifest until the middle or late stages of the problem. The earlier treatment begins, naturally, the easier it will be. Table 12.1 cites some of the more common signs and symptoms of alcoholism. A person could experience some isolated incidents of such drinking problems without necessarily being an alcoholic. However, alcohol abuse usually results in declining job performance.

Signs of Drug Dependency

Drug dependencies also produce observable changes in employees' work performance. The **signs of drug dependency,** however, are not always obvious. Some managers have mistaken an employee's euphoric appearance for the "look of love." Some of the symptoms

TABLE 12.1   Common Signs and Symptoms of Alcohol Dependency.

- Early-morning drinking
- Drinking to calm nerves, forget worries, or reduce depression
- Getting drunk often (more than three or five times during a year)
- Going to work intoxicated
- Drinking alone with increased frequency
- Injuring oneself, or someone else, while intoxicated
- Lying about drinking habits
- Gulping drinks and drinking too fast
- Loss of interest in food
- Driving a motorized vehicle while intoxicated
- Regularly acting irritable, resentful, or unreasonable when not drinking
- Doing something under the influence of alcohol that one avows would never occur without alcohol
- Absenteeism, especially on Monday mornings and after holidays
- Hand tremors
- Occasional complaints from customers of the company
- Decline in work performance

TABLE 12.2 Possible Warning Signs Related to Drug Abuse.

- Anxiety reactions and states of panic
- Accidents due to impaired judgment and distorted perceptions of space or time
- Attitudes of paranoia or excessive suspicion of others
- Mental confusion, loss of contact with reality, and lapses of memory
- Indifferent, apathetic, and sometimes compulsive behavior
- Dilated pupils, a flushed face, and a feeling of being chilly
- Chronic sniffles
- Occasional convulsions
- A deterioration of values
- Falling asleep on the job, drowsiness
- Abscesses, needle marks, and "tracks" (discolorations along the course of veins in the arms and legs)
- The regular wearing of dark sunglasses indoors (to protect dilated pupils)
- An unhealthy appearance because of poor diet and personal neglect

associated with alcoholism could also be related to drug dependency. Some of the principal warning signs related to drug use are listed in Table 12.2.

No one person would necessarily have all or any of the symptoms cited in Table 12.2. And a supervisor should guard against assuming that the presence of one or more symptoms is conclusive proof of alcohol or drug abuse. Symptoms will likewise vary with the *stage of alcoholism* or the *type of drug used* as well as with the *experience of the drug user.* Samples of employees' urine have indicated the taking of certain drugs in quantities that would kill less experienced users, yet the users went undetected until examined medically.

What can influence the symptoms?

GETTING TOUGH WITH SUBSTANCE ABUSERS: EMPLOYEE DRUG TESTING

Make that "getting testy" with substance abusers!

Nearly three quarters—74.5 percent—of the 1200 companies surveyed in a 1992 study by the American Management Associations said they now test employees for drugs. The number that carry out random drug testing increased tenfold between 1987 and 1992.[21] What these figures mean is that if you abuse drugs or alcohol, you are more likely than ever before to get caught by your employer. Testing for abuse problems is becoming increasingly widespread in U.S. industry as losses to the economy continue to mount. Workplace substance abuse has been estimated to cost employers $120 billion a year.[22]

TABLE 12.3   Common Methods for Uncovering the Use of Substances in the Workplace.

- The use of undercover agents
- The use of dogs trained to smell certain types of drugs (not only German shepherds but also springer spaniels and golden retrievers)
- The use of employees to "sniff-and-squeal" (sometimes a requirement that selected employees sign an "S & S" agreement, which makes the signer responsible for all others in the work group who violate alcohol and drug rules)
- The testing of bodily fluids (saliva, blood, urine)
- The testing of a person's hair (shows not only *if* drugs have been taken but also *when* they were taken)

Types of Tests

Some of the more common methods for uncovering the use of substances are listed in Table 12.3. The *physiological* tests—those involving body-fluid samples, hair, or (less frequently) patches attached to the skin—are the ones most often used. There are also paper-and-pencil tests that are said to be able to measure or predict the use of drugs or alcohol. One of the most recent, and least well known, developments is impairment-based screening, such as tests of eye-hand coordination. Some who criticize urinalysis on the grounds of inaccuracy or invasion of privacy have recommended greater reliance on measuring impairment in a suspected substance abuser's actions and skills.

Types of Testing Programs

There are three basic types of testing programs. *Random testing* (used by about nine percent of employers with drug-screening programs, according to a recent survey) involves tests of employees without regard to whether they are suspected of having drug or alcohol problems. The goal is to keep anti-substance-abuse awareness continuously high among all employees because of the possibility of having to submit to a test at any time. Employees to be tested can be chosen in a variety of ways—for example, by department or employee number or through the use of a computer—as long as the selection is random. *Fitness-for-duty testing* is done to find out whether a person is capable of performing a job. This type of test is most often done as part of the preemployment-screening process. *"For cause" testing* (used by about 74 percent of recently surveyed companies that tested for drugs) is the most common kind of program. The employer requires a test only if it has a reasonable suspicion or cause to believe that an employee is involved in drug use. Given these options, how are companies actually doing drug testing in the "real world" of work?

High *awareness,* not high *employees!*

"Real-World" Drug Testing Programs

The Texas Instruments Company (TI) is one employer that has chosen the random-testing route to combat drugs. Its "Universal Random Testing" program gives all 39,000 TI employees "from the boss to the janitor" the opportunity to be selected in a computer-based process. TI officials claim that production has increased and accident frequency has declined since the program was inaugurated.[23]

Trump Shuttle, an air transportation company, was required to test certain employees in safety-sensitive positions under federal guidelines. In early 1989, however, Trump Shuttle extended drug testing to all employees, including "nonregulated" ones (e.g., clerical workers, reservations agents, sky caps, and managers). The company takes the for-cause approach with its nonregulated workers. They are informed at the outset that they are subject to testing if there is reasonable suspicion that they are using drugs. They are also told about the company's EAP. If an alcohol- or drug-abusing employee goes to the EAP voluntarily for help, the EAP is left alone to handle the matter on a confidential basis. Employees who do not admit a substance-abuse problem, show signs of substance abuse on the job, and receive confirmed positive test results are terminated. Terminated workers can go through an appeals process, but the company's experience has been that employees caught in this way have not appealed when confronted with the evidence.[24]

Long Island Lighting Company, a New York utility, also has no patience with "high fliers." It recently extended its at-random program to employees who had not previously been covered by federal drug-testing requirements. Under the expanded program, which was negotiated with the company's unions, urine tests are to be conducted monthly. An employee testing positive the first time would get a five-day suspension. Second-offenders lose their jobs. The same types of testing required by government regulations would be carried out after accidents, for reasonable cause, before hiring, and for rehabilitation testing.[25]

Weighing the Pros and Cons of Testing

Drug testing in the workplace is a subject of debate. Some employees and employers feel that mandatory random drug testing is incompatible with their basic philosophies. They believe that such programs run the risk of encroaching on the civil and privacy rights of employees by the use of methods that might be construed as accusatory. Further, the U.S. Drug Enforcement Administration warns that there exist disreputable firms offering cheap, but inconclusive, analyses. The validity of urine test results has long been a target of critics. The cost of drug testing may be one reason why testing programs are still fairly rare among smaller firms. The average cost per examination is around $70. On the plus side, though, research has shown that some

A QUESTION
OF
ETHICS

Nothing Casual About Motorola's Anti–Substance Abuse Program![c]

Most employees whose reflexes and judgment on the job are consistently impaired from the abuse of drugs or alcohol would probably not be welcomed by employers concerned with total quality management. However, what about the casual user of, say, marijuana—the person who smokes an occasional joint on weekends for "recreational purposes" but not on a regular basis? Should that person's job be in jeopardy?

It is at Motorola, a high-tech company with a substance testing program that shows favoritism to no one. Everyone is included, from senior executives to mid-managers to supervisors to operating employees. In fact, the company's employees themselves rejected the notion of selective testing, believing in the ethos of "good for one, good for all," including the bosses and those in noncritical positions.

Anyhow, back to casual use: Gary Howard, the employee-relations director overseeing Motorola's program, says, "We're not particularly as concerned about impairment [on the job], although we're concerned about it, as we are about having a work force that doesn't use drugs." He believes it *is* the company's business if an employee uses marijuana on weekends. Howard contends, "Our stated objective is to become the finest company in the world. You can't be the finest company in the world if you don't have the best people in the world, what we refer to as the 'best in class' in Motorola. Best-in-class people, to us, don't use drugs."

A Question of Ethics: So . . . what do you think? Should a company have the right to control a person's casual use of drugs? Why or why not? When does "casual use" become "drug abuse"?

employers may see significant returns on the dollars they spend on drug screening, as much as $800 per new employee, according to one recent study based on Postal Service hiring data.[26] Table 12.4 summarizes some of the principal arguments against and in favor of drug testing in the workplace.

The Supreme Court has upheld the right of certain employers to test employees for substance abuse. In 1989, it upheld the constitutionality

SOURCE: Reprinted by permission of UFS, Inc. & NEA, Inc.

TABLE 12.4   Arguments Against and in Favor of Drug Testing in the Workplace.

Arguments against drug testing:
- Administration costs may outweigh benefits
- Invasion of privacy
- Abuse of employee civil rights
- Possible negative effects on employee morale
- Potential inaccuracy and inconclusiveness of test results
- Lack of universal agreement as to what constitutes drug abuse

Arguments in favor of drug testing:
- Reduced accident rate and materials waste
- Reduced absenteeism
- Reduced employment costs, such as for recruitment, training, and employee turnover
- Motivator for problem employees to seek rehabilitation
- Possible enhanced employee pride as a result of working in "drug-free work environment"
- Creates opportunities for firm to obtain government contracts

of drug testing for a broad array of Customs Service and transportation industry employees. Justice Anthony Kennedy, who wrote opinions in two relevant cases, contends that the government's interest in regulating railroad and other transportation employees to ensure the safety of the traveling public and the employees themselves justifies the tests.[27]

Because of the controversial nature of drug tests in the workplace many firms have solicited legal advice on the matter. Seventeen states have passed laws concerning drug testing, and some state constitutions—for example, California's—have privacy provisions that have already figured in court cases. Table 12.5 provides a list of guidelines for the employers considering the use of tests on employees for detecting drug use. The application of these guidelines could help to minimize future organizational problems related to drug testing.[28] Information is also available from the Institute for a Drug-Free Workplace, which publishes an annual *Guide to State Drug Testing Laws and Legislation.*

TABLE 12.5   Guidelines for Employers Considering Testing Employees for Drugs.

1. Explain to employees why drug testing is necessary. (Safety of the work force is a primary reason.)
2. Choose a competent testing laboratory. (The avoidance of inaccurate results is essential to gain acceptance of the program.)
3. Give employees advance notice. (The goal is not to catch or punish employees but to have a safe, drug-free environment.)
4. When a drug user is identified, provide rehabilitation. (Employees should be assisted when they are willing to stop abusing drugs.)
5. Consider using fitness-for-duty, rather than urine, tests. (Random urine tests may create legal complications. Fitness-for-duty tests—such as eye exams and coordination tests—can identify employees likely to have drugs in their systems. They can then be given urine tests.)

TABLE 12.6   Legislation Related to Drugs and the Workplace.

- **Executive Order 12564, September 15, 1986:**
  Order that mandated federal agencies to formulate a drug-free workplace plan which would include drug testing among other critical components.
- **Public Law 100-71, Supplemental Appropriations Act, July 11, 1987:**
  Specified the conditions under which the Executive Order would be implemented.
- **Mandatory Guidelines for Federal Workplace Drug Testing Programs, Federal Register, April 11, 1988:**
  Set forth the standards for all aspects of drug testing and procedures in the federal government program.
- **Department of Defense Regulations, Federal Register, November 14, 1988:**
  Requires drug testing of more than 4 million employees in safety and security jobs in all major modes of transportation.
- **Nuclear Regulatory Commission, Federal Register, June 7, 1989:**
  Requires licensees authorized to operate or construct a nuclear power reactor to implement fitness-for-duty programs.
- **Public Law 100-690, Drug-Free Workplace Act of 1988, November 1988:**
  Requires most federal grantees and contractors procuring property or services valued at more than $25,000 from any federal agency to establish a drug-free workplace.

BEING DRUG FREE IS GOOD BUSINESS

As a part of the omnibus legislation passed by Congress—the **Drug-Free Workplace Act of 1988**—contractors or receivers of grants from any federal agency must certify that they will maintain a "drug-free workplace," or in the case of a grantee who is an individual, must certify that his or her "conduct" will be drug free. The act further requires the employer to notify all employees about the consequences of distributing or possessing illegal drugs on the job.

What happens if the employer or grantee doesn't maintain a drug-free workplace? The act calls for suspension of payments under the government contract or grant, plus "debarring" the employer or grantee from receiving any further contracts or grants for up to five years.[29] Significant legislation related to drugs and the workplace are summarized in Table 12.6.

SUMMARY

This chapter has provided an overview of the broad, complex, and changing problems of alcohol and drug abuse. No longer are the non-identical twin problems of alcoholism and drug addiction looked upon solely as the responsibility of the courts; both are now recognized by most authorities as diseases that are "caught" by individuals either through the influence of their peers or through attempts to reduce the stress and tension of their environment.

A number of concerned managers have developed organizational policies and programs designed to deal with problem drinkers and substance users on their payrolls. However, patience has at times run thin, and an increasing number of organizations are now screening applicants and existing employees through the use of substance-abuse testing, an activity that is not fully accepted in a society in which concerns for individual rights of privacy are so prevalent. However, there are others who contend that the public's right to use safe facilities and the employer's right to a drug-free working environment outweigh certain rights of privacy. What do you think?

TERMS AND CONCEPTS TO REMEMBER

alcoholic

Hughes Act (Comprehensive Alcohol Abuse and Alcoholism Prevention, Treatment, and Rehabilitation Act of 1970)

National Institute of Alcohol Abuse and Alcoholism

recovering alcoholic

drug abuse (drug addiction)

drug

treatable disease

Employee Assistance Programs (EAPs)

constructive coercion

sham approach

signs of alcohol dependency

signs of drug dependence

Drug-Free Workplace Act of 1988

QUESTIONS

1. What are some individual behaviors that could indicate that a person has a drinking problem?

2. How does the chapter define an *alcoholic?* How does the definition differ from that of a *social drinker?*

3. What are some of the principal *economic costs* associated with drug abuse?

4. What generally can cause a person to "catch" the diseases of alcoholism or drug dependency?

5. What is meant by the "stigma of alcohol or drug programs"? How might such stigmas be overcome?

6. What are the major types of drugs currently being used and abused? Which kinds are most prevalent among employees?

7. Why is it desirable for organizations to establish official alcohol and drug abuse policies and programs?

8. What is meant by the statement: "Drug use has a sort of public invisibility"?

9. What is meant by the concept of "constructive coercion"? How do you personally feel about its use?

10. How might a supervisor avoid being duped by an employee's use of the "sham approach"?

11. Should employees ever be discharged for substance abuse? Explain.

12. How do you feel about the use of urine tests as a method of drug-use detection?

13. What are the major "shoulds" associated with the administration of an organization's alcohol or drug abuse program?

14. Why should supervisors not attempt personally to diagnose alcohol or drug problems, nor counsel individuals with them?

15. Assume that you are a personnel manager facing some skeptical supervisors who feel any person with drinking or drug problems should be fired on the spot. Prepare a logical argument designed to convince the supervisors that dismissal should be a last—not first—resort.

16. What is the purpose of the Drug-Free Workplace Act of 1988? Do you favor or oppose its existence? Why?

APPLICATIONS

12.1 The Case of Johnny Ballantine

Johnny Ballantine, a sales representative for MedSolutions Software for the past three years, is directly accountable to Joseph Jenever, the sales manager in the branch office in Raleigh, North Carolina. Ballantine's principal responsibility is to sell computer programs to hospitals and doctors' offices for the management of medical records, health insurance claims, and other administrative tasks.

About eight months ago, Ballantine and his wife, Nivaria, were returning to Raleigh from a weekend visit with friends in Chapel Hill. During the trip Ballantine fell asleep at the wheel, the automobile careened off the highway, and Nivaria was critically injured. She died two days later, leaving Ballantine with the full responsibility of raising their two daughters, Rosa, age nine, and Rioja, age fourteen.

In recent months Jenever has begun to notice some significant changes in Ballantine's activities and behavior. For example, there has been a marked increase in Ballantine's entertainment expense account. When questioned about the change earlier this month, Ballantine explained, "I've got to drink a lot when I'm out with customers; it's good business."

Jenever noticed another unusual situation relating to Ballantine's territory. Every two weeks, he is required to submit an itinerary, a list of the customers he intends to contact on particular days. Recently, on two separate occasions, Jenever discovered that Ballantine had not followed his proposed itinerary. The first time, Jenever had reason to call the customer in an effort to locate Ballantine because of an emergency involving Rioja, his elder daughter. The second time, an important account urgently wanted to discuss a "bug" in a customized appointment-manager system MedSolutions had just installed. In neither case was Ballantine where his itinerary indicated he would be. Nor was he even expected by his customers on those days.

In addition, Ballantine's behavior when he is in the office has changed significantly lately. He often avoids Jenever and frequently becomes belligerent with the office staff. During the past month and a half, Ballantine has had two accidents with his company car, both involving his having driven into parked cars. Also, it appears to Jenever that Ballantine's hands have developed mild tremors in recent weeks.

Jenever suspects that Ballantine is drinking to excess, but he is not quite certain how to handle what he believes to be an exceedingly difficult and delicate situation.

Questions

1. What, in your judgment, is the primary problem in this case?

2. What should Jenever do about the problem?

12.2 The Producer Who Couldn't Say No

Patti Rocque, 29, produces and directs "Hot Nights in the City," a 90-minute entertainment show that airs in the late-night time slot every Saturday on a suburban Chicago cable television station. Modeled on the MTV format, "Hot Nights" features musical performances and comedy, as well as the latest work by video artists. Rocque has even pioneered poetry readings, avant-garde drama, and interviews with painters and sculptors on her show, innovations that have attracted the attention of the national music-video channels. Though "Hot Nights" mainly spotlights local "Chicago-land" talent, the show, because of its large and loyal following in a major U.S. media market, has been able in recent months to attract internationally known performers to its studio.

Patti Rocque created "Hot Nights," built it into a respected and important program in the Midwest, and continues to pour all her energy into it to take it to the next level—perhaps national syndication. But her real joy comes from scouting new artists to present to her audience. Because these artists are principally musicians, comedians, and actors, scouting means spending many evenings in clubs—and that means being around alcohol for more than a few hours almost every day.

As is the custom in her position, Patti entertains prospective "Hot Nights" guests and their agents at her table, picking up the tab for their drinks as well as her own. Many of those she meets with seem to be fairly heavy drinkers during these informal get-togethers.

Patti frequently finds herself in a difficult situation. Her mother was an alcoholic who died in a tragic automobile accident while under the influence of alcohol. As a young girl, Patti swore that she would never let booze get the best of her. She vowed to herself that she would always be a moderate drinker.

During the early phases of working on the show, Patti was fairly successful in controlling her intake of alcohol. As the program became more popular, however, and the pressure increased to bring on more, better known performers, she found herself making occasional exceptions to her two-a-day limit. She even stashed a container of odorless mixed drinks in her desk drawer at the station. When asked about it, Patti said it contained the results of her experiments with a new juicing machine she had received for her birthday.

Unfortunately, Patti lost control of her intake. She recognized that she had developed a serious alcohol problem after a recent discussion with her doctor. Her health was becoming dangerously affected. On her doctor's advice, Patti decided to attend a recovery clinic. She was told at the clinic that she could never be fully cured—that it would be easy to lapse into alcoholism again if she didn't totally abstain. She said that she understood and would comply with the advice after her recovery.

Patti still must spend long evenings in clubs scouting talent. She finds herself surrounded by people who drink and expect her to do the same. She feels embarrassed by always ordering bottled water, especially since many of her associates have started kidding her about being a teetotaller. She wants to be sociable and accepted by others, but she finds herself in a dilemma. Her counselors have warned her that any drinking could start her back on the dreary path to alcoholism, and she sincerely desires to avoid that fate.

Questions

1. How can a person know when he or she is making the transition from a moderate social drinker to a person approaching alcoholism?

2. If you were to advise Patti with her "peer-pressure problem," what would you try to get her to do? Be specific.

12.3 Drug Testing—Solution or Threat?

Jack Ramirez is director of human resources for the Direct to You Company, a large mail-order retailer of unisex sports clothes. Recently, Ramirez discovered that there was a significant substance-abuse problem among Direct to You's employees, especially those fielding customer calls on the 24-hour telephone sales lines. Several workers were recently suspended for having smoked marijuana on company premises. Two additional employees were discharged after having displayed erratic behavior on the job and being absent excessively. Both employees, according to the grapevine, were crack cocaine abusers. Several other employees regularly appeared to return intoxicated from lunch. Jack realized that something had to be done about the problem.

Jack recently learned that Tie-Dye Fashions, one of Direct to You's major suppliers, had begun a program of substance detection through the use of urinalysis. All of Tie-Dye's employees are now tested in an effort to identify and confront substance abuse in the workplace. After obtaining senior management's approval, Jack decided to confer with first-line supervisors and the company's medical adviser about instituting a similar program at Direct to You.

Jack called for a meeting and distributed a planned agenda in advance in the hope of eliminating any surprised reactions from the participants. Jack began the meeting by detailing the substance-abuse problems that Direct to You had been experiencing. He then proposed that all employees submit to periodic urinalysis testing to determine who might be substance abusers.

Several of the supervisors favored the idea. "It would sure simplify matters for us if we had hard data to act on," said Suzie Quefoote. She added, "As it is now, we have to play both narc and doctor to figure out who's on what, and whether customer complaints about ordering and shipping problems are due to organizational deficiencies or 'high' workers."

The company medical adviser, Dr. Nightengale, was next to speak. "We certainly could perform the tests, but I'm not sure we should. First, the tests aren't 100 percent reliable. Second, unless someone has a high concentration of alcohol in his or her body at the time of the test, alcohol won't show up. It would seem that employee performance alone would be enough to indicate alcohol intoxication on the job. You should also realize that many of the other drugs we can test for may show up days after a person used one of them. Medical ethics dictate that medical procedures should be for the benefit of the patient. I'm not sure that these tests meet that criterion."

Some of the other supervisors were even more adamant in their reactions. "It's an invasion of everyone's privacy!" exclaimed George Ghanjini. "If a person is performing badly on the job, a test might be okay. But to test everybody without cause is against our civil rights!"

"I agree," said Danielle Darngood. "Someone who is a good worker might have smoked a joint on Friday evening, and it could still show up on the test on Monday afternoon. It's none of our darned business unless the worker's performance in the workplace is being impaired."

"A union would never stand for it," said Horace Hoffman. "You're in for a fight if you try to institute testing of all employees without specific cause."

"I think that employees should be tested," asserted Myrtle Munger. "All our jobs depend on providing quality service. We can't afford to ignore the effects that someone's behavior might have on output. Besides, someone who breaks the law and takes drugs on weekends probably doesn't abide by company policies and rules either."

Questions

1. How do you feel about the testing of employees for the use of substances? Are such tests ever justified? Explain.

2. Should all new applicants for positions be tested? Should all employees, whether applicants or long term, be tested? Or should only those employees whose performance is below standards be tested? Explain.

3. Assume that a testing program is instituted at the Direct to You Company. What should a supervisor do when an employee is tested positive, that is, shows evidence of the use of substances?

NOTES

1. From a University of Michigan study reported by the National Institute on Drug Abuse, a study prepared and reported by Parents Resource Institute for Drug Education, and *The World Almanac and Book of Facts 1992* (New York: Pharos Books, 1991), p. 249.

2. Carlos Alcala, "Teen Drug Use, Smoking Rates Up," *Oakland Tribune,* June 9, 1992, p. A-5.

3. "Alcoholism Rising Among Elderly," Cox News Service as reported in *Stars and Stripes,* February 6, 1992, p. 6.

4. "Out in the Open," *Time.* November 30, 1987, pp. 42–50; National Institute on Drug Abuse, "Drugs in the Workplace," *USA Today/International Edition,* October 12, 1989, p. 1; and see note 1, *The World Almanac and Book of Facts 1992,* pp. 940, 941, 951.

5. Minda Zetlin, "Corporate America Declares War on Drugs," *Personnel,* 68 (August 1991), p. 8.

6. Michael M. Harris and Laura L. Heft, "Alcohol and Drug Use in the Workplace: Issues, Controversies, and Directions for Future Research," *Journal of Management,* 18 (June 1992), p. 239.

7. "ABC Fights Drug-Alcohol Abuse," *Contra Costa Times/Times-Plus Real Estate,* December 15, 1985, p. 9.

8. "Drugs, Vandalism Plague Atomic Units in U.S., Group Says," *Stars and Stripes,* January 12, 1992, p. 7.

9. "Three Pilots Who Flew Drunk Sentenced to Prison," *San Francisco Chronicle,* October 27, 1990, p. A-3; and Margaret Zack, "Drunken Airline Crew Sentenced," *San Francisco Examiner,* October 27, 1990, p. A-9.

10. Richard Behar, "Joe's Bad Trip," *Time/International Edition,* July 24, 1989, pp. 46–51.

11. "AMA Concern About Alcoholism Detailed," *NIAAA Information and Feature Service,* National Clearinghouse for Alcohol Information, October 19, 1980, p. 2.

12. "Bush's War on Drugs in Retreat, Survey Says," *New York Times,* as reported in *Stars and Stripes,* December 20, 1991, p. 6.

13. "Drug Abuse Patients on Rise in Emergency Rooms," *Jet,* July 13 1992, p. 38.

14. "Anti-Drug Effort Must Focus on Habitual Users, Feds Say," *New York Times,* as reported in *Stars and Stripes,* December 21, 1991, p. 6.

15. See note 5, p. 1.

16. See note 8.

17. "Marijuana Now a Major Factor in Truck Accidents," *Contra Costa Times,* August 12, 1989, p. B-2.

18. "Study Finds More Women Using Drugs," *Contra Costa Times,* August 20, 1989, p. B-7; and Jack Anderson and Dale Van Atta, "'Drug Babies' May Be a Fiscal Time Bomb," *San Francisco Chronicle,* November 29, 1989, p. B-3.

19. "Questions and Answers About Drug Abuse," *Prudential Health Series* (Rockville, MD: National Clearinghouse for Drug Abuse Information, August 1971), p. 6.

20. Frederick Willman and Mary Ellen Kane, *The Kemper Approach to Alcoholism, Drug Addiction, and Other Living Problems* (Long Grove, IL: Kemper Group, 1986), pp. 12, 13.

21. American Management Associations survey results presented on *NBC Nightly News,* April 2, 1992.

22. Rob Brookler, "Industry Standards in Workplace Drug Testing," *Personnel Journal,* 71 (April 1992), p. 128.

23. See note 21.

24. See note 22, p. 130.

25. "Drug Testing Extended at NY Utility," *Monthly Labor Review,* June 1992, p. 60.

26. See note 6, p. 249.

27. "Drug Tests Upheld for Two Groups," *USA Today/International Edition,* March 22, 1989, p. 1.

28. "Lawyers Advise Firms, Employees Facing Tests," *Contra Costa Times,* July 26, 1987, p. B-5.

29. "Drug-Free Workplace Requirements; Notice and Interim Final Rules," *Federal Register,* Vol. 54, No. 19, January 31, 1989, pp. 4947–4952.

BOX NOTES

a. Adapted from Peter Jennings, *NBC Evening News,* April 2, 1992; and *The World Almanac and Book of Facts 1992.* (New York: Pharos Books, 1992), pp. 452, 453.

b. Adapted from Diane Summers, "Efficiency Gains Are on the Cards," *Financial Times,* February 3, 1992, p. 10; and Dan Sperling, "More Employees Help Foot the Detox Bill," *USA Today/International Edition,* March 31, 1989, p. 8.

c. Adapted from Tim W. Ferguson, "Motorola Aims High, So Motorolans Won't Be Getting High," *The Wall Street Journal,* June 26, 1990, p. A-17.

EXPERIENTIAL EXERCISE

Don't Say Yes

Anyone concerned about alcohol abuse should ask himself or herself the following questions (any *yes* answers could be an indication of a current or potential alcohol problem):

Yes	No	
____	____	1. Do you drink to feel better about yourself?
____	____	2. Do you turn to alcohol when you have troubles?
____	____	3. Do you make excuses for the reasons you drink?
____	____	4. Do you feel guilty after drinking?
____	____	5. Do you drink to help you sleep?
____	____	6. Do you often have diarrhea, indigestion, or nausea due to drinking?
____	____	7. Have you had other health problems related to drinking?
____	____	8. Have you ever fallen down or burned yourself while you were drinking?
____	____	9. Do you feel worried, anxious, or depressed most of the time?
____	____	10. Do you find yourself not realizing you are repeating things while drinking?
____	____	11. Have you ever put yourself or others in danger by driving after drinking?
____	____	12. Have you ever missed work or put off work because of drinking?
____	____	13. Have you had financial or legal problems in which drinking was involved?
____	____	14. Do you drink alone? Do you drink less with others?
____	____	15. Do you feel isolated and alone?

_____ _____   16. Do you often feel the need to telephone people when you are drinking?

_____ _____   17. Have you changed friends to be around people who drink like you do?

_____ _____   18. Do you hide your drinking from your spouse or children?

_____ _____   19. Have others told you that they think you drink too much?

_____ _____   20. Is your parent or your spouse a heavy drinker?

_____ _____   21. Do you think you drink too much?

_____ _____   22. Do you plan activities around being able to drink?

_____ _____   23. Do you find yourself thinking of drinking in-between times?

_____ _____   24. Have you failed in promises to yourself to cut down on your drinking?

_____ _____   25. Are there times when you don't drink because you're afraid you'll lose control of yourself?

_____ _____   26. Do you drink and use other drugs?

Part Four

Organizational Health, Ethics, and Globalization

CHAPTER 13 Developing and Maintaining a Less Stressful Life

CHAPTER 14 The Challenges Facing Individuals in Organizations

CHAPTER 15 Organizational Ethics and Responsibilities Toward Society

CHAPTER 16 On a Global Scale

CHAPTER 13

Developing and Maintaining a Less Stressful Life

Stress Kills!

**When you finish this chapter,
you should be able to:**

1
Understand the nature and effects of stress on individuals.
2
Identify the types of adjustive reactions that can be caused by frustration.
3
Reduce the likelihood of "catching" the burnout disease.
4
Describe the nature of faith and the stress-inducing
consequences of its absence.
5
Describe several ways of more effectively managing
your career- and non-career-related stress.
6
Distinguish between the schools of *behavioristic* and *humanistic* psychology.
7
Recognize the types of personal behavior that could cause your work
associates to become stressed.
8
Explain why the concepts of happiness and success may have different
meanings to different people.

> Happiness is not achieved by the conscious pursuit of happiness. It is generally the by-product of other activities.
>
> *Aldous Huxley, Novelist*

> The problem is not stress. Rather, it is how we *react* to stress. Emotions—not events—cause stress-related events.
>
> *Michael Morrison, Author*

Pressures, demands, and changes—these are all conditions that exist in a person's environment and often result in a condition called **stress.** There seems to be no shortage of stress these days in people's lives, both on and off the job. Stress-causing events can happen with little warning, even when people are seeking pleasure. Imagine, for example, the stress that was suddenly felt by the 62,000 anxious World Series fans at Candlestick Park in San Francisco on October 17, 1989, when an earthquake measuring about seven on the Richter scale suddenly hit the area. Or can you visualize being the owner of one of the 3000 houses or apartments destroyed by a furious blaze that caused more than $2 billion in damage to the Oakland/Berkeley, California, hillsides on October 20, 1991? Or can you put yourself in the rain-drenched oxfords of the any of the 250,000 people left homeless by the severest natural disaster in U.S. history, Hurricane Andrew, a storm that ripped through Florida and Louisiana with a vengeance in late August 1992, destroying or damaging more than 90,000 homes and causing nearly $20 billion in property damage alone. Events such as these doubtlessly cause stress for those affected by them.

 We are never going to remove stress completely from our lives, nor really should we try. As Dr. Lawrence Lamb has stated, "It is not so much stress, within reason, but how you meet the stress, that counts in life."[1] Dr. Lamb's statement is important in that he suggests that the way we *manage* our stress determines how it affects us. In this chapter, we will discuss the nature of stress, typical reactions to stress, including *burnout,* and various proven techniques for managing stress.

THE NATURE OF STRESS

It's important to realize that not all stress is harmful; in proper amounts it's actually helpful. Stress is a lot like your body temperature. Without a temperature (I didn't say fever!), you would be dead. Only when temperatures rise above or fall below so-called normal—about 98.6°F or about 37°C—do we become concerned about it. As with temperatures, as long as you have not crossed over your own personal threshold level of stress and reached a danger point, you need not be unduly concerned; you often even benefit from the stress you experience.

Two Types of Stress—Eustress and Distress

Stress actually comes in two flavors: **eustress** and **distress.** Eustress is the type of tension that helps you hold your body erect; it helps you stay awake in a lecture hall or church; it helps you to meet your deadlines and accomplish your goals. It even accompanies good experiences, like being told you were promoted or won the lottery. Distress, on the other hand, especially over long periods of time, is likely to cause disease, such as ulcers, asthma, arthritis, or allergies. It can lead to heart attacks, as well as alcohol and drug abuse. (Tables 13.1 and 13.2 summarize some of the principal types of on- and off-the-job causes of distress.)[2]

The Three Stages of Stress

The human mind and body are a lot like a metal spring. A spring has a certain tolerance for stress. It can be strained up to certain limits (depending on its strength and construction) and then will return to its original shape. We are much like a spring; we can be pressured up to certain limits, and generally we will rebound.

TABLE 13.1   Career-Related Causes of Stress

- Performance anxiety (e.g., caused by new job or promotion)
- Poor planning or goal setting
- Unclear job requirements
- Little recognition of performance
- Insufficient authority to make decisions
- Peer pressure
- Conflict with others
- Excessive work demands
- Underuse of skills
- Work overload or underload
- Low morale
- Insecurity (regarding job responsibilities, future, etc.)
- Lack of needs satisfaction
- Misunderstanding and ineffective communication
- Formal performance appraisals
- Working conditions
- Equipment
- Organizational politics
- Inconsistent managers
- Unsupportive boss
- Receiving criticism in front of others
- Rapid change

TABLE 13.2   Off-the-Job Causes of Stress

- Family problems
- Financial difficulties
- Poor health
- Substance abuse (alcohol, cigarettes, or hard drugs)
- Traffic violations
- Automobile problems
- Neighbors
- Current events
- Insomnia (can also be a result of stress)
- Home maintenance problems

Dr. Jere E. Yates points out that there are actually three different stages, or points, that humans can experience with stress.[3] As you can see in Figure 13.1, the first, the **yield point,** is the stage that reveals itself as a slight change from "normal" behavior. We will reach this point from time to time.

The next stage—an extremely critical point—is called our **elastic limit.** Dr. Yates has described this point as kind of an early-warning device that tells us when we are near our stress threshold. We can function reasonably well between our yield point and our elastic limit. However, if "bent out of shape"—that is, pressed beyond our elastic limit—neither a spring nor a human being will rebound easily.

Like a herniated rubber band!

Once we cross over our elastic limit, we may reach our **rupture point,** which can cause some severe and permanent mental and physical damage if we don't manage our stress properly. We'll discover shortly some of the methods that can be used for preventing or reducing the harmful effects of distress.

FRUSTRATION—A RESPONSE TO STRESS

Socrates regularly suggested to his friends and acquaintances that perhaps they should attempt to know their *own selves* a bit better. His advice was a succinct, "Know thyself." To his friends with more time to spare, he would sometimes add, "Know your strengths and your weaknesses; your potentialities, your aims and purposes; take stock of yourself." Socrates, one of the best and the brightest of his time, believed that before individuals could really understand how to deal effectively with the problems of others, they first had to look within and become better acquainted with themselves.

Attempting to know one's own self well is not a simple task. We are so close to ourselves, both physically and mentally, that absolute

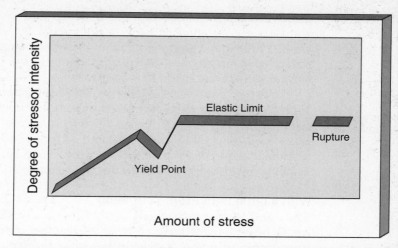

Figure 13.1 The three stages of stress. Yield point represents a slight change from "normal" behavior. Elastic limit represents danger zone that results in greater change in "normal" behavior. Rupture results in severe mental and physical damage (nervous breakdown). Adapted from Jere E. Yates, *Managing Stress* (New York: American Management Association, 1979), p. 23.

objectivity is well-nigh impossible. For example, have you ever looked at your reflection in a mirror and attempted to perceive yourself as others might see you? It's difficult to do, isn't it? Some persons prefer not to know how others perceive them; they may feel—either consciously or unconsciously—that ignorance provides them with a protective shield.

What do *you* see when looking in a mirror?

Reasonably well-adjusted persons, however, generally have a better knowledge and understanding of their own sentiments and behavior. They are usually aware that life is beset with stress, strain, anxieties, and frustration, but they attempt to gain greater insight into their feelings so that they can cope with them more effectively. Other, less-well-adjusted persons tend to create their own tensions and frustrations and to lose faith in themselves and in others. In the section that follows you will learn about the nature of frustration along with some typical reactions that individuals occasionally experience when attempting to cope with life's many stressors. Managers should be on the lookout for these among their employees and, if necessary, refer individuals with such symptoms to a counselor.

The Nature of Frustration

Have you ever observed a young child—assume a little boy—who was unable to have what he wanted? Do you remember his reactions? He may have tugged and pulled interminably on Mommy's dress or

Daddy's aching hand, whining, shrieking, and crying until either his wants were satisfied or he was distracted by something else. The young child was experiencing what could be termed **frustration,** *the feeling of insecurity and dissatisfaction arising from unresolved problems or unsatisfied needs and wants.*

What was your last frustrating experience?

You, too, have undoubtedly experienced frustration from time to time. Perhaps you've been rejected by someone of whom you were quite fond. Or maybe you were turned down for a job you wanted. Or you may have been bypassed for a particular job promotion to which you had anxiously aspired. Problems often arise when the needs of organizational members, either on or off the job, go unsatisfied for a long time.

With a Little Help From Your Mind

The *mind,* either consciously or subconsciously, generally attempts to *cause* behavior designed to help the frustrated person adjust to an unresolved situation, a type of behavior termed an **adjustive reaction** or **defense mechanism.** Some adjustive reactions are *positively directed* while others may be *negative.*

Some frustrations may result in *mild* adjustive reactions; other reactions may be *extreme* and *emotional.* The intensity of a particular adjustment generally depends on two factors: the *type* of frustration *activity* and the *previous experience* of the frustrated *person.* Psychologists have developed a variety of terms to describe the numerous types of adjustive reactions to frustration.

REACTIONS TO FRUSTRATION

An understanding of psychological concepts, such as adjustive reactions, certainly won't enable you to lie on your cozy make-believe psychiatrist's couch, skillfully playing the role of a psychotherapist while sensitively treating your own complex mental problems or those of others. Any person with chronic or severe problems should seek professional assistance. However, an awareness of the major adjustive reactions, or defense mechanisms, may enable you to deal more effectively with the relatively normal stresses and strains of everyday living that can affect both you and others in your organization. When you recognize some of the adjustive responses in others, you should be able to empathize with them more fully and understand behavior that previously may have made you angry, frustrated, or disappointed.

The adjustive reactions with which we'll be primarily concerned are:

1. Rationalization
2. Compensation

3. Negativism

4. Resignation

5. Flight

6. Repression

7. Pseudostupidity

8. Obsessive thinking

9. Displacement

10. Conversion

Rationalization

"Shoot . . . I didn't really want that crummy promotion anyhow. Besides, that job will be nothing but problems for the geek who got it. Actually, I'm darn lucky I didn't get it."

Doesn't that statement remind you of the story your parents might have read to you when you were a child—Aesop's fable about the fox who couldn't reach the grapes? You might remember that the fox wore himself out trying to reach some juicy grapes hanging high on a trellis. He finally gave up and sighed something like, "I didn't really want those suckers anyhow. Besides, I'll bet they're sour!"

"Sour grapes" comments like the one about the promotion bypass mentioned earlier are quite common. Individuals may actually mean what they say, but often their remarks are excuses for deeper, subconscious feelings. The psychological adjustive reaction involved here is termed **rationalization,** which exists when an individual attempts to give plausible (rational)—but not necessarily true—explanations for specific and often undesirable behavior.

Another example of rationalization is provided by the person who says, "Everybody else cheats on exams, expense accounts, income taxes, and in politics; so why shouldn't I?" But does *everybody else* cheat? Not likely, but such a belief is a defense mechanism that tends to make the person feel that his or her behavior is more acceptable. Even if you feel that the ethical values of an increasing number of individuals have deteriorated, should you follow suit? If someone else were to punch him- or herself continually on the nose, and if you realized that such an activity was foolish and undesirable, would you feel that you had to do the same thing? Imitating behavior that you feel is undesirable merely because "everyone else does it" is logically equivalent to saying, "If I don't smoke, somebody else will."

In effect, the person who attempts to justify behavior that he or she feels is undesirable—either consciously or subconsciously—is engaging in rationalization.

Why might some people *rationalize* their behavior?

Aim That at Me, You Little Squirt, and You're a Goner![a]

Talk about your "adjustive reactions." A toy water gun called the "Super Soaker" made a splash in the toy stores of America in early 1992, but it seemed to dampen the spirits of some persons who seemed not yet proficient in the activity of stress management. The toy water gun was linked to some violent reactions including real shootings and resulted in a proposed ban by a Michigan legislator, Gilbert DiNello. He called for outlawing the sale and use of the toys, which hold nearly a half-gallon of water and can shoot water up to fifty feet.

Here are some of the reactions of individuals frustrated by the guns:

- In New York, a man retaliated for a squirt gun attack with a handgun, wounding two teens.

- In Boston, a boy was shot and killed when a squirt gun fight escalated into a brawl.

- Also in Boston, a woman and her son said they were burned by youths squirting bleach.

- In New Castle, Pennsylvania, a teen was shot in the hand after someone in the truck in which she was riding squirted water into a crowd.

- In Southfield, Michigan, where numerous incidents occurred, students were told they would be suspended if caught with squirt guns.

A Question of Ethics: So, what do you think? Since the water guns seem to bring out some nasty reactions in certain people, should they be banned? Even if not officially banned, do you feel it is ethical for stores to continue selling such toys?

Compensation

You've probably heard of people with physical limitations who went on to achievements far beyond the capabilities of many individuals without similar misfortunes. Well known are Franklin D. Roosevelt, former president; John Milton, poet; Ray Charles, Stevie Wonder, José Feliciano, musical performers; and Stephen Hawking, an almost totally paralyzed, speechless and wheel-chair-bound physicist and author of a best-selling book, *A Brief History of Time*. In reality, many organizational members who strive with unusual zeal to attain certain self-imposed goals are exhibiting a form of adjustive reaction.

We are referring to the concept of **compensation** when we discuss a situation in which individuals with feelings of inadequacy—either real or imagined—exert extra effort in an attempt to overcome the insecure feelings.

What might determine whether a compensation is positive or negative?

Some forms of compensation may be quite beneficial, or *positive,* while others are harmful, or *negative.* Positive compensation might be found in a person whose child died from a birth defect and who expends an inordinate amount of energy on helping children with physical or intellectual challenges. Employees who feel that their abilities are inferior to those of co-workers may work particularly hard on certain projects to prove that they can do as well. Often the best college term papers received by professors are prepared by students who lack a certain degree of confidence but who labor with extra vigor on their projects. The best students seldom seem to feel that they have expended sufficient time on assignments.

Some people may react in a *negative* fashion because of their feelings of inadequacy. They may become aggressive, pushy, overcritical, and sometimes even power-hungry. Some historians believe that Napoleon's ambitious military conquests may have been related to feelings of inadequacy brought about by his short stature.

Negativism

An anonymous philosopher is alleged to have claimed, "If we all would only admit that we are insecure, then we would probably be less insecure." Individuals with typical insecurities tend to believe that other mortals don't feel the same as they do; but few of us are totally secure, regardless of outward appearances.

The promotion on TV of many products is directed toward the normal insecurities most people tend to have, such as the fear of rejection by others ("Spray one armpit and half the world will love you!"). Many high achievers are driven by a fear of failure that makes them insecure.

How might others be affected by a person's negativism?

One of the unfortunate by-products of some people's insecurities can be termed **negativism,** *the subconscious resistance to other persons or objects.* Take, for example, the hypothetical case of a supervisor named Hattie Ferndowner whose ideas at a particular supervisors' meeting had been totally rejected. Hattie originally thought that her proposals were good, but as a result of their rejection, she felt disappointed and frustrated. A reasonably secure and well-adjusted person might have either attempted to analyze the rejection of the ideas or merely dismissed the situation from her mind and gone on to other important matters.

Hattie, however, returned to her department, and for the rest of the day caustically picked apart nearly everything that her subordinates did. At the end of the day, Hattie regretted her actions even though she didn't fully understand the reasons for her negative behavior. In one sense, Hattie was not only "belittling"; she also was "being little" Some years ago Charles Reigner wrote an essay that may illuminate Hattie's behavior:

Life is too short to be little. Every one of us has his share of rebuffs and disappointments. When somebody says or does something that hurts us, our first impulse is to try to return the hurt. We want to fight back: but when we do we are just lowering ourselves to the plane of the attacker. When we exhibit littleness, we show that we have not attained maturity in our thinking and acting.

It is those people who are in love with their work who get the greatest measure of happiness and satisfaction in life. They are ready at all times to join hands with others in a good cause. Such people have passed the adolescent state of dependence or near-dependence on others.

Individuals who get worthwhile things done will have some people say cutting and unkind things about them. Their motives will be belittled and their actions questioned. The worst thing they can do under such circumstances is to brood on the unkind things said about them.

Because we play small parts in the scheme of things is no warrant for our ever being little in our attitudes. A friend of mine who was once unjustly attacked said, "I have enough pride not to give my attacker the satisfaction of knowing that what was said hurt me."

Until people and nations actually mature in their thinking and acting, we are going to have tension and war. What can we as individuals do? Well, we can resolve not to be little ourselves. We can act like mature people, for life is too short to be little.[4]

Resignation

"You can't fire me, J. B. You know why? Because *I quit,* that's why!" This statement to J. B. is the ultimate in resignation by an organizational member but is only one of various types. The psychological term, **resignation,** generally refers to a deep-seated, extremely intense type of frustration sometimes experienced by individuals. The condition may be long-lasting or temporary. Resignation can be defined as the state of giving up or withdrawing from one's involvement with a particular situation.

An example with which some students might identify concerns a term paper assignment. Assume that you have a ten-page term project due only two days from now. Let's also assume that you've already done all of the necessary background reading and research, but you are finding it extremely difficult to "put it all together." And the excessive noise coming from a nearby room doesn't help a bit; it only tears apart any ideas flowing through your head.

You've sat in front of your notebook computer for two hours, but you've produced only two paragraphs, both of which provide you with no personal satisfaction—and they'll probably please your professor even less! Finally in disgust, you shout, "To heck with it! I'll bat this darn thing out tomorrow night." You then lie down on your flotation system—and it's not even water bedtime. Your decision to stop working and to do a less than adequate job tomorrow evening is a form of resignation.

You might have adjusted more positively to the situation. You might have asked the people in the next room to be quieter, or you might have attempted to change your environment by going to a library or to another room, if possible. Sometimes, however, the act of resignation appears, at least temporarily, to be the easy way out, but it neither gets your tasks completed nor provides you with feelings of achievement.

How might *resignation* seem to be the easy way out?

Another example: An employee—let's call him Joe—has received little comment on the progress he had made on a company project assigned to him. This lack of reinforcement—either positive or negative—has frustrated Joe and has resulted in his no longer caring whether he does a good job. Joe could have asked his boss for comments but instead chose resignation as an easier way out.

Flight

The adjustive reaction to frustration or conflict termed **flight** could be confused with that of *resignation*. Flight, however, goes somewhat farther and involves the actual leaving, or running away from, a particular situation that causes frustration or anxiety. Resignation may involve an apathetic, "don't-give-a-darn" attitude about the problem but, unlike flight, doesn't necessarily involve leaving the source of conflict or frustration.

According to the Census Bureau, nearly one in five Americans change residences each year.[5] Of course, not all moves could be considered adjustive reactions. Flight may result in a person's taking a new job as a means of getting away from home, daydreaming, or even excessive drinking or the taking of drugs. A person exhibiting a flight reaction either consciously or subconsciously wants to avoid a situation and assumes that things will be better "anywhere but here."

Can you run away from yourself?

Frequently, persons trying to run away or attempting to free themselves from what they believe to be the causes of their frustrations and tensions are, in reality, attempting to run from themselves. Unfortunately, one's own self always seems to follow. For example, let's take the hypothetical case of a young woman named Ms. Frieda Phlier who felt extremely dissatisfied with certain aspects of her job. Her love life, too, had not been all that she had hoped for in recent months. So Frieda decided to quit her job in Kansas City and head out to the Coast. Frieda found what she believed to be a good job in San Francisco, some of whose conditions were much better than those of her former place of employment, and the men in the "Bay Area," she discovered, "are absolutely super dreamy."

Soon, however, Frieda found that her new job was even worse than the old one and that *not all* those men were so super dreamy after all. After several months in her western "utopia," Frieda left her job and once more began searching, not realizing that utopia is really in the "eye of the beholder." Instead of attempting to flee from that which cannot be left behind, a person might do better to try to follow the advice to "know thyself" and discover how to adapt more readily to present conditions. Sometimes in our obsessive quest for greater freedom, we actually forgo more freedom than we attain.[6] As one wise guy once said, "Never leave hold of what you've got until you've got hold of something else." Have you ever noticed that employed people seem to find new jobs more easily than unemployed people?

Repression

"Oops! I'm sorry, boss, but I completely forgot to tell you about the Purdy Upsett Company. That big order they placed a while back, you remember? Well they canceled it last week."

This example of a lost account illustrates that a person may "forget" something, especially something psychologically disturbing, because of the sense of anxiety or guilt that it might arouse. When individuals unknowingly exclude certain experiences or feelings from their consciousness, they are experiencing an adjustive reaction called **repression.**

Not all repression is necessarily negative. The human mind is a miraculous instrument whose tendency to repress the unpleasant aspects of many experiences is often beneficial. For example, years after a vacation, family members may remember the events that gave them pleasure, but they tend to repress, or forget, the less pleasant parts, such as the flat tire when they had no spare, the high prices at the gas stations, the biting mosquitoes, and the upset stomachs.

I don't remember any "ants."

Persons who have experienced many tragedies during their lives, such as accidents or the unexpected deaths of their loved ones, often appear later not to be excessively disturbed by the events. Nevertheless, they may have been profoundly affected by the experiences when they occurred. The mind tends to repress unpleasant events, and the individual who continually focuses on distressing past experiences often finds little enjoyment in the present.

Why is it not necessarily undesirable to forget some things?

Pseudostupidity

In some cases the act of forgetting, instead of being the unconscious repression of events, is intentional and used as a means of avoiding certain types of activities. Referred to as **pseudostupidity,** it is exhibited by some individuals who *consciously* attempt to give the impression of being forgetful or inept. Let's look at the case of Freddie Fergessen. He's frustrated, let's assume, at what he perceives to be an excessive work load. He's also sick and tired of attending all those company meetings that do nothing, he feels, but waste his time. In general, he's considered to be a competent employee, but everyone around him is well aware of his "absentmindedness." They actually expect him to forget— which, in reality, is his goal. However, there are certain things that Freddie never forgets, such as who borrowed lunch money from him!

Obsessive Thinking

Another adjustive reaction is **obsessive thinking.** The term refers to the behavior of a person who enlarges out of all realistic proportion specific problems or situations that he or she has experienced.

For example, individuals employed in dull, monotonous jobs requiring little in the way of active thinking or concentration may continually mull over personal or company problems in their minds. Perhaps the particular problems are not especially grave, but the obsession with them can create an exaggerated effect, making the problem appear gigantic.

How might obsessive thinking be avoided in work situations?

A mind that is kept occupied, however, has little opportunity for obsessive thinking. If the job could be redesigned, or if the person could be allowed to talk with other employees, the chances for obsessive thinking might be diminished.

Let's look at another example: Assume that you have a subordinate whose spouse is critically ill and currently bedridden in a hospital. The doctors doubt whether the patient will survive. Would telling the employee to take the week off necessarily serve as a release of tensions? Probably not. It's unlikely that the employee would be permitted to spend entire days at the hospital. It's more likely that he or she would be home thinking obsessively about little other than the problem. The opportunity to interact with others during periods of severe stress often helps individuals to focus their minds on topics other than their own personal problems.

Displacement

What personal motives might have caused the following immoderate (to say the least!) types of behavior?

A disgruntled employee shot four supervisors Friday at a battery plant, police said.

A man was accused of slashing his girlfriend with a broken beer bottle and trying to suck her blood after watching a vampire movie.

A man was beaten to death by four men in what his family said was an argument over a $3 babysitting fee, authorities said.

An airline passenger was arrested after putting his hands around the throat of a flight attendant who spilled a drink on him, officials said.

A disgruntled employee opened fire Monday in the factory where he worked, killing three colleagues, police said.

An elderly women has been arrested for setting her husband on fire after he ate her chocolate Easter bunny, police said.

An upset bank customer was arrested after he stripped off his clothes and quacked like a duck when his loan application was denied.

We all react to frustration, but, one hopes, our reactions are far less psychotic than the examples cited above. The incidents seem more like fiction than truth, but each appeared as an opening sentence in a newspaper article. These events could have been extreme examples of **displacement,** *the psychological process of redirecting pent-up feelings toward objects other than the main source of the frustration.*

When a particular situation affects a person's feelings of security, he or she may react by lashing out verbally (or, as we have seen, physically) at others. Prejudice toward other groups is often the result of an individual's own insecurities and can be a form of displacement. **Scapegoating,** *blaming others for one's own problems or insecurities,* is also a type of displacement. Some of our negative reactions to others

FRANK AND ERNEST · by Bob Thaves

TWO EACH OF EVERYTHING, EXCEPT WE'LL TAKE AS MANY SCAPEGOATS AS WE CAN GET.

SOURCE: Reprinted by permission of UFS, Inc. & NEA, Inc.

may really be our own psyches telling us (and others) something about ourselves. Remember, when Clarence talks about Suzie, we may learn a lot about Clarence and very little about Suzie. People who are reasonably well adjusted and secure tend to perceive positive traits in others. Unfortunately, those who are insecure and fail to accept their shortcomings tend to perceive others in a negative light.

Here's another brief example of displacement: Assume that you reject, abruptly and without any explanation, an employee's request for a particular afternoon off. What might have caused your reaction? Perhaps you were reprimanded earlier in the day by your own boss about something you had, or had not, done. You may be attempting to release your own frustrations and tensions by hassling your employee. Such behavior on your part is likely to create even more tension for you later.

Conversion

The mind and the body are inextricably related and significantly affect each other. A healthy body tends to facilitate the existence of a healthy mind, and healthy mental attitudes often make for healthier bodies.

Some bodily disorders, for example, are **psychosomatic** in origin; they are physical symptoms of inner mental conflict. The term **conversion** is used to symbolize a psychological process whereby emotional frustrations are expressed in bodily symptoms of pain or malfunction.

For example, assume that a person whom we'll call Walter Worry, an unusually conscientious employee with your organization, was assigned the responsibility of presenting at a meeting next Monday a detailed forecast of his department's production for the next six months. Let's also assume that Walter's cousins, whom he has not seen for five years, unexpectedly dropped in for the entire weekend on the way to Bangor for their annual vacation.

Were Walter's cousins a pain?

As a result of the surprise visit, Walter was unable to complete his project on time. Instead of explaining to his boss why he had not completed the task, Walter developed a painful headache and called in sick on the morning of his scheduled presentation. The pain may have been real to Walter, but it could have been caused by his mental frustrations. Many aches and pains result primarily from anxieties.

BURNOUT—THE DISEASE OF HIGH ACHIEVERS

Have you ever noticed what typically occurs when you've run a machine too long and too hard? It may burn out. High achievers sometimes do the same to themselves: They run themselves too long and too hard. A similar phenomenon often occurs—a condition psychologists refer to as **burnout,** *the complete exhausting of a person's physical and intellectual resources caused by excessive efforts to attain certain unrealistic, job-related goals.*

Who Are Candidates for Burnout?

Burnout candidates tend to be people with extremely high aspirations. They are typically idealistic and self-motivated high achievers. They usually start projects with a high degree of enthusiasm. Even though their schedules tend to be jam-packed with projects, they still have difficulty saying "no" to new opportunities or tasks that come their way. They also tend to do more than their share of work when working on team projects.[7]

What Are the Symptoms of Burnout?

The goals that burnout candidates set for themselves tend to be unrealistic and unattainable. As a result, such individuals usually become frustrated and lose much of their earlier enthusiasm. They tend to become apathetic toward their jobs and develop feelings of wanting to "get away from it all"—*the flight syndrome* discussed earlier.

Individuals suffering from burnout frequently feel that they are working harder and harder and accomplishing less and less. They also tend to feel tired much of the time. In addition, they are likely to feel irritable, develop aches and pains, pull away from friends and loved ones, and lose their sense of humor. Table 13.3 summarizes some of the major symptoms of burnout.

What Is the Cure for Burnout?

If not "cured" in time, burnout victims frequently find their stress-related problems compounded. Their unhappiness with their stressful situations may lead to divorce, the abuse of drugs, nervous break-

TABLE 13.3   Symptoms of Burnout.

Individuals experiencing burnout have the tendency to:
1. Become apathetic toward their work responsibilities.
2. Engage in the *flight syndrome.*
3. Feel that they are working harder and accomplishing less.
4. Feel irritable.
5. Develop physical pains.
6. Withdraw from friends and loved ones.
7. Lose their senses of humor.
8. Feel tired much of the time.
9. May consume greater quantities of alcohol than in the past.

---

downs, and even fatal strokes. Assuming that you are a high-achieving person, what can you personally do to prevent your "catching" the burnout disease, or at least to reduce its negative effects? The sections that follow provide some useful suggestions for dealing with pressure and stress. Carefully study them along with the guidelines listed in Table 13.4, and you may be able to help yourself develop immunity to the "disease." In addition, you might want to reflect on the words of humorist Ken Hubbard, who said: "Do not take life too seriously; you will never get out of it alive."[8]

THE NEED TO MANAGE STRESS WITH FAITH

Unmanaged stress, as we know, can cause problems for the individual. In the following sections we examine the various ways in which you might cope with and control the effects of stress. In this section we explore the concept of **faith** and investigate some of the stress-inducing consequences of its absence.

With violence, terrorism, international conflict, and a reported 24,703 murders in the U.S. in a recent year (an average of between eight and nine per day during the month of August 1992 in Los Angeles County alone); with air pollution, child neglect and broken homes, high unemployment, fear of acquiring the AIDS virus, and fellow Americans attempting to survive while living in cardboard boxes or under highway overpasses; with the *terra firma,* as pictured on the six o'clock news, seemingly crumbling a bit more each day beneath our shores, the maintenance of faith and positive attitudes is no mean feat. The list of negative events to which we are exposed is enormous and mind-boggling. Yet, maintaining *faith* is essential for one's mental and physical well-being.

The Meaning of Faith

The word *faith* has many meanings. To some persons faith is a belief and trust in and loyalty to God or a belief in the traditional doctrines of a formal religion. To others it may be an absolute allegiance to something concrete, such as one's country, or something abstract, such as the symbolic meanings of the American flag or the phrase "family values."

Other types of faith that individuals may have are in *themselves,* in *humanity,* or in their *own futures.* Without the existence of some positive beliefs, a person has little to look forward to. People who lose all or most of their faith often turn to negative, and frequently destructive, styles of behavior.

For example, individuals who lose faith, are thus aimless and pessimistic about the future, may abuse alcohol or drugs; they may

TABLE 13.4   Guidelines for Maintaining and Developing the Faith Necessary to Cope With the Pressures of Living.

1. Try to establish a *balance* between work and leisure activities, which is essential to preventing destructive tensions.
2. Learn how to slow down or *unwind.* Individuals whose tensions are excessive and prolonged sometimes discover that mama nature assists the slowing down process with heart attacks and increased accidents. Furthermore, prolonged periods of job stress, particularly with deadline pressures, are believed to be major factors associated with drinking problems. A bit morbid, but too often true, is some graffiti philosophy felt-penned onto a washroom wall in San Francisco: "Death is nature's way of telling you to slow down." Think about those words.
3. When you are already fully committed, learn how *to say no* tactfully to new opportunities and requests from others that do little for you other than increase your tensions and anxieties.
4. Learn how to *relax.* Hobbies and athletics do *not* always help work addicts if they pursue those activities with the same fanatic zeal that they do their work.
5. Try to find yourself some *alone time,* a relaxing period when you either do nothing or perhaps read or work on a hobby. The focus, however, should be on yourself without any outside responsibilities.
6. Learn to enjoy being with other *people,* especially friends with interests that help you to relax.
7. Make the effort to *smile.* The act of smiling is believed to trigger different chemical reactions in the body that directly influence our emotional state. When you feel blue, make the effort to smile at someone (even yourself!), and you'll begin to feel better.
8. Be sure to *rest.* A good night's sleep will help to prepare you for the challenges of tomorrow. You'll function and handle pressures much better if you feel rested.
9. *Take regular vacations.* Some psychologists advise taking frequent short vacations or easing into long vacations by cutting down gradually in your work. Don't take a briefcase filled with work or studies. A book of short stories, easily put aside, can be an enjoyable "escape."
10. Plan your *next vacation* soon after finishing one. Such planning gives you something to look forward to instead of the feeling that you are back in your usual routine or travail.
11. Plan some *weekends* exclusively with your family, friends or "significant other." During such periods, attempt not to have work readily accessible.

What types of behavior might "faithless" persons engage in?

believe that violence and theft are reasonable; they may develop negative attitudes about almost everything, including xenophobic attitudes toward immigrants. They may develop the tendency to make wisecracks during serious situations, or they may develop an unhealthy "Who cares? What difference does it make?" philosophy.

The Need for Situational Faith

What has caused the prevalent erosion of trust?

"You can't trust anyone," is a comment made regularly by many individuals. A prevalent attitude among numerous Americans is their lack of faith in their fellow humans, a sort of adversarial, us-versus-them syndrome, with groups of people doubting other groups of people.

When individuals live in an unhealthy atmosphere of distrust, they tend to become apprehensive of all their associates. Perhaps, instead, we need to develop the ability to apply what might be called **situational faith.** Historically, we have put forward the belief that in our democratic system a person is innocent until proven guilty. Perhaps we should attempt to develop a similar conviction that a person is worthy of our trust until we have positive evidence to the contrary.

Could distrust actually create untrustworthiness?

If you are a manager, for example, you must have a certain amount of trust in your employees; you cannot reasonably search all the workers as they leave for home each day. Excessive restriction of employees might even create a challenge for them to see what they can get away with, since a person's behavior often becomes what others expect it to be—the *Pygmalion effect,* as we've learned earlier.

Is any person an island?

Also, individuals who have been hurt by someone for whom they cared deeply may develop bitterness, doubt, and disbelief toward others. Even with such feelings of distrust, which are difficult to discard, we must retain a certain degree of *vulnerability*—to be realistic in our feelings but vulnerable in our behavior. We will risk being hurt again, but too much protection may isolate us from satisfying experiences in the future.

Establish Ethical Values

Although there are exceptions, most reasonable people have a conscience. Those who engage in unethical practices often discover that their conscience can be a tremendous stress producer.

We've already touched upon the necessity of faith and trust both in yourself and in others. A significant way to maintain greater trust is to be trustworthy yourself. Any discussion of the nature of trust runs the risk of sounding "goodie-goodie" or possibly even prudish, but think seriously about the following: If you continually engage in unethical practices with others, say your associates, your organization, or members of the general public, two principal problems might confront you. The first is *the added stress you create for yourself caused by your own conscience,* and the second is *the tendency to assume that others are as unethical in their dealings as you are,* which is not necessarily the case. The major point, for now, is that unethical practices can be an unnecessary stress-inducer. We'll discuss more on ethics in Chapter 15.

Cockeyed Idealists

Is there anything more
ideal than idealism?

Those who retain hope while half-submerged in a sea of despair are sometimes accused of being cockeyed idealists. But isn't idealism likely to be a far more positive and constructive approach than pessimism?

Optimism and faith in humanity do not necessarily imply naiveté. On the contrary, psychological studies point out that hopeful people are more likely to overcome barriers, that hope plays a significant role in giving people a measurable advantage in areas such as academic achievement, withstanding stress on the job, and coping with tragic illness. Dr. Charles R. Snyder, who devised a scale to assess a person's hope, contends that hope is not merely the feeling that everything will turn out all right. Instead, Snyder asserts that "having hope means believing you have both the will and the way to accomplish your goals."[9]

An idealist, of course, should always keep one foot on the ground —or at least one little toe! The realistic person striving for a better world, reaching eagerly for a piece of that proverbial "pie in the sky," might at least discover a "treasure in the attic." To some persons, the "pie" always seems to be tastier in another neighborhood, so they become nomads, not really certain of what they are searching for.

MANAGING CAREER-RELATED STRESS

A study conducted by the Northwestern National Life Insurance Company revealed that 46 percent of Americans in 1991 believed that their jobs were highly stressful, up from 20 percent in 1985.[10] Think, if you will, about your own life. Assuming that you have an eight-hour workday (probably a low estimate, considering travel and preparation time or jobs with differing responsibilities), you will spend roughly 1912 hours a year at your job. In a lifetime of about forty years of employment, you will have spent at least 76,480 hours (9560 work-days) in your job. If during your entire career you dread your work because of the stress it causes you, a substantial part of your lifetime will seem beset by dullness and drudgery. Is this what you really want out of life? Of course not. In this section we examine the nature of work followed by some specific suggestions that can aid you in coping with career-related stress, as listed in Table 13.5.

The Meaning of Work

Is *work* really a nasty
four-letter word?

Some persons, when asked what the word *work* means to them, will give a negative definition. To many individuals, work is equated with drudgery—a dull, unpleasant, and irksome set of activities—which mainly serves as the means (the paycheck?) to far more satisfying ends (a notebook computer or some new skis?).

TABLE 13.5   Selected Guidelines for Managing Career-Related Stress.

- Develop readily attainable goals.
- Select a satisfying occupation.
- Have faith in yourself and seek opportunities.
- Establish and practice ethical values.
- Take the "workaholic" cure—learn how to unwind.
- Take stock of yourself—analyze your feelings that may be causing stress.
- Don't succumb to Parkinson's Law. (See p. 503)
- Don't succumb to Kossen's Law. (See p. 504)
- Learn how to avoid the 2:1 Rule. (See p. 505)

To many other persons work has no such unfavorable connotations. They not only look forward to paydays but also look forward with eager anticipation to nearly every day. Open your eyes widely, look intently, and you will see persons who truly enjoy their work.

Why is there so significant a difference in reactions toward work? The *nature* of a particular job has some influence, but an even more important reason could be individual *attitudes,* especially since two individuals in similar positions with the same organization may perceive their own activities from completely different viewpoints.

Assume that, if given a choice, you would prefer to experience a more positive work situation. What might you do—and it *is* principally up to *you*—to acquire a more positive attitude toward your occupation? If you were to make a sincere effort to attempt to improve your understanding of yourself, you could probably develop, better than anyone else, a list of factors that would influence in a positive manner your own attitudes toward work and living in general. To aid you, consider the following suggestions and attempt to pick out those that might be useful to you.

Develop Readily Attainable Goals

One activity that can assist you in reducing career-related stress is the development of readily attainable short-range goals. Flexible long-range goals, such as the desire to be a corporate executive, an office manager, a lawyer, or a physician, can be beneficial since they tend to give you a sense of direction. But as essential as any long-range goal are relatively easily attained shorter-range goals, which tend to provide you with periodic feelings of self-accomplishment. For example, your plans may include the acquisition of a Bachelor's or Master of Business Administration degree. Shorter-range goals could include the satisfactory completion of each college course in which you have enrolled along the way, as well as a two-year Associate's degree. Working toward the two-year degree, for example, could

Why are attainable goals beneficial for the mind?

Time Out for Stress Reduction![b]

Tell a European that you as an American or Canadian with one year of service with a company receive only two weeks of vacation each year, and he or she will be shocked. And North Americans may be equally astounded when told that workers in Sweden, Denmark, Brazil, and Austria can relax with thirty paid days off. Americans begin to catch up to the rest of world as they build up seniority. However, because they switch employers fairly often, most never achieve equality with their foreign counterparts.

People sometimes need a drastic change from their usual routines as a means of "recharging their rundown batteries." An increasing number of organizational consultants contend that an *extended leave* from work periodically allows employees to recover from the stresses of the job. As a result, some organizations now enable employees to take extended breaks, some with full or partial pay and others without compensation, to pursue personal interests that may or may not be directly related to the job.

The idea of periodic leaves has substantial merit. It may avoid job burnout, which is, in effect, something of a "forced" leave, since people don't perform their jobs up to standards when they are stressed.

According to New Ways to Work, sabbatical leaves are more common in Australia and the U.S. than they are in the United Kingdom. More than 13 percent of U.S. companies offer employees some form of paid sabbatical leave. McDonald's, for example, both in its American and in its European operations, offers sabbaticals of eight weeks after ten years of service. This time can be attached to the normal five weeks' annual holiday, giving a block of three months. The extended leave applies to *all* full-time staff. Prudential, the United Kingdom's largest life insurer, restricts its extended breaks to managers, three days being awarded for each year of service as a manager. ICI and IBM sponsor individuals on foreign two-year placements. ICI, for example, allowed a manager to teach science in Tonga, and IBM enabled an employee to act as a training officer in the ministry of finance in Malawi. However, some persons hesitate taking extended leaves, fearing that they may not be missed or that someone else will step into their shoes during their absence.

enable you to feel the satisfaction of accomplishment and even provide stimulation for your longer-run efforts.

Too frequently, however, we tend to wish away our lives, often in segments. Some young people while in high school may wish those years away so that they can be "free" from what they feel is its drudgery. If they serve in the military, those years are often wished away. If they begin apprenticeship training in a trade, they tend to wish those months or years away. If they are in occupational positions with promotional possibilities, they may go on wishing their time away. Some persons awaken one day, look at their aging faces in the mirror, and suddenly realize that they have wished away substantial portions of their irreversible lives.

Do you wish to wish your entire life away?

Perhaps instead of wishing your life away, you could retain greater mental health by attempting to derive as much personal satisfaction as possible out of each moment in the day. Think about the words of Henry Van Dyke: "There is only one way to get ready for immortality, and that is to love this life and live it as bravely and faithfully and cheerfully as we can."[11]

If you gotta do it, why not enjoy it?

Select a Satisfying Occupation

An important consideration, especially for a younger person, is the *choice of occupation*. If you have the opportunity to take a wide variety of college courses, you may, as a result, tap previously unknown interests. When you discover a particular field that excites you, interview other individuals who work in the occupation. Ask them *open questions* and attempt to uncover their true feelings about their occupations. You might ask them such questions as "What do you like least (most) about your position?" Wait for answers, listen carefully, and you may discover relevant and useful information. The first step toward maintaining a positive attitude in a work situation is to choose a field that truly interests you.

Why not choose what you like?

Have Faith in Yourself and Seek Opportunities—A Fish Story

Someone once conducted an experiment with fish to determine if cold-blooded aquatic vertebrates could be made to lose faith, as does *Homo sapiens*. The experimenter obtained a medium-sized tank, filled it with fresh water, and divided it in half with a glass partition. Into one side of the tank was placed a hungry fish about 14 inches long, and on the other side were placed five fish small enough to be readily devoured by their piscatorial superior.

Do fish have faith?

The ravenous larger fish suddenly observed what she believed to be her *petit déjeuner* and mightily swam toward the little snacks. As you might have expected, each time the larger fish streaked toward the smaller ones, she smashed her tender mandible into the clear glass barrier.

Hungry and not eager to give up, she enthusiastically but abortively endured the same frustrating experience for fifteen minutes until she finally abandoned her tiresome efforts.

Then the experimenter lifted the glass barrier from the center of the tank, thus making accessible the small fish to the large one. What would you guess happened then?

A fish called resignation?

The large, hungry fish hardly budged. The tender little morsels, however, curiously swam near her, occasionally within gill's length. The large fish did nothing, even though she now could begin her meal with no difficulty. She had given up—*resigned*—assuming that the opportunity wouldn't be hers even when the small fish brushed against her pectoral fins.

This true fish story has its human equivalent: Some individuals who have had one opportunity after another slip away, or who have felt certain barriers to be insurmountable, may also develop an "I don't care" attitude, as did the fish, and give up. These attitudes are understandable; however, such persons might close their despondent eyes to real opportunity when it comes along. As anthropologist Ashley Montague has said, "The deepest personal defeat suffered by human beings is constituted by the difference between what one was capable of becoming and what one has in fact become."

"You mean *I* can do it?"

Do you remember our discussion of the Pygmalion effect in Chapter 6? We learned that a person's expectations of an event or certain types of behavior can actually cause the event to occur. The concept could be modified to relate to a person's expectations or belief in himself or herself, something that we'll call an **inner-directed Pygmalion effect.** Far too frequently, many people develop a defeatist attitude that becomes deeply cemented into their subconscious. They have become programmed to believe that they would never do some of the things that others have done.

How might you make your job more satisfying?

The negative inner-directed Pygmalion—that is, the pessimistic person—like our despondent aquatic friend, often passes up opportunities that come very near. There are numerous things that you can do, however, to make your job seem more interesting, challenging, satisfying, and less stressful. For example, periodically you might analyze the methods currently being used on your job to determine how they might be improved, which is far more satisfying than mere criticism with little positive action. You might enter company slogan or name-a-product contests. Or perhaps you might volunteer for special projects or temporary assignments. Company publications usually need interesting material. Perhaps you have the latent interest and ability to apply some of your inactive literary talents to writing an article. You might be amazed at how such efforts help to satisfy your higher-order needs. The major point, regardless of the activity you choose, is that there are infinite ways in which you can make your own job and life more interesting and less stressful if you seek out fresh, realistic opportunities and convince yourself that you can accomplish those things.

Take the "Workaholic" Cure

Have you ever found that you tend to create some of your own tensions and pressures? Many individuals do. They are unable to relax even when they have some spare time. They tend to fill up every available moment of their waking hours with work activities. They are in a continual struggle against time and frequently have a false sense of urgency. They are punctual people and are enraged at anyone who is late. They frequently do several things simultaneously. They gulp down meals. They drink too fast. They drive too fast, too close to the cars in front of them, and are continually irritated at the driver who cruises along at the speed limit. They are, in effect, work addicts. People with these characteristics are what cardiologists Meyer Friedman and Ray Rosenman have labeled as having **Type A personalities.**[12]

A Type A personality may be useful in rising up an organizational ladder to higher management positions. However, Friedman and Rosenman feel that people, in order to cope more effectively with life's innumerable pressures and frustrations, should learn to turn off "A" periodically and become **Type B personalities.** Type B people may have some of the same characteristics as Type A's, but B's are less likely to have characteristics that are chronic, incessant, or constantly overdone. They ordinarily attempt to enjoy a reasonable amount of leisure. Many individuals, however, find the use of their spare time extremely difficult. For example, a surprisingly large number of managers and professional people in organizations are suffering from an affliction believed to be worse in some respects than excessive drinking. Its name? **Work addiction,** often called **workaholism.** Some persons apparently overwork for the same reason that alcoholics overdrink: to escape (they hope) from frustration.

There are *parallels* between the alcoholic and the Type A workaholic. Both *crave* their activities—excessive drinking for one and excessive work activity for the other. Both develop a *capacity*—some alcoholics "enjoy" at least an 18-drink day, whereas some managers regularly work an 18-hour day. Both can develop *withdrawal symptoms*—the alcoholic develops tensions and anxieties without his or her beverage; the person addicted to work often develops tensions and anxieties on weekends or vacations.

Perhaps burying oneself in work is an activity similar to *flight*. Work may serve to shield the work addict from other, less-satisfying activities.

Learn when to be "B."

What are the similarities between the alcoholic and the workaholic?

"I know I need to relax, but relaxation makes me tense!"

SOURCE: From *The Wall Street Journal*—permission, Cartoon Features Syndicate

What is the major difference between the work addict and the hard worker?

Many persons in organizations are *hard workers,* but the major difference between them and the *Type A work addict* is that the addict feels *guilty* when not working; the hard worker does not. Type A individuals, especially when their goals are unrealistic, are often ripe candidates for *burnout,* a condition previously discussed.

Any obsessive-compulsive worker should attempt to learn how to enjoy leisure. Some psychologists feel that workaholics need help just as do alcoholics. Both must first recognize that they have problems. Both engage in destructive behavioral patterns that have to be unlearned so that their energies can be channeled into more positive directions. The late Bertrand Russell once advised, "To be able to fill leisure intelligently is the last product of civilization."

Type A work addiction can lead to trouble. For example, it can lead to dreadful careers, destructive family relationships, drug and alcohol abuse, and even early death. Without work, the work addict starts coming unglued. There might be a little workaholic in each of us. Wouldn't you prefer, however, to try to recognize the warning signs of addiction and cope with them before it's too late?

If you are an obsessive-compulsive worker and not really deriving the satisfaction from living that you would like, examine the guidelines in Table 13.4 and consider if they might assist you to maintain or develop the faith and hope that we have been discussing.

Take Stock of Yourself

We all feel nervous, anxious, and tense from time to time. Turmoil in one's life can be exhausting and make coping with work and personal responsibilities extremely difficult. H. Randall Hicks, M.D., suggests that when experiencing anxiety, a person can take some immediate steps to deal with the problem. Dr. Hicks suggests, "Find a quiet space in your home and sit down with your thoughts. Write down the things you think may be causing your nervousness. Put them in rank order and write down a plan of how you can effectively deal with them." Dr. Hicks also recommends talking out your feelings with someone you trust, taking a long, soothing bath, going for a walk, doing a physical workout, or getting lost in a novel. "These activities can give you a sense of control," explains Dr. Hicks. "They can dissipate some of your stress and they can divert your mind from troubling thoughts."[13]

How rank can they get?

Your computer can also provide you with therapeutic value when you feel stressed about something. The mere act of inputting your frustrations and feelings into your nonjudgmental word processing system (or writing them by hand) can provide release of tension and solutions to problems as effectively as would a visit to a therapist or doctor.

Break the Law of Parkinson

Have you ever noticed before embarking on a vacation or business trip that you were concerned about not having enough time to pack your luggage? If you've taken trips regularly, you may have noticed that the preparations for them tend to expand to fill your available time. If you have three days to prepare, you may spend much of those three days getting ready, whereas if you have only half an hour advance notice, you still manage to pack in time.

Can you actually have less time when you have more time?

Were you ever amazed at how fast you readied yourself for work or school on mornings on which you overslept? Some people ordinarily allow about two hours in which to ready themselves, yet 20 minutes will suffice when they oversleep.

The point of the previous examples is expressed by C. Northcote Parkinson in his famous **Parkinson's Law,** which states that *work expands to fill the time available for its completion.*[14] Although individuals differ, many people work far more efficiently when they are pressed for time. When individuals have excessive amounts of time, they often find less important tasks or time wasters to do. According to an old adage with a grain or two of truth in it, "If you want something done right, then give the task to a busy person."

A modification of Parkinson's Law could be applied to such situations as the use of storage space. For example, let's assume that you find your storage space at work (this illustration could also apply to storage space in your home) is woefully inadequate. So you contract with a cabinetmaker to build you some additional shelves. Finally, you assume, there will be no more problems since you now have far more space than you could ever use. Within a relatively short period of time, however, you are in a state of utter disbelief for you have now discovered that you and your employees have completely filled the new shelves with additional materials.

An intelligent use of time, accompanied by adequate planning and the establishment of objectives, can enable you to break Parkinson's Law not only with impunity but also with the rewards of accomplishment. These feelings of accomplishment tend to reduce feelings of stress and tension that usually accompany many tasks. To combat "Parkinson's peril," however, you must be willing to overcome some of your deep-seated habits.

Break Kossen's Law

"I'm so organized I can't get anything done!"

Let's assume that you're well aware of the stresses that can develop when you fail to organize. You know about the pitfalls of Parkinson's Law, so you carefully plan your activities right down to the month, the week, the day, the hour—even the minute. You don't look for additional work to fill any gaps in your time; in fact, you feel that you don't even have any time gaps!

Unfortunately, you may find that your sophisticated and highly developed state of organization hasn't really reduced your stress level much. Additional activities, tasks, responsibilities, and interruptions seem to come your way. This particular stumbling block is termed **Kossen's,** or **K's, Law** and is defined as follows:

> Regardless of your state of organization, new tasks and interruptions will seek you out, thereby expanding your responsibilities, commitments, and work load.

The only thing that surprises me are people who are surprised by surprise factors!

There are ways, however, to break Kossen's Law without getting arrested. One way is to allow for *surprise factors,* which are those unexpected interruptions that continually upset the well-structured plans that people have made. However, should you really be *surprised* when your boss or one of your employees develops the urgent need to discuss something with you? Should you really be *surprised* when one of your customers has an unscheduled serious problem that demands your immediate attention? Should you really be *surprised* when you didn't allow for an unexpected traffic jam, and the rush-hour traffic has you tense and upset because you have an important appointment on the other side of town? Overscheduling your activities—not allowing for the unexpected—can cause you to experience continual frustration and stress. To avoid the disquieting effects of Kossen's Law, allow a reasonable amount of slack time for those not-so-surprising surprise factors that never seem to be out of sight for long.

"I know you're in there. I can hear you thinking!"

There are other ways to break Kossen's Law and reduce your stress level. Another method is to develop a periodic *closed-door, no-incoming-telephone-calls-please policy*. This approach runs the risk of irritating people who want to talk to you. However, such problems can be minimized if you make your intentions clear and yourself accessible at specified times.

How to break the law.

What can you do if you are asked to take on new tasks and responsibilities that you know can't be comfortably worked into your already overcrammed schedule? Be honest with the person. Point out that you would sincerely like to help, but that your present commitments prevent you from doing a satisfactory job on the project. You could also indicate that, rather than do a lousy job, you'd rather not take on any additional responsibilities at this time.

In some instances, you might maintain a better personal image with the requester if you indicate that you'd like to give the request some careful consideration before deciding. Then, within two or three days, contact the requester and indicate that your present schedule doesn't allow you to take on any additional responsibilities. Don't let too much time elapse, however, between the request and your response. If you do, you might begin to develop guilt feelings that could interfere with your normal work activities.

Of course, as we'll learn in the following chapter, like it or not you should consider the "political" implications of your turning down a new task or opportunity. Your career path might be damaged in some instances if you fail to make certain adjustments in your schedule to show your boss that you are willing to accept additional assignments.

Take Two, They're Large—The "2:1 Rule"

Another stressor faced by managers develops out of the tendency to misjudge how much time a project will take or how much a project will cost. Often time and cost estimates run low.

For example, let's assume that you have a term paper assignment for a college class. You estimate that the project will take a specific number of hours to complete. Even if Kossen's Law gives you a break by not following on your heels, you may still find that certain information you need takes about twice as long to look up as you expected. The typing of your term paper also takes much longer than you anticipated. This phenomenon is so commonplace in organizations that many managers refer to it as the **2:1 rule,** *the tendency for activities and projects to take in time or cost of materials approximately twice the original estimate.* Some managers believe that even a 2:1 ratio is too conservative.

Why never "twice as short"?

Is there any solution to this time-cost overrun stress inducer? One possibility is to seek advice from experienced people on how much time or money a project is likely to cost. Also attempt to make certain that your estimates are realistic and not solely based on a "wishing-it-were-so" philosophy (see Chapter 2). Experienced managers tend to become more realistic in their estimates, although frequently their realism results from several years of bad experience with estimates.

DON'T BITE THE HAND THAT NEEDS YOU——
MANAGING STRESS OFF THE JOB

Is there any part of your life you would prefer not to live over again?

How would you answer the following question: "Would you be willing to live your life—every bit of it—all over again?" Your response would provide considerable insight into how you perceive your past experiences.

Life seems to become more complex and stressful as civilization advances. Our houses, factories, and offices are now filled with labor-saving gadgets and devices, yet we are continually frustrated by mechanical failures and breakdowns. A large proportion of American families possess houses and automobiles, yet at times they've wondered if there would be enough fuel to heat their houses or to operate their automobiles. The events of the day—ranging from violent crime, natural disaster, stock market crashes, hostile takeovers, the loss of jobs, and the erosion of public services—add to the frustrations and tensions we experience in work organizations.

How will *you* cope with the continually increasing stresses of life? Some people, as we've already observed, react to stress and frustration by engaging in the adjustive reaction of *flight*—the attempt to run from problems. Flight is seldom a successful solution to such problems since utopia seems to exist only in the eye of the beholder. Therefore, a key question is, "What can we do to adapt more readily to our present environment?"

Two Schools of Thought

The school of **behavioristic psychology,** championed by such psychologists as B. F. Skinner and James. V. McConnell, argues that we mortal beings have little real influence over our destinies. The controversial **behaviorists** further assert that most of our actions are determined or controlled without our knowledge—not unlike those of caged rats or birds in a laboratory experiment—by the people and institutions around us. Our activities, they feel, are primarily conditioned responses to the stimuli we receive.

What is the future of ratkind?

An opposing school of psychological thought—**humanistic psychology**—pioneered by **humanists** Abraham Maslow, Carl Rogers, and Rollo May, believes that strong individuals will always step forth from the "conditioned mass." Humanistic psychology argues that individuals can actively shape their own lives and that at least some human responses are not conditioned, or controlled, by other forces.

A Melange of Both Schools?

There is little doubt that much of your behavior *is*, as the behaviorists argue, conditioned by our experiences. We are aware, for example, that many persons respond in an almost knee-jerk fashion to others with certain styles of haircuts, shapes of noses, or manners of handshaking, even when unacquainted with them. Many of our normal reactions do appear to be conditioned responses.

How can you influence your moods?

However, we are also capable of independent thought. We're able to influence our moods by altering our environment (music, for example, can change moods), and we can influence our lives by altering such factors as our attitudes (see Table 13.6). Let's now discover how we can prevent ourselves from acting solely as laboratory rats would in a behavioral psychologist's maze, beginning first with a short story about identical twin sisters.

Recognize the Positive

Once upon a time there was a small community, and residing in this community was a family with identical twin daughters. One daughter was a pessimist and the other an optimist. One year when their birthday rolled around, a friend of the family—the town psychiatrist—and the girls' parents decided to conduct an experiment. For her birthday, the mother and father gave the pessimistic daughter a shiny new bicycle, a water gun, and a colorful hat. The optimistic child was given a room full of fresh horse manure and a small green shovel.

About 15 minutes later, the psychiatrist and the anxious parents went into the pessimist's room and enthusiastically asked her how she liked her presents. The sulking young girl snapped, "The bicycle is no good, the water gun doesn't shoot far enough, and the hat is too small." Then they went into the optimist's room and asked her how she liked her gifts. Within the room busily and excitedly shoveling horse manure about was the optimistic child, who looked up and cheerfully replied, "It's a lot of work, but I know there's a pony in here somewhere!"

What effect does your attitude have on how you cope with pressures?

A corny story—agreed—but it does help to illustrate the important fact that our *attitudes* strongly influence how we cope with our environmental pressures. Some individuals, such as the pessimistic daughter, continually focus on the negative—and they can usually find it, for there always seem to be undesirable aspects in any situation. As James Cabell wrote in *The Silver Stallion:* "The optimist proclaims that we live in the best of all possible worlds; and the pessimist fears this is true."

TABLE 13.6   Selected Guidelines for Managing Stress Off the Job.

- Recognize the positive aspects of situations.
- Vary your activities.
- Influence others positively.
- Exercise regularly.
- Learn how to wait without being stressed.
- Seek help from qualified friends and professionals.

A characteristic that helps many persons to see the brighter aspects of situations and overcome stresses and frustrations more readily is a *sense of humor.* An anonymous humorist once paradoxically exclaimed, "The only way that I can retain my sanity is to act crazy!" Persons who can laugh at their own shortcomings are often more healthy-minded individuals than those who can't.

Vary Your Activities

Everyday stresses seem far easier to cope with for those who regularly have new experiences to look forward to, that is, a wide variety of interests. During a television interview the late Bertrand Russell once caustically remarked, "Some individuals' interests consist of no more than sitting in their water closets all day powdering their noses while observing the looking glass and wondering about the reason for their boredom!"

Perhaps our jobs aren't the only activities that need occasional enriching. In fact, as industrial psychologist David Sirota cautions, "A normal healthy person has three aspects of life: Work, play, and love."[15] We could all probably benefit from what might be called **life enrichment.** The enrichment of lives is really each person's own individual responsibility. Men and women must develop their own cures for loneliness, boredom, and loss of faith.

How might you enrich your life?

Simple activities can sometimes enrich at least portions of your life. For example, you may feel that you're in a rut—following the same pattern every day—driving to work and then driving the same way back home again. If so, why not vary your route? Does it really matter if another road takes ten minutes or so longer? The opportunity to see different scenery, different neighborhoods, even different traffic signals, all contribute to the variety of your life.

Many persons feel that most life enrichment activities are too costly; as a result, they spend much of their idle time dozing in front of the TV. Many interests, however, aren't that expensive. Unfortunately, many persons have not yet discovered, developed, or acquired them.

What are some leisure
activities that aren't too
expensive?

For example, have you ever considered taking an evening course in music at a community college? "Not particularly interested in music," you say? Are you really certain? With little or no knowledge of a specific area, an individual has no way of knowing his or her potential interest. An evening course in classical guitar isn't likely to enable you to take over where the late Andrés Segovia left off, but you might be amazed at how it can expand your appreciation of polished professional artists.

Contributing your talents to such activities as little theater groups—if not by acting, then perhaps as a stage assistant—can be another enjoyable experience. You will have the opportunity to meet and mix with other people, and you would be assigned certain responsibilities that might give you feelings of participation and contribution.

Evening courses and little theater groups are only two illustrations of the wide variety of inexpensive activities that could enrich your life. *You,* however, have to discover for *yourself* what might enhance your own happiness.

Influence Others Positively

Another activity that is beneficial to one's own mind is the exertion of a positive and helpful influence over others. As only one person in a nation of about 250 million, you may at times feel somewhat powerless to exert influence over others. However, you may have considerably more influence on others than you imagine. Sometimes you may not even realize for years afterward how you may have assisted someone with your comments or attempts to help. For example, a public school speech therapist attempted once a week for two years to assist a young child to overcome a speech impediment, with little result. During a summer vacation, the child and his parents moved to another state, and the young boy finally decided to try to apply what the therapist had attempted so diligently to teach. Within a matter of weeks, the speech difficulty disappeared, but the persistent therapist never knew that her persevering efforts had succeeded. Frequently, people have assisted us without having ever known about it.

Parents influence their children's values far more than they realize. If you have children, you may have noticed that almost all of what they learn and do within their first few years is the result of direct imitation of you and your spouse. You may not always be a first-hand witness of the results of many of your efforts to influence others, but your influence may be felt nonetheless.

Will you always find out the effects of your efforts?

Exercise—The Shape of Things to Come

We've already mentioned that your mind can affect your body's wellbeing. The reverse—the body affecting the mind—is equally important. The relationship between the two is sometimes referred to as the **holistic effect.** As we grow older, or as we assume positions with greater responsibility but less physical activity, we can generally find an infinite variety of excuses for not exercising. "I'm too tired." "I'm too busy." "It's too early." "It's too late." "I really *should* start exercising." "Maybe next week, *if* it's not raining."

Almost without our awareness the condition of our bodies can begin to deteriorate, a process that can take place with amazing speed in the inactive person. Of course, you may live to a ripe old age

Is inactivity broadening?

in spite of not taking proper care of your body. But put your feet into the well-worn slippers of the sickly 88-year-old person who said, "If I had only known I was going to live this long, I would have taken better care of myself!"

Evidence that more Americans feel *they* are "going to live that long" exists in a Gordon S. Black Corporation survey that found 82 percent of those polled to say they regularly exercise 1 or more hours a week.[16] Another study of men over a 27-year period found that Americans' quest for healthier lifestyles has paid off in a 25 percent reduction in the incidence of heart attacks among men. After many years of increase, the death rates from coronary heart disease—mostly heart attacks—started dropping sharply in 1968. Since then death rates have fallen by more than 30 percent. Exercise, along with cutting out cholesterol, giving up cigarettes, and keeping control of high blood pressure are all believed to be contributors to the declining number of heart attacks.[17]

However, a disquieting countertrend seems to have developed among younger people in the U.S. According to the National Centers for Disease Control, only about a third of American high school students get enough exercise to keep them physically fit. The survey reports that only 36 percent of students in grades 10 through 12 participate in vigorous physical activity for at least twenty minutes three or more days per week. The percentage was higher—61 percent—in 1984. The survey also reveals that students who are vigorously active spend less time watching television than those who did not exercise.[18]

Chapter 8 discussed wellness programs offered by many companies. Your use of company facilities, such as exercise rooms or running tracks, can provide a convenient way for maintaining your physical condition and releasing tensions. If you have to travel occasionally overnight on business, you no longer have a valid excuse for not exercising. Many hotels now provide exercise rooms and swimming pools that enable you to maintain your physical (and mental) fitness away from your home base.

Before undertaking a strenuous exercise program yourself, check with your doctor; then find out what sort of *regular* exercise will benefit you. Physical activity can be of value to practically every part of your body and can make a big difference in whether you feel sluggish or energetic, stressed or unstressed. One of the greatest benefits of exercise is to the *mind,* for exercise can be a form of relief for the man or woman beset by anger, pressures, worries, or distress.

Why Wait When You Have to Wait?

Another cause of stress and frustration in individuals is the recurring experience of **forced waiting.** Dentists and doctors make you wait; post office personnel make you wait; automobile repair firms make

Work It on Out![b]

One of the major benefits of exercise is that of enabling you to deal with stress more effectively. Dr. Michael McGannon, director of the Insead Business School health course, suggests that your road back to physical (and mental) fitness should proceed according to the following simple rules:

- Enjoy the exercise you are doing. The obvious moral pleasure is not enough to keep you at it.
- Exercise frequently. That means about three times a week.
- Exercise for a short, sustained period of, say, thirty minutes per session.
- Exercise at the right intensity. Your training heart rate (THR) may be a useful measure. To calculate it, subtract your age from 220, and multiply this figure by 75 percent. For example if you are twenty, and fairly sedentary, your THR will be 150: (220–20) x 0.75.
- Choose an activity you really enjoy—walking, gardening, rowing, swimming, roller skating—and do it three times a week for thirty minutes.
- Stop making excuses for why you can't exercise today.

you wait; banks make you wait; even gas stations make you wait. Everybody seems to make you wait—it almost seems like a conspiracy! In fact, if on the average you spend 45 minutes of each day idly waiting for something, you have allowed over 270 of your hours in a year to melt away into oblivion.

If waiting frustrates you, *why wait when you have to wait?* You probably know by now what sorts of situations are likely to require idly biding your time. Why not figuratively don your old girl or boy scout sombrero and "be prepared," as the motto suggests, for forced waiting.

For example, if you have an appointment for your periodic physical examination, take along something that interests you, perhaps the article or book you've been waiting to read but have never had quite enough time to start. Or maybe you could take some letter writing materials with you. How about that letter from Uncle Horace that you haven't yet answered, and it's been three years since he wrote!

How about that letter
to Uncle Horace?

Or if you are a salesperson who calls on customers, you may experience the frustrations of clients not seeing you promptly. Most salespeople, like yourself, have regular and substantial amounts of paperwork to prepare. Instead of complaining about how many forms you have to fill out each evening on your own time, why not accomplish what you can while waiting?

Arthur Brisbane on the subject of the use of idle time once stated: "Time is the one thing we possess. Our success depends upon the use of our time, and its by-product, the odd moment."

Waiting actually can be a delightful part-time experience if you make it so. The above discussion has been aimed more at those with a reasonably strong work ethic. You might prefer, however, merely encouraging your mind to wander and engage in free or creative thinking, a pastime that you may seldom have time for otherwise. If the fact of waiting usually bothers you, and if you go to your waiting situations prepared with activities you find interesting, you are likely to find that time will pass more quickly than you desire.

"Use" Your Friends *and* the Pros

Your friends can often be quite helpful in assisting you through some difficult and distressful periods, especially if they have developed the art of empathetic listening. Unfortunately, however, friends typically lack the professional training necessary to help others "get back in shape" after they have reached their stress threshold.

Well-meaning friends frequently tell their distressed companions something like, "Don't worry about your problems; everything's going to be all right." Or a well-intentioned friend may relate similar experiences that she or he has had. These are not the approaches that a truly distressed person needs. A stressed-out person needs an empathetic listener who is capable of guiding him or her into making rational decisions.

Why not get help when you need it?

Don't be afraid to seek out the professional help of a counselor or therapist. There are a number of functions that a professional can perform. In times of distress—that is, crises, relationship difficulties, transitions, loss of loved ones, or other specific problems—the therapist serves as a sounding board, a neutral third party, who can guide you in seeing other perspectives in a particular situation. The professional counselor can aid you in discovering your true feelings and possible remedies for your condition.

Some churches offer support with "in-transition groups" that provide distressed individuals the opportunity to share their problems with others. The opportunity of "getting things off your chest," plus seeing that you are not the only person in the world with such feelings, can be very helpful in returning your "spring" to its original shape.

It's never too late to be depressed.

There may be times, such as late in the evening, when you are deeply distressed and do not have easy access to a support system.

We hope that this will never occur, but if you ever feel so depressed that you are contemplating suicide, go immediately to the telephone and dial a local **Suicide Prevention and Crisis Intervention Service,** a community agency staffed with individuals trained to assist you through difficult and emotional situations. You can find the number in your local telephone directory. As we've already learned, often the mere opportunity to speak with an empathetic listener enables us to focus on our own problems more clearly.

CAUSING ASSOCIATES TO BECOME DISTRESSED

So far, we've discussed the various ways to manage stress related to your own career and personal life. If you are a manager, you may, at times, be guilty of creating stress in others, such as associates in your organization who are accountable to you. They may encounter some of the same types of stressors that you periodically experience. Try to be sensitive to any observable symptoms of stress in your associates, such as chronic headaches or continual tiredness.

Since employees tend to follow as they are led, you should attempt to set a good example for your associates. If you look unsettled, fraught with pressure, and act in a short-tempered manner, you may cause your associates to behave in a similar way. Table 13.7 lists six guidelines for avoiding employee tension and stress.

TABLE 13.7   Guidelines for Avoiding Employee Tension and Stress.[19]

1. Don't set impossibly high goals in the mistaken belief that they will make employees try more earnestly.
2. Don't criticize employees for not spending enough time at their desks getting work done after you've called frequent, lengthy meetings.
3. Don't put employees on the spot, especially in front of others. Give them time to research answers to your questions.
4. Don't continually take employees off one project to work on others, requiring them to juggle numerous projects at the same time. Often it is better to allow them to concentrate and finish one project at a time.
5. Don't involve the entire staff in every problem or crisis, especially when some of the individuals can do nothing to alleviate the difficulty.
6. Don't bring up employees' past mistakes when you are correcting them for current mistakes.

HAPPINESS AND SUCCESS ARE . . . ?

If you conscientiously apply the concepts you've read about so far in this chapter, you should be able to find that you are able to cope with and control your distress level more effectively. Related to the topic of stress management are the concepts of *happiness* and *success,* twin topics of great importance to many individuals living in a high-achieving society.

A Hundred Years From Today . . .

Life in our space capsule Earth is relatively brief. As the Romans would say, *tempus fugit,* or "time flies." Do you remember that when you were in grade school summers seemed nearly endless? And have you noticed that each summer since has seemed to grow shorter and shorter? Time has a stealthy habit of creeping up on us. One morning you may wake up, look in the mirror, and suddenly realize that the person you see is not the person you saw 20 years before.

Mirror, mirror, on the wall . . . ?

Each of us has more influence than we might imagine on whether we will be able to look back on our lives as generally having been happy experiences. But what actually is this thing called *happiness?* Happiness is different things to different people. There are some ingredients, however, that make for more gratifying circumstances. Look at the following list and decide which statements are integral parts of your present situation. Are there any factors that you might add to the list that could contribute to your personal pleasure? If some of the items on the list could make you happier but aren't a part of your present situation, what might you do to utilize them?

What would make your life a happier experience?

I have enjoyable feelings about my job.

I have reasonably good physical and mental health.

I feel good about myself, that is, my self-esteem is reasonably good.

I am free from economic want, that is, my basic needs are reasonably satisfied.

I have some close friends whose company I regularly enjoy.

I have a fairly good sense of humor.

I try to understand the points of view of others and to accept them as they are, not as I want them to be.

I am engaged in an activity that I feel is useful to society.

I feel that I know how to enjoy my leisure.

I feel that my life has a sense of purpose and includes some specific, but flexible, goals.

The Concept of Success

One of the premises of this chapter has been that the maintenance or restoration of faith *is possible* if society's members—that means *us*—are willing to cease venting their insecurities, frustrations, and emotions on their fellow human beings.

Although it may sound contradictory, we must learn *to feel more secure with our insecurities.* As we acquire more education, we tend to realize that we cannot know or do everything and, as a result, may feel more secure with this knowledge. The hope that many persons have lost can be restored if they are willing to educate themselves to face reality—to perceive things as they truly are, not as they've never been or as they appear to be on the screen of a television set—and to attempt to engage in activities that improve the lot of their fellow human beings.

How can you feel more secure with your insecurities?

An ancient Chinese seer once advised, "A journey of a thousand miles begins with a single step, and it is taking that step today." *Success* is another word that means many things to many people. Numerous persons feel that success is important to them, but they are not quite certain what the concept means.

What is "success"?

If you were to observe each day on your way to work an old man dressed in ragged clothes sitting on the grass in a city park merely whiling away the time feeding bread to the pigeons, would you say that he is a success? Who can really say for certain? Perhaps you would have to ask him before you could know.

Is a person in possession of two cars, two houses, a boat, and a responsible executive position necessarily a success? Once again, perhaps you must obtain an honest answer from the person before you can know. Individuals' *attitudes,* far more than their possessions, determine the feelings of success. Material objects in themselves can either contribute to or detract from a person's feeling of faith and success. A worthwhile way to conclude this chapter might be with a comment that Henry Ford once made about these concepts. Read his words and see how they might relate to you:

We begin as pensioners. Some people live two-thirds of their lives on the provision made for them by others. We graduate into cooperators, earn our own living, hold up our own end of the job, produce a little extra for the pensioners that are coming on behind us. A few enter the third stage, where they do something more for the world than the world does for them. They put the world in their debt by making every man's living better, or his hope larger, or his opportunity wider. Just to hold up one's end of the load is a great and satisfactory thing; it makes one a man. However, it only squares the account. But to do for the world more than the world does for you—that is success.[20]

SUMMARY

In this chapter we explored the nature and effects that stress can have on individuals. We looked at stress from different standpoints—eustress (positive) and distress (negative), career-related and off-the-job related—along with how to avoid causing stress in associates.

We also examined some of the main types of reactions that individuals may experience in their attempts to adjust to everyday stresses and frustrations. *Adjustive reactions* range from the normal mild kinds to the psychotic extreme. Some high achievers are like machines that have been run too long and too hard—they sometimes burn out. We examined some of the typical symptoms and cures for the condition of burnout experienced by some persons.

Faith in one's self, in humanity, and in the future are essential if individuals are to derive personal satisfaction from living. Individuals with little faith or hope tend to be restless in their behavior, changing schools, jobs, addresses, and mates with excessive frequency. The search for utopia is difficult since many of the problems from which individuals are attempting to escape tend to follow them to each destination.

We further inspected some useful methods for living with and managing stress. We also examined how friends and counselors can help us when we are approaching, or have passed through, our stress threshold. And finally we analyzed some of the essential ingredients of those nebulous concepts, happiness and success.

We customarily spend much of our lives in work situations. Consequently, the choice of a satisfying occupation, as well as an enjoyable personal life imbued with a variety of interests, can aid the individual in achieving a more satisfying existence and in maintaining a reasonable degree of faith and hope in both the present and the future.

TERMS AND CONCEPTS TO REMEMBER

stress	conversion
eustress	burnout
distress	faith
yield point	situational faith
elastic limit	inner-directed Pygmalion effect
rupture point	Type A personalities
frustration	Type B personalities
adjustive reaction (defense mechanism)	work addiction (workaholism)

rationalization	Parkinson's Law
compensation	K's (Kossen's) Law
negativism	2:1 rule
resignation	behavioristic psychology
flight	behaviorist
repression	humanistic psychology
pseudostupidity	humanists
obsessive thinking	life enrichment
displacement	holistic effect
scapegoating	forced waiting
psychosomatic	Suicide Prevention and Crisis Intervention Service

QUESTIONS

1. Evaluate the following statement: "We should do everything within our power to remove stress from our lives completely."

2. What is the difference between *eustress* and *distress?*

3. Explain the significance of the terms *yield point, elastic limit,* and *rupture point* as they relate to stress.

4. Why is the process of "knowing thyself" so difficult?

5. When a person becomes frustrated, why does he or she tend to experience what is termed *adjustive reactions?*

6. Do you feel that the defense mechanism of *rationalization* is *beneficial* or *harmful* to the person who experiences it? Explain.

7. What is one of the major problems associated with attempting to run away from the causes of frustration and stress?

8. What is your own personal definition of *faith?* Could a person have faith and yet not believe in a formalized religion? Explain.

9. Explain the meaning and significance of the term *situational faith.*

10. How might an excessive distrust of employees by managers work to the detriment of the organization?

11. Assuming that you are fed up with your studies, family, and friends, what sort of personal behavior might help to restore some of your faith and hope?

12. Singer and actress Dolly Parton, a lady not necessarily noted for her philosophical musings, once advised, "The way I see it, if you

want the rainbow, you have to put up with the rain." Provide a real-world example of how Parton's "homespun philosophy" applies to your own life.

13. What do you think of when you hear the word *work?* What do you believe influenced your thoughts?

14. Explain the significance of the "fish story" cited in the chapter.

15. What is the difference between Type A and Type B personalities? Which one do you think you are? Which is better? Why?

16. What tends to cause burnout? What can be done to "cure" the burn-out disease?

17. How can a person successfully "break" Parkinson's Law?

18. Describe Kossen's Law. How might its implications be avoided?

19. What is the significance of the 2:1 rule? How can its implications be avoided?

20. Explain the apparent conflict between the behavioristic and humanistic schools of psychology. What arguments might you offer to show the relevance of both schools of thought?

21. The chapter suggests that a sense of humor can help you overcome stresses and frustrations. What is the difference between having a "sense of humor" and being a "joke teller"?

22. If forced waiting frustrates you, how might you develop a situation in which it is not necessary for you to wait when you have to wait?

23. Should a person be ashamed to admit that he or she has called a Suicide Prevention and Crisis Intervention Service? Would you be? Explain.

24. How might you avoid stressing your associates if you are a manager?

APPLICATIONS

13.1 The Rat Race

Dear Uncle Brian:

I know I haven't written to my favorite uncle for a long, long time. Frankly, I haven't felt like doing much of anything lately. I've really been fed up with most things these days.

Well, it's Friday evening again. Another week shot to hell. The weekends just can't roll around too fast for me. Don't you dread Monday morning? I sure as heck do. But I've got quite a bit of sick leave accumulated so I've started taking off every other Monday, and I spend nearly the whole darned day in bed. Man, what a waste, but it's one heckofa lot better than going to that dull office in town. Besides, I really haven't been feeling too well lately, terrible headaches most of the time. Probably from that rotten music my sons play on their blasted CD players or listen to on MTV. How come you hardly ever hear Barry Manilow any more?

Cripes, driving is getting to be a drag. You know, I spend about two miserable hours a day on that big hunk of concrete they call a highway, and I can only creep along at ten miles an hour. At times I feel like I'm living with those wimps in the cars on both sides of me.

You remember that Gladys and I moved out to good old Surreptitious Valley to get away from all that crap and smog in the city. But things out here just aren't like they used to be. Kids getting stopped by the police for cruising up and down Maple Street or for speeding, teachers getting beat up, burglaries, the whole shmear. I even had my bowling ball stolen out of the back seat of my Chrysler last week.

We decided to take Jason and Jeffery out of that public school jungle. Their school used to be a good one until they started open enrollment and let those trouble makers from the other side of town go to *our* public school. Why can't those people stay with their own kind where they belong? Some things just aren't supposed to mix, you know, like water and grease.

So we're now sending our boys to that private school about thirty miles from our house. Man, does that cost us a bundle. Even had to buy Gladys a car to drive them. Now we've got three cars in the family. Gives us status. But we spend a small fortune just trying to maintain them and paying for gas.

Uncle, am I ever glad it's Friday. Life has really become a rat race. Same old crap, day in and day out. Wash the cars, and they get dirty all over again. Mow the lawn, and it grows right back in five days, paint the house, and it needs painting again in two years. Every Sunday morning either Jeffery or Jason accidentally trip the burglar alarm and scare the living daylights out of the neighbors. Back and forth, back and forth, every day on the same highway. Every darned day I'm chained to that desk down at the office, except for my morning coffee breaks, 45 minutes for lunch, and a couple of trips to the restroom. You know, during the week the big event of my day is hopping onto the couch after dinner, watching 20-year old documentaries on the social life of monkeys, and then falling asleep.

I guess I should hope that I stay "chained" to my desk. The company's been going through some of that "restructuring" stuff, and nobody's sure if they're going to be working or not a month from now. I hate those welfare leaches, but sometimes I feel like joining them. I'm more entitled to a handout than they are.

I have to hurry on this letter. I'm going bowling with my good old buddies again tonight. Do it every Friday night. That's about the only real pleasure I get these days—that and drinking beer watching the games on TV on Saturdays, Sundays, and Monday evenings. Does Gladys ever get peeved with those sports programs! At least I keep telling myself it's fun.

By the way, I guess I didn't tell you what Gladys and I might do. I'm so sick of this darned rat race, we might buy a little motel up in Twain Harte. We'll get a lot of fresh air up there and get away from the hustle-bustle routine down here. I think it will be kind of fun being one of those entrepreneurs. (How do you like that word, unc?)

Well, Uncle Brian, I gotta get going now. The guys will be coming by soon to pick me up for Friday night bowling. Such a life, eh? By the way, be sure to give Aunt Fanny my regards.

Your nephew,
Quentin

Questions

1. What do you feel is troubling Quentin?

2. What adjustive reactions discussed in the chapter does Quentin appear to be experiencing?

3. How might Quentin improve his attitude toward living?

13.2 A Search for Utopia

Twenty-five idealistic young Canadians from Victoria, British Columbia, have decided to leave what they feel to be the depressing weather of western Canada to establish new lives on a South Sea island to prove that their dreams of a utopia can come true.

"We will live on the island for the rest of our lives," said 20-year-old waitress, Barbara Broadway, one of six women who will make the trip.

The originator of the trip, Joseph Centerfielder, a computer programmer, said that he and the group hope to find sun, security, romance, and escape from the frustrations and tensions of modern industrial life. Centerfielder explained that the twenty-five persons will establish a share-and-share-alike island family community.

None of the women are single, and there are six married couples. The remaining members are men. The average age of the group members is 33. Among the group are an accountant, a stockbroker, a law-enforcement officer, a firefighter, a plumber, and a social worker.

Their intentions are to depart after the first of next year to settle on an eight-square-mile island off the west coast of Queensland, Australia. Currently, they are negotiating with the government of Queensland to acquire a renewable ten-year lease for $900,000.

Questions

1. What, in your opinion, are the twenty-five persons "looking for" on the island?

2. Do you feel that they will achieve their goals? Explain your answer.

3. What sort of problems might evolve in the following areas: (1) lack of leadership, (b) morale, (c) status, and (d) personal property?

13.3 The Case of the Overworked American

According to my estimates, the average employed person is now on the job an additional 163 hours, or the equivalent of an extra month a year. . . . Hours have been increasing throughout the twenty-year period (1969–1987) for which we have data. The breakdown for men and women shows lengthening hours for both groups, but there is a "gender gap" in the size of the increase. Men are working nearly one hundred (98) more hours per year, or two and a half extra weeks. Women are doing about three hundred (305) additional hours, which translates to seven and a half weeks, or 38 added days of work each year. The research shows that hours have risen across a wide spectrum of Americans and in all income categories—low, middle, and high. The increase is common to a variety of family patterns—people with and without children, those who are married, and those who are not. And it has been general across industries and, most probably, occupations.

The extra month of work is attributable to both longer weekly schedules and more weeks of work. . . . As long as work is available, people are on the job more steadily throughout the year. This factor accounts for over two-thirds of the total increase in hours. It has been especially important for women, as they are increasingly working full-time and year round. Women now take less time off for the birth of a child and are not as likely to stop working during the summer recess in order to care for children. For better or worse, the pattern of women's employment is getting to look more and more like men's.

Weekly schedules are also getting longer, by about one hour per week (54 minutes, to be exact). This is the first sustained peacetime increase in weekly hours during the twentieth century. What is especially surprising is that it is not just women whose days are getting longer, but men as well. And after twenty years of increase, the proportion of employees on long schedules is substantial. In 1990, one-fourth of all full-time workers spent at least 49 hours on the job each week. Of these, almost half were at work 60 hours or more.

So what's pushing up hours? One factor is moonlighting—the practice of holding more than one job at a time. Moonlighting is now more prevalent than at any time during the three decades for which we have statistics. As of May 1989, more than seven million Americans, or slightly over 6 percent of those employed, officially reported having two or more jobs, with extremely high increases occurring among women. The real numbers are higher, perhaps twice as high—

as tax evasion, illegal activities, and employer disapproval of second jobs make people reluctant to speak honestly. The main impetus behind this extra work is financial. Close to one-half of those polled say they hold two jobs in order to meet regular household expenses or pay off debts. As one might expect, this factor has become more compelling during the 1980s, with the disappearance of stable positions that pay a living wage and the increase of casual and temporary service sector employment.

A second factor, operating largely on weekly hours, is that Americans are working more overtime. After the recession of the early 1980s, many companies avoided costly rehiring of workers and, instead, scheduled extra overtime. Among manufacturing employees, paid overtime hours rose substantially after the recession, and by the end of 1987, accounted for the equivalent of an additional five weeks of work per year. One automobile worker noted, "You have to work the hours, because a few months later they'll lay you off for a model changeover and you'll need the extra money when you're out of work. It never rains but it pours—either there's more than you can stand, or there isn't enough." While many welcome the chance to earn premium wages, the added effort can be onerous. Older workers are often compelled to stretch themselves, because many companies calculate pension benefits only on recent earnings. [From Juliet B. Schor, *The Overworked American: The Unexpected Decline of Leisure* (New York: BasicBooks, 1991), pp. 29–31.]

Questions
1. What stresses are implied by this description of recent changes in Americans' hours of work? Are there any elements of eustress involved?

2. What steps can be taken to manage or reduce time-related stress on the job?

NOTES

1. Dr. Lawrence Lamb, "Stress and How It Affects People," *Contra Costa Times,* January 18, 1986, p. 7-B.

2. Stan Kossen, *Supervision, 2nd ed.* (St. Paul, MN: West Educational Publishing, 1991), pp. 149, 150.

3. Jere E. Yates, *Managing Stress* (New York: American Management Associations, 1979), pp. 23, 24.

4. Charles G. Reigner, "Mature Thinking," Reproduced from the March 1966 issue of *The Rowe Budget,* p. 17, by special arrangement with,

and permission of the author, Charles G. Reigner, and the publisher, The H.M. Rowe Company, Baltimore and Chicago.

5. "U.S. Mobility Slows, Report Says," *The Washington Post,* December 20, 1991, p. 22.

6. For a thorough discussion of the concept of freedom, see the classic works by Erich Fromm, *Escape from Freedom,* (New York: Holt, Rinehart and Winston, 1941); and Ashley Montague, *The Humanization of Man* (New York: Grove Press, 1962), pp. 66–78.

7. Barbara S. Cohen, "Burnout: The Malaise That Affects Growing Numbers of Super-Achievers," *World of Work Report,* November 1981.

8. Michael Hudson, "Job Burnout: Cause and Cure," *American Business,* February 1981, p. 22.

9. "Hopeful People More Likely to Overcome Barriers, Study Says," *The New York Times,* December 23, 1991, p. 27.

10. From a study conducted by Northwestern National Life Insurance Company and reported by Ray Brady, "The Money Crunch," on the *CBS Evening News,* February 20, 1992.

11. Margherita Osborne, ed., *The Book of Success* (Joliet, IL: P.F. Vollard, 1927), p. 9.

12. Meyer Friedman and Ray H. Roseman, *Type A Behavior and Your Heart,* (Greenwich, CT: Fawcett Publications, 1974); and Cathy Trost, "Like Mother, Like Baby, Type-A Study Says," *The Wall Street Journal,* March 6–7, 1992, p. 4.

13. Ellen Michaud and Lila L. Anastas, *Listen to Your Body* (Emmaus, PA: Rodale Press, 1988), p. 263–265.

14. C. Northcote Parkinson, *Parkinson's Law* (Cambridge, MA: The Riverside Press, 1957), pp. 2–12.

15. Beth Brophy, "Workaholics Beware: Long Hours May Not Pay," *U.S. News & World Report,* April 7, 1986, p. 60.

16. Ben Brown, "Fitness Boom Has No Sign of Fatigue," *USA Today/ International Edition,* July 21, 1989, p. 9, 10.

17. "Health Craze Linked to Drop in Heart Attacks," *Contra Costa Times,* April 18, 1985, p. 17-C.

18. "Exercise by High School Students Declining, Survey Says," *San Francisco Examiner,* January 24, 1992, p. 26.

19. Adapted from F.J. McGuigan, director of the Institute for Stress Management at United States International University, as reported in "Inefficient Bosses May Contribute to Employee Stress Disorders," *Contra Costa Times/Business,* February 10, p.

20. Osborne, *The Book of Success,* p. 52.

21. Adapted from "Testing for Type-A Personality Traits," The Jenkins Activity Survey, Job Involvement Scale, *The Wall Street Journal Europe,* March 6–7, 1992, p. 4.

BOX NOTES

a. Adapted from Ron Prichard, "Squirt Guns Spur Outpouring of Concern," *USA Today/International Edition,* June 10, 1992, p. 3A.

b. Adapted from Michael J. Mandel, "Economic Trends—U.S. Workers Suffer from A Time-Off Gap," *Business Week/ International Edition,* August 12, 1991, p. 9; and Diane Summers, "When a Change Is as Good as a Rest," *Financial Times,* March 6, 1992.

c. Adapted from Dr. Michael McGannon, "Making a Strong Case for Getting Physical," *Financial Times,* May 20, 1992, p. 10.

EXPERIENTIAL EXERCISES

Mechanisms for Personal Defense

Recognition of defense mechanisms can often make adaptation to them easier. Think back on your experiences. How have you used the following adjustive reactions at various times in your life? What caused them to occur?

Defense Mechanism

Rationalization
Example _____
Cause_____

Compensation
Example _____
Cause_____

Negativism
Example _____
Cause_____

Resignation
Example _____
Cause_____

Flight
Example _____
Cause_____

Repression
Example _____
Cause_____

Pseudostupidity
Example _____
Cause_____

Obsessive Thinking
Example _____
Cause_____

Displacement
Example _____
Cause_____

Conversion
Example _____
Cause_____

Are You a Candidate for Burnout?

Answer either *yes* or *no* to the following statements. Your answers should be considered *general* responses.

Yes   No

____ ____   1. I feel really tired most of the time.

____ ____   2. I even feel tired after I have had seven or more hours sleep.

____ ____   3. I am much less patient and short-tempered with my associates than I used to be.

____ ____   4. I seldom feel that I am meeting my deadlines.

____ ____   5. I am not exercising regularly nor spending as much time on hobbies as I did in the past.

____ ____   6. I am spending much less time with my family and friends than I did in the past.

_____ _____ 7. I seldom feel that I have accomplished enough work.

_____ _____ 8. I seldom feel that I have time to relax.

_____ _____ 9. I am drinking _or_ taking drugs more than I did in the past.

_____ _____ 10. I generally become quite annoyed when the automobile in front of me is traveling too slowly and I can't pass.

Instructions: Count the number of _yes_ responses. If you have five or more _yes_ responses you are a potential candidate for burnout. If you had eight or more the chances are that you already feel burned out much of the time. If so, review the concepts in Chapter 13 and try your best to apply them to your own life.

Are You an "A" or a "B"?[21]

Instructions: Print the number of your choice in the space to the left of the item number. Add their totals when you are finished.

10 1. Do you ever have trouble finding time to get your hair cut or styled? Never (1); Occasionally (10); Almost always (12).

34 2. Your everyday life is filled mostly by: problems needing solution? (34); challenges needing to be met? (37); a rather predictable routine of events? (3); not enough time to keep you interested or busy? (13).

1 3. How often do you actually "put words in a person's mouth" in order to speed things up? Frequently (9); Occasionally (10); Almost never (1).

3 4. If you tell your spouse or a friend that you will meet somewhere at a definite time, how often do you arrive late? Once in a while (18); Rarely (18); Never late (3).

10 5. When you have to wait in line at the post office, a restaurant, or a store, what do you do? Accept it calmly (2); Feel impatient but not show it (10); Feel so impatient that someone can tell you are restless (12); Refuse to wait in line, and find ways to avoid such delays (12).

6. *(handwritten: 6)* How do you feel about competition on the job or in outside activities? Prefer to avoid it (1); Accept it because it's a necessary evil (6); Enjoy it because it's stimulating (13).

7. *(handwritten: 5)* How was your temper when you were younger? Fiery and hard to control? (5): Strong but controllable (26); No problem (26); I almost never got angry (32).

8. *(handwritten: 11)* Would people you know well agree that you tend to get irritated easily? Definitely yes (4); Probably yes (11); Probably no (21); Definitely no (11).

9. *(handwritten: N)* Would people you know well agree that you have less energy than most people? Definitely yes (4); Probably yes (16); Probably no (11); Definitely no (13).

10. *(handwritten: 19)* Would people you know well agree that you enjoy a "contest" (competition) and try hard to win? Definitely yes (16); Probably no (10); Definitely no (1).

11. *(handwritten: 3)* When you are in a group, how often do other people look to you for leadership? Rarely (0); About as often as they look to others (3); More often than they look to others (5).

12. *(handwritten: 36)* How much schooling did you receive? High school graduate (11); Trade or business school (13); Some college (18); Graduated four-year college (36); Postgraduate work (38).

13. *(handwritten: 33)* When you were in school, were you an officer of any group, such as student council, glee club, 4-H club, sorority or fraternity, or captain of an athletic team? No (3); Yes, I held one such position (33); Yes, I held two or more such position (33).

14. *(handwritten: 9)* How often do your daily activities motivate you into working harder? Less often than most people's activities (1); About average (9); More often than most people's activities (17).

15. *(handwritten: 17)* Do you ever keep two jobs moving forward at the same time by shifting back and forth rapidly from one to the other? Never (2); Yes, but only in emergencies (17); Yes, regularly (36).

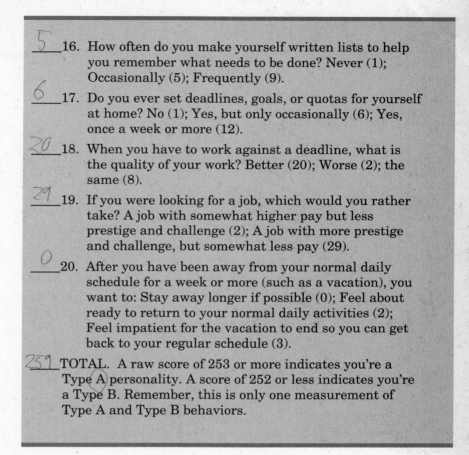

_5_ 16. How often do you make yourself written lists to help you remember what needs to be done? Never (1); Occasionally (5); Frequently (9).

_6_ 17. Do you ever set deadlines, goals, or quotas for yourself at home? No (1); Yes, but only occasionally (6); Yes, once a week or more (12).

_20_ 18. When you have to work against a deadline, what is the quality of your work? Better (20); Worse (2); the same (8).

_29_ 19. If you were looking for a job, which would you rather take? A job with somewhat higher pay but less prestige and challenge (2); A job with more prestige and challenge, but somewhat less pay (29).

_0_ 20. After you have been away from your normal daily schedule for a week or more (such as a vacation), you want to: Stay away longer if possible (0); Feel about ready to return to your normal daily activities (2); Feel impatient for the vacation to end so you can get back to your regular schedule (3).

_253_ TOTAL. A raw score of 253 or more indicates you're a Type A personality. A score of 252 or less indicates you're a Type B. Remember, this is only one measurement of Type A and Type B behaviors.

CHAPTER 14

The Challenges Facing Individuals in Organizations

Without Individuals,
Where Would We Be?

When you finish this chapter,
you should be able to:

1

Explain why a certain degree of conformity among
organizational members is desirable.

2

Describe the major classifications of conformity related to privacy, company
resources, off-the-job activities, workplace affairs, dress, and smoking.

3

Evaluate the three general areas in which many employers
believe that they have the "right to know."

4

Practice sound concepts for disciplining employees.

5

Summarize some typical challenges that individuals may
have with themselves in organizations.

6

Describe the nature and purpose of organizational politics.

> Essentially the social transaction of employment is a two-way
> street with mutual responsibilities between the individual
> and the organization.

Keith Davis, Professor of Organizational Behavior

> One person's innovation is another person's failure.

Richard Foster, Management Consultant

Individuals, we've already learned, are unique. Although there are similarities among all people, each individual has a distinctive personality and a set of values that was established long before joining a formal work organization. Although they may go along with current fads and trends, most individuals seem to enjoy, and even need, feelings of uniqueness. Few people want to be treated impersonally, as if they were just numbers or members of a faceless mass.

The successes of participative management help to substantiate the need individuals have for a feeling of personal contribution and involvement. Many persons want to believe that others value their individual opinions.

Does a person have to give up some individuality upon becoming a member of a work group? What happens when the individual's philosophy and needs seem not to meld with those of the organization? To what extent do employees have the right to privacy? How should discipline be applied when a person's behavior deviates from accepted organizational standards? What are some of the typical challenges faced by individuals whose personal aspirations exceed their capabilities? What can an individual do when promoted to a position the demands of which exceed his or her present skill level? Should errors ever be admitted or are they better covered up? Does an individual member of an organization have to be "political" to achieve personal goals? What are some of the typical "political" activities that take place in organizations?

The answers to these important questions, which can help you understand some of the critical issues and challenges facing the individual in organizations, will be discussed in this chapter. This chapter, along with the previous one, provides you with information that can assist your own adjustment to organizational—as well as personal—life.

TO BE OR NOT TO BE? THE QUESTION OF CONFORMITY

Is there room for nonconformity in organizations? Many organizational members are intensely individualistic, yet they continue to be cooperative and capable members of their work groups. Other employees find it difficult to conform to the standards of their organizations and seem to be miserable in their jobs.

Is conformity necessary for organizational members? If it is, then to what degree does an organization have the right to expect—or even require—you to conform? For example, as an organizational member, should you be told what to think, what to wear, and what to do? Or should you have the right to do whatever you believe is right whenever you want? Let's now explore the problem of conformity versus individualism in organizations.

Problems of Individualism

One of the difficulties besetting individuals—whether managers or nonmanagers—is that of reconciling the desire for *being one's self* with the necessity of *being an effective team member* of an organization. As with individuals, organizations develop philosophies and values. Do you remember an earlier chapter where you learned about *organizational culture?* Organizational members are generally expected to match their own personal cultures with the culture of their employer and subscribe to philosophies of the organizations for which they work. Robert N. Hilkert, a banker, once expressed an attitude that still commonly prevails in organizations:

Can I be me or must I be he?

> Our decisions are contained within the framework of our philosophy. By "our philosophy" I mean that of the institution we serve and that which is our own, *provided that our personal philosophy does not for long conflict with that of the institution which we serve.* If we cannot live with the philosophy of our employer, and if we cannot bring our employer around to ours, then our days in that organization are numbered. We must decide whether to leave before we are requested to do so.[1]

At first glance, Mr. Hilkert's philosophy may seem somewhat crass. However, regardless of your personal reaction to his words, it's important for you to remember that organizations have unique personalities and values. Some organizations follow the general practice of aggressively introducing new products and establishing new programs. Others take a "wait-and-see" approach, preferring to let competitors "stick their necks out." Some firms are highly structured and expect rules to be followed to the letter. Others are relatively informal, allowing considerable variation in practices and procedures. There is no single type of organization that serves as the model for all others.

Because organizations differ, before accepting a position with a particular organization you should attempt to "know thyself" *and* "thy organization." Do you know what sort of personality exists in the organization you are considering for a career position? Are your expectations toward the organization realistic? If not, you may soon discover that philosophically the relationship is incompatible.

Is Conformity a Sellout?

How do you personally feel about **conformity?** Do you feel that conforming to an organization's standards is akin to "selling out"? Most of us probably desire to retain our individuality. Yet the word *conformity* might have connotations that are somewhat harsher than reality. Don't we voluntarily *conform* to many things each day out of need and our own interest in survival? For example, not conforming to the directive of a one-way sign on a road could result in the loss of your life. Not conforming to no-smoking rules near combustible or explosive materials could do the same. Perhaps conforming to organizational standards is also related in certain ways to our survival.

What choices do you have?

Of course, the likelihood that you'll be willing to conform and approve of everything about a particular organization is slight. What are your alternatives when your values differ from those of the organization? In the extreme, you could *quit,* but that's not always a practicable solution. You might also try to *change* the organization's standards, but you may discover that some standards in organizations change slowly and that your efforts are largely unappreciated. You can also continue to work with the organization and *maintain a negative attitude* that makes your organizational life miserable.

Is being a rebel always worth it?

A more useful approach than either quitting or being perpetually negative might be to ask yourself some important questions: In general, do I like my job? Does it ordinarily satisfy my basic needs as well as my ego needs? Do my desired opportunities for advancement exist in this organization? Will I necessarily find a better job elsewhere? If you feel that, in general, the advantages of your job outweigh the disadvantages, perhaps you should attempt to *adjust your standards* to those of the organization.

Types of Conformity

Areas of conformity can be classified in a variety of ways. For example, conformity can be categorized as either **legitimate** or **nonlegitimate.** It can concern either *thoughts* or *behavior* and can involve either *on-the-job* or *off-the-job* situations. Each of these sets of factors relates to the other.

Most of us are willing to conform in areas that to us seem *legitimate.* For example, we probably would agree that we should conform to the practice of honesty—that it would be wrong for us to "dip into the till" and steal our employer's money. On the other hand, we would probably disagree with a company practice that "forced" us to vote for a particular candidate or to attend a particular church.

Oliver North appeared to face the dilemma of legitimate versus nonlegitimate issues in the notorious "Iran-*Contra*gate" scandals of the late 1980s in which he was accused of indirectly diverting government and private funds illegally to aid the *Contras* in their efforts to overthrow the Sandinista government of Nicaragua. Of course, not everyone agreed whether his "merely following orders" of superiors was legitimate or should be considered a criminal act because of their illegal outcome. Marine Lieutenant Colonel North was perceived as a hero by some members of the general public (legitimate conformity) and as a criminal (nonlegitimate conformity) by others. Thirty-two percent of the polled public believed that North should go to jail for his actions, and 53 percent felt that he shouldn't. As a result of his trial, he theoretically could have been imprisoned for up to ten years and fined $750,000 for his actions.[2]

What, then, makes conformity standards on and off the job *legitimate* or *nonlegitimate?* Frequently, their legitimacy is gauged by how job related the standards of conformity are. For example, arriving to work on time is a fairly clear-cut job-related standard of legitimate conformity. Not punching your boss, Judith, in the nose when she turns down your request for a raise is another. Many other routine types of activities are also typically accepted as necessary for the organization to function effectively.

Punchin' Judy not allowed!

The legitimacy of some areas, however, is far less clear, especially when they involve the personal values of an employee. Let's now examine five of these areas separately: the *use or misuse of company resources, off-the-job activities, workplace affairs, standards of appearance,* and *smoking.*

Can I Do What I Want With Company Resources?

You probably recall from Chapter 2 that not everyone perceives situations in the same fashion. Some employees, for example, will "borrow" company equipment or supplies, such as pencils, pens, and paper, for use at home. Others misuse company computers by infringing on copyrights through the copying of proprietary software for personal use.

"But that's different!"

Do you perceive these actions as legitimate? Would you approve of such actions if you were the owner of a company whose employees used your firm's materials for their personal gain? Not very likely. Yet some employees have rationalized their behavior by saying that the items they "borrow" are insignificant and that the company will never miss them. Others may assert: "I've worked here for a long time; the company owes it to me. Besides, the company can afford it better than I can." Such rationalizations, however, fail to make the activities legitimate.

Because of excessive occurrences of employee theft of company information, some organizations, such as IBM and Xerox, have established policies related to computer use by employees. The firms have also attempted to restrict employee access to certain types of information.

Formal policies, it is believed, tend to discourage employees from using company property, such as computers, for personal purposes like creating betting pools or preparing resumés for themselves and friends.

United Airlines discovered that some employees used the computer system to overbook seats under phony names to provide available seats for themselves under a travel-free, space-available program the company offers to employees. In an effort to reduce the incidence of such abuses, United now requires new employees to sign forms saying they have read the company's computer policy.

Some companies have purchased expensive monitoring systems that enable them to know which employees are misusing computers and telephones. Unfortunately, such activities smack of "Big Brotherism" to some observers who feel it is an invasion of employees' privacy, a topic to be discussed in a later section. Nonetheless, courts have usually ruled in favor of employers, since the employee's activities involved the misuse of company property. However, Alan Westin, a professor at Columbia University, is opposed to strong controls in these areas, stating that: "A company that treats people like prisoners subject to strip searches won't get excellence." IBM and Xerox, apparently concerned with the privacy issue, attempt to give employees advance notice of a computer audit.[3]

What I Do on My Own Time Is WHOSE Business?

Employees in some fields must regularly be "on call"; that is, they may not be required to be physically present at the workplace, but they must be available when needed. Medical doctors, for example, make arrangements to be on call periodically—such as every third weekend—so that medical attention can be provided to the patient whose own doctor is unavailable. Customer service representatives with some manufacturing companies, such as a manufacturer of computer mainframes, are on call periodically to ensure that assistance will be available if a customer's computer malfunctions.

Let's assume that your job responsibilities require you to be on call occasionally. Let's also assume that one evening when you are on call, you and your spouse are entertaining friends at your home. It should be fairly apparent that during your on-call period you really aren't free to do anything you might desire. For example, if your beeper warns you to call your company and you're told that you have to make a quick trip to the office of an important customer, you certainly wouldn't enhance your company's image by arriving at the customer's site intoxicated.

But what if your position doesn't require you to be on call? Are you then free to do whatever you want on your own time? Although the line between what you can and can't do off the job isn't always clear-cut, most managers would contend that you shouldn't engage in

Can you expect to do whatever you want?

behavior away from the job that would be damaging to the organization that pays your salary. Assume, for example, that you work for the pharmaceutical firm, Sterling Drug Company. Is it likely that your boss would approve of your entering a wet t-shirt contest, attended by *Penthouse* magazine photographers, while wearing a shirt with the slogan "Sterling Drug Company managers are *crack* performers!" emblazoned across its front? Probably not, although some managers might not object—and might even consider it good publicity. It's important for you, therefore, to know the boundaries of behavior that are acceptable to your particular employer, recognizing, of course, that not all companies adhere to the same standards of acceptability and unacceptability.

Let's take one more example. Assume that you are an office systems salesperson who calls principally on major accounts in a particular territory. You've worked in the same territory for five years, and you've discovered that you can meet your sales quota without having to work full-time. Although you could probably expand your sales volume by putting in a full day's work, you've decided to use your "spare time" to operate your own business on the side. You've heard that many doctors have tropical fish tanks in their waiting rooms to "entertain" their waiting patients. So you've decided to start your own business and to spend two hours of each working day calling on doctors' offices to promote your line of tropical fish and aquarium supplies. You are meeting the sales quota agreed upon with your primary employer. Therefore, is it legitimate for you to carry on a business on the side? Most sales managers would contend that such behavior is outside the boundaries of legitimacy. They would be more likely to believe that your full allegiance during a normal working day must be to your primary employer.

"But boss . . . Don't you believe in free enterprise?"

What's Wrong With Workplace Affairs?

Nobody should tell you whom you can date, *right?* The answer *right* to that question would certainly appear to be logical. Unfortunately, however, **workplace affairs**—*the dating or romancing between two adults employed in the same work situation*—can create challenges for supervisors attempting to maintain productivity standards and morale.

"It's nobody's affair but my own!"

In general, two types of affairs can exist in the workplace, each of which may have adverse effects on productivity and morale. One type of workplace affair occurs when either one or both persons is married to someone else. The two individuals discover a mutual attraction and begin dating. The second type exists when two unmarried individuals working in the same department share common interests and begin dating.

So—how about it? Should the supervisor put an emphatic stop to such departmental liaisons? Professors Mondy and Premeaux of McNeese State University contend that workplace romances are a personal matter and that a supervisor *does not have the right* to bring

Don't Go There With an "Attitude"![a]

So your company is going to assign you to one of its branches in Saudi Arabia. Sounds like an exciting adventure, doesn't it? However, you might find a few challenges and frustrations along the way, especially since you are probably used to a completely different culture.

Here are a few tips: First of all, don't plan to transact any business at government offices on Thursdays and Fridays—those are official holidays. Private businesses, however, typically work from Saturday to Thursday.

Working hours will also take some getting used to. Government offices are typically open from 7:00 A.M.. to 2:30 P.M. Businesses normally are open from 8:00 A.M. to 7:00 or 8:00 P.M., with a long break in the afternoon. Business also ceases during prayer times, which are published in local papers.

If you are a woman, you can forget about driving a car. Only men are allowed to drive. And men, don't get into an auto accident. Accidents are not easily resolved, and the police can detain all parties involved until an amicable settlement has been reached. And another thing, ladies: Take care to dress in public in accordance with Saudi ideas of modesty. Dresses should be at least calf-length, fastened to the neck, and loose fitting, with elbow-length sleeves. A headscarf and an *abiyah* cloak are advisable during Ramadan and Haji. Also remember that women are advised not to take a taxi on their own.

How about that little "nightcap" you're accustomed to? Well, you might want to consider going on the wagon, because the Saudi government prohibits the manufacture and drinking of alcohol. Offenders can be severely penalized.

Shaking hands is the custom on meeting and departure. Food and drink should be taken with the right hand only. And no pictures, please, in public. These are merely a few of the individual challenges to expect on your assignment to Saudi Arabia.

the workers' behavior in line with the supervisor's own personal beliefs. However, Mondy and Premeaux believe that the supervisor *does have an obligation* to become involved when workplace affairs cause productivity to decline or morale of other employees to suffer.[4]

How can such workplace entanglements affect productivity? One way may occur when the lovers spend an inordinate amount of work time concentrating on each other rather than on their job responsibilities. Further, co-workers who observe the "lovebirds" consuming company time planning their upcoming weekend together at Lake Tahoe may become upset at having to carry their workload.

Another potential problem exists when one or the other is married and a spouse discovers the romantic link, as frequently happens. Many disgruntled mates have been known to create havoc on the work scene either by perpetually telephoning the department or by furiously bursting onto the work site in person.

Supervisors whose departments experience workplace affairs should remember that their major concern should be with job performance, not personal lives. Prior to any interviews with the participants, the supervisor should carefully document any adverse effects the romance has had on behavior. If performance or morale have deteriorated, the supervisor should hold separate interviews with each party and concentrate on performance, not the affair. The supervisor should stress that the affair is the business of the participants, but that productivity and morale are the responsibility of everyone in the department. The participants should be given ample time to clear up productivity problems on their own. Previously announced disciplinary action may have to be taken if improvement is not forthcoming.

Performance counts!

Can't I Wear What I Like?

To what extent should we have to conform to an organization's standards of appearance? Shouldn't we be "free" to dress and look however we want as long as we're carrying out our job responsibilities? After all, it has long been suggested that a book should never be judged by its cover, so why should human beings be judged by their clothing?

"Don't judge me by my cellophane necktie."

Progressive thinkers might believe that their personal appearance should be nobody's business but their own. Ideally, perhaps they're right. Unfortunately, however, what *should be* and what *is* are often two different things in the real world. Research conducted by Robert Half, a financial recruitment agency, revealed that 55 percent of the impact a person makes on others is based on appearance.[5] Some companies, such as IBM and SAFECO Insurance Company, have fairly stringent employee dress codes that emphasize a "neutral look," one that tends not to detract from any message employees may present to members of the public.

"Imprisoned by my quest for freedom?"

Some employees, in their intense desire to be free, actually tend to imprison themselves by conforming to what may be their own unrealistic standards. The desire for freedom or nonconformity can become so much of a fetish that it actually prevents some persons from opening doors of opportunity that might otherwise be there for them.

Of course, there are no hard and fast rules for dress that can apply to every situation. What might be an acceptable standard of dress in Manhattan's financial district might seem bizarre in the small town of Twin Forks, Montana. Some organizations, for example, prefer that their employees—especially those who contact customers—conform to a relatively conservative image. Others are fairly loose in their standards of dress. Certain standards tend to persist over time, such as dressing in a low-key manner that tends not to draw undue attention to your appearance. However, each organization has its own expectations about what constitutes sound standards.

But There ARE Individual Differences

There are some organizational hazards associated with assuming that everyone's behavior and values in an organization should conform to a predetermined and precise set of standards. Creative ideas, for example, can be squelched by an excessively homogeneous atmosphere. Furthermore, not all employees share the same types of self-image and aspirations.

For example, managers are sometimes guilty of unrealistic role expectations toward certain employees. Some managers may be surprised when an employee refuses an offer to be promoted to a supervisory position. But does everyone necessarily want to become a manager?

To illustrate, let's look at a person whom we'll call Jim. He has worked for fourteen years, let's assume, in a branch office of a large bank. He knows the technical aspects of his job better than most of the other employees and has a personal style with the public that enhances the bank's image. Each time promotional opportunities have arisen, however, Jim has turned them down. Some of his fellow workers have difficulty understanding Jim's attitude. Think back, however, to the motivational concepts discussed in Chapter 5. Each individual, as you may recollect, has different needs. Only Jim himself really knows why he doesn't want a promotion. Perhaps he is confident in his present position and believes he would lose some of his feelings of security if he became a manager.

Not everyone wants to lead.

Regardless of Jim's personal motives, if he is carrying out his job responsibilities satisfactorily, is there any particular reason for not permitting him to remain in his present position? Some companies even give special recognition to individual contributors, such as Jim, as a means of helping to satisfy some of their ego needs.

Can't We Have a Smoke-Free Environment?

In a "free society," shouldn't those who want to smoke have the right to do so? Although *freedom* is a revered concept in the United States,

"Do you smoke?"
"Only passively!"

unfortunately *passive smoking*—breathing cigarette smoke wafting through the air—tends to restrict the freedom of nonsmokers. It also tends to have an adverse effect on the health of both smokers and nonsmokers alike.[6]

For example, smoking leads to about 400,000 U.S. deaths a year. An Environmental Protection Agency (EPA) study involving lung-capacity tests on 2100 people examined over a ten-year period indicated that the effects of long-term exposure to *environmental tobacco smoke,* or *ETS,* on the lungs of nonsmokers were about the same as the effects of smoking one to ten cigarettes a day. The EPA also emphasized that "substantial evidence shows nonsmokers are at risk of cancer from secondary tobacco smoke. Roughly 3000 additional lung cancer cases can be attributed to secondary smoke annually." As if those statistics weren't scary enough, the American Heart Association (AHA) declared that passive tobacco smoke is a major risk factor for heart disease. AHA studies report that exposure to secondhand smoke raises the risk of dying from heart disease 30 percent and causes more than 50,000 deaths a year. The AHA has found that environmental tobacco smoke is one of the leading sources of indoor pollution.[7]

Studies by the EPA indicate that secondhand smoke is also extremely hazardous to children. EPA researchers said, "Exposure to secondhand tobacco smoke accounts for thousands of serious respiratory ailments, such as pneumonia, bronchitis and emphysema, in young children, especially infants."[8]

With smoking being the leading preventable cause of death and disease in the United States, it should not come as a surprise that an increasing number of firms have adopted smoking policies in recent years. For example, Pacific Northwest Bell Telephone Company put its 15,000 employees on notice that after three months, smoking would no longer be permitted at work. Some managers feared protest,

SOURCE: Reprinted by permission of UFS, Inc. & NEA, Inc.

lawsuits, and even resignations. None of that occurred. Within six months, 350 of the company's 4000 smokers even stopped smoking altogether, and most of the others cut down considerably. More and more companies have adopted the policy that employees do not have the right to "pollute" the workplace with smoke. Firms that have tightened their policies include Heinz USA, Texas Instruments, Boeing, and Du Pont. Some firms have even considered lowering medical insurance deductibles for nonsmokers as an incentive.[9]

Loss of pollution rights!

Motivation for employers to ban smoking on the job has frequently come from the employees themselves. Any organizations contemplating the elimination of smoking from the workplace are likely to enjoy greater success if they consult with their employees rather than just confiscate all ashtrays one Monday morning. According to a survey by a British employment research group, most organizations go through the following stages on the way to banning or restricting smoking.[10]

What is a logical "banning" procedure?

Consulting the Work Force. An essential first step in preventing an employee backlash, or a mutiny, by those addicted to smoking is to utilize surveys, ballots, questionnaires, meetings, and negotiations with employee unions or associations. The results are often surprisingly favorable, even from smokers.

Determining the Degree of Restriction. A complete ban throughout an organization is likely to create some difficult withdrawal problems for those addicted to smoking. The British-based newspaper *Financial Times* has overcome this problem by providing smoking employees with "sin bins," specially designated, well-ventilated areas on each floor where employees can continue to practice their habit.

Phasing in of Policies. Anti-smoking programs tend to be accepted more readily when they are gradually introduced, or at least when an ample period of warning, say, twelve weeks is provided, before implementation. A gradual transition tends to reduce the likelihood of employee resentment or legal entanglements. One organization, for example, phased in its program over a four-month period. Smoking was first prohibited before 10:30 A.M., then before noon, 2:00 P.M., 4:30 P.M., and finally throughout the entire day.

Helping Employees to Stop Smoking. Some companies provide assistance for employees who would like to stop smoking, such as time off for "stop smoking" classes. IBM, for example, has even offered acupuncture and hypnotherapy, as well as counseling and classes.

In much of the world, smokers still don't take kindly to employers that encroach on their alleged rights to smoke at the workplace. However, in the United States, where a much smaller proportion of adults continue to smoke, many organizations now have little choice as to whether they should implement a nonsmoking policy. As of 1992, forty-four states and the District of Columbia limited smoking in public workplaces, and fifteen states banned smoking in private workplaces. There was no smoking even at the Republican convention during the summer of 1992, since Houston banned smoking at the Astrodome.[11]

What if an employee rebels and refuses to comply with an organization's no-smoking policy? Of course, the same practices related to employee discipline discussed in other sections of the text should be applied.

No moralist can—or should—attempt to shame a person into breaking the smoking habit; an individual must be both willing and able to break it on his or her own. Organized groups have been formed in some cities to aid persons who sincerely want to begin tasting food and breathing fresh air again. One such organization, the Kaiser Permanente Health Center in Oakland, California, regularly conducts Stop Smoking classes. Included in the advice and assistance offered to class members are the ten tips listed in Table 14.1. If you seriously desire or intend to quit smoking, you ought to take a thoughtful look at the suggestions. If you've never smoked, you might think long and hard before you start. It is much more difficult to stop than start smoking. Mark Twain, tongue in cheek, once said, "To quit smoking is the easiest thing I've ever done. I ought to know; I've done it thousands of times."

What can you do to stop smoking?

TABLE 14.1   Guidelines for Stopping Smoking.

- Don't stock up. Never buy by the carton; wait until one pack is finished before buying another.
- Change brands with each pack for a week or two before quitting.
- Always ask yourself: "Do I *really* want this cigarette?"
- Each day try to put off lighting your first cigarette.
- Only smoke half of each cigarette.
- Be *aware* of your smoking. Ask yourself: "Why do I need to smoke right now?"; "What is this cigarette doing for me?"; "What would I do if I didn't smoke this cigarette?"
- Don't smoke while involved in another activity, that is, while you are on the phone, reading, watching TV, or talking. Concentrate on the cigarette.
- Look forward to the time you will be quitting and able to think of yourself as a nonsmoker.
- Tell people around you that you're going to quit smoking.
- If you have physical symptoms that might be related to your smoking, relieve your mind by discussing them with your doctor. It is easier to quit when you know your health status.

DO EMPLOYEES HAVE THE RIGHT TO PRIVACY?

A question of right versus right!

To what extent does the individual in an organization have the right to privacy? Opinions differ, since what an employee may perceive as an "invasion of the right of privacy" may be believed by an employer to be merely the "right to know." The United States Constitution protects citizens from intrusion by the government, but it says nothing about employment situations. A growing concern related to personal rights has developed as a result of employers' expanding their activities in the area of what they feel they have the right to know about employees.

What Do Employers Want to Know?

The Human Resource Management Association surveyed its members and asked what activities they believed their companies had the right to engage in to uncover necessary information about employees. The three general activities most reported were:[12]

1. Employee testing
2. Collection of information
3. Surveillance

The *A Question of Ethics* box, "The Boss is Watching!" summarizes some of the principal findings of the report. The section that follows briefly examines each of these three major activities.

Testing Employees

We've already discussed in Chapter 12 the use of such devices as urinalysis and saliva testing for the detection of drug and alcohol use. There are other areas of controversy related to testing and the privacy issue, and these areas are discussed next

Lie Detector Tests. An area of concern related to the privacy issue has been whether an employer should have the legitimate right to require individuals to take a **polygraph,** or **lie detector, test** as a condition of employment. Because of their widespread abuse and questionable reliability, pressure against polygraph tests began to build during the latter 1980s. As a result, legislation was passed to make illegal the use of polygraphs by private-sector companies as a tool for employee screening or dismissals. The bill, called the **Employee Polygraph Protection Act of 1988,** has certain exceptions. Employers can ask an employee to submit to a polygraph test only when they reasonably suspect that the employee was involved in a workplace theft or other incident causing economic loss to the employer.

?

A QUESTION
OF
ETHICS

The Boss Is Watching![b]

Sheribel F. Rothenberg, a Chicago lawyer who specializes in employment matters for both employees and employers, believes that increased instances of invasion of workers' privacy are a "sign of the times." Rothenberg says, "Rights of privacy are being eroded across the board." He adds, "I think it's open season for employers."

Although not everyone would agree with Mr. Rothenberg's negative tone, a recent study by the Human Resource Management Association seems to assert that its member employers are increasingly exercising their "right to know" about applicants for positions and existing employees. Here are some of the findings of the study:

- *Employee testing:* Drug tests are deemed necessary by 91.8 percent of the respondents; alcohol tests, 88.1 percent; medical tests, 80 percent; psychological tests, 57.4 percent; AIDS tests, 37.7 percent; and pregnancy tests, 8.1 percent.
- *Collection of information:* 87.9 percent said criminal records must be checked; 53.8 percent would check previous substance abuse; 44.7 percent back credit-rating checks; 34.2 percent would check on drug and alcohol use outside of work; and 32.6 percent would check psychiatric history.
- *Surveillance:* 57 percent approve of monitoring VDT keystroke rates; 49.2 percent would record employees' phone calls; 45 percent think it's permissible to search employees' offices, desks, or lockers; 38.7 percent approve of using secret video cameras to monitor employees; 18.8 percent think it's all right to open employees' mail; and 17.6 percent would listen to phone conversations.

A question of ethics: So, what's your opinion? Do you think employers should be permitted to use such devices as polygraphs, integrity tests, credit checks, spotters, and HIV examinations as tools in the employment process? Is such activity a legitimate way of ensuring that employees meet organizational standards and fit into the organization's culture, or, instead, are such techniques an invasion of employee privacy? What do *you* think?

The act also permits the use of lie detector tests on the following categories of workers: government employees; utility workers directly involved in the production and transmission of electrical power; many private security company employees; pharmaceutical workers handling controlled substances, such as prescription drugs that are addictive; and people working in child-care centers.

How do I know that the integrity test has integrity?

Integrity Tests. Now barred from using lie detector tests to screen employees, some firms have turned to various types of **integrity tests** as alternatives. One of these is a pencil-and-paper honesty test, which seeks to gauge integrity through multiple-choice questions on ethical dilemmas.[13] Questions that have appeared on pencil-and-paper tests include:

1. Do you always tell the truth?
2. What would you do if you observed your boss stealing company supplies?
3. Did you ever make a false insurance claim?
4. Have you ever gotten really angry at someone for being unfair to you?
5. Do you blush often?

A person who says "No, I never have" to number 4 is probably distorting the answers to other questions, according to users of such questions. Question 5 is said to be a type of question thrown in as a change of pace.[14]

Graphology Testing. Some employers have turned to the use of **graphology,** which involves the analysis of handwriting. Supporters of graphology testing contend that it can be used as a means of character testing. Of course, as with any employment tests, employers may be required to prove that graphology tests are valid and job related. As an interesting aside, a professor was once told by a colleague that writing downhill on the chalkboard was an indication of a lack of confidence. From that point on the professor made certain that his chalkboard writing always went upwards in a confidence-building direction!

I'm the uphill champion!

HIV Testing. Another area of controversy related to the right of privacy is **HIV testing,** that is, examining employees for HIV, the AIDS virus. Testing specifically for HIV by private companies is not yet common, although detection may occur during a physical examination. The U.S. Army screens recruits and rejects those who are HIV-positive, and it retests all servicemen and -women about every eighteen months.[15]

Ericsson, the Swedish electrical multinational, tests managers who must travel to other countries where the HIV risk is great because HIV infection impairs resistance to other diseases. In the United Kingdom, companies such as Unilever test managers recruited in high-risk areas on the grounds that they may travel to countries that require a negative HIV test before a work permit is granted.[16]

A fear expressed by some authorities related to HIV testing concerns the stigmatization and ostracism that often follow revelation of HIV-positive status. Likewise, HIV tests do not guarantee that applicants are or will remain HIV free, since the most commonly used tests detect only antibodies, and these may take months or longer to appear after a person becomes infected.

Collection of Information

A wide variety of information may be desired by employers, ranging from criminal records to psychiatric history. An increasingly prevalent method of looking into the private lives of present employees or applicants for jobs is a technique that employees may never even know is being used—**credit checks.** As an alternative to the use of polygraph tests, many employers today routinely run credit checks on applicants for employment, contending that they are a good measurement of a person's integrity. Employers who use credit records argue that the way an applicant handles bills, loans and other financial obligations helps predict whether he or she is likely to steal, sell company secrets, or otherwise act irresponsibly on the job.

Does having no *credit mean you're honest?*

Nordstroms Incorporated, a department store chain, runs credit checks on finalists for "sensitive" jobs in its security, financial and credit departments. Abbott Laboratories, a Chicago-based maker of medical supplies, evaluates credit reports as "part of the routine reference-checking on everybody," according to Ellen Walvoord, director of corporate communications. She adds, "If a person had serious financial problems as revealed in their credit report, it could affect their suitability for certain positions."[17]

Surveillance of Employees

Almost 60 percent of the company representatives polled in the Human Resources Management Association survey cited earlier approve of some types of surveillance of employees, even including searching employees' offices, desks or lockers. Some of the methods of surveillance are fairly sophisticated, as can be seen by the discussion that follows.

Workplace Monitoring. According to information revealed during a Senate Labor and Human Resources Committee employment and productivity subcommittee hearing, about ten million American workers are affected by **workplace monitoring;** that is, they are monitored by covert electronic surveillance devices at job sites across the United States, often without their knowledge or permission. The Communications Workers Union president, Morton Bahr, contends that employer snooping violates workers' privacy rights. Bahr also states that studies have shown such monitoring adversely affects workers' health by increasing the incidence of stress-induced ailments.[18] Reacting to pressure from the Communications Workers union, Northern Telecom became the first major corporation in the U.S. to prohibit secret voice, computer, and video monitoring. The union has also been lobbying Congress to pass legislation banning secret monitoring and requiring warnings of covert surveillance to employees and the public.[19]

*But, boss . . .
I'll break out in a rash.*

Spies. Some employers have resorted to hiring spotters who spy on employees as a means of checking on employee integrity. Employers say monitoring enables them to better train employees, measure productivity, and ensure that proper procedures are followed. Three Chicago hotels—the Palmer House, the O'Hare Hilton, and the Westin—formerly hired spotters who acted as employees but spied on workers for drug use, theft, and other rules- or law-breaking acts. The hotels have since ceased the practice because of pressure from the union.[20]

*"Spots before
my eyes!"*

Access to Personnel Records

Should employees have the right to see their own personnel records? An increasing number of organizations now permit their employees to have access to the files. Do employees also have the right to feel that limitations should be placed on the access that third parties have to such records? The trend appears to be in the direction of greater rights of privacy regarding third-party access to information in employee records.

Set the record straight!

Some states have passed legislation giving employees the right to see their personnel files, and some—such as Connecticut—also restrict release of the contents of these files to outsiders. Apparently goaded by the Business Roundtable and the Department of Commerce, many firms have adopted formal privacy policies on their own. A sample policy formulated by Chase Manhattan is presented in Table 14.2.

THE CHALLENGE OF DISCIPLINING EMPLOYEES

An activity that affects individuals and their behavior in organizations is disciplinary action. Traditionally, **discipline** has been considered a negative activity aimed at punishing employees who fail to meet organizational standards. Although in some cases punitive

TABLE 14.2   Privacy Policy of Chase Manhattan Bank.

Employees	Customers
May see any "individually identifiable" information in their personnel files except for that about future planning	Will be the primary source of any information collected about them
Will have sensitive information—such as medical files—kept separate from personnel files	Will be told what outside sources are tapped for data
Must give prior O.K. for release of any data to outsiders except to confirm employment dates	Will not have their names and addresses sold to outsiders
Will be told the reason for any information collected about them	Can block disclosure of information to outsiders unless in response to a subpoena or credit inquiry
Will have nothing in their files irrelevant to "job-related decisions"	Will be told of subpoenas for personal information before it is turned over, unless a court prohibits it
Will have any customer relationship with the bank kept separate from the employee relationship	Will have all discussions of their banking relationship confined to bank employees "directly concerned"
Are assured that files are open only to Chase personnel with a "need to know"	Will have the opportunity to verify all information and correct inaccuracies

Courtesy: Chase Manhattan

actions may be unavoidable, a more modern managerial philosophy looks at discipline as a constructive opportunity *to correct* rather than *to punish* a person's behavior.

The Nature of Discipline

The word *discipline* stems from Latin and means *teaching* or *learning*. Since most employees don't intentionally deviate from a manager's standards, perhaps they need the "Latin" approach of attempting to modify, improve, or correct employee behavior. After all, isn't your concern as a manager to return the situation to normal as rapidly as possible? Managers who attack the employee rather than the situation generally find that their troubles intensify.

Attack the problem— not the person!

Being "Progressive"

Today, many managers employ a form of **progressive discipline,** an approach that follows the philosophy that the severity of disciplinary measures requiring some degree of punishment should increase each time an employee must be disciplined. Typically, the first stage of progressive discipline is an *oral warning,* followed by a *written warning* for the next infraction. The third step may be a *disciplinary layoff.* The ultimate in discipline—the last step—is *discharge,* which should only be considered after all reasonable efforts at correcting the employee's

A progressive approach.

behavior have failed. Some authorities contend that discharge should *not* be considered a part of the disciplinary process but is actually the result of *the failure to have disciplined in an effective manner.*

Can You Document It?

Write it down!

Once again, the importance of full **documentation** related to any disciplinary measures can't be overstressed as a means of protecting you—a manager—and your company against false charges by a disgruntled employee. Also important is that disciplinary measures be applied in a consistent fashion throughout every department of an organization to avoid employees' charges of discrimination or unfair treatment. Remember to document even positive accomplishments of employees. Documentation of both positive and negative employee performance assists you in preparing formal performance reviews. Trying to maintain an incident file in your mind, especially considering all the other information vying for brain space, is indeed a difficult task.

Do It in Private

In an earlier chapter we learned about the need that people have for self-esteem. The manner in which you as a manager discipline an employee will significantly influence how well this need is satisfied.

"Jones, I wonder if I could see you in the closet for a moment."

Have you ever been "chewed out" by your boss in front of your co-workers? If so, how did it feel? Such experiences can seriously damage a person's feeling of self-worth. The embarrassment of being disciplined in front of peers can act as a demotivating force on an employee. A general guideline, therefore, is to try to obtain a physical setting for discussing problems with employees that will result in a positive, rather than negative, outcome.

Just Like a Red-Hot Stove!

"Boss, I'd really prefer a microwave oven if you don't mind."

In these modern times when microwave ovens are so common, there may be some individuals who aren't familiar with "stoves." Nonetheless, as a further means of reducing troubles associated with disciplinary action, it is sometimes recommended that managers employ what has been termed the **red-hot stove rule,** a concept that equates disciplinary action with touching a hot stove. Think of what happens when a person touches a red-hot stove. The person near the the object receives *ample warning* (the redness of the stove). The discipline is *immediate* (the person receives immediate feedback!). The discipline is *consistent* (everyone who touches it is treated equally—they get burned!). The discipline is *unemotional* (a stove doesn't lose its temper). And finally, the discipline is *impersonal* (the severity of the discipline depends on how much or how long the person touched the stove, not on the personality or characteristics of the person who touched it).

Situational Discipline Should Be Applied

Of course, managers should be consistent and treat everyone equitably when administering disciplinary action. However, there are some circumstances in which the nicely laid out four steps of the progressive disciplinary model might not apply. For example, numerous fire departments have strict rules related to reporting to work drunk. If a firefighter abuses the rule, the disciplinary act is one of immediate dismissal. This type of discipline, therefore, tends to take the form of a *penalty*. It does have the effect of discouraging firefighters from being intoxicated during working hours. In general, the major factors that should be considered in determining the disciplinary action needed are:

What influences disciplinary action?

- Seriousness of the offense.
- Past record of the employee.
- Elapsed time since the last offense.
- Circumstances surrounding the particular case.
- Company practice in similar past cases.

Enforcing Rules

Disciplinary measures, whether corrective or punitive, are usually taken as a result of nonstandard performance; that is, an employee has failed to meet planned organizational objectives. Is it really fair to discipline a person who has not been given the opportunity to learn an organization's standards?

Managers are expected to enforce **rules,** which can be defined as *statements of precisely what activity or conduct is or is not to be engaged in.* An illustration of a rule is, "Coffee breaks are to be not in excess of fifteen minutes and are to begin at 10:15 A.M. and 2:15 P.M. daily."

Does it make sense?

Managers are likely to have trouble enforcing rules that don't make sense to employees. Rules should continually be reevaluated to ascertain whether they are applicable to changing organizational conditions. Employees tend to lose respect for rules that either seem illogical and out of date or are not enforced. Also, rules must be communicated to and understood by the employees. Rules should always be enforced equitably, promptly, and consistently or they will lose their effectiveness.

For example, assume that a firm has a company parking lot with special places nearer to the plant for senior executives of the organization. For the past six months, about ten operating employees have parked regularly in the reserved spaces, but nothing has ever been said to them by management. On one particularly dreary, rainy Monday morning, an executive arrived at the parking lot a bit late and couldn't find a parking space near the plant. He became enraged at the prospect of becoming soaked by the downpour. On discovering that two of the reserved spaces were occupied by workers' cars, he determined who they were and suspended them for two days without pay for the infraction of the rules.

The punished pair could become hostile for a number of reasons and might even submit a grievance to their union steward, if there is one. The rules hadn't been enforced previously so the workers had reason to believe that the rule, in effect, didn't exist. Also, the punished individuals were only two of about ten persons who had used the executive spaces during the past six months, yet the others weren't disciplined. Was it fair to enforce the rule without advance notice after it had been ignored for six months? Morale problems and labor unrest could develop from what might seem like an insignificant event.

The San Francisco Employers Council developed a useful checklist of questions for supervisors to ask themselves before taking disciplinary action against employees for infractions of rules (see Table 14.3).

"Dehiring" Employees

News item: Lockland, Ohio. A disgruntled worker opened fire during a [name of company] disciplinary meeting, killing two employees and wounding another two. Police identified the assailant as [name], a three-year employee. The employee was being told of his dismissal, police said.

TABLE 14.3   Checklist to Review Before Taking Disciplinary Measures Against Employees.

- Have I found out all the facts before taking disciplinary action?
- Is the employee getting the same treatment others have received for the same offense?
- Is the rule that has been violated a reasonable one?
- Did the employer know the rule?
- Have the proper preliminary procedures been followed?
- In appropriate cases, has the employee been warned in writing and given lesser penalties, according to past practice or work rules? (This doesn't apply to major violations of which there is absolute proof.)
- Am I being fair and impartial? Or am I reacting against the employee because he or she has challenged my authority?
- What is the employee's past disciplinary record and length of service?
- Does the employee have a reasonable excuse for violating the rule?
- Can the employee's guilt be proven by direct objective evidence or only by circumstantial evidence?
- Does the company have a past record of strict rule enforcement? If not, were employees notified of management's intention to crack down on violations of this type?

Whew! Quite a heavy reaction to dismissal, wasn't it? Fortunately, not all discharges result in such extreme behavior. Nonetheless, firing employees is one of the most painful and difficult chores managers may ever have to face, one that taxes their organizational behavior skills to the utmost. So difficult is the firing of employees that many managers have eliminated the word *firing* from their vocabularies and in its place substituted less emotional words such as *termination, dehiring, separation, outplacement,* and even *disemployment.* But regardless of what they call it, managers must at times face the unpleasant task of firing employees. As can be seen from the *Box of Interest,* "The `Opportunity' to Quit!" the task of dealing with departing employees became increasingly common recent years.

Ready, aim, dehire!

Employees should be dismissed only as a last resort, after other reasonable efforts at correction or discipline, such as additional training, oral warnings, or suspensions, have failed. Some traditional managers feel that if a person has done something serious enough to warrant discipline, he or she should be fired immediately. A more constructive and modern attitude is that the *situation* or *employee's behavior* should be *corrected* rather than the *employee punished.*

Why is correction more desirable than punishment?

There are occasions, however, when employees must be dismissed, especially during economic recessions when organizational restructuring activities take place to cut costs. In such cases, some organizations have attempted to assist the discharged employees in obtaining employment elsewhere by inviting prospective employers to job fairs for the purpose of interviewing the employees. **Outplacement consultants** are sometimes used to assist discharged executives.

There is no simple way to fire employees, but there are some useful tips that can make dismissal somewhat easier on people:

1. *Come directly to the point.* Don't beat around the bush and be so tactful that the employee doesn't really understand your intentions.

2. *Timing is extremely important.* The bad news will probably be less disastrous if presented to the employee late in the working day. To save the employee unnecessary embarrassment, be certain that other employees do not overhear you. Related to the question of proper timing is the individual's personal situation. Can your decision be postponed in the event of a serious family illness? Can your decision be timed to avoid sentimental holidays, such as Christmas or the employee's birthday or personal anniversary?

3. *Let the employee know why* he or she is being dismissed. The dismissal may be necessitated by cost-cutting measures rather than the employee's own performance. By informing

The "Opportunity" to Quit![c]

"GM to eliminate 120,000 jobs during the decade." "Digital seeks 7,000 job cuts." "Giant merger of BankAmerica, Security Pacific to eliminate 10,000 to 12,000 jobs." "Boeing warns of 2438 more layoffs." "General Electric Company aircraft engine business to cut 2800 more jobs." "Computerized cash registers to cut 7000 jobs at Sears." "AT&T to plan further layoffs, close 31 offices." "United Technologies will eliminate 13,900 jobs." "IBM sets plan to encourage certain workers to leave, will reduce staff by 40,000 worldwide." These are merely a small sample of similar ominous headlines that could be read during a recent year.

Employees who face the prospect of being laid off or "encouraged" to quit can become challenges for managers. Employees may become depressed and demotivated while awaiting the "verdict" of who will leave and who will remain. How is it best to deal with employees who work for companies that announce, in effect, that they are going on a "lean and mean fitness diet" of restructuring, "de-layering," and "outplacing" numerous employees?

Employee morale tends to be enhanced if employees are notified well in advance of impending layoffs and can be involved in the planning, design, and implementation of an outplacement program. Worker attitudes are substantially better in situations where employees feel reassured that services are established to meet their needs. A company's reputation can be severely damaged in the community if massive layoffs are ineptly handled.

Some organizations hire outplacement consultants to assist outgoing employees in finding new jobs. Some organizations also offer generous financial incentives to employees who voluntarily quit. IBM, for example, recently offered two weeks severance pay for every year of employment—up to one year's pay—to employees who quit. To employees over age fifty who took early retirement Digital Equipment offered twenty-six weeks' salary as a lump-sum payment in addition to retirement benefits. Some employees find that early retirement is sometimes a "blessing in disguise."

the employee of the reason, you will help eliminate feelings of self-doubt that often result from a dismissal. An employee fired for a negative reason can benefit from knowing what types of behavior should be avoided in the future. Also, be certain to have factual documentation to support your decision to discharge an employee.

4. *Don't encourage retaliation* during the termination interview by losing your temper, even if the employee becomes belligerent. Angry employees will occasionally attempt to take revenge against you or the organization. Do you remember our news item at the beginning of this section?

5. *Allow time for the terminated employee to respond* while maintaining control of the interview.

6. *Terminate the employment as soon as possible* after the decision to fire has been made. Often, even if two weeks' notice is mandatory, immediate dismissal with two weeks' salary paid in advance is preferable to retaining the employee for the two weeks. Employees are frequently not very productive during their last days with an organization and, if disgruntled about the firing, can sow the seeds of discontent among other employees.

CHALLENGES WITH ONE'S SELF

There's a human tendency when we experience problems to look for external causes. We often feel more secure if we can convince ourselves that someone or something else can be blamed for any troubles we've experienced. Unfortunately, however, such attitudes are sometimes out of tune with reality.

A more effective approach is first to satisfy ourselves that we aren't the cause of the problems before we blame others. For example, the job performance of Harriet—one of your employees, let's assume—has recently deteriorated. Your immediate reaction might be to assume that she is entirely the cause of her changed behavior. However, could the *reprimand* that you gave her last week in front of her peers have had a demotivating effect on her? By first looking within yourself you may discover the true causes of some problems.

Let's now examine some typical challenges that some individuals may have with themselves.

Wants Beyond Capabilities

Not everyone has the aptitude to become a neurosurgeon. The desire to pursue a particular profession isn't usually sufficient in itself. Let's

Could *you* fly around
Saturn?

take a look at the hypothetical case of a young man named Bob whose father happens to be a well-known neurosurgeon. Bob and his family have for some time assumed that he would follow in Dad's footsteps. Although bright in many ways, Bob unfortunately lacks the aptitude and abilities to be a surgeon. Bob, however, refuses to recognize his limitations and, having the "right connections," has been accepted by a medical school. Bob is highly motivated, a factor that sometimes offsets lesser ability, but in his case motivation fails to get him through medical school. Bob flunks out.

What has occurred in Bob's case is a problem that sometimes develops when an individual's aspirations are greater than his or her capabilities. Although many management skills can be developed, not everyone, for example, has the capabilities to direct and coordinate a division of a large corporation. Frustration often results when a person fails to heed the admonishment "know thyself" sufficiently and believes that he or she has capabilities that don't exist. However, in cases where potential capabilities do exist, individuals with a "blind faith" in themselves have sometimes dived in and succeeded where excessive caution might have caused them to seek lower-level opportunities.

The Problem of "Making It"

Sometimes an individual who has strived hard to achieve his or her present position feels dissatisfaction rather than accomplishment shortly after reaching it. Why might this occur? Do you remember our discussion of Maslow's motivational and needs concepts from Chapter 5? There we learned that a satisfied need ceases to motivate; that is, the motivation no longer exists for the pursuit of a particular goal once you've achieved it. Perhaps the person at the head of a large corporation—the chief executive officer—doesn't feel as successful as many people might imagine. The manager's goal, once attained, may not offer precisely the satisfactions expected, especially if expectations were unrealistic. If so, reevaluation of one's present situation and the establishment of new goals is desirable.

After you've made it,
then what?

Getting in Over Your Head

Problems can also develop for individuals whose higher-order, or ego, needs are quite strong. Let's take the case of Heidi, who has performed well in every position that she has ever held in her firm. If Heidi has done a reasonable job, the chances are fairly good that she'll be promoted to a higher level. If she does well in the higher position, then she'll probably be promoted over time to an even more responsible position.

Can you visualize what might occur? Heidi has performed admirably in position A. As a result she is promoted to position B. After an outstanding and conscientious performance in position B, Heidi

Did Heidi get too high on the job?

is promoted to position C. But—alas! She now discovers that she is grappling for her very existence in position C. She finds that she can't perform as well as she did in her previous positions, so she is likely either to remain in position C indefinitely, to be demoted, or to be terminated.

Who knows? Perhaps one day you will be promoted to a position in which you feel insecure. If so, what should you do? Flee? Resign? Try to avoid your boss and your associates? Devour a box of calorie-filled candy? Pinch the snout of your Doberman pinscher? Or couldn't you pursue a more positive approach? Whenever you feel somewhat insecure in a new position, you might first try to discover what your deficiencies actually are and then develop a specific plan and timetable for overcoming them. Perhaps your only deficiency is a *temporary feeling* of uncertainty about your ability to perform your new job, which is a normal reaction when faced with new challenges. You certainly needn't be destined for a lifetime of feeling insecure solely because of a promotion.

Fear of Admitting Errors

Are managers human?

Assume that you are a manager in an organization. As a manager, you shouldn't make mistakes, should you? If you agree, you have crowned managers with undeserved glistening golden halos (untarnished!). Managers, too, are human and will make mistakes occasionally, although naturally they can't afford to err excessively. Managers also have egos and, like most individuals in organizations, may be embarrassed when they make errors in judgment. For example, assume that an office manager purchased a large quantity of the wrong size printer ribbon. Some managers in a similar situation might become excessively defensive and try either to cover up their mistakes or to "pass the buck." However, as a sign on the late President Harry S Truman's desk candidly stated: "The buck stops here."

SOURCE: From *The Wall Street Journal*—permission, Cartoon Features Syndicate.

Individuals in organizations, whether leaders or workers, will generally earn far more respect by admitting when they are wrong or don't know something. Attempts at concealment generally fail in the long run. However, some employees are mentally set to believe that their managers should know everything. And some managers seem to believe that there is no room for error among their associates. Perhaps such individuals would benefit from exposure to the realities of human fallibility.

Can anyone know everything?

The Question of Ethics for Individuals in Organizations

Individuals sometimes have to make difficult choices as members of organizations, difficult because of their potential impact on income and career paths. Imagine, for example, that you work as a sales representative for a steel supply company and that you have called on one of your customers who wants to place an unusually large order. This morning you learned that in five days your company intends to make substantial price reductions on the materials that your customer wants to buy. You have at least two options: You can take the order for the materials at today's prices, or you can inform your customer that the price is about to drop, thus saving her or him a considerable amount of money. If you enable your customer to purchase at next week's lower price, your commission, or earnings, would also be substantially lower.

Is life a one-shot deal?

What should you do? For some individuals the choice would be difficult. But need it be? Presumably your responsibility is not merely to push through "one-shot deals." Regular repeat business if far more desirable and profitable to your firm and to you over the long run. If your customer discovers that you sold materials at higher prices than necessary, what will probably be her or his attitude toward you and your company in the future? Ethical company representatives generally learn that they have far more regular, loyal, and profitable accounts when their customers are treated responsibly.

Have you ever found yourself caught in that devilish position between a rock and the deep blue sea?

Another situation that could strain your ethical values might be if your boss were to direct you to do something that you believe is either unethical or illegal. For example, assume that you are an accountant and your boss, Mr. Nomore Straight, asks you to keep a separate set of books—one with padded expense figures—for income tax purposes. In a figurative sense you have been placed between the Scylla of willful disobedience and the Charybdis of ethical or legal responsibility.* There could be negative consequences whether you fulfill or don't fulfill the request.

When confronted with such dilemmas, you have to make a decision. Do you let your personal financial responsibilities influence or

---

*Scylla in ancient mythology was a rock on the Sicilian coast (personified as a female monster) opposite a whirlpool called Charybdis. Mariners were believed to have to sail between these two equally hazardous alternatives. A more modern expression with a similar meaning is *caught between a rock and a hard place.*

change your decision? What are your alternatives? One alternative is *to do as you are directed.* However, if you do, you may be as legally responsible (or as criminally negligent) as your boss. Further, your conscience may create unpleasant stress-inducing reactions that could affect other aspects of your life.

A second choice is to refuse to carry out your boss's request. However, if you don't do as directed, you also run risks since your boss determines your pay raises and promotions. However, if you are caught, and the chances are fairly good that you will be, how might your career be affected?

A third alternative is to attempt to reason with your boss as to why you can't carry out the act. In some cases, you may be able to convince him or her to scuttle the decision by stressing the consequences of the illegal activity. You might even point out to your boss that you really can't allow yourself to be put into a situation in which you are jeopardizing your career and personal life by breaking the law. You could even say something like, "If I broke the law in favor of our company, isn't it likely that I would be the type of individual who would also break the law against our company? Boss, I want you to know that I prefer to deal ethically both *for* and *with* our company."

Realistically, such pleas could fall on deaf ears. A fourth alternative that has been used successfully by some organizational members is to merely give the request "lip service," that is, say, "Okay, boss. I'll do the best I can on that" and then ignore the request. In some cases, the need for such unethical behavior may fade away. Of course, in some cases it won't, and you have to either give your boss more lip service, or make a different decision.

The fifth alternative is the extreme one. If you find that if more positive approaches don't work, and that your conscience cannot live with the unethical practices of your boss or firm, then you may have to make the ultimate decision of resigning. Such an act takes a lot of courage, since it may adversely affect your financial situation. Others, however, have made such choices and felt better about themselves as a result.

You should continually remind yourself when confronted with certain temptations that *ethical values are not necessarily obsolete.* You will discover that you can live a far more confident existence if, in your mind, your activities do not border on the unethical or illegal.

HAVE YOU EVER CONSIDERED GOING INTO POLITICS?

Up with organizational politics?

How do you react to the phrase *the need to play organizational politics?* The words have a negative tone, don't they? Yet many managers today, especially those in larger organizations, believe that politics is a way of organizational life. There are many managers, for example, who have failed in their attempts to rise in the organizational hierarchy because they were politically inept.

The Nature of Organizational Politics

Organizational politics is the manner in which *individuals obtain and hold onto power,* which enables them to influence events and other people. Organizations differ. Each has its own political philosophy, just as do national political parties. If you are a "member" of an organizational political group, you will accomplish more of your objectives by acquiring the political skills necessary to gain and maintain the power that you require. Professor Jeffrey Pfeffer, author of *Managing with Power,* contends that individuals who want to succeed, and often even survive as managers, must learn the craft of politics. Pfeffer states, "To get things done, you need power—more power than those whose opposition you must overcome—and thus it is imperative to understand where power comes from and how these sources of power can be developed."[21]

Political activities aren't necessarily complex or abstract, nor should they be dysfunctional for the organization. They include such behavior as *not embarrassing your boss, willingly accepting certain assignments and invitations, compromising and trading off* during decision-making activities and with resources where necessary, and *having close relationships with others who have power* in the organization. Regardless of your own personal views on the need to "play politics" in organizations, a certain degree of political astuteness is essential for those who aspire to rise in many organizations.

In an earlier chapter, we discussed the *Pygmalion effect.* It suggested that your expectations toward others influence the results you are likely to attain from them. Doesn't your boss also have the need for recognition and self-esteem, as do you and other employees? The higher anyone rises in an organization, the lonelier it may become. Even presidents of corporations need regular reassurance and support from their subordinates. Supporting your boss is politically wise and is likely to reap benefits for you. Showing support for your boss is also likely to cause him or her to show much more support for you. Furthermore, by working hard to enable your boss to be promoted, you are at the same time helping to create a space for your own advancement. Since you're unlikely ever to have the perfect boss, you may as well try to adapt to the one you do have—or be prepared to be frustrated on your job.

Bosses Aren't Necessarily Self-Supporting

You have probably noticed that your boss is anything but an invincible, godlike figure who never makes a mistake. On the contrary, you have probably observed that bosses have insecurities and human

**A BOX
OF
INTEREST**

Is Whistle-Blowing by Modem the Answer?[d]

"Whistle-blowers," employees who publicly reveal waste or mismanagement by their employers, have frequently had to whistle a different tune after their employers fired them for various reasons unrelated to their revelations. Federal employees need fear no more since they are now protected by whistle-blower legislation—the Whistle-blower Protection Act—passed in April 1989. In theory, at least, federal employees can now "squeal" on their bosses with an increased chance of survival.

Prior to the passage of the law, employees had to prove that their whistle blowing was a *substantial* or *predominant* factor for employer retaliation. The protection law states that employees only have to prove that the whistle-blowing was a *contributing* factor, and the burden of proof has been shifted to the employer to prove that it was not a factor.

However, life for whistle-blowers continues to be fraught with risks. According to the *Dallas Morning News,* some military whistle-blowers have been forced to undergo psychiatric evaluations and been sent to mental wards as intimidation or reprisal. And in another case, a senior technician at a government laboratory was reassigned by his boss to a room filled with radioactive chemicals after he questioned plant safety. Concerned about such retaliatory measures, Senator David Pryor of Arkansas has said, "We're still shooting the messenger."

Perhaps one solution to this problem is to bring whistle-blowing into the computer age, which has been done recently. Now whistle-blowing hackers can connect to a computer bulletin board to anonymously report cases of government waste, fraud, or other abuses. By using passwords and pseudonyms, whistle-blowers can communicate via computer with the House Government Operations Subcommittee on Information, Justice, and Agriculture. In a downloading of modem morality, government employees can now communicate without giving their names and possibly endangering their careers.

Thus far, whistle-blowers in private industry are not protected by legislation. Should they be? Assume that you fly regularly with a particular airline. Would you object to one of the carrier's mechanics blowing the whistle on the firm if it was drastically cutting corners on maintenance?

frailties like everyone else. Because your boss occasionally goofs, you could find your own confidence beginning to sag, which might make you less supportive of him or her. However, is it realistic (or politically astute) for you to expect the impossible from your boss? If we believe that bosses aren't supposed to make errors, then our expectations are probably out of tune with reality.

The impossible takes a bit more time—even for bosses!

The Politics of Innovation and Limited Resources

A firm usually has a limited amount of funds available for operational expenses. It generally budgets and allocates specific amounts of these funds to each department to enable them to operate. Members of one department often feel they are competing with other departments for pieces of the budgetary pie.

Organizations today, in order to survive in national and international markets, must *innovate*. **Innovation** is the creation of a new idea and guiding it through various stages for the purpose of developing a new service, procedure, or product. Innovation requires financial and physical resources.

Most senior managers contend that they want innovative employees. Unfortunately, however, the act of innovation by individuals in one department is often resented by those in another department. The reason relates to consultant Richard Foster's quote at the beginning of this chapter: "One person's innovation is another person's failure."[22] People in other departments frequently perceive that the innovating department is robbing them of their rightful share of the limited financial resources. There are some politically astute ways of confronting interdepartmental rivalry and resentment. Techniques include *the use of think tanks, the use of interfunctional teams, and companywide commitment*.

"We really wish those guys would *out*-ovate!"

The Use of Think Tanks. What are the politically astute ways of confronting interdepartmental rivalry and resentment? One method applied by some organizations is to establish **think tanks,** geographically separated *groups located away from the traditional work environment whose function is to engage in intensive research and development*. They are typically located apart from corporate headquarters in the belief that their isolated location has a less inhibiting influence on the innovators' activities.

"Send in the tanks!"

The Use of Interfunctional Teams. We discussed the usefulness of teams in earlier chapters. As a way of reducing interdepartmental rivalry, some organizations have established **innovation teams** consisting of individuals from different functional areas, such as design, manufacturing, marketing, and finance. Involving members of various departments can be an effective way to develop new ideas with a

Innovation teams—a good idea for good ideas?

minimum of friction. In some cases, a charismatic individual is assigned to aid the team by serving as a coordinator or facilitator whose responsibility is to locate resources and run political interference for the team.

Companywide Commitment. Separate think tanks and interfunctional teams are not always feasible, nor are they necessarily the complete answer to political problems. A critical factor for successful innovation is the commitment and active support of senior management. Management must attempt to develop and maintain an organizational climate that both fosters and rewards creative thinking.

Employees should be shown tangible evidence of how they, too, can profit from such creative activities. For example, employees in every department should be made aware that future company revenues, and thus the security of their continued employment plus future raises in pay, are highly dependent on the outcome of the innovators' efforts.

Selling Your Ideas

A lot of people react negatively to the concept of selling, but if you think about it, haven't you been selling all your life? Selling—another "political" tool—is basically the art of influencing and persuading others to "buy" an idea, product, or service. From childhood on, haven't you been trying to persuade others to go along with your point of view? If you have any children, haven't they consistently and untiringly tried to persuade you to buy them the latest in stylish garments? Don't sweethearts, husbands, and wives, as well as bosses, try to sell (persuade) others to behave in a certain manner? Learning the basics of selling can help foster your own organizational activities and opportunities with your boss as well as your peers. Let's examine two guidelines for attempting to sell your point of view to others in the organization.

Doesn't everyone try to sell something?

Focus on Benefits, Not Features. If you are trying to sell your boss or your peers on an idea, don't sell solely yourself, although your own features are certainly important. When attempting to sell an idea, you should demonstrate how the other person and the organization are going to *benefit* from the idea, that is, how it will *satisfy their wants and needs.*

"Here is what's in it for you . . . "

Would a printer salesperson, for example, be likely to say to a prospective customer, "If you buy this Bullet 650 laser-quality printer, my husband and I will be able to afford that trip to Martinique that we've been longing for"? Not likely. The salesperson would first try to find out what was important to the prospective buyer and then relate her product's features to the *customer's needs.* Can you see how this approach could help you sell your boss on giving you a raise?

Test the Waters First. Another approach to selling your ideas to your boss or a peer is to use what has been termed the *trial balloon approach.* You might, for example, merely say to the other person, "I got an idea the other day that I'd like to share with you." You briefly discuss the idea and then possibly change the subject. What you've done, so to speak, is planted a seed that might very well grow. If, instead, you had pushed for an on-the-spot decision, you might have received immediate resistance. People frequently develop negative attitudes toward new ideas that require adjustments in their thinking or behavior. After they have had the chance to mull over the ideas without the pressure of having to make an immediate decision, they frequently become more receptive.

Try a balloon for size.

Accentuate YOUR Positives

Assume that you've invited some friends over for dinner. Let's also assume that you like to work around the house. Before dinner, one of your guests, Irma, says, "I heard you put up some new wood paneling in your family room. Could I see it?" You show your recently completed do-it-yourself project to Irma, who then says, "You did a great job. Your paneling looks fantastic. Was it hard to put up yourself?" In an unpolitical manner, you then reply, "It really didn't come out as well as I had hoped. Do you see that gap between the molding and the ceiling? I'm really not pleased with the job." Irma agrees, "Now that you mention it, I do see the gap. Hmmm, too bad."

Then comes dinner time. Irma's husband, Manuel, says to you. "This dish that you prepared is outstanding. I'm really enjoying it." And what do you say to Manuel? "Do you *really* like it? Actually, I put too much oregano in it. I personally think it's too spicy." Manuel thinks for a moment and then says, "Yes, now that you've mentioned it, it does taste a bit spicy."

Take this oregano, please!

Perhaps your responses wouldn't be precisely like those in the above illustrations, but you have probably heard many similar responses. How are these illustrations relevant to your own "political" activities on the job? They suggest that you might develop a better image in the minds of others if you didn't talk about your small problems and drawbacks. To further illustrate, let's assume that on your job you are currently facing a few minor obstacles that you know can easily be worked out. You may receive unexpected reactions from your boss when you "advertise" such problems to him or her. Because of your boss's high degree of concern for the department's operations, he or she may overreact to something that is actually quite trivial.

A more politically astute way to develop and maintain a good image is to say something like "Fine, thanks," when your boss asks you how things are going. Naturally you want to keep the boss attuned to any problems that are going to demand his or her attention, but an application of the exception principle can benefit you in situations of this type. And when someone compliments you for work well done, try to avoid putting yourself or your work down by saying, "You mean you like it?" A simple "thank you" will do wonders for your image.

SUMMARY

A certain degree of conformity is necessary in most organizations to provide predictability and stability and to accomplish organizational goals. Most employees whose individual philosophy differs markedly from that of their employers' must make some significant choices. They have to decide whether to quit, to try to change the organization, to continue working but with a negative attitude, or to try to adapt to the organization's standards.

Conformity can be classified as *legitimate* or *nonlegitimate*. Employees can be asked to conform in the way they think and in the way they *behave*. The concepts of conformity also apply to both *on-* and *off-the-job* activities. Efforts by managers to create a conforming atmosphere should not overlook individual differences. The right to privacy and management's use of tests, collected information, and surveillance of employees were also discussed in the chapter.

Leaders face the challenge from time to time of having to discipline some employees. Following accepted guidelines tends to make the task more effective. Individuals in organizations often have problems associated with their own attitudes and activities. For instance, their wants may exceed their capabilities, they may become dissatisfied after achieving goals, they may discover that they have gotten in "over their heads," they may have difficulty admitting errors, and they may occasionally face ethical dilemmas.

"Playing politics" appears to be a basic part of contemporary organizational life and is not necessarily a negative set of activities, except when its presence hinders the organization and its members.

TERMS AND CONCEPTS TO REMEMBER

conformity	workplace monitoring
legitimate areas of conformity	discipline
nonlegitimate areas of conformity	progressive discipline
workplace affairs	documentation

polygraph (lie detector) test

Employee Polygraph Protection Act of 1988

integrity tests

graphology

HIV testing

credit checks

red-hot stove rule

outplacement consultants

rules

organizational politics

innovation

think tanks

innovation teams

QUESTIONS

1. Should an individual member of an organization be expected to conform to all of its standards and policies? Explain.

2. What is the difference between *legitimate* and *nonlegitimate* forms of conformity? Give examples of each. Ask another person if he or she agrees with your classifications.

3. What are the potential dangers to organizations that encourage excessive conformity among individual employees?

4. Since the company you work for can afford it better than you, is there anything really wrong with occasionally taking home some paper, pencils, and paper clips?

5. Should your manager have any right to tell you what you can't do on your own, off-the-job, time? Explain.

6. Should *workplace affairs* between consenting adults be permitted? Explain.

7. Assume that you are a supervisor in a commercial bank. The standards of dress of one of your associates has recently deteriorated significantly. Specifically, what would you say to the employee?

8. What are some important decisions and activities that should be included as a part of any program intended to ban smoking from the workplace?

9. Assume that you have successfully stopped smoking. Why might an acquaintance of yours be unappreciative of any crusading efforts on your part to persuade him or her to quit?

10. How does *passive smoking* affect the nonsmoker?

11. Do you feel that employee testing, credit checks, and the use of surveillance techniques, as described in the chapter, invades the privacy of employees? Explain your position.

12. Should employees be permitted to have access to their own personnel records? Explain. How do you feel about third-party access?

13. Some companies have used "sniffer dogs" to randomly spot-check employees on duty for drugs and marijuana. Some employees were fired as a result. How would you rule on the legality of such practices if you were a federal judge? Would your decision be any different if the employees worked in a nuclear plant or were a part of the passenger train, bus, or airlines industries?

14. What is the purpose and nature of the progressive disciplinary process?

15. What is the significance of the red-hot stove rule?

16. When should an employee be fired?

17. How is documentation related to the disciplinary process?

18. When might a manager have trouble enforcing rules?

19. What potential problem exists when a person's wants are beyond his or her capabilities?

20. Why doesn't a person necessarily feel satisfied once he or she has attained a lofty goal?

21. Why do many leaders tend to find it difficult to admit mistakes?

22. Explain the meaning of a sentence in the chapter that states: "In a figurative sense you have been placed between the Scylla of willful disobedience and the Charybdis of ethical or legal responsibility."

23. What is meant by the term *organizational politics?* Do you feel that it is a favorable part of organizational life?

24. Why is it considered politically astute to be supportive of your boss?

25. Prepare a specific message attempting to "sell" an idea to your boss using one of the techniques discussed in the chapter.

26. What is probably one of the most desirable responses you can make to a person who has just complimented you? Why?

APPLICATIONS

14.1 Caught on Two Horns of a Dilemma

Wanda Wohri, a representative of a pharmaceutical company, has the responsibility of calling on druggists and doctors to promote the products of the S.S. Crowlow Company, Inc. Wanda is a voracious reader, and recently she learned from a foreign publication that a

German governmental agency in Bonn has banned the sale of a drug that her company currently manufactures and distributes under a different brand name in the United States and Canada. The Bonn governmental agency has uncovered what it believes to be positive evidence that the drug can cause birth defects.

Not long after reading the German report, Wanda was requested by her boss, Mr. Fred Finchpenny, to come to his office. During the session, Mr. Finchpenny informed Wanda that the sale of a particular drug, which the Crowlow Company has been marketing under the brand name of Encrouchonol, has not been particularly good in her territory. He also suggested that she begin to promote Encrouchonol to her accounts with greater vigor.

Encrouchonol is the Crowlow Company's name for the drug that was removed from the German market. Wanda explained this to Finchpenny, who glossed over the German experience and mumbled something about those "dumb foreigners." He informed her of the tremendous capital investment that Crowlow has sunk into the research, development, and advertising of Encrouchonol. "If we don't recover our investment," warned Finchpenny, "all of us are going to suffer financially here at Crowlow. The recession hit us hard, and so we have to start generating more income or we're going to be in serious trouble!"

Wanda was disturbed by Finchpenney's attitude, and she told him that the company should not be promoting a drug that might cause harm. Finchpenny stressed again that the firm has hardly begun to recover the tremendous investment already made. He also made allusion to her being a widow with a $150,000 house mortgage and two children whom she currently supports financially at an out-of-state university. Finchpenny closed the discussion with the comment, "I expect to see some positive results on your next monthly production statement!"

Questions

1. What sort of a problem does Wanda face?

2. What are the various choices Wanda could make regarding the problem?

3. If you were in Wanda's position, what would you do now? What are the implications of your decision?

14.2 A Rebel With or Without a Cause?

Randy Kaufman has been a sales representative for the Photo-Made Office Products Company for the past 9 months. Although he has generally attained or surpassed his monthly sales quotas, Randy seems to be experiencing some difficulty in adjusting to organizational life.

Randy has never been much of a conformist. While in college, he was generally outspoken in opposing American foreign policies. He continually bragged that he would go to prison before he would fight an "imperialistic war" in such places as Iraq or Somalia. During holiday dinners, such as Thanksgiving, he typically argued with some of his relatives about a wide variety of issues. His caustic, somewhat combative manner of discussing issues tended to alienate others.

Randy is accountable to Teri Titeship, the district sales manager. Titeship follows a practice of applying close controls on his sales staff. For control purposes, the sales representatives are required to submit the following reports:

1. Monthly sales projection, submitted monthly

2. Weekly sales projection, submitted weekly

3. Production sheets, submitted weekly, that indicate the following:
    a. Number of telephone survey calls
    b. Number of telephone appointment calls
    c. Number of actual product demonstrations
    d. Number of cold calls on prospects
    e. Number of leads obtained
    f. Monthly goals report projecting sales and describing methods for achievement (partially overlaps number 1 and above)

4. A weekly planner, indicating scheduled product demonstrations

5. A "hotlist" report, summarizing past activity with a listing of prospects that are likely to make a purchase within the next 60 days, submitted daily.

6. A postproduct demonstration report, submitted at the end of each day.

In addition, the sales representatives are required to report to the office each morning at 8:00 A.M. and spend a minimum of two hours on the telephone making survey calls and setting up appointments. They are required to check back into the office between 4:00 P.M. and 5:00 P.M. each afternoon. They aren't permitted to leave the office before 5:15 P.M. The sales representatives must prepare paperwork and sales proposals on their own time, that is, not during official working hours. They also are required to attend evening meetings lasting until 10:00 P.M. for which they receive no compensation. Since they work on a straight commission, their earnings depend solely on their sales.

Most of the sales representatives in the office feel that the paperwork demanded by Titeship is greater than that imposed upon sales representatives at other companies. However, they comply with Titeship's requirements, complaining only to each other and to their spouses rather than to Titeship.

Randy, however, has been complaining quite openly both to Titeship and to others in the office. Titeship has frequently warned Randy that his negative attitude must change and that his complaints are damaging to the morale of the other employees. Randy's behavior, however, has not changed. This morning Randy was given a written warning that placed him on probation. He was told that he would be discharged if his attitude did not improve substantially during the next two months.

Questions

1. In your opinion, are the demands for conformity that Titeship has placed on his sales force legitimate or nonlegitimate? Explain.

2. How do you feel about Titeship's decision to place Randy on probation?

3. What are some of the choices of action available to Randy in relation to the standards that he has found difficult to accept?

14.3 We All Want to March to Different Drummers

The claims department of Protection Insurance Company, Inc., employs twelve clerks whose job it is to carefully and completely fill out the forms necessary to process claims from customers. The work requires great attention to detail, as even the slightest error can delay customers' claims for days. All twelve clerks work in one large room, and between the sound of the printers and the piped-in background music the room can be very noisy.

One of the clerks, Seth Warmath, decided he'd had enough of the noise in the office and began bringing in and wearing his own stereo headphones as he worked. He found that use of his headphones allowed him to drown out all the other sounds, listen to the kind of music he preferred, and enhance his concentration. After two weeks of wearing the headphones as he worked, he realized that his output and accuracy rates were substantially improved. Several of the other clerks in the office decided to try wearing headphones, too, and they had similar results.

Danielle Trevino, supervisor of the clerks, looked the other way when it came to the headphones. She realized that the insurance company was a relatively conservative employer with strict dress codes and employee rules. But since there was no specific rule regarding headphones and the company provided music in the office, she saw no problem in allowing employees to use them as long as the work was getting done.

Jane Garfunkel, vice president of operations, entered Danielle's area on a routine tour of facilities. As she and Danielle walked among the clerks, Garfunkel noticed the headphones and asked, "Since when are you folks doing transcriptions down here?"

"Transcriptions?" Danielle replied.

"Yes. Aren't those headphones part of the transcribing equipment?"

"Well, no," Danielle answered sheepishly. "Several of our clerks have found that they work better to their own music. It can get pretty noisy in here."

Danielle could see that Garfunkel was not impressed. Garfunkel tapped Seth on the shoulder. As he looked up, removing his headphones, he said, "Yes, Ms. Garfunkel, can I help you?"

"What do you think you're doing with those things in the workplace?" she asked angrily.

"These? Oh, I concentrate better if I can drown out all the other noise," Seth responded.

"We provide piped-in music for you workers, and that should be adequate. How can you hear the phone or respond to co-workers with them on? I want them removed at once, permanently!" she said to Danielle as she stormed out of the office.

"Sorry, folks," Danielle said to the clerks. "I guess that's it for the headphones."

"Wait a minute, Danielle," said Seth. "What I put into my ears is *my* business so long as I get the job done!"

"That's right," agreed some of the others. "This way we can each listen to what we want instead of that piped-in garbage."

"Besides," said another, "it's so noisy in here that I rely on my phone light, not the sound, to know when I have a call."

"That lady's nuts!" remarked another. "We're not supposed to talk to one another; we're supposed to key in data. Even if I needed to talk to someone in the office, I'd have to go over to that person to be heard. I don't see how the headphones hamper our ability to do our jobs one bit."

"Absolutely," said another. "We've all noticed an improvement in our work since we started using the headphones. Surely, you've noticed it, too, Danielle. You need to talk to Ms. Garfunkel again and see if you can get her to change her mind."

Questions

1. What would you do now if you were Danielle? What political risks exist in this incident?

2. Assume that Danielle wants the employees to be able to continue the use of headphones. How might she gain approval of the idea?

3. How do you feel about Seth's remark, "What I put into my ears is my business so long as I get the job done"?

NOTES

1. From an address delivered by Robert N. Hilkert, while first-president of the Federal Reserve Bank of Philadelphia, at the Annual Convention of the American Institute of Banking, May 30, 1961, in Seattle Washington (emphasis added).

2. "A Partial Vindication," *Time/International Edition,* May 15, 1989, pp. 21-32.

3. Laurie P. Cohen, "Internal Security," *Wall Street Journal,* September 16, 1985, p. 24C.

4. R. Wayne Mondy and Shane R. Premeaux, "People Problems: The Workplace Affair," *Management Solutions,* November 1986, pp. 36-39.

5. Charles Batchelor, "No More Than a Whisker Away From Success," *Financial Times,* November 1, 1991, p. 14.

6. Janice M. Horowitz, "Why Quitting Means Gaining," *Time,* March 25, 1991, p. 61; and Tim Friend, "Passive Smoke Seen as 'Toxin,'" *USA Today,* June 11, 1992, p. 1-A.

7. "Second-Hand Smoke: Take a Look at the Facts," a pamphlet published by the American Lung Association, n.d.; Tim Friend, "EPA: Indoor Smoking is Big Pollutant," *USA Today/International Edition,* June 21, 1989, p. 1; Tim Friend, "Passive Smoke Seen as 'Toxin,'" *USA Today/International Edition,* June 11, 1992, p. 1-A; Diane Summers, "Doctor Warns on Passive Smoking Danger," *Financial Times,* July 8, 1991, p. 6; and Paul Raebur, "Second-hand Smoke Lethal, Report Warns," *Contra Costa Times,* May 30, 1991, p. 1-B.

8. "EPA Says Secondhand Smoke Harms Children, *Oakland Tribune,* June 19, 1992, p. A-2.

9. "A Sign of the Times: Smokers Need Not Apply," *Business Week,* July 27, 1987, p. 42.

10. Diane Summers, "Ashes to Ashes as Smoking Bites Dust," *Financial Times,* January 17, 1992, p. 7.

11. Protect Non-Smokers from Risks of Smoke," *USA Today,* June 11, 1992, p. 14A.

12. Carol Kleiman, "What Privacy Rights Do Workers Have? Very Few," *San Francisco Examiner,* September 15, 1991, p. 2-B.

13. "Honestly, Can We Trust You?," *Time/International Edition,* January 23, 1989, p. 35; and Daniel Seligman, "Lying," *Fortune/International Edition,* March 27, 1989, p. 127.

14. Susan Tompor, "More Employers Attempt to Catch a Thief By Giving Job Applicants 'Honesty' Exams," *The Wall Street Journal,* August 3, 1981.

15. Rex Winsbury, "A Testing Dilemma," *Financial Times Weekend,* July 25/26, 1992, p. 8.

16. See note 15.

17. Gilbert Fuchsberg, "More Employers Check Credit Histories Of Job Seekers to Judge Their Character," *The Wall Street Journal,* May 30, 1990, p. B-1.

18. Arlee C. Green, "Big Brother Is Watching, Pressuring U.S. Workers," *AFL-CIO News,* April 16, 1990, p. 11; Arlee C. Green, "VDT Monitoring Increases Health Woes, Study Finds," *AFL-CIO News,* October 29, 1990, p. 2; and "Workplace Monitoring," *AFL-CIO News,* September 30, 1991, p. 3.

19. "CWA Applauds Historic Ban on Monitoring," *AFL-CIO News,* February 17, 1992, p. 9.

20. Patricia Amend, "How Companies Keep an Eye on Their Workers," *USA Today/International Edition,* March 15, 1990, p. 9-A; and Jeffrey Rothfeder, Michele Galen, and Lisa Driscoll, "Is Your Boss Spying on You?" *Business Week/International Edition,* February 26, 1990, pp. 72BE-72GE.

21. Jeffrey Pfeffer, *Managing with Power* (Boston, MA: Harvard Business School Press, 1992).

22. Walter Kiechel III, "The Politics of Innovation," *Fortune/International Edition,* May 16, 1988, p. 87.

BOX NOTES

a   Adapted from *Business Profile Series: Saudi Arabia, Fifth Edition,* provided by the Saudi British Bank, June 1991.

b. Adapted from Carol Kleiman, "What Privacy Rights Do Workers Have? Very Few," *San Francisco Examiner,* September 15, 1991, p. 2-B.

c. Adapted from "White-Collar Lay-Offs in America—A Lot More than You Would Think," *The Economist,* February 2, 1992, pp. 68, 69; "Jobs Are Still the Chief Worry," *Business Week/International Edition,* February 10, 1992, p. 12; "IBM Sets Plan to Encourage Certain Workers to Leave," *The Wall Street Journal Europe,* May 23, 1991, p. 3; "Bank Mergers Should Take

Workers Into Account, UFCW Says," *AFL-CIO NEWS,* October 4, 1992, p. 4; and David Stipp, "Digital Equipment Sweetens Retirement Offer to Cut Jobs," *The Wall Street Journal Europe,* March 3, 1992, p. 3.

d. Adapted from "Whistle-Blower Boon," *Christian Science Monitor,* March 3/16-22, 1989, p. 20; "Whistle-Blower Measure Urges Better Protection," *USA Today/International Edition,* May 16, 1989, p. 4; Bob Dart, "U.S. Creates Whistleblowing by Computer," *Contra Costa Times,* March 19, 1992, p. 26; and Pete Yost, "Whistle-Blowers Still Fielding Flak," *The Los Angeles Times,* March 22, 1992, p. 18.

EXPERIENTIAL EXERCISES

Declining Ethics?

Read the following paragraph:

Today's younger generation has views somewhat like those of the young student, Raskolnikov, in Dostoevski's classic novel, *Crime and Punishment,* who believed that the "end justified the means." As long as Raskolnikov achieved his goals, he believed, it mattered little what he did in pursuing them. Many of America's contemporary youth have been equated with the student. They are considered by some observers as "the least morally anchored generation ever." Young people today tend to believe that the only important consideration is winning and "looking out for *numero uno.*" As with Raskolnikov, they are willing to do whatever it takes to accomplish their own personal goals.

Activity: Show the paragraph to at least ten young people under twenty-five years old. Ask them an open question, such as, "What is your reaction to the comments?" Did the young people you interviewed agree or disagree with the views presented? If they disagreed, what were their reasons for disagreeing? What did your informal survey tell you about the current values of some young people? How do you personally feel about their responses?

How Willing Are You to Conform?

Read the statements below. Then rank on a zero to 10 scale your degree of acceptance of the statements **related to your career job,** zero representing a *complete lack of willingness to conform* to the requirements of the statement and 10 a *complete willingness.* After you have finished ranking the statements, get together with four or five class members and compare each other's responses. Ask each other why the particular statement was ranked in a particular way.

Rank   **Statement**
(0-10)

_____   1. I would willingly wear a dark, somber-looking suit on the job.

_____   2. I would willingly get my hair cut each week (if a man) or have my hair styled professionally twice a month (if a woman).

_____   3. If requested by my boss, I would be willing to make up a phony invoice.

_____   4. I would be willing to play on the company volleyball team even if I did not like playing volleyball.

_____   5. If requested by my boss, I would be willing to stop dating a co-worker.

_____   6. A person unwilling to accept a promotion should not be allowed to maintain his or her job with an organization.

_____   7. A ban on smoking in the workplace is an acceptable requirement.

_____   8. Employers have the right to use secret video cameras to monitor employees.

_____   9. A person must "play politics" to succeed on the job.

_____ 10. My boss has the right to control my behavior off the job.

CHAPTER 15

Organizational Ethics and Responsibilities Toward Society

It All Relates to the Bottom Line

When you finish this chapter, you should be able to:

1

Explain what has caused some people to develop negative attitudes toward business corporations.

2

Recognize the risks associated with low standards of organizational ethics.

3

Contrast two prevalent philosophies—profit quest and social accountability—of the proper role of business.

4

List at least seven areas of managerial social responsibility.

5

Summarize some of the guidelines designed to enhance the success of organizational social programs.

> A peace above all earthly dignities,
> A still and quiet conscience.

Shakespeare

> Greed can be good when it spurs profitable and productive growth.
> But it can also be bad when it outpaces all other considerations.

Franco Modigliana, Economist

The business community has had considerable positive influence on American society, providing jobs and helping to create high levels of living standards for many people. However, well-publicized scandals and some business practices have periodically tarnished its image and adversely affected the public's attitudes toward business and its behavior. Such attitudes have fluctuated over the years, at times being highly critical and at other times notably supportive.

Perhaps even more important than what attitudes have been in the past, and even what they currently are, is what they are likely to be in the future. Many businesspeople today are concerned with the question of ethics and other factors that are apt to mold future attitudes toward business. Many observers of the social scene believe that the way in which business managers perceive and discharge their ethical, legal, and moral responsibilities toward society will significantly influence future public attitudes toward business.

What does the word *ethics* actually mean. Developing a working definition provides us with little difficulty. Developing illustrations is a more challenging task, as we'll see. Basically, **ethics** deals with the standards of conduct or morals established by the current and past attitudes and moods of a particular society. In simple terms, business ethics relates to standards of "right" and "wrong."

But reality is seldom simple. Not everyone agrees on the "proper" ethical and social roles of business. A complicating factor is that what is considered wrong by one person, firm, industry, or country may be considered right or even desirable by another.

Traditionally the role of business has been solely to turn a profit. However, managers who ignore public pressures regarding ethical and social issues may find themselves in more difficult situations over time. The business community experienced an environment with looser governmental reins during the deregulatory period of the 1980s. Because of certain abuses during this so-called decade of excess, demands for re-regulation have occurred in certain areas in the 1990s. Thrift institutions serve as a vivid example. Congressional calls for greater regulation of the industry occurred after numerous thrifts recklessly abandoned investment caution during the "deregulatory 1980s."

Chapter 14 discussed the question of ethical standards for individuals in organization. The major purpose of this chapter is to provide you with an overview of the social pressure and ethical responsibilities that business organizations and their managers are likely to confront. In addition, we'll examine some specific guidelines that managers should consider if they are sincerely interested in fulfilling their organizational behavior responsibilities, not only to the business owners but also to society and its environment.

HAVE STANDARDS OF BUSINESS ETHICS DECLINED?

Many managers today are highly concerned about maintaining the public's faith in private institutions, and possibly even serving as role models for the citizens of the struggling Eastern European nations. Neither is a simple task. Although attitudes of young people toward business improved during the 1980s, a fair amount of prejudice and negativism continue to exist in relation to the business community. In 1990, for example, a Roper poll indicated that a small proportion of Americans believe U.S. corporations are paying proper attention to the interests of their workers (only 6 percent), customers (11 percent), and "the nation as a whole" (5 percent), while catering too much to the interests of executives (43 percent) and stockholders (40 percent).[1]

As we know, prejudice involves making judgments before gathering ample facts, which seems to be a fairly common human tendency. It shouldn't come as too much of a surprise, therefore, that people who have had little association with business have present notions and tend to make sweeping generalizations about the motives and activities of "those businesspeople."

Will more makeup help?

The television medium has not been particularly kind toward businesspeople. Many executives blame television for the bad image some people have about business leaders, arguing that most business managers are portrayed as being crooked, greedy, and foolish. "Soaps," for example, have often portrayed the businessperson as a noncaring, ruthless moneygrubber. Films, too, have often characterized executives as the villains. Nor has the popular press been much of a benefactor of business, having focused primarily on negative rather than positive business activities.[2]

Prejudices Transferred Into Reality

Unfortunately, not all negative attitudes toward the business community can be blamed on blind and emotional prejudice. Highly publicized events such as Wall Street scandals and disastrous oil spills have done little to enhance the image of business. Exxon Corporation's

March 24, 1989, oil spill at Valdez, Alaska—240,000 barrels of oil pouring into scenic Prince William Sound—played havoc on the environment and helped to tarnish the petroleum industry's image, especially in light of Exxon's management having reassured environmentalists that such a disaster was impossible.[3]

The image of the business community became further tarnished during the past decade as reports of business scandals appeared in the news with increasing frequency. Aiding in such discoloration

were accounts of certain "highly respected" millionaires, such as Ivan Boesky, Dennis Levine, Michael Milken, Robert Maxwell, and Clark Clifford, who became known as "profit-at-any price criminals." They were accused of such wrongdoing as racketeering, mail fraud, abuse of employee pension funds, taking bribes, and other infractions of the law. Such individuals have not been exactly the best of role models for young people aspiring to attain a career in business.

Does Anything Go?

An unethical attitude of "go for it," that the achievement of large financial gain outweighs the risk of being caught, seems to have prevailed in recent years not only in the financial community but in other industries as well, resulting from penny stock scams, junk bond abuses, overcharging the government on defense contracts, and money-laundering scandals. A government agency, the Department of Housing and Urban Development (HUD), was accused of allowing private escrow agents to embezzle millions of dollars from its coffers.[4] And even 355 present and former U.S. legislators in the House of Representatives were accused in 1992 of having misused their over-

draft privileges with the House bank over extended periods.[5] This sort of behavior could not readily be considered a positive "role model" for the youth of today.

Commercial transactions have long been built on a foundation of trust. Contracts, for example, do not have to be in writing to be legal and enforceable. Transactions occur regularly this way. However, increasingly prevalent have become attitudes such as that of private investor and dean of the Fordham Business School, Arthur Taylor: "I can't do transactions on the telephone any more because people do not keep their word."[6]

Have consciences eroded in recent decades? Businesspeople have never been considered absolute angels in their dealings with others, at times subscribing to the philosophy of **caveat emptor,** "let the buyer beware." At times, the pendulum seems to swing toward a philosophy of **caveat vendor,** "let the seller beware," with purchasers of goods attempting to take advantage of those who sell them. Some observers feel that an erosion of values has taken place. Abraham

Zaleznik, psychoanalyst and Harvard Business School professor, asserts, "Conscience is a fragile thing. It needs support from institutions, and that support is weakening."[7]

Judged by Ethical Actions

Accusing all businesspeople of unethical practices would be unfair. Many business managers maintain consistently high standards of ethical behavior. Consequently, much of the recent criticism has been aimed at specific business firms and their practices. Nonetheless, business managers must be concerned—as many actually are—with public attitudes, since the future of business enterprise is linked closely to these attitudes. Business managers who ignore public sentiment over time are likely to find that a disenchanted public can exert pressure through its elected representatives, who may create regulations that force business to display greater social responsibility.

There are some other important reasons why business has been criticized in recent decades. Let's look briefly at a few of them.

The Effects of Acquisitions and Restructuring Activities

Some people have developed an antipathy toward business because of the frequent waves of *leveraged buyouts (LBOs), mergers,* and *hostile takeovers.* Periods of "merger mania" have been recurring in recent decades, during which smaller, or weaker, companies have been purchased by larger, or more powerful, organizations. During these periods, many employees watched with uncertainty as giant companies gobbled up the firms that employed them.

Trading equity for equity.

Leveraged buyouts enable managers to borrow sizable amounts of funds on their firm's equity, which can then be used to purchase equity in other firms. The managers can then sell parts of the acquired businesses at a handsome profit. Most acquiring companies divest portions of their newly acquired assets within a year, often with devastating effects on employees. The motive for breaking an acquired firm into parts is pure profit, since the total value of its parts sold separately is usually greater than the value of the entire firm when intact.

Billions of dollars have changed hands in mergers and acquisitions during the past decade. A few of the permanent acquisitions included KKR buying RJR/Nabisco ($25 billion), Chevron buying Gulf Corporation ($13.4 billion), Philip Morris buying Kraft ($13 billion), and AT&T buying McCaw Cellular Communications ($12.4 billion). Many of the acquisitions of one company by another have been considered **hostile (unfriendly) takeovers,** that is, the acquired company did not want to be taken over by the acquiring firm.

In several instances, the managers taking over the acquired firms lacked the expertise to run them, which sometimes resulted in the failure of these firms or their being sold soon after acquisition. Many employees in the acquired firm often felt that the new management showed little humane concern for them. Employees tended to feel that they were not unlike pawns in a chess game or real estate in a game of Monopoly. As business journalist Timothy Schellhardt has observed, "In the corporate acquisition game, the conquerors keep their jobs and often win larger fiefdoms. The defeated find themselves job hunting."[8]

"There goes your pay-check mate!"

Some firms have attempted to defend themselves from hostile takeovers by establishing employee stock option plans (ESOPs), or by purchasing their own stock on the open market so that would-be acquirers would be unable to purchase a controlling share of stock. Other firms that anticipated unfriendly takeovers developed **golden parachute** programs for existing executives whose positions were likely to be terminated after the acquisition. A golden parachute is a severance agreement *with executives* that guarantees two or three years of their annual pay plus possible benefits, such as stock purchase options, if they lose their jobs as a result of an acquisition. For example, Union Carbide established a $28 million golden parachute severance protection program for 42 of its executives. Under the terms of the agreement, each executive would receive payments equal to about three years of their average annual compensation plus additional benefits in the event of a hostile takeover.[9]

The frenzied pace of leveraged buyouts during the 1980s peaked in 1989, when federal bank regulators starting pressuring commercial banks and savings and loans to stop lending to companies whose bonds

"The board sent over this parachute, but I'm not sure it's golden."
SOURCE: From *The Wall Street Journal*—permission, Cartoon Features Syndicate.

What goes up . . .
must come down.

had become "junk" because of their excessively high debt ratios. A counter-trend during the early 1990s has been to **deleverage,** that is, to swap high-cost debt for cheaper financial obligations. The low interest rates of the early 1990s contributed heavily toward this trend.[10]

In spite of the current abatement of corporate acquisition activities, **restructuring** continues to be common among a large proportion of Fortune 500 companies. Restructuring activities include spinning off businesses, laying off employees, and reducing costs drastically. AT&T, for example, announced in 1992 its intention to cut 6000 more jobs in addition to the 133,000 lost since the sell-off of its regional operations. IBM soon followed with an announcement that its work force would shrink by at least 32,000 during 1992. Unlike the restructuring of the mid-1980s, the recent one has also hit America's service industries—ranging from banking to fast-food outlets. Service firms recently involved in restructuring activities include Citicorp and American Express.[11]

"Guess what! I've been
restructured!"

Tremendous amounts of uncertainty and anxiety tend to develop among the employees of the acquired and restructured firms. A three-year study found that acquisitions and restructuring activities often fail because companies place too much importance on financial information and spend too little time planning for the stressful effects of change on their staff. Employees typically have become uncertain of the future direction of their careers, resulting in lower productivity, higher employee turnover and absenteeism, worse strike records, and poorer accident rates.[12]

A sorry result of the excessive leveraging of the 1980s has been the necessity on the part of many organizations to sell off assets, close down plants that should be modernized, terminate pension funds, and seek wage and benefits reductions.

Lack of Sufficient Concern for the Environment

Part of the public's attitude toward the business community has resulted from the latter's reluctance to show concern for the environment unless pressured by government agencies. The public tends to be cynical when it *hears* business executives talk about their social responsibility but *observes* what appears to be contrary behavior.

"Raindrops keep falling
on my head. Does that
make me an
acid head?"

Stirred by reports of acid rain, dirty air, filthy lakes and rivers, global warming, ozone depletion, nuclear and toxic wastes, and the disastrous *Exxon Valdez* oil spill, the public appears to desire a reversal of the trend of the lax Reagan years by calling for more environmental regulation.

Some businesspeople are concerned about the cost of complying with new regulations, while environmentalists argue that the economic cost is well worth it in terms of healthcare costs alone.

A QUESTION
OF
ETHICS

Do Employees Have the Right to Feel Secure?[a]

A study of more than thirty corporations revealed that employees are easier to manage when they feel secure, that is, don't have to worry about losing their jobs. Companies such as Hewlett-Packard, Honeywell, Advanced Micro Devices, and Dana Corporation have had formal "no-layoff" policies. Some companies use "buffers" to protect full-time employees by employing temporary employees and subcontractors and by spreading out the work. The added job security that employees feel, according to the study, allows them to adapt more readily to new ideas and change.

Jack Barry, president of the International Brotherhood of Electrical Workers union, emphasized during negotiations with AT&T management in April 1992 that without job security it would be hard for his members to continue cooperation with management at the plant-floor level. Barry contended that employees had lost job security in recent years because of the many layoffs resulting from downsizing and restructuring. "Workers whose jobs are secure are not threatened by change," Barry said during the formal opening of negotiations with management.

AT&T was due to cut 6000 more jobs—in addition to 133,000 lost since the sell-off of its regional operations—but it agreed that employees declared "surplus" could choose to take special unpaid leave of up to two years to pursue career or personal interests while the company paid all benefits, including tuition assistance. Employees with at least five years of service had the opportunity to take temporary jobs in the company with no loss of pay for two years.

A Question of Ethics: Do you feel that organizations have a moral obligation to provide security to their employees? If so, what types of security should they provide?

Will Defensiveness Really Help?

Far too frequently, the initial business response to criticism has been excessively defensive, with strident denials of guilt or threats of shortages, higher prices, and unemployment. For example, Robert Stemple, former head of General Motors Corporation, accused the media of being hostile and the cause of consumer criticism of its products.[13] Industry has also consistently lobbied against consumer protection and environmental legislation. As a result, the damage to the image of business has been so extensive that considerable remedial action—more than mere propaganda—is necessary if business is to operate in an atmosphere of public faith and confidence. However, as we shall soon see, attitudes among business leaders on the proper role of business differ greatly.

TWO PHILOSOPHIES: PROFIT QUEST VERSUS SOCIAL ACCOUNTABILITY

How do you feel about profits? Most observers of society today would probably agree that the quest for profits is not, in itself, an evil activity. However, there exists incomplete agreement as to what degree the maximization of profits should be the concern of business managers. There actually are two principal schools of thought on the subject: the **trustee-of-profit** philosophy and **enlightened self-interest** philosophy.

The classical trustee-of-profit viewpoint contends that the corporation's *sole responsibility is to produce profits* and that any expenditure on corporate social goals amounts to a hidden tax on workers, customers, and shareholders.

The second, and more modern, philosophy—enlightened self-interest—argues that *social goals* should not be considered as competition for profits but instead as *one of the overall goals of management*. As Professor David Vogel has written, "Profitability can be regarded as a necessary condition of responsible social performance."[14]

The two points of view, which typify the opposition that has long prevailed among philosophers, are sometimes referred to as the *profit-quest* and the *social-accountability* approaches. Let's examine each briefly.

The Profit-Quest Approach

Although many families were hit badly by the "triple-dip" recession of the early 1990s, Americans continue to enjoy one of the highest material standards of living in the world. Those who subscribe to the **profit-quest** approach argue that the attainment of such standards has been largely a result of the private (more aptly called *mixed*) enterprise system in the United States. Although there are other nations with high standards of living, few offer their citizens as wide a choice of different consumer products as exists in the United States. Trends in other countries—both Eastern and Western—have frequently emulated developments in American technology and marketing. Americans

"But not without my MTV!"

could survive quite well without automatic icemakers, palmtop computers, fax machines, compact disc players, and talking scales, but the existence of such goods has generally been assured by the consuming public's consistent flow of "dollar votes."

Why have profits been important to the American system?

Much of America's wide choice of products and reasonably well-paying jobs has been dependent on the earning of *profits* by the business community. Reasonable profits themselves—unless you happen to subscribe to Marxian philosophy—aren't necessarily evil. Many of America's past and present social ills were caused not so much by the making of profits as by what was done with the nation's resources.

However, many corporations seem to have the notion that they aren't obliged to do anything but turn a profit. Some firms *profess* social concern but, as we have seen, *don't appear* to mean it. At times their efforts have seemed merely to be a part of a well-publicized public relations fad with little apparent significance.

As the chapter on leadership styles showed, there is more than one philosophy or way of perceiving others; some managers perceive individuals positively, whereas others stress the negative. The same thesis holds true for the way in which business managers perceive the general public vis-à-vis their social responsibilities. Some managers feel that their only concern need be with the quest for profits. "We *aren't* social workers!" some business leaders exclaim.

The Social-Accountability Approach

Of course, not all organizations hold an exclusive trustee-of-profit philosophy. For many organizations, **social accountability,** that is, an attitude of responsibility toward society, is a major concern. Corporate goals still include earning profits, but many executives today also feel that making a good product, offering it at a good price, and earning a decent profit are not enough; many corporations also have a **social conscience.**

Does your *social conscience* bother you?

Enlightened executives display their social consciences in a variety of ways. In the following section you will read about the areas of public concern that receive attention from the business community.

AREAS OF SOCIAL RESPONSIBILITY

We shall now move onto a controversial topic, the *special areas of social responsibility* that the business community should face. Our list of concerns will be neither complete nor absolute. Keep in mind that issues that seemed almost radical during one era sometimes become commonplace during another. Conversely, issues that were significant during one period become unnecessary during another if the specific problems no longer exist.

The following discussion is intended to illustrate the various types of social responsibilities with which some managers are concerned. The list should be modified as social conditions change. Among current managerial concerns are responsibilities:

- To employees
- To consumers
- To the environment
- To provide information
- To assist special employment groups
- To help small businesses
- To contribute money and talent

Responsibility to Employees

One of the primary social responsibilities of an organization should be its *own employees,* and much of what we've already covered in this text concerns employee relations. From the standpoint of improving the corporate image, employees are exceedingly important since they are an influential *communication link* to the general public. Information regarding either favorable company practices or the distribution of shoddy products and unfair management tactics will readily be transmitted to the general public through employees' communication networks.

What are some ways that organizations show social responsibility to employees?

Some firms have the reputation of being concerned with employees' attitudes, their personal problems, and other factors that influence both on-the-job performance and public attitudes toward the organization. Some firms, for example, encourage employees to *further their educations* by assisting them with the costs of attending night colleges or universities. Others assist employed parents by providing them with *day-care nurseries* for their children. As we've already learned, many firms now provide *counseling services* for employees with such problems as alcoholism, drug abuse, and emotional difficulties. Others provide workshops that offer advice on how to cope during stressful periods of plant closings or relocations. Some companies, such as Digital Equipment, Federal Express, Lincoln Electric, and Hewlett-Packard, have maintained a long-standing commitment to their employees, either formally or informally, through **no-layoff policies.**[15] Surplus staff is either retrained and deployed to other departments or reduced through attrition, early retirement, and limitations on hiring when economic conditions require a reduction in personnel.

IBM, too, has long subscribed to a no-layoff, "full-employment," policy. For example, IBM maintained its no-layoff tradition during a recent recessionary year, 1992, when 40,000 jobs had to be cut.

Have you ever been
"voluntarily
transitioned"?

Instead of layoffs, IBM employed a procedure referred to as a "voluntary transition program" that allowed employees to retire early or to receive financial incentives to quit. Some employees were able to maintain their employment by relocating or learning new skills. However, IBM's substantial decline in profits in 1991 and 1992 created such a financial strain on the company that John Akers, IBM chairman announced, "If business conditions do not improve significantly, it is likely that some business units will be unable to maintain full employment."[16] Unfortunately, attempting to maintain no-layoff policies during prolonged economic slumps can prove costly for organizations.

General Motors, in contrast, placed several communities and thousands of employees in a state of shock early in 1992 when it suddenly announced plant closings and cutbacks affecting twelve plants. Some employees expressed anger at the company's decision to transfer some of its production facilities to Toluca, Mexico.[17]

Some firms enable their employees to take paid **social service leaves.** IBM and Xerox are among those firms with programs that allow employees to take up to one year off, generally with full salaries and employee benefits, for socially constructive tasks.

Social-service leaves are expensive to the company. However, a Xerox executive, Harold Davis, typified the attitudes of some companies when he stated, "More companies are going to have to be doing this, because you have to put something back into the communities—you can't just extract profits. And this is not bad for business, either."[18]

Responsibility to Consumers

A company's customers are its bread and butter, so to speak. Without customers there are no revenues and thus no profits. The principle of *caveat emptor* already mentioned is less prevalent today than in the past. Once again the change resulted in part because an outraged public pressured its elected representatives into passing legislation to protect the unwary consumer.

Satisfied consumers
pay company salaries!

Any company's survival over the long run is highly dependent on its ability to provide consumers with the goods and services they want, at a price they're willing to pay, and of a quality they consider reasonable. Firms that have failed to do so have usually lost business to those that have attempted to satisfy the public's needs. The total quality management movement discussed in Chapter 7 is a positive step in the direction of focusing on customer wants and needs.

The whole enchilada
in just 2 days!

Taco Bell Corporation showed its concern for consumers and the community soon after the destructive Los Angeles riot that occurred on April 30, 1992. While many managers decided not to rebuild their destroyed structures, Taco Bell launched a construction marathon to build a Compton outlet in just 48 hours to replace the $500,000 site that was destroyed during the riots. Calling their efforts "From Rubble to Re-Employment in Two Days," Taco Bell executives agreed to provide some business and job opportunities to minorities during rebuilding. Five of the ten members of the construction consortium were minority-owned contractors, and minorities accounted for 168 of the 255 workers on the job site.[19]

Responsibility to the Environment

Unfortunately, America's gigantic economy has produced not only an *affluent,* but also an *effluent* society, one with polluted rivers, foul air, and an urban atmosphere that generates fear, tension, and sometimes misery.

Not everyone agrees on the extent to which businesses can afford to be involved with protecting the environment. Some executives have contended, for example, that the increased costs resulting from the installation of antipollution devices can price their products out of consumer markets.

Federal legislation requires any company or individual that accidentally spills chemicals to report the accident to the Environmental Protection Agency (EPA). Anyone who violates the EPA's spill-reporting requirements faces criminal prosecution and substantial fines.

Is concern for the environment costly? A valid question relates to how much additional costs a firm can afford and still remain competi-

"My father is an industrial polluter. What does yours do?"

SOURCE: From *The Wall Street Journal*—permission, Cartoon Features Syndicate.

tive and profitable, especially for smaller firms. However, over the long run, it is doubtful that more stringent environmental concerns and controls will have a significant influence on industry's costs. Historically, some of the most profitable firms have been those most concerned with the environment. Those who oppose such controls principally on the grounds of cost should not overlook an essential point: Society reaps substantial benefit from a pollution-free environment. Of course, a free economy does produce a lot of wealth, and wealth is a social good. But so is *health,* which is attainable only with the sacrifice of some types of freedoms, such as the freedom to pollute.

Many firms have shown a concern for the environment. Some firms place emphasis on *waste prevention* and the *recycling of waste materials,* rather than on *waste disposal.* In fact, so many companies have become involved with recycling activities that the U.S. recycling business became plagued in 1992 by distribution bottlenecks and regional gluts of collected materials. Consequently, more than two dozen large U.S. corporations have formed a voluntary alliance to develop and expand markets for recycled products. The group calls itself the "Buy Recycled Business Alliance" and includes such companies as McDonald's Corporation, Sears, Roebuck & Company, 3M Corporation, Safeway Incorporated, and Bell-South. Most member companies have committed senior managers to the effort; at least five are corporate vice-presidents.[20]

Too much of a good thing?

Another example—this one showing a global concern for the environment—is Herman Miller, a furniture maker in Zeeland, Michigan, that no longer uses tropical woods, such as rosewood, from endangered rain forests in its office desks and tables. The company has switched to cherry, which does not come from the endangered tropical rain forests.[21]

Responsibility to Provide Information

What types of information can organizations provide?

Another socially beneficial approach taken by some organizations is the dissemination of practical information to the general public or to other businesses. For example, Metropolitan Life Insurance Company has consistently made available free brochures providing information on health and hygiene. Naturally, the longer people live, the longer they will pay insurance premiums to insurance companies such as Metropolitan Life. This factor, however, need not detract form the social usefulness of such efforts.

As we've already seen, another firm the Kemper Financial Group, has actively distributed free information to companies concerned with establishing drug and alcohol abuse programs.

Utility companies, too, have provided free counseling on how to insulate houses. Some have also provided low-interest loans to allow homeowners to purchase energy-saving items such as solar heating units.

Some companies, however, take an opposite tack. In fact, in recent years, there has been a trend to "hide" or exclude unfavorable information in less obvious sections of annual reports. According to Sid Cato, publisher of a Waukesha, Wisconsin, newsletter on annual reports, "More than ever, companies are trying to tell it like it ain't." Many companies use slick color graphics, and tend to gloss over problems and focus on less important, but positive, items. William P. Dunk, a consultant on annual reports, has contended, "Most annual reports excel more in communications than in disclosure. This makes many annual reports read like Truman Capote novels in fiction."[22]

Responsibility to Assist Special Employment Groups

Considerable space in this text has already been devoted to the hiring of individuals who have been discriminated against for various reasons. Many organizations have shown an awareness of their responsibilities to special employment groups in recent decades. Some firms actively promote their equal employment opportunity hiring practices to increase the proportion of minorities, women, and individuals with mental or physical challenges in their organizations. Others have developed innovations in employment, such as the use of computer terminals at home, so that individuals with disabilities can be gainfully employed.

Recessions are depressing. . . .

Many members of special employment groups tend to have less seniority than other employees, since many of the former are newer to the work force. As a result, recessions frequently result in the undoing of much of the progress achieved in the area of equal employment opportunity. Newer employees are usually laid off or discharged during recessions. "Last hired, first fired" has been a well-known expression to many minorities and women during economic recessions. Restructuring activities resulting from hostile takeovers have frequently affected minorities and women in the same manner as recessions.

Responsibility to Help Small Businesses

Some business executives have made contributions to society by assisting small business managers. For example, the **Service Corps of Retired Executives (SCORE)** is a volunteer organization of over 3000 *retired* senior managers who advise business owners. Business owners can request the assistance of a SCORE advisor from the Small Business Administration. An advisor whose expertise fits the nature of the problem (marketing, personnel, finance) meets with the owner to analyze the problem and develop a solution. The advice is free.

Do small businesspeople know the SCORE?

Would you like to be an ACE?

The related organization is the **Active Corps of Executives (ACE),** a volunteer organization of *active* professionals who supplement SCORE's services to small business owners with expert, up-to-date advice. ACE also works though the Small Business Administration.

Ben and Jerry—Two Modern-Day Robin Hoods?[b]

Eating ice cream has become a virtuous and socially responsible act, thanks to two baby-boomers, Ben Cohen and Jerry Greenfield, makers of "Vermont's Finest All-Natural Ice Cream" since 1978. Their success has been phenomenal, now second only to Haagen Dazs in the super-premium ice cream market. Having graduated from "America's class clowns" to "national role models for corporate responsibility," their goal is to make first-rate products *and* profits in a socially responsible manner. According to Ben, the question is, "How much do we benefit the community and how much money do we make?"

Here are a few of Ben and Jerry's progressive activities: Executive salaries are limited to only seven times the lowest wage, recently a maximum of $130,000 including benefits, thus freeing more money for socially responsible activities. The brownies in the Chocolate Fudge Brownie product are made at Greystone Bakery in Yonkers, New York, a firm that reinvests profits in jobs and training for the homeless. Berries for Wild Maine Blueberry ice cream comes from the Passamaquoddy Indians to support traditional elements of their economy. Profit from the nut brickle candy in Rain Forest Crunch assists rain forest and environmental preservation. A shop was opened in Harlem, an innercity debut intended to plow back 75 percent of its profit to HARKhomes, a shelter and community center for the homeless. Most of the ten part- and full-time jobs are filled by homeless people.

So two guys who were the fattest boys in their high school gym class haven't done badly in spite of their meager beginnings. Ben dropped out of college, and Jerry was twice rejected from medical school. Jerry enrolled in a $5 correspondence course in ice cream making when they couldn't afford the equipment to make their other favorite food—bagels. They started making the ice cream in a converted garage on $12,000 of mostly borrowed funds. They now earn high profits selling expensive premium ice cream to upscale customers and redistribute most of the profits to the less fortunate. Robin Hood is alive and well!

ACE volunteers typically are business executives, officers of trade associations, management professors, lawyers, and accountants. As with SCORE, there is no fee to the small businessperson for this service.

Responsibility to Contribute Money and Talent

Although portions of the previous section have illustrated examples of undesirable behavior on the part of the business community, there are numerous positive examples of corporate behavior as well. Many firms, of course, show a high degree of concern for society's needs by contributing money and talent. You need only read the newspapers for examples of social concern regularly displayed by some members of the business community. Ben and Jerry's provides us with an example of a socially progressive company that became one of the world's largest purveyors of ice cream. Their concern for the community and the environment is traced in *A Box of Interest* entitled "Ben & Jerry—Two Modern-Day Robin Hoods?"

No "Rocky Road" to social responsibility!

The National Volunteer Center in Arlington, Virginia, estimates that 600 companies in the United States have some sort of formal volunteer program that encourages employee participation. Ralston Purina of St. Louis, Missouri, for example, supports an employee volunteer network to match employee interests with nonprofit groups' needs. Oakland-based Clorox Company sponsors a well-established public service program that encourages employees to volunteer their services to charitable and community-service organizations.[23] Clorox has also developed and published a formal policy on its responsibilities to the community (see Figure 15.1).

GUIDE TO SOCIAL ACTION

One of the primary functions of management is that of *planning*. Yet managers concerned with social programs often neglect this important function. Instead, they too frequently have been involved with "putting out fires" ignited by disgruntled members of the public.

Social programs developed in a *calm and thoughtful atmosphere* tend to convey greater sincerity and are more likely to succeed than those hastily conceived in an atmosphere of crisis. Too frequently, pressured and harried executives have developed and employed programs before analyzing their implications, thus creating distrust—rather than appreciation and respect—in the general public.

Naturally, no magic formulas can guarantee the success of any program, but some approaches tried by various organizations have been effective. The purpose of the following section, therefore, is to offer a *set of guidelines* (see Table 15.1) that can result in more successes than a helter-skelter approach of haste, indecision, and uncertainty.

Community Relationships

We endeavor to build and maintain excellent relationships with the communities in which we have a presence. Our relationships are based on two fundamental beliefs:

As corporate citizen, we have the same obligations as does the individual citizen who enjoys the community's services and amenities.

The well-being of the Company and our employees is inseparably tied to the well-being of the community.

We, therefore, respect the rights of our immediate neighbors and of other members of the community. This includes operating our facilities safely and in compliance with applicable environmental regulations, and taking those additional steps, as necessary, to make our operations positive contributors to their communities.

We look for ways to improve the quality of work life in our communities, working in partnership with local government, business and charitable organizations, as well as through the contribution of funds to qualified organizations and projects whose purpose in community betterment. We also encourage our employees to participate in civic affairs and activities of their interest, recognizing that volunteer work is highly commendable and valuable form of community service.

Figure 15.1 The Clorox Company's formal policy on community relations.
SOURCE: By permission of the Clorox Company

Management Must Be Committed

Why is senior management support especially important?

One of the most important guidelines for social action is that *managers*—from the chief executive to the supervisors—*must have firm, sincere commitments* to a corporation's social programs. These commitments should be a part of the ongoing goals and operations of the organization. A few token dollars spent here or there on temporary programs do not make a company socially responsible in the eyes of the public.

Why the need for long-term consistency?

The commitment must first be *well thought out* and above all *consistent* and *long term*. For example, people will generally be turned off by programs that receive funding one year and are put on a bare-bones budget the next. Consistency should pervade the entire company so that employees in one branch will not be saying or doing one thing while others are saying or doing something else.

TABLE 15.1   Suggested Guidelines Related to Employing Socially Responsible Programs.

- Management must be committed.
- The program should be integrated into regular operations.
- The program must be communicated.
- The program must be credible.
- Participants should be concerned with action.
- Failures should not be discouraging.

The Program Should Be Integrated Into Regular Operations

Why shouldn't programs be separated from normal operations?

To prevent the appearance of window dressing, no program should be considered separate and apart from an organization's regular operations. A firm sincerely concerned with social responsibility should not grandstand its efforts but should instead attempt to incorporate its obligations to society into the basic structure of the organization.

The Program Must Be Communicated

All levels of an organization must understand the program if it is to be as effective as possible. As we have learned, employees provide a significant communications link with the public, and their misinterpretation of a program can cause untold damage.

What are ways to communicate a program to employees?

Some firms use *videotapes, movies,* or *slides* to help explain the objectives of a program as well as details of the employees' responsibilities to it. *Company schools* are sometimes established so that interested employees can learn about environmental subjects. *Public service awards* can motivate employees to participate in such programs.

The Program Must Be Credible

Why is credibility essential?

Those directing the programs should be concerned with *credibility.* Few activities will ever be 100 percent successful. Although negative aspects shouldn't be accentuated when company activities are discussed, efforts to gloss over shortcomings may result in the entire program's being mistrusted. In other words, companies should be honest about their programs.

Participants Should Be Concerned With Action

Which speaks louder and clearer— actions or words?

Little is gained by managers who speak eloquently before civic or other groups about the need for social action yet are not themselves actively and sincerely involved with specific programs. The public can generally see through such rhetoric.

Some firms, as we have learned, permit their employees to be genuinely involved by encouraging them to volunteer for work in the community—often on company time. Some firms offer their employees paid sabbaticals; others allow a half day each week for such activities as counseling minority businesses.

Those Virtuous Europeans![c]

According to a recent survey by the Henley Centre for Forecasting, European employers are a fairly virtuous lot, or at least that's what they claimed when asked a number of questions about their social responsibility activities. The Henley Centre queried 500 employers across sectors in the European Community (Common Market) about their employment practices. Here are some of their findings:

- Thirty-two percent of the organizations—half of them in the public sector—say they have a woman on the board of directors or in a similar top function.
- Job sharing is offered by 48 percent of the companies.
- Career breaks—such as leaves for service—are offered by 59 percent.
- Maternity leave beyond legal requirements is provided by 40 percent.
- Only 9 percent of the companies provided on-site childcare.
- An additional 16 percent have off-site provision for childcare.
- Dissatisfaction with employers' childcare facilities is especially high in the United Kingdom, France, and Germany.
- Eighty-seven percent provide formal management development programs.
- Eighty-five percent subsidize employees' studies.
- Sixty-six percent offer retraining programs.
- Forty-two percent offer extended study leave.

The report points out that an increasing proportion of companies are trying to impress the public with their concern for the environment. About 70 percent of the European Community countries either have carried out environmental checks on their activities or intend to carry out such audits.

The Henley report concludes that employment practices and conditions in Europe's largest companies are fairly responsible. However, the report did warn that without increases in childcare facilities, there is likely to be scant growth in the proportion of women attaining executive and management positions.

Failures Should Not Be Discouraging

As you may know, the Ford Motor Company's Edsel automobile was something of a failure. Undaunted, Ford managers went on to develop two bestsellers, the Mustang and the Maverick.

A similar spirit should prevail among those involved with social programs. Not all programs will succeed. Managers, however, should examine the entire picture before deciding that a program has failed and abandoning it. A modification of certain aspects might improve the programs' overall effectiveness.

Should you be discouraged by an occasional Edsel? It may become a collector's item!

SUMMARY

In an earlier chapter, we examined the nature and causes of prejudice. We learned that prejudice is a form of judgment made with insufficient facts. Although some business managers have neglected sound ethical practices and social responsibilities in the past, much prejudice toward the business community has resulted from the general public's lack of understanding of business and its place in society.

Business managers are generally concerned with effective communication *within* their organizations; more and more managers have developed an awareness of organizational behavior techniques, such as job enrichment, designed to motivate employees. Perhaps there is an additional need for managers to develop programs of "social enrichment" *outside* their organizations.

Organizational leaders have done little in the past to modify the many erroneous concepts and prejudices about business held by the general public. Too often managers have either been *excessively defensive* or have placed excessive stress on how *right* everything is. In far too many instances management has been reluctant to talk about its problems candidly, and as a result, the public frequently feels that business has something to hide. Annual reports, for example, have customarily been filled with puffery, window dressing, and glad tidings, instead of honest appraisals of things as they really are.

Management must learn that talk alone will not convince a skeptical general public of the desirability of private organizations. True, zealots have at times thrown uninformed and biased rhetorical rocks at the business community. In the long run, however, management will fail to get its message across by fighting rhetoric with rhetoric. To quote an old cliché, "You can try to fight fire with fire, but firefighters usually use water!"

The general public also has certain responsibilities. Rather than being blindly and emotionally prejudiced toward business in general, it should strive to become better informed about the actual activities of the business community and to realize that many organizational contributions toward society cannot be made *unless* firms are able to earn reasonable profits.

The solutions needn't involve a battle between business and the general public. Instead, business leaders must establish *long-term commitments* to social action. Too often, programs have been ill-conceived, hastily adopted, and then hastily dropped. Management must be willing not only to anticipate the need for change but also to employ programs with foresight *before* it is pushed "up against the corporate wall," as it has been during some turbulent periods of the past. Some citizens have argued that aggressive and hostile attacks upon business are the only effective way to get its attention. The public must be convinced otherwise—not through the use of clever managerial rhetoric or propaganda campaigns in the mass media but by a display of sincere concern for the well-being of American society by organizations.

Finally, management should profoundly examine the ethical aspects of all its actions. The temptation is sometimes great to pursue ethically questionable practices because they benefit the cash flow or profit positions of a company. The long-run effects of such actions, however, not only could be disastrous but could ultimately sound the death knell of American private enterprise. As one Bank of America official has asserted: "In the long pull, nobody can expect to make profits—or have any meaningful use for profits—if our society is wracked by tensions."

TERMS AND CONCEPTS TO REMEMBER

ethics

caveat emptor

caveat vendor

leveraged buyouts (LBOs)

hostile (unfriendly) takeovers

golden parachute

deleverage

restructuring

trustee-of-profit

enlightened self-interest

profit-quest

social accountability

social conscience

no-layoff policies

social service leaves

Service Corps of Retired Executives (SCORE)

Active Corps of Executives (ACE)

QUESTIONS

1. Do you feel that business managers are more or less ethical now than they were in the past? Explain your viewpoint.

2. How do you feel about the image of the business community that the television and film media have frequently displayed?

3. What image-damaging activities by the business community have you heard about? How might such adverse publicity have been avoided?

4. What effect does a hostile takeover have on the managers of an acquired company? Are golden parachute programs desirable or undesirable as an approach for aiding executives? Explain.

5. What is *restructuring?* Does it tend to have a positive or negative effect on organizations? Explain.

6. Evaluate the following statement: "All this talk about pollution control and safer products is understandable, but if the public wants all those things, it had better be prepared to pay for them in the form of higher-priced products."

7. Explain how the profit-quest and social-accountability philosophies differ regarding the public responsibilities of business organizations.

8. Explain the following statement: "The actual dollars-and-cents value of social responsibility programs is difficult to determine."

9. What are some of the major social responsibilities some managers are concerned with? How do you feel about these concerns?

10. Under what conditions might a socially responsible organization not be able to maintain a no-layoff policy?

11. What are the probable long-run consequences of business organizations' ignoring their responsibilities to the general public?

12. Why is the commitment of senior management toward any organizational program essential for its success?

13. Explain the suggested guidelines that should be followed by the business community as a means of enhancing the success of social programs.

14. In May 1993, Levi Strauss & Company announced that it was phasing out clothing purchases from China because of what the company called pervasive human rights violations there. The decision affected 30 contractors who produced two percent of Levi Strauss' output.[24] Do you agree or disagree with this decision? Why or why not?

APPLICATIONS

15.1 Whose Responsibility Is Social Responsibility?

Magnum Rubber Products, a producer of specialized rubber parts, employed nearly seventy people. Tim Magnum, the previous owner, founded the firm ten years ago on a shoestring. He had been the type of manager who wasn't afraid of getting his hands dirty; he generally worked right alongside of his employees.

Magnum Rubber Products had always provided its employees with above-average pay and benefits for the industry and was considered to have had excellent working conditions. The firm had also been commended for its outstanding employee safety programs and safety record. Morale had generally been high among employees, who openly appreciated the responsible way that the company had treated them. There had also been considerable pride among employees because of their belief that they produced some of the highest quality products on the market.

Last year Tim Magnum unexpectedly died. Most employees began to fear that the company might close and that they would lose their jobs. Their fears were allayed, however, when a nationally known rubber company, U.S. General Rubber, acquired Magnum and retained most of its employees. One of U.S. General's corporate managers, Joan Robbins, was transferred from corporate headquarters to serve as general manager of Magnum Rubber Products, which was now considered to be a division of U.S. General. Ms. Robbins soon developed the reputation of being an effective manager and an enthusiastic corporate team player. The Magnum division's employees, pleased to still be holding their jobs, continued to enjoy high morale.

At a recent supervisors' meeting, Ms. Robbins, asked each supervisor to motivate their subordinates into supporting the company's annual United Way campaign. Ms. Robbins explained, "Our company is a leader in an industry that must demonstrate social responsibility. We demonstrate our attitudes in part by showing a strong commitment to our local communities. U.S. General will match the direct contributions of each employee, or give any employee ten hours free time a month to perform a community service for organizations supported by the United Way. This company *is* its people. This company requires a commitment and assistance from each one of its employees. It is the responsibility of each employee to participate. We've prepared packets for each employee explaining the need for their help and a card authorizing us to deduct a contribution from their paychecks. All employees have to do is merely indicate the amount of their contribution and sign the card."

Ms. Robbins added, "Those who prefer taking release time rather than making a financial contribution can work with any of the agencies on the list. You, the supervisor, will have to sign the release form. That way you can work it out together as to the least disruptive way to schedule their absences. If there are no questions I would like to conclude by saying that this is our first chance to show corporate headquarters that we're team players. I'm counting on all of you to really pitch this campaign to your workers!"

As the group was leaving the meeting, several of the supervisors began grumbling to each other. One supervisor exclaimed, "Welcome to corporate America! I'll bet most of my people will resent even being asked to contribute. Mr. Magnum never tried to tell us what we had to do about charity donations. It's a personal matter!"

"I personally think it's a great idea," asserted another. "And pretty generous of the company to match the gifts or give release time. I can't help but wonder, however, if all this do-gooder stuff isn't possibly related to the bad press U.S. General got last week about cost overruns on government contracts."

"Yeah," added another supervisor. "I've heard of social responsibility to the employees, but never corporate responsibility *from* the employees. What a lot of bull!"

"I'm with you," interjected another supervisor. "If the company wants to give to charity, it should do so with profits, not out of the pockets of its employees!"

"Well, one thing's for sure," said another supervisor. "I sure can't afford to have half my staff absent ten hours a month if I'm going to meet my deadlines and objectives. My job is to produce rubber products, that's all!"

Questions

1. Assuming that you were one of the affected supervisors, how would you present Ms. Robbins's directive to your employees?

2. What effect would the bad publicity that the company recently received have on your attitude toward the new campaign?

3. What is your reaction to the following comments of Joan Robbins? "This company *is* its people. This company requires a commitment and assistance from each one of its employees. It is the responsibility of each employee to participate."

15.2 Hiring and Firing on the Same Day

Two years ago, the Kelman Company, a large manufacturer of power tools and small household appliances began a voluntary employee retraining program designed to prepare existing employees for potentially more complex jobs that were likely to develop in the future.

Kelman had followed a no-layoff policy in the past and has always had an exceptionally stable work force. Sandy McFerran, Director of Human Resources, hoped to maintain such stability even as the company's personnel needs changed. Kelman's strategy was to incorporate greater use of programmable automated equipment, which would require fewer production workers. Sandy recognized that available positions in the future would require a much greater need for highly skilled technicians, computer programmers and operators, and other higher-skilled employees.

Sandy's hope was to be able to retrain and retain, rather than to layoff, most of Kelman's current employees as the company's needs changed. She publicized the series of retraining programs in company publications and posted monthly fliers on the bulletin boards about anticipated personnel needs. She also held meetings with supervisors for the purpose of promoting employee participation in the programs. While Sandy wanted to encourage participation in the retraining programs, she didn't want to risk endangering overall morale by disclosing how far-reaching and extensive the company's modernization would be. Her major hope was that an ample number of workers would take advantage of the retraining opportunity before it was too late.

Sandy was disappointed at the poor employee response to the retraining programs. Only 15 percent of the company's 4000 operations employees participated in the programs. Most of the participants were younger employees who saw the programs as a way of advancing with the Kelman Company. Many of the older employees seemed largely unconcerned about the impending changes. They felt satisfied with their current jobs and believed that the no-layoff policy and seniority rights would protect them as the company's modernization program unfolded.

Today is the day Sandy has been dreading. Kelman's automation program has been installed and is now operational. As a result, the company has no further need for nearly 300 of its employees. Layoff notices have been prepared for workers employed in areas undergoing staff reductions. The changes mean that some senior employees, especially those with outdated skills, will no longer be needed and will be discharged. Other less senior employees who received retraining will be retained. In addition, there are 180 new positions for which no existing employees are qualified. Sandy has placed an advertisement in the local newspaper announcing these openings.

Questions

1. What is your opinion as to why so few workers participated in the Kelman Company's retraining program?

2. What do you think will be the reaction of the laid-off employees?

3. How do you feel about the way Sandy handled the personnel activities discussed in this case? Should the employees have been told that their chances of being laid off in the future were enhanced if they didn't volunteer for retraining?

4. What can you conclude about your own career future from this case?

NOTES

1. "Most Americans Endorse Import Curbs, Roper Poll Finds," *AFL-CIO News,* June 25, 1990, p. 8.

2. "Bad Guys Wear Pinstripes," *Business Week,* October 21, 1988, pp. 61, 66.

3. Mike McQueen and Rae Tyson, "Exxon Trying to 'Set Matters Right,'" *USA Today/International Edition,* May 4, 1989, p. 3; and "A Backlash Against Business?" *Business Week/International Edition,* February 6, 1989, pp. 22–23.

4. "HUD Embezzlement Probe Ordered," *USA Today/International Edition,* June 13, 1989, p. 3.

5. David Ellis, "Nobody Here but Us Chickens," *Time,* March 23, 1992, p. 25; and David Ellis, "Time to Clean House," *Time,* March 30, 1992, p. 29.

6. Myron Magnet, "The Decline and Fall of Business Ethics," *Fortune,* December 8, 1986, p. 65.

7. See Note 5, p. 66.

8. Timothy D. Schellhardt, "Merged Firms Often Fire Workers the Easy Way—Not the Best Way," *The Wall Street Journal,* February 24, 1986, p. 35.

9. "Union Carbide Protects Execs with 'Golden Parachutes'," *Contra Costa Times,* December 26, 1985, p. 19C.

10. Nikki Tait, "The Number of Leveraged Buy-Outs Is in Sharp Decline," *Financial Times,* October 1, 1991, p. VII; and Anne B. Fisher, "The Big Drive to Reduce Debt," *Fortune/International Edition,* February 10, 1992, pp. 70–74.

11. Martin Dickson, "US Business Turns Leaner and Meaner," *Financial Times,* February 11, 1992, p. 17, Nancy Dunne, "AT&T Agrees Three-Year Pay Deal," *Financial Times,* July 3, 1992, p. 4; and "IBM to Slash Work Force by Minimum 32,000 in 1992," *The Wall Street Journal Europe,* July 29, 1992, p. 3.

12. Diane Summers, "Management Stress Can Lead to Merger Breakdown," *Financial Times,* January 8, 1992, p. 8.

13. "GM Chairman Blames Bad Press for Pessimism About U.S. Autos," *Oakland Tribune,* January 19, 1992, p. 27.

14. Thornton Bradshaw and David Vogel, *Corporations and Their Critics* (New York: McGraw-Hill, 1980).

15. "A Japanese Import That's Not Selling," *Business Week,* February 26, 1990, p. 42.

16. Thomas McCarroll, "The Humbling of a Computer Colossus," *Time,* May 20, 1991, pp. 42–44; "IBM Sets Plan to Encourage Certain Workers to Leave," *The Wall Street Journal Europe,* May 23, 1991; "IBM Expects to Cut 40,000 Jobs Through Buyouts, Early Retirement," *Los Angeles Times,* September 29, 1992, p. 62; and Louise Kehoe, "Big Blue Turns Mean and Lean to Survive Recession," *Financial Times,* December 16, 1992, p. 15.

17. "GM to Shut, Trim 12 Plants Following $4.5 Billion Loss," *The Washington Post,* February 24, 1992, p. 21.

18. Jeffrey A. Tannenbaum, "Paid Public-Service Leaves Buoy Workers," *The Wall Street Journal,* May 6, 1981, p. 25.

19. George White, "Taco Bell Rushes to Set Example in City Hit by Riots," *Los Angeles Times,* June 10, 1992, p. D-1.

20. Frank Edward Allen, "Big U.S. Corporations Form Alliance to Spur Recycling," *The Wall Street Journal,* September 4, 1992, p. 7.

21. Susan Caminiti, "The Payoff From a Good Reputation," *Fortune/International Edition,* February 10, 1992, pp. 49–53.

22. Lee Berton, "Firms' Annual Reports Are Short on Candor, and May Get Shorter," *The Wall Street Journal,* September 9, 1987, p. 24.

23. Zachary Schiller, "Doing Well by Doing Good," *Business Week/International Edition,* December 5, 1988, pp. 118–120; and Patricia Amend, "More Companies Lend a Hand," *USA Today/International Edition,* December 1, 1989, p. 15.

24. "Levi Strauss To Drop China-made Clothing," *The San Francisco Examiner,* May 6, 1993, p. 3-B; and Louis Kehoe, "Bold Fashion Statement," *Financial Times Weekend,* May 8–9, 1993, p. 9.

25. Adapted from a *Business Week/Harris Poll:* "Is An Antibusiness Backlash Building?" *Business Week,* July 20, 1987, p. 71.

BOX NOTES

a. Adapted from "Job-Security Pledges Can Benefit Both Workers and the Boss," *The Wall Street Journal,* May 14, 1985, p. 1; "Job Security Major Issue at AT&T Contract Talks," *The Washington Post,* April 1, 1992, p. 21; and Nancy Dunne, "AT&T Agrees Three-Year Pay Deal," *Financial Times,* July 3, 1992, p. 4.

b. Adapted from Peter Nulty, "Global Warming: What We Know," *Fortune/International Edition,* April 9, 1990, p. 71; and Karen Fricker, "The Robin Hoods of the Ice Cream World," *Financial Times/Weekend,* July 4/5, 1992, p. XV.

c. Adapted from Diane Summers, "In the Very Best of Company," *Financial Times,* May 11, 1992, p. 14.

EXPERIENTIAL EXERCISES

Are You "Backlashing" Toward Business?[25]

Your answers to the following questions will give an indication of your attitude toward the business community. After you've completed the questionnaire, have ten other persons answer the questions and compare their responses with yours. What do you believe influenced the responses you received?

Questions	*Answers (Check one)*	
1. How would you rate the ethical standards of business executives?	Excellent	_____
	Fairly good	_____
	Only fair	_____
	Poor	_____
	Not sure	_____
2. Do you think white-collar crime is very common, somewhat common, not very common, or not common at all?	Very common	_____
	Somewhat common	_____
	Not very common	_____
	Not common at all	_____
	Not sure	_____
3. During the past decade, there was a massive wave of mergers and acquisitions that swept the country. In general, how do you feel they have been for the country?	Good for the country	_____
	Bad for the country	_____
	Not made much difference	_____
	Not sure	_____

4. Some takeovers are friendly and others are hostile. Critics have argued that there should be new government restrictions on hostile takeovers. Do you favor or oppose such restrictions?

Favor _____
Oppose _____
Not sure _____

5. Do you think companies should be required by law to notify their workers and the local community in advance that they are planning to shut down an operation?

Should be required _____
Should not be required _____
Not sure _____

6. Federal regulation of business has been too lax, but now it has gone too much the other way and is too tough.

Agree _____
Disagree _____
Not sure _____

7. When the government largely deregulated a number of services, such as trucking, airlines, and telephone companies, the overall results were positive.

Agree _____
Disagree _____
Not sure _____

8. As a result of federal deregulation, job safety, environmental quality, and product safety have all declined.

Agree _____
Disagree _____
Not sure _____

9. Even though it has some drawbacks, privatization of government-owned enterprises is necessary to improve their efficiency.

Agree _____
Disagree _____
Not sure _____

10. Suppose one candidate in the upcoming presidential election had strong business backing while another candidate was strongly opposed by business. If you had to choose, which candidate would you say is better qualified to be president?

Candidate with business backing _____
Candidate opposed by business _____
Not sure _____

11. Which party, the Republicans or the Democrats, do you feel is better able to put the interests of the country ahead of the interests of business?

Republicans _____
Democrats _____

The Commencement Speaker

Assume that you've been extended an invitation to be the commencement speaker at this year's graduation exercises at Harde Nocks University. You've been requested to discuss "What's Wrong with Ethics in American Society?" Prepare a ten-minute address expressing a viewpoint that you believe would be of interest to graduating students and their guests.

CHAPTER 16

On a Global Scale

It's a Small, Small World

**When you finish this chapter,
you should be able to:**

1

Recognize the increased concern of organizations
for global, transnational operations.

2

Identify the various factors that influence the
culture and operations of global organizations.

3

Reduce the effects of culture shock related to foreign job assignments.

4

Avoid some of the problems associated with repatriation.

> For many major companies, going global is a matter
> of survival, and it means radically changing the way they work.
>
> *Jeremy Main, Management Writer*

"Big Macs" hawked in Moscow, Russia; "Finger-lickin'-good Kentucky Fried Chicken" sold in Beijing, China; Fords manufactured in England; General Motors automobiles manufactured in Germany; Coca-Cola bottled in Santa Cruz de Tenerife, the Canary Islands, Spain; Pepsi bottled in Bombay, India; Marlboro cigarettes produced in Russia; Toys 'R' Us operating in Tokyo; and "genuine original riveted" Levi Strauss denim jeans made in Hungary. Business operations have indeed become increasingly *global* in recent decades. **Globalism** has become a hot topic among corporate directors and managers who realize that in many instances the very survival of their firms has become dependent on how well they apply their managerial talents on a transnational, rather than solely domestic basis.

OPPORTUNITIES AND CHALLENGES ON A GLOBAL BASIS

Many senior executives have tended to view their firms as "American," a fairly natural attitude that is changing rapidly, however, with

"My client wants the jury to know that the getaway car was American made."

SOURCE: From *The Wall Street Journal*—permission, Cartoon Features Syndicate

the "new guard" of managers directing today's organizations. For example, numerous contemporary chief executive officers, such as Rockwell's Donald Beall, Whirlpool's David Whitwam, and Motorola's George Fisher, feel right "at home" in foreign environments, each having spent considerable time in overseas posts. Theirs is a global point of view. They expect their firms to operate as **transnationals,** without loyalty to a particular home. For many organization members, this trend requires an entirely new way of thinking, one that views the entire world as one market. The transnational organization manufactures, conducts research, raises capital, and buys supplies wherever it can do the job best, unlike the *multinational* or *international* firm that may operate overseas but remains firmly anchored in its home country.[1]

A Rapidly Changing World

The world has been changing at mind-boggling speed during the 1990s. In spite of some setbacks in 1992 related to the acceptance of the *Maastrict treaty* on economic and political union, the **European Economic Community (EEC),** or *Common Market,* consisting of twelve Western European nations,* continues in its attempts to move toward a "borderless Europe" with the goal of gradually breaking down most of its traditional economic barriers.

Would a
Trojan horse help?

Some U.S. leaders fear that the EEC nations are developing a "Fortress Europe," which could block the importation of American goods. As a result, an increasing number of U.S. firms have established, or intend to establish, operations within the EEC as a means of being a part of the action. In some instances, American firms have purchased European firms: Ford bought the British car-maker Jaguar, General Motors acquired half of Sweden's Saab-Scania's passenger car operations, Businessland acquired Böwe Systemvertrieb, a German personal computer dealer, Pfizer bought Swiss Medivent, AT&T obtained 20 percent of Italy's Italtel, and Emerson Electric secured France's Leroy-Somer.[2]

Americans have sometimes been accused by other nationalities of being **ethnocentric,** which means having the belief that virtually everything in the United States is better than what exists in other countries. True, many things are better—but not all. In reality, many things that we think are American are not, and determining what nationality a product is these days has become downright difficult. Did you know, for example, that some GM cars have more Japanese components than some Japanese cars do? Did you also know that a

---

*Belgium, Denmark, Germany, Greece, Spain, France, Ireland, Italy, Luxembourg, Netherlands, Portugal, and the United Kingdom. Other nations, such as Norway and Austria, have applications for membership pending.

Ford Probe is really a Mazda MX-6 and that a Mitsubishi Eclipse is a Plymouth Laser? Did you further know that Zenith TVs are made in Mexico and Mitsubishi TVs are made in Santa Ana, California? And finally, did you realize that 40 percent of all Japanese-brand vehicles sold in America are actually *made in the USA?*[3] So what really is a "foreign" product? The distinction has become so fuzzy that *Forbes,* a business publication, has rated Honda Motor Company as the most efficient "American" car company![4]

Looking Beyond Domestic Borders

The world of the 1990s barely resembles the world of prior decades. Merely ask the cartographers (map makers) for substantiation of this premise. Intense competition from, and investment opportunities in, Asian countries and the collapse of communism in the Eastern countries have motivated American managers into taking a second look at their methods of management, production, and marketing.

Furthermore, managers from a variety of nations have noted the significant changes in attitudes toward private enterprise by officials in China and have increasingly looked beyond their domestic borders for business opportunities. In addition, trade agreements between Canada, Mexico, and the United States will create both hurdles and opportunities for American managers and their employees. Some companies now find that a high proportion of their operating income comes from outside their home countries. For example, 80 percent of the Coca-Cola Company's operating profits before expenses comes from outside the United States.[5] Table 16.1 lists some recent examples of investments made in other countries.

Gyrations and crises in the exchange rates of the American dollar, Japanese yen, English pound, Italian lira, and other currencies create additional challenges, risks, and pressures for the transnational business manager.

A South *and* North of the Border—A Foot in Each

¡Hola, amigos! Here's an additional trend that combines U.S. efforts with those of its neighbor to the south—Mexico. The **maquiladora industry,** based on low-cost Mexican labor and border-zone assembly plants, tripled in activity during the 1980s.[6] By 1989, some 1500 U.S. firms were operating *maquiladora* plants on the Mexican side of the 2000 mile border that stretches from Brownsville, Texas, to San Diego, California. They employed an estimated 370,000 workers—and there are predictions that employment will have grown to more than a million workers by 1995 along the border strip.[7]

The concept of *maquiladora* is supposed to involve "twin plants," one on each side of the border, thus providing American firms with the economic advantages of both locations. However, critics of the

¡Trabajodores baratos!

TABLE 16.1   Examples of Foreign Investments by U.S. Companies During the 1990s.

- McDonald's Canadian division engaged in a joint venture with Russia to open in Moscow the world's largest fast-food outlet (700 seats).
- Pizza Hut engaged in a joint venture with Russia to open outlets.
- Kentucky Fried Chicken opened outlets in Beijing and Shanghai.
- Honeywell began operations in Czechoslovakia.
- Avis, Hertz, and Budget established car rental agencies in Poland.
- General Motors engaged in a joint venture to build cars in the eastern part of Germany.

activity argue that the vast majority of workers are on the Mexican side of the border, where wages are cheap, and only "shelter" operations are maintained on the U.S. side.[8]

Although such global activities are not unusual in our world today, such ventures by American companies have become a hot political issue in recent years, especially in light of the **North American Free Trade Act (NAFTA)**—legislation that proposes to reduce substantially the trade barriers between the United States, Mexico, and Canada. A *Box of Interest,* "South of the Border . . . Down Mexico Way!" discusses some of the issues associated with NAFTA. Many firms have long benefited from doing their designing and engineering in one country, manufacturing of certain components in various countries, assembling in still other countries, and marketing wherever possible. Such activities are likely to continue in the probable future absence of trade barriers.

A Need to Understand Global Organizational Behavior

As more U.S. firms become global in their operations, more of them will require managers and employees who are global in their outlook.

Global O.B. all over the globe!

The concepts that you have already studied in this text will have to be adapted to what could be termed **global organizational behavior.** Such OB concepts as communication, motivation, leadership, morale, and adaptation to change are especially important to managers of global operations. The ability to apply OB concepts situationally to cultures that are foreign is becoming increasingly important for American managers.

ORGANIZATIONAL CULTURES IN A GLOBAL ENVIRONMENT

As we learned earlier, each organization has its own distinct culture. Culture is important in establishing and maintaining the value of its

A BOX OF INTEREST

South of the Border . . . Down Mexico Way![a]

The North American Free Trade Act (NAFTA)—legislation that proposes to break down the trade barriers between the United States, Mexico, and Canada—has generated a lot more heat than light in recent years. U.S. free traders and supporters of NAFTA contend that Mexican and Canadian markets will open up, resulting not only in increased exports of American-made products to Canada and Mexico but also in the creation of additional jobs in the United States. Opponents of NAFTA contend that the only thing exported will be American jobs and that many companies will merely move their plants south to take advantage of lower-paid Mexican labor.

Would it really be logical for American companies to leave the U.S. and move to Mexico? Labor quality couldn't be as good as in America when the average Mexican has only a sixth-grade education and only 3 percent of Mexicans have college degrees—could it? Well, don't be too sure. Senior executives from IBM, Ford, Procter & Gamble, A.O. Smith, Kohler, GE, and Caterpillar have nothing but praise for the quality of the workers in their Mexican plants. *No es todo:* An MIT study in 1990 reported that Ford's Mercury Tracer plant in Hermosillo was the highest-quality assembly plant in the world.

But the major issue is whether the law will reduce American employment. The head of Eastman-Kodak says no. He claims that after Eastman expanded in Mexico, every three jobs there resulted in one additional support person in the United States. However, U.S. union officials snap back by presenting a long list of companies that closed or laid off workers from U.S. plants to move production to Mexico. Examples: Zenith closed its last television manufacturing facility in the United States. American Car, a freight car producer, previously employed 4000 in St. Louis. Jolly Green Giant went from 12,000 to 115 workers after its move. Jeans maker Farah Co. had employed 3750 in the early 1980s and went down to 410.

members. A significant challenge faced by American global managers is determining how to blend established American organizational cultures with the cultures that exist within organizations in other nations. The task is not easy. However, the task is less difficult after

TABLE 16.2   **Selected Factors That Influence the Culture and Operations of Global Organizations.**

- Customs
- Language and communications styles
- Attitudes toward time
- The work force
- Differences in pay scales
- Labor laws
- Standards of ethics
- Political climate
- Variations in foreign exchange rates

Americans learn what significant types of differences exist in various regions of the world. It is beyond the scope of this text to cover each cultural difference that exists in each region of every country. The following discussion is intended to reveal some of the *types of factors* that vary among peoples of the world. Keep in mind, however, the dangers of generalizing about any culture. Each nation has wide variations within it. Merely travel through Sweden and Italy and you will soon discover that not all Swedes are blond nor Italians brunette!

A variety of factors influence the culture and operations of global organizations (see Table 16.2). Each of these is briefly discussed below.

Differences in Customs

"What's wrong with *these* people. Don't they know that the way *we do it* in America is much better than the way they do it? And why do they keep asking me, 'Which one, North, South, or Central?' when I say I'm from America? Those other people aren't Americans; they're Canadians, Salvadorans, or Peruvians—not Americans."

Some U.S. citizens receive a rude cultural awakening when they first "hit the shores," so to speak, of a foreign land. Many of them experience something known as **culture shock,** a state of confusion and anxiety that can affect individuals when they are first exposed to an unfamiliar culture. They find no round-the-clock convenience stores, few—if any—laundromats, and high-speed driving habits that are often stress-inducing, and they sometimes develop new health problems, such as first-time asthma, insomnia, changes in sexual behavior, sinus headaches, or constipation.[9] Americans, of course, aren't the only people afflicted with culture shock. Japanese managers and their families who have moved to the United States have also experienced this malady. Some Japanese firms have even established separate schools for the children of Japanese employees located in the United States.

"185 KPH on the autobahn stressful?"
"Jawohl!"

Psychiatrist Raymond A. Sleszynski, who has worked with many *expatriates* overseas, believes that Americans have a more difficult time adapting to different cultures because they come from a gigantic culture of their own. (An **expatriate** is a person who lives and works in a country other than his or her native country.) Americans also tend to shy away from learning foreign languages and often have a provincial attitude regarding other countries and cultures. Sleszynski believes that "the Dutch are the most adapted of all, because they're from a small country and, of course, no one speaks Dutch other than the Dutch, so they have to learn English, German, and French. As a result, they feel comfortable and at home with all these cultures."[10]

Up to the First Floor. Confusion is somewhat natural at first for transplanted expatriates of any nationality. To add to their bewilderment, new arrivals find things much different from the way they were back home. For example, they may discover that in some countries the first floor is not synonymous with the ground floor, or lobby, as it typically is in the United States. In many countries, such as France, Italy, and Spain, what an American perceives as the second floor is actually the first.

"Montez au premier étage, s.v.p."

Time Zones a Hassle. Merely coping with differences in time zones can be a veritable hurdle. For example, American managerial expatriates are often on the phone calling corporate headquarters in the United States just past midnight or right before dawn. However, with the advent of sophisticated fax machines, faxes can now be stored and scheduled to transmit at any future date and time to take advantage of international time differences and low rates.

Foreign Expatriates in the United States. A large proportion of all foreign-owned industry in the United States was acquired during the 1980s and early 1990s. Consequently, just as with American managers abroad, foreign expatriates working in the United States likewise have adjustments to make. Some of them working for the first time in the United States feel uncomfortable in the "foreign" American environment. For example, Japanese managers attending an American classroom training environment need encouragement before they will readily speak out. Many Japanese believe it to be impolite to be as outspoken as their American counterparts in training sessions. Hispanic transplants, too, have their differences. For example, they tend to feel it to be impolite to start a business meeting before engaging in a certain amount of relaxed small talk. American managers, on the other hand, believe such sociability is a waste of valuable time.[11]

"We've only got time for big talk."

Employee relations is sometimes more of a challenge for foreign managers located in the U.S. For example, Ian Martin, a British businessperson, contends that "dealing with the question of race and gender is different. The U.S. seems further down the road than Europe." Martin is head of Grand Metropolitan's American operations, a British company that acquired the Pillsbury foods group, which incudes such companies as the Burger King fast-food chain, as well as Green Giant canned corn.[12]

Differences in Language and Communication Styles

Communication and language are areas where significant differences exist among cultures. Such factors as conversational styles vary substantially in different countries. For example, Latins, especially some South Americans, tend to speak mere millimeters away from the faces of their listeners. Non-Latins often feel uncomfortable in such situations. Latins, in general, also tend to touch each other more than do many Americans and Northern Europeans. (People from Italy, France, Spain, and Portugal are also considered to be Latins.)

¡Hablan muy circa!

Words also have different meanings in different cultures, and it is important to have a complete knowledge of slang and idiomatic expressions. For example, Otis Engineering Company once shocked potential customers at a Moscow trade fair when its posters promised that Otis oil well completion equipment would do wonders for improving a person's sex life! Parker Pen Company's managers' faces also turned a bright red after their company blitzed Latin America with an advertising campaign that—much to their chagrin—implied that its new ink would help to prevent unwanted pregnancies![13] Some common names for American products, such as the *Fig Newton* cookie or the *fanny pack* worn by skiers, joggers, and tourists, are considered obscene words in Germany and Great Britain, respectively. And when former President George Bush visited Australia in 1992, he later learned that the "V" sign he flashed to the crowds with his fingers is considered an obscenity there!

"V" for Vulgarity?

Differences in Attitudes Toward Time

Attitudes toward time vary among different cultures. Americans, in general, tend to be relatively punctual for business engagements. Swiss businesspeople usually expect you to be precisely on time for an appointment. The spectrum shifts markedly in some cultures, however, where businesspeople may not even show up for the first or second appointment. When they do finally appear, they convey the impression that punctuality was not one of their priorities. Such persons may have expected you to wait for them for one-half to a full hour. These illustrations are not intended to be critical nor presented as "rights" and "wrongs." They are merely intended to illustrate cultural differences. You will save yourself considerable stress and aggravation if you learn and attempt to accept the attitudes and

Why do today what you can put off until tomorrow?

customs of nationals in the countries where you may work. Expecting everything to be just as it was back home is unrealistic.

Differences in the Work Force

The global work force is anything but homogeneous. Employees' attitudes and value systems vary greatly in a wide variety of important ways. One of these ways is *productivity*. Few firms can compete effectively on a global basis unless productivity, the level of output per employee, is comparable to that of their competitors.

In some cultures, managers and employees alike are interested primarily in getting the job done, with little concern for how long it takes or how productive their efforts are. Such relaxed attitudes probably don't lead to burnout, but they also don't do much to assist the bottom lines of global concerns. A serious problem faced by companies that want to establish operations in the eastern region of Germany, formerly the Communist sector, is that productivity there is estimated to be only one-third to one-half of the productivity levels of the western part, yet wages in the east are nearly as high as in the west.[14]

Here's some surprising information: According to a study made by Professors John Paul MacDuffie and Thomas Kochan of twenty-four companies around the world, European workers are usually better trained than American ones yet are still far less productive. The authors of the study contend that European car plants are not managed well enough according to the principles of flexible—or lean—production to make the best use of their well-educated work force. Conversely, the U.S. plants are relatively good at extracting value from poorly prepared workers. U.S. employee productivity, however, was far less than Japan's, where plants are better organized for lean production.[15] Table 16.3 summarizes some of the major differences in work forces around the world.

Differences in Pay Scales

Employee wages also vary substantially from country to country. Frequently, those who are opposed to free trade with other nations use the argument that American firms confront unfair competition from foreign organizations that have cheaper labor. This premise is not entirely true. According to the U.S. Department of Labor, factory workers in twelve industrialized nations earned more in 1990 than their counterparts in the United States. The average hourly wages of factory workers in Norway and Germany, for example, the top two countries in terms of wages, were $21.86 and $21.53, respectively, while the average American factory workers received only $14.77. Table 16.4 lists the countries whose average wages were above and below those in the U.S.

"Your results are great . . . but awfully late!"

TABLE 16.3   **Major Types of Differences in Work Forces on a Global Basis.**

- *Supply of workers*—plentiful in some areas, scarce in others
- *Skill level*—skill levels high in some areas, low in others
- *Level of productivity*—high levels lacking in some cultures
- *Level of motivation*—work ethic weaker in some cultures
- *Attitudes toward leadership*—participative approach expected in some cultures, not related to in others
- *Attitudes toward achievement*—high achievement not important in some cultures where poverty is not looked upon negatively
- *Reaction to discipline*—less accepted among some cultures
- *Expectations of job security*—high levels of job security expected and required in some cultures
- *Attitudes toward status and rank*—significant class distinctions in some cultures
- *Attitudes toward women and people of various races*—sexism and racism more prevalent in some cultures

Differences in Labor Laws

Labor laws related to such factors as vacations, family leave, compensation, discharge, and taxation also differ considerably from country to country. Mangers are expected to conform to the regulations of the countries in which they operate.

Labor legislation also tends to reflect the values of host countries. For example, not all cultures seem to promote the work ethic to the extent prevalent in Japan and the United States, where vacations tend to be relatively short and sometimes not even taken. In contrast, labor laws in many Western European nations require that employers provide employees no less than four to six weeks annual vacation, paid holidays, and sick and family leaves. In reality, therefore, European workers make more per actual hours worked because they generally work fewer hours and receive longer vacations than their American counterparts. German auto workers, for example, work 1600 hours a year compared to workers at Toyota in Japan who work about 2300 hours a year, while General Motors Corporation employees in the U.S. typically put in about 2000 hours a year. European workers straight out of high school receive at least thirty days paid vacation a year, while only two weeks is not uncommon for American workers.[16]

Each country also varies in the ease or difficulty with which employees can be lawfully discharged. For example, job security tends to be more assured in many European countries than it is in general for employees in the United States.

The degree of employee participation in managerial decision making also varies among countries. In some nations **codetermination,**

TABLE 16.4   Countries With Average Hourly Factory Worker Wages Above and Below Those in the U.S. in 1990.

Average hourly wages higher than in the U.S.	Average hourly wages lower than in the U.S.
• Norway, $21.86	• Great Britain, $12.97
• Germany, $21.53	• Australia, $12.43
• Sweden, $20.93	• Japan, $12.64
• Switzerland, $20.83	• Ireland, $11.76
• Finland, $20.76	• Spain, $11.61
• Belgium, $18.94	• Israel, $8.55
• The Netherlands, $18.22	• New Zealand, $8.33
• Austria, $17.01	• Taiwan, $3.95
• Denmark, $17.85	• South Korea, $3.82
• Italy, $16.41	• Singapore, $3.78
• Canada, $16.02	• Hong Kong, $3.20
• France, $15.23	• Mexico, $1.80

Source: U.S. Dept. of Labor

Some employees get "board" on the job.

worker representation on the board of directors, is legally required. German firms provide an interesting example of codetermination. German managers are generally noted for their more authoritarian approach to leadership in comparison with their American or Japanese counterparts, yet employees are, by law, entitled to have representatives serve on the executive committees of large corporations. Worker representatives are also elected to serve on management committees. Worker representatives are expected to make managerial decisions that are in the best interest of the organizations and the workers. As a result of codetermination, labor strife in Germany has typically been substantially less than in the past. (Codetermination continues to be voluntary in the U.S. but is likely to be utilized to a greater extent in the future.)

Managers of global firms are responsible for complying with the various labor laws that exist in their host countries. Learning, absorbing, and adapting to the various differences that exist among different countries can be a frustrating experience at times. Many European countries are more accustomed than the United States to regulated employment and labor relations and have more comprehensive social benefits. In some instances, social legislation in other countries comes in direct conflict with U.S. law.[17]

Differences in Ethical Standards

The issue of ethics is also important in global organizational behavior. Some American firms had difficult times with this topic some

?

"If We Can't Sell It Here, Then Let's Sell It There!"[b]

We live in an appearance-conscious society. One is supposed to "dress for success." Therefore, people wear clothes that are supposed to reflect their current or desired positions in an organization. Creams, ointments, oils, perfumes, and various products *ad infinitum* are purchased to influence appearance and, therefore, how people respond to the individual. Related to such attempts at image building is an operation that two million women have received: silicone breast implants.

Unfortunately for the recipients, however, some of the implanted devices made by four companies in the U.S. have developed leaks, after which the chemical attempted to circulate throughout the body. In 1992, a federal judge upheld a record $7.34 million damage award against Dow Corning Corporation, one of the manufacturers of the devices, to a woman whose silicone breast implant ruptured. The court ruled that there was ample evidence that the rupture caused her to contract a painful disease called *mixed-connective tissue disorder.*

Discovered in 1992 were Dow Corning company documents revealing that the firm was aware more than twenty years prior to this case that its silicone gel implants could leak and that the fluid could cause medical problems. The incident caused a shake-up at Dow Corning, the product was removed from the market, and two of its top executives were replaced.

The U.S. Food and Drug Administration declared a moratorium on selling the devices in the U.S. However, the three other manufacturers, Bioplasty, Inc., Mentor Corp., and the McGhan Medical unit of Inamed Corp., continued to push the devices in foreign markets. When asked why, their spokespeople stated that they were complying with the U.S. Food and Drug Administration not to *import* the silicone implants. Company representatives said that they were selling them out of their plants located *abroad.*

A question of ethics: In your judgment, since they were doing nothing illegal, were the three companies acting in an unethical manner by continuing to sell the product in foreign countries after it had been banned in the U.S.?

years ago. During the 1970s, the general public and U.S. trading partners abroad lost considerable confidence in the ethical standards of certain American businesspeople because of their behavior with foreign officials. As a result, Congress enacted the **Foreign Corrupt Practices Act of 1977** to help restore lost faith. The act was an outgrowth of a reported 450 U.S. companies having bribed foreign government officials to aid their overseas marketing. The act prohibits paying any official of a foreign government for the purpose of influencing any decision in order to obtain or retain business.

Although the business community has generally opposed the act from its inception, suggesting that it has been a major cause of U.S. lack of competitiveness in many markets abroad, there are other observers who disagree. For example, Professor Kirk Davidson of Golden Gate University in San Francisco, contends, "Our business managers, after all, are entrepreneurial and innovative and creative kinds of people, so it seems to me that the law is loose enough that there are many ways, while not disobeying the act, it can be circumvented. The law certainly is not a major factor in our competitive problems."[18]

Here's that "rock and a hard place" again!

Nonetheless, American managers conducting business abroad sometimes find themselves on the horns of a dilemma. They contend that the bribing of foreign officials and businesspeople to acquire sales contracts is standard practice in some countries, that such activities are considered to be "financial favors" by locals, not unlike giving a hairdresser a tip in appreciation for a job well done. Some American managers contend that they must engage in **situational ethics,** the application of moral standards that relate to the attitudes and laws in a particular social and cultural environment. However, to American government officials the offering of financial favors—that is, **bribes** to foreign officials and businesspeople—to acquire or maintain business is illegal.

Differences in Political Climate

The political climate of a nation has a considerable effect on ex-pats and other employees in an organization. Certain types of events can be disrupting to business activity. For example, the U.S. Government has in the past sometimes imposed *sanctions* on countries whose behavior was considered undesirable. **Sanctions** are coercive measures adopted against a country whose behavior is considered unacceptable.

Well . . . maybe a hot dog!

Assume, for example, that you recently accepted an important position with your firm in Beijing, China. You've attended a four-week crash course in the Chinese language and have learned how to say "hello," "good-bye," "thank you," "happy new year," and "where's the bathroom?" You've made two trips to Beijing to arrange living accommodations for your family, convinced your spouse that you and the kids absolutely will never eat grilled dog, and have even obtained your flight tickets on China Airlines. Imagine the uncertainty and anxiety you might develop upon learning that the president of the United States is considering imposing sanctions on China and canceling China's most-favored-nation trade status because Chinese authorities have recently crushed another student demonstration in Tiananmen Square, killing 400 students, wounding 500 others, and arresting 2000. This sort of event sometimes occurs.

"Come home . . . immediately!"

There have been other cases in which American employees have been ordered by the U.S. government to leave their jobs and return to the United States. This situation occurred in January 1986 when then-President Ronald Reagan signed an executive order banning trade and travel to Libya. He also ordered all Americans in Libya to leave. Reagan's sanctions were aimed at Libyan political Colonel Muammar Gadaffi for his alleged support of international terrorism. Americans were especially prevalent in the petroleum and construction industries at the time. The Bush administration acted similarly toward Libya in March 1992, when it urged the estimated 1000 Americans there to depart before the United States-led United Nations Security Council sanctions and boycotts were to be imposed. The actions were a response to United States and British requests for the surrender of two Libyan agents wanted in connection with the bombing of Pan Am flight 103 in 1988 over Lockerbie, Scotland, in which 270 people died.[19] You can see, therefore, how the political climate of a nation can influence the activities of employees with global firms.

Fluctuations in Foreign Exchange

Although not directly involved with the topic of organizational behavior, *foreign exchange* can have a significant effect on the profitability of companies operating globally. **Foreign exchange** deals with the relationship of the currency of one country to that of another. This relationship changes over time.

Exchange for less!

To illustrate the effect of foreign exchange, let's look at the case of an American firm, Ford Motor Company, that has manufacturing facilities in Great Britain. On September 1, 1992, the rate of foreign exchange between Great Britain and the U.S. was £1.00 equaled $2.00. Slightly less than three months later, the value of one British pound was only $1.51, about a 25 percent decline in the value of the British pound. Assuming that Ford desired to repatriate some of its British profit to the U.S., it would have found that its British pounds had dropped substantially in value. Such losses can negatively influence a company's ability to maintain its work force and invest in new plant and equipment. There are methods, however, that skilled international money managers can use to hedge, or offset, potential risks. But the activity is fraught with risk. The topic of foreign exchange is far more complicated than illustrated in our brief discussion.

Harley Does it . . . Toys 'R' Us Does It
Why Can't Good Old Federal Express Do It?[c]

"Two out three," as they say, "ain't bad." That is, unless you happen to be the third in a triad of global success/failure stories. Have you ever wondered why some U.S. companies, such as Federal Express, fail miserably when they attempt to "go global," while others, such as Harley-Davidson and Toys 'R' Us, seem to develop the right stuff?

Federal Express began operations slightly more than two decades ago and currently enjoys 50 percent of the U.S. market for overnight deliveries. It carries over 3 million items each day. Federal Express' attempt to transfer its domestic success to Europe in 1985 didn't make it. So it reduced its work force in Europe in 1992 by 6600 persons and now uses local subcontractors for all deliveries between European cities or countries because its overnight volume was a piddling 100,000 packets a day—nothing compared with the potential market. Some sources contend that Federal Express' major mistake was not understanding the different requirements in running a business in Europe.

The American motorcycle manufacturer, Harley-Davidson, in contrast, can't seem to do anything wrong with a current worldwide demand for "bikes" that has been outweighing supply. Once deemed about "out of gas," Harley-Davidson now ships its powerful, shiny "hogs" to many corners of the earth.

Toys 'R' Us is another organization that doesn't seem to be toying around in its global endeavors. It had 166 stores outside the United States in early 1993, including stores in Australia and Japan. An interesting sidelight is that Toys 'R' Us also operates abroad somewhat the way it has in the United States, buying its stock directly from manufacturers, a practice that keeps its prices low. Most Japanese toy stores buy their stock directly from wholesalers.

Time will tell if one year's success stories become another year's case of the blahs.

EASING THE TRANSITION FOR INNOCENTS ABROAD

¡Deseo tenir mi MTV!

A **cultural leveling effect** has been taking place throughout the world as a result of increased international travel, global satellite TV, short-wave radio, popular music, and films. Worldwide communication now takes place with ease through direct-dial portable telephone systems, palmtop computers with built-in modems, and fax machines. Yet, in spite of such leveling trends, there remain specific cultural differences that make adjustment for the expatriate a continual challenge. Certain practices, however, can ease the transition for "innocents abroad." These include:

1. Selecting the right people for the right place
2. Allowing orientation visits
3. Providing training opportunities
4. Using foreign nationals
5. Providing extras

Each practice is now described briefly.

Selecting the Right People for the Right Place

As with any position, sound selections for assignments overseas, or across borders, are essential. The "my-country, right-or-wrong" type of individual usually doesn't adapt well to foreign environments. Some Americans abroad have damaged both their company's and their country's image by conveying an attitude of **cultural arrogance,** a concept similar to the *ethnocentric* trait discussed earlier. As with ethnocentrism, cultural arrogance exists when a person conveys the attitude that his or her own culture is superior to another's.

Romans don't speak *pig latin!*

Some employees do not function well in a foreign environment. The "right people" should, of course, be competent in their specialty. In addition, people should be selected on the basis of their desire to work and live in a foreign culture. Where possible, persons with a knowledge of a foreign language or those who have already traveled or lived in other countries, especially the host country, should be seriously considered. The attitudes of the employee's spouse and children toward living in a foreign country should also be taken into account, since the employee's family often makes or breaks the assignment.

The "right place" depends on the employee's willingness and ability to adapt to the foreign environment. Some firms attempt to make the American employee's first assignment easier to adapt to by sending him or her to a country that closely reflects the employee's own cultural background.

Allowing Orientation Visits

An employee's adjustment to a first assignment in a foreign country can be facilitated and apprehensions reduced if he or she can make one or two orientation visits to the new location before actually assuming job responsibilities. Levi Strauss International, for example, allows its managers to spend some time in the new environment arranging housing for their families and schools for their children. Levi Strauss also assumes the responsibility of disposing of the employee's U.S. housing if desired.

Care to check it out first?

Providing Training Opportunities

Cross cultural training for employees soon to be assigned to foreign countries is essential if they are to get off to a good start. Many firms feel that involving employees' spouses in certain aspects of training programs allows for easier adjustment. Some companies provide their soon-to-become ex-pats and their spouses with orientation related to the customs and cultural differences in the host country. Employees should learn as much as they can in advance about the host country's laws, business practices, and customs. They should also be familiar with the U.S. laws that affect global operations.

Spouses get shocked, too!

Some global companies provide opportunities for their employees to take an intensive course in the host-country's language. Kai Lindholst, a director with Egon Zehnder, a management recruiting firm, believes that "languages are important, especially a working knowledge of French and Spanish, and perhaps even Portuguese, for working overseas."[20] An Accountemps survey of corporate vice-presidents and personnel directors indicated that a knowledge of Spanish and Japanese has become increasingly important to a successful business career in recent decades.[21] Although expertise in a foreign language is unlikely as a result of a three- to six-week crash course, it does give the trainee a better feel for the new culture and may aid in avoiding some misunderstandings.

Sayonara, amigo!

General Electric Medical Systems Company puts a lot of effort into assisting and training ex-pats. The company has adapted a "Global Leadership Program," developed and administered by an international business school faculty at the University of Michigan, for use by its staff. In order to give managers a better feel of other cultures, top leaders from the General Electric's global division meet on three different continents for several days at a time to learn more about each other. Between sessions, the managers work on three-way task forces intended to deal with specific and practical problems. The various nationalities working together on such projects learn to understand each other better in addition to solving problems.[22]

Use Foreign Nationals

Look for some
local talent!

Knowing all the "ins and outs" of a foreign culture is difficult for American managers. Natives of a particular country, of course, tend to have a much greater sense of their own lands than do managers sent from the United States. Many U.S. firms, therefore, hire a substantial amount of local talent, either as full-time employees or part-time consultants. The nationals should also be immersed in the corporate culture of the American company as well. American firms operating abroad sometimes send their foreign managers to the United States to gain a greater awareness of the company's domestic corporate culture.

Providing Extras

Chapter 5 discussed various concepts of human needs. Sometimes in a foreign environment these needs are more difficult to satisfy. Language barriers, for example, create a certain degree of insecurity. Prices may be substantially higher than at home, or currency fluctuations may reduce purchasing power, thus making the satisfaction of certain basic needs more arduous. Further, the absence of an employee's complete family, usual friends, and convenient facilities can also cause frustration for some. In some regions, political instability, war, or the prevalence of terrorism can create anxiety, insecurity, and stress.

Exxxtraaa! Exxxtraaa!

To help offset some of these inconveniences, some firms provide their ex-pat managers with certain "extras," ranging from housing allowances and chauffeurs to private school tuition for their children. Some firms also pledge to give ex-pats a comparable position upon their return to the United States, which helps to reduce potential job insecurities.

REPATRIATION—RETURNING HOME

Home, shock, home!

"I had no idea going back home would be such a shock!" These are words that may be difficult to appreciate if you have not spent considerable time living in another culture. Once ex-pats adjust to their new environments, however, they often grow to appreciate the "best of both worlds." As one manager living and working in Asia enthusiastically put it, "Living here is so stimulating, it's almost out of control. I love it!"[23]

A Period of Readjustment

Repatriation, *bringing an employee back to the home country,* may require considerable adjustment. After returning home, the employee sometimes discovers that something is "missing" from the American culture. Certain "extras" on which they became somewhat dependent, such as a chauffeur, maid, or premium pay, are not provided in the

You can't step twice on the same Wienerschnitzel.

domestic assignment. Their hometown and circle of friends may also be different. "Things just don't seem the same at home anymore," is a common attitude of repatriates. In some cases, things were never as the employee idealized while in the overseas post.

Company Guidance and Counseling

To ease the transition of returning home some firms provide their employees with counseling, which should begin before the repatriation actually takes place.

Candid communication with the repatriates is also important. Returning employees want, and are entitled to know, what their new job assignments will be, in which direction their careers are now headed, and how their promotional opportunities have been affected by their stint overseas. A **repatriation agreement** that spells out in advance specifically what the new job assignment will be can also help to reduce anxiety.

SUMMARY

Many managers of firms throughout the world believe that operating on a global basis is essential to ensure their survival in the highly competitive world of business today. Opportunities continue to exist throughout the rapidly changing world in spite of economic crises and tribal conflicts in many regions. An understanding of *global organizational behavior* and how cultures differ is essential for employees of global concerns.

A number of factors influence the culture and operations of global organizations. These include customs, language and communication styles, attitudes toward time, the work force, differences in pay scales, labor laws, standards of ethics, and political climate.

Although a cultural leveling has occurred throughout the world, there remain numerous differences in various regions and countries. The transition from working in a home country to working abroad can be eased by effective selection and assignments, orientation visits, adequate training, the use of foreign nationals, and providing expatriates with extras to enable them to satisfy their needs.

Repatriation—the bringing home of ex-pats—may also require adjustment. Providing counseling, along with a repatriation agreement that clarifies future job assignments, can ease the "shock" of returning home after an extended stint abroad.

TERMS AND CONCEPTS TO REMEMBER

globalism

transnationals

European Economic Community (EEC)

ethnocentric

maquiladora industry

North American Free Trade Act (NAFTA)

global organizational behavior

culture shock

expatriate

codetermination

Foreign Corrupt Practices Act of 1977

situational ethics

bribes

sanctions

foreign exchange

cultural leveling effect

cultural arrogance

cross-cultural training

repatriation

repatriation agreement

QUESTIONS

1. What effect has the concept of a "Fortress Europe" had on the decisions of some American managers?

2. What is the purpose of the *maquiladora* industry?

3. Economic history has shown us that free trade, as envisioned by the North American Free Trade Act (NAFTA), tends to expand economic activity among trading nations over the long run. However, in the short run, industries sometimes shift operations to lower-cost countries and some jobs may be eliminated. Unemployed workers often have to seek employment in different industries. In your opinion, is the tradeoff between increased long-term economic activity and higher short-term unemployment worth it? What might be done to ease the transitional stage? By whom?

4. Comment on the following attitude:

   "I'm glad I was transferred back to the states. The personnel practices those guys over there have are absolutely ridiculous. Everybody gets five weeks vacation per year; they even get a year's family leave to take care of their babies; and I've never seen a country with so many holidays. I don't see how firms in countries like that ever get anything done!"

5. What is *culture shock?* What can be done to reduce its effects?

6. Is an American working for a U.S. company in Spain subject to Spanish laws? Explain.

7. Why was the Foreign Corrupt Practices Act of 1977 passed?

8. How might a country's political climate affect American expatriates?

9. What are *sanctions?* Do you feel that governments should apply sanctions that affect international trade? Explain.

10. What are some methods that can be employed to ease the transition of the person assigned to an overseas position?

11. Why can culture shock develop from *repatriation?*

APPLICATIONS

16.1 "Why Didn't They Tell Me It Would Be Like This?"

Janet Juguete, president of Progeny, Inc., a manufacturer of children's toys located in Sioux City, Iowa, decided to begin attempting to market the firm's products in other countries. Many organizations when starting to market their products abroad prefer to work through local export agents, who are local representatives in the foreign country representing a variety of manufacturers. Juguete, however, decided not to utilize export agents since they also represent competing firms. She believed that Progeny could have better sales results by establishing its own sales branches abroad.

A Sales Office in the Canary Islands

Based on the recommendations of an American consultant, Juguete decided to begin a pilot project in the Canary Islands, an archipelago consisting of seven islands situated in the Atlantic Ocean about 125 miles west of Morocco. The islands form two provinces of Spain. Juguete was informed that Las Palmas, Gran Canaria, the largest city in the archipelago, with a population in excess of 350,000 would be a desirable base of operations. Canarian families tend to be large. Canary Islanders also have the reputation for showering their children with toys. The city has one of the world's busiest deep-water shipping ports and an international airport with regular flights to continental Europe. In winter, many Northern European tourists come to the island with their children to escape the frigid northern climes. The climate of the Canary Islands is referred to as one of "eternal spring," with temperatures in the 70s and 80s practically every day. Transportation is adequate among the several islands, consisting of hydrofoil ferries and shuttle airplanes.

Green Offered the Position

Juguete circulated a notice throughout the company announcing the opening of a marketing manager position in Las Palmas. Ringo Green, one of Progeny's top sales representatives, was the only applicant for the position. Green had been having personal problems recently and was depressed as a result of his wife's divorcing him, which had come as a deep shock to him. He believed that getting "as far away from Sioux City and my 'ex' as possible" would help him adapt to his new life and be good for reducing his stress level. Because of Green's past sales record, Juguete accepted his application for the position.

Green had studied a semester of Spanish while in high school, but had never had the opportunity to use the language. His experience traveling in foreign countries was limited to a two-week vacation in Winnipeg, Canada. He attended a community college for one year.

Juguete informed Green that he would be responsible for developing a sales office in Las Palmas. Juguete also said that she would locate two American salespersons who would be sent to the islands after Green located office facilities.

Culture Shock Sets In

After his arrival in Las Palmas, Green received a real shock. He had believed before his arrival that everyone would speak English. He had heard that English was practically an international language. Apparently the islanders hadn't heard that, since Green discovered that very few of the people whom he met spoke English. His high school Spanish didn't seem to help much either, other than to assist him in ordering a cup of coffee at a restaurant. He had even forgotten the words for sugar and milk! He did remember the names for potatoes (*patatas*) and bus (*autobus*) in Spanish, but he soon discovered that Canary Islanders used different words—*papas* and *guagua,* respectively.

Green had hoped to find an established American community so that he wouldn't feel like a foreigner. There was none, however. He did find out that although the person who was said to have discovered America—Christopher Columbus—stopped off at Las Palmas on his way to the "New World," not many Americans had yet discovered the Canary Islands. (By the way, hadn't Native Americans already "discovered" America by the time Chris got there?) He should have realized this before he left Sioux City, when most of his friends asked him, "What part of the Caribbean are the Canary Islands in?"

Obtaining Permits

Trying to set up an office was an even greater challenge. He was told neither he nor any of his future staff could work on the island, or in any part of Spain, without first acquiring a residence visa and a work permit. Working without these would result in immediate expulsion. To obtain the permits, he would have to obtain documentation from his banker that he was financially responsible and was "unlikely to become an economic burden upon the state." He also had to obtain a character reference from an American Embassy, which meant a flight to Madrid. He also had to arrange for the Sioux City Police Department to send a document testifying that he had no criminal record. Plus, he had to submit health documents indicating the results of a recent physical examination. He realized that these things would have been easier for him to take care of in the United States prior to his departure. The same requirements existed for any additional Americans who would be working for him. Green wrote to Juguete to have her arrange for the new sales representatives to take care of such documentation before coming to the islands.

Green was further informed by the island authorities that, assuming there were no complications, he would receive his visa and work permit no less than three months from the time he submitted all of the necessary documents. He was also told that the two Americans he intended to bring over would not necessarily be permitted to work unless he could prove that they were not taking work away from Spanish people.

Becoming Homesick

Green found the Canary Islanders friendly and willing to give him information. Unfortunately he couldn't always understand what they were saying. He was beginning to develop remorse about having taken the position. He was continually frustrated in his dealings with the local bureaucracy. He couldn't believe how many copies of every form were necessary. Green also was becoming a bit homesick. He thought often about his two young children, who were living with his former spouse, and missed the opportunity to visit with them regularly.

A Phone Call from Headquarters

He recently received a phone from Juguete, who asked him how things were going. The following is his response:

"Janet, where in the world did you send me? Everything here is so different from what I'm used to. Can you believe that most of the businesses still have *siesta* hours. They're closed between 1:00 P.M. and 4:00 P.M. All the things I have to do seem to take so long to accomplish. Sometimes it takes me a half hour merely to get through to you on the telephone. The post office system and banks also seem to operate so differently from what I'm used to. Airmail letters that you send, for some reason, take up to three weeks to arrive from Iowa. And you should see some of the stores. Hardware stores and *supermercados* are more like the ones that existed 40 years ago in the United States. Power failures occur at least twice a month. And I can't even drink the water."

Improvements Over Time

Green recently met a German businessperson who told him, "You should have been on the islands ten years ago. Many regions didn't even have electricity. I know people in some of the smaller villages who have never taken a hot shower or bath in their lives. To them, having only cold water is normal. But the islands are improving, *poco a poco!*"

They hadn't changed fast enough for Green's tastes. One day after experiencing additional frustrations attempting to find out how his visa and work permit applications were progressing, Green asked himself, "How did I get here? What was I thinking when I accepted this position? Why didn't they tell me it would be like this?"

Questions

1. In your opinion, was it a mistake for Juguete to have selected the Canary Islands as a location for a pilot project?

2. What is your reaction to her having selected Green for the assignment?

3. If you had been responsible for setting up the foreign operations, what would you have done differently from the way Juguete and Green arranged things?

16.2 "What We Need Is a Consultant!"

Bowery International is a large manufacturer of cleaning supplies for households, businesses, and institutions. Two years ago the company decided to expand globally and developed manufacturing facilities in Asia, Western Europe, and South America. Bowery's head of international operations, Harry Warner, has cautioned all foreign marketing directors by letter that they must comply with the corporate policy related to gratuities, the offering of gifts to customers. Company representatives are not to offer customers "any gifts of merchandise, payments, tangible or intangible things of value, either directly or indirectly through relatives or friends in order to acquire or maintain business." Warner also warned company representatives in other countries that violation of the Foreign Corrupt Practices Act of 1977 subjects company directors to fines of up to $10,000 and up to five years imprisonment.

William Mordido is in charge of South American operations. He and his marketing representatives have been frustrated in their attempts to gain a foothold in governmental institutions, which typically are large purchasers of the types of product Bowery manufactures. Mordido is certain that his competitors have obtained sizable contracts by offering "financial favors" to the government purchasing agents. In fact, one customer, Ricardo Schmidt, whose purchases have been minimal, has on two occasions suggested that $50,000 deposited in his personal saving account might make it easier for him to decide to expand his purchasing. William explained his company's policies regarding gratuities and "financial favors." Purchases from Schmidt continued to be small.

Recently Schmidt phoned Mordido and requested that he come to his office to discuss an idea for expanding his purchases from Bowery. Mordido agreed. The following is what Schmidt said to Mordido:

> William, you know that I control the purchases for all the public buildings in this district. The purchases amount to a lot of money. I can understand how you have to go along with your corporate policies regarding "financially assisting" customers. However, I have an idea that might enable you to increase your sales substantially. You don't have to *give* me a thing. Instead, you *hire* me as an *outside consultant* for a $50,000 fee. I will then advise you on ways in which you can increase your sales volume to my department. I know that you have the authority to hire people. And there's no law against utilizing consultants. Companies do it all the time. What do you say, William?

Question

1. If you were William Mordido, what would you say and do now?

NOTES

1. John Hillkirk, "Globalism Replaces Nationalism," *USA Today/International Edition,* March 14, 1990, pp. 9-B, 10-B; and Jeremy Main, "How to Go Global—and Why," *Fortune/International Edition,* August 28, 1989, pp. 54–58.

2. Blanca Riemer et al., "The New Rush to Europe," *Business Week/International Edition,* March 26, 1990, pp. 20–23.

3. George F. Will, "All-American Cars Are a Vanishing Breed," *The Washington Post,* as reported in *The Stars & Stripes,* February 12, 1992, p. 13.

4. "Forbes Releases Survey of Most Efficient Firms," *Associated Press,* as reported in *The Stars & Stripes,* December 27, 1991, p.16.

5. Roger Cohen, "For Coke, World Is Its Oyster," *The New York Times,* November 21, 1991, p. IV–16.

6. "Charlie Crowder Sees Utopia, and It's a Border Town," *Business Week/International Edition,* July 31, 1989, pp. 29–30.

7. Dave Kent, "Firms Strike Gold South of Border," *AFL-CIO News,* February 4, 1991, p. 7.

8. See note 6.

9. J. L. Komilnicki, "Losing Touch," *Sunday,* a *Stars & Stripes Magazine,* November 24, 1991, pp. A1–A5.

10. See note 9.

11. Amanda Bennett, "American Culture Is Often a Puzzle for Foreign Managers in the U.S.," *Wall Street Journal,* February 12, 1986, p. 1; and William McWhirter, "Special Report: I Came, I Saw, I Blundered," *Time/International Edition,* October 9, 1989, pp. 40–41.

12. Martin Dickson, "Selling Hamburgers to Americans," *Financial Times,* November 1, 1991, p. 14.

13. Stan Kossen, *Creative Selling Today,* 3rd ed., (New York: Harper-Collins, 1989), p. 447.

14. Richard E. Smith, "East German's Jobs Riddle," *International Herald Tribune,* April 2, 1990, pp. 9, 13.

15. John Gapper, "In Pursuit of a Lean Machine," *Financial Times,* January 22, 1992, p. 8; and "U.S. Still Ahead in Something . . . Yes, Productivity," *International Herald Tribune,* October 14, 1992, p. 1.

16. Timothy Aeppel, "In Europe's Car Plants, Pay Is High and Hours Are Fewer," *The Wall Street Journal Europe,* February 27, 1992, p. 8.

17. David Goodhart, "American Business Fear Social Legislation," *Financial Times,* December 4, 1991, p. 2.

18. "Foreign Corrupt Practices Act—Necessary Law or Needless Hurdle," *GGU Magazine,* February 1987, pp. 5–6.

19. "Americans Urged to Leave Libya," *Financial Times,* March 20, 1992, p. 4; and "U.S. Citizens Urged to Leave Libya as Embargo Sought," *Oakland Tribune,* March 19, 1992, p. 2.

20. Elizabeth M. Fowler, "Foreign Experience, Languages Boost Hopefuls Up the Corporate Ladder," *Contra Costa Times/Business Times Section,* December 30, 1985, p. 12.

21. Sam Ward, "Business of Foreign Languages," *USA Today/International Edition,* October 20, 1989, p. 20.

22. Jeremy Main, "How to Go Global—and Why," *Fortune/International Edition,* August 28, 1989, pp. 54–58.

23. Ford S. Worthy, "The Good Life of Yanks in Asia," *Fortune/International Edition,* April 23, 1990, p. 96.

BOX NOTES

a. Adapted from Nancy J. Perry, "What's Powering Mexico's Success," *Fortune/International Edition,* February 10, 1992, pp. 65–67; Nancy Dunne, "U.S. Labor Fears Mexican Role in the Revolution," *Financial Times,* June 26, 1992, p. 6; and Sidney Weintraub and Rogelio Ramirez de la O, "Where Mexico Should Draw the Line," *Financial Times,* June 15, 1993, p. 17.

b. Adapted from Bruce Ingersoll, "Official Seeks Criminal Probe of Dow Corning on Implants," *The Wall Street Journal Europe,* February 14, 1992, p. 4; and Robert L. Rose, "Most U.S. Makers of Silicone Breast Implants Are Selling Overseas Despite Halt at Home," *Wall Street Journal Europe,* March 3, 1992, p. 9.

c. Adapted from Nikki Tait, "FedEx Wraps Up Its European Dream," *Financial Times,* March 23, 1992, p. 17; Robert Ball, "America the Dutiful," *Time,* April 20, 1992, p. 47; "Sales Rise at Harley-Davidson," *Financial Times,* April 23, 1992, p. 21; Martin Dickson, "Hog Wild in Milwaukee," *Financial Times Weekend,* June 12/13, 1993, p. 11; "U.S. Toy Store Draws Kudos in Japan," *Contra Costa Times,* December 22, 1991, p. 22; and Nikki Tait, "Toys 'R' Us Boosts Sales and Profits," *Financial Times,* March 12, 1992, p. 20.

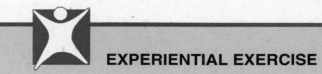

EXPERIENTIAL EXERCISE

A Cultural Quiz

Answer the following questions either *generally yes* or *generally no.*

Generally Yes	Generally No	PART I
_____	_____	1. I enjoy eating foods that some people consider "weird."
_____	_____	2. I have friends from a variety of ethnic backgrounds.
_____	_____	3. I can converse in at least one foreign language.
_____	_____	4. I have traveled to a foreign country at least once.
_____	_____	5. I can visualize myself retiring in a foreign country.
_____	_____	6. I can imagine myself living without television.

PART II

Generally Yes	Generally No	
_____	_____	1. I believe that foreigners, like the Japanese, should not be allowed to buy American companies and real estate.
_____	_____	2. I believe that French people generally do not like Americans.
_____	_____	3. I believe that "Yankee ingenuity" is, and always will be, the best in the entire world.
_____	_____	4. I believe that soccer matches could never seem as exciting as American football games.
_____	_____	5. The Japanese could never have developed all those fancy electronic gadgets unless they had copied all of America's products.

_____   _____   6. I believe it is important for me to
                              spend significant amounts of time
                              with people of my own religious,
                              ethnic, racial, and national
                              background.

Total *generally yes* responses, Part I _____.

Total *generally no* responses, Part II _____.

Key: Get together with four or five other members of your class.
Compare your answers. How many of your responses in Part II
were *generally yes?* How many of your responses in Part II
were *generally no?* If you answered five in Part I *generally yes*
and you answered five in Part II *generally no,* you might be a
favorable candidate for an overseas assignment with a global
company because of your apparent adaptable attitudes toward
different things and cultures.

   This exercise is not definitive. There are far more factors
that would influence the success of an overseas assignment
than inherent in these questions.

Glossary

The number following each definition indicates the chapter in which it is discussed.

Absenteeism and turnover records: Personnel documentation that relates to employee attendance and separations (5).

Accountability: The answerability of organizational members to their bosses; sometimes used interchangeably with *responsibility* (6).

Accountability-for-results principle: The assertion that bosses are still held answerable for results even when authority to achieve objectives has been assigned to their subordinates (7).

Achievement needs: See *Needs, achievement* (5).

Active Corps of Executives (ACE): A volunteer organization of active managers who supplement SCORE's services to small business owners with the most current expertise and techniques (15).

Acquired immune deficiency syndrome (AIDS): A disease acquired by a virus that affects the immunity of the human body; transmitted in specific ways from one person to another (11).

Action-oriented: As related to the study of organizational behavior, showing a concern for *what to do about problems* among people in groups (1).

Ad hoc committee: A body of persons temporarily established to work on a specific task (2).

Adjustive reaction (defense mechanism): Conscious or unconscious forms of behavior that assist the individual in adapting to frustrating situations; may be either positively or negatively directed (13).

Affiliation: See *Needs, social* (4, 5).

Affirmative action program (AAP): Attempts by an organization to ensure equitable treatment of minorities and women in employment; efforts to ensure fair recruitment, hiring, and promotion practices (10).

Age bias: Discrimination against individuals solely on the basis of their age, rather than on their qualifications (11).

Age Discrimination in Employment Act of 1967: Legislation that prohibits employers from discriminating against individuals 40 to 70 years old in any area of employment because of age (11).

Alcoholic: A person who habitually lacks self-control in the use of alcoholic beverages, or who drinks to the extent that his or her health is adversely affected, or whose social or economic functioning is significantly disrupted (12).

Americans with Disabilities Act of 1990 (ADA): Legislation that broadens the scope of the Rehabilitation Act of 1973 by requiring private, as well as public, employees to provide persons with disabilities the same protection against discrimination provided by other civil rights legislation (11).

Approval needs: See *Needs, approval* (5).

Asch conformity studies: A study conducted by Solomon Asch that illustrated the apparent need people have to conform to group standards (4).

Attitudes: Feelings or emotions towards people and things (2).

Authority: The *right* of people in organizations to make decisions, act, and direct others to act; power that flows down the organizational hierarchy (6).

Autocratic (authoritarian) leadership: A style of leadership in which managers keep decisions and controls to themselves (6).

Autonomy: A core job dimension that enables employees to feel responsible for their actions (8).

Baldrige award: See *Malcolm Baldrige National Quality Award* (7).

Behavioristic psychology: A school of psychology that emphasizes observable behavior as opposed to unobservable conscious processes; the belief that human beings have little real influence over their actions, which are primarily conditioned responses to stimuli they receive (13).

Behavior modification The activity of influencing human behavior through the use of positive or negative reinforcement techniques (5).

Belongingness: The feelings of identity and unity with group members desired by many persons; see also *Needs, social* (4).

Benchmarking: The continuous process of obtaining accurate information about how others, such as competitors, handle similar quality problems (7).

Body language: A nonverbal form of communication that goes beyond what people say; meaning that is transmitted through glances, posture, or various types of body movements (3).

Boiled-frog syndrome: A concept that helps to explain how individuals sometimes fail to recognize the gradual deterioration of certain conditions until after a crisis has set in (9).

Bona fide occupational qualification (BFOQ): A provision of the Civil Rights Act of 1964 that permits employers to discriminate against employees in hiring practices in certain "reasonably necessary" instances (10).

Bottom-up assessment (upward appraisal): A system that allows the evaluation of managers by their associates (employees) (8).

Brainstorming: A group problem-solving or idea-generating activity in which members can express themselves freely, regardless of the nature of their ideas, to other group members (4).

Brainwriting: A group idea-generating process in which group members usually sit around a table and each person writes ideas on paper; similar to *brainstorming,* but has certain advantages over the latter (4).

Bribes: Efforts to stimulate sales by offering kickbacks or elaborate gifts to customers (16).

Burnout: The complete exhausting of a persons' physical and intellectual resources caused by excessive efforts to attain certain unrealistic job-related goals (13).

Buzz (gripe or deep-sensing) sessions: The management practice of allocating certain amounts of time for obtaining feedback from employees related to their attitude toward their jobs (5).

Cafeteria-style benefit program (flexible-benefit plan): A benefits program in which employees can choose a combination of insurance and other options best suited to their personal desires and individual and family situations (8).

Carpal tunnel syndrome (CTS): An inflammation of the tendons, nerves, blood vessels, and ligaments around the hand, forearm, and shoulder caused by repetitive motions, such as those made on a computer keyboard, also termed *repetitive strain injury (RSI)* (8).

Caveat emptor: An outdated and illegal business philosophy that means "let the buyer beware"; a belief that when goods were sold without an express warranty, the buyer had to take the full risk of loss from potential defects in the goods (15).

Caveat vendor: A philosophy that means "let the seller beware"; a belief that a buyer is entitled to "get away with" anything possible when dealing with a seller of goods or services (15).

Change management: The activities associated with the effective introduction of change (9).

Changing: As a part of the change process, the activity of learning new ideas and habits so that desired behavior can be engaged in (9).

Charismatic authority: The power and ability developed by some individuals to influence and win the devotion and respect of others, frequently because of personality traits and mannerism (5, 6).

Civil Rights Act of 1866: Legislation established that all persons regardless of race shall have the same right to make and enforce contracts related to employment as enjoyed by white citizens (10).

Civil Rights Act of 1966—Title VII: Legislation that prohibits employers, labor unions, and employment agencies from discriminating against persons on the basis of color, religion, sex, or national origin (10).

Civil Rights Act of 1991: Legislation that overturned several Supreme Court rulings that made it difficult for minority and female workers to gain legal remedies for workplace discrimination; expanded the rights of victims of sexual harassment and discrimination to sue for damages (10).

Closed questions: Questions that typically can be answered with only a yes or no (3).

Cluster chain: The transmission of informal communication in a manner in which one person tells several others and some of them tell one or more persons (4).

Committee: A body of persons formed to consider, investigate, take action, or report on issues related to an organization; referred as to *ongoing* or *standing* when considered permanent (4).

Communication: A two-way process resulting in the transmission of information and understanding between individuals (3).

Comparable worth: The argument that asserts that women should be paid as much as men for performing tasks in other occupations requiring comparable (not identical) skills, training, responsibilities, hazards, and effort (10).

Compensation: A situation in which an individual with feelings of inadequacy—either real or imagined—exerts extra effort in an attempt to overcome the insecure feelings (13).

Competence needs: See *Needs, competence* (5).

Compressed work week: The shortening of the work week so that it involves more hours of work per day for fewer days per week, such as a four-day, forty hours system (8).

Conceptual (administrative) skills: The ability to think abstractly and see relationships between seemingly separate entities (6).

Condition response: A learned or acquired reaction to a particular situation (5).

Conformity: Activity that complies with established standards (14).

Constructive coercion: A blunt supervisory approach to handling substance abuse problems to make the employee aware of the consequences of continuing such behavior (12).

Contingency (situational) leadership: An approach to management recognizing that no one style of management fits all situations, that the "best" approach to management depends on a variety of factors (6).

Contingent workers: Includes temporary, part-time, and leased employees, plus the self-employed (8).

Continuous improvement teams (CITs): Small groups that meet regularly to work on developing methods for the development and maintenance of quality (7).

Conversion: A psychological process whereby emotional frustration and tensions are expressed in bodily symptoms of pain or malfunction (13).

Codetermination: Worker representation on an organization's board of directors (16).

Core job dimensions: As developed by Hackman and Oldham, the factors that are essential ingredients of any job if the benefits of job enrichment are to be derived (8).

Creativity: Any reasoning process that solves a problem in an original and useful way; the developing of new methods for doing things by examining older methods; the ability to see useful relationships between dissimilar things (2).

Credibility gaps: The chasm of disbelief that can develop between individuals when promises are made but not kept (3).

Credit checks: An employment activity that investigates the credit records of prospective or current employees on the belief that such records are an indication of their integrity (14).

Cross-cultural training: Training often provided for persons soon to be assigned to foreign countries related to the customs and cultural differences in the host country (16).

Cross-training: The human resource management practice of training employees in other positions as a means of employee development and job enrichment; also termed *multiskilling* (8).

Cultural arrogance: Conveying an attitude that one's own country or culture is superior to any other's (16).

Cultural diversity: A situation in which members of a group are varied in their beliefs, value systems, behavior patterns, and thought characteristics (4).

Cultural leveling effect: A tendency for various cultures in different countries to assume a certain degree of similarity because of ease of communication and transportation (16).

Culture shock: The state of confusion and anxiety that can affect individuals when they are first exposed to an unfamiliar culture (16).

Delegation: The act of giving rights or assigning tasks and responsibilities to others (7).

Delegation-by-results principle: The assertion that any person to whom the authority is delegated should be provided sufficient rights to accomplish expected objectives (7).

Deleverage: The swapping of high-cost debt for cheaper financial obligations (15).

Delphi method: A group decision-making process in which each participant is given a problem or questionnaire to work on independently; the results are turned in to a coordinator who distributes them to all members, who then revise their original analyses and resubmit them (4).

Derived X (I've-been-burned theory): A negative attitude toward employees held by some managers who believe themselves to be positively oriented but who have had negative experiences (real or imagined) causing them to shift their assumptions (6).

Descriptive questionnaires: Forms that ask open-ended questions intended to elicit more than a yes or no response; frequently used for morale surveys and exit interviews (5).

Discipline: A managerial activity intended to correct work-related behavior that deviates from established standards; also used as an employee development tool (14).

Discrimination: An action directed either against or in favor of something or someone (10).

Displacement: The psychological process of redirecting pent-up feelings toward objects other than the main source of the frustration (13).

Distress: A negative type of stress that, if not managed properly, can cause a variety of diseases and mental depression (13).

Documentation: Maintaining records of incidents related to an employee's behavior; necessary to back up disciplinary action and promotions (14).

Doublespeak: The use of words in an evasive, ambiguous, or stilted manner for the purpose of deceiving or confusing the reader (3).

Double standards of supervision: Treating certain individuals or special employment groups differently from other employees; considered to be an unfair method of managing (10).

Downward communication: Communication that conveys messages from higher to lower levels of an organization, such as from supervisors to workers (3).

Drug: A substance that has an effect on the body or mind (12).

Drug abuse (drug addiction): An activity by individuals who habitually lack the ability to control their intake of drugs (12).

Drug-Free Workplace Act of 1988: Legislation requiring contractors and grantees of the federal government to certify a drug-free workplace as a precondition for receiving a contract or grant (12).

Dual-career families: Households in which both spouses have established positions with organizations (9).

Dual command: A situation in which one subordinate is accountable to more than one boss; an abuse of the unity-of-command principle (7).

Economic guarantees: Financial commitments made to employees for the purpose of reducing or eliminating their resistance to change (9).

Elastic limit: A stage in the stress process that serves as warning that a person is near his or her stress threshold (13).

Emergent system: See *Informal system* (1).

Employee counselors: Staff individuals whose principal function is to assist employees with their problems and complaints (5).

Employee Assistance Programs (EAPs): Formal personnel programs designed to aid employees with personal problems—such as drug and alcohol abuse or psychological problems—that tend to affect their job performances (12).

Employee involvement (EI): See *Participative (democratic) leadership* (6).

Employee Polygraph Protection Act of 1988: Legislation intended to make illegal in most instances the use of polygraphs by private-sector companies as a tool for employee screening or dismissals (14).

Empowerment: Providing employees with greater authority to make decisions on their own (6).

Enlightened self-interest: A managerial belief that a concern for social goals should be a basic part of the overall goals of an organization (15).

Equal Employment Opportunity Commission (EEOC): An agency created by Title VII of the Civil Rights Act of 1964 to administer civil rights legislation and investigate complaints related to violations of the law (10).

Equal Pay Act of 1963: Legislation requiring employers to provide equal pay to women and men for performing substantially similar work (10).

Equity theory: Developed by J. Stacy Adams, an expectation theory of motivation that focuses on *fairness* and especially on what people expect to get out of their jobs in relation to what they put into them (5).

Ergonomics: Designing products and workplaces in a manner that makes them more suitable for employees (8).

ERG theory of needs: A categorization of needs that includes three levels: existence, relatedness, and growth (5).

Escape reinforcement: See *Reinforcement, escape* (5).

Ethics: Standards of conduct or morals established by the current and past attitudes and moods of a particular society (15).

Ethnocentric: Having the belief that virtually everything in one's home country is superior to what exists in other countries (16).

European Economic Community (EEC): A group of twelve Western European nations whose purpose is to remove most traditional economic barriers among its nations; also known as the *Common Market* (16).

Eustress: A positive type of stress that enables a person to function and accomplish goals (13).

Exception principle: The assertion that regular and recurring decisions should be delegated to employees and that nonroutine decisions be handled at a higher level (7).

Existence needs: See *Needs, existence* (5).

Exit interviews: Sessions with departing employees, especially with those who resign, to determine reasons for leaving and to uncover possible organizational problems (5).

Expatriate: A person who lives and works in a country other than his or her native country (16).

Expectancy theory: The theory that individuals will be motivated by their belief that specific behavior on their part will lead to a desired outcome (5).

Extinction: The reduction in the effects of a conditioned response as a result of repeated *non-reinforcement* (5).

Facilitator: An organization development specialist assigned the responsibility of serving as consultant to others in carrying out an organizational diagnosis and analysis (9).

Fact: Something with the quality of being actual; that which can be established by observation or experience (2).

Faith: A concept with various meanings; such as a belief and trust in and loyalty to God; a belief in the traditional doctrines of a formal religion; an absolute allegiance to something concrete, such as one's country, or in something abstract, such as in the concept of freedom; a belief in oneself or in humanity (13).

Fallacy of composition: The assumption that what is true for one person or situation is necessarily true for all people or situations (2).

Fallacy of division: The assumption that what is true for the whole is necessarily true for each of its parts (2).

Family leave: The provision of time off for parents to care for newborn or adopted children and for family medical emergencies (10).

Father of human relations: Elton Mayo, credited with having established organizational behavior (then known as "human relations") as a separate field as a result of research studies conducted in 1927 at the Hawthorne works of the Western Electrical Company (1).

Father of scientific management: F. W. Taylor, famous for his concerns for technical efficiency in organizations (1).

Feedback: A core job dimension that enables employees to consistently receive information on how they are performing; the activity that makes communication a two-way process; an activity that enables the effectiveness of communication to be determined; a response to the behavior or communication of others; see also *Two-way communication* (3, 8, 9).

Filtering: The straining out of ingredients in a message that are essential to more complete understanding of its meaning (3).

Flexplace: An employment practice in which employees are allowed to work at home rather than in an office or plant (8).

Flextime (flexible working hours, glide time): A condition in which employees may, with prior approval of their supervisors, alter their usual working hours (8).

Flight: Leaving or removing oneself from a particular situation that causes frustration or anxiety (13).

Forced waiting: A condition of uncontrollable delays as a result of having to wait for others (13).

Foreign Corrupt Practices Act of 1977: Legislation intended to discourage the making of any payments to foreign officials by U.S. businesspeople for the purpose of influencing any decision in order to obtain or retain business (16).

Foreign exchange: The relationship of the currency of one country to that of another (16).

Formal communication: Official communication that is transmitted through the structured organizational network (3).

Formal leader: A manager who has been officially delegated particular rights, power, or authority over others in an organization (4).

Formal organization: The planned structure of an organization; relates to the official lines of authority; responsibility, and accountability ranging from the board of directors and chief executive officer to the operating workers (1).

Formal (required) system: The planned structure that consists of individuals who are positioned and coordinated by management to attain predetermined organizational goals and objectives (4).

Freedom to fail: A supportive condition in which employees feel able to make risk decisions without fearing excessive repercussions from their bosses (6).

Free-rein (*laissez-faire*) leadership: A style of leadership in which the leader serves more to facilitate than to directly lead the group, which works out its own techniques for accomplishing organization goals (6).

Frustration: The feeling of insecurity and dissatisfaction arising from unresolved problems or unsatisfied needs and wants (13).

Future shock: A term coined by author Alvin Toffler to describe our reaction when change occurs more rapidly than our ability to absorb and cope with it (9).

Gainsharing: Organizational change programs of employee involvement, with an organization-wide financial formula; the practice of providing employees with periodic cash bonuses for developing ways in which the organization can enjoy cost savings (8).

Gatekeepers: Individuals who determine what information is received by key decision makers (3).

Glass ceiling: A condition in which certain individuals, such as minorities and women can see the next step up in a typical career path, but they never receive the opportunity to assume it (10).

Globalism: Applying business activity on a transnational, rather than solely domestic basis, with little concern for the impact on the home country's economy (16).

Global organizational behavior: The application of organizational behavior concepts to global organizations (16).

Goal accomplishment: The achievement of sought-after wants; one of the reasons that people become members of groups (4).

Golden parachute: A severance agreement with executives that guarantees two or three years of their annual pay plus possible benefits if they lose their jobs as a result of an acquisition (15).

Gossip chain: The transmission of informal communication from one person to everyone else in the network (4).

Grapevine: The network of informal relationships through which facts, half-truths, and rumors are transmitted (3, 4).

Graphology: The analysis of handwriting (14).

Grid organization development method: An OD technique for analyzing existing managerial approaches to production and people for the purpose of improving future managerial effectiveness (9).

Group: Two or more people who interact personally, or through communication networks, with each other, usually sharing similar goals, experience, or needs (4).

Group cohesion: The emotional closeness that group members have for each other and their groups (4).

Group decision making: Efforts at generating ideas that involve two or more persons (4).

Group interview: An evaluation session in which several managers, or members of a board or panel, observe, challenge, and pool their impressions of an interviewee; may also involve several managers questioning and observing several candidates for a particular position as a group (4).

Groupthink: The process of deriving negative result from group decision-making efforts; a concept popularized by author Alvin Toffler (4).

Growth needs: See *Needs, growth* (5).

Habits: Activities that are performed unconsciously as result of frequent repetition (9).

Halo effect: Assuming that a person good at one activity will do well at most other activities (2).

Handicapped individual: See *Individuals with disabilities* (11).

Hawthorne effect: Any improvement in worker performance that is the by-product of attention and feelings of self worth (1).

Hidden agenda: Refers to the attitudes and feelings that group members bring to, or develop at, a meeting (4).

Hierarchy of needs: A categorization of needs from lower- to higher-order (5).

HIV testing: An employment practice that examines prospective or current employees for HIV, the AIDS virus (14).

Holistic effect: The relationship between the separate parts of an object and their effect on the whole project, as in the relationship between the human mind and the body and its effect on the entire person (13).

Horizontal communication: Communication that takes place between departments or people on the same level in an organization (3).

Horizontal loading: A form of job enlargement that pushes earlier work stages and pulls later work stages into the job (8).

Hostile (unfriendly) takeovers: An acquisition of one company by another when the acquired company did not want to be taken over by the acquiring firm (15).

Hughes Act (Comprehensive Alcohol Abuse and Alcoholism Prevention, Treatment, and Rehabilitation Act of 1970): Legislation that created the National Institute of Alcohol Abuse and Alcoholism, whose purpose is to engage in research and to provide assistance to those concerned with establishing alcohol rehabilitation programs (12).

Human immunodeficiency virus (HIV): A virus that can affect the body's normal defense against illness may develop into acquired immune deficiency syndrome (AIDS) (11).

Humanist: A person who subscribes to the humanistic school of psychology (13).

Humanistic psychology: A school of psychology that emphasizes the uniqueness, self-esteem, and dignity of the individual (13).

Human resource approach: An approach to organizational behavior that emphasizes individual involvement in decisions made in the organization (1).

Human resource management skills: The ability to work effectively with and through people; includes accurate perception, effective communication, empathy, and the ability to motivate others (6).

Individuals with disabilities: Any person who has a physical or intellectual impairment that substantially limits one or more of that person's major life activities (11).

Inference: A judgment made without facts and going beyond what one observes (2).

Informal communication: Unofficial communication that supplies information to supplement information that is transmitted through the formal network (3).

Informal (emergent) system: The natural self-grouping that results from the psychological and social needs of individuals (4).

Informal leader: A person who is able to influence other group members because of age, knowledge, social skills, or personal strength (4).

Informal organization: The natural self-grouping of individuals according to their personalities and needs rather than to any formal plan (1).

Inner-directed Pygmalion effect: The tendency for a person's expectations about him- or herself to actually cause the expected behavior to occur (13).

Innovation: The creation of a new idea and guiding it through various stages for the purpose of developing a new service, procedure, or product (14).

Innovation teams: Groups consisting of individuals from different functional areas, such as design, manufacturing, marketing, and finance, for the purpose of developing new ideas (14).

Integrity tests: Devices for screening employees for honesty and use of illegal substances (14).

Interventions: Activities engaged in by OD specialists to assist group members in effecting change (9).

Interviewing: The activity of consulting with others for the purpose of evaluating, informing, training, or obtaining information (4).

Interviews and questionnaires: The activities of consulting with others, either orally or in writing, for the purpose of uncovering employee attitudes and opinions toward their work environments (5).

Intuition: Arriving at conclusions on the basis of feelings rather than logic and facts (2).

Job bank: Organized groups of retired personnel who are subject to recall on a part-time or full-time basis during periods of peak work loads (11).

Job enlargement: The process of increasing the complexity of a job to appeal to the higher-order needs of workers; also termed *Whole job concept* (8).

Job enrichment: A form of changing or improving a job to create a more motivating work environment (8).

Job rotation: The shifting of employees from one job to another to create a more motivating work environment (8).

Job sharing (twinning): An approach to job enrichment that allows two employees to share a full-time position (8).

K.I.S.S. concept: The notion that communications should be delivered in an understandable fashion; an acronym that symbolizes either *Keep It Simple, Stupid*, or *Keep It Short and Simple* (3).

K's (Kossen's) Law: Regardless of your state of organization, new tasks and interruptions will seek you out, thereby expanding your responsibilities, commitments, and work load (13).

Law of effect: Actions repeated or avoided as a consequence of certain previous actions (5).

Leadership: A set of developed skills that attempts to influence or change the behavior of others to accomplish organizational, individual, or personal goals (6).

Legitimate areas of conformity: Standards of employee behavior, both on- and off-the-job, that tend to affect the job and the workplace (14).

Leveraged buyouts (LBOs): A procedure that enables managers to borrow sizable amounts of funds on their firm's equity, which can then be used to purchase equity in other firms (15).

Life enrichment: Gaining personal satisfaction not only from one's job but also from one's total existence, resulting in the reduction or elimination of feelings of loneliness, boredom, and loss of faith (13).

Listening: The act of hearing with thoughtful attention; requires a certain degree of tension to be active (3).

Listening responses: Various methods for showing interest in what a speaker is saying (3).

Maintenance activities: Behaviors related to social and emotional needs employees bring to the job, such as the opportunity to "clown around" (4).

Maintenance (hygiene) factors: Factors, according to Frederick Herzberg, that tend to have a neutral effect on the work environment but are likely to cause dissatisfaction if not met; they include salary, employee benefits, interpersonal relationships, working conditions, company rules and policies, and job security (5).

Malcolm Baldrige National Quality Award: An annual award to companies for excellence in quality, two given in each of three categories—manufacturing, service, and small business (7).

Management: The process of combining human and technical resources to achieve organizational goals; involves the application of the management functions of planning, organizing, coordinating, leading, and controlling (6).

Management by objectives (MBO): A management activity whereby a supervisor and his or her subordinates jointly establish goals and objectives; involves regular follow-up appraisal activities to see if objectives have been accomplished or are in need of modification (9).

Managerial grid: A device, developed by Robert R. Blake and Jane S. Mouton, utilized for dramatizing the various managerial concerns for either production or people or various combinations of both (9).

Maquiladora **industry:** The combination of U.S. industry with Mexican; based on low-cost labor and border-zone assembly plants (16).

MBWA (*Management by Wandering Around*): A managerial technique intended to make a manager more accessible to employees ideas and feelings; involves the activity of informal discussions with employees (3).

Meetings: A group activity intended to provide information or solve problems (4).

Mental set: A tendency to make up one's mind first, then look for evidence to support that position; the tendency to see (hear, smell, or taste) what we expect while remaining unaware of the things we don't expect (2).

Mission statement: A general statement that relates closely to the culture and philosophical objectives of an organization; an expression of an organization's purpose (7).

Mommy track: An employment scheme that distinguishes between men and women by establishing secondary tracks for women who desire to combine careers with raising children; can be used to the detriment of women in employment (10).

Morale: The atmosphere created by the attitudes of the members of an organization (5).

Morale surveys: Devices used to uncover employee attitudes and opinions toward their work environments (5).

Motivation: The various forces or drives within individuals that cause them to behave in a specific manner (5).

Motivation-maintenance model: A theory developed by Frederick Herzberg that describes two sets of factors in the workplace, one set tending to motivate employees and the other tending to create dissatisfaction if withdrawn (5).

Motivational (satisfiers) factors: Factors, according to Frederick Herzberg, that tend to motivate and cause job satisfaction, such as achievement, recognition, challenging work, growth and advancement possibilities, and responsibility (5).

Multiple careers: The trend for older employees to establish new careers in their later or "retired" years; some employers provide older employees the opportunity to acquire additional training and counseling that help prepare them for career changes (11).

Multiskilling: See *Cross training* (8).

Multivalued reasoning: The recognition that in most situations or problems there may be more than two sides (2).

National Institute of Alcohol Abuse and Alcoholism: An organization that engages in research and provides assistance to managers in establishing alcoholism programs (12).

Needs: The feeling of deprivation; that which motivates a person into action designed to obtain relief or satisfaction; can be physiological (food or drink), security-related (medical insurance), social (friends) or psychological (self-esteem, status, and feelings of achievement) (5).

Needs, achievement: Personal desires concerned with accomplishing something successfully (5).

Needs, approval: Personal desires concerned with being regarded favorably (5).

Needs, competence: Personal desires concerned with performing tasks in a high-quality manner (5).

Needs, existence: The first level in the ERG theory of needs developed by Alderfer; concerned with physical and material human needs (5).

Needs, growth: The third level in the ERG theory of needs developed by Alderfer; concerned with the needs for self-esteem and self-realization (5).

Needs, power: Personal desires concerned with possessing control, authority, or influence over others (5).

Needs, relatedness: The second level in the ERG theory of needs developed by Alderfer; concerned with one's relationship to others, both on- and off-the-job (5).

Needs, safety and security: Personal desires concerned with feelings of safety and security, such as union or association membership, unemployment compensation, seniority rights, and retirement programs (4, 5).

Needs, self-esteem: Personal desires concerned with feelings of self-worth and dignity (4, 5).

Needs, social: Feelings that are usually learned, such as the desire to belong and to enjoy peer acceptance (4, 5).

Negativism: An adjustive reaction; the unconscious resistance to other persons or objects (13).

Networking: The use of all possible personal connections as a source of job information (10).

No-layoff policies: An organizational practice in which surplus staff, instead of being forcibly separated, is reduced by attrition and retirement (15).

Nonlegitimate areas of conformity: Expectations of employee behavior, both on- and off-the job, that seem not to affect or be related to the job and workplace (14).

Nonverbal communication: Objects or conditions that convey meaning without words, such as voice tones, physical expressions, gestures, body posture, and the use of time (3).

Nonverbal symbols: Objects or conditions that convey meaning without words, such as space, height, and status symbols (3).

North American Free Trade Act (NAFTA): Legislation that substantially reduces trade barriers among the United States, Mexico, and Canada (16).

Objective questionnaires: A technique for surveying attitudes that asks multiple-choice questions (5).

Obsessive thinking: A condition that exists when a person enlarges out of realistic proportion specific problems or situations that he or she has experienced (13).

OD practitioner (change agent or OD consultant): A practitioner of organizational development; may be a member of an outside consulting firm or an in-house consultant who is assigned to a personnel department; a change agent who attempts to diagnose specific organization problems, provide feedback to organizational members about findings, and then assist members in developing strategies of interventions for improving the total organization (9).

Older worker: As arbitrarily defined by the Age Discrimination Act, a person age 40 and older (11).

One-way communication: A message flowing in one direction with no feedback or certainty of understanding involved (3).

Open-door policy: The practice by some managers of permitting others to drop by their offices without appointments (3).

Open questions: Questions that cannot be answered with a simple yes or nor response; intended to elicit greater response from an interviewee (3).

Organization: A group of individuals structured by specialized activities and levels of authority for the purpose of accomplishing specific goals and objectives effectively (1).

Organization chart: A diagram that illustrates the official chain of command, shows the various levels of management, and presents the official titles of each department or individual (1, 6).

Organization development: A group problem-solving process intended to bring about planned and orderly change for the purpose of improving the effectiveness of the entire culture of an organization (9).

Organizational behavior (OB): The study of the behavior of people and their relationships in organizations to attempt to meld personal needs and objectives with the overall needs and objectives of the organization (1).

Organizational culture: The values that influence the environment in which people work (1, 6).

Organizational diagnosis (organizational analysis): An activity that applies techniques intended to uncover the causes of problems in an organizational environment (9).

Organizational politics: See *Politics, organizational* (14).

Outplacement consultants: Advisors employed by organizations to assist separated employees in obtaining new employment (14).

Parkinson's Law: The assertion, developed by C. Northcote Parkinson, that work activities tend to expand to fill the time available for their completion (13).

Participative (democratic) leadership: A style of leadership that involves employees in decision making that affects them; tends to develop greater commitment toward organizational goals from employees (6).

Peer effect: The influence that associates have on an individual's perception and judgment (2).

Perceptual filters: The tendency to block out certain portions of the environment from our perception and to see or hear what we are set to see or hear (2).

Performance appraisal interview: A conference between the manager and an employee to discuss the employee's past performance and plans for improvement (8).

Performance-related payment plan (incentive payment system): A method of rewarding employees for their efforts rather than paying them on a fixed basis regardless of their achievements (5).

Phased retirement: A gradual reduction in the hours worked by older employees rather than the complete elimination of their working opportunities (11).

Physical access: As related to individuals with disabilities, conditions that allow those with limitations to make use of facilities that would ordinarily be inaccessible to them (11).

Physical and intellectual challenges: See *Individuals with disabilities* (11).

Planned agenda: A predetermined set of activities to be presented and discussed during a meeting; serves to reduce the amount of time wasted during a meeting (4).

Politics, organizational: The manner in which managers obtain and hold onto power; skills that enable the individual to accomplish goals more effectively; sometimes perceived as a negative activity (14).

Polygraph (lie detector) test: Examinations of employees with devices designed to detect false statements made by them; their use now illegal in most instances (14).

Position power: See *Power, position* (5).

Positive reinforcement: See *Reinforcement, positive* (5).

Post hoc, ergo propter hoc (fallacy of false cause): The assumption that when one event precedes another, the first event necessarily causes the second (2).

Power: Possession of control, authority, or influence over others (4).

Power needs: See *Needs, power* (5).

Power, position: A degree of influence a person has over others that is affected by his or her position in an organization (5).

Profit quest: The belief by some managers that their sole responsibility is to make a profit for their firms (15).

Pregnant Maslow needs mix: A modification of the traditional Maslow hierarchy of needs concept; illustrates the probably relative weight of the various categories of needs for society in general (5).

Prejudice: An attitude that results in the making of judgements based on insufficient evidence; prejudging (10).

Preventive maintenance: As related to organizational behavior, activities that involve anticipating potential problems and needs and modifying conditions to prevent their occurring (3).

Preventive prejudice: Exists when individuals prejudge the intention of others and thus react first on the basis of an often unfounded belief that an action is going to be taken against them (10).

Probability chain: The transmission of informal messages on a random, or unpredictable, basis (4).

Production-based compensation plans: See *Gainsharing* (8).

Progressive discipline: An approach in which the severity of disciplinary measures increases each time an employee must be disciplined (14).

Projection: The tendency to apply to others some of our own faults and motives (2).

Proportional employment: Hiring practices that attempt to match the percentages of particular groups in the local work force (10).

Protected classes of workers: Employment groups affected by civil rights legislation (10).

Pseudostupidity: The intentional act of forgetting or feigning ignorance as a means of avoiding certain types of activities and responsibilities (13).

Psychological distance: The mental attitudes of supervisors toward employees regarding the closeness of the working relationship (6).

Psychosomatic: As related to physical disorders, those maladies that have their origin, at least in part, in mental stress or other psychological factors (13).

Punishment reinforcement: A type of behavior modifications that involves the withholding of rewards, or outcomes, from an employee because of past undesirable behavior (5).

Pygmalion Effect: The concept that suggests that the expectations of an event or certain types of behavior can actually cause the event or behavior to occur; the *self-fulfilling prophecy* (6).

Qualified individuals with disabilities: Persons who are capable of performing particular jobs with reasonable accommodation to their disability (11).

Quality circles (QCs): A method used for attempting to improve the quality and quantity of output; consist of rank-and-file employees with a common concern who form a group to exchange information for mutual improvement; QCs typically consist of five to ten members and a leader to guide each group (4).

Quality of work life (QWL): Refers to how effectively the job environment meets the needs and expectations of employees (1, 8).

Rationalization: The attempt by an individual to give plausible, but not necessarily true, explanations for specific, often undesirable behavior (13).

Reasonable accommodations: Working faculties arranged so that individuals with disabilities will not face insurmountable obstacles (11).

Recovering alcoholic: Refers to a person who has gone through rehabilitation as a result of alcohol abuse; a person who is more able to control his or her use of alcohol but not considered completely cured (12).

Red-hot stove rule: A concept that equates disciplinary action with touching a red-hot stove; involves such factors as *prior warning, immediacy, consistency,* and *impersonality* (14).

Refreezing: As a part of the change process, the attempt to apply on a regular basis what one has learned (9).

Rehabilitation Act of 1973: An act that requires federal contractors to take affirmative action to hire and advance persons with disabilities (11).

Reinforcement, escape: A somewhat negative technique intended to motivate a person into performing in a favorable manner to *escape from,* or *avoid,* a particular situation (5).

Reinforcement, positive: The creation of an external environment that encourages the repetition of certain behavior (5).

Reinforcement theory: A theory of motivation that assumes that certain actions will be repeated or avoided in the future because of past consequences of such behavior (5).

Relatedness needs: See *Needs, relatedness* (5).

Reliability: A necessary requirement related to testing that means a test measures the same factors over and over (10).

Repatriation: The activities associated with transferring an employee back to his or her home country (16).

Repatriation agreement: A contract between employers and employees working abroad that spells out in advance specifically what subsequent job assignments will be upon return to the home country (16).

Repression: A defense mechanism that involves the unknowing exclusion of certain experiences or feelings from one's consciousness (13).

Required system: See *Formal (required) system* (1).

Resignation: A defense mechanism characterized by a person's giving up, or withdrawing, from a particular environmental situation (13).

Responsibilities: Specific *tasks* or *duties* that have been assigned to an organizational member (6).

Responsibility: The *obligation* that organizational members have to perform assigned work or to make certain that someone else performs it in a prescribed manner (6).

Restructuring: The process of analyzing an existing organization and modifying it for the purpose of meeting new demands, as during a merger or for enhancing efficiency (15).

Reverse discrimination: Discrimination against nonminorities that results from attempts to overcome past hiring inequities of minorities (10).

Right-side-up organization: A non-traditional organizational structure that perceives the customers on top, followed by operating employees supported by first-line managers, who in turn are supported by middle managers and senior executives (8).

RIO process: A technique of applying management by objectives, RIO being an acronym for *Responsibilities, Indicators,* and *Objectives* (9).

Risk decisions: The opportunity for employees to make decisions on their own without the excessive fear of the consequences of making errors (8).

Robotics: The use of mechanical equipment (*universal transfer devices*) that duplicates human physical motions for the purpose of reducing or eliminating human labor (1).

Role assuming: Sometimes called *role playing;* the concept of creating a more realistic situation, usually one of human problems and conflicts, and then acting out the various parts without worrying about behavioral consequences (1).

Role expectation: The way in which individuals are mentally set to perceive the behavior of others (5).

Rules: Statements of precisely what activity or conduct is or is not to be engaged in; generally related to disciplinary action (14).

Rumors: Information transmitted through the grapevine, usually without a known authority for its validity (3, 4).

Rupture point: A stage of stress that can cause some severe and permanent mental and physical damage if therapeutic assistance is not obtained (13).

Rusty halo effect: The prejudicial tendency to feel that a person who performs poorly in one activity will perform poorly in most other activities (2).

Sanctions: Coercive measures adopted by one country against another country whose behavior is considered unacceptable (16).

Scalar principle: The assertion that authority and accountability in an organization should flow in a clear unbroken line through the organizational hierarchy (7).

Scapegoating: An adjustive reaction, also a form of *displacement,* that involves blaming a particular person for one's own problems or insecurities (13).

Security: See *Needs, safety and security* (4, 5).

Selective placement: Matching the physical abilities of a person with disabilities with the physical demands of a particular job (11).

Selective reception: The tendency to hear or see only what one is set to hear or see and to tune out much of the rest of a message or image (3).

Selective X-Y: An approach that assumes attitudes towards employees are not fixed but may vary with a person's past experiences and current prejudices (6).

Self-esteem: The pride that a person has in him- or herself; see also *Needs, self-esteem* (4).

Seniority systems: A plan used in connection with selecting, promoting, or otherwise considering employees on the basis of their length of employment with an organization (10).

Service Corps of Retired Executives (SCORE): A volunteer organization of retired executives who advise small business owners in conjunction with the Small Business Administration (15).

Seven-step system: A logical procedure for more effective decision making and problem solving (2).

Sexual harassment: Unwelcome sexual advances, requests for sexual favors, and other verbal or physical conduct of a sexual nature (10).

Sham approach: A technique used by some substance-abusing employees to placate their bosses; the act of merely making the pretense of seeking professional help (12).

Signs of alcohol dependency: Overt indications that a person may be abusing alcohol (12).

Signs of drug dependency: Overt indications that a person may be abusing drug substances (12).

Single-strand chain: The transmission of informal messages from one person to the following person in the chain (4).

Situational ethics: The applications of morale standards that relate to the attitudes and laws in a particular social and cultural environment (16).

Situational faith: The belief that a person is worthy of trust until there is ample evidence to the contrary (13).

Situational thinking: A decision-making process that involves drawing on similar past experiences when analyzing present problems but recognizing that each situation is unique and thus may require a distinct solution (1).

Snap judgments: Hastily conceived first impressions of people and things (2).

Social accountability: An attitude of responsibility toward society by corporate managers (15).

Social norms: Standards of behavior or beliefs that group members tend to follow to be accepted by the group (4).

Social reality: A factor influencing group membership; a form of "reality" created by group members as a means of reinforcing their own perception and attitudes (4).

Social service leave: A program offered by some companies that enables employees to take time off from their regular jobs with regular pay and benefits for the purpose of engaging in temporary community service activities (15).

Span-of-control principle: The assertion that, in general, the larger the number of employees reporting to one manager, the more difficult it is for him or her to supervise effectively (7).

Span-of-empowerment principle: the assertion that the greater the degree of employee empowerment, or assignment of right to make decisions, the greater the number of employees can be supervised effectively (7).

Special employment group: Individuals who are treated differently because they are members of a special group, such as the aging, and not for reasons related to their skills or aptitudes (10).

Standards: Predetermined goals and objectives that employees are expected and able to meet (7).

Statistical process control (SPC): The use of statistical techniques that aid in analyzing a process and its output and in determining the activities necessary for improvement (7).

Status: A person's perceived social ranking relative to his or her fellow employees (9).

Status symbols: Visible indicators of a person's rank or position in an organization (3).

Strategies: Carefully thought decisions that help organizational members develop action plans for achieving the end results established by a mission statement; as related to OD, the development of plans to enable the carrying out of organization development interventions (7, 9).

Stress: See *Distress and Eustress* (13).

Stress interview: A questionable interviewing technique in which the interviewee is intentionally placed in a tense—and sometimes abusive—situation to observe the person's response to stress (4).

Structured (directive) interview: A technique that usually follows a predetermined pattern with the interviewer asking a specific set of questions taken from a detailed form; useful in helping the interviewer move toward desired objectives (4).

Suggestion systems: A feedback mechanism used to encourage upward communication in organizations (3).

Suicide Prevention and Crises Intervention Service: A community agency staffed with persons trained to assist distraught individuals through difficult and emotional situations (13).

Synergism: The interaction of two or more independent parts, the effects of which are different from that which would be attained by each part individually (4).

Task activities: Specific behaviors that directly affect the accomplishment of goals, such as running a fax machine (4).

Task force: A body of persons temporarily established for the purpose of accomplishing a specific objective; a term sometimes used instead of *ad hoc committee* (2, 4).

Task identity: A core job dimension that enables employees to have a *more complete job* with which he or she can identify, rather than a minute, repetitious job that seems to have little relationship to a whole (8).

Task significance: A core job dimension that enables employees to feel that the job they perform *has an impact on others* (8).

Task variety: A core job dimension that enables employees to perform a wide variety of operations requiring both *thinking* and *doing* types of activities (8).

Technical skills: A person's ability to apply techniques, utilize processes, and understand procedures necessary for carrying out specific tasks (6).

Telecommuting: An employee practice in which employees are allowed to work at home and submit their work through computer terminals (8).

Testing requirement exception: A provision of the Civil Rights Act of 1964 that authorizes the use of professionally developed ability tests in employment if they are not "designed, intended, or used to discriminate" (10).

Theory X: See *X theory* (6).

Theory Y: See *Y theory* (6).

Think tanks: Geographically separated groups located away from the traditional work environment (14).

Third age: Considered to be everyone over 50 and under 75 years of age (11).

Total quality management (TQM): An ongoing process that expects everyone in an organization to be motivated toward the goal of continuous improvement and to be oriented toward meeting the needs of customers; concerned with improving the quality of the organizations activities (1; 7).

Transnationals: Organizations that manufacture, conduct research, raise capital, and buy supplies wherever they can do the job best (16).

Treatable disease: The attitude that drug and alcohol abuse are diseases and thus can be treated by proper counseling and medical attention (12).

Trustee-of-profit: The belief that a corporation's sole responsibility is to produce profits and that any expenditure on corporate social goals amounts, in essence, to a hidden tax on workers, customers, and shareholders (15).

2:1 rule: The tendency for activities and projects to take in time or cost of materials approximately twice the original estimate (13).

Two-valued reasoning: The belief that situations or people are either right or wrong, good or bad, with no possibilities in between (2).

Two-way communication: A necessary ingredient of communication that helps to ensure understanding has taken place; see also *Feedback* (3).

Type A Personalities: Relates to individuals afflicted with a tendency toward work addiction and an obsession with time and achievement (13).

Type B Personalities: Relates to individuals who do not experience work addiction tendencies (13).

Unfreezing: As a part of the change process, the discarding of old ideas and habits in order to learn new ones (9).

Union: An association of workers that has as its major objective the improvement of conditions related to employment (1).

Unity-of-command principle: The assertion that, since instructions or orders from two or more bosses may conflict, no employee should be accountable to more than one boss (7).

Unstructured (nondirective) interview: A technique that attempts to avoid influencing the interviewee's remarks; broad, general questions are typically asked, and the interviewee is encouraged to answer in some depth (4).

Upward communication: Communication that flows from lower to higher levels of an organization, such as from worker to supervisor or from supervisor to middle-manager (3).

Upward Pygmalion Effect: The influence that an employee's expectations have on the behavior of his or her boss; see also *Pygmalion effect* (6).

Validity: A requirement related to testing that means a test measures what it was designed to measure (10).

Verbal cocoon problem: The tendency for some managers, especially those who perceive their role as authoritative, to filter out incoming communication from associates (3).

Verbal communication: Forms of communication involving words, such as oral conversations and printed messages (3).

Verbal symbols: Words that are used in either oral conversations or printed messages (3).

Vertical loading: Enriching work by pulling down responsibilities from above and pushing certain tasks of a job down to a lower job classification (8).

Video display terminals (VDTs): Screens attached to computers for displaying data (8).

Wellness programs: Fitness programs sponsored by employers for the purpose of maintaining and improving employee's physical health, sense of well-being and productivity (8).

Well pay: The provision of an extra reward to employees for those who show up to work regularly as expected (8).

Wishing it were so: The tendency to see and believe the things we want to see and believe (2).

Work addiction (workaholism): A compulsive type of behavior displayed by persons who experience withdrawal or guilt feelings when they are not working (13).

Workplace affairs: The dating or romancing between two adults employed in the same work situation (14).

Workplace monitoring: The observation of employees on the job; sometimes through the use of covert electronic surveillance devices (14).

Xenophobia: An unreasonable fear or hatred of foreigners or people who are "different" (10).

X theory: Developed by Douglas McGregor, a traditionally negative set of assumptions held by some managers toward employees (6).

Yield point: The stage of stress that reveals itself as a slight change from "normal" behavior (13).

Y theory: Developed by Douglas McGregor, a positive set of assumptions held by some managers toward employees (6).

Index

Subject Index

Absenteeism, 185, 186, 188
Accountability, defined, 206
Accountability-for-results principle, 266
Achievement needs, 160, 169
Acquired immune deficiency syndrome (AIDS), 326, 412–13, 416–21
Action-oriented, 7
Ad hoc committee, 130
Adjustive reaction, 482
Administrative skills, 229, 230
Affairs, at workplace, 537
Affirmative action programs (AAP), 362
  unwanted problems associated with, 367
Age bias, 399
Age Discrimination in Employment Act of 1967, 400, 404
Agenda
  hidden, 128
  planned, 128, 133
Aging
  employment problems of, 399–401
  process, variability of, 399–400
AIDS, (acquired immune deficiency syndrome), 326, 412–13, 416–21
  and co-worker pressure, 420
  hiring people with, 418
  hotline, 420
  legal aspects in the workplace, 418
  risks in the workplace, 419–20
Alcohol and drug abuse
  major causes, 447–49
  organizational approaches to, 449
  programs, 450–53
  treatable diseases, 449
Alcohol
  dependency, signs of, 457
  alcohol problem, extent of, 438–41

Alcoholic
  defined, 440
  recovering, 442
Alcoholism
  health insurance coverage, 452
  trend toward rehabilitation, 441–42
Americans with Disabilities
  Act of 1990 (ADA), 410, 412, 415, 418, 419, 424, 442
Appearance, standards of, 539–40
Approval needs, 160
Asch conformity studies, 119
Assessment centers, 231
Attitude surveys, 189
Attitudes, 35
Authoritarian (autocratic) leadership, 218–20
Authority
  charismatic, 161
  defined, 206
Autocratic (authoritarian) leadership, 218–20
Autonomy, related to core dimensions, 284

Babies, born addicted to drugs, 447
Bakke v. University of California Medical School at Davis, 367
Behavior modification, 173, 176
Behavioristic psychology, 506
Behaviorists, 506
Belongingness, 119
Benchmarking, 254
Benefits, employee, 163
Body language, 82
Boiled-frog syndrome, 323, 324
Bona fide occupational qualification (BFOQ), 365
Bosses, support by employees, 560–62
Bottom-up assessment, 302
Brainstorming, 128
Brainwriting, 128
Bribes, 622

Burnout, 491–93
  candidates for, 492
  symptoms of, 492
  cure for, 492–93
Buying committee, 113
Buzz sessions, 188, 189

Cafeteria-style benefit program, 301
Carpal tunnel syndrome (CTS), 289, 290
Caveat emptor, 580, 588
Caveat vendor, 580
Certainty of misery, 324
Chains
  cluster, 126
  gossip, 125
  networks, 124–26
  probability, 125
  single-strand, 124
Change, as a three-step process, 328, 329
  effects of, 318, 319
  factors that obstruct its introduction, 319–27
Change agent, 334
Change management, 327
Charismatic authority, 161
  defined, 208
Child-care facilities, 287
Civil rights
  for gays and lesbians, 362
  religious beliefs, 361
  key legislation, 360, 361
  sexual preferences, 362
Civil Rights Act of 1866, 360–61
Civil Rights Act of 1964, 359, 377
  related to,
    BFOQ exception, 365
    testing requirements, 365–66
    seniority systems, 366
Civil Rights Act of 1991, 360
Climate surveys, 189
"Closed-door" policy, 505
Closed questions, 92
Cluster chain, 126

Coaching, 231
Codetermination, worker representation, 619
Cohesion, group, 119, 121
Committees, 130–31
    ad hoc, 130
    ongoing, 130
Communication
    barriers to, 85–88
    breaking down barriers, 93–99
    downward, 78, 79
    electronic forms, 80
    essential ingredients, 71
    feedback, 71
    filtering of, 79
    formal versus informal, 77
    grapevine, 77
    horizontal, 79
    leadership, 204
    listening, 88–93
    nature of, 71, 72
    nonverbal forms, 82–85
    one-way, 71
    responsibility for effective, 72
    selective reception, 78, 79
    spoken versus written, 80, 81
    two-way process, 71
    upward, 77
    verbal, 81
Company resources, the "right" to
    borrow, 535–36
Comparable worth, 371
Compensation, 484–85
Competence, needs, 161
Compressed work week
    advantages of, 295
    disadvantages of, 295, 296
Conceptual skills, 229, 230
Conditioned response, 174
Conformity
    approaches to, 534
    Asch conformity studies, 119
    versus individualism, 533
    legitimate conformity, 534
    nonlegitimate conformity, 534
    as a sellout, 534
Conformity studies, Asch, 119
Constructive coercion, 455
Content theories, of motivation, 173
Contingent workers, 297
Continuous improvement teams
    (CITs), 257
Conversion, 491
Core job dimensions, 283–84
Counselors, employee, 188
Creativity
    aids to, 57, 58
    meaning of, 56

Credibility gaps
    avoiding, 96
    barrier to communication, 86, 87
Credit checks, 547
Cross-training, 286
Cultural arrogance, 625
Cultural diversity
    in groups, 121, 122
    in the workplace, 352–83
Cultural leveling effect, 625, 626
Culturalization, effects of, on values
    toward women, 370
Culture, organizational, 17, 233
Culture shock, 615
Customers
    external, 254
    internal, 254

Decision making
    brainstorming, 128
    brainwriting, 128
    committees, 130–31
    Delphi method, 129
    deficiencies in group, 131–33
    group, 127
    in organizations, 18
    pitfalls to, 54–56
    quality circles (CQs), 129
    task force, 130
Deep-sensing, 188, 189
Defense mechanism, 482
Delegation, 264–66
Delegation-by-results principle, 264
Deleveraging, 583
Delphi method, 129
Deming Prize, 262
Democratic (participative) leadership, 220–23
Derived X (I've-been-burned) Theory, 213, 214, 265
Desert Storm military intervention, 120
Directive (structured) interviews, 137
Disabilities, individuals with, 398
    advantages of hiring, 421
    managing, 422–25
    problems of persons with, 408–13
Discipline, 548–55
    dismissal, 552–53, 555
    documentation of, 550
    nature of, 549
    privacy and, 550
    progressive, 549
    red-hot stove rule, 550
    rules, enforcement of, 551–52
    situational, 551
Discrimination
    defined, 355

nature of, 354–62
    reverse, 366–68
Dismissing employees, guidelines
    for, 553–54
Displacement, 489–91
Distress, 479
Double standards of supervision,
    363
Doublespeak, 74–75
Downward communication, 78, 79
Drinking problems, among work
    force, 440–41
Drug, defined, 444
Drug-Free Workplace Act of 1988,
    442, 463
Drug abuse, defined, 442
    economic cost, 448–49
    prevalence of, 442–46
    public invisibility, 448
Drug addiction, 442
Drug and alcohol abuse
    recognizing symptoms, 456–58
    supervisory guidelines, 456
    supervisory responsibilities,
        453–56
Drug dependency, signs of, 457–58
Drug testing
    of employees, 458–63
    guidelines for, 463
    pros and cons of, 460–62
    types of, 459–60
Drugs
    legislation related to, 464
    major types of, 444
    and the workplace, 445–46
Dual command, 264

Earnings of minorities, as a percentage of white males,
    368–69
Economic guarantees, 332
Elastic limit, 480
Emergent organization, 123
Emergent system, 17, 117, 183
Emotions, as a barrier to communication, 86
Employee assistance programs
    (EAPS), 451–52
Employee benefits, 163
Employee counselors, 188
Employee involvement (EI), 220,
    221
Employee Polygraph Protection Act
    of 1988, 544
Employee Retirement Income Security Act of 1974, 419
Employee surveys, 189
Empowerment, 158, 224, 440

Enlightened self-interest philosophy, 585
Entry-level positions, 286
Environmental tobacco smoke (ETS), 541
Equal Pay Act of 1963, 359, 371
Equity theory, 178, 179
ERG theory of needs, 166
Ergonomics, 289
Errors, admitting, 557
Escape reinforcement, 174
Ethical values, 495
Ethics
    defined, 578
    employee, 558–59
    organizational, 578–97
    situational, 622
Ethnic minority managers, challenges faced by, 382–83
Ethnocentric, 611
Eustress, 479
Exception principle, 266, 277
Exercise, 510–11
    breaks, 289
    making it enjoyable, 291
Existence needs, 166
Exit interviews, 189, 190
Expatriate, 616
Expectancy theory, 176–78
Extinction theory, 175

Facilitator, in organization development, 34
Facts
    definition, 38
    versus inferences, 38–42
Faith
    developing, 494
    a fish story, 499–500
    guidelines for maintaining meaning of, 493
    in one's self, 499–501
    situational, 495
Fallacies, see logical fallacies
Fallacy
    of composition, 47, 48
    of division, 48
Family leave, 372
Father of scientific management, 9
Faulty translations, as a barrier to communication, 86
Feedback, 71, 80, 89, 94, 33, 170, 284, 334
Filtering, of communication, 79
Flexecutives, 299
Flexible-benefit plan, 301
Flexible working hours, 293
Flexplace, 295–96

Flextime, 293–94
Flight, 487–88, 492, 501
Forced waiting, 511
Foreign-owned industry in the United States, 616
Foreign Corrupt Practices Act of 1977, 622
Foreign exchange, 623
Foreign nationals, 627
Formal communication, 77
Formal leader, 119
Formal organization, 8
    reason for existence, 117
Four C's of written communication, 98, 99
Free-rein (laissez-faire) leadership, 223, 224
Freedom to fail, 234
Frustration, nature of, 480–82
Frustration, reactions to, 482–91
    compensation, 484–85
    conversion, 491
    displacement, 489–91
    flight, 487–88
    negativism, 485
    obsessive thinking, 489
    pseudostupidity, 489
    rationalization, 483
    repression, 488
    resignation, 486–87
Future shock, 332, 333

Gainsharing, 292
Gatekeepers, as a barrier to communication, 88
Glass ceiling, defined, 363, 365, 423
Glide time, 293
Global organizational behavior, 613
Global organizational cultures, 613–23
    attitudes toward time, 617
    customs, differences in, 615
    ethical standards, 620, 622
    labor laws, 619–20
    language differences, 617
    pay scale differences, 618
    political climate, differences in, 622–23
    work force, differences in, 618
Global organizations
    employee orientation visits, 626
    extras provided for employees, 627
    selection of employees for, 625
    time zones, coping with, 616
    training for, 626
Globalism, 610
Goals
    developing readily attainable, 497, 499

problems associated with achieving, 556
Golden parachute, 582
Gossip chain, 125
Grapevine, 77, 122–23, 126
Graphology tests, 546
Grid organization development method, 334
Gripe sessions, 188, 189
Group
    cohesion, 119
    decision making, 127
    deficiencies in, 131
    defined, 113
    interviews, 137
Groups
    behavior of, 118–22
    cultural diversity in, 121
    formal, nature of, 116–17
    influence of members, 118–19
    why people join, 113
Groupthink, 131, 132
    illusion of unanimity, 132
Growth needs, 166

Habits, 321, 323
Halo effect, and perception, 46
Handicapped, as an outdated term, 408, 414
Happiness, concept of, 515
Hawthorne,
    effect, 11
    studies, 11
Hereditary factors, and perception, 43
Hidden agenda, 128
Hierarchy of needs concept, Maslow's, 162–65
HIV (human immunodeficiency virus), 326, 416–21
    how transmitted, 416–17
    tests, 546–47
Holistic effect, 510
Horizontal communication, 79, 80
Horizontal loading, 285
Horizontal promotions, 233
Hostile (unfriendly) takeovers, 581, 591
How many Fs? exercise, 37
Hughes Act (Rehabilitation Act of 1970), 442
Human immunodeficiency virus (HIV), 326, 411, 412, 413, 416–21
Human relations, father of, 11
Human resource management, (HRM), 12
    skills, 229

Humanistic psychology, 506–07
Hygiene (maintenance) factors, 167–69

Identical twins story, 507
In-transition groups, 513
Individuals in organizations, challenges facing, 531–65
Inactivity, as communication, 83
Incentive payment system, 177
Individuals with disabilities, defined, 411
Inferences
    versus facts, 38–42
    probability and, 40
Influencing others positively, 510
Informal communication, 77
Informal groups
    grapevine, 122
    work arrangement influence on, 120–21
Informal leader, 119
Informal organizations, 9, 117–18, 123
Informal system, 183
Inner-directed Pygmalion effect, 500
Innovation, 562
    teams, 562–63
Institute for a Drug-Free Workplace, 462
Integrity tests, 546
Interventions, in organization development, 333
Interviewing, 136–40
    disciplinary, 454
    exit, 189, 190
    group, 137
    guidelines for being interviewed, 139, 140
    guidelines for conducting, 138, 139
    for morale surveys, 189
    stress, 138
    structured (directive), 137
    styles of, 136
    unstructured (nondirective), 137
Intuition, 53, 54
Inverted Maslow needs mix, 166
"Iran-Contragate" scandals, 535

Japan-bashing, 4
Job banks, 407
Job enlargement, 285
Job enrichment, 283–93, 440
Job rotation, 233, 286
Job sharing, 301
Johnson & Johnson, 290

K.I.S.S. concept, 97
Kossen's Law (K's Law), 504

L.A. riots of 1992, 5, 558
Laissez-faire (free-rein) leadership, 223, 224
Law of effect, 173
Leaders
    as benevolent autocrats, 219
    characteristics of, 208
    importance of, 207
Leadership
    attitudes, 209
    autocratic (authoritarian), 218–20
    "best" style, 224, 226
    defined, 204
    democratic (participative), 220–23
    formal, 119, 206
    (free-rein) laissez-faire, 223, 224
    functions and characteristics of, 204–09
    in a global environment, 209
    informal, 119
    laissez-faire (free-rein), 223, 224
    negative, 214
    participative (democratic), 220–23, 380
    positive, 214, 215
    situational (contingency), 224, 226
    as a skill, 227–30
    skills, development of, 230–33
    styles of, 217–24
    traditional, 214
    versus management, 205
Learned needs, 159
Learning tips, 19
Leveraged buyouts, 581, 582, 583
Life enrichment, 508
Listening, 88–93
    empathetic, 99
    responses, 91–93
Loading
    horizontal, 285
    vertical, 284
Logical fallacies
    of composition, 47, 48
    of division, 48
    post hoc fallacy, 48–50
    two-valued reasoning, 50, 51
    wishing-it-were-so philosophy, 50
Long-term memory, 20
Los Angeles riots of 1992, 5, 588

Maintenance (hygiene) factors, 167–69
Maintenance activities, 121
Malcolm Baldridge National Quality Award, 261–63
Management
    defined, 205
    modern, 214
    by objectives (MBO), to effect change, 335–37
    versus leadership, 205

Management by Wandering Around (MBWA), 95
Managerial grid, 335
Maquiladora industry, 612
Maslow's
    hierarchy of needs concept, 162–65
    inverted, 166
    pregnant, 165
MBO (management by objectives, 335–37
McGann v. H&H Music, 419
Meetings
    elements of good, 136
    purpose of, 127
Mental set, 35
    as applied to perceiving ethnic minorities, 362–63
Metric Conversion Act of 1975, 328
Mission statement, 253
Modeling-identification-socialization process, 355
Mommy track, 372
Mommy trackers, 300
Monitoring, of workplace, 547–48
Moonlighting, 298
Morale
    defined, 181
    evaluating, 187–91
    factors that affect, 182–85
    in organizations, 179–82
    and productivity, 181, 182
    surveys, 189
    warning signs of low, 185, 187
Motivation
    content theories, 173
    defined, 157
    equity theory, 178, 179
    ERG theory of needs model, 166, 167
    expectancy theory, 176, 177
    fear and, 214
    hierarchy of needs model, 162–64
    motivation-maintenance model, 167–73
    process theories, 173
    reinforcement theory, 173
Motivation-maintenance model, 167–73
Motivational (satisfiers) factors, 168, 169–71
Motivational model, 158–60
"Move it" syndrome, 337
Multiple careers, 406
Multiskilling, 286
Multivalued reasoning, 51
My Fair Lady, 216
Myths, effect of, 325, 326

NAFTA (North American Free Trade Act), 613
Need
  for achievement, 160
  for approval, 160
  defined, 156
Needs
  competence, 161
  existence, 166
  growth, 166
  learned, 159
  power, 161
  priority of, 162–164
  relatedness, 166
  theories, comparison of, 172
Negativism, 485
Networking, 377
Networks, communication, 124, *see also* chains
No-layoff policies, 332, 587–88
Noise, as a barrier to communication, 87
Nondirective (unstructured) interviews, 137
Norms, social, 118
North American Free Trade Act (NAFTA), 613

Objectives, in MBO, 338
Obsessive-compulsive behavior, 502
Obsessive thinking, 489
Occupation, selecting a satisfying, 499
OD consultant, 334
OD practitioner, 334
Oil spill, Valdez, Alaska, 580
Old-young woman quiz, 35, 36
Older women, problems of unemployment, 400
Older workers, 399
  attitudes toward, 400–03
  defined, 400
  myths and realities associated with, 401
  need for counseling, 404
One-way communication, 71
Ongoing committees, 130
Open-door policies, 95
Open questions, 92
Opinion surveys, 189
"Oppressed majority," 358
Organization
  chart, 8, 206
  effect of personal needs on, 16
  emergent, 123
  formal, 8
  human side of, 10, 11
  informal, 9, 123
  need for order and predictability, 16

Organization development (OD), 333, 334
Organizational analysis, 334
Organizational behavior (OB)
  history of, 9
  recent trends in, 12
  what it is, 6
  what it is not, 7
Organizational culture, 17, 233
Organizational diagnosis, 334
Organizational needs, 16
Organizations, decision making in, 18
Outplacement consultants, 553
Overeagerness to respond, as a barrier to communications, 87

Pan Am Lockerbie flight Number 103, 623
Parkinson's Law, 503
Part-time employees, 300
Participation, employee, 331, 332
Participative (democratic) leadership, 220–23, 380
Passive smoking, 541
Peer pressure, 45
People, concern for, 335
People with physical and intellectual challenges, 408
Perception
  as a barrier to communication, 85, 86
  environmental background, related to, 43–45
  filters, 35
  halo effect and, 46
  hereditary factors and, 43
  mental set, 35
  peer pressure and, 45
  projection, 45
  rusty halo effect and, 47
  snap judgments and, 45
Performance-related payment plan, 177
Performance appraisal interview, 284
Persons with physical or intellectual challenges, 414
Phased retirements, 407
Physical access, 410
Physical and mental disabilities, causes of, 409
Physical examinations, 422
Physically and intellectually challenged, common attitudes toward, 413–14, 416
"Pig-in-a-poke" riddle, 323
Pink-and-blue syndrome, 379
Planned agenda, 128

Policies, 16
Politics, organizational, 559–60, 562–65
Polygraphs, use of, 544
Position power, 161
Positive reinforcement, 174, 175, 286
Post hoc fallacy, 48–50
Power, position, 161
Power needs, 161
Pregnant Maslow needs mix, 165
Prejudice, 382
  defined, 355
  in favor of others, 356, 357–58
  as a learned response, 355
  nature of, 354–62
  preventive, 358
Preventive maintenance, listening as a form of, 91
Pride in work, 187
Principles of organizations, summary of major, 267
Priority of needs, 162–64
Privacy issue, 544–48
  credit checks, 547
  graphology tests, 546
  HIV tests, 546–47
  integrity tests, 546
  personal records, 548
  polygraphs, use of, 544
  spies, 548
  surveillance, 547
  testing employees, 544
  workplace monitoring, 547–48
Probability chain, 125
Problem solving
  intuition, 53, 54
  seven-step system, 51–53
  scientific method, 51–53
Process theories of motivation, 173
Production, concern for, 335
Production-based compensation plans, 292
Profit-quest approach, 585
Projection, 45
Promotions, horizontal, 233
Proportional employment, 367
Protected classes of workers, 359
Pseudostupidity, 489
Psychological distance, 184, 225
Psychosomatic, 491
Pygmalion Effect, 215–17, 495, 560
  upward, 217

Qualified individuals with disabilities, 411
Quality circles (CQs), 121, 129, 250
Quality of work life (QWL), 12, 249
  defined, 281

factors that influence, 281, 282
greater concerns over, 280, 281
improving the, 282–92
limitations, 291
Quality standards, 255
Questionnaires
descriptive, 190
for morale surveys, 189
objective, 190
postexit, 190
Questions
closed, 92
open, 92

Rationalization, 13–7
Reasonable accommodation, 361, 410, 422, 424
Recognition, 174
needs for, 170
Records, employee, use of, 548
Recovering alcoholic, 442
Rehabilitation Act of 1973, 409–10, 418
Reinforcement theory, 173–76
father of, 173
Reinforcement
escape, 174
positive, 174, 175
Relatedness needs, 166
Reliability, related to testing, 366
Religious beliefs, 361
Repatriation, 627–28
agreement, 628
Repetitive strain injury (RSI), 289
Repression, 488
Required systems, 17, 116
Resignation, 486–87
Responsibility, 171
defined, 206
Rest breaks, 289
Restructuring, 583, 591
effect of leadership, 209
Results management, 336
Retirement, easing the transition, 406–07
Reverse discrimination, 366–68
Right-side-up organization, 303, 304
RIO process, 336, 337
Risk decisions, 287
Robotics, 14
Role assuming, 21
Rules, 184
Rumors, 77
defined, 122
Rupture point, 480
Rusty halo effect, and perception, 47

Sabotage, 187
Sanctions, 622

Satisfiers (motivational) factors, 168, 169–71
Scalar principal, 263
Scapegoating, 490–91
Scientific management, father of, 9
Scylla and Charybdis, 558
Sedatives (downers), 444
Selective placement, 422
Selective reception, 78, 79
Selective X-Y attitudes, 212, 213
Self-esteem, 170, 174
Self-fulfilling prophecy, 216
Seniority, 400
systems, 366
Sense of humor, need for, 508
Seven-step system, approach to problem solving, 51–53
Seven Deadly Diseases, Deming's, 262
Sexual harassment, 373, 375–76
guidelines related to, 377
Sexual preferences, 362
Sham approach, 455
Short-term memory, 20
Single-strand chains, 124
Situational ethics, 622
Situational thinking, 18
Skills
administrative, 229, 230
conceptual, 229, 230
human resource management, 229
technical, 229
Smoking, 540–43
methods for restricting, 542   543
Snap judgments, and perception, 45
Social-accountability approach, 586
Social action, guide to, 593–95, 597
Social contact, 288
Social norms, 118
Social responsibility, areas of, 586–93
consumers, 588–89
employees, 587–89
environment, 589–90
information, providing, 590–91
money and talent, contributing, 593
small business, aid to, 591–93
special employment groups, 591
Social service leaves, 588
"Sour grapes" rationalization, 483
Spaced repetition, 20
Span-of-control principle, 267, 268
Span of empowerment, 268
Special employment groups, 354, 398
Spies, in the workplace, 14–19
Standards, of quality, 255

Statistical process control (SPC), 260
Status, 321
symbols, as communication, 83
Stimulants (uppers), 444
Strategies, 256
in organization development, 334
Stress
acquiring, 514
career-related
causes, 479
managing, 496–506
causing associates to acquire, 514
elastic limit, 480
interviews, 138
managing, 478–516
nature of, 478–80
off the job
causes, 480
guidelines for, 508
managing, 506–14
rupture point, 480
three stages of, 479–80
yield point, 480
Strikes, 187
Structured (directive) interviews, 137
Substance abuse, problems of, 438–64
Success, concept of, 516
Suggestion systems, 94
Suicide Prevention and Crisis Intervention Service, 514
Superstitious beliefs, 325
Supervising women, guidelines for, 376
Surprise factors, allowing for, 504
Surveillance, of employees, 547
Surveys, morale, 189
Symbols, as communication, 82
Synergism, 116, 331, 332

Tardiness, 186
Task
activities, 121
force, 130
identity, 284
significance, 284
variety, 283
Teams, 288
innovation, 562
Technical skills, 229
Telecommunication device for the deaf (TDD), 414
Telecommuting, 296
Teleworking, 296
Temporary employees (temps), 297, 299, 300
Testing employees, 544

Testing requirement exception, 365–66
Theory X
  attitudes, 211, 212
  managers, 325
Theory Y attitudes, 211, 212
Think tanks, 562
Third age, 408
Tiananmen Square demonstrations, 623
Time, as communication, 85
Timing, in communicating, 98, 99
Titanic, sinking of, 36, 37
Title VII, of the Civil Rights Act of 1964, 359
Total quality management (TQM), 12, 249
  defined, 250, 251
  reasons for utilizing, 249
  supportive culture needed, 251
Touching, as communication, 84, 85
Training, for quality, 256
Trial balloon approach, 564
Trustee-of-profit philosophy, 585
Turnover, 186, 188
Twinning, 301
2:1 rule, 505
Two-valued orientation or reasoning, 7, 50, 51, 166
Two-way process, communication as a, 71, 72
Type A and B personalities, 501

Understudy assignments, 232
Unemployment, long-term, of the aging, 400
Union, 12
  harder-line bargaining, 15
  membership trends, 14
Unity of command, 264
Unstructured (nondirective) interviews, 137
Upward appraisal, 302
Upward communication, 77, 94–95
Upward Pygmalion effect, 217

Valdez, oil spill incident, 441, 583
Validity, related to testing, 366
Verbal cocoon problem, 89, 188
Vertical loading, 284
Video conferencing, 135
Video display terminals (VDTs), 289
Vision, as a mission, 253
Voice, as communication, 83, 84
Vroom-Yetton model, 226, 227

Wants, beyond capabilities, 555–56
Watergate scandal, 4
Well-pay, 287

Wellness programs, 290
Whistle-blower Protection Act of 1989, 561
Whistle-blowing, 561
Whole job concept, 284, 285
Wishing-it-were-so philosophy, 50–51, 216, 506
Women, in management, challenges faced by, 378–82
Women employees, supervising, 373
Word interpretation, affected by doublespeak, 74–75
Words
  as inexact symbols, 73
  international meaning, 73–74
  meanings affected by tone, 78
  nature of, 72–76
  new meaning, 74
  newly developed, 78
  regional meaning, 73, 74
Work, meaning of, 496–97
Work addiction, 501
Workaholism, cures for, 501–02
Worker teams, 121

X Theory, 211, 212
Xenophobia, 354, 361, 364, 494

Y Theory, 211, 212
Yield point, 480

Name Index

Adams, J. Stacy, 178
Akers, John, 588
Alderfer, Clayton, 166
Amman, Fritz, 356
Argyle, Michael, 120

Bahr, Morton, 548
Baldridge, Malcolm, 261
Barry, Jack, 584
Beall, Donald, 611
Beatty, Warren, 399
Belous, Richard, 301
Bernstein, Aaron, 352
Bickerton, Richard, 453
Blake, Robert, 335
Blyth, Myrna, 372
Boesky, Ivan, 580
Bolick, Clint, 368
Bonaparte, Napoleon, 485
Bovee, Christian, 318
Bowen, David, 224
Brenner, M. Harvey, 406
Brisbane, Arthur, 513
Brown, Arnold, 127

Burdick, Walton E., 177
Bush, George, 5, 353, 375, 400, 443, 617

Cabell, James, 507
Capote, Truman, 591
Cato, Sid, 591
Catt, Stephen E., 204
Chaplin, Charlie, 280
Charles, Ray, 484
Cicero, 70
Clifford, Clark, 580
Clinton, Bill, 333, 362, 367, 375
Cohen, Ben, 592
Cohen, Stanley L., 220
Cohn, Jonathan, 411
Cole, K. C., 370
Coulter, Steve, 296
Cratylus, Greek philosopher, 318
Cronin, David, 434
Crowne, D. P., 160

Davidson, Kirk, 622
Davis, Harold, 588
Davis, Keith, 123, 532
Deming, W. Edwards, 178, 252, 262
Devey, Donald, 398
DiNello, Gilbert, 484
Dostoevski, Fyodor, 574
Drucker, Peter, 4, 53, 268
DuBrin, Andrew, 294
Dunk, William P., 591
Durenberger, David, 373

Feliciano, José, 484
Fisher, George, 611
Fletcher, Arthur, 353
Ford, Henry, 516
Foster, Richard, 532, 562
Friedman, Meyer, 501
Fromm, Erich, 398
Furnham, Adrian, 4

Gadaffi, Muammar, 623
Gantt, Henry L., 9
Garbo, Greta, 112
Gilbreth, Frank B.
Gilbreth, Lillian M.
Goldstein, Irwin L., 175, 176
Gorbachev, Mikhail, 5
Greenfield, Jerry, 592
Gregory, Richard L., 34
Guinier, Lani, 367

Hackman, J. Richard, 283
Hahn, Carl, 226
Hammer, Stuart, 210
Harrison, Bennett, 221
Hassenfeld, Alan G., 156

Hawking, Stephen, 484
Hazelwood, Joseph, 441
Hendrik van Loon, 131
Heraclitus, Greek philosopher, 318
Herzberg, Frederick, 156, 167
Hicks, H. Randall, 503
Higashi, Kan, 280
Hilkert, Robert N., 533
Hill, Anita, 373
House, Robert J.
Howard, Gary, 461
Hubbad, Ken, 493
Hughes, Howard, 112
Huxley, Aldous, 478

Ingebritson, Miriam, 438
Inouye, Daniel, 373
Irvin, Milton, 352

Jagger, Mick, 399
Janis, Irving L., 112
Johnson, Magic, 416, 420
Jones, Andrew, 308

Karr, Alphonse, 318
Keen, Karlyn, 378
Kelley, Maryellen, 221
Kennedy, Anthony, 462
Kennedy, John F., 209, 327
King, Rodney, 353
Kochan, Thomas, 618
Krantz, K. Theodor, 248

Lamb, Lawrence, 478
Lavetti, Al, 255
Lawler, Edward, 176, 224
Levine, Dennis, 580
Lindholst, Kai, 626
Lopez, José Ignacio, 356
Lubbers, Ruud, 415
Lutz, William, 74

MacDuffie, Paul, 618
Main, Jeremy, 610
Manilow, Barry, 520
Manz, Charles, 259
Marlowe, D., 160
Martin, Ian, 616
Maslow, A. H., 162, 506
Maxwell, Robert, 114
May, Rollo, 506
Mayo, Elton, 11
McCartney, Paul, 399
McClelland, David C., 161
McConnell, James V., 506
McGann, John, 419
McGannon, Michael, 512
McGregor, Douglas, 211
Megalli, Mark, 75

Merson, Michael, 417
Michaelson, Marc, 406
Milken, Michael, 580
Miller, Donald S., 204
Milton, John, 484
Minor, John B., 120
Modigliana, Franco, 578
Mondy, R. Wayne, 537
Montague, Ashley, 500
Morrison, Michael, 478
Mouton, Jane, 335

Nader, Ralph, 75
Nair, Keshavan, 204
Nietzsche, Friedrich, 133
Nixon, Richard, 4
Nolte, Nick, 399
Noriega, Manuel, 445
North, Oliver, 535

Oldham, Greg R., 283
Ornstein, Robert, 323
Orwell, George, 75

Packwood, Bob, 373
Parkinson, C. Northcote, 503
Parton, Dolly, 518
Pauling, Linus, 112
Pavlov, Ivan Petrovich, 174
Pfeffer, Jeffrey, 560
Pfeiffer, Eckhard, 356
Porter, Lyman, 176
Premeaux, Shane R., 537
Pryor, David, 561

Raskolnikov, 574
Reagan, Ronald, 209, 623
Reigner, Charles, 486
Richards, Phillip, 303
Roethlisberger, F. J., 11
Rogers, Carl, 506
Roosevelt, Franklin D., 325, 484
Rosenman, Ray, 501
Rosenthal, A. M., 248
Rothenberg, Sheribel F., 545
Rubin, Vera, 370
Russell, Betrand, 34, 36, 502

Sanders, Harland, 400
Schellhardt, Timothy, 582
Schor, Juliet, 164
Schreyer, William, 44
Schroeder, Patricia, 375
Schwartz, Felice, 372
Segovia, Andrés, 509
Shakespeare, 578
Sharman, Graham, 255
Shaw, George Bernard, 21
Sheldon, Lou, 418

Skager, Rodney, 439
Skinner, B. F., 173, 506
Sleszynski, Raymond A., 616
Sloan, Alfred P., 232
Snyder, Charles R., 496
Socrates, 480
Spenley, Paul, 251
Spiegel, Larry, 248, 263
Spinoza, Baruch, 45
Sprenger, Paul, 372
Steers, Richard M., 176
Stein, Stan, 403
Stempel, Robert, 324, 584

Takeuchi, Hirotaka, 90
Taylor, Arthur, 580
Taylor, F. W., 9
Thomas, Clarence, 373
Toffler, Alvin, 332
Toffler, Barbara Ley, 337
Torrington, Derek, 178
Truman, Harry S., 557
Turney, John R., 220
Twain, Mark, 543

Van Dyke, Henry, 499
Vogel, David, 585
Vroom, Victor, 176, 226

Walton, Richard, 282
Walvoord, Ellen, 547
Webber, Ross A., 291
Weber, Max, 303
Westin, Alan, 536
Whitwam, David, 611
Wilcox, V., 83
Wilson, Pete, 353
Wonder, Stevie, 484
Wright, David McCord, 324

Xue, Lan, 221

Yates, Jere, 480
Yetton, Philip, 226

Zaleznik, Abraham, 580–81

Organization Index

A. O. Smith, 614
Abbot Laboratories, 547
Active Corps of Executives (ACE),
    591
Advanced Micro Devices, 584
Al-Anon, 452
Alcoholics Anonymous, 442, 452
American Association of University
    Women, 370

American Council for Drug Education, 446
American Enterprise Institute, 378
American Express, 583
American Heart Association (AHA), 541
American Medical Association, 442, 446
American Petroleum Institute, 75
American Quality Foundation, 255
Ashridge Management Research Group, 210
Associated Builders and Contractors, 440
AT&T, 261, 373, 416, 424, 554, 581, 583, 584, 611
Avis Corporation, 613

BankAmerica Corporation, 123, 296, 554, 598
Bell-South, 590
Ben and Jerry's, 592, 593
Bethlehem Steel, 220
Bioplasty, Inc., 621
Boeing Aircraft Company, 542, 554
Böwe Systemvertrieb, 441
Budget Rent-A-Car, 613
Burger King, 617
Business Roundtable, 548
Businessland, 611
Buy Recycled Business Alliance, 590

California State Department of Vocational Rehabilitation, 413, 414
Caterpillar Corporation, 15, 180, 280, 614
Chase Manhattan, 548
Chevron Corporation, 294, 581
Chrysler Corporation, 74, 228
Church's Fried Chicken, 403
Citicorp, 583
Clorox Company, 593, 594
Coca-Cola Company, 612
Cocaine Anonymous, 452
Common Market, 611
Communications Workers Union, 548
Compaq Computers, 356
Conference Board, 297
Conrail-Amtrak, 446
Control Data Corporation, 294
Courtaulds Fibres Company, 13

Dana Corporation, 259, 584
Department of Health and Human Services, 443
Department of Housing and Urban Development (HUD), 580

Digital Equipment, 554, 587
Dow Corning Corporation, 621
Du Pont Company, 376, 424, 542

Eastman-Kodak, 178, 614
Economic Intelligence Unit (EIU), 210, 249
Egon Zehnder, 626
Emerson Electric, 611
Environmental Protection Agency, 541, 589
Equal Employment Opportunity Commission (EEOC), 359, 375, 377, 410, 425
Equitable Life Assurance Company, 377
Ericsson, 547
Esprit de Corp., 356
EuroDisney, 322
European Economic Community (EEC), 611
European Foundation for Quality Management, 262
Exxon Corporation, 124, 441, 579

Farah Company, 614
Federal Express, 587, 624
Ford Motor Company, 178, 210, 228, 254, 293, 597, 611, 614, 623
Frito-Lay, 298

General Electric Company, 259, 554, 614
General Electric Medical Systems Company, 626
General Motors Corporation, 11, 124, 178, 228, 232, 248, 261, 263, 293, 324, 356, 554, 584, 588, 611, 613, 619
Georgia Power Company, 403
Goodrich and Sherwood Company, 133
Gordon S. Black Corporation, 511
Grand Metropolitan, 617
Green Giant, 617
Greyhound Lines, 15
Greystone Bakery, 592
GTE-Michigan, 416
Gulf Corporation, 581

H&H Music, 419
HARKhomes, 592
Harley-Davidson, 624
Hasbro Corporation, 156
Heinz USA, 542
Henley Centre for Forecasting, 596
Herman Miller Furniture, 590
Hertz, 613
Hewlett-Packard, 259, 293, 294, 424, 584, 587

Honeywell Corporation, 376, 584, 613
Honda Motor Europe, 308, 612
Human Resource Management Association, 544, 547

IBM, 124, 177, 178, 254, 259, 298, 416, 498, 535, 536, 539, 542, 554, 583, 587, 588, 614
ICI, 498
ICR Survey Research Group, 248
Imperial Food Products, 17
Inamed Corporation, 621
Insead Business School, 512
Institute for a Drug-Free Workplace, 462
Institute of Manpower Studies, 183
International Brotherhood of Electrical Workers, 584
Italtel, 611

J.C. Penney, 403
Jaguar, 611
Japanese Union of Scientists and Engineers, 262
Job Accommodation Network (JAN), 424
Johnson & Johnson, 287, 290
Jolly Green Giant, 614

Kaiser Permanente Health Center, 543
Kemper Financial Group, 590
Kemper Insurance Group, 450
Kentucky Fried Chicken (KFC Corporation), 400, 613
Kohler, 614
Kraft, 581

Leroy-Somer, 611
Levi Strauss & Company, 96, 599, 626
Lincoln Electric Company, 178, 587
Link Resources, 295
Long Island Lighting Company, 460
Louis Harris and Associates, 422

Manpower, Inc., 9–25, 300
Marriott Corporation, 424
McCaw Cellular Communication, 581
McDonald's Corporation, 402, 403, 498, 590
McDonald's of Canada, 613
McGhan Medical, 621
McKinsey & Company, 255
Medivent, 611
Mentor Corporation, 621
Merrill Lynch & Company, 44

Metropolitan Life Insurance Company, 294, 590
Mothers Against Drunk Drivers (MAAD), 439
Motorola, Inc., 286, 461, 611

National Academy of Sciences, 289
National Airlines, 74
National Association of Manufacturers, 258
National Centers for Disease Control (CDC), 416, 420, 511
National Council on Alcoholism, 440, 441
National Institute on Alcohol Abuse and Alcoholism, 438
National Institute on Drug Abuse, 443
National Transportation Safety Board, 446
National Volunteer Center, 593
New Ways to Work, 498
Nordstroms, Inc., 547
Northern Telecom, 548
Northwest Airlines, 440
Northwestern National Life Insurance Company, 496
Nuclear Regulatory Commission, 440

Office of Federal Contract Compliance, 359–60
Organization for Economic Cooperation and Development (OECD), 13
Otis Engineer Company, 617

Pacific Bell, 296
Pacific Northwest Bell Telephone Company, 541
Parents Resource Institute for Drug Education, 438
Parker Pen Company, 617
Parsons Pine Products, 287
PepsiCo, 298
Pera International, 251
Pfizer, 611

Philip Morris, 581
Pillsbury, 617
Pizza Hut, 613
President's Committee on Employment of the Handicapped (PCEH), 424
Procter & Gamble, 614
Professional Air Traffic Controllers Organization (PATCO), 15
Prudential Insurance Company, 447, 498
Public Citizen, 440

Ralston Purina, 593
Rank Xerox, 262
Republic Steel Company, 11
Riviera Hotel, 400
Robert Half Recruitment Agency, 539
Rockwell Corporation, 611

Saab-Scania, 611
Safeco Insurance Company, 296, 539
Safeway Stores Inc., 253, 368, 403, 590
San Francisco Employers Council, 552
Sears, Roebuck & Company, 554, 590
Seattle Mariners, 364
Securities and Exchange Commission, 44
Security Pacific Corporation, 124, 554
Service Corps of Retired Executives (SCORE), 591
Sheraton Hotels, 363
Small Business Administration, 591
Students Against Drug Drivers (SAAD), 439
Suicide Prevention and Crisis Intervention Service, 514

Taco Bell Corporation, 588, 589
Technica U.S., 255
Tektronix, 300

Texas Instruments Company, 414, 460, 542
3M, 259, 590
Tobacco Institute, 75
Toledo Edison Company, 424
Toyota Motor Corporation, 254, 619
Toys "R" Us, 5, 624
Traditional Values Coalition, 418
Travelers Insurance Company, 300, 301, 407
Trump Shuttle, 460
TRW, 259

U.S. Commission on Civil Rights, 353
U.S. Department of Health and Human Services, 410
U.S. Department of Labor Employment Standards Administration, 411
U.S. Drug Enforcement Administration, 460
Unilever, 547
Union Carbide, 582
United Airlines, 536
United Auto Workers Union, 11, 228
United States Justice Department, 447
USX Corporation, 293, 360

Velcro USA, 248
Volkswagen, 228, 356

Wage and Salary Administration and Research Institute, 44
Walt Disney Company, 322
Western Electric Company, 11
Whirlpool Corporation, 611
World Health Organization (WHO), 416, 417

Xerox Corporation, 188, 535, 536, 588

Zenith, 614